Macroeconomics: Theories and Policies

PRENTICE HALL SERIES IN ECONOMICS

EIGHTH EDITION

Macroeconomics

Theories and Policies

Richard T. Froyen
University of North Carolina

PEARSON
Prentice
Hall

Upper Saddle River, New Jersey 07458

Library of Congress Cataloging-in-Publication Data

Froyen, Richard T.
   Macroeconomics : theories and policies / Richard T. Froyen.—8th ed.
     p. cm.
   Includes bibliographical references and index.
   ISBN 0-13-143582-5
    1. Macroeconomics.   2. Keynesian economics. I. Title.

HB172.5.F76 2004
339 — dc22   2004049274

AVP/Executive Editor: David Alexander
VP/Editorial Director: Jeff Shelstad
Project Manager: Marie McHale
Editorial Assistant: Katy Rank
Media Project Manager: Peter Snell
Executive Marketing Manager: Sharon M. Koch
Marketing Assistant: Melissa Owens
Managing Editor (Production): Cynthia Regan
Production Editors: Kerri M. Tomasso and Denise Culhane
Permissions Supervisor: Charles Morris
Production Manager: Arnold Vila
Manufacturing Buyer: Michelle Klein
Cover Design: Kiwi Design
Composition/Full-Service Project Management: GGS Book Services/Atlantic Highlands
Printer/Binder: Phoenix Color Corp.
Typeface: 10/12 Times Roman

To Linda,
Katherine, Sara, and Andrea

Credits and acknowledgments borrowed from other sources and reproduced, with
permission, in this textbook appear on appropriate page within text.

Pearson Education LTD.   Pearson Education Australia PTY, Limited
Pearson Education Singapore, Pte. Ltd Pearson Education North Asia Ltd
Pearson Education, Canada, Ltd   Pearson Educación de Mexico, S.A. de C.V.
Pearson Education–Japan   Pearson Education Malaysia, Pte. Ltd

10 9 8 7 6 5 4 3 2 1
ISBN 0-13-143582-5

Brief Contents

CONTENTS

PART II CLASSICAL ECONOMICS AND THE KEYNESIAN REVOLUTION   35

PREFACE

Macroeconomics emerged as a major branch of economics during the world depression of the 1930s. The severe economic problems of the time lent importance to the subject matter of macroeconomics—the behavior of the economy as a whole. A book by John Maynard Keynes, *The General Theory of Employment, Interest, and Money*, developed a framework in which to systematically consider the behavior of aggregate economic variables such as employment and output. During the two decades following World War II, Keynes's followers elaborated and extended his theories. From the first there were skeptics, perhaps most notably Milton Friedman, but Keynesian economics became the orthodox mode of thinking about macroeconomic questions.

The years since the late 1960s, however, have witnessed major challenges to Keynesian economics. In the 1970s there was increased interest in *monetarism*, the body of theory Milton Friedman and others had developed beginning in the 1940s. A new school of macroeconomic theory, the *new classical* economics also came on the scene during the 1970s. In the 1980s, Keynesian policy prescriptions came under attack from a group called the *supply-side* economists. The 1980s also witnessed the development of two new lines of macroeconomic research: the *real business cycle* theory and the *new Keynesian* economics.

Many of the post-1970 developments in macroeconomics have been the result of dissatisfaction with the Keynesian theory and the policy prescriptions that follow from it. In addition to controversy, however, the past three decades have seen what all would agree is progress in our theories of the macroeconomy. There have been significant improvements in the handling of expectations, in our understanding of labor market institutions, in accounting for the macroeconomic implications of various market structures, in the modeling of open economies, and in accounting for the ultimate sources of economic growth.

In this book I have tried to explain macroeconomics, inclusive of recent developments, in a coherent way but without glossing over the fundamental disagreements among macroeconomists on issues of both theory and policy. The major modern macroeconomic theories are presented and compared. Important areas of agreement as well as differences are discussed. An attempt is made to demonstrate that the controversies among macroeconomists center on well-defined issues that are based on theoretical differences in the underlying models.

FEATURES

Distinguishing features of the approach taken here include the following:

- An up-to-date summary of the Keynesian position, including research that has come to be called the new Keynesian economics.

- A detailed analysis of the challenges to the Keynesian position by the monetarists, new classical economists, and real business cycle theorists.
- An extensive treatment of monetary policy that considers both optimal tactics (the instrument problem) and possible optimal strategies (e.g., inflation targets). For both monetary and fiscal policy questions, policy issues are closely related to the theories we consider.
- An analysis of the post-1970 slowdown in U.S. output growth, capital formation, and growth in labor productivity. Within this context of intermediate-run growth the views of the supply-side economists and their critics are examined. Also within this context of the determinants of rates of intermediate-run economic growth, we consider whether there are signs that the productivity slowdown of the 1970s has been reversed. Is there a "new economy" developing for the new century?
- A consideration of the determinants of long-run economic growth. Both the neoclassical growth model and recent models of endogenous growth are discussed.
- Consideration of foreign exchange rate determination and the International Monetary System. Monetary and fiscal policy effects in the open economy are analyzed within the framework of the Mundell–Fleming model.

ORGANIZATION

Part I (Chapters 1–2) discusses the subject matter of macroeconomics, recent behavior of the U.S. economy, and questions of measurement. Part II (Chapters 3–9) begins our comparison of major macroeconomic models. We start with the classical system and then go on to the Keynesian model. Part III considers challenges to the Keynesian system and rebuttals to these challenges. Chapter 10 examines monetarism and the issues in the monetarist Keynesian controversy. Chapter 11 examines the monetarist view of the unemployment inflation trade-off and the *natural rate* theory, as well as the Keynesian view of the same topics. Chapter 12 presents the new classical theory with its central concepts of *rational expectations* and market clearing. In Chapter 13 two recent directions in macroeconomic research are examined. One, very strongly rooted in the classical tradition, is the real business cycle theory. The second, the new Keynesian economics, is, as its name suggests, firmly in the Keynesian tradition. Chapter 13 summarizes and compares the different models considered in Parts II and III.

Part IV considers open-economy macroeconomics. Chapter 15 focuses on exchange rate determination and the international monetary system. Chapter 16 utilizes the Mundell–Fleming model to examine the effects of monetary and fiscal policy in the open economy.

Part V deals with macroeconomic policy. Chapters 17 and 18 focus on monetary policy. Chapter 19 considers fiscal stabilization policy. Chapter 20 discusses policies to promote economic growth, many of which are also fiscal in nature.

In Part VI we go into the microeconomic foundations of some relationships employed in the models in previous chapters. Chapter 21 is a detailed analysis of consumption and investment demand. Chapter 22 considers the demand for money and other financial assets.

NEW IN THE EIGHTH EDITION

- There has been one major change in organization. Material on long-run equilibrium growth has been expanded and put as a separate chapter following the chapters on the classical economics (Chapter 5). Discussion of intermediate-run economic growth and the supply-side economics that was part of the previous chapter on growth is now a separate chapter (Chapter 20) in the section on economic policy. This change will make it easier to consider one timeframe without the other and to emphasize theoretical or policy issues.
- Many new perspectives have been added covering a large range of topics, including: labor productivity in the recent "jobless recovery," Taylor rules for monetary policy, Robert Lucas on real business cycles, the sustainability of U.S. current account deficits, and the national income accounts for England and Wales in 1688.
- Chapters on economic policy have been thoroughly updated to cover subjects such as: the Bush administration tax cuts, the recent crisis in state and local government finance, and the return of large structural federal budget deficits.
- In terms of pedagogy, I have continued the attempt made in the previous revision to simplify where possible. This was done by pruning some examples and elaborations, especially in the core chapters. None of the changes are major ones, but hopefully taken together they will make the book more student friendly. Also, a number of new questions and problems have been added.

ANCILLARIES

- *Instructor's Manual with Test Bank:* This resource manual provides the instructor with detailed chapter summaries, answers to end-of-chapter questions, and a complete test bank. For each chapter, there are 50 to 70 multiple-choice questions as well as 10 to 15 problems and essay questions. The Instructor's Manual is available for download at http://www.prenhall.com/froyen. Further resources for both students and instructors may also be found on the companion website.
- *Study Guide:* Each chapter contains a detailed overview with a tips section on equations and graphs called *Techniques in Depth*. The Study Guide also provides a self-test with 30 multiple-choice questions and 10 problems and essay questions.

ACKNOWLEDGMENTS

I am especially grateful to Sharon Erenburg, Eastern Michigan University, for extensive comments and contributions that helped in revisions for this edition as well as the previous one. Reviewers recruited by Prentice Hall also provided many useful suggestions. These reviewers are: Peter Hess, Davidson College; Brice Sutton, St. Louis University; Darryl Getter, U.S. Naval Academy; Charles R. Britton, University of Arkansas; Lara Bryant, University of North Carolina, Chapel Hill; Anthony J. Laramie, Boston College; Masha Rahnama, Texas Tech University; and Kristin A. Van Gaasbeck, University of California, Davis.

Many people have been helpful in preparing the various editions of this book. I have benefited from comments by Roger Waud, Art Benavie, Alfred Field, and Pat Conway, all from the University of North Carolina, as well as by Lawrence Davidson and Williard Witte, Indiana University; Dennis Appleyard, Davidson College; Alfred Guender, University of Canterbury; Homer Erekson, Miami University; Allin Cottrell, Wake Forest University; David Van Hoose, Baylor University; Michael Bradley, George Washington University; Art Goldsmith, Washington and Lee University; Sang Sub Lee, Freddie Mac; David Bowles, Clemson University; Michael Loy and Lawrence Ellis, Appalachian State University; and Rody Borg, Jacksonville University.

I am also grateful for editorial assistance with this revision. I wish to thank Rod Banister, David Alexander, Gladys Soto, and Katy Rank at Prentice Hall and Sandra Krausman at GGS Book Services, Atlantic Highlands.

Part

I

Introduction and Measurement

CHAPTER 1

Introduction

CHAPTER 2

Measurement of Macroeconomic Variables

*P*art I discusses the subject matter of macroeconomics, the behavior of the U.S. economy, and the measurement of macroeconomic variables. Chapter 1 defines macroeconomics and traces the macroeconomic trends in the United States since World War II. The chapter then poses some central questions in macroeconomics. Chapter 2 deals with measurement and defines the main macroeconomic aggregates. Central to this task is an examination of the U.S. national income accounts.

Chapter 1

Introduction

1.1 WHAT IS MACROECONOMICS?

This book examines the branch of economics called *macroeconomics*. The British economist Alfred Marshall defined economics as the "study of mankind in the ordinary business of life; it examines that part of individual and social action which is most closely connected with the attainment and with the use of the material requisites of well-being."[1] In macroeconomics, we study this "ordinary business of life" in the aggregate. We look at the behavior of the economy as a whole. The key variables we study include total output in the economy, the aggregate price level, employment and unemployment, interest rates, wage rates, and foreign exchange rates. The subject matter of macroeconomics includes factors that determine both the levels of these variables and how the variables change over time: the rate of growth of output, the inflation rate, changing unemployment in periods of expansion and recession, and appreciation or depreciation in foreign exchange rates.

Macroeconomics is policy oriented. It asks, to what degree can government policies affect output and employment. To what degree is inflation the result of unfortunate government policies? What government policies are *optimal* in the sense of achieving the most desirable behavior of aggregate variables, such as the level of unemployment or the inflation rate? Should government policy attempt to achieve a *target level* for foreign exchange rates?

For example, we might ask to what degree government policies were to blame for the massive unemployment during the world depression of the 1930s or for the simultaneously high unemployment and inflation of the 1970s. What role did "Reaganomics" play in the sharp decline in inflation and rise in unemployment in the early 1980s? Were government policies during the Clinton administration responsible for the simultaneously *low* levels of unemployment and inflation achieved during the late 1990s?

---

[1] Alfred Marshall, *Principles of Economics*, 8th ed. (New York: Macmillan, 1920), p. 1.

Economists disagree on policy questions. In part, the controversy over policy questions stems from differing views of the factors that determine the key variables mentioned previously. Questions of theory and policy are interrelated. Our analysis examines different macroeconomic theories and the policy conclusions that follow from those theories. It would be more satisfying to present *the* macroeconomic theory and policy prescription. Satisfying, but such a presentation would be misleading because there are fundamental differences among schools of macroeconomists. In comparing different theories, however, we see that there are substantial areas of agreement as well as disagreement. Controversy does not mean chaos. Our approach is to isolate key issues that divide macroeconomists and to explain the theoretical basis for each position.

We analyze the macroeconomic orthodoxy as it existed when the 1970s began, what is termed *Keynesian economics*. The roots of Keynesian theory as an attack on an earlier orthodoxy, *classical economics*, are explained. We then examine the challenges to the Keynesian position, theories that have come to be called *monetarism* and the *new classical economics*. Finally, we consider two recent directions in macroeconomic research. One, strongly rooted in the classical tradition, is the *real business cycle theory*. The other, the *new Keynesian theory*, is, as its name suggests, in the Keynesian tradition. How each theory explains the events from the 1970s to the present, as well as the policies each group of economists propose to provide for better future economic performance, is a central concern of our analysis.

1.2 POST-WORLD WAR II U.S. ECONOMIC PERFORMANCE

Our tasks here are to sketch the broad outline of U.S. macroeconomic performance over the post–World War II period and to suggest some central questions addressed in our later analysis.

Output

Figure 1.1 shows the growth rate of output for the United States for the years 1953–2002. The output measure in the figure is *real* **gross domestic product (GDP)**.[2] Gross domestic product measures current production of goods and services; *real* means that the measures in Figure 1.1 have been corrected for price change. The data measure growth in the quantity of goods and services produced.

gross domestic product (GDP)

a measure of all currently produced final goods and services

The data in the figure show considerable variation in GDP growth over the past five decades. During the 1960s, there was steady, relatively high growth in GDP. In all other decades, there were years of negative growth; GDP declined in at least one year.

---

[2]Gross domestic product is one of two widely reported measures of aggregate output. The other, gross national product, is introduced in Chapter 2, where the difference between the two is explained.

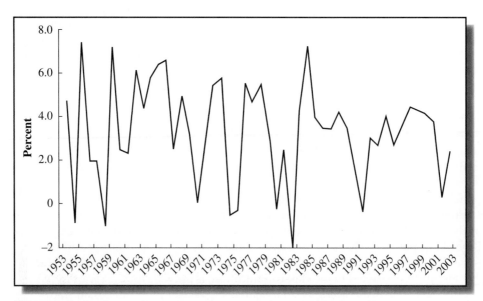

Figure 1.1 Annual Percentage Change in Real GDP, 1953–2002

Table 1.1 summarizes growth trends over these decades. The table indicates a decline of about 1 percentage point in the rate of growth of GDP during the post-1970 period. The data for the late 1990s seemed to signal a reversal of this decline but GDP growth again slowed early in the new century.

Unemployment

unemployment rate
the number of unemployed persons expressed as a percentage of the labor force

Figure 1.2 shows the U.S. **unemployment rate** for each year since 1953. The unemployment rate is the percent of the labor force that is not employed. For example, in 2003, 146.5 million people were in the labor force and 8.8 million, or 6.0 percent, of these were unemployed.

The slower output growth in the post-1970 period is reflected in rising unemployment during these years, as can also be seen from Table 1.2, which shows average unemployment rates for selected periods. In the late 1990s there seemed to be a reversal of this trend as the unemployment rate fell to a 30 year low of just under 4 percent. Then as output growth slowed after 2000, the unemployment rate rose to nearly 6 percent. Although this rate is not especially high by the standard of previous recessions, unemployment did remain high even as output growth picked up in 2003–04, causing talk of a "jobless recovery."

Table 1.1
Real GDP Growth in the United States, Average Percentage Change for Selected Periods

YEARS	PERCENT
1953–69	3.8
1970–81	2.7
1982–95	3.0
1996–99	4.0
2000–02	2.1

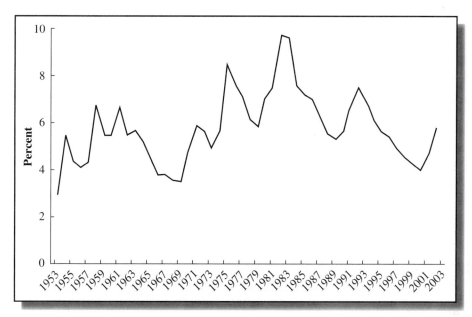

Figure 1.2 U.S. Unemployment Rate, 1953–2002

Inflation

Figure 1.3 shows the rate of **inflation** for 1953–2002. To calculate the rate of inflation, we use a **price index** that measures the aggregate (or general) price level relative to a base year. The inflation rate is then computed as the percentage rate of change in the price index over a given period. In Figure 1.3 the inflation rate is measured by the **consumer price index (CPI)**; other price indices are considered in the next chapter. The CPI measures the retail prices of a fixed "market basket" of several thousand goods and services purchased by households.

It can be seen from the figure and also from Table 1.3 that the inflation rate was low and relatively stable in the 1950s and early 1960s. In the late 1960s, an upward trend in inflation is apparent. This upward trend continued and intensified in the 1970s. The early 1980s were a period of *disinflation*, meaning a decline in the inflation rate. The inflation rate remained fairly low throughout the 1980s. There was an upward blip in the inflation rate in 1990, partly due to a sharp rise in energy prices after Iraq's invasion of oil-rich Kuwait. This was reversed as energy prices fell

inflation
a rise in the general level of prices

price index
a measure of the aggregate price level relative to a chosen base year

consumer price index (CPI)
a measure of the retail prices of a fixed "market basket" of several thousand goods and services purchased by households

Table 1.2
U.S. Unemployment Rate, Averages for Selected Periods

YEARS	PERCENT
1953–69	4.8
1970–81	6.4
1982–95	6.9
1996–99	4.7
2000–02	4.9

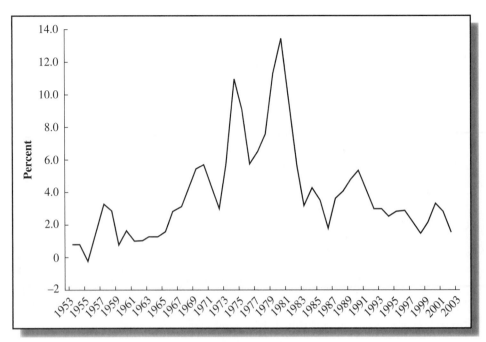

Figure 1.3 U.S. Inflation Rate, 1953–2002

with the allied victory in the Persian Gulf War in early 1991. Inflation then remained low, falling below 2 percent in 1997 and again in 2002.

Inflation and Unemployment

Figure 1.4 plots the annual unemployment rate for 1953–2002 with the annual inflation rate during that same time period. It is interesting to note that in the early portion of this period, through the late 1960s, a negative relationship between the inflation rate and unemployment rate is obvious; years of relatively high rates of inflation are years of relatively low unemployment. In the period since 1970, no such simple relationship is evident. During parts of the 1970s—for example, 1973–75—the unemployment and inflation rates both rose sharply. In the early 1980s, the negative relationship seemed to return, with unemployment rising sharply as inflation declined. Later in the 1980s, the inflation rate remained low while the

Table 1.3
U.S. Inflation Rate, Averages for Selected Periods

YEARS	PERCENT
1953–60	1.4
1961–69	2.6
1970–81	8.0
1982–95	3.8
1996–02	2.4

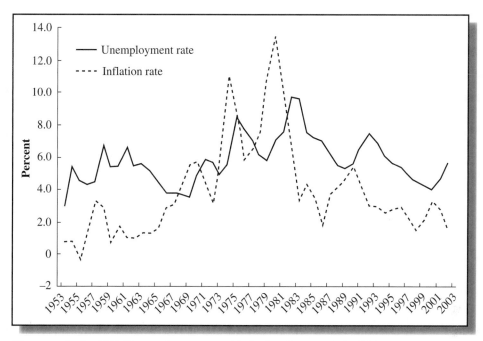

Figure 1.4 U.S. Unemployment and Inflation Rates, 1953–2002

unemployment rate steadily declined. Between 1990 and 1991, the unemployment rate rose and the inflation rate fell, but the behavior of the inflation rate appears to have been due to factors connected with the Persian Gulf War, rather than any underlying unemployment-inflation relationship. From 1992 to 1999, both the inflation and unemployment rates fell. Then beginning in 2001 unemployment rose as the inflation rate fell.

These changes in the relationship between the inflation rate and the unemployment rate can be seen in Figure 1.5. In both graphs, the inflation rate is measured on the vertical axis, and the unemployment rate is on the horizontal axis. Graph *a* is for the years 1953–69, and the negative relationship between the two variables is evident. Graph *b* is for 1970–2002, and for these years there is no apparent relationship between inflation and unemployment.

The U.S. Federal Budget and Trade Deficits

The performance of the U.S. economy over the past two decades has on average been quite good, certainly when measured against the decade of the 1970s. For much of the period, however, there has been concern over two structural imbalances: large federal budget deficits and a skyrocketing foreign trade deficit.

Figure 1.6 plots the **federal budget deficit** for the years 1953–2002. In the 1950s and 1960s, budget deficits were small, and sometimes the budget was actually in surplus. Budget deficits were somewhat larger in

federal budget deficit
federal government tax revenues minus outlays

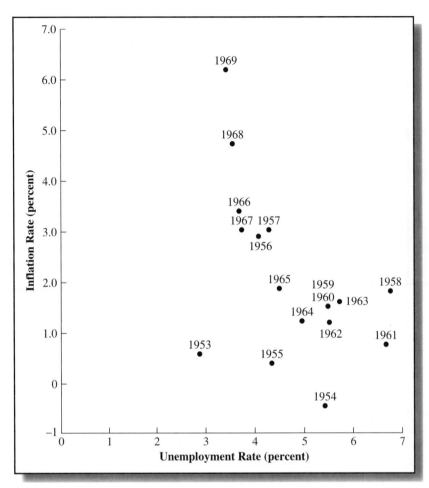

Figure 1.5a Relationship Between Inflation and Unemployment, 1953–69

the 1970s, particularly during periods of recession. It was in the 1980s and early 1990s that very large deficits emerged. For example, the deficits of 1985–86 and 1990–91 each totaled approximately 5 percent of GDP, a level unseen since World War II. Then beginning in 1993 a combination of government spending cuts and tax increases began to reduce the deficit and by 1998 the budget moved into surplus. Early in the new century, however, the budget moved dramatically back into deficit, with deficits similar in magnitude to those of the 1980s and 1990s predicted out to 2010.

trade deficit
the excess of imports over exports

Figure 1.7 shows the U.S. merchandise **trade deficit** for the years since 1953. The trade deficit is the excess of U.S. imports over exports. We began to run trade deficits in the 1970s, but as with federal budget deficits, it was in the 1980s that the trade deficit ballooned, rising to over $150 billion in 1988. The trade deficit then declined for a few years, but it began to rise in the mid-1990s, exceeding $260 billion by 1999, rising to over $300 billion in 2000, then to $500 billion by 2003.

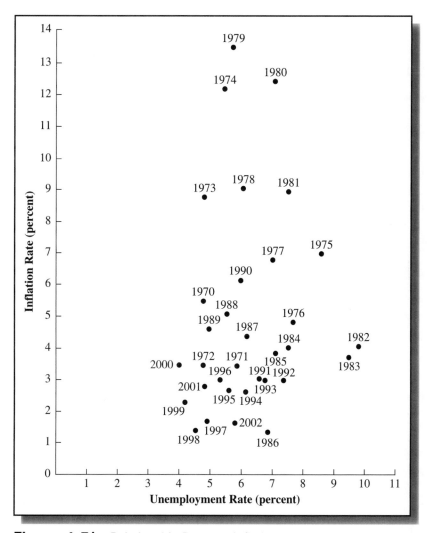

Figure 1.5*b* Relationship Between Inflation and Unemployment, 1970–2002

1.3 CENTRAL QUESTIONS IN MACROECONOMICS

The data in the foregoing tables and figures suggest some important macroeconomic questions.

Economic Instability

Why did output, employment, and inflation become more unstable in the period after 1970? In contrast, what factors explain the steady expansion of output in the 1960s or the price stability of the 1950s and 1990s? Answering those questions

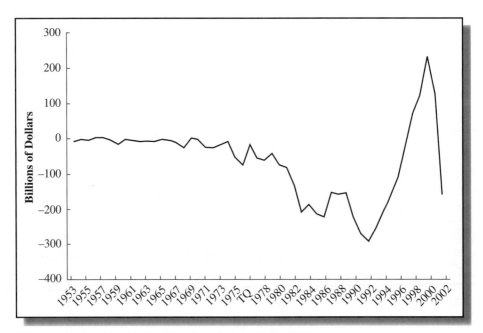

Figure 1.6 U.S. Federal Budget Deficit, 1953–2002

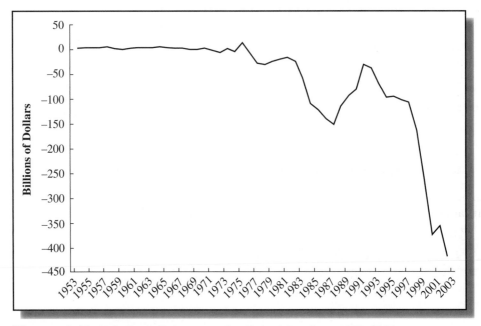

Figure 1.7 U.S. Trade Balance on Goods and Services, 1953–2002

requires a general explanation of the determinants of output, employment, and the price level over periods of several years, collectively termed the *cyclical* behavior of the economy. The macroeconomic theories in Parts II and III attempt to explain those determinants.

The Output-Inflation Relationship

What relationship exists between unemployment and inflation? Why were both the unemployment rate and the inflation rate so high during much of the 1970s? What became of the negative relationship that existed between these two variables in the 1950s and 1960s (see Figure 1.5*a*)?

The presence of both high inflation rates and high unemployment rates during the 1970s was especially puzzling to macroeconomists. The experience of the 1950s and the 1960s had led economists to explain substantial inflation as a symptom of too high a level of total demand for output. Substantial unemployment was considered the result of inadequate demand. Such an explanation is consistent with the negative relationship between inflation and unemployment during the 1953–69 period, as shown in Figure 1.5*a*. When demand was high, the inflation rate was high and unemployment was low; when demand was low, the inflation rate was low but unemployment was high. But this line of reasoning cannot explain simultaneously high unemployment and high inflation. Total demand for output cannot be both too high and too low.

The events of the 1970s caused economists to reconsider and modify earlier theories of inflation and unemployment, as we see in the analysis that follows. An important part of this reconsideration of existing theory concerns the role of total demand for output, what is termed **aggregate demand**, in determining output, employment, and inflation.

Additional questions about the relationship between inflation and unemployment were raised by the behavior of the two variables in the mid- to late 1990s. As the unemployment rate fell to low levels, many economists expected rising inflation. Instead, the inflation rate remained low. Why?

aggregate demand
the sum of the demands for current output by each of the buying sectors of the economy: households, businesses, the government, and foreign purchasers of exports

All in all, the relationship between unemployment and inflation has been much more complex in the post-1970 period than in earlier years. The macroeconomic theories we consider try to explain why.

A Growth Slowdown and Turnaround?

What explains the decline in the growth rate in output, as measured by GDP, over the years after 1970? As we saw in Table 1.1, output grew at an average annual rate of 3.8 percent for the 1953–69 period, compared with 2.7 percent for 1970–81 and 3.0 percent for 1982–95. Accompanying the decline in output growth were declines in growth in labor productivity and real wages. By the mid-1990s, many Americans, especially young people, were complaining about the shortage of good jobs.

Over much of the period, there was also the question of the shortage of jobs per se. Together with the slower growth in the post-1970 period, the unemployment rate was higher than in the 1950s or 1960s. It should be noted, however, that the rise in the average unemployment rate in the United States in the post-1970 period was much less marked than in most of Europe. In fact, by 2000, the U.S. unemployment rate had returned to below 5 percent, whereas unemployment rates in countries such as Germany, France, and Italy were still at near post–World War II record highs.

Moreover, in the United States during the late 1990s, sometimes referred to as the "roaring nineties," it seemed that the trends toward slower growth and higher unemployment were being reversed. Then, beginning in 2001 there was a recession followed by a slow recovery returning the economy to slow growth and rising unemployment. Were the late 1990s an aberration or truly the beginning of an era of more rapid economic growth?

Implications of Deficits and Surpluses

As U.S. federal budget deficits rose rapidly in the 1980s, observers speculated as to their effects. The *Financial Times* asked whether the economy was headed for a "rendezvous with disaster." Others believed that the deficit posed problems of a subtler, long-term kind more akin to "termites in the basement" than "the wolf at the door." As the budget moved into surplus in the late 1990s, the problem receded. There was actually concern about the huge projected surpluses, which implied that the national debt would be retired completely by 2012. The concern was unwarranted.

Today the concern is again with huge current and projected future deficits. Given the debt the country will pile up, how will the government commitment to the retiring baby boom generation, in terms of Social Security benefits and Medicare, be financed? Will government borrowing to finance the deficits raise interest rates and retard investment and growth?

The rapidly growing U.S. trade deficit has also been a cause of concern. The United States effectively borrows from abroad to finance the deficit. Thus, continuing deficits have been mirrored by a growing U.S. foreign debt. Many worry about the effects of the deficits and debt on the future stability of the dollar and of U.S. asset markets.

1.4 CONCLUSION

There is no shortage of questions. The chapters that follow present theories that try to explain the data discussed here and provide answers to the questions we have raised. Prior to examining these theories, in Chapter 2 we consider the measurement of the major macroeconomic variables that will be of interest.

KEY TERMS

- gross domestic product (GDP) 3
- unemployment rate 4
- inflation 5
- price index 5
- consumer price index (CPI) 5
- federal budget deficit 7
- trade deficit 8
- aggregate demand 11

REVIEW QUESTIONS AND PROBLEMS

1. What are some of the important variables that constitute the subject matter of macroeconomics? How does macroeconomics differ from microeconomics, the other major branch of economic theory?
2. Summarize the behavior of the inflation rate and unemployment rate since 1980. Did the movements of the inflation and unemployment rates over this period more closely resemble those of the 1970s or those of the 1950s and 1960s?
3. There appear to have been several shifts in the output-inflation relationship over the 1953–2002 period. Explain the nature of these shifts.
4. Using the *Economic Report of the President* or other sources for the most recent years, update the data in Tables 1.1 to 1.3.
5. Summarize the behavior of U.S. federal government budget deficits and U.S. merchandise trade deficits over the years since 1953. Does this behavior suggest a relationship between the two deficits? Perhaps at sometimes and not at others?

Chapter 2

Measurement of Macroeconomic Variables

Now what J want is, Facts. Teach these boys and girls nothing but Facts. Facts alone are wanted in life. Plant nothing else, and root out everything else. You can only form the minds of reasoning animals upon Facts; nothing else will ever be of any service to them. . . . Stick to the Facts, sir![1]

*J*n subsequent chapters we examine several macroeconomic models. These models are simplified representations of the economy that attempt to capture important factors determining aggregate variables such as output, employment, and the price level. Elements of such models are theoretical relationships among aggregative economic variables, including policy variables. As a prelude to understanding such theoretical relationships, this chapter begins by defining the real-world counterparts of the variables in our models. It also considers some accounting relationships that exist among these variables because we use these relationships to construct our theoretical models. We begin by describing the key variables measured in the national income accounts.

---

[1]Charles Dickens, *Hard Times* (New York: Norton, 1966), p. 1.

2.1 THE NATIONAL INCOME ACCOUNTS

Economists read with dismay of Presidents Hoover and then Roosevelt designing policies to combat the Great Depression of the 1930s on the basis of sketchy data such as stock price indices, freight car loadings, and incomplete indices of industrial production. Comprehensive measures of national income and output did not exist at that time. The Depression emphasized the need for such measures and led to the development of a comprehensive set of national income accounts.[2]

Like the accounts of a business, national income accounts have two sides: a product side and an income side. The product side measures production and sales. The income side measures the distribution of the proceeds from sales.

On the product side there are two widely reported measures of overall production: gross domestic product (GDP), which we looked at in Chapter 1, and gross national product (GNP). They differ in their treatment of international transactions. GNP includes earnings of U.S. corporations overseas and U.S. residents working overseas; GDP does not. Conversely, GDP includes earnings from current production in the United States that accrue to foreign residents or foreign-owned firms; GNP excludes those items. For example, profits earned in the United States by a foreign-owned firm would be included in GDP but not in GNP.

For the United States, there is little difference between these two measures because relatively few U.S. residents work abroad, and the overseas earnings of U.S. firms are about the same as the U.S. earnings of foreign firms. The difference between GNP and GDP is large for a country such as Pakistan, with a large number of residents working overseas, or Canada, where there is much more foreign investment than there is Canadian investment abroad. In 1991, the U.S. national income accountants shifted emphasis from GNP to GDP. Our explanation of the product side of the national accounts therefore concentrates on GDP. The GNP concept enters into the discussion at a later point.

On the income side of the national accounts, the central measure is national income, although we also discuss some related income concepts.

2.2 GROSS DOMESTIC PRODUCT

Gross domestic product (GDP) is a measure of all currently produced final goods and services evaluated at market prices. Some aspects of this definition require clarification.

gross domestic product (GDP)
measure of all currently produced final goods and services

---

[2]Nobel Prize–winning economists Simon Kuznets and Richard Stone played pioneering roles in the development of national income accounting. See Simon Kuznets, *National Income and Its Composition, 1919–38* (New York: National Bureau of Economic Research, 1941). During World War II, the Commerce Department took over the maintenance of the national income accounts. National income accounts data are published in the *Survey of Current Business*. A description of recent revisions in the national income accounts is "Preview of the Comprehensive NIPA Revision: Changes in Definitions and Classifications," *Survey of Current Business* (June 2003), pp. 17–34.

Currently Produced

GDP includes only currently produced goods and services. It is a flow measure of output per time period—for example, per quarter or per year—and includes only goods and services produced during this interval. Such market transactions as exchanges of previously produced houses, cars, or factories do not enter into GDP. Exchanges of assets, such as stocks and bonds, are examples of other market transactions that do not directly involve current production of goods and services and are therefore not in GDP.

Final Goods and Services

Only the production of final goods and services enters GDP. Goods used to produce other goods rather than being sold to final purchasers—what are termed intermediate goods—are not counted separately in GDP. Such goods show up in GDP because they contribute to the value of the final goods they are used to produce. Counting them separately is double counting. For example, we would not want to count the value of flour used in making bread separately, and then again when the bread is sold.

However, two types of goods used in the production process are counted in GDP. The first is currently produced **capital goods**—business plant and equipment purchases. Such capital goods are ultimately used up in the production process, but within the current period only a portion of the value of the capital good is used up in production. This portion, termed **depreciation**, can be thought of as embodied in the value of the final goods that are sold. Not including capital goods separately in GDP would be equivalent to assuming that they depreciated fully in the current time period. In GDP, the whole value of the capital good is included as a separate item. In a sense this is double counting because, as just noted, the value of depreciation is embodied in the value of final goods. At a later point we will subtract out depreciation to construct a *net* output measure.

capital goods
capital resources such as factories and machinery used to produce other goods

depreciation
portion of the capital stock that wears out each year

The other category containing intermediate goods that is part of GDP is *inventory investment*—the net change in inventories of final goods awaiting sale or of materials used in the production process. Additions to inventory stocks of final goods belong in GDP because they are currently produced output. These additions should be counted in the current period as they are added to stocks to get the timing of national product correct; they should not be counted later when they are sold to final purchasers. Inventory investment in materials similarly belongs in GDP because it also represents currently produced output whose value is not embodied in *current* sales of final output. Notice that inventory investment can be negative or positive. If final sales exceed production—for example, because of a rundown of inventories (negative inventory investment)—GDP will fall short of final sales.

Evaluated at Market Prices

GDP is the value of goods and services determined by the common measuring rod of market prices. This is the trick to being able to measure apples plus oranges plus railroad cars plus. . . . But this does exclude from GDP goods that are not sold in markets, such as the services of homemakers or the output of home gardens, as well as nonreported output from illegal activities, such as the sale of narcotics, gambling, and prostitution.[3] Also, because it is a measure of the value of output in terms of market prices, GDP, which is essentially a quantity measure, is sensitive to changes in the average price level. The same physical output will correspond to a different GDP level as the average level of market prices varies. To correct for this, in addition to computing GDP in terms of current market prices, a concept termed *nominal GDP*, the national income accountants also calculate *real GDP*, which is the value of domestic product in terms of constant prices from a base year. The way the latter calculation is made is discussed later in this chapter.

GDP can be broken down into the components shown in Table 2.1. The values of each component for selected years are also given in the table. The data in the table suggest a number of trends and patterns that will be of interest to us later.

The **consumption** component of GDP consists of the household sector's purchases of currently produced goods and services. Consumption can be further broken down into consumer durable goods (e.g., automobiles, televisions), nondurable consumption goods (e.g., foods, beverages, clothing), and consumer services (e.g., medical services, haircuts). Consumption is the largest component of GDP, comprising between 60 and 70 percent of GDP in recent years.

consumption
household sector's demand for output for current use

Table 2.1 Nominal Gross Domestic Product and Its Components, Selected Years (billions of dollars)

	Gross Domestic Product	Consumption	Investment	Government Purchases of Goods and Services	Net Exports
1929	103.7	77.5	16.5	9.4	0.4
1933	56.4	45.9	1.7	8.7	0.1
1939	92.0	67.2	9.3	14.7	0.8
1945	223.0	119.8	10.8	93.2	−0.9
1950	294.3	192.7	54.1	46.9	0.7
1960	527.4	332.3	78.9	113.8	2.4
1970	1,039.6	648.9	152.4	237.1	1.2
1980	2,795.6	1,762.9	477.9	569.7	−14.9
1990	5,803.2	3,831.5	861.7	1,181.4	−71.4
2000	9,824.6	6,683.7	1,755.4	1,751.0	−365.5
2002	10,446.2	7,303.7	1,593.2	1,972.9	−423.6

Note: Components may not sum to total due to rounding error.

Source: Bureau of Economic Analysis, Department of Commerce.

---

[3]For some services that are not actually sold on the market, the Commerce Department does try to *impute* the market value of the service and include it in GDP. An example is the services of owner-occupied houses, which the Commerce Department estimates on the basis of rental value.

investment

part of gross national product purchased by the business sector plus residential construction

The **investment** component of GDP in Table 2.1 consists of three subcomponents. The largest of these is business fixed investment. Business fixed investment consists of purchases of newly produced plant and equipment—the capital goods discussed previously. The second subcomponent of investment is residential construction investment, the building of single- and multifamily housing units. The final subcomponent of investment is inventory investment, which is the change in business inventories. As noted, inventory investment may be positive or negative. In 2002, inventory investment was $3.9 billion, meaning that there was an increase of that amount of inventories during that year.

Over the years covered by the table, investment was a volatile component of GDP, ranging from 3.0 percent of GDP in 1933 to 18.4 percent of GDP in 1950. This volatility of investment behavior has implications for the macroeconomic models considered later.

The figures in Table 2.1 are *gross* rather than net, meaning that no adjustment for depreciation has been made. The investment total in the table is gross investment, not net investment (net investment equals gross investment minus depreciation). In 2002, for example, depreciation, which is also called the capital consumption allowance, was $1,393.5 billion. Therefore, net investment was $199.7 billion (1,593.2 − 1,393.5).[4]

government purchases

goods and services that are the part of current output that goes to the government sector—the federal government as well as state and local governments

The next component of GDP in the table is **government purchases** of goods and services. This is the share of the current output bought by the government sector, which includes the federal government as well as state and local governments. It is important to note that not all government expenditures are part of gross domestic product because not all government expenditures represent a demand for currently produced goods and services. Government transfer payments to individuals (e.g., Social Security payments) and government interest payments are examples of expenditures that are not included in GDP. From the table it can be seen that government's share in GDP has increased in the post–World War II period relative to the prewar period. In 1929, government purchases of goods and services were 9.1 percent of total output. Not surprisingly, in 1945, the government component of output, swollen by the military budget during World War II, rose to 42 percent. In the postwar period, the government sector did not return to its prewar size. Government purchases of goods and services were approximately 20 percent of GDP in 1960 and 1990. Between 1990 and 2002, there was a slight decline to 18.9 percent of GDP. Trends in the size of the government budget—both purchases of goods and services and other components not included in the national income accounts—are analyzed in a later chapter when we consider *fiscal* or government budget policy.

net exports

total (gross) exports minus imports

The final component of GDP given in Table 2.1 is **net exports**. Net exports equal total (gross) exports minus imports. These items represent the direct contribution of the foreign sector to GDP. Gross exports are currently produced goods and services sold to foreign buyers. They are a part of GDP. Imports are purchases by domestic buyers of goods and services produced abroad

---

[4]In 1933, depreciation was $7.6 billion. Because gross investment was only $1.7 billion, *net* investment was negative. This means that the capital stock declined in that year because gross investment was insufficient to replace the portion of the capital stock that wore out.

GDP is the most comprehensive measure of a nation's economic activity. Policymakers use GDP figures to monitor short-run fluctuations in economic activity as well as long-run growth trends. It is worthwhile, however, to recognize important limitations of the GDP concept.

NONMARKET PRODUCTIVE ACTIVITIES ARE LEFT OUT

Because goods and services are evaluated at market prices in GDP, nonmarket production is left out. (As noted earlier, for instance, homemaker services are left out.) Intercountry comparisons of GDP overstate the gap in production between highly industrialized countries and less-developed nations, where largely agrarian nonmarket production is of greater importance.

THE UNDERGROUND ECONOMY IS LEFT OUT

Also left out of GDP are illegal forms of economic activity and legal activities that are not reported to avoid paying taxes, the *underground economy*. Gambling and the drug trade are examples of the former. Activities not reported for purposes of tax avoidance take many forms; for example, repairmen who are paid in cash for services may underreport or fail to report the income. It is hard to estimate the size of the underground economy for obvious reasons. Rough estimates for the United States range from 5 to 15 percent of GDP.

GDP IS NOT A WELFARE MEASURE

GDP measures production of goods and services; it is not a measure of welfare or even of material well-being. For one thing, GDP gives no weight to leisure. If we all began to work 60-hour weeks, GDP would increase, yet would we be better off?

GDP also fails to subtract for some welfare costs to production. For example, if production of electricity causes acid rain, and consequently water pollution and dying forests, we count the production of electricity in GDP but do not subtract the economic loss from the pollution. In fact, if the government spends money to try to clean up the pollution, we count that too!

GDP is a useful measure of the overall level of economic activity, not of welfare.

and should not be counted in GDP. Imported goods and services are, however, included in the consumption, investment, and government spending totals in GDP. Therefore, we need to subtract the value of imports to arrive at the total of domestically produced goods and services. Net exports remain as the (net) direct effect of foreign-sector transactions on GDP. As can be seen from the table, net exports were strongly negative in 2002, reflecting a large excess of imports relative to exports.

Read Perspectives 2.1.

2.3 NATIONAL INCOME

We turn now to the income side of the national accounts. In computing national income, our starting point is the GNP total, not GDP. The reason is that, as explained earlier, GNP includes income earned abroad by U.S. residents and firms but excludes earnings of foreign residents and firms from production in the United States. This is the proper starting point because we want a measure of the income of U.S. residents and firms.

To go from GDP to GNP, we add foreign earnings of U.S. residents and firms. We then subtract earnings in the United States by foreign residents and firms. This calculation results in a GNP of $10,436.7 billion compared with a GDP of $10,446.2 billion. As noted previously, there is little difference between these two production measures for the United States.

national income

sum of the earnings of all factors of production that come from current production

National income (NI) is the sum of factor earnings from current production of goods and services. Factor earnings are incomes of factors of production: land, labor, and capital. Each dollar of GNP is one dollar of final sales, and if there were no charges against GNP other than factor incomes, GNP and national income would be equal. There are, in fact, some other charges against GNP that cause national income and GNP to diverge, but the two concepts are still closely related. The adjustments required to go from GNP to national income, with figures for the year 2002, are shown in Table 2.2.

The first charge against GNP that is not included in national income is depreciation. The portion of the capital stock used up must be subtracted from final sales before national income is computed; depreciation represents a cost of production,

net national product

gross national product minus depreciation

not factor income. Making this subtraction gives us **net national product**, the net production measures referred to earlier. From this total, both indirect taxes—sales and excise taxes—and the net amount of some additional items labeled "other" in the table are subtracted to yield national income.

An indirect tax such as a sales tax represents a discrepancy between the market price of a product, which includes the tax (the amount entered in GNP), and the proceeds of the seller, from which factor incomes are paid. The "other" category in Table 2.2 includes minor adjustments for additional discrepancies between factor earnings and the market prices of items included in GNP.[5]

Table 2.3 shows the components of national income and the level of each component in 2002. Compensation of employees, which includes wages and salary payments as well as supplementary benefits, is the largest element in national income, 71.6 percent in 2002. Corporate profits were 9.4 percent of national income in that year. The next item in the table, proprietors' income, is the income of unincorporated business. In 2002, this amounted to 9.1 percent of national income. The final two items are (net) rental income of persons and net interest income, which together totaled 9.9 percent of national income.

Table 2.2
Relationship of Gross National Product and National Income, 2002 (billions of dollars)

Gross national product	10,436.7
Minus: Depreciation	1,393.5
Net national product	9,043.2
Minus: Indirect taxes and other	703.1
National income	8,340.1

Source: Bureau of Economic Analysis, Department of Commerce.

---

[5]An example of the type of item included in the "other" category is bad debts to the business sector. Because such debts are uncollected, they are not factor earnings, yet they represent sales included in GNP.

Table 2.3
Components of
National Income,
2002 (billions of
dollars)

Compensation of employees	5,969.5
Corporate profits	787.4
Proprietors' income	756.5
Rental income of persons	142.5
Net interest	684.2
	8,340.1

Source: Bureau of Economic Analysis, Department of Commerce.

2.4 PERSONAL AND DISPOSABLE PERSONAL INCOME

National income measures income earned from current production of goods and services. For some purposes, however, it is useful to have a measure of income received by *persons* regardless of source. For example, consumption expenditures by households would be influenced by income. The relevant income concept would be all income received by persons. Also, we would want a measure of income after deducting personal tax payments. **Personal income** is the national income accounts measure of the income received by persons from all sources. When we subtract personal tax payments from personal income, we get disposable (after-tax) personal income.

personal income
measure of income
received by persons from
all sources

To go from national income to personal income, we subtract elements of national income that are not received by persons and add income of persons from sources other than current production of goods and services. The necessary adjustments are shown in Table 2.4. The first items subtracted from national income are the portions

Table 2.4   Relationship of National Income, Personal Income, and Disposable Income, 2002 (billions of dollars)

National income	8,340.1
Less	
Corporate profits tax payments, undistributed profits, and valuation adjustment	353.8
Contributions to Social Security	746.5
Plus	
Transfer payments to persons	1,288.0
Personal interest income	394.4
Personal income	8,922.2
Less	
Personal taxes	1,111.9
Personal disposable income	7,810.3

Source: Bureau of Economic Analysis, Department of Commerce.

of the corporate profits item in the national income accounts that are not paid out as dividends to persons. These portions include corporate profits tax payments, undistributed profits (retained earnings), and a valuation adjustment made by the Commerce Department to correct for a distortion of reported profits figures because of inflation. The first two should require no explanation. The details of the valuation adjustment need not concern us here except to recognize that, because this adjustment was made to the corporate profits entry in the national income, but did not actually affect profits that can be paid out to persons, it must be subtracted in computing personal income. Also subtracted from national income in computing personal income are contributions to Social Security by the employer and employee. Such payroll taxes are included in the employee compensation term in national income but go to the government, not directly to persons.

The items added in going from national income to personal income are payments to persons that are not in return for current production of goods and services. The first of these are *transfer payments*. These are predominantly government transfer payments such as Social Security payments, veterans' pensions, and payments to retired federal government workers. There is also a small amount of business transfers, for example, gifts to charities. The other item added in going from national income to personal income is personal interest income—mainly, interest payments by the government to persons. Government interest payments are made on bonds previously issued by federal, state, and local governments. Personal interest payments here do not include interest payments by corporations. These are considered payments for factor services and included in national income. With these adjustments, we can calculate personal income. We then subtract personal taxes to get personal disposable income.

Table 2.5 shows how U.S. residents used their disposable income in 2002. Most of it, 93.5 percent, was spent for consumption, the household sector's purchases of goods and services. There were two other expenditures. The first was interest paid to business (installment credit and credit card interest). The second, a very small component of personal expenditures, was transfers to foreigners (e.g., gifts to foreign relatives). Personal saving is the part of personal disposable income that is not spent. In 2002, personal saving was $285.9 billion, or 3.7 percent of personal disposable income.

Read Perspectives 2.2.

Table 2.5

Disposition of Personal Disposable Income, 2002 (billions of dollars)

Personal disposable income	7,810.3
Less	
Personal consumption expenditures	7,303.7
Interest paid to business	188.4
Personal transfer payments to foreigners (net)	32.3
Personal saving	285.9

Source: Bureau of Economic Analysis, Department of Commerce.

PERSPECTIVES 2.2
National Income Accounts for England and Wales in 1688

National income accounts provide a profile of the economic life of a country. Although it is only in the post–World War II years that governments systematically kept these accounts, there are estimates from previous eras. These are of interest in charting the changes that economies have undergone.

Tables 2.6 and 2.7 show the national product and income accounts for England and Wales (combined) for the year 1688, the year of the Glorious Revolution. They were compiled by Gregory King and more than a century passed after 1688 before administrative records allowed such calculations to be repeated. In terms of completeness and consistency, his calculations remained unique until the twentieth century.[a]

From Table 2.6 we see that for England and Wales in 1688 relative to the 2002 United States economy, consumption was a much larger fraction of total national product (90 percent versus 70 percent). Investment and government spending were much smaller fractions of output. Imports and exports were each about 10 percent of GNP,

somewhat smaller than most modern economies. Still, this was an "open" economy with significant foreign trade.

The figures in Table 2.7 for the components of national income show that in England and Wales in 1688, wages and salaries comprised a much smaller fraction and rents, profits, and interest a much larger one relative to the U.S. economy today. Wages and salaries were 37 percent of national income versus a current 71 percent. Rents, profit, and interest were nearly three times higher as a share of national income in England and Wales in 1688 than in the United States today.

Overall, the picture of England and Wales in 1688 is one of an agrarian economy. It is estimated that 70 to 80 percent of the population was engaged in agriculture. But it was an open economy and there was significant investment. The picture is not one of a subsistence economy. Estimates from other sources suggest that per capita income at the time was perhaps one-eighth of that for England and Wales today.

Table 2.6 Gross National Product of England and Wales, 1688 (millions of pounds)

Consumption	46.0
Investment	1.7
Government purchases	2.4
Exports	5.1
Less imports	−4.4
Gross national product	50.8

Table 2.7 Components of National Income for England and Wales, 1688 (millions of pounds)

Wages and salaries	17.7
Rents	13.0
Profits and interest	14.7
Cottagers and paupers	2.6
National income	48.0

---

[a]The estimates in the tables are taken from Phyllis Deane and W. A. Cole, *British Economic Growth: 1688–1959* (London: Cambridge University Press, 1967, p. 2). The estimates are based on King's original manuscripts and worksheets as well as other contemporaneous sources.

2.5 SOME NATIONAL INCOME ACCOUNTING IDENTITIES

The interrelationships among gross domestic (or national) product, national income, and personal income form the basis for some accounting definitions or *identities* that are used to construct the macroeconomic models considered in later chapters. In deriving these identities, we simplify the accounting structure by ignoring a number of items discussed previously. The resulting simplified accounting structure is carried over into several of the models in the next part.

The simplifications we impose are as follows:

1. The foreign sector will be omitted. This means that we drop the net exports term from GDP (see Table 2.1) and the net foreign transfers item from personal outlays in breaking down the disposition of personal income (see Table 2.5). The foreign sector is reintroduced into our models later, when we consider questions of international macroeconomics. In excluding the foreign sector, we also exclude foreign earnings of U.S. residents and firms, as well as U.S. earnings of foreign residents and foreign-owned firms. GNP and GDP are thus equal. The terms GNP and GDP are used interchangeably except where we reintroduce the foreign sector.

2. Indirect taxes and the other discrepancies between GNP and national income are ignored (see Table 2.2). We assume that national income and national product or output are the same. *The terms* national income *and* output *are used interchangeably throughout this book.*

3. Depreciation is also ignored (except where explicitly noted). Therefore, gross and net national product are identical.

4. Several simplifications are made in the relationship between national income and personal disposable income (see Table 2.4). We assume that all corporate profits are paid out as dividends; there are no retained earnings or corporate tax payments, and there is no valuation adjustment (see Table 2.4). We assume that all taxes, including Social Security contributions, are assessed directly on households. Also, business transfer payments are ignored. Consequently, we can specify personal disposable income as national income (or output) minus tax payments (Tx) plus government transfers (Tr), which include government interest payments.[6] Letting *net* taxes (T) equal tax payments minus transfers,

$$T \equiv Tx - Tr \tag{2.1}$$

we have (personal) disposable income Y_D equal to national income (Y) minus net taxes:

$$Y_D \equiv Y - Tx + Tr \equiv Y - T$$

With these simplifications, we have the following accounting identities. Gross domestic (or national) product (Y) is defined as

$$Y \equiv C + I_r + G \tag{2.2}$$

---

[6]Government transfers exclude that part of personal interest income in Table 2.4 that is not paid to households by the government.

that is, as consumption (C) plus *realized investment* (I_r) plus government purchases of goods and services (G).[7] The subscript (r) on the investment term is included because we want to distinguish between this realized investment total that appears in the national income accounts and the *desired* level of investment spending.

From the income side of the national income accounts, again using simplifications 1 to 4 *and ignoring interest paid to business* (in Table 2.5), we have the identity

$$Y_D \equiv Y - T \equiv C + S \tag{2.3}$$

which states that, with the simplifying assumptions we have made, all disposable income, which equals national income (Y) minus *net* tax payments (T = tax payments minus transfers), goes for consumption expenditures or personal saving (S). We can write (2.3) as

$$Y \equiv C + S + T$$

and, because Y is both national income and output, we can combine (2.2) and (2.3) to write

$$C + I_r + G \equiv Y \equiv C + S + T \tag{2.4}$$

This identity states that expenditures on GDP ($C + I_r + G$) must by definition be equal to the dispositions of national income ($C + S + T$) and will be useful in the construction of the Keynesian macroeconomic model.

2.6 MEASURING PRICE CHANGES: REAL VERSUS NOMINAL GROSS DOMESTIC PRODUCT

So far the figures we have been discussing are for **nominal GDP**, which measures currently produced goods and services evaluated at current market prices. GDP is the value of currently produced goods and services measured in market prices, so it will change when the overall price level changes as well as when the actual volume of production changes. For many purposes, we want a measure of output that varies only with the quantity of goods produced. Such a measure would, for example, be most closely related to employment; more workers are not needed to produce a given volume of output simply because it is sold at a higher price.

nominal GDP
gross domestic product measured in current dollars

The GDP measure that changes only when quantities, not prices, change is termed *real GDP*. The traditional way of constructing real GDP is to measure output in terms of constant prices from a base year. Using 1996, for example, we can compute the value of GDP in 1960, 1980, or 2002 in terms of the price level or value of the

---

[7]It is important to distinguish identities such as (2.1) and (2.2), which are indicated by the three-bar symbol ($\equiv$), and equations, which are indicated with the usual equal sign (=). Identities are relationships that follow from accounting or other definitions and therefore hold for any and all values of the variables.

dollar in 1996. Changes in GDP in 1996-valued dollars then provide a measure of quantity changes between these years. The procedure of measuring real GDP in terms of prices from a base year, however, has several shortcomings, which we will discuss. Consequently, in 1995 the U.S. Bureau of Labor Statistics began to construct an alternative real GDP measure called *chain-weighted real GDP*. We consider the two procedures in turn.

Real GDP in Prices from a Base Year

Column 1 of Table 2.8 shows nominal GDP for selected years. Column 2 shows the value of real GDP as measured in 1996 prices for each of these years. In 1996, real and nominal income are the same because base-year prices are current prices. In prior years, when current prices were lower than 1996 prices, real GDP was higher than nominal GDP. Conversely, in the years after 1996, when prices were higher, nominal GDP exceeded real GDP.

Table 2.8 shows that real GDP often behaves quite differently from nominal GDP. Nominal GDP changes whenever the quantity of goods produced changes *or* when the market price of those goods changes; real GDP changes only when production changes. Therefore, when prices are changing dramatically, the movements of the two measures diverge sharply. It can be seen from the table, for example, that while nominal GDP rose by approximately $250 billion from 1973 to 1975, real GDP actually declined between those two years. Again, between 1979 and 1980, there was a rapid increase in nominal GDP but a fall in real GDP. In both periods, real GDP

Table 2.8 Nominal GDP, Real GDP, and Implicit GDP Deflator, Selected Years

	NOMINAL GDP (BILLIONS OF CURRENT DOLLARS)	REAL GDP (BILLIONS OF 1996 DOLLARS)	IMPLICIT GDP DEFLATOR ((COLUMN 1/COLUMN 2)*100)
1960	527.4	2,376.7	22.2
1970	1,039.7	3,578.0	29.1
1973	1,385.5	4,123.4	33.6
1974	1,501.0	4,099.0	36.6
1975	1,635.2	4,084.4	40.0
1979	2,566.4	4,912.1	52.2
1980	2,795.6	4,900.9	57.0
1990	5,803.2	6,707.9	86.5
1996	7,813.2	7,813.2	100.0
1998	8,781.5	8,508.9	103.2
2001	10,082.2	9,215.9	109.4
2002	10,446.2	9,439.9	110.7

Source: Bureau of Economic Analysis, Department of Commerce.

declined because the actual production level of goods and services declined. Prices, however, rose rapidly enough in these inflationary years to make nominal GDP rise.

Now consider the numbers in column 3 of Table 2.8, which gives the ratio of nominal GDP to real GDP (nominal GDP ÷ real GDP), where the ratio is multiplied by 100 (following the procedure in the national income accounts). The ratio of nominal GDP to real GDP is a measure of the value of current production in current prices (e.g., in 2002) relative to the value of the *same* goods and services in prices for the base year (1996). Because the same goods and services appear at the top and bottom, the ratio of nominal GDP to real GDP is just the ratio of the current price level of goods and services relative to the price level in the base year. It is a measure of the aggregate (or overall) price level, which in the previous chapter we called a **price index**. This index of the prices of goods and services in GDP is called the **implicit GDP deflator**.

price index
measures the aggregate price level relative to a chosen base year

We measure changes in the aggregate price level by comparing values of the implicit GDP deflator in different years. First, compare the implicit price deflator between the base year, 1996, and 2002. In the base year, real and nominal GDP are the same, and the implicit price deflator has a value of 100. From Table 2.8 we see that in 2002 the value of the implicit GDP deflator was 110.7. This means that GDP at current prices in 2002 (nominal GDP) was 10.7 percent higher than the same goods and services valued at 1996 prices. The aggregate price level, as measured by the GDP deflator, rose 10.7 percent between 1996 and 2002.

implicit GDP deflator
index of the prices of goods and services included in gross domestic product

We can also use the implicit GDP deflator to measure price changes between two years, neither of which is the base year. Between 2001 and 2002, the implicit GDP deflator rose from 109.4 to 110.7. As measured by this index, the percentage rise in the aggregate price level (or rate of inflation) between 2001 and 2002 was

$$[(110.7 - 109.4) \div 109.4] \times 100 = 1.19\%$$

Before going on, consider how the GDP deflator got its name. The ratio of nominal to real GDP is termed a *deflator* because we can divide nominal GDP by this ratio to correct for the effect of inflation on GDP—to deflate GDP. This follows because

$$\text{GDP deflator} = \frac{\text{nominal GDP}}{\text{real GDP}}$$

$$\text{real GDP} = \frac{\text{nominal GDP}}{\text{GDP deflator}}$$

Less obvious is why the adjective *implicit* is attached to the name of this price index. The GDP deflator is an implicit price index in that we first construct a quantity measure, real GDP, and then compare the movement in GDP in current and constant dollars to gauge the changes in prices. We do not *explicitly* measure the average movement in prices. Two examples of explicit price indices are considered in the next section.

Chain-Weighted Real GDP

Two problems arise when real GDP is measured using prices in a base year. One problem is that every time the base year changes, the weights given to different sectors are changed and history is rewritten. When, for example, the base year was changed from 1987 to 1996, the recessions of the 1970s took on a slightly different pattern.

A second, more serious problem involves changes in relative prices and consequent substitutions among the product categories contained in GDP. For example, in the years since 1996, the relative price of personal computers has been falling, and consumers have shifted expenditures toward computer purchases. If in calculating real GDP we use the higher 1992 prices to weight the computer component, computers will be overestimated as a GDP component.

To address these problems, the BEA (Bureau of Economic Analysis), the government agency that maintains the national income accounts, in 1995 introduced a new chain-weighted measure of real GDP. Instead of using prices in a base year as weights, the chain-weighted measure uses the average of prices in a given year and prices in the previous year. Thus, real GDP in 1997 is calculated using 1996 and 1997 prices as weights. In effect, the base moves forward each year to eliminate the problem caused by relative-price–induced substitutions such as those in the computer example. Moreover, history will not be rewritten by arbitrary changes in the base year. Once the chain-weighted measure has been calculated, it remains fixed.

The chain-weighted measures do not differ greatly from previous measures that used the base-year method. The chain-weighted measures show somewhat slower growth for more recent years and somewhat more rapid growth back in the 1960s. Thus, the growth slowdown discussed in Chapter 1 is more pronounced in the chain-weighted series.

2.7 THE CONSUMER PRICE INDEX AND THE PRODUCER PRICE INDEX

Because the GDP deflator measures changes in the prices of all currently produced goods and services, it is the most comprehensive measure of the rate of price change. Two other price indices are widely reported, however, and have their uses and advantages.

consumer price index (CPI)
measures the retail prices of a fixed "market basket" of several thousand goods and services purchased by households

The **consumer price index (CPI)** measures the retail prices of a fixed "market basket" of several thousand goods and services purchased by households. The CPI is an explicit price index in the sense that it directly measures movements in the weighted average of the prices of the goods and services in the market basket through time. The CPI is the price index most relevant to consumers because it measures the prices of only goods and services directly purchased by them. Many government pensions, including Social Security benefits, and some wage rates are indexed to the CPI, meaning they have provisions for automatic increases geared to increases in the CPI.

producer price index (PPI)
measures the wholesale prices of approximately 3000 items

Another widely reported explicit price index is the **producer price index (PPI)**, which measures the wholesale prices of approximately 3,000 items. Because items sold at the wholesale level include many raw materials and semifinished goods, movements in the producer price index signal future movements in retail prices, such as those measured in the CPI.

Figure 2.1 Three Measures of the Inflation Rate, 1967–2002

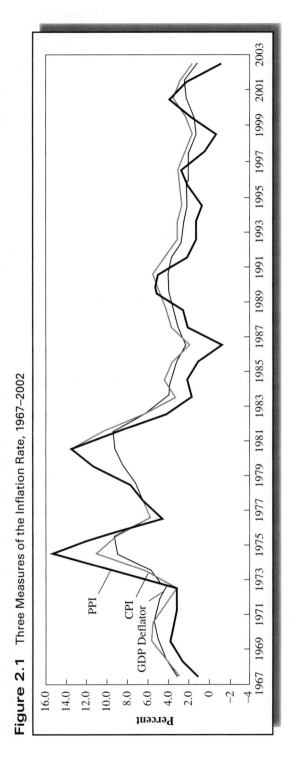

Both the consumer price index and the producer price index have the advantage of being available monthly, whereas the implicit GDP deflator is available only quarterly.

Figure 2.1 shows the annual inflation rates for the years 1967–2002 as measured by the three price indices we have discussed. In terms of broad movement in the inflation rate, the three indices show similar patterns. The acceleration of inflation in the 1973–75 and 1979–80 periods is evident in each series, as is the disinflation in the post-1980 years. There are, however, some differences in the three series that reflect their different composition. The producer price index, for example, gives a larger weight to raw materials than either of the others and therefore rose substantially more than the CPI or GDP deflator in 1973 and 1974, when agricultural and crude oil prices skyrocketed. Conversely, when these raw material prices declined during the 1982–86 period and again in 1996–97, the decline in the inflation rate registered by the producer price index was the largest among the three inflation measures.

Read Perspectives 2.3.

2.8 MEASURES OF CYCLICAL VARIATION IN OUTPUT

Most of this book focuses on short-run, or cyclical, movements in output and employment—fluctuations over periods of perhaps one to four years. In these short-run periods, fluctuations in output and employment come primarily from variations in actual output around **potential output**, where potential output is defined as the level of real output that the economy could produce at high rates of resource utilization. Such short-run movements in output consist of changes in the utilization rates of labor and capital. It is in the longer run that growth of potential output, which implies growth in the available quantity of factors of production (capital and labor), becomes an important determinant of the growth of output. We have already discussed the measurement of actual real output (GDP); what remains is to explain the measurement of potential real output and thus the deviations of *actual* GDP from *potential* GDP.

potential output
level that would be reached if productive resources (labor and capital) were being used at benchmark high levels

A problem arises in measuring potential output. What are sustainable high levels of resource allocation? In the 1960s, the President's Council of Economic Advisors, which at the time compiled the official estimates of potential output, simply estimated the level of output that corresponded to a 4 percent unemployment rate. In later years, economists and policymakers concluded, in part on the basis of the experience of the 1960s, that 4 percent was too low an unemployment rate to be sustained without a buildup of inflationary pressure. In the 1980s, an unemployment rate in the range of 5.5 to 6 percent was often put forth as a benchmark high-employment level. But in recent years, there has been less certainty that any one unemployment rate is an appropriate benchmark; by 2000, for example, the unemployment rate had dipped below 4 percent without any apparent development of inflationary pressures.

Fortunately for our current purpose of broadly describing the cyclical movements in output over recent decades, the precise measure of a benchmark high-employment level, and thus of potential output, is not important. For policy questions concerning

PERSPECTIVES 2.3
Upward Bias in the Consumer Price Index

Many economists and policymakers have argued that the CPI overstates increases in the cost of living. If such overstatement is significant, there are important consequences because many government transfer payments, the most important of which are Social Security benefits, are indexed to the CPI. An upward bias in the CPI would mean overindexation at the cost of many billions of dollars to the U.S. Treasury.

Several possible sources of upward bias have been identified. The major ones are substitution bias, quality adjustment, and new products.

SUBSTITUTION BIAS

The CPI measures prices of a *basket* of commodities, with the weights given to each category fixed in a base year. The weights are based on the Consumer Expenditure Survey and are changed approximately every 10 years. But within this period, as relative prices change, consumers shift away from items whose relative prices rise to items whose relative prices fall. Using weights from the base year will then overweight the items whose price has risen fastest and overstate inflation.

QUALITY ADJUSTMENT

The Bureau of Labor Statistics, which maintains the CPI, tries to distinguish between changes in the underlying price of goods and changes in quality. In some cases, this distinction is relatively straightforward. If the memory of a personal computer

doubles and its price rises only slightly, the price of computing services has actually fallen. But many changes in quality are hard to measure, and observers believe that the CPI understates quality changes. For example, in medicine, the results from certain surgical procedures have probably improved in recent years while at the same time the procedures have become more expensive, but it will be several years before the success rates are known and adjustment can be made for quality change.

NEW PRODUCTS

New products often decline sharply in price in the first years after they are introduced. Examples are air conditioners in the 1950s, VCRs in the 1980s, and cellular phones in the 1990s. These products, however, are not added to the market basket until years after they are introduced, so these price declines are never recorded (as of 1998, cell phones were still not in the CPI).

In 1996, an advisory commission appointed by the Senate Finance Committee estimated that, because of these distortions, the CPI overstates inflation by 1.1 percentage points per year. The commission recognized that there was uncertainty in this estimate and judged that the plausible range of the overstatement was 0.8 to 1.6 percentage points. Since 1996, there have been a number of changes in the method of computing the CPI. These changes have reduced the index's overstatement of inflation by perhaps one-half.[a]

[a]See Robert Gordon, "The Boskin Commission Report and its Aftermath" (NBER Working Paper, October 2000).

how low we might expect the unemployment rate to be reduced, the proper benchmark unemployment rate is important.

Figure 2.2 shows plots of actual and potential GDP, where potential GDP is measured simply by the trend (or average) rate of growth in GDP. Because, as discussed in Chapter 1, there was a slowdown in trend growth in the post-1970 period, we restrict our discussion to the 1970–2002 period.

The brief recession of 1970 was followed by a robust recovery that pushed output above the trend line by 1973. Then came the severe recession of 1973–74, when

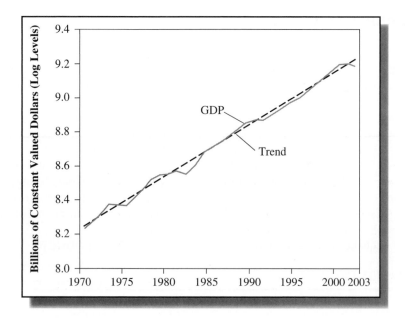

Figure 2.2
Potential (Trend) and Actual GDP

output fell nearly 5 percent below potential output. There was another sharp drop when trend output fell below potential output during the recession of 1981–82. This was followed by a long period of expansion and then a less severe recession in 1990–91. The period 1991–2000 was one of sustained expansion. GDP then declined in a recession in 2001.

Fluctuations in actual output around potential output, as illustrated in Figure 2.2, together with the associated variations in other macroeconomic aggregates, form the subject matter for much of the analysis to come.

Read Perspectives 2.4.

2.9 CONCLUSION

monetary policy
central bank's use of control of the money supply and interest rates to influence the level of economic activity

money
whatever is commonly accepted as payment in exchange for goods and services (and payment of debts and taxes)

We have now discussed the real-world counterparts to the central variables that appear in the models of the next section—with one exception. The exception is money. The quantity of money is a key variable in all the models we consider later. Control of the quantity of money through **monetary policy** is one important type of stabilization policy. The definition of money turns out to be somewhat more complicated than it seems at first glance and is best put off until later, when questions of money supply and demand are examined in detail. For now, it is adequate to use the term **money** in our models to mean the stock of currency plus "checkable" deposits (deposits on which checks may be written).

We return to questions of measurement at several later points. In addition to further discussion of the empirical definition of money (see Chapter 17), we also need to consider foreign exchange rates and measures

PERSPECTIVES 2.4
Dating Business Cycles

We have talked about recessions as periods when output falls well below potential output and unemployment rises above the high-employment benchmark, but precisely how do we measure when recessions begin and end? For example, if output begins to decline in January, rises a bit in February, and then begins a sustained decline in March, did the recession begin in January or in March? Also, the date when unemployment begins to increase may not coincide with the start of the output decline.

There is no precise way to date recessions or expansions. Judgments must be made. In the United States, the closest we come to an official dating of business cycles is that done by the Business Cycle Dating Group of the National Bureau of Economic Research (NBER), a private research organization. Table 2.9 shows the NBER dating of post–World War II U.S. business cycles. The *peak* measures the end of an expansion, and the *trough* gives the end of each recession. On average, expansions lasted just less than 50 months and recessions just over 10 months. None of the postwar recessions came near the 43-month contraction period that began the Great Depression of the 1930s. The economic expansion that began in March 1991 and ended in March 2001 was the longest of the post–World War II period (120 months).

Table 2.9 Postwar U.S. Business Cycles

PEAK	TROUGH	LENGTH (MONTHS) EXPANSION	RECESSION
November 1948	October 1949	37	11
July 1953	May 1954	45	10
August 1957	April 1958	39	8
April 1960	February 1961	24	10
December 1969	November 1970	106	11
November 1973	March 1975	36	16
January 1980	July 1980	58	6
July 1981	November 1982	12	16
July 1990	March 1991	92	8
March 2001	November 2001	120	8

of our international transactions (see Chapter 15) and go into more detail concerning the federal government budget (see Chapter 19). Some other variables (e.g., the wage rate and the interest rate) are defined as they are encountered in our analysis.

This chapter began with one of Charles Dickens's characters admonishing a teacher to "Stick to the Facts." But Conrad's Lord Jim complains "They wanted facts. Facts! They demanded facts from him, as if facts could explain anything." At this point we turn to explaining, rather than just measuring, the behavior of macroeconomic variables.

KEY TERMS

- gross domestic product (GDP) 15
- capital goods 16
- depreciation 16
- consumption 17
- investment 18
- government purchases 18
- net exports 18
- national income (NI) 20
- net national product 20

- personal income 21
- nominal GDP 25
- price index 27
- implicit GDP deflator 27
- consumer price index (CPI) 28
- producer price index (PPI) 28
- potential output 30
- monetary policy 32
- money 32

REVIEW QUESTIONS AND PROBLEMS

1. Define the term *gross domestic product*. Explain carefully which transactions in the economy are included in GDP.
2. What is the difference between GNP and GDP?
3. Define the term *national income*. Why is NI not equal to GNP?
4. Define the terms *personal income* and *personal disposable income*. Conceptually, how do these income measures differ from national income? Of what usefulness are these measures?
5. Three price indices were considered in this chapter: the GDP deflator, the consumer price index, and the producer price index. Explain the differences among these different measures of the price level.
6. Using the data in Table 2.8, compute the percentage change in the price level between 1960 and 1970; between 1973 and 1996; between 1960 and 2002.
7. Explain the concept of chain-weighted real GDP. What problems with the previous measure of real GDP led to the introduction of this new measure?

Part II

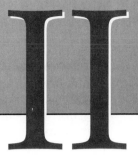

Classical Economics and the Keynesian Revolution

CHAPTER 9

The Keynesian System (IV): Aggregate Supply and Demand

The chapters in this Part begin our analysis of macroeconomic models. We start with the classical model and then turn to the Keynesian model which developed as an attack on the classical system—as the so-called Keynesian revolution. One chapter in this Part (Chapter 5) is our first consideration of long-run economic growth.

Chapter 3

Classical Macroeconomics (I): Equilibrium Output and Employment

3.1 THE STARTING POINT

The term *macroeconomics* originated in the 1930s. That decade witnessed substantial progress in the study of aggregative economic questions. The forces that determine income, employment, and prices had been receiving greater attention since the turn of the century, after a long period in which microeconomic questions dominated the field of economics. The world depression that began in 1929 added urgency to the study of macroeconomic questions. The products of this research were theories of the "business cycle" and policy prescriptions for stabilizing economic activity. One theory and set of policy conclusions swept the field and became a new orthodoxy in macroeconomic thought. The book containing this theory was *The General Theory of Employment, Interest and Money*, by John Maynard Keynes, and the process of change in economic thinking that resulted from this work has been called the Keynesian revolution. But revolution against what? What was the old orthodoxy? Keynes termed it "classical economics," and it is this body of macroeconomic thought that we study in this chapter and the next.

The ideas that formed the Keynesian revolution, as well as the evolution of these ideas in the post-Keynesian period, are central to our analysis. A prerequisite for this analysis is a knowledge of the classical system that Keynes attacked. Classical theory also plays a positive role in the later development of macroeconomics. Although many early Keynesian writers viewed the classical theory as ready for the scrap heap of out-moded ideas, overreaction subsided with time, and modern Keynesian economics contains many ideas that originated with the classical economists. The classical model also provides the starting point for challenges that have been mounted against the Keynesian theory by *monetarists, new classical economists,* and *real business cycle theorists.*

Keynes used the term *classical* to refer to virtually all economists who had written on macroeconomic questions before 1936. More conventional terminology distinguishes between two periods in the development of economic theory before 1930. The first, termed classical, is the period dominated by the work of Adam Smith (*Wealth of Nations*, 1776), David Ricardo (*Principles of Political Economy*, 1st ed., 1817), and John Stuart Mill (*Principles of Political Economy*, 1st ed., 1848). The second, termed the neoclassical period, had as its most prominent English representatives Alfred Marshall (*Principles of Economics*, 8th ed., 1920) and A. C. Pigou (*The Theory of Unemployment*, 1933). The theoretical advances distinguishing the classical and neoclassical periods were related primarily to microeconomic theory. Keynes felt that the macroeconomic theory of the two periods was homogeneous enough to be dealt with as a whole.

To classical economists, the equilibrium level of income at any time was a point of *full employment* or, in terms of the variables described in Chapter 2, a point when actual output was equal to potential output. Equilibrium for a variable refers to a state in which all the forces acting on that variable are in balance and, consequently, there is no tendency for the given variable to move from that point. It was an important tenet of classical economists that only full-employment points could be positions of even short-run equilibrium. Away from full employment, classical economists assumed that forces not in balance were acting to bring output to the full-employment level. Classical equilibrium economics examined the factors that determined the level of full-employment output along with the associated levels of other important aggregates, such as employment, prices, wages, and interest rates.

3.2 THE CLASSICAL REVOLUTION

Classical economics emerged as a revolution against an earlier orthodoxy, a body of economic doctrines known as mercantilism. Mercantilist thought was associated with the rise of the nation-state in Europe during the sixteenth and seventeenth centuries. Two tenets of mercantilism were (1) bullionism, a belief that the wealth and power of a nation were determined by its stock of precious metals, and (2) the belief in the need for state action to direct the development of the capitalist system.

Adherence to bullionism led countries to attempt to secure an excess of exports over imports in order to earn gold and silver through foreign trade. Methods used to secure this favorable balance of trade included export subsidies, import duties, and development of colonies to provide export markets. State action was assumed to be necessary to cause the developing capitalist system to act in line with the interests of the state. Foreign trade was carefully regulated, and the export of bullion was prohibited to serve the ends of bullionism. The use of state action was also advocated on a broader front to develop home industry, to reduce consumption of imported goods, and to develop both human and natural resources.

In contrast to the mercantilists, classical economists emphasized the importance of *real* factors in determining the "wealth of nations" and stressed the optimizing tendencies of the free market in the absence of state control. Classical analysis was primarily *real* analysis; the growth of an economy was the result of increased stocks of the factors of production and advances in techniques of production. Money played a role only in facilitating transactions as a *means of exchange*. Most *real* questions in economics could be answered without analyzing the role of money. Classical economists mistrusted government and stressed the harmony of individual and national interest when the market was left unfettered by government regulations, except those necessary to see that the market remained competitive. Both of these aspects of classical economics—the stress on real factors and the belief in the efficacy of the free-market mechanism—developed in the course of controversies over long-run questions, concerns about the determinants of economic development. These classical positions on long-run issues were, however, important in shaping classical economists' views on short-run questions.

The attack on bullionism led classical economists to stress that money had no intrinsic value. Money was held only for the sake of the goods it could purchase. Classical economists focused on the role of money as a means of exchange. Another role money had played in the mercantilist view was as a spur to economic activity. In the short run, mercantilists argued, an increase in the quantity of money would lead to an increase in demand for commodities and would stimulate production and employment. For classical economists to ascribe this role to money in determining real variables, even in the short run, was dangerous in light of their deemphasis of the importance of money.

The classical attack on the mercantilist view of the need for state action to regulate the capitalist system also had implications for short-run macroeconomic analysis. One role for state action in the mercantilist view was to ensure that markets existed for all goods produced. Consumption, both domestic and foreign, must be encouraged to the extent that production advanced. The classical response is stated by John Stuart Mill:

> In opposition to these palpable absurdities it was triumphantly established by political economists that consumption never needs encouragement.[1]

As in other areas, classical economists felt that the free-market mechanism would work to provide markets for any goods that were produced: "The legislator, therefore, need not give himself any concern about consumption."[2] The classical doctrine was that, in the aggregate, production of a given quantity of output will generate sufficient demand for that output; there could never be a "want of buyers for all commodities."[3] Consequently, classical economists gave little explicit attention to factors that determine the overall demand for commodities, which in Chapter 1 we termed **aggregate demand**, or to policies that regulate aggregate demand.

Thus, two features of the classical analysis arose as part of the attack on mercantilism:

aggregate demand
sum of the demands for current output by each of the buying sectors of the economy: households, businesses, the government, and foreign purchasers

1. Classical economics stressed the role of real as opposed to monetary factors in determining real variables such as output and employment. Money had a role in the economy only as a means of exchange.
2. Classical economics stressed the self-adjusting tendencies of the economy. Government policies to ensure an adequate demand for output were considered by classical economists to be unnecessary and generally harmful.

---

[1] J. S. Mill, "On the Influence of Consumption on Production," in *Essays on Economics and Society*, vol. 4 of *Collected Works* (Toronto: University of Toronto Press, 1967), p. 263.
[2] Ibid., p. 263.
[3] Ibid., p. 276.

We turn now to the model constructed by classical economists to support these positions.

3.3 PRODUCTION

production function
summarizes the relationship between total inputs and total outputs assuming a given technology

A central relationship in the classical model is the aggregate **production function**. The production function, which is based on the technology of individual firms, is a relationship between the level of output and the level of factor inputs. For each level of inputs, the production function shows the resulting level of output and can be written as

$$Y = F(\overline{K}, N) \tag{3.1}$$

where Y is real output, $\overline{K}$ the stock of capital (plant and equipment), and N the quantity of the homogeneous labor input.[4] For the short run, the stock of capital is assumed to be fixed, as indicated by the bar over the symbol for capital. The state of technology and the population are also assumed to be constant over the period considered. For this short-run period, output varies solely with variations in the labor input (N) drawn from the fixed population.

The numbers in Table 3.1 illustrate the fundamental relationship between a change in labor input and the resulting change in output, holding the capital stock constant, $\overline{K}$. The values from Table 3.1 are plotted in Figures 3.1a and 3.1b.

In Figure 3.1a, the production function, $Y = F(\overline{K}, N)$, indicates the output that would be produced by the efficient utilization of each level of labor input. As drawn, the production function has several characteristics. At low levels of labor input, the function is a straight line. The slope of the line gives the increase in output for a given increment in labor input, so this straight-line (constant-slope) portion of the production function exhibits constant returns to scale. For very low levels of labor utilization, it might be presumed that additional workers could be applied to a given amount of plant and equipment without a fall in the productivity of the last worker hired. For the most part, however, we consider situations where adding additional labor will result in increased total output, but where the size of the increases to output declines as more labor is employed. This portion of the production function exhibits diminishing returns to scale. Negative returns to scale occur when additional labor input results in decreased total output. Firms would not operate on this portion of the production function, since hiring additional labor results in a decrease in total output.

marginal product of labor (MPN)
the addition to total output due to the addition of a unit of labor (the quantity of other inputs being held constant)

In Figure 3.1b, we plot the change in output given a change in labor input. This is the **marginal product of labor (MPN)**. The marginal product of labor is the slope of the production function ($\Delta Y / \Delta N$) in Figure 3.1a.[5]

---

[4]Functional notation such as that used in (3.1) will be used at numerous points in our analysis. In each case, such equations mean that the function involved (in this case F) is a relationship that determines a unique value of the left-hand variable (in this case Y) for each combination of the levels of the *arguments* of the function (in this case K and N).

[5]The differencing symbol Δ (delta) indicates the change in the variable it precedes (e.g., ΔY is the change in Y).

Table 3.1 The Relationship Between Output, Fixed Capital Stock, and Labor

	N = Labor	Y = Output	$\Delta Y/\Delta N$ = MPN	
A	0	0		
B	1	10	10	Constant returns
C	2	20	10	
D	3	28	8	Diminishing returns
E	4	33	5	
F	5	34	1	
G	6	32	−2	Negative returns

On line A,   0 units of labor (N) are hired, and total output (Y) is 0.

On line B,   1 unit of labor (N) is hired, and total output (Y) is 10 units.

$\Delta Y/\Delta N$ the change in output given a change in labor, is 10/1 = 10.

This is the marginal product of labor. The MPN of worker 1 is 10, since output increased by 10 units when labor increased by 1 unit.

On line C,   2 workers are hired, and total output (Y) is 20 units.

$\Delta Y/\Delta N$ the change in output given a change in labor, is (20 − 10)/1 = 10.

The marginal product of labor of worker 2 is the same as the marginal product of labor of worker 1, since output increased by 10 units when labor increased by one unit.

This is the area of constant returns to scale.

On line D,   3 workers are hired, and total output (Y) is 28 units.

$\Delta Y/\Delta N$ the change in output given a change in labor, is (28 − 20)/1 = 8.

The MPN of worker 3 is 8 units. The increase in output when worker 3 was hired is less than the marginal product of worker 2.

This is the area of diminishing returns to scale. In this area on the production function, total output increases as an additional unit of labor is hired, but marginal output diminishes.

Output increases at a diminishing rate due to the law of diminishing returns.

This law states that as variable inputs (in this case, homogeneous labor) are added to a fixed input (the capital stock, which is being held constant), beyond some point, the amount by which output increases will diminish.

On line E,   4 workers are hired, and output (Y) is 33 units. The MPN of worker 4 is 5 units.

On line F,   5 workers are hired, and output (Y) is 34 units. The MPN of worker 5 is 1 unit.

On line G,   6 workers are hired, and output (Y) is 32 units. This is the area of negative returns. The MPN of worker 6 is negative (−2). At this point, both total output and marginal output decreased. Firms would not hire in the area of negative returns to scale.

In the range of constant returns to scale, as N increases, the slope of the line is flat. As more workers are hired, however, the slope becomes negative, indicating that while the marginal product of each worker hired is positive, it is less than the marginal product of the previous worker. This area represents diminishing returns to scale. The marginal product of the additional worker is below the horizontal axis in the area of negative returns to scale.

The short-run production function plotted in Figure 3.1a is a technological relationship that determines the level of output given the level of labor input (employment). The capital stock, along with the existing level of technology and skill level of the

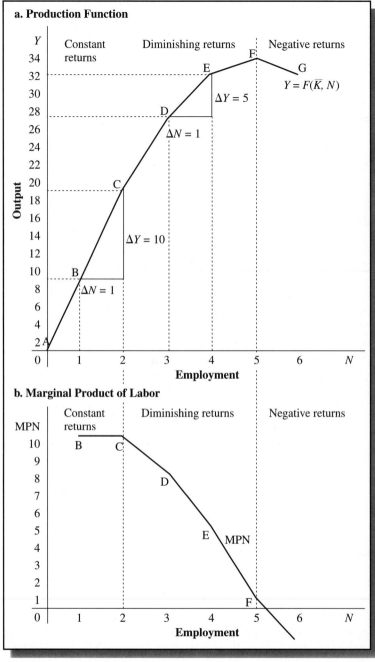

Figure 3.1 Production Function and Marginal Product of Labor Curves

workforce, is being held constant. Classical economists assumed that the quantity of labor employed would be determined by the forces of demand and supply in the labor market, as explained in the next section.

3.4 EMPLOYMENT

The hallmark of classical labor market analysis is the assumption that the market works well. Firms and individual workers optimize. They have perfect information about relevant prices. There are no barriers to the adjustment of money wages; the market *clears*.

Labor Demand

On the demand side of the market, purchasers of labor services are firms that produce commodities. To see how the aggregate demand for labor is determined, we begin by considering the demand for labor on the part of an individual firm, denoted the ith firm. In the classical model, perfect competitors are firms that choose their output level so as to maximize profits. In the short run, output is varied solely by changing the labor input so that choice of the level of output and quantity of the labor input are one decision. The perfectly competitive firm will increase output until the marginal cost of producing a unit of output is equal to the marginal revenue received from its sale. For the perfectly competitive firm, marginal revenue is equal to product price (P).[6] Because labor is the only variable factor of production, the marginal cost of each additional unit of output is the marginal labor cost. Marginal labor cost equals the money wage divided by the number of units of output produced by the additional unit of labor. We defined the units of output produced by the incremental unit of labor employed as the marginal product of labor (MPN). Thus marginal cost for the ith firm (MC_i) is equal to the money wage (W) divided by the marginal product of labor for that firm (MPN_i).[7]

$$MC_i = \frac{W}{MPN_i} \tag{3.2}$$

---

[6]A perfectly competitive firm faces a horizontal product demand curve. By assumption, the firm is so small a portion of the market that its increase in output can be sold without depressing product price. The analysis could be reformulated for the firm facing a downward-sloping demand curve without substantially changing the conclusions that we reach in this chapter. The question of whether firms are in fact perfect competitors does, however, have important implications at future points in our analysis.

[7]The i subscript does not appear on the price or wage variables because these are uniform across firms. The marginal product of labor for each firm (MPN_i) is derived from the production function for each firm, assumed to be identical over all firms; that is,

$$Y_i = F(\overline{K}_i, N_i)$$

for each firm.

The condition for short-run profit maximization in the purely competitive market is:

$$P = MC_i \qquad\qquad (3.2a)$$

Substituting the expression for marginal cost (MC) from (3.2) into (3.2a) shows the short-run profit-maximizing position for the firm buying labor in the market for inputs:

$$P = W/MPN_i \qquad\qquad (3.3)$$

In the input market, firms maximize profits by hiring labor services up to the point where MR = MC; in this market, where $P = W/MPN_i$, multiplying both sides of equation (3.3) by MPN and dividing both sides by P gives the expression:

$$\frac{W}{P} = MPN_i \qquad\qquad (3.4)$$

The profit maximization condition in (3.4) can be explained as follows: The firm will hire up to the point where the additional output obtained by hiring one more worker (MPN) is just equal to the real wage (W/P) paid to hire that worker.

The condition for profit maximization in equation (3.4) is illustrated in Figure 3.2. The demand for labor schedule for the firm, plotted against the real wage, is the marginal product of labor schedule. The labor demand curve is downward-sloping due to the law of diminishing returns. In Table 3.2, using a product price of $1, the data from Table 3.1 are used to indicate how much labor the firm will hire. At a real wage such as $8 (e.g., a money wage of $8 and a product price of $1), the firm will hire 3 workers. At a quantity of labor below 3, say 2, the marginal product of labor (10) exceeds the

Figure 3.2 Labor Demand for a Firm in Real Terms

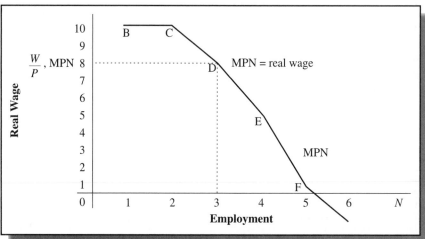

The condition for profit maximization is met at the point where the real wage (W/P) is equated with the marginal product of labor (MPN), as shown in equation (3.4). If the real wage is $8, then the firm will maximize profits by hiring 3 workers, since the marginal product of labor, (MPN), is 8. This is shown at point D on the graph of the demand for labor, MPN. In order to get the firm to hire more labor, the real wage must fall since the additional output produced by each additional worker is declining.

Table 3.2 Profit-Maximizing Position of a Firm Hiring Labor

	$N = $ LABOR	$Y = $ OUTPUT	MPN	$P = $ PRICE
A	0	0		
B	1	10	10	$1
C	2	20	10	$1
D	**3**	**28**	**8**	**$1**
E	4	33	5	$1
F	5	34	1	$1
G	6	32	−2	$1

The condition for profit maximization is met at the point where the real wage (W/P) is equated with the marginal product of labor (MPN), as shown in equation (3.4). If the real wage is $8, then the firm will maximize profits by hiring 3 workers, since the real wage of the third worker is $8 and the marginal product of the third worker is 8 units. This is shown in line D, which is in bold.

real wage (8.0). The payment to the worker in real terms is less than the real product produced. Profits will be increased by hiring additional units of labor. Alternatively, at quantities of labor input above 3, if the real wage is $8, the real wage is above the marginal product of labor. The payment to labor exceeds the real product of the marginal worker, and marginal cost exceeds product price. The firm will reduce labor to increase profit.

Thus, the profit-maximizing quantity of labor demanded by a firm at each level of the real wage is given by the quantity of labor input that equates the real wage and the marginal product of labor. The marginal product curve is the firm's demand curve for labor. The implication is that labor demand depends inversely on the level of the real wage. The labor demand curve is downward-sloping due to the law of diminishing returns. The higher the real wage, for example, the lower the level of labor input that will equate the real wage to the marginal product of labor. In Figure 3.2, if the wage were $5, instead of $8, labor demand would be 4 instead of 3. The demand curve for labor is an economy-wide aggregation of the individual firms' demand curves. For each real wage, this curve will give the sum of the quantities of labor input demanded by the firms in the economy. We write this aggregate labor demand function (N^d) as

$$N^d = f\left(\frac{W}{P}\right)$$

$$(-)$$

(3.5)

where in the aggregate, as with individual firms, an increase in the real wage lowers labor demand.

Labor Supply

The last relationship necessary for determining employment and output in the classical system is the labor supply curve. Labor services are supplied by individual workers in the economy. Classical economists assumed that the individual attempts to maximize utility (or satisfaction). The level of utility depends positively on both real income, which gives the individual a command over goods and services, and leisure. There is, however, a trade-off between the two goals because income is increased by work that reduces available leisure time.

Consider, for example, how individual j allocates one 24-hour period between leisure hours and hours worked: (N_j^s), is the individual's supply of labor. Figure 3.3 illustrates the choice facing the individual. On the horizontal axis, we measure hours of leisure per day. The maximum, of course, is 24 hours. The horizontal intercept, where the individual chooses no labor and all leisure, is 24. The number of hours worked are, therefore, 24 minus the number of hours of leisure selected. Real income is measured on the vertical axis and is equal to the real wage, W/P, multiplied by the number of hours the individual works. Each vertical intercept is the real wage multiplied by 24 hours in the day, which would occur if the individual chose all labor and zero leisure—i.e., $(W/P \cdot 24)$. The curved lines in the graph (labeled U_1, U_2, U_3) are indifference curves. Points along one of these curves are combinations of income and leisure that give equal satisfaction to the individual; hence, the person is indifferent as to which point along a given curve is selected. The slope of the indifference curve gives the rate at which the individual is willing to trade off leisure for income—that is, the increase in income the person would have to receive to be just as well off after giving up a unit of leisure. In fact, the cost of choosing each hour of leisure is the real wage, W/P, since the individual is choosing not to work for each hour of leisure. In addition, all points along U_2, for example, yield greater satisfaction to the individual than any point on U_1, since any point on an indifference curve that sits farther to the right indicates a larger income, given leisure (or the same number of hours worked). Therefore, the individual attempts to achieve the "northern-most" possible indifference curve. The higher the real wage, the higher the satisfaction the individual can select (represented by an indifference curve that sits farther to the right).

The straight-line rays originating at the point of 24 hours on the horizontal axis give the budget lines facing the individual. Starting from 24 hours (no work, all leisure), the individual can trade off leisure for income at a rate equal to the hourly real wage, W/P. The slope of the budget line is the real wage. The higher the real wage, the steeper the budget line, reflecting the fact that at a higher real wage, an individual who increases hours of work by one unit (moves one unit to the left along the horizontal axis) will receive a larger increment of income (move farther up the vertical axis along the budget line) than he or she would have received at the lower real wage. Three budget lines, corresponding to real wage rates of 2.0, 3.0, and 4.0, are shown in Figure 3.3a. Notice that at a higher real wage, the individual can choose an indifference curve that yields greater satisfaction.

In Figure 3.3b, we construct the labor supply curve for the jth individual. This supply curve consists of points such as A, B, and C from Figure 3.3a, giving the amount of labor the individual will supply at each real wage. This aggregate labor supply curve can be written as:

$$N^s = g\left(\frac{W}{P}\right)$$

$$(+)$$

(3.6)

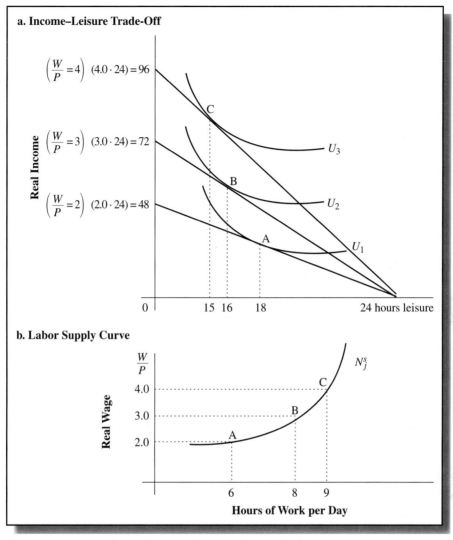

a. Income–Leisure Trade-Off

$\left(\dfrac{W}{P}=4\right)$ $(4.0 \cdot 24) = 96$

$\left(\dfrac{W}{P}=3\right)$ $(3.0 \cdot 24) = 72$

$\left(\dfrac{W}{P}=2\right)$ $(2.0 \cdot 24) = 48$

Real Income

C

B

A

U_3

U_2

U_1

0   15 16   18   24 hours leisure

b. Labor Supply Curve

$\dfrac{W}{P}$

N_j^s

Real Wage

4.0 ---------------------------- C

3.0 ----------------------- B

2.0 --------------- A

6   8   9

Hours of Work per Day

Figure 3.3 Individual Labor Supply Decision

Part *a* depicts the individual's labor–leisure choice. The individual will supply labor (N_j^s) up to the point where the rate at which labor may be traded for leisure in the marketplace, which is given by the real wage (W/P), is equated with the rate at which the individual is willing to trade labor (give up leisure) in return for income, which is measured by the slope of the individual's indifference curves (U_1, U_2, U_3). At a real wage of 2.0, the individual will choose 18 hours of leisure, point A on the Income–Leisure trade-off graph. Hours of work chosen will then be 6 (24 hours in the day − 18 hours of leisure). This is shown at point A on the labor supply curve. At a real wage of 3.0, the individual will choose 16 hours of leisure, point B on the Income–Leisure trade-off graph. Hours of work chosen will then be 8 (24 hours in the day − 16 hours of leisure). This is shown at point B on the labor supply curve. At a real wage of 4.0, the individual will choose 15 hours of leisure, point C on the Income–Leisure trade-off graph. Hours of work chosen will then be 9 (24 hours in the day − 15 hours of leisure). This is shown at point C on the labor supply curve.

Two features of the classical labor supply theory require further comment. First, note that the wage variable is the real wage. Labor supply is determined by the real wage, not the money wage. The worker receives utility ultimately from consumption, and in making the labor–leisure decision, the individual is concerned with the command over goods and services received for a unit of labor. For example, starting at point C on the income–leisure trade-off graph: If the money wage is $4 and the price is 1.0, the real wage is $4 $\left(\frac{4}{1}\right)$ and the individual will choose 15 hours of leisure and work 9 hours (point C on the labor supply curve). If the money wage is still $4, but the price is now 2.0, the individual's real wage is $2 $\left(\frac{4}{2}\right)$. The individual will now select point A on the income–leisure trade-off graph, choosing 18 hours of leisure. Hours of work decrease to 6 (24 − 18), which is point A on the labor supply curve. Clearly, as the *real wage increases* (decreases), leisure decreases (increases) and *hours of work increase* (decrease). This is the significance of equation (3.6). Since the real wage (W/P) is measured along the vertical axis on the labor supply curve, if either the money wage or price (or both) change, the number of hours worked are determined by moving along the labor supply curve.

Second, by the construction of Figure 3.3, the labor supply curve is positively sloped; more labor is assumed to be supplied at higher real wage rates. This relation reflects the fact that a higher real wage rate means a higher price for leisure in terms of forgone income. At this higher price, we assume that the worker will choose less leisure. This effect is analogous to the "substitution effect" in the theory of consumer demand. There is another effect: the equivalent of the "income effect" in consumer demand theory. As the real wage increases, the worker is able to achieve a higher level of real income. At higher levels of real income, leisure may become more desirable relative to further increments in income. With successive increases in the real wage, a point may be reached at which the worker chooses to supply less labor as the real wage increases and consumes more leisure. At this point, the income effect outweighs the substitution effect; the labor supply curve assumes a negative slope and bends back toward the vertical axis. Almost certainly, at extremely high wage rates, we would reach a backward-bending portion of the labor supply curve, and perhaps wage rates need not be so "extremely" high. Although the empirical evidence on this question is inconclusive, we will assume that for wage rates that have been observed in industrialized nations, the aggregate labor supply curve does have a positive slope; the substitution effect outweighs the income effect.

3.5 EQUILIBRIUM OUTPUT AND EMPLOYMENT

So far, the following relationships have been derived:

$$Y = F(\overline{K}, N) \text{ (aggregate production function)} \qquad (3.1)$$

$$N^d = f\left(\frac{W}{P}\right) \text{ (labor demand schedule)} \qquad (3.5)$$

$$N^s = g\left(\frac{W}{P}\right) \text{ (labor supply schedule)} \qquad (3.6)$$

These relationships, together with the equilibrium condition for the labor market,

$$N^s = N^d \qquad \qquad \text{(3.7)}$$

determine output, employment, and the real wage in the classical system. In common terminology, output, employment, and the real wage are designated as the *endogenous variables* in the model to this point, where an endogenous variable is one that is determined within the model.

Equilibrium within the classical model is illustrated in Figure 3.4. Graph *a* shows the determination of the equilibrium levels of employment (N_0) and the real wage $(W/P)_0$ at the point of intersection between the aggregate labor demand and labor supply curves. This equilibrium level of labor input (N_0) results in an equilibrium level of output (Y_0) given by the production function, as shown in Figure 3.4*b*.

The Determinants of Output and Employment

We now consider which factors are the ultimate determinants of output and employment in the classical theory. What are the *exogenous variables* that, when changed, in turn cause changes in output and employment, where exogenous variables are those determined outside the model? In the classical model, the factors that determine output and employment are those factors that determine the positions of the labor supply and demand curves and the position of the aggregate production function.

The production function is shifted by technical change that alters the amount of output forthcoming for given input levels. As graphed in Figure 3.4*b*, the production function also shifts as the capital stock changes over time. The labor demand curve is the marginal product of labor curve, the slope of the production function. Consequently, the position of the labor demand curve will shift if the productivity of labor changes because of technical change or capital formation. From the derivation of the labor supply curve, one can see that this relationship would change as the size of the labor force changes. Population growth would, for example, shift the labor supply curve out to the right. The labor supply curve would also shift with changes in individuals' preferences regarding labor–leisure trade-offs (i.e., U_1, U_2, U_3 in Figure 3.3*a*).

A common feature of the factors determining output in the classical model is that all are variables affecting the supply side of the market for output—the amount firms choose to produce. *In the classical model, the levels of output and employment are determined solely by supply factors.*

Because the supply-determined nature of output and employment is a crucial feature of the classical system, it is worthwhile to demonstrate this property more formally. To do so, we further consider the properties of the labor supply and demand functions just discussed. Figure 3.5*a* reproduces the aggregate supply and demand curves for labor. Figure 3.5*b* plots labor supply and labor demand as functions of the money wage (W). We first consider the form of each of the latter relationships. For labor supply, we can draw a positively sloped curve such as $N^s(P_1)$, which gives the amount of labor supplied for each value of the money wage, *given that the price level is P_1*. The curve is upward-sloping because at the given price level a higher money wage is a higher real wage. Workers are interested in the real wage, so each

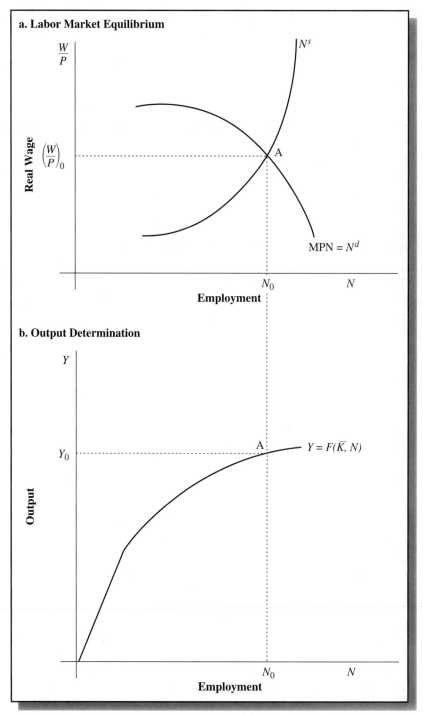

Figure 3.4 Classical Output and Employment Theory

Part a depicts labor market equilibrium at real wage $(W/P)_0$ at equilibrium point A. In the aggregate, labor supply equals labor demand, $N^d = N^s$. Equilibrium employment is N_0. Substitution of equilibrium employment into the production function in part b, determines equilibrium aggregate output, Y_0 at point A.

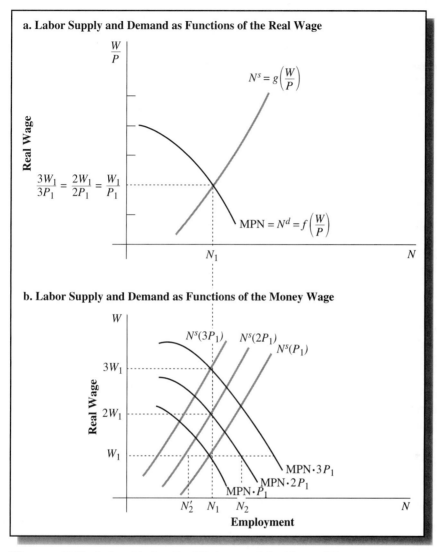

a. Labor Supply and Demand as Functions of the Real Wage

$$N^s = g\left(\frac{W}{P}\right)$$

$$\frac{3W_1}{3P_1} = \frac{2W_1}{2P_1} = \frac{W_1}{P_1}$$

$$MPN = N^d = f\left(\frac{W}{P}\right)$$

N_1

N

b. Labor Supply and Demand as Functions of the Money Wage

$N^s(3P_1)$ $N^s(2P_1)$ $N^s(P_1)$

$3W_1$

$2W_1$

W_1

$MPN \cdot 3P_1$

$MPN \cdot 2P_1$

$MPN \cdot P_1$

N_2' N_1 N_2

N

Employment

Figure 3.5 Labor Market Equilibrium and the Money Wage

Part *a* shows the determination of equilibrium employment (at N_1) where labor supply equals labor demand. In part *b* labor supply and demand are plotted as functions of the money wage. Increases in the price level (from P_1 to $2P_1$, then to $3P_1$) shift the labor supply and demand schedules upward proportionately. The money wage rises proportionately with the price level (from W_1 to $2W_1$, then to $3W_1$). The real wage and level of employment are unchanged.

price level will have a different curve. For a given money wage each price level will mean a different real wage and, hence, a different amount of labor supplied. At a price level of $2P_1$, or twice that of P_1, the labor supply curve in Figure 3.5*b* shifts to $N^s(2P_1)$; less labor is supplied for any money wage because at the higher price level a given money wage corresponds to a lower real wage. A rise in the price level shifts the labor supply curve (plotted against the money wage) upward to the left. That the individual worker is interested *only* in the real wage can be seen from the fact that the same level of labor (N_1) is supplied at a money wage of W_1 and a price level of P_1 (real wage W_1/P_1) as at money wage and price combinations of $2W_1, 2P_1$, or $3W_1, 3P_1$ (real wage = W_1/P_1 at both points). *Equiproportional increases (or decreases) in both money wages and the price level leave the quantity of labor supplied unchanged.*

Now consider the labor demand curve plotted against the money wage, where in Figure 3.5 we use the fact that the labor demand [$f(W/P)$] and marginal product of labor (MPN) schedules are equivalent. Recall that the condition met at all points along the labor demand curve is

$$\frac{W}{P} = \text{MPN} \qquad (3.8)$$

If we want to know the quantity of labor that will be demanded at any money wage, as was the case for the quantity supplied, the answer depends on the price level. Given the money wage, the firm will choose the level of employment at which

$$W = \text{MPN} \cdot P \qquad (3.9)$$

At successively higher price levels ($P_1, 2P_1, 3P_1$) the labor demand curve plotted against the money wage shifts to the right (from $\text{MPN} \cdot P_1$ to $\text{MPN} \cdot 2P_1$ to $\text{MPN} \cdot 3P_1$). For a given money wage, more labor is demanded at higher price levels because that money wage corresponds to a lower real wage rate.[8] *The demand for labor depends on the real wage.* Equiproportional increases in the money wage and the price level from (W_1, P_1) to ($2W_1, 2P_1$) and ($3W_1, 3P_1$) leave labor demand unchanged at level N_1. They leave the real wage unchanged at W_1/P_1, which corresponds to the demand N_1 in Figure 3.5a.

The information in Figure 3.5 is useful in constructing the classical **aggregate supply function**—a relationship that makes clear the supply-determined nature of output in the classical model. The aggregate supply curve is the macroeconomic analog to the microeconomic concept of the firm's supply curve. For the firm, the supply curve gives the output forthcoming at each level of the product price. For the perfectly competitive firm, profits are maximized, as we have seen, where marginal cost (W/MPN_i for the ith firm) equals product price (P), or equivalently where

aggregate supply function

macroeconomic analog to the individual market supply curve, which shows the output forthcoming at each level of product price. The aggregate supply curve shows the total output firms will supply at each value of the aggregate price level

$$\text{MPN}_i = \frac{W}{P} \qquad (3.10)$$

the marginal product equals the real wage. The individual firm takes the money wage as given in deciding on the optimal output to supply and therefore the quantity of labor to hire. One firm would not expect its effort to hire more labor to cause the money wage to change because the firm is a small part of the overall market. Because the money wage is assumed to be fixed, the output supply curve for the firm is positively sloped. Higher prices mean lower real wages, and

---

[8]Equation (3.9) has a simple interpretation. For profit maximization, the money wage paid to the incremental worker (W) must just equal the worker's contribution to the firm's revenue. The worker's contribution to money revenues equals his or her marginal product multiplied by product price ($\text{MPN} \cdot P$), which is termed the marginal revenue product.

consequently the firm demands more labor and produces more output. In constructing the aggregate supply curve for the economy, we cannot assume that the money wage remains fixed as output and labor input are varied. The money wage must adjust to maintain equilibrium in the labor market. With this important difference, the aggregate supply curve addresses the same question as its microeconomic analog: How will the level of output supplied vary when we change the product price?

In Figure 3.6 we construct the classical aggregate supply function. Consider output supplied at the three successively higher price levels, P_1, $2P_1$, and $3P_1$, which were plotted in Figure 3.5. At price level P_1 and money wage W_1, employment was N_1 and we assume that the resulting output is Y_1, as shown in Figure 3.6.[9] How will output supplied vary as we go to a price level of $2P_1$? At a price level of $2P_1$, *if* the money wage remained at W_1, we can see from Figure 3.5*b* that labor demand would increase to N_2. The higher price would mean a lower real wage, and firms would try to expand both employment and output. The money wage will not, however, remain at W_1. At a price level of $2P_1$ the labor supply curve in Figure 3.5*b* will have shifted to N^s ($2P_1$), and at a money wage of W_1, labor supply will be only N_2' units. There will be an excess demand for labor equal to $(N_2 - N_2')$ units and the money wage will rise.

Figure 3.6 Classical Aggregate Supply Curve

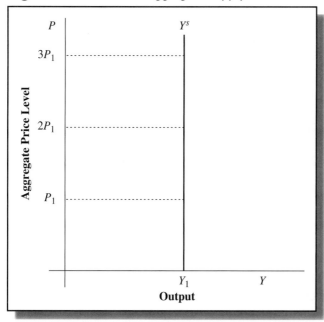

The vertical classical aggregate supply curve reflects the fact that higher values of the price level require proportionately higher levels of the money wage for labor market equilibrium. The real wage, employment, and therefore level of output are the same at P_1, $2P_1$ and $3P_1$. The vertical aggregate supply curve implies that output is supply-determined in the classical system.

---

[9]This output level is read from the production function given in Figure 3.4.

The process at work here is one of some firms responding to higher prices by attempting to expand employment and production. To expand employment, they raise money wages in an effort to bid workers away from other firms. Firms that lag in the process of raising money wages suffer higher quit rates and lose workers. This process of rising money wages will stop only when the money wage has increased sufficiently to reequilibrate supply and demand in the labor market. As can be seen in Figure 3.5b, reequilibration occurs at a money wage of $2W_1$, where the money wage has increased proportionately with the price level. At this point the initial real wage is restored and employment is back at its original level. Consequently, output supplied at price level $2P_1$ is equal to Y_1, the output level for price level P_1. At a still higher price level of $3P_1$, the money wage rises to $3W_1$, but again output is unchanged at Y_1. The aggregate supply curve is vertical. Higher prices provide a spur to output only if they are not matched by proportionately higher money wages—only if they lower the real wage. Given the assumptions we have made, however, equilibrium in the labor market requires that money wages rise proportionately with prices to maintain the equilibrium real wage in that market.

The vertical aggregate supply curve illustrates the supply-determined nature of output in the classical model. An aggregate demand curve could be constructed and added to Figure 3.6, but whatever the shape and position of such a curve, it would clearly not affect equilibrium output. For output to be in equilibrium, we must be on the supply curve; output must be at Y_1.

Factors That Do Not Affect Output

It is of interest to consider the factors that will *not* affect output and employment in the classical model. Because output and employment are supply-determined, the level of aggregate demand will have *no* effect on output. As John Stuart Mill advised the legislator, "He need not give himself concern over the demand for output." Factors such as the quantity of money, level of government spending, and level of demand for investment goods by the business sector are all demand-side factors that have no role in determining output and employment. The case of government tax policy is more complex. Changes in taxes, to the degree that they affect the demand side, will not affect output or employment. But changes in tax rates also have incentive or supply-side effects that do matter for output and employment, as we will see in Chapter 4.

Read Perspectives 3.1.

Factors That Do Affect Output

In the classical system, we have seen that changes in price do not affect any of the real variables in the system: the real wage, employment levels, or real output. How does output change in this system? Figure 3.7 gives an example of how a change in the capital stock affects the aggregate production function, labor market and thus output.

We start at equilibrium point A on the production function, labor market, and with the aggregate supply curve Y_1^s, with equilibrium levels of the real wage, $(W/P)_1$, employment, N_1, and output, Y_1. Suppose new capital is purchased that has

It was argued in section 3.5 that the determinants of output in the classical model are all supply-side variables. The traditional view had been that these supply-side variables change only slowly over time. But if output is determined by variables that change only slowly, how can the classical model explain sharp cyclical movements in output? Real GDP, for example, fell by 2.5 percent in 1982, rose by 6.8 percent in 1984, and fell by 30 percent between 1929 and 1933. This apparent failure of the classical equilibrium model to explain cyclical movements in output led to the Keynesian revolution.

In the post-1980 period, however, some economists have argued that the business cycle *is* caused by changes in *real* supply-side variables, much along classical lines. These economists do not accept the view that supply-side factors change only slowly over time. They believe that changes in technology and shocks that affect capital formation and labor productivity, as well as disturbances that influence the availability and prices of natural resources, can explain the short-run fluctuations in output as well as its long-run growth path. The models these economists have constructed are called *real business cycle* models.

In the model in this chapter, the real business cycle theorists see fluctuations in real output and employment as resulting from shifts in the production function and labor demand schedules in Figure 3.4. If preferences of workers change, the labor supply schedule could also shift.

Events such as the OPEC (Organization of Petroleum Exporting Countries) oil-price shock in 1974 led all economists to recognize that at times supply-side shocks can affect the cyclical behavior of output. Still, the view that real supply-side factors can fully explain the business cycle is controversial. We will consider real business cycle models in detail in Chapter 13.

higher levels of technology and increases the marginal product of each worker. This will shift the production function upward, since the output of each additional worker will be greater. The new production function is specified as $Y = F(\overline{K}_2, N)$. Since the marginal product of labor (MPN) increases, the demand for labor increases (holding price constant). In the labor market, as the demand for labor shifts up and to the right, equilibrium changes from point A to point B. Because the real wage increases, workers will be willing to work more hours, and equilibrium employment increases from N_1 to N_2. Substituting the new level of employment, N_2, into the production function shows that output increases to Y_2. In Figure 3.7c, the aggregate supply curve shifts from Y_1^s to Y_2^s. Real output increases from Y_1 to Y_2.

3.6 CONCLUSION

The striking feature of the classical model is the supply-determined nature of output and employment. This property follows from the vertical aggregate supply curve. The classical aggregate supply curve is vertical because of the assumptions we have made about the labor market. It is worthwhile to recognize explicitly the nature of these assumptions. In general, the foregoing portrayal of the labor and product markets can be characterized by the term auction market. Labor and output are assumed to be traded in markets that are continually in equilibrium and in which all

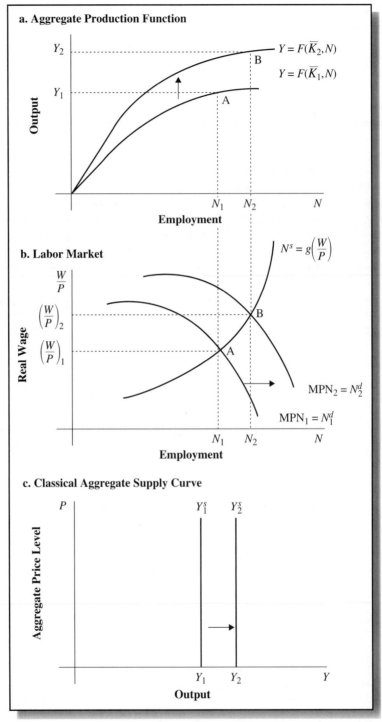

Figure 3.7 The Effect on Output, the Real Wage, and Employment of an Increase in the Capital Stock in the Classical System

participants make decisions based on announced real wage rates and product prices. Two assumptions implicit in this classical representation of the labor market are as follows:

1. Perfectly flexible prices and wages.
2. Perfect information on the part of all market participants about market prices.

For whatever time period we assume that the equilibrium model determines employment and output, equilibrium must be achieved. If such a model is to explain employment and output in the short run, prices and wages must be perfectly flexible in that time period.

The auction market characterization of the labor market also requires that market participants have perfect information about market prices. Both suppliers and purchasers of labor must know the relevant trading prices. This condition requires that when selling and buying labor at a given money wage (W), both workers and employers know the command over commodities that will result from such a wage (W/P).

These two assumptions, essential for the nature of the classical equilibrium theory of employment and output, are the elements of the classical theory that Keynes attacked. Before considering that attack, we discuss other major elements of the classical theory.

KEY TERMS

- aggregate demand 39
- production function 40

- marginal product of labor (MPN) 40
- aggregate supply function 52

REVIEW QUESTIONS AND PROBLEMS

1. In what respects was the classical attack on mercantilism important in shaping classical economists' views on macroeconomic questions?
2. Explain the concept of an aggregate production function. How would you expect the production function in Figure 3.1 to be affected by an increase in the average and marginal productivity of labor for a given output level, owing, for example, to increased education of the labor force? How would such a shift in the production function affect the levels of output and employment in the classical model?
3. Explain the classical theories of labor supply and demand. Why is the labor demand schedule downward-sloping when plotted against the real wage, whereas the labor supply schedule is upward-sloping on the same graph?
4. Suppose that the public's taste changes in such a way that leisure comes to be more desirable relative to commodities. How would you expect such a change to affect output, employment, and the real wage in the classical model?
5. We termed the classical view of the labor market an *auction market*. What assumptions underlie this characterization?

6. In microeconomics, we would expect the supply curve for the firm to slope upward to the right when drawn against price. The classical aggregate supply curve is based on this microeconomic theory of the firm but is vertical. Why?
7. What factors are the major determinants of output and employment in the classical system? What role does aggregate demand have in determining output and employment?

Chapter 4

Classical Macroeconomics (II): Money, Prices, and Interest

*I*n this chapter we complete our discussion of the classical model. We analyze the classical theory of aggregate price level determination, which brings in the demand side of the model. Determination of the interest rate is also discussed. Next, we consider the policy conclusions that emerge from the classical model—classical views on monetary and fiscal policy.

4.1 THE QUANTITY THEORY OF MONEY

To understand the determination of the price level in the classical system, we analyze the role of money. In the classical theory, the quantity of money determines aggregate demand, which in turn determines the price level.

The Equation of Exchange

The starting point for the classical **quantity theory of money** is the equation of exchange, an identity relating the volume of transactions at current prices to the supply of money times the turnover rate of each dollar. This *turnover rate* for money, which measures the average number of times each dollar is used in transactions during the period, is called the **velocity of money**. In the form used by the prominent American quantity theorist, Irving Fisher, this identity is expressed as

$$MV_T \equiv P_T T \qquad (4.1)$$

where M is the quantity of money, V_T the transactions velocity of money, P_T the price index for the items traded, and T the volume of transactions. This relationship is an identity because of the *ex post*

quantity theory of money
classical theory stating that the price level is proportional to the quantity of money

velocity of money
rate at which money *turns over* in gross domestic product transactions during a given period: that is, the average number of times each dollar is used in gross domestic product transactions

definition of velocity. If, for example, over a given period the value of transactions in current dollars (P_TT) were \$3,600 billion and the money stock (M) were \$300 billion, we define the transactions velocity (or turnover rate) of money as the number of times the average dollar was used in transactions:

$$V_T \equiv \frac{P_TT}{M} = \frac{3,600}{300} = 12 \qquad \textbf{(4.2)}$$

The transaction variable (T) includes not only sales and purchases of newly produced goods but also exchanges of previously produced goods and financial assets. Another expression of the equation of exchange focuses only on income transactions:

$$MV \equiv PY \qquad \textbf{(4.3)}$$

M is again the quantity of money, and V is now the income velocity of money, the number of times the average dollar is used in a transaction involving current output. The price index for currently produced output is given by P, and the level of current output by Y. Again, this relationship would be an identity as long as income velocity was defined residually, as the level necessary to make the equality hold:

$$V \equiv \frac{PY}{M} \qquad \textbf{(4.4)}$$

In equation (4.3), the variables are easier to measure and more central to our concerns, so we focus on this form of the equation.

The equation of exchange is a truism and does not explain the variables it contains. Fisher and other quantity theorists, however, postulated that the *equilibrium* values of the elements in the equation of exchange, with the exception of the price level, were determined by other forces. Thus, the equation of exchange served to determine the price level. As Fisher put it:

> We find that, under the conditions assumed, the price level varies (1) directly as the quantity of money in circulation (M), (2) directly as the velocity of its circulation (V), (3) inversely as the volume of trade done by it (T). The first of these three relations is worth emphasis. It constitutes the "quantity theory of money."[1]

Output (or transactions) is a measure of real economic activity. As we saw in Chapter 3, classical economists regarded this variable as supply-determined. Most simply, money was assumed to be a metallic money such as gold, but considering paper money and bank deposits does not seriously complicate the analysis. The important assumption was that the quantity of money was exogenously controlled by the monetary policy authority.

Fisher argued that, in equilibrium, the velocity of money was determined by the payment habits and payment technology of society. For example, factors such as the average length of the pay period, the practice of using charge accounts or bank charge cards, and the prevalence of trade credit among businesses all affect the velocity of circulation. Shorter pay periods lead to smaller average money holdings over

---

[1]Irving Fisher, *The Purchasing Power of Money* (New York: Macmillan, 1922), p. 29.

the pay period for any given income level, hence an increase in velocity. Frequent use of charge accounts by consumers or trade credit by businesses also increases velocity, the number of transactions per unit of money. According to Fisher and other quantity theorists, *the equilibrium level of velocity was determined by such institutional factors and could be regarded as fixed for the short run.*

If velocity is predetermined and not simply defined residually to equate MV and PY, the equation of exchange is not merely a definition. With output fixed from the supply side, the equation of exchange now expresses a relationship of proportionality between the exogenously given money supply and the price level:

$$M\bar{V} = P\bar{Y} \tag{4.5}$$

or

$$P = \frac{\bar{V}}{\bar{Y}} M \tag{4.6}$$

The bar over the V and Y indicates that these terms can be taken as given. Equation (4.6) indicates the dependence of the price level on the supply of money. A doubling of M doubles P, or a 10-percent increase in M leads to a 10-percent increase in P. This is the basic result of the quantity theory of money: *The quantity of money determines the price level.*

The Cambridge Approach to the Quantity Theory

The mathematics of the quantity theory may be clear from equations (4.5) and (4.6), but what about the economics? How do changes in the money supply affect the price level? This question can be answered more easily after considering another variant of the quantity theory, the Cambridge approach.

The **Cambridge approach**, named after Cambridge University, the academic home of its originators Alfred Marshall and A. C. Pigou, also demonstrated a proportional relationship between the quantity of money and the aggregate price level. The foundation of this relationship was, however, less mechanistic than the transactions, or Fisherian (after Irving Fisher), version of the quantity theory. Marshall began by focusing on the individual's decision on the optimal amount of money to hold. Some money will be held because of the convenience that money provides in transactions compared with other stores of value. Money also provides security by lessening the possibility of inconvenience or bankruptcy from failing to meet unexpected obligations. But as Pigou noted, "Currency held in the hand yields no income," so money will be held only insofar as its yield in terms of convenience and security outweighs the income lost from not investing in productive activity or the satisfaction lost by not simply using the money to purchase goods to consume. On these criteria, how much money will it be optimal to hold?

> **Cambridge approach**
> a version of the quantity theory of money that focuses on the demand for money ($M^d = kPY$)

Marshall and the other Cambridge economists assumed that the demand for money would be a proportion of income. The Cambridge equation is written as

$$M^d = kPY \tag{4.7}$$

Money demand (M^d) is assumed to be a proportion (k) of nominal income, the price level (P) times the level of real income (Y). The primary desirable property of money is its usefulness for transactions, so it follows that the demand for money depends on the level of transactions, which may be supposed to vary closely with the level of income. The proportion of income that would be optimal to hold in the form of money (k) is assumed to be stable in the short run, depending, as in the Fisherian formulation, on the payment habits of the society.

In equilibrium, the exogenous supply of money must equal the quantity of money demanded:

$$M = M^d = kP\overline{Y} \tag{4.8}$$

With k treated as fixed in the short run and real output ($\overline{Y}$) determined, as before, by supply conditions, the Cambridge equation also reduces to a proportional relationship between the price level and money supply. As in the Fisherian approach, the quantity of money determines the price level.

The formal equivalence of the Cambridge equation and Fisher's version of the equation of exchange can be seen by rewriting (4.8) as

$$M \frac{1}{k} = P\overline{Y} \tag{4.9}$$

By comparing this with Fisher's equation (4.5), we can see that the two formulations are equivalent, with V equal to $1/k$. For example, if individuals wish to hold an amount equal to one-fourth of the nominal income in the form of money, the number of times the average dollar is used in income transactions will be four.

Although the two formulations of the quantity theory are formally equivalent, the Cambridge version represents a step toward more modern monetary theories. The Cambridge focus was on the quantity theory as a theory of the demand for money. The proportional relationship between the quantity of money and the price level resulted from the fact that the proportion of nominal income people wished to hold in the form of money (k) was constant and the level of real output was fixed by supply conditions. Following up on Pigou's analysis of the alternatives to holding wealth in the form of money, Keynes attacked the quantity theory by providing a new theory of money demand. Monetarists, as we will see, also take the Cambridge form of the quantity theory as the starting point for their theory of money demand.

In addition, the Cambridge focus on money demand leads to an answer to the question about the way money affects the price level. Let us suppose that we begin at equilibrium and then consider the effects of doubling the quantity of money. Initially, there is an excess of money supply over the amount demanded. Individuals try to reduce their money holdings to the optimal proportion of their income by putting this excess into alternative uses of consumption and investment. They increase their demand for commodities. This increased demand for commodities puts upward pressure on prices. In the language of classical economists, there is too much money chasing too few goods. If output is unchanged, as it would be in the classical model, and k is constant, a new equilibrium will be reached only after the price level is doubled. At that point, nominal income, and hence money demand, will have doubled. This was the link in the classical system between money and prices; an excess supply of money led to increased demand for commodities and upward pressure on the price level.

The Classical Aggregate Demand Curve

The quantity theory was thus the *implicit* theory of the aggregate demand for output within the classical system. We can use the quantity theory to construct the classical aggregate demand curve in Figure 4.1. For concreteness, we assign numerical values to the variables with which we are concerned. Let the value of k be one-fourth so that velocity is 4. Initially, let the supply of money be 300 units. In order for either equation (4.8) or (4.5) to hold, $P \times Y$ (nominal income) must be equal to 1,200 (4 × 300). In Figure 4.1, with price on the vertical axis and real output on the horizontal axis, the line labeled Y^d ($M = 300$) connects all the points where $P \times Y$ equals 1,200 units.[2] Points lying on the schedule, for example, are real income levels of 300 and 600 with accompanying price levels of 4.0 and 2.0, respectively.

Now consider a higher value of the money supply of, for example, 400 units. To satisfy either equation (4.8) or (4.5), with k still equal to one-fourth ($V = 4$), $P \times Y$ must

Figure 4.1 Classical Aggregate Demand Curve

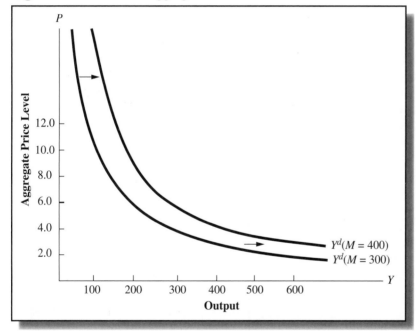

The classical aggregate demand curve plots combinations of the price level (P) and output (Y) consistent with the quantity theory equation $PY = M\bar{V}$, for a given money supply (M) and fixed velocity ($\bar{V}$). With $M = 300$ and velocity assumed to be 4, points such as $P = 12.0$ and $Y = 100$ or $P = 6.0$ and $Y = 200$ ($PY = 1,200 = MV$ in each case) lie along the aggregate demand curve. An increase in the money supply to $M = 400$ shifts the aggregate demand curve to the right.

---

[2]The schedule Y^d($M = 300$) and other such aggregate demand curves are constructed so that the product of the value of the variable on the vertical axis times the value of the variable on the horizontal axis ($P \times Y$) is equal at all points along the schedule. Such a curve is a rectangular hyperbola.

now equal 1,600. The schedule Y^d ($M = 400$) corresponding to a value of M equal to 400 lies above and to the right of the Y^d ($M = 300$) schedule and shows all $P \times Y$ combinations of 1,600. *An increase in the money supply shifts the aggregate demand curve to the right.*

For a given supply of money, we trace out a downward-sloping aggregate demand curve that can be put together with the vertical aggregate supply curve in Figure 3.6 to illustrate the determination of price and output in the classical model. This is done in Figure 4.2.

Figure 4.2 reproduces the vertical aggregate supply curve (Y_1^s) from Figure 3.6 and shows several aggregate demand curves [$Y^d(M_1)$, $Y^d(M_2)$, $Y^d(M_3)$] drawn for successively higher values of the money supply (M_1, M_2, M_3). As just explained, increasing the money supply shifts the aggregate demand curve upward to the right. Because the supply curve is vertical, increases in demand do not affect output. Only the price level increases. Also note that for a given value of k (or V), *a change in the quantity of money is the only factor that shifts the aggregate demand curve.* Because the equilibrium value of k (or V) was considered to be stable in the short run, aggregate demand varied only with the supply of money.

The classical theory of aggregate demand has been termed an *implicit* theory, and it is worthwhile to consider its nature more carefully. The theory is not explicit in the sense that it focuses on the components of aggregate demand and explains the factors that determine their level. Instead, in the classical theory, a given value of MV [or M ($1/k$)] implies the level of $P \times Y$ that is required for equilibrium in the money market—for money demand to equal the existing money supply. If money demand exceeds (falls short of) money supply, there will be a spillover to the commodity market as individuals try to reduce (increase) their expenditures on commodities. Points along the Y^d schedule are points at which firms and households are in equilibrium

Figure 4.2 Aggregate Supply and Demand in the Classical System

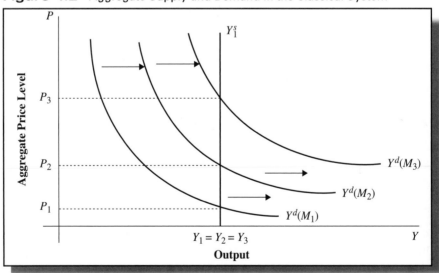

Successive increases in the money supply, from M_1 to M_2 and then to M_3, shift the aggregate demand curve to the right, from $Y^d(M_1)$ to $Y^d(M_2)$ to $Y^d(M_3)$. The price level rises from P_1 to P_2 to P_3. Output, which is supply-determined, is unchanged ($Y_1 = Y_2 = Y_3$).

with regard to their money holdings and, therefore, are also at equilibrium rates of expenditures on commodities.

Read Perspectives 4.1.

PERSPECTIVES 4.1
Money in Hyperinflations

The relationship between money and the price level postulated by the quantity theory can be seen clearly during hyperinflations. A hyperinflation is a period when the price level explodes. The inflation rate reaches astronomical levels. When this happens, the money supply *always* explodes as well. This can be seen from Table 4.1, which shows the monthly inflation rates and growth rates in the money supply from four hyperinflations. In each case, the extremely high inflation rate (19,800 percent per month for Hungary) is matched by an extremely high rate of growth in the money supply (12,200 percent for Hungary).

Table 4.2 shows inflation and money growth rates for several countries that have experienced high and sustained inflation rates during a more recent period. Here again there is a strong positive relationship between inflation and money growth.

As we will see in later chapters, many economists do not accept the quantity theory of money as applied to economies in normal circumstances. The data in Tables 4.1 and 4.2 do, however, illustrate an implication of the quantity theory on which there is general agreement: Sustained very high inflation rates require accommodating high money growth rates.

Table 4.1 Inflation and Money Growth in Four Hyperinflations

	TIME PERIOD	INFLATION RATE (MONTHLY, PERCENT)	MONEY GROWTH RATE (MONTHLY, PERCENT)
Germany	August 1922 to November 1923	322	314
Greece	November 1943 to November 1944	365	220
Hungary	August 1945 to July 1946	19,800	12,200
Poland	January 1923 to January 1924	81	72

Source: Philip Cagan: "The Monetary Dynamics of Hyperinflation," in Milton Friedman, ed., *Studies in the Quantity Theory of Money* (Chicago: University of Chicago Press, 1956), p. 26. Reprinted by permission of the University of Chicago Press.

Table 4.2
Inflation and Money Growth in Several High Inflation Economies, 1985–95

	INFLATION RATE (ANNUAL, PERCENT)	MONEY GROWTH RATE (ANNUAL, PERCENT)
Nicaragua	962	836
Brazil	875	996
Peru	399	389
Argentina	256	258

Source: World Bank.

4.2 THE CLASSICAL THEORY OF THE INTEREST RATE

In the classical system, the components of commodity demand—consumption, investment, and government spending—play their explicit role in determining the interest rate. It is, in fact, the interest rate that guarantees that exogenous changes in the particular components of demand do not affect the aggregate level of commodity demand.

The equilibrium interest rate in the classical theory was the rate at which the amount of funds individuals desired to lend was just equal to the amount others desired to borrow. For simplicity, we assume that borrowing consists of selling a standard bond, a promise to pay certain amounts in the future. Lending consists of buying such bonds. Later, we consider the properties of bonds in more detail, but for now the simplest assumption is that the standard bond is a "perpetuity," a bond that pays a perpetual stream of interest payments with no return of principal. The rate of interest measures the return to holding bonds and, equivalently, the cost of borrowing. The interest rate depends on the factors that determine the levels of bond supply (borrowing) and bond demand (lending).

In the classical system, the suppliers of bonds were the firms, which financed all investment expenditures by the sale of bonds, and the government, which might sell bonds to finance spending in excess of tax revenues.[3]

The level of the government deficit (excess of spending over revenues) as well as the portion of the deficit the government might choose to finance by selling bonds to the public are exogenous policy variables. In the classical model, the level of business investment was a function of the expected profitability of investment projects and the rate of interest. The expected profitability of investment projects was assumed to vary with expectations of product demand over the life of these projects, and the state of these expectations was subject to exogenous shifts.

For a given expected profitability, investment expenditures varied inversely with the interest rate. Classical economists explained this relationship as follows. A firm would have a number of possible investment projects offering various expected returns. It could rank these projects in order of the level of expected profits. The rate of interest represents the cost of borrowing funds to finance these investment projects. At a high interest rate, fewer projects will be profitable, net of interest costs. At successively lower rates of interest (lower borrowing costs), more and more projects will become profitable net of interest costs, and investment will increase. We look at investment in more detail later but obtain the same general result. Investment depends inversely on the rate of interest. Thus, on the supply (borrowing) side of the bond market, government bond supply is exogenous, and the business supply of bonds equals the level of investment expenditure. Investment varies inversely with the interest rate and is also influenced by exogenous shifts in the expected profitability of investment projects.

---

[3]The word *might* is used concerning the government's sale of bonds to finance a deficit because, as will be explained in section 4.3, the alternative of financing the deficit by printing money is available to the government. Also note that *investment* refers to expenditure by firms on plant, durable equipment, and inventories—investment in the national income accounts sense. The term *investment* does *not* refer to the purchase of financial assets such as bonds.

On the demand (lending) side of the bond market are the individual savers who purchase the bonds. In the classical model, saving was taken to be a positive function of the rate of interest. The act of saving is the act of forgoing current consumption to have a command over goods in a future period, a trade-off of current consumption for future consumption. As the interest rate increases, the terms of the trade-off become more favorable. A dollar saved today will earn a higher interest return for the saver, a greater command over consumption goods in future periods. Classical economists assumed that individuals would take advantage of this more favorable trade-off; they would save more at higher rates of interest.

But saving need not go into bonds; money is also a potential store of wealth. Because money paid no interest, classical economists assumed that bonds would be preferred as a store of wealth. As discussed previously, some money would be held for the convenience and security it offered. However, wealth accumulated through new saving would be held in bonds. Classical economists believed that people might shift their wealth into the form of money in times of severe general economic distress. At such times, with bank panics and bankruptcies prevalent, people might worry about bond default and "hoard" money, but for normal times the classical assumption was that saving was a demand for bonds.

Determination of the interest rate is illustrated in Figure 4.3. Saving (S) is plotted as an upward-sloping function of the rate of interest. Saving provides the demand for bonds, or as the classical economists called it, the *supply of loanable funds*. Investment (I) is a negatively sloped schedule plotted against the interest rate. Investment plus the exogenously determined government deficit (G − T), all of which we assume to be financed by selling bonds, equals bond supply. In classical terminology, this is the

Figure 4.3 Interest Rate Determination in the Classical System

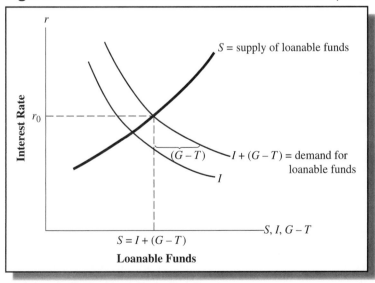

The equilibrium interest rate r_0 is the rate that equates the supply of loanable funds, which consists of saving (S), with the demand for loanable funds, which consists of investment (I) plus the bond-financed government deficit (G − T).

demand for loanable funds. In the diagram, r_0 is the equilibrium interest rate, the rate of interest that equates the demand and supply for loanable funds.

The interest rate plays a stabilizing role in the classical system, as can be seen by examining the effects of a change in the expected profitability of investment. Recall that in the short run, investment depends on the interest rate and the expected future profitability of investment projects. Let us suppose that as a result of an exogenous event (e.g., fear of a future war), business managers in general lower their expectation about future profits from investment. The effect would be reduced investment and, hence, a reduced demand for loanable funds *at each interest rate.*

Figure 4.4 illustrates the effect of this autonomous decline in investment demand. For simplicity, we assume that the government budget is balanced ($G = T$), so there is no government borrowing. Investment is the only source of the demand for loanable funds. The fall in expected profitability of investment projects is shown as a shift in the investment schedule downward from I_0 to I_1. At a given rate of interest, the amount of the decline in investment is measured by ΔI in Figure 4.4.

Figure 4.4 Autonomous Decline in Investment Demand

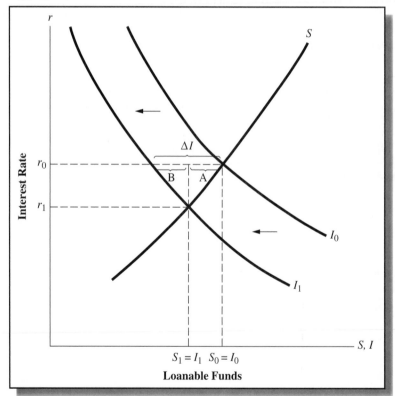

An autonomous decline in investment shifts the investment schedule to the left from I_0 to I_1—the distance ΔI. The equilibrium interest rate declines from r_0 to r_1. As the interest rate falls, there is an interest-rate–induced increase in investment—distance B. There is also an interest-rated–induced decline in saving, which is an equal increase in consumption—distance A . The interest-rate–induced increases in consumption and investment just balance the autonomous decline in investment.

At the initial equilibrium interest rate of r_0, after the fall in investment, the supply of loanable funds exceeds demand, putting downward pressure on the rate of interest. As the rate of interest declines, two adjustments occur. First, saving declines; thus, consumption (C) increases. The amount of this decline in saving and the equal increase in current consumption demand is given by the distance marked A in Figure 4.4.[4] Second, investment is somewhat revived by the decline in the interest rate. This interest-rate–induced increase in investment is measured by the distance B in Figure 4.4. Equilibrium is restored at interest rate r_1 with saving (the supply of loanable funds) again equal to investment (the demand for loanable funds). At the new equilibrium, the increase in consumption (fall in saving) plus the increase in investment caused by the drop in the interest rate, the distance A + B in Figure 4.4, is just equal to the original autonomous decline in investment demand, the distance ΔI in Figure 4.4. Because of the adjustment of the interest rate, the sum of private-sector demands (C + I) is unaffected by the autonomous decline in investment demand.

This stabilizing role of the interest rate is important to the classical system. The interest-rate adjustment is the first line of defense for full employment. Shocks that affect consumption demand, investment demand, or government demand will *not* affect the demand for output as a whole. These shocks will not shift the aggregate demand curve in Figure 4.2. Even if they did, there would be no effect on output or employment because of the self-adjusting properties of the classical labor market as reflected in the vertical aggregate supply curve—the second line of defense for full employment.

4.3 POLICY IMPLICATIONS OF THE CLASSICAL EQUILIBRIUM MODEL

In this section we analyze the effects of fiscal and monetary policy actions within the classical model. We consider the effects that various policy shifts will have on output, employment, the price level, and the interest rate.

Fiscal Policy

Fiscal policy is the setting of the federal budget and thus comprises decisions on government spending and taxation. In considering the classical view of fiscal policy, it is convenient to begin with government spending.

Government Spending

Consider the effects of an increase in government spending. The question of how the increased spending is financed arises first. Like a business or household, the government has a budget constraint, the condition that all expenditures must be financed from some source. The government has three sources of funds: taxation, selling bonds to the public (borrowing funds from the public), or creating new money. The creation of new money can take several forms, but in our discussion of the classical

---

[4]It is important to note that as saving declines there is a dollar-for-dollar increase in current consumption. Real income is fixed, as are taxes, so *all* changes in saving are mirrored in changes in current consumption.

system, it will do no harm to assume that the government simply prints new currency to finance its spending.

To increase spending, then, the government must increase taxation, sell additional bonds to the public, or increase the money supply. For now, to avoid bringing in a monetary policy change, we assume that the money supply is fixed. We also assume that tax collections are fixed. The increased government expenditures are therefore assumed to be financed by selling bonds to the public.

It follows from our analysis to this point that a bond-financed increase in government spending will *not* affect the equilibrium values of output or the price level. This must be the case, because we constructed both the aggregate demand and aggregate supply curves, which together determine output and the price level, without reference to the level of government spending. Output is not affected by changes in government spending, so employment must also be unaffected. To understand these results, we examine how a change in government spending affects the interest rate.

Figure 4.5 shows the effect in the loanable funds market of an increase in government spending financed by a sale of bonds to the public. If government spending is greater than tax revenue, then $(G - T)$ is positive, where G is total government spending, T is tax revenue, and $(G - T)$ is the government deficit. We assume that before the increase in government spending the government budget was in balance—that is, $(G = T)$. The government deficit is then equal to the increase in

Figure 4.5 Effect of Increase in Government Spending in the Classical Model

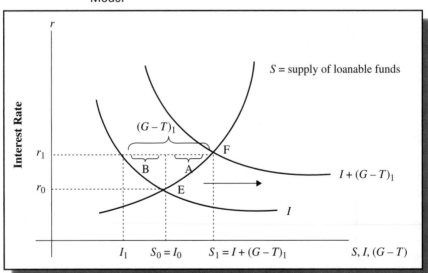

At equilibrium point E, the interest rate r_0 is the rate that equates the supply of loanable funds, S, with the demand for loanable funds, I. Adding government deficit spending, $(G - T)_1$, shifts the demand for loanable funds to the right. The equilibrium interest rate rises from r_0 to r_1 at equilibrium point F. The increase in the interest rate causes a decline in the quantity of investment from I_0 to I_1, a distance B, and an increase in saving, which is an equal decline in consumption, from S_0 to S_1, a distance A. The decline in investment and consumption just balances the increase in government deficit spending.

government spending, $(G - T)_1$. Initially, with no government deficit, the loanable funds market is in equilibrium at point E. Assuming there is no government borrowing, the equilibrium interest rate, r_0, equates the supply of loanable funds with the demand for loanable funds. Initially investment, I, is the only source of demand for loanable funds. If the increase in government spending is financed by selling bonds, then total demand for loanable funds includes both investment, I, and government borrowing, $(G - T)_1$. The increase in demand for loanable funds is shown as a rightward shift in demand, from I to $I + (G - T)_1$, moving from equilibrium point E to equilibrium point F. Note that the distance of the horizontal shift in the curve measures the amount of the increase in government deficit spending. This amount is measured by the distance $(G - T)_1$ in Figure 4.5.

The increase in government spending creates an increased demand for loanable funds as the government sells bonds to the public to finance the new spending. This creates an excess of borrowers over lenders at the initial interest rate r_0, and the interest rate is pushed up to r_1. The increase in the interest rate has two effects. Saving increases from S_0 to S_1; this is the distance A in Figure 4.5. As was explained in the preceding section, an increase in saving is mirrored by an equal decline in consumption. Second, the quantity of investment declines with the higher interest rate. At r_1, we can read the new level of investment as I_1, along the I schedule. The investment decline is the distance B in Figure 4.5.

The figure shows that the amount of the decline in consumption, which equals the amount of increased saving (distance A) plus the decline in investment (distance B), just equals the amount of the increase in government spending $(G - T)_1$. The increase in government spending financed by selling bonds to the public pushes the interest rate up by enough to "crowd out" an equal amount of private expenditure (consumption plus investment). Private expenditures are discouraged because the higher interest rate causes households to substitute future consumption for current consumption—in other words, to save more. Investment declines because fewer projects appear profitable with higher borrowing costs. It is this crowding out that keeps aggregate demand from increasing when the government component of demand rises. Because aggregate demand is not changed, increases in government expenditures financed by bonds do not affect the price level.

What are the effects of an increase in government spending if, alternatively, the government prints money to finance the new spending? Here, because the quantity of money is changed, the price level will change proportionately. We have previously analyzed the way an increase in the money supply shifts the aggregate demand curve up along the vertical aggregate supply curve, raising the price level (see Figure 4.2). In the classical system, the source of the increase in the money supply does not matter. A given change in the money supply has the same effect whether it enters the economy to finance an increase in government spending or in another manner. Put differently, and this is the crucial point, *the increase in government spending has no independent effect on aggregate demand.*

Tax Policy

Demand-Side Effects. As long as we consider only the effects on demand, analysis of a change in taxes produces results that are analogous to those for government spending. For example, by increasing the disposable income of households, a tax cut would stimulate consumption. If, however, the government sold bonds to the public to replace the revenues lost by the tax cut, the same crowding-out process would follow, as in the case of a bond-financed increase in government spending. The equilibrium interest rate would rise, investment would fall, and there would also be an interest-rate–induced rise in saving, meaning that consumption would fall back toward the pre–tax-cut level. In the case of a tax cut, as with an increase in spending, aggregate demand would not be affected.

If revenues lost because of the tax cut were replaced by printing new money, then, as with an increase in government spending, the money creation *would* increase aggregate demand, and the tax cut would cause the price level to rise. Again, though, it would simply be the increase in the money supply that affected the price level. The tax cut would have no *independent* effect on aggregate demand.

Supply-Side Effects.   If the tax cut were a lump-sum cut, meaning, for example, that every household received a tax cut of $100, then the demand-side effects would be all that we would need to consider.[5] But suppose the tax cut was in the form of reduced income tax rates. Suppose the marginal income tax rate were cut from an initial rate of 40 percent to a new rate of 20 percent. Instead of 40 cents of every additional dollar being taken as a tax payment, only 20 cents would be taken. In the classical model, such a change would have an incentive effect on labor supply. The change would affect the supply side of the model and would affect output and employment.

Figure 4.6 illustrates the effect of a cut in the marginal income tax rate within the classical model. Part *a* shows the effects in the labor market. A cut in the tax rate would increase labor supply at any value of the (pretax) real wage and shift the labor supply schedule out to the right. This shift follows because the worker is concerned about the *after-tax* real wage, which in this case is $(1 - t^y)\,W/P$, where t^y is the marginal income tax rate. If we had included an income tax in our classical model in Chapter 3, the labor supply function would have been

$$N^s = g\left[(1 - t^Y)\,\frac{W}{P}\right] \tag{3.6}$$

For a given pretax real wage (W/P), a cut in the income tax represents an increase in the after-tax real wage and therefore increases labor supply.

In Figure 4.6*a*, as the marginal income tax rate falls from 0.40 to 0.20, the labor supply schedule shifts from N^s $(t^y = 0.40)$ to N^s $(t^y = 0.20)$. Equilibrium employment increases from N_0 to N_1. Part *b* of Figure 4.6 shows the aggregate production function. The increase in employment from N_0 to N_1 as a result of the increase in labor supply leads to an increase in output from Y_0 to Y_1.

In part *c* of the figure, this increase in the supply-determined level of output (from Y_0 to Y_1) is shown as a shift to the right in the aggregate supply curve from Y^s $(t^y = 0.40)$ to Y^s $(t^y = 0.20)$. Because the level of aggregate demand is unchanged

---

[5]Because the tax cut would affect wealth, which in turn might influence the labor–leisure choice, even a lump-sum tax cut could affect the supply side. We are neglecting wealth effects here as being of secondary importance.

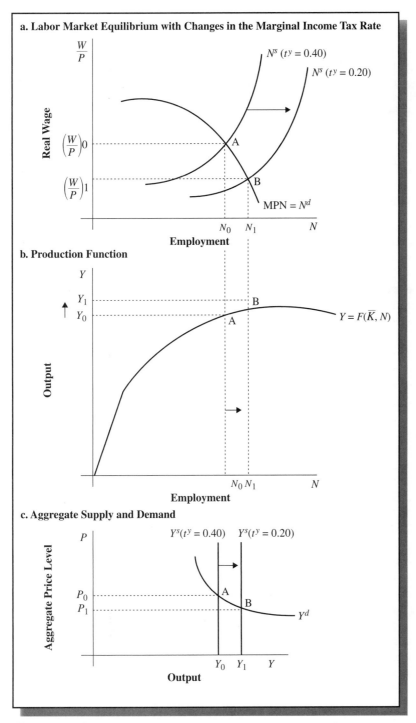

a. Labor Market Equilibrium with Changes in the Marginal Income Tax Rate

N^s $(t^y = 0.40)$

N^s $(t^y = 0.20)$

$\left(\dfrac{W}{P}\right)0$

$\left(\dfrac{W}{P}\right)1$

$MPN = N^d$

N_0 N_1 N

Real Wage

Employment

b. Production Function

Y

Y_1

Y_0

$Y = F(\overline{K}, N)$

Output

$N_0 N_1$ N

Employment

c. Aggregate Supply and Demand

$Y^s(t^y = 0.40)$ $Y^s(t^y = 0.20)$

P

P_0

P_1

Y^d

Y_0 Y_1 Y

Aggregate Price Level

Output

Figure 4.6 The Supply-Side Effects of an Income Tax Cut

In part *a* , a reduction in the marginal income tax rate (from 0.40 to 0.20) increases the after-tax real wage for a given value of the pretax real wage. The labor supply curve shifts out to the right. Equilibrium moves from point A to point B. Employment and output increase, as shown in part *b* of the graph, moving from point A to point B on the production function. This increase in output is represented by the shift to the right in the vertical aggregate supply curve in part *c*.

(determined by the level of the money supply), this increase in aggregate supply results in a fall in the price level.[6]

In summary, changes in government spending or taxes have no independent effects on aggregate demand because of the interest-rate adjustment and resulting crowding-out effects on components of private-sector demand. Changes in marginal income tax rates have additional supply-side effects. A reduction in the marginal income tax rate, for example, stimulates labor supply and leads to an increase in employment and output.

Read Perspectives 4.2.

Monetary Policy

In the classical system, the quantity of money determines the price level and, for a given real income, the level of *nominal* income. In this sense, monetary policy was quite important to classical economists. Stable money was a requirement for stable prices.

In another sense, money was not important. The quantity of money did not affect the equilibrium values of the real variables in the system: output, employment, and the interest rate. The supply-determined nature of output and employment was the subject of Chapter 3. The theory of the equilibrium interest rate we have constructed here is a real theory that did not mention the quantity of money. Factors determining the interest rate were real investment demand, real saving, and the real value of the government deficit—what the classical economists called the forces of "productivity and thrift."

To classical economists, money was a "veil" that determined the nominal values in which we measure such variables as the level of economic activity, but had no effect on real quantities.

4.4 CONCLUSION

Classical economists stressed the *self-adjusting tendencies of the economy.* Free from destabilizing government actions, the private sector would be stable, and full employment would be achieved. The first of these self-stabilizing mechanisms is the interest rate, which adjusts to keep shocks to sectoral demands from affecting aggregate demand. The second set of stabilizers consists of freely flexible prices and money wages, which keep changes in aggregate demand from affecting output. Flexibility of prices and wages is crucial to the full-employment properties of the classical system. The inherent stability of the private sector led classical economists to *noninterventionist* policy conclusions. To be sure, many of the interventionist mercantilist policies that classical economists opposed (tariffs, trading monopolies, etc.) were a far cry from the macroeconomic stabilization policies of today, but the model itself argues for nonintervention in a very general sense.

---

[6]The aggregate demand curve is fixed as long as revenues that were lost because of the cut in the income tax rate are replaced by increased bond sales to the public. If lost revenue were instead replaced by printing money, the aggregate demand curve would shift to the right, and the price level might not fall.

PERSPECTIVES 4.2
Supply-Side Economics—A Modern Classical View

Classical economists in the nineteenth and early twentieth centuries did not give much attention to the supply-side effects of changes in income tax rates. At the time, the marginal income tax rate was low and pertained only to the relatively wealthy. As can be seen from Table 4.3, in the United States, the average marginal income tax rate (averaged across each tax bracket) in 1920 was only 4.6 percent and by 1929 had declined to 3.5 percent. Moreover, in the 1920s fewer than 15 percent of U.S. households had incomes high enough to require filing an income tax return.

As can also be seen from Table 4.3, the situation was different in the post–World War II period. By 1980, the average marginal income tax rate was above 30 percent, and a large majority of U.S. households had incomes high enough to be subject to the income tax. In the 1970s, a group that became known as the *supply-side economists* argued, much along the lines of the analysis in this subsection, that such taxes formed a "wedge" between the real wage paid by employers

and that received by the worker. Reducing the size of that wedge, they argued, would increase the incentives to supply labor and result in higher output and employment, as illustrated in Figure 4.6.

By the late 1970s, economists such as Robert Mundell of Columbia University and Arthur B. Laffer, then at the University of Southern California, had popularized the idea that tax cuts would have strong favorable "supply-side" effects. Then Representative Jack Kemp and Senator William Roth accepted the supply-siders' argument, and in 1977 they introduced a bill calling for across-the-board cuts of 10 percent in personal income tax rates in each of three successive years. In 1980, Ronald Reagan endorsed the Kemp–Roth proposal, and in 1981 the Reagan–Kemp–Roth tax bill, calling for a 23-percent across-the-board income tax cut over three years, was passed. Later, the Tax Reform Act of 1986 further reduced marginal income tax rates.

The effects of these tax cuts, as well as later supply-side policies, are considered in Chapter 20.

Table 4.3
Average Marginal
Tax Rate, Selected
Years (Percent)

1916	1.2	1950	19.6
1920	4.6	1970	24.3
1929	3.5	1980	30.4

Source: Robert J. Barro and Chaipat Sahasakul, "Measuring the Average Marginal Tax Rate from the Individual Income Tax," *Journal of Business* 56 (October 1983), pp. 434–35, Table 2. Reprinted by permission of The University of Chicago Press.

A second central feature of the classical system is the *dichotomy between the factors determining real and nominal variables*. In the classical theory, real (supply-side) factors determine real variables. Output and employment depend primarily on population, technology, and capital formation. The interest rate depends on productivity and thrift. Money is a veil determining the nominal values in which quantities are measured, but monetary factors do not play a role in determining these real quantities.

In the next theoretical system that we consider—Keynesian theory—we will see policy conclusions that are much more interventionist. We will also see that monetary and real variables are much more interrelated in the Keynesian system.

KEY TERMS

- quantity theory of money 59
- velocity of money 59
- Cambridge approach 61

REVIEW QUESTIONS AND PROBLEMS

1. Explain the role of money in the classical system. Specifically, in the classical model, what role does money have in determining real output, employment, the price level, and the interest rate? Explain how money affects these variables; or, if money has no effect on some of them, explain why.
2. What are the differences between the Fisherian and Cambridge versions of the quantity theory of money?
3. Define the term *velocity of money*. What factors determine the velocity of money in the classical system? What is the relationship between the velocity of money and the Cambridge k?
4. Explain how aggregate demand is determined within the classical model. What would be the effects on output and the price level of an increase in aggregate demand?
5. Classical economists assumed that velocity was stable in the short run. But suppose that, because of a change in the payments mechanism—for example, greater use of credit cards—there was an exogenous rise in the velocity of money. What effect would such a change have on output, employment, and the price level within the classical model?
6. Explain how the interest rate is determined in the classical theory.
7. Explain how the interest rate works in the classical system to stabilize aggregate demand in the face of autonomous changes in components of aggregate demand such as investment or government spending.
8. Within the Cambridge form of the quantity theory, the demand for money is given by

$$M^d = kPY \qquad (4.7)$$

Suppose that income (Y) is given at 300 units and the money supply (M) is fixed at 200 units. Also suppose the value of k initially is $1/4$; initially individuals wish to hold money balances equal to one-fourth of their income. Then assume that individuals increase money demand to one-third of their income; k rises to $1/3$.

How does this increase in money demand affect the equilibrium value of the aggregate price level (P)? What was the initial equilibrium price level? What is the value after the increase in money demand? Explain the process that leads to the change in the aggregate price level.

9. In deriving the labor supply curve in Figure 3.3, we implicitly assumed that the marginal income tax rate (t^y) was equal to zero. Assume instead that $t^y = 0.20$. Redraw the figure with this modification and compare the resulting labor supply curve with the present one in Figure 3.3b.

10. Within the classical model, analyze the effects of an increase in the marginal income tax rate. Explain how output, employment, and the price level are affected. Consider cases when the increased revenue produced by the tax increase results in a decline in bond sales to the public and when it results in lower money creation.

11. What are the major policy conclusions of classical economics? Explain how these policy conclusions follow from the key assumptions of the classical theoretical system.

Chapter 5

Long-Run Economic Growth: Origins of the Wealth of Nations

*A*s pointed out in Chapter 3, the main focus of the classical economics was the long-run growth of nations. Adam Smith, the first academic economist, was writing during the early stages of the industrial revolution. He witnessed the expansion of industrial capitalism and tried to explain the process that was beginning to sustain economic growth in some, but not all parts of the world. In this chapter, as in Smith's famous book, the subject is "the nature and causes of the Wealth of Nations."

Living standards across countries vary greatly. Wealth is spread very unequally among nations. Using official measurements of prices and exchange rates, per capita incomes in the United States and wealthy European countries are about 50 times those of the poorest African and Asian countries. This is surely an overstatement, but even correcting for such factors as more nonmarket economic activity in poor countries, per capita income estimates are still 20 times larger in the richest relative to the poorest countries. Within the developed nations, the standard of living has also improved greatly over time. Between 1870 and 2000 in the United States, national income grew at an annual rate of 3.5 percent. Over the same period, per capita income grew at an annual rate of 1.8 percent. The latter figure implies that per capita income doubled approximately every 40 years.

Even small variations in growth rates have large effects when compounded over time. If, for example, U.S. per capita income had grown at only 0.8 percent over this time period, in 2000 per capita income would have been 2.8 times rather than 10 times the 1870 level. The growth rate matters.

Here we examine the determinants of output growth over the long run. These are the factors responsible for the sustained growth in the now-wealthy countries. Variations in such factors are the source of the enormous income disparities among nations. In the other chapters in this part we will see that much controversy exists over the relative importance of aggregate supply and demand as determinants of output. In long-run equilibrium economic growth, supply factors—those determining the growth of potential output—are of predominant importance. Substantial output growth over long periods has been the result of the growth of factor supplies (the labor force and capital stock) and changes in technology that increase output per unit of factors employed. These were the factors central to the classical model.

5.1 GROWTH AND THE AGGREGATE PRODUCTION FUNCTION

As just noted, over the period 1870–2000, national income in the United States increased at an annual rate of 3.5 percent. Per capita output increased at an annual rate of 1.8 percent. What factors account for such sustained growth? One way to approach this question employs the *aggregate production function* seen in the previous two chapters. The aggregate production function relates the level of output to the level of factor inputs.

For the purposes of this chapter, the aggregate production function can be written as

$$Y = A(t)F(K, N) \qquad\qquad (5.1)$$

Equation (5.1) differs from expressions for the short-run aggregate production function in Chapter 3 in two respects. First, there is the additional term $A(t)$. This term represents technological change, which is for now taken simply to depend on time; that is, as time passes, the $A(t)$ term increases, meaning that more output will be produced for a given amount of factor inputs. In equation (5.1), the $A(t)$ term enters multiplicatively. With this specification, technological change is assumed not to affect the relative marginal productivities of the two factors, as determined by the $F(K, N)$ part of the production function. In other words, technological change results in equal increases in the productivities of both factors. Such technological change is termed *neutral* (favoring neither capital nor labor) technological change. Robert Solow, studying shifts in the aggregate production function over time, found evidence that, for the United States, technological change had in fact been neutral. We restrict our analysis to this case.[1]

A second difference between equation (5.1) and previous specifications of the production function is the absence of the bar over the K variable, indicating that here

---

[1]See Robert Solow, "Technical Change and the Aggregate Production Function," *Review of Economics and Statistics*, 39 (August 1957), pp. 312–20. Also relevant to the discussion here is Solow's book, *Growth Theory*, 2nd ed. (London: Oxford University Press, 2000).

we are not assuming that the capital stock is constant. This difference reflects the fact that we are now dealing with the long run.

On the basis of equation (5.1), we follow Solow's method in the previously mentioned study and write the following specification for the growth in output over time:

$$\frac{\dot{Y}}{Y} = \frac{\dot{A}}{A} + w_k \frac{\dot{K}}{K} + w_n \frac{\dot{N}}{N} \tag{5.2}$$

where the dot over a variable indicates the time rate of change in that variable (e.g., $\dot{N}$ is the rate at which the labor force is increasing). Equation (5.2) specifies the proportional rate of increase in output ($\dot{Y}/Y$) as depending on the proportional rate of technological change ($\dot{A}/A$) and the proportional rates of change in the capital stock and number of workers employed ($\dot{K}/K$) and ($\dot{N}/N$). The weights (w_k, w_n) attached to these latter two variables are their shares in national output, reflecting their importance in the production process. Equation (5.2) indicates that the growth in output depends on the rate at which technological progress occurs over time and the rate at which factor supplies are growing over time.

constant returns to scale means that increasing all inputs by a certain proportion (e.g., only 100 percent) will cause output to rise by the same proportion (100 percent)

If the production function given by equation (5.1) exhibits **constant returns to scale**, it can be written in an alternative form that will provide some insights into the way each factor enters into the growth process. Constant returns to scale mean that if all inputs rise in some proportion, output will increase in the same proportion. A doubling of the amount of both capital and labor used in production would, for example, just double the amount of output produced. With constant returns to scale, it follows that for a given technology, fixing $A(t)$, output per worker (Y/N) will depend only on the amount of capital employed per worker, the capital/labor ratio.[2] Letting q equal output per worker (Y/N) and k equal capital per worker (K/N), we can rewrite (5.1) as

$$\frac{Y}{N} = A(t)f\left(\frac{K}{N}\right)$$

or

$$q = A(t)f(k) \tag{5.3}$$

where $f(k)$ is the function relating output per worker to the capital/labor ratio, for a given technology—what is called the *intensive* form of the aggregate production function.

The relationship given by equation (5.3) is shown in Figure 5.1. The state of technology is assumed to be $A(t_0)$, which fixes the position of the production function relating output per worker to capital per worker. As we move out to the right along the production function, output per worker increases with the increase in capital per worker (k). The shape of the production function in Figure 5.1 reflects the assumption

---

[2]With constant returns to scale, output per worker (Y/N) does not depend on the level of output. Therefore, with technology fixed, once we fix the capital/labor ratio (K/L), no other variable affects output per worker; Y/N is also fixed.

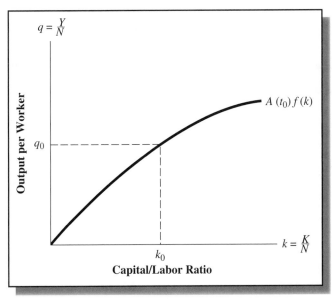

Figure 5.1 Aggregate Production Function: Equation (5.3)

The intensive form of the production function shows output per worker ($q = Y/N$) corresponding to each capital/labor ratio ($k = K/N$) for a given technology [$A(t_0)$]. As the capital/labor ratio rises, output per worker increases but at a declining rate, reflecting diminishing returns to increases in capital per worker.

that there are diminishing returns to increases in capital per worker. The increment to output per worker declines with successive increases in capital per worker.[3] At an assumed initial capital/labor ratio of k_0, output per worker would be q_0 in the figure.

Figure 5.2 illustrates the process of growth in output per worker between two points of time, t_0 and t_1. Technological change causes the production function to shift upward from $A(t_0)f(k)$ to $A(t_1)f(k)$. By itself, this technological change would increase output per worker, at the initial capital/labor ratio k_0, from q_0 to q_1' in Figure 5.2. In addition, however, we assume that the capital/labor ratio increases over time, a process called **capital deepening**. This is illustrated in the graph by a movement to a capital/labor ratio k_1. As a result, output per worker increases further to q_1.

capital deepening is the process when capital grows at a faster rate than labor and the capital/labor ratio rises

The framework illustrated in Figure 5.2 [the graph of equation (5.3)] suggests that the growth of output per worker is the result of two factors:

1. Technological change, which increases output per worker for a given capital/labor ratio.
2. Capital deepening, as the capital/labor ratio increases.

---

[3]Notice that this assumption of diminishing returns to increases in capital intensity is not at odds with the assumption that the production process exhibits constant returns to scale. The latter assumption refers to the effect of proportional increases in *all* factors of production. Diminishing returns to increases in capital intensity refer to the effects of increases in the amount of one factor (capital) per unit of the other factor (labor).

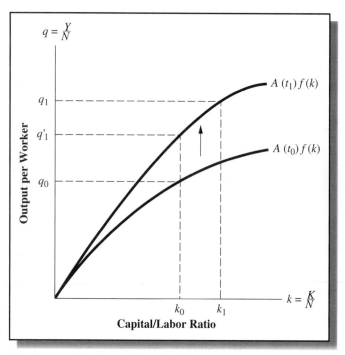

Figure 5.2 Growth in Output per Worker

Output per worker increases from q_0 to q_1' when, as the result of technological progress, the production function shifts upward from $A(t_0)f(k)$ to $A(t_1)f(k)$. There is a further increase in output per worker from q_1' to q_1 as a result of an increase in the capital/labor ratio from k_0 to k_1.

If we are considering the growth rate in total output, as opposed to output per worker, growth in the labor force is an additional source of growth.

5.2 SOURCES OF ECONOMIC GROWTH

The framework in the previous section, developed by Robert Solow and others in the 1960s, is referred to in the literature as the *neoclassical growth model*. In this section, we consider the sources of economic growth within this model. The next section examines recent developments in growth theory and their implications for sources of growth.

The factors that determine a country's long-run equilibrium growth rate are those that affect the rate of technological change, labor force growth, and rate of capital formation. Influences on these magnitudes are the ultimate sources of economic growth. We begin with a somewhat paradoxical result: Within the neoclassical growth model, the long-run equilibrium growth rate does not depend on a nation's saving rate ($s = S/Y$).

The independence of a nation's growth rate from the saving rate is at first surprising, because we would expect the saving rate to affect the rate of capital

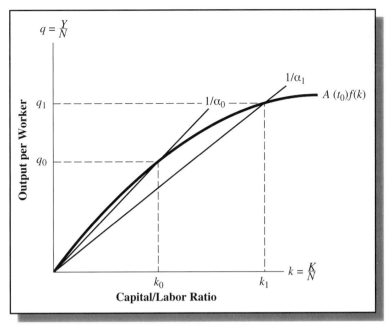

Figure 5.3 Effects of an Increase in the Saving Rate

As a result of an increase in the saving rate, the capital/labor ratio increases from k_0 to k_1. Output per worker increases from q_0 to q_1. The capital/output ratio rises from α_0 to α_1. Once q_1 is reached, there is no further increase in output per worker. The initial equilibrium growth rate in output is restored.

formation and therefore the equilibrium growth rate. To see why the equilibrium growth rate does not depend on the saving rate within the neoclassical model, let us analyze the effect of an increase in the saving rate within the production function framework of the preceding section.

In Figure 5.3, assume that initially the saving rate is s_0 and that the economy is in equilibrium, with the capital/labor ratio k_0 and output per worker equal to q_0. Consider the ray marked $1/\alpha_0$ coming from the origin and intersecting the production function at a level of output per worker equal to q_0. Each point along the line corresponds to a constant ratio of the variable on the vertical axis Y/N to the variable on the horizontal axis K/N—that is, a constant output/capital ratio—because

$$\frac{Y}{N} \div \frac{K}{N} = \frac{Y}{K} = \frac{1}{\alpha}$$

where α is the capital/output ratio (K/Y). Initially, the capital/output ratio is α_0 in Figure 5.3.

Now consider an increase in the saving rate to some higher value, s_1 (say, 15 percent of income as opposed to 10 percent of income). Initially, the economy was assumed to be in equilibrium at the capital/labor ratio k_0; capital and labor were growing at the same rate. With the increase in the saving rate, the rate of capital formation will initially increase. To see this relationship clearly, we need to specify the relationship between capital formation and the saving rate. The rate of capital formation can be written as

$$\frac{\dot{K}}{K} = \frac{I}{K} - \frac{D}{K} \tag{5.4}$$

where I is gross investment and D is depreciation. In long-run equilibrium, output will grow as supply grows, so we ignore the problem of inadequate demand. We assume that all saving (S) is channeled into investment ($I = S$). We also assume that depreciation is a constant fraction (δ) of the capital stock. Using these facts, we can rewrite equation (5.4) as

$$\frac{\dot{K}}{K} = \frac{S}{K} - \frac{\delta K}{K} = \frac{sY}{K} - \frac{\delta K}{K} \tag{5.5}$$

where the second equality follows from the fact that saving is equal to the saving rate times the level of income. From equation (5.5) it follows that an increase in the saving rate (s) will *initially* increase the rate of capital formation.

Because the rate of capital formation has increased with no change in the rate of growth in the labor force, the capital/labor ratio will rise. A new equilibrium will be reached, as shown in Figure 5.3, at capital/labor ratio k_1 and with higher output per worker, q_1. After this adjustment, however, there will be no further increase in output per worker and, because labor force growth is unchanged, the equilibrium growth rate will return to its initial level.

To see why, look at the ray labeled $1/\alpha_1$, which crosses the production function at the new level of output per worker, q_1, in Figure 5.3. As explained previously, each point along such a ray corresponds to a fixed capital/output ratio. The $1/\alpha_1$ ray is flatter than the initial $1/\alpha_0$ ray, indicating that the ratio of Y/N to K/N, the output/capital ratio, is lower after the increase in the saving rate. The capital/output ratio (K/Y) is therefore *higher*. At a higher capital/output ratio, a larger saving rate ($s = S/Y$) is required just to maintain a constant growth rate in the capital stock. Once the capital/output ratio has reached α_1, capital formation will have returned to the initial equilibrium rate equal to the growth rate in the labor force. There will be no further increases in output per worker or the capital/labor ratio.

The effect on the rate of economic growth is shown in Figure 5.4. Assume that the equilibrium growth rate for income is g. If the rise in the saving rate occurs at time t_0, the growth rate ($\dot{Y}/Y$) will rise temporarily as the economy moves from the initial level of output per worker, q_0, to the higher level of output per worker, q_1. At this new higher level of output per worker, the growth rate will return to g, as shown at time t_1 in Figure 5.4. The increased saving rate causes a temporary period of faster growth but does not affect the equilibrium growth rate.

None of the preceding discussion implies that the saving rate is unimportant in the neoclassical growth model. The temporary period during which a change in the

Figure 5.4
Effect on the Growth Rate of an Increase in the Saving Rate

At time t_0, the saving rate increases. Initially the rate of growth in output rises. This is the period when output per worker is increasing from q_0 to q_1, as shown in Figure 5.3. At time t_1, when output per worker has reached q_1 in Figure 5.3, the initial equilibrium growth rate g has been restored.

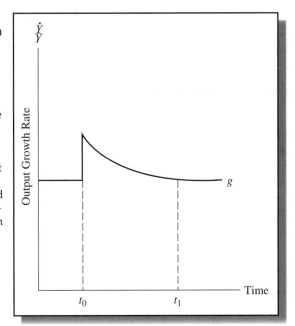

saving rate does affect the growth rate (from t_0 to t_1 in Figure 5.4) may be a long period in calendar time. Also, notice that even after the full adjustment to a change in the saving rate (after we reach t_1 in Figure 5.4 and k_1 and q_1 in Figure 5.3), the higher saving rate has resulted in a *permanent* increase in both capital and output per worker. An economy with a higher saving rate will therefore have a higher standard of living due to a more capital-intensive production process.

5.3 RECENT DEVELOPMENTS IN THE THEORY OF ECONOMIC GROWTH

After an active period in the 1950s and 1960s, interest in the theory of long-run economic growth declined in the 1970s. Interest in the theory had declined because of doubts about whether it really told us much about growth. The neoclassical growth model explained the dynamics of the growth process, but it ended up telling us that the long-run equilibrium growth rate depended on two exogenous variables: the rate of population growth and the rate of technological change. Because these were exogenous, the theory did not isolate the fundamental sources of long-run growth. For this reason, few policy conclusions came out of the traditional theory of long-term growth.

The latter part of the 1980s witnessed a resurgence of interest in growth theory. Paul Romer, one of the developers of the new growth theory, states: "From the point of view of policy advice, growth theory had little to offer. In models with exogenous technological change and exogenous population growth, it never really mattered what the government did."[4]

Endogenous Growth Models

Recent research extends the traditional analysis by making the rate of technological change or of population growth (or both) endogenous. Having done this, we can ask what factors will speed up or impede the growth process. How will various government policies affect the growth in these variables? The new growth theory is not an attack on the traditional theory. It is, rather, an extension that goes more deeply into the ultimate sources of growth. To see the lines along which this research is proceeding, we examine a model of endogenous technological change.[5]

Read Perspectives 5.1.

PERSPECTIVES 5.1
Growth Accounting for the United States: An Example

Edward Denison carefully studied economic growth in the United States. Table 5.1 summarizes his findings concerning the sources of growth in U.S. output for 1929–82. As the table indicates, real output grew at an annual rate of 2.9 percent over this period. The other numbers in the table show the percentage (proportion of the total) contribution to the growth rate of several factors. These factors are broken into two groups.

The first group, containing one factor, is growth in labor input. This is growth in output due to the increase in the quantity of labor. Denison estimated that 32 percent, approximately one-third, of the growth in output between 1929 and 1982 came from this source.

The other sources of growth are factors that increase the amount of output per unit of labor input (referred to as output per worker in the previous section)—in other words, factors that increase *labor productivity*. Let us consider each in turn.

EDUCATION PER WORKER

The first of these other sources of growth listed in Table 5.1 is education per worker. As explained by Denison:

Educational background decisively conditions both the types of work an individual is able to perform and his proficiency in any particular occupation. The distribution of American workers by highest school grade completed has shifted upward continuously and massively, and this shift has been a major growth source.[a]

Denison estimated that 14 percent of U.S. economic growth is due to increased education of the labor force.

[4]Paul Romer, "Capital Accumulation and Long-Run Growth," in Robert J. Barro, ed., *Modern Business Cycle Theory* (Cambridge, Mass.: Harvard University Press, 1989), p. 51. Keep in mind that we are discussing the long run. In the previous subsection, we saw that the saving rate could affect the growth rate, perhaps for a substantial period of time. There are certainly government policies that can influence saving. Only the long-run equilibrium growth rate was exogenous.

[5]For a model of endogenous population growth, see Gary Becker, Kevin Murphy, and Robert Tamua, "Human Capital, Fertility and Economic Growth," *Journal of Political Economy*, 98 (October 1990), pp. 512–37.

Table 5.1
Sources of U.S.
Economic Growth,
1929–82 (percent)

Annual growth rate of output (percent)	2.9
Percentage of growth due to:	
Growth in labor input	32
Growth in labor productivity	
Education per worker	14
Capital formation	19
Technological change	28
Economies of scale	9
Other factors	−2

Source: Edward F. Denison, *Trends in American Economic Growth, 1929–82* (Washington, D.C.: The Brookings Institution, 1985), p. 30.

CAPITAL FORMATION

Denison estimated that capital formation was responsible for 19 percent, just less than one-fifth, of U.S. economic growth between 1929 and 1982.

TECHNOLOGICAL CHANGE

The next factor in Table 5.1 is *technological change*. This includes changes in technological knowledge (e.g., ways to employ robots in the production process) as well as new knowledge about how to organize businesses (managerial strategies). In Denison's estimates, technological change accounted for 28 percent of growth and was the most important influence on labor productivity.

ECONOMIES OF SCALE

Denison found that, rather than the constant return to scale we assumed in the previous section, the United States has experienced *economies of scale*; even given the state of technology, an increase in the quantity of inputs has resulted in a more than proportional increase in output. Denison estimated that 9 percent of U.S. growth from 1929 to 1982 resulted from this source.

OTHER FACTORS

Denison considered other factors that either stimulate or retard the growth process (e.g., changes in allocation of resources among industries, effects of weather on farm output, work stoppages). Taken together, these factors had a net negative effect equal to 2 percent of economic growth.

[a]Edward F. Denison, *Trends in American Growth 1929–82* (Washington, D.C.: The Brookings Institution, 1985), p. 15.

To consider an endogenous technology, we modify the production function in (5.1) as follows:[6]

$$Y_t = F(K_t, N_t, A_t) \tag{5.6}$$

As before, output (Y) depends on the levels of the capital (K) and labor (N) inputs. Output also depends on the level of technology (A), which now appears inside the production function as one of the endogenous inputs. The relationship between

[6]This specification is taken from the Arrow–Romer model described in Romer, "Capital Accumulation and Long-Run Growth," pp. 98–100.

output and technology is, however, different from that with the other inputs. We can see this difference by looking at the production function for an individual firm, denoted by the subscript i:

$$Y_{it} = F(K_{it}, N_{it}, A_t) \tag{5.7}$$

The firm's output depends on its own level of capital (K_{it}) and labor (N_{it}) but also on the economy-wide level of technology (A_t). Advances in the state of knowledge are therefore assumed to increase the productivity of all firms.[7]

The level of technology is not assumed to grow exogenously. In one type of endogenous growth model, the growth of technology depends on the growth of capital. New investment fosters inventions and improvements in the machines that constitute the stock of capital. There is also assumed to be momentum to advances in knowledge. Inventions and productivity advances themselves lead to more knowledge by a "learning by doing" process.

In other models, increases in the labor input also increase the stock of knowledge by a process one author describes as: "The greater the level of the labor input, the greater is the scope for learning and acquisition of new skills. A higher level of labor input also requires more intensive use of factors fixed in the short run, thus raising the incentive to eliminate waste and bottlenecks."[8] This is, again, a process of learning by doing.

Policy Implications of Endogenous Technological Change

Consider the effects of an increase by all firms in their employment of labor and capital inputs in a model with endogenous technological change. Suppose, for example, firms increase capital and labor by 5 percent. We will assume that this increase by itself would cause output to rise proportionately by 5 percent. This is the traditional neoclassical assumption—constant returns to increases in capital and labor. As just discussed, however, the increases in capital and labor advance the economy-wide technology (A_t rises). This advance leads to an additional rise in output. Models with endogenous technological change therefore exhibit increasing returns to scale, once we take account of the effects of increased capital and labor on technology.[9] Increasing returns to scale has important policy implications.

With increasing returns, changes in the saving rate and therefore in the rate of capital formation can permanently affect the long-run equilibrium growth rate. This result contrasts with neoclassical growth theory, in which the effect of changes in the saving rate on the growth rate is temporary (see Figure 5.4).

In the neoclassical model, an increase in the rate of capital formation causes a less than proportionate increase in the growth rate of output. The reason is that, with constant returns to scale, the growth rate in the labor input would have to increase by the same amount as that of capital in order for output growth to rise proportionately. We are assuming the growth rate in the labor input will be fixed. Whereas the growth rate

---

[7]Some models do allow for technological advances (e.g., patents), the benefit of which accrues only to the firm that finances them. Still, there are some advances that benefit all firms.

[8]George Stadler, "Business Cycle Models with Endogenous Technology," *American Economic Review*, 80 (September 1990), pp. 763–68.

[9]Notice that this is consistent with Denison's finding of economies of scale in the U.S. growth experience. (Perspectives 5.1.)

in output rises less in proportion to the increase in the growth rate in capital, depreciation rises proportionately because, in both the traditional and newer growth models, depreciation is simply a fraction of the stock of capital, δ in the previous subsection. With the growth rate in output rising less than proportionately while the growth rate in capital and the depreciation rate are rising proportionately, depreciation becomes a larger fraction of output and eventually absorbs the higher saving. The rate of capital formation and the growth rate in output return to their initial levels.

With increasing returns, it is possible that *taking account of the positive effect that capital formation has on the level of technology (A)*, an increase in the saving rate and therefore in the rate of capital formation will result in a proportionate increase in the growth rate in output. If so, depreciation will not increase as a fraction of output and will not absorb the higher level of saving. The rate of capital formation and the growth rate in output will be permanently higher.

It follows, then, that with endogenous technological change and therefore increasing returns to scale, policies that affect the saving rate and thus the rate of capital formation affect the long-run equilibrium growth rate. Because many government policies have potential effects on these variables, what the government does now matters for long-run growth.

5.4 INTER-COUNTRY INCOME DIFFERENCES REVISITED

Let us return to where we began this chapter: considering huge inter-country differences in per capita incomes that must be due to differences in past rates of economic growth. How do the theories we have examined explain these differences? What do these theories predict about the future distribution of the wealth of nations?

Much of the discussion of these questions has focused on the hypothesis of *convergence*, the idea that per capita income levels across countries will tend to converge over time with richer countries growing more slowly than poorer ones.

The neoclassical growth model provides support for the idea of convergence. In that model, an economy that is below the steady state capital/labor ratio and therefore the steady state capital/output ratio will have a relatively high growth rate as it moves to the long-run equilibrium growth path. If production functions, saving rates and investment in human capital were the same across countries and technology could move freely across country boundaries, different countries would be converging to the same steady state. Current inter-country differences in per capita income would in this case be the result of shocks that had taken place in the past. Past wars or colonial domination would have displaced an economy from its steady state equilibrium. An economy subject to such a negative shock would then grow more rapidly than one that had not been affected as it returned to its steady state equilibrium.

What does empirical evidence reveal about convergence? First, consider Figure 5.5, which looks at 21 OECD members, a sample of highly industrialized countries. In the figure the average annual growth rate in GDP (gross domestic product) for 1960–97 is measured along the vertical axis and the initial (1960) GDP level is on the horizontal level. The scatter of points has the negative slope consistent with the convergence

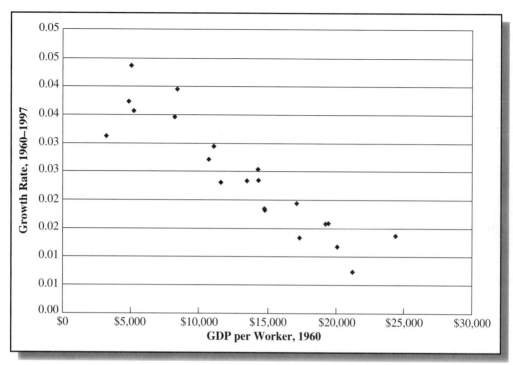

Figure 5.5 Convergence in the OECD, 1960–97

hypothesis: Countries with the highest initial GDP per capita had lower growth rates than countries that were poorer at the outset.

An examination of data for U.S. states, which compares post-1880 growth in per capita income with the 1880 income level, also provides support for convergence.[10] The states with the highest 1880 income levels grew more slowly in subsequent years.

But now look at Figure 5.6. Here we examine a broader sample of countries. In addition to the OECD countries considered in Figure 5.5, the sample includes middle income countries and some very poor countries, 71 countries overall. As can be seen from the figure, this data set does not support convergence. Notice in particular that some of the countries with the lowest initial levels of per capita income had low and in some cases negative rates of growth in subsequent years.

How should we interpret the disparate findings about convergence? One interpretation of the data from OECD countries and U.S. states is that the assumption that these groups had similar economic features is reasonable. Thus, they may have the same steady state equilibrium income levels. Countries or states with lower initial income levels were below their steady state equilibrium point. The economic infrastructure in some OECD countries, for example, certainly sustained more damage in World War II than in others. In the case of U.S. states, the economies of southern states were devastated by the Civil War while those of the northern states were not.

---

[10]See Robert J. Barro and Xavier Sala-i-Martin, "Convergence," *Journal of Political Economy*, 100 (April 1992), pp. 223–51.

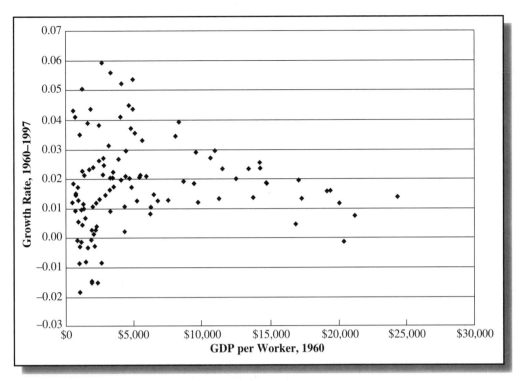

Figure 5.6 Convergence in OECD and Non-OECD Countries, 1960–97

When we go to the broad sample of countries, the assumption of similar economic structures across countries may become untenable. Thus, these countries have very different steady states. Consequently, they are not moving to any one capital/labor or capital/output ratio. Their income levels are not converging.

The concept of convergence we have considered so far is called *absolute* convergence. Countries with lower initial income will have higher subsequent growth rates period. A weaker concept is *conditional* convergence. An economy will grow more rapidly if it is below its own steady state per capita income level. Steady state levels will, however, differ across countries due to the different features of their economies. Conditioned upon these different economic features, countries with higher initial income levels will have lower growth rates in later years.

A number of studies have found support for conditional convergence across a broad set of countries such as that in Figure 5.6.[11] Important control variables, those that influence the steady state income level across countries, include the level of human capital per capita, adherence to the rule of law, the degree of openness to foreign trade, and some macroeconomic variables such as inflation rates and government consumption ratios. Given these variables, the initial income level has the expected negative effect. Still, these studies indicate that convergence is a slow process occurring over many decades.

---

[11]See, for example, Robert J. Barro, and Xavier Sala-i-Martin, *Economic Growth* 2nd edition (New York: McGraw Hill, 2004, Chapter 12.)

5.5 Conclusion

The neoclassical growth model implies that the rate of technological change is the primary determinant of the steady state equilibrium rate of growth in per capita income. The saving rate and therefore rate of investment in both physical and human capital will affect the growth rate for a considerable period of time and will also influence the steady state capital/labor and capital/output ratios. In endogenous growth models the saving rate and thus the rate of capital formation can have permanent effects on a nation's growth rate.

Because of inter-country differences in these variables, there have been large differences across countries in growth experiences. Past "shocks" such as wars, civil unrest, rapacious dictators, and colonial domination no doubt also influenced cross-country differences in growth rates. Consequently, there are very large disparities in per capita income levels across countries. The gains that could be made in a country by a generation of rapid growth are huge. Per capita income in Taiwan grew by 6.4 percent per year between 1960 and 2000. This growth increased the level of per capita income by a factor of 13. Singapore, Hong Kong, and South Korea all had growth rates of over 5 percent per year. This is what has been called the "Asian miracle." In contrast, in the Democratic Republic of Congo, per capita income *fell* at an annual rate of 3.2 percent over these years and the level of per capita income by 2000 was at one-third the level of 1960.

Concerning the factors that lead to rapid growth in some countries and stagnation in others, Robert Lucas has written, "The consequences for human welfare involved in questions like these are simply staggering: Once one starts to think about them, it is hard to think about anything else."[12]

Key Terms

• constant returns to scale 80

• capital deepening 81

Review Questions and Problems

1. Explain why, in the neoclassical growth model with exogenous technological change, the long-run equilibrium rate of growth in output is independent of the saving rate (S/Y).
2. Explain why, in a model with endogenous technological change, a rise in the saving rate may lead to a permanent rise in the long-run growth rate in output.
3. According to Denison's estimates, which factors were the most important in accounting for the growth in real output over the 1929–82 period?
4. What features of the neoclassical growth model led to the criticism that the model did not really *explain* the processes that generated economic growth? How do endogenous growth models try to remedy this possible weakness of the neoclassical model?
5. Explain the convergence hypothesis. How does the hypothesis of absolute convergence differ from that of conditional convergence?

---

[12]Robert Lucas, Jr., "On the Mechanics of Economic Development," *Journal of Monetary Economics*, 22 (July 1988), pp. 3–42.

Chapter **6**

The Keynesian System (I): The Role of Aggregate Demand

6.1 THE PROBLEM OF UNEMPLOYMENT

Keynesian economics developed against the background of the world depression of the 1930s. The effect of the Depression on the U.S. economy can be seen in Figure 6.1, which shows the annual unemployment rates for the years 1929–41. The unemployment rate rose from 3.2 percent of the labor force in 1929 to 25.2 percent in 1933, the low point for economic activity during the Depression. Unemployment remained at over 10 percent throughout the decade. Real gross national product (GNP) fell by 30 percent between 1929 and 1933, and did not reach the 1929 level again until 1939.

The British economist John Maynard Keynes, whose book *The General Theory of Employment, Interest and Money* is the foundation of the Keynesian system, was more heavily influenced by events in his own country than those in the United States. In Great Britain, high unemployment began in the early 1920s and persisted into and throughout the 1930s.[1] The high unemployment in Great Britain led to a debate among economists and policymakers over the causes and the proper policy response to increased unemployment. Keynes was a prominent participant in this debate, during the course of which he developed his revolutionary theory of macroeconomics.

According to Keynes's theory, high unemployment in Great Britain and the United States (as well as in other industrialized countries) was the result of a deficiency in *aggregate demand*. Aggregate demand was too low because of inadequate investment demand. Keynes's theory provided the basis for economic policies to combat unemployment by stimulating aggregate demand. At the time of the Depression, Keynes favored fiscal policy measures, primarily government spending on public works projects, to stimulate demand. More generally, the Keynesian theory

---

[1] The unemployment rate in Great Britain was above 10 percent as early as 1923 and remained above 10 percent, except for one brief fall to 9.8 percent, until 1936, the year *The General Theory* was published.

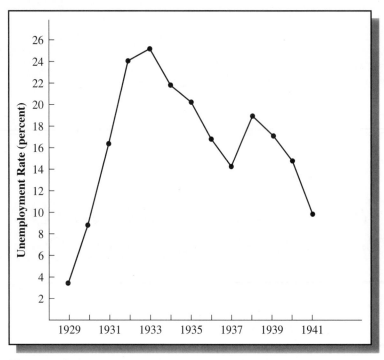

Figure 6.1 U.S. Unemployment Rate, 1929–41

advocates using monetary and fiscal policies to regulate aggregate demand. To understand the revolutionary nature of this theory, consider the state of macroeconomic thinking about unemployment as an economic policy question at the time Keynes's thought was developing.

Classical economists recognized the human cost of unemployment, as stated, for example, by Alfred Marshall:

> Forced interruption to labour is a grievous evil. Those, whose livelihood is secure, gain physical and mental health from happy and well-spent holidays. But want of work, with long continued anxiety, consumes a man's best strength without any return. His wife becomes thin; and his children get, as it were, a nasty notch in their lives, which is perhaps never outgrown.[2]

But Marshall had little to say about the causes of unemployment. He noted that unemployment existed in early times and argued that knowledge was the cure, in that it would increase the skills of labor and also keep laborers and firms from making poor economic decisions that would result in business failures and unemployment. When Marshall suggested ways to diminish fluctuations in employment, the following was the first given:

> Those causes of discontinuity which lie within our scope, and are remediable, are chiefly connected in some way or other with the want of knowledge;

---

[2]Alfred Marshall, *Money, Credit and Commerce* (London: Macmillan, 1922), p. 260.

but there is one which is willful: it is fashion. Until a little while ago only the rich could change their clothing at the capricious order of their dressmakers: but now all classes do it. The histories of the alpaca trade, the lace trade, the straw hat trade, the ribbon trade, and a multitude of others, tell of bursts of feverish activity alternating with deadening idleness.[3]

To the modern reader, this analysis must appear quaint; it was hardly a basis for meaningful solutions to the unemployment problem of Britain in the 1920s. Marshall and the other economists relying on the classical theory had little else to offer.

Much of the debate over economic policy in Great Britain at that time focused on the desirability of government spending on public works as a cure for unemployment, what we would now term an expansionary fiscal policy action. Keynes and others argued that such actions would increase output and employment. Such expenditures would act both directly and indirectly because they would increase the income and hence consumer expenditure of those employed by the public works projects, thus generating secondary employment.

Those arguing against Keynes's view drew primarily on the classical analysis we have presented in Chapters 3 and 4. Increases in government expenditure, unless financed by money creation and thus changes in monetary policy, would not affect either employment or the price level. If public works projects were financed by creating money, the price level but not the levels of output or unemployment would be affected. This classical theory was the basis for the official position of the Conservative Party in Great Britain, which was in power for most of the 1920s and early 1930s. As Winston Churchill explained, "It is the orthodox Treasury dogma, steadfastly held, that whatever might be the political or social advantages, very little employment can, in fact, as a general rule, be created by state borrowing and state expenditure."

In the United States, classical policy prescriptions were also influential. Far from trying to raise demand and stimulate output and employment during the height of the Depression in 1932, the administration of Herbert Hoover engineered a large tax *increase*. Hoover's reason for increasing tax rates was to balance the federal budget in the wake of falling tax revenues as income declined. Because, in the classical system, fiscal policy had no effect on income, prudent budget management had come to mean simply balancing spending with tax revenues.[4] When Franklin Roosevelt ran against Hoover for the presidency in 1932, he attacked Hoover for failing to balance the budget and argued for *cuts* in government spending. Bernard Baruch, an advisor to several presidents, expressed the conventional policy prescription as follows:

Balance budgets, stop spending money we haven't got. Sacrifice for frugality and revenue. Cut government spending—cut it as rations are cut in a siege. Tax—tax everybody for everything.[5]

---

[3]Ibid.

[4]This ignores the supply-side effects of a change in the tax rate, discussed in section 4.3. As explained there, the classical economists gave little consideration to those effects, though they have become an important policy consideration in recent years.

[5]Arthur M. Schlesinger, *The Crisis of the Old Order* (New York: Houghton Mifflin, 1957), p. 457.

Would not the increase in taxes or cut in government spending lower aggregate demand, output, and employment? Not in the classical system, because output and employment were supply-determined. In any case, in the classical model, fiscal policy did not affect aggregate demand. As we will see, such a tax increase or spending cut is just the opposite of the "correct" policy action indicated by the Keynesian model.

In sum, the situation in the early 1930s was one of massive unemployment that was not well explained by the classical system and for which classical economics provided no remedy. Many economists and political figures argued in favor of various policy actions, including public works projects, to try to increase aggregate demand. Such policies would not work in the classical system, where output and employment were not demand-determined. As Keynes pointed out: "The strength of the self-adjusting school depends on its having behind it almost the whole body of organized economic thinking and doctrine of the last hundred years."[6] Keynes ranged himself among the "heretics" to the classical view of the self-adjusting properties of the economy. Of the heretics, he wrote: "They are deeply dissatisfied. They believe that common observation is enough to show that facts do not conform to the orthodox reasoning. They propose remedies prompted by instinct, by flair, by practical good sense, by experience of the world—half right, most of them, half wrong."[7] Keynes felt that the heretics would never prevail until the flaw in the orthodox classical theory had been found. He believed that flaw to be the lack of an explicit theory of the aggregate demand for output and, hence, of the role of aggregate demand in determining output and employment. We discuss next the theory provided by Keynes and his followers to fill this gap.

Read Perspectives 6.1.

PERSPECTIVES 6.1
Macroeconomic Controversies

In this part we consider different schools of macroeconomics. This puts the emphasis on controversies. It should be kept in mind though that we are interested in fundamental differences, which are rooted in macroeconomic models not in partisan policy disputes. The dividing line between the two is not always clearly drawn but to see that the line exists consider the following.

Lionel Robbins was a prominent exponent of the classical economics. Dismissing some critics of that theory he wrote:

> On this plane, not only is any real knowledge of the classical writers non-existent but further their place has been taken by a set of mythological figures, passing by the same names, but not infrequently invested with attitudes almost exactly the reverse of those which the originals adopted. These dummies are very malignant creatures indeed. . . . They can conceive of no function for the state than that of the night watchman. . . . Hence, when a popular writer of the day wishes to present his own point of view in a specially favourable setting, he has only to point the contrast with the attitude of these reprehensible people and the desired effect is produced.[a]

Robbins, however, conceded the need to critically reexamine the writings of the classical economists to see, "to what extent is their theory of the market sustained by the results of more recent analysis? How far were they justified in the hope

---

[6]John M. Keynes, *Collected Works*, vol. 13 (London: Macmillan, 1973), p. 489.
[7]Ibid., pp. 488–89.

that financial controls (about the exact nature of which they never reached agreement) were sufficient to maintain the stability of the envelope of aggregate demand? Were the Classical Economists right in their apprehensions of over-all collectivism?"[b]

That to Robbins Keynes was no popular writer of the day but rather a very serious critic can be seen from a description he provided in a different context.

Keynes was in his most lucid and persuasive mood; and the effect was irresistible. At such moments, I often find myself thinking that Keynes must be one of the most remarkable men that ever lived—the quick logic, the birdlike swoop of intuition, the vivid fancy, the wide vision, above all the incomparable sense of the fitness of words, all combine to make something several degrees beyond the limit of ordinary human achievement. . . . He uses the classical style of our life and language, it is true, but it is shot through with something which is not traditional, a unique unearthly quality of which one can only say that it is pure genius.[c]

The quote shows the awe in which Keynes was held (at least at times) even by those he attacked. I also use it to indicate that Keynes's arguments with the classical economists and the later criticisms of Keynes's theory by economists such as Milton Friedman and Robert Lucas are contributions by some of the major intellectual figures of our age.

---

[a]Lionel Robbins, *The Theory of Economic Policy* (London: Macmillan, 1952), p. 5.
[b]Ibid., p. 206.
[c]Quoted from Robert Skidelsky, *John Maynard Keynes, Fighting For Freedom, 1937–1946* (New York: Viking, 2001).

6.2 THE SIMPLE KEYNESIAN MODEL: CONDITIONS FOR EQUILIBRIUM OUTPUT

A central notion in the Keynesian model is that an equilibrium level of output requires that *output be equal to aggregate demand*. In our model, this condition for equilibrium can be expressed as

$$Y = E \tag{6.1}$$

where Y is equal to total output (GDP) and E equals aggregate demand or desired expenditures on output. Aggregate demand (E) consists of three components: household consumption (C), desired business investment demand (I), and the government sector's demand for goods and services (G). Thus, in equilibrium we have

$$Y = E = C + I + G \tag{6.2}$$

The simple form of (6.2) and of the identities discussed later results from neglecting some complexities in the definitions of GDP and national income. These simplifications, discussed in Chapter 2, are noted here briefly again. Exports and imports do not appear in equation (6.2). For now, we are dealing with a "closed" economy, neglecting foreign trade. The roles of imports and exports in the simple Keynesian model will be considered in section 6.7. Notice that for a closed economy we need not distinguish between gross domestic product and gross national product, the other output measure defined in Chapter 2. Depreciation is also neglected, so we do not need to distinguish between GDP and net national product. We also assume that GDP and national income are equivalent. This means we do not include items in the model that cause a discrepancy between the two totals (primarily indirect business taxes). A final assumption relates to the units in which each of the variables is measured. For this chapter, we assume that *the aggregate price level is fixed*. All variables are *real* variables, and all changes are changes in real terms.

With national product Y also measuring national income, we can write

$$Y \equiv C + S + T \tag{6.3}$$

Equation (6.3) is an accounting definition, or identity, stating that national income, all of which is assumed to be paid to households in return for factor services (wages, interest, rents, dividends), is either consumed (C), paid out in taxes (T), or saved (S).[8] In addition, from the fact that Y is national product, we can write

$$Y \equiv C + I_r + G \tag{6.4}$$

Equation (6.4) defines national product as equal to consumption plus *realized* investment (I_r) plus government spending.[9]

Using the definitions given in equations (6.3) and (6.4), we can rewrite the condition for equilibrium income given in equation (6.2) in two alternative ways, which will help us understand the nature of equilibrium in the model. By (6.2), Y must equal $(C + I + G)$ in equilibrium, and from (6.3), Y is defined as $(C + S + T)$; *in equilibrium* therefore,

$$C + S + T \equiv Y = C + I + G$$

or, equivalently,

$$S + T = I + G \tag{6.5}$$

In similar fashion, from equations (6.2) and (6.4) we can see that in equilibrium

$$C + I_r + G \equiv Y = C + I + G$$

or, by canceling terms,

$$I_r = I \tag{6.6}$$

There are then three equivalent ways to state the condition for equilibrium in the model:

$$Y = E = C + I + G \tag{6.2}$$
$$S + T = I + G \tag{6.5}$$
$$I_r = I \tag{6.6}$$

To help interpret these conditions, we turn to the flowchart in Figure 6.2. Each magnitude in the chart (each of the variables in our model) is a *flow* variable. The magnitudes are measured in dollars per period. In the national income accounts, they are measured as billions of dollars per quarter or year. The flow marked with the uppermost arrow in the diagram is the flow of national income from the business

---

[8]The model does not allow for retained earnings. All profits are paid out as dividends. Also, firms are assumed to make no tax payments; all taxes are paid by households.
[9]Recall from Chapter 2 that *realized* investment is the total that appears in the national income accounts whether or not that investment was desired by firms.

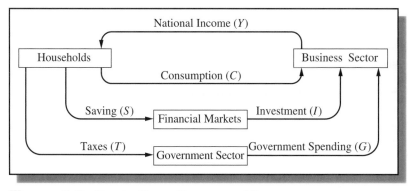

Figure 6.2 Circular Flow of Income and Output

sector to the household sector. This flow consists of payments for factor services. Such payments sum to national income, which is equal to national product. There is a corresponding flow from the household sector to the business sector, consisting of the factor services supplied by the household sector. This flow and similar flows are not shown in the diagram because they are not money flows.

National income is distributed by households into three flows. One is a flow of consumption expenditures that goes back to the business sector as a demand for the output. Thus the inner loop of our diagram depicts a process whereby firms produce output (Y), which generates an equal amount of income to the household sector, which in turn generates a demand for the output produced (C).

Not all national income returns directly to the firms as a demand for output. There are two flows out of the household sector in addition to consumption expenditure—the saving flow and the flow of tax payments. If we regard the inner loop of our diagram, linking the households (as suppliers of factor services and demanders of output) and the business sector (as suppliers of output and demanders of factor services) as the central income- and output-generating mechanism, the saving and tax flows are *leakages* from this central loop.

The saving leakage flows into financial markets, which means that the part of income that is saved is held in the form of some financial asset (currency, bank deposits, bonds, equities, etc.). The tax flow is paid to the government sector. The tax flow in the diagram is *net* taxes—that is, gross tax payments minus transfer payments from the government to the household sector (Social Security benefits, welfare payments, unemployment compensation, etc.). Consequently, in later discussions, a tax increase or a tax cut can be interpreted equivalently as a change in the opposite direction in the level of transfer payments.

Although each dollar of output and, hence, national income does not directly generate one dollar of demand for output on the part of the household sector, this does not mean that total demand must fall short of output. There are additional demands for output on the part of the business sector itself for investment and from the government sector. In terms of the circular flow, these are *injections* into the central loop of our diagram. The investment injection is shown as a flow from financial markets to the business sector. The purchasers of the investment goods are actually the firms in the business sector themselves. These purchases must, however, be financed by borrowing. Thus the dollar amount of investment represents an equivalent flow of funds lent to the business sector. Government spending is a demand for the output of the business sector and is shown as a money flow from the government to the business sector.

We can now examine the three equivalent expressions for equilibrium given by equations (6.2), (6.5), and (6.6). Production of a level of output, Y, generates an equivalent amount of income to households. A portion of this income, equal to consumption demand (C), returns directly to the firms as a demand for output. The level of output will be at equilibrium if this directly generated demand (C), when added to desired investment expenditures of firms (I) and government spending (G), produces a total demand equal to Y—that is, if

$$Y = E = C + I + G \tag{6.2}$$

From the second version of the condition for equilibrium income

$$S + T = I + G \tag{6.5}$$

we see that a flow rate of output will be an equilibrium rate if the leakages ($S + T$) from the central loop of our diagram are just balanced by injections ($I + G$) into this central income and output circular flow. This rate ensures that the amount of income households do not spend on output ($S + T$), and therefore the amount of output that is produced but not sold to households ($Y - C \equiv S + T$), is just equal to the amount the other two sectors wish to buy ($I + G$). This is equivalent to saying that total output equals aggregate demand and is thus also equivalent to the first way of stating the condition for equilibrium.

The third way of expressing the condition for equilibrium, equation (6.6) ($I = I_r$), states that in equilibrium desired investment must equal realized investment. What does it mean for desired investment to differ from realized investment? The GDP accountant computes investment as the total volume of business spending on plant and equipment, plus inventory investment, the increase (or decline) in inventories.[10] We assume that desired spending on plant and equipment equals actual spending as recorded by the GDP accountant. It is in the last category, inventory investment, that desired and realized totals may differ. The GDP accountant will record all goods that are produced by a firm and not sold as inventory investment—*whether such investment was intended or not.*

To see how realized and intended inventory investment can differ, consider what happens when a level of output ($Y \equiv C + I_r + G$) is produced that exceeds aggregate demand ($E = C + I + G$). In this case,

$$Y > E$$
$$C + I_r + G > C + I + G \tag{6.7}$$
$$I_r > I$$

where $I_r - I$ is the *unintended inventory accumulation.* The amount by which output exceeds aggregate demand ($I_r - I$) will be unsold output over and above the amount

---

[10]Here, to keep the discussion simple, we are ignoring residential construction investment. In Chapter 7, the investment concept will be broadened.

of inventory investment the firm desired. This excess is unintended inventory accumulation.

In the reverse situation, in which aggregate demand exceeds output, we have

$$E > Y$$
$$C + I + G > C + I_r + G \qquad\qquad (6.8)$$
$$I > I_r$$

where $I - I_r$ is the *unintended inventory shortfall*. Demand is greater than output, and firms sell more than was planned. Inventories end up at less than the desired level. The equilibrium point ($I = I_r$) is a level of production that, after all sales are made, leaves inventory investment at just the level desired by firms. As can be seen from equation (6.7) or (6.8), this is the level at which output equals aggregate demand and hence is equivalent to the other two ways of expressing the condition for equilibrium.

This third way of expressing the condition for equilibrium in the model shows clearly why there cannot be an equilibrium at any other point. If, at a given level of output, firms are accumulating undesired inventories or are seeing their inventories depleted, there is a tendency for output to change. If production exceeds demand ($Y > E$), firms are accumulating unwanted inventories ($I_r > I$), and there is a tendency for output to fall as firms cut production to reduce the level of inventories. If, alternatively, demand is outstripping production ($E > Y$), there is an inventory shortfall ($I_r < I$) and a tendency for output to rise as firms try to prevent further falls in inventories. Only when aggregate demand equals output will firms be satisfied with their current level of output. There is neither an unintended inventory buildup nor a shortfall and, therefore, no tendency for output to change. This situation is what is meant by equilibrium.

6.3 THE COMPONENTS OF AGGREGATE DEMAND

We have expressed the condition for equilibrium in the simple Keynesian model in terms of the components of aggregate demand. To see the factors that determine the level of income, we consider the factors that affect the components of aggregate demand: consumption, investment, and government spending. Saving and taxes also enter into our discussion.

Consumption

Consumer expenditure is the largest component of aggregate demand, amounting to between 60 and 70 percent of GDP in recent years.

Keynes believed that the level of consumer expenditure was a stable function of disposable income, where disposable income (Y_D) in our simple model is national income minus net tax payments ($Y_D = Y - T$).[11] Keynes did not deny that variables other than income affect consumption, but he believed that income was the dominant

---

[11]Recall here that T is net taxes (i.e., gross tax payments minus transfer payments). Disposable income ($Y_D = Y - T$) is therefore national income minus gross taxes plus transfer payments.

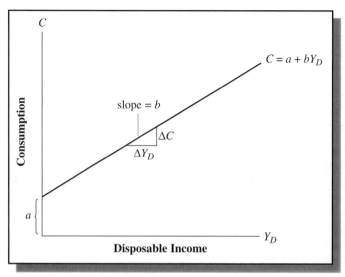

Figure 6.3 Keynesian Consumption Function

The consumption function shows the level of consumption (C) corresponding to each level of disposable income (Y_D). The slope of the consumption function ($\Delta C / \Delta Y_D$) is the marginal propensity to consume (b), the increase in consumption per unit increase in disposable income. The intercept for the consumption function (a) is the (positive) level of consumption at a zero level of disposable income.

factor determining consumption. In a first approximation, other influences could be neglected.

The specific form of the consumption–income relationship, termed the **consumption function**, proposed by Keynes was as follows:

consumption function
the Keynesian relationship between income and consumption

$$C = a + bY_D, \qquad a > 0, \qquad 0 < b < 1 \qquad \textbf{(6.9)}$$

Figure 6.3 graphs this relationship. The intercept term a, which is assumed to be positive, is the value of consumption when disposable income equals zero. As such, a can be thought of as a measure of the effect on consumption of variables other than income, variables not explicitly included in this simple model. The parameter b, the slope of the function, gives the increase in consumer expenditure per unit increase in disposable income. In notation, we frequently use

$$b = \frac{\Delta C}{\Delta Y_D} \qquad \textbf{(6.10)}$$

marginal propensity to consume (MPC)
the increase in consumption per unit increase in disposable income

where, as in Chapter 3, the differencing symbol, Δ, indicates the change in the variable it precedes. The value of the increment to consumer expenditure per unit increment to income (b) is termed the **marginal propensity to consume (MPC)**. The Keynesian assumption is that consumption will increase with an increase in disposable income ($b > 0$) but that the increase in consumption will be less than the increase in disposable income ($b < 1$).

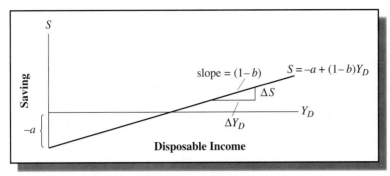

Figure 6.4 Keynesian Saving Function

The saving function shows the level of saving (S) at each level of disposable income (Y_D). The slope of the saving function is the marginal propensity to save ($1 - b$), the increase in saving per unit increase in disposable income. The intercept for the saving function ($-a$) is the (negative) level of saving at a zero level of disposable income.

From the definition of national income,

$$Y \equiv C + S + T \qquad (6.3)$$

we can write

$$Y_D \equiv Y - T \equiv C + S \qquad (6.11)$$

which shows that disposable income is, by definition, consumption plus saving. Thus a theory of the consumption–income relationship also implicitly determines the saving–income relationship. In the case of the Keynesian theory, we have

$$S = -a + (1 - b)Y_D \qquad (6.12)$$

If consumption is a units with Y_D equal to 0, then *at that point*

$$S \equiv Y_D - C = 0 - a$$
$$= -a$$

If a one-unit increase in disposable income leads to an increase of b units in consumption, the remainder ($1 - b$) is the increase in saving:

$$\frac{\Delta S}{\Delta Y_D} = 1 - b \qquad (6.13)$$

This increment to saving per unit increase in disposable income ($1 - b$) is called the **marginal propensity to save (MPS)**. The graph of the saving function is shown in Figure 6.4.

marginal propensity to save (MPS)
the increase in saving per unit increase in disposable income

Investment

Investment was also a key variable in the Keynesian system. Changes in desired business investment expenditure were one of the major factors that Keynes thought were responsible for changes in income.

As noted previously, Keynes believed that consumption was a stable function of disposable income. This view did not imply that the level of consumption expenditures would not vary over time. It did imply that, in the absence of other factors that caused income to change, consumption expenditures would not be an important independent source of variability in income. Consumption was primarily *induced* expenditure, meaning expenditure that depends directly on income.

To explain the underlying causes of movements in aggregate demand and, hence, income, Keynes looked to the *autonomous* components of aggregate demand. These components were determined, in large part, independently of current income. When these expenditure components varied, they caused income to vary. Keynes believed that investment was the most highly variable of the autonomous components of aggregate demand. He believed that variable investment spending was primarily responsible for income instability.

Table 6.1 contains figures for investment and consumption as percentages of gross national product in selected years. The data contrast investment and consumption spending in prosperous years (1929, 1955, 1973, 1979, 1989) with corresponding spending in subsequent depression or recession years (1933, 1958, 1975, 1982, 1991). Investment spending does appear to be more volatile and is a logical choice as a factor explaining income variability. The question remains: What determines investment?

Keynes suggested two variables as primary determinants of investment expenditures in the short run: the interest rate and the state of business expectations.

In explaining the relationship between investment and the rate of interest, Keynes's analysis did not differ from the classical view. The level of investment is assumed to be inversely related to the level of the interest rate. At higher interest rates, fewer investment projects have a prospective return high enough to justify borrowing to finance them. This link will be important in Chapter 7. For now, because we have not explained how the interest rate is determined in the Keynesian model, we neglect the effect of the interest rate on investment. We focus on the second factor determining investment, the expected yield on investment projects.

Business managers' expectations about the future profitability of investment projects are a central element in Keynes's analysis. Keynes emphasized the "uncertain knowledge" upon which expectations of the future must be based. In planning

Table 6.1
Consumption and Investment as a Percentage of Gross National Product, Selected Years

YEAR	INVESTMENT	CONSUMPTION
1929	15.7	74.8
1933	2.5	82.1
1955	17.1	63.5
1958	13.8	64.5
1973	16.1	62.6
1975	12.5	64.0
1979	16.0	62.7
1982	13.1	65.3
1989	11.0	67.1
1991	9.6	68.5

the profitability of a project that will produce output over 20 or 30 years, a manager needs a great deal of knowledge about the future. He needs to know the future demand for the product, which requires knowledge about future consumer tastes and the state of aggregate demand. He needs knowledge about future costs, including money wages, interest rates, and tax rates; a well-grounded forecast of such variables cannot be made for 20 or 30 years into the future.

Nevertheless, investment decisions are made. Keynes felt that rational managers faced with the need to make decisions under such extreme uncertainty formed expectations using the following techniques:

1. They tended to extrapolate past trends into the future, ignoring possible future changes, unless there was specific information about a prospective change.
2. "Knowing that our own individual judgment is worthless, we endeavor to fall back on the judgment of the rest of the world which is perhaps better informed. That is, we endeavor to conform with the behavior of the majority or the average. The psychology of a society of individuals each of whom is endeavoring to copy the others leads to what we may strictly term a *conventional* judgment."[12]

Keynes believed that an expectation formed in this manner would have the following property.

In particular, being based on so flimsy a foundation, it is subject to sudden and violent changes. The practice of calmness and immobility, of certainty and security, suddenly breaks down. New fears and hopes will, without warning, take charge of human conduct. The forces of disillusion may suddenly impose a new conventional basis of valuation. All these pretty, polite techniques, made for a well-panelled board room, are liable to collapse. At all times the vague panic fears and equally vague and unreasoned hopes are not really lulled, and lie but a little way below the surface.[13]

In summary, expectations of the future profitability of investment projects rested on a very precarious base of knowledge, and Keynes felt that such expectations could shift frequently, at times drastically, in response to new information and events. Consequently, investment demand was unstable. Investment expenditure is the main component of autonomous expenditures that Keynes believed to be responsible for income instability.

Government Spending and Taxes

Government spending (G) is a second element of autonomous expenditures. Government spending is assumed to be controlled by the policymaker and therefore does not depend directly on the level of income.

We assume that the level of tax receipts (T) is also controlled by the policymaker and is a policy variable. A more realistic assumption is that the policymaker sets the tax rate, and tax receipts vary with income. This assumption would complicate

---

[12]John M. Keynes, "The General Theory of Employment," *Quarterly Journal of Economics* (February 1937), p. 214.
[13]Ibid., pp. 214–15.

our calculations but would not change the essential conclusions (more complex tax structures are discussed in Chapter 19, where we consider fiscal policy in more detail).

6.4 DETERMINING EQUILIBRIUM INCOME

We now have all the elements needed to determine equilibrium income (output).[14] The first form of the condition for an equilibrium level of income is

$$Y = E = C + I + G \qquad (6.2)$$

Equilibrium income (Y) is the *endogenous* variable to be determined. The *autonomous* expenditure terms I and G are given, as is the level of T; these are the *exogenous* variables determined by factors outside the model. Consumption is, for the most part, *induced* expenditure determined *endogenously* by the consumption function

$$C = a + bY_D = a + bY - bT \qquad (6.9)$$

where the second equality uses the definition of disposable income ($Y_D \equiv Y - T$).

Substituting the equation for consumption given by (6.9) into the equilibrium condition (6.2), we can solve for $\overline{Y}$, the equilibrium level of income, as follows:

$$
\begin{aligned}
Y &= C + I + G \\
Y &= a + bY - bT + I + G \\
Y - bY &= a - bT + I + G \\
Y(1 - b) &= a - bT + I + G \\
\overline{Y} &= \frac{1}{1 - b}(a - bT + I + G)
\end{aligned}
\qquad (6.14)
$$

Figure 6.5 depicts the determination of equilibrium income. Income is measured along the horizontal axis, and the components of aggregate demand are measured along the vertical axis. The 45° line is drawn to split the positive quadrant of the graph. All points along this line indicate that aggregate expenditures equal aggregate output. The value of the variables measured on the vertical axis, ($C + I + G$), is equal to the value of the variable measured on the horizontal axis, (Y). The consumption function ($C = a + bY_D$) is shown on the graph, and we have also plotted the ($C + I + G$) or aggregate expenditure (E) schedule, which is obtained by adding the autonomous expenditure components, investment and government spending, to consumption spending at each level of income. Because the autonomous expenditure components (I, G) do not depend directly on income, the ($C + I + G$) schedule lies above the consumption function by a constant amount.

As shown in Figure 6.5b, the line plotting these autonomous expenditure components alone, the $I + G$ line, is horizontal because their level does not depend on Y. The

---

[14]Recall that national output and income are identical under the assumptions we have made. These terms are used interchangeably in our discussion.

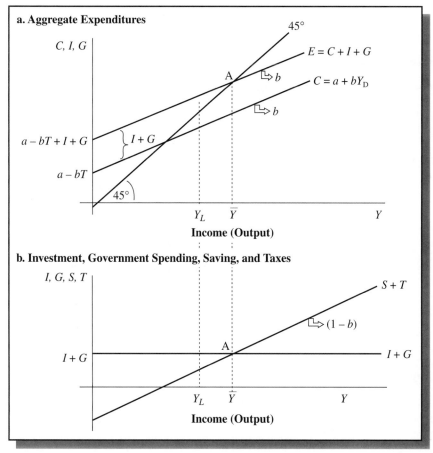

a. Aggregate Expenditures

Figure 6.5 Determination of Equilibrium Income

In part *a*, the equilibrium level of income is $\overline{Y}$, at point A where the $C + I + G = E$ schedule intersects the 45° line. At that point, aggregate expenditures equal output, $(C + I + G) = Y$. At point A in part *b*, at the equilibrium level of output, $\overline{Y}$, the $S + T$ and $I + G$ schedules intersect, so $S + T = I + G$. At the level of income Y_L, which is less than equilibrium output $\overline{Y}$, aggregate demand exceeds output, $(C + I + G) > Y$. At points greater than equilibrium output $\overline{Y}$, output exceeds aggregate demand.

upward-sloping line, marked $S + T$ in the graph, plots the value of saving plus taxes. This schedule slopes upward because saving varies positively with income.

In Figure 6.5*a*, the equilibrium level of income is shown at the point where the $(C + I + G)$ schedule crosses the 45° line, and aggregate demand is therefore equal to income $(\overline{Y})$. This intersection illustrates the equilibrium condition expressed in equation (6.2). In equilibrium, it must also be true that the $(S + T)$ schedule intersects the $(I + G)$ horizontal schedule. This intersection, shown in Figure 6.5*b*, illustrates the equilibrium condition expressed in equation (6.5).

The understanding of the properties of an equilibrium level of income is aided by considering why other points on the graph are not points of equilibrium. Consider a level of income below $\overline{Y}$, for example, the point marked Y_L in Figure 6.5*a*.

A level of income equal to Y_L generates consumption as shown along the consumption function. When this level of consumption is added to the autonomous expenditures $(I + G)$, aggregate demand exceeds income; the $(C + I + G)$ schedule is above the $45°$ line. Equivalently, at this point $I + G$ is greater than $S + T$, as can be seen in Figure 6.5b. It also follows that with demand outstripping production, desired investment will exceed actual investment at points such as $Y_L (C + I + G > Y \equiv C + I_r + G$; therefore, $I > I_r)$. There will be an unintended inventory shortfall at such points below $\overline{Y}$ and therefore a tendency for output to rise.

Conversely, at levels of income above $\overline{Y}$ in Figure 6.5a, and 6.5b, output will exceed demand (the $45°$ line is above the $C + I + G$ schedule), and unintended inventory investment will be taking place ($Y \equiv C + I_r + G > C + I + G$; therefore, $I_r > I$), and there will be a tendency for output to fall. It is only at Y that output is equal to aggregate demand; there is no unintended inventory shortfall or accumulation and, consequently, no tendency for output to change.

Returning to our expression for equilibrium income, equation (6.14), we can rewrite this equation in a form that gives the essence of Keynes's view of income determination. Our expression for equilibrium consists of two parts:

$$\overline{Y} = \frac{1}{1-b}(a - bT + I + G)$$

$$\overline{Y} = \left(\begin{array}{c} \text{autonomous expenditure} \\ \text{multiplier} \end{array} \right) \times \left(\begin{array}{c} \text{autonomous} \\ \text{expenditures} \end{array} \right)$$

(6.15)

autonomous expenditure multiplier
gives the change in equilibrium output per unit change in autonomous expenditures (e.g., government spending)

The first term, $1/(1 - b)$, is called the **autonomous expenditure multiplier**. Note that b is the fraction of any increment to disposable income that goes to consumption—the marginal propensity to consume (MPC). The term $1/(1 - b)$ or $1/(1 - \text{MPC})$ is then 1 divided by a fraction and, hence, some number greater than 1. Some examples are as follows:

$$b = 0.5: \quad \frac{1}{1-b} = \frac{1}{1-0.5} = \frac{1}{0.5} = 2$$

$$b = 0.8: \quad \frac{1}{1-b} = \frac{1}{1-0.8} = \frac{1}{0.2} = 5$$

$$b = 0.9: \quad \frac{1}{1-b} = \frac{1}{1-0.9} = \frac{1}{0.1} = 10$$

We call this term the autonomous expenditure multiplier because every dollar of autonomous expenditure is multiplied by this factor to get its contribution to equilibrium income.

autonomous expenditures
are expenditures that are largely determined by factors other than current income

The second term in the expression is the level of **autonomous expenditures**. We have already discussed two elements of autonomous expenditures, investment (I) and government spending (G). The first two terms $(a$ and $-bT)$ require a few words of explanation. These terms measure the autonomous component of consumption expenditures (a) and the autonomous effect of tax collections on aggregate demand $(-bT)$, which also works through consumption. Consumption is, for the most part, induced expenditures, as explained previously. The two terms $(a$ and $-bT)$, however, affect the amount of consumption *for a given level of income* (Y). In terms of Figure 6.5, they determine the height of the consumption function. Like G and I, they affect the amount of aggregate demand for a given level of income rather than being themselves directly determined by income. They are thus appropriately included as autonomous factors affecting aggregate demand.

Keynes's theory in its simplest form can be stated as follows. Consumption is a stable function of income; that is, the marginal propensity to consume is stable. Changes in income come primarily from changes in the autonomous components of aggregate demand, especially from changes in the unstable investment component. A given change in an autonomous component of aggregate demand causes a larger change in equilibrium income because of the multiplier, for reasons we explain later. Equation (6.15) makes clear that, in the absence of government policies to stabilize the economy, income will be unstable because of the instability of investment. From equation (6.15) one can also see that by appropriate changes in government spending (G) and taxes (T), the government could counteract the effects of shifts in investment. Appropriate changes in G and T could keep the sum of the terms in parentheses (autonomous expenditures) constant even in the face of undesirable changes in the I term.

6.5 CHANGES IN EQUILIBRIUM INCOME

Consider the effect on equilibrium income of a change in autonomous investment demand. We assume that the other determinants of autonomous expenditures, the other items in parentheses in equation (6.15), are fixed. We solve for the change in equilibrium income from equation (6.15) as follows:

$$\Delta \bar{Y} = \frac{1}{1-b} \Delta I \qquad \text{(6.16)}$$

or

$$\frac{\Delta \bar{Y}}{\Delta I} = \frac{1}{1-b} \qquad \text{(6.17)}$$

A one-unit change in investment causes a change in income of $1/(1-b)$ units. If b is 0.8, for example, Y changes by five units for each one-unit change in investment. Why does income change by a multiple of the change in investment, and why by the precise amount $1/(1-b)$?

One analogy to the process behind the multiplier is the "ripple effect" of a stone dropped in a pond. There is the initial effect as the stone disturbs the water. Added to this is the effect on the rest of the water surface as the water displaced by the stone spreads out to the adjoining water, with intensity that diminishes with the distance from the initial point of impact. The investment change is the initial disturbance; let us assume this equals 100 units. As some firms experience increased demand as a result of this increased investment, their output increases. In consequence, their payments to factors of production (wages, rents, interest, dividends) increase. To the households, this is an increase in income and, because taxes are fixed, an equal increase in disposable income. Consumption will then increase, although by less than the increase in income. This is the beginning of the indirect effects of the shock. With ΔI equal to 100 as assumed, if the MPC were 0.8, for example, there would now be an additional 80 units of consumer demand.

The process does not stop here; the 80 units of new consumer expenditure, with the resulting increase in production, generate a second-round increase in income for some households of 80 units. There will be a further increase in consumer demand (64 units if the MPC is 0.8). Thus, the reason that income rises by more than the autonomous rise in investment is that the rise in investment leads to induced increases in consumer demand as income increases.

Why is the increase in income per dollar increase in investment just equal to $1/(1 - b)$? With the other elements of autonomous expenditures fixed, we can write the change in equilibrium income as investment varies as

$$\Delta Y = \Delta I + \Delta C \tag{6.18}$$

Restoring the equality of income and aggregate demand requires that equilibrium income rise by an amount equal to the increase in investment (ΔI) plus the income-induced increase in consumer demand. Rearranging terms in equation (6.18), we have

$$\Delta Y - \Delta C = \Delta I$$

or[15]

$$\Delta S = \Delta I \tag{6.19}$$

Equation (6.19) also follows from our second way of expressing the condition for equilibrium income:

$$S + T = I + G \tag{6.5}$$

With T and G fixed, to restore equilibrium, S must rise by the amount of the increase in I, as required by equation (6.19). Restoring equilibrium requires that income rise by enough to generate new saving equal to the new investment.

Because ΔS is equal to $(1 - b)\Delta Y$, we have, from equation (6.19),

$$(1 - b)\Delta Y = \Delta I$$

$$\frac{\Delta \overline{Y}}{\Delta I} = \frac{1}{1 - b} = \frac{1}{1 - \text{MPC}} = \frac{1}{\text{MPS}} \tag{6.20}$$

For example, if b equals 0.8, the marginal propensity to save (MPS = $1 - b$) is equal to 0.2. Each dollar increase in income will generate 20 cents worth of new saving, and a five-dollar increase in income will be required to generate the one dollar of new saving to balance a one-dollar increase in investment. The value of the multiplier in this case is 5.

The effect of an increase in autonomous investment is illustrated in Figure 6.6. Initially, with investment at I_0 and government spending and taxes at G_0 and T_0, equilibrium income is at $\overline{Y}_0$. Now let investment increase to the higher level, I_1. The aggregate demand (E) schedule shifts up by the amount ($\Delta I = I_1 - I_0$), from $E_0 (= C + I_0 + G_0)$ to $E_1 (= C + I_1 + G_0)$. The ($I + G$) schedule shifts up by the same amount. Equilibrium is restored at $\overline{Y}_1$, where income is now equal to the higher value of aggregate demand. Note that the increase in income is equal to the initial increase

---

[15]Note that tax collections are fixed, so $\Delta Y = \Delta Y_D$. Thus, $\Delta Y = \Delta Y_D \equiv \Delta C + \Delta S$ and, therefore, $\Delta Y - \Delta C = \Delta S$.

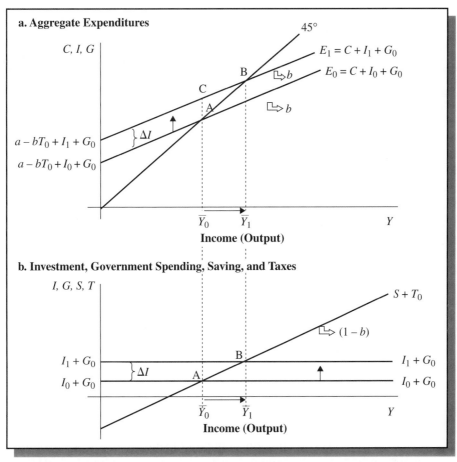

Figure 6.6 Effect of an Increase in Autonomous Investment on Equilibrium Income

In part *a*, beginning at equilibrium A, an increase in autonomous investment, from I_0 to I_1 shifts the aggregate expenditure schedule upward from $E_0 = C + I_0 + G_0$ to $E_1 = C + I_1 + G_0$. Equilibrium income increases from point A to point B, $\overline{Y}_0$ to $\overline{Y}_1$. The increase in income is equal to the initial increase in investment (shown as an increase in the intercept), I_0 to I_1, *plus* an income-induced increase in consumption. This increase in consumption is shown as we move along the higher expenditure function, E_1, from point C to point B. In part *b*, beginning at equilibrium A, the $I + G$ schedule shifts up from $I_0 + G_0$ to $I_1 + G_0$. Equilibrium income increases from point A to point B, $\overline{Y}_0$ to $\overline{Y}_1$.

in investment plus an induced increase in consumption (ΔC), as shown in the graph. Note also that at the new equilibrium, saving has increased by the same amount as investment ($\Delta S = \Delta I$).

The multiplier concept is central to Keynes's theory because it explains how shifts in investment caused by changes in business expectations set off a process that causes not only investment but also consumption to vary. The multiplier shows how shocks to one sector are transmitted throughout the economy. Keynes's theory also implies that other components of autonomous expenditure affect the overall level of equilibrium income. The effect on equilibrium income of a change in each of the two policy-controlled elements of autonomous expenditures, government spending and taxes, can be calculated from equation (6.15).

We proceed just as we did in considering the effects of a change in investment and let one component of autonomous expenditures change while each of the others is held constant. For a change in government spending (G), we have

$$\Delta \bar{Y} = \frac{1}{1-b} \Delta G$$

$$\frac{\Delta \bar{Y}}{\Delta G} = \frac{1}{1-b}$$

(6.21)

For a change in taxes, we have

$$\Delta \bar{Y} = \frac{1}{1-b} (-b) \Delta T$$

$$\frac{\Delta \bar{Y}}{\Delta T} = \frac{-b}{1-b}$$

(6.22)

For government spending, a one-dollar increase has the same effect as a one-dollar increase in investment. Both are one-dollar increases in autonomous expenditures. The multiplier process, whereby the initial increase in income generates induced increases in consumption, is the same for an increase in government spending as for investment.

In terms of Figure 6.6, in part a, an increase in government spending of ΔG would shift up the expenditure schedule by the same amount as an *equal* increase in investment. In this case, the intercept would shift up due to an increase in government spending. In part b, an increase in government spending of ΔG would shift up the $I + G$ schedule from $I_0 + G_0$ to $I_0 + G_1$, the same amount as an *equal* increase in investment. In both figures, ΔY will be the same; $\bar{Y}_0$ to $\bar{Y}_1$.

From equation (6.22) we see that the effect of an increase in taxes is in the opposite direction to those of increased government spending or investment. A tax increase lowers the level of disposable income $(Y - T)$ for any level of national income (Y). This effect shifts the aggregate demand schedule down because it reduces consumption spending *for any level of national income*. The effect on equilibrium income from a tax increase is illustrated in Figure 6.7. We assume that taxes rise by ΔT from T_0 to T_1. The aggregate demand schedule shifts from $(C + I + G)_0$ down to $(C + I + G)_1$. This is the consequence of the downward shift in the consumption function caused by the rise in taxes from T_0 to T_1. Equilibrium income falls from $\bar{Y}_0$ to $\bar{Y}_1$.

Notice that the aggregate demand schedule shifts down by $(-b\Delta T)$, that is, by only a fraction (b) of the increase in taxes. The reason is that, at a given level of income, a one-dollar increase in taxes reduces disposable income by one dollar but lowers the consumption component of aggregate demand by only b dollars. The rest of the decline in disposable income is absorbed by a fall of $(1 - b)$ dollars in saving. Unlike changes in government expenditures and investment, which have a dollar-for-dollar effect on autonomous aggregate demand, a one-dollar change in taxes

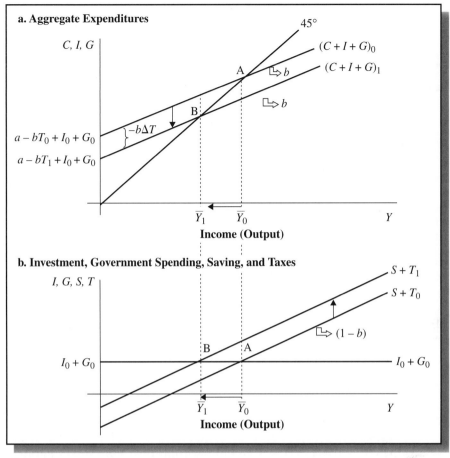

Figure 6.7 Effect of an Increase in Taxes on Equilibrium Income

An increase in taxes from T_0 to T_1 shifts the aggregate expenditure schedule downward in part *a*, from $(C + I + G)_0$ to $(C + I + G)_1$ to equilibrium point B, since taxes are in the intercept. Equilibrium income falls from $\overline{Y}_0$ to $\overline{Y}_1$. In part *b*, starting at equilibrium point A, the saving plus taxes schedule shifts up, from $S + T_0$ to $S + T_1$. Equilibrium moves from A to B.

shifts the aggregate demand schedule by only a fraction $(-b)$ of one dollar. This fraction $(-b)$ times the autonomous expenditure multiplier, $1/(1 - b)$, gives the effect on equilibrium income of a one-dollar change in taxes, $-b/(1 - b)$.

There is a relationship between the absolute values of tax and government expenditure multipliers, which can be seen in the following examples:

$$b = 0.5: \quad \frac{1}{1 - b} = \frac{1}{1 - 0.5} = 2; \quad \frac{-b}{1 - b} = \frac{-0.5}{1 - 0.5} = -1$$

$$b = 0.8: \quad \frac{1}{1 - b} = \frac{1}{1 - 0.8} = 5; \quad \frac{-b}{1 - b} = \frac{-0.8}{1 - 0.8} = -4$$

$$b = 0.9: \quad \frac{1}{1 - b} = \frac{1}{1 - 0.9} = 10; \quad \frac{-b}{1 - b} = \frac{-0.9}{1 - 0.9} = -9$$

The tax multiplier is one less in absolute value than the government expenditure multiplier. This fact has an interesting implication for the effects of an increase in government spending accompanied by an equal increase in taxes, a balanced-budget increase. To find the effects of such a combination of policy changes, we add the two policy multipliers to get the following expression:

$$\frac{\Delta \overline{Y}}{\Delta G} + \frac{\Delta \overline{Y}}{\Delta T} = \frac{1}{1-b} + \frac{-b}{1-b} = \frac{1-b}{1-b} = 1$$

A one-dollar increase in government spending financed by a one-dollar increase in taxes increases equilibrium income by just one dollar. This result, termed the **balanced-budget multiplier**, reflects the fact that tax changes have a smaller per-dollar impact on equilibrium income than do spending changes. The value of 1 for the multiplier results because the tax multiplier is one less in absolute value than the spending multiplier. The latter result does not carry through in many more complex models, but the result that tax changes affect aggregate demand by less per dollar than changes in government spending is quite general.

balanced-budget multiplier
gives the change in equilibrium output that results from a one-unit increase or decrease in *both* taxes and government spending

6.6 FISCAL STABILIZATION POLICY

Because equilibrium income is affected by changes in government spending and taxes, these fiscal policy instruments can be varied to stabilize the total of autonomous expenditures and, therefore, equilibrium income, even if the investment component is unstable.

An example of fiscal stabilization policy is illustrated in Figure 6.8. The economy is assumed to be in equilibrium at a potential level $\overline{Y}_P$, with aggregate demand at E_P equal to $(C + I_0 + G_0)$. We assume that from this point autonomous investment declines from I_0 to I_1, as a result of an unfavorable change in business expectations. In the absence of a policy action, aggregate demand declines to E_L, equal to $(C + I_1 + G_0)$. The new level of equilibrium income is below potential output at $\overline{Y}_1$.

Within the model, an appropriate fiscal policy response would be to increase government spending by an amount sufficient to restore equilibrium at $\overline{Y}_P$. In the graph, a rise in government spending from G_0 to G_1 shifts the aggregate demand curve back up to E_P, now equal to $(C + I_1 + G_1)$. Alternatively, a tax cut could be used to restore the initial level of aggregate demand. Because the tax multiplier is smaller, the appropriate tax cut would be larger than the required spending increase.

Read Perspectives 6.2.

6.7 EXPORTS AND IMPORTS IN THE SIMPLE KEYNESIAN MODEL

Both imports and exports have been growing as shares of GDP over recent decades. In 1960, U.S. imports of goods and services totaled 4.4 percent of GDP. By 2003, this figure was 13.8 percent of GDP. Exports rose from 4.9 percent of GDP in 1960 to

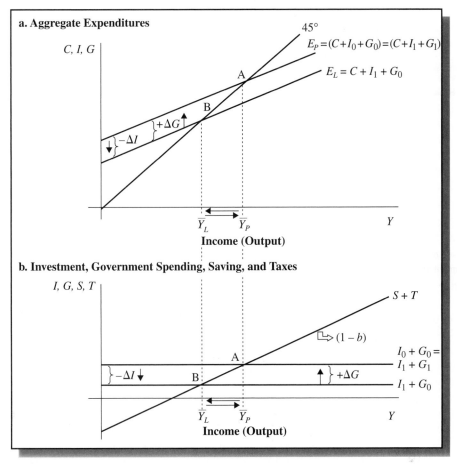

Figure 6.8 An Example of Fiscal Stabilization Policy

Beginning at equilibrium point A in part *a*, a decline in autonomous investment expenditure from I_0 to I_1 shifts the aggregate expenditure schedule downward from $E_p = (C + I_0 + G_0)$ to $E_L = (C + I_1 + G_0)$, moving to equilibrium point B. A compensating increase in discretionary government spending from G_0 to G_1 shifts the aggregate expenditure schedule back to equilibrium point A where $(C + I_1 + G_1) = E_p = (C + I_0 + G_0)$. Equilibrium income is again at $\overline{Y}_P$. In part *b*, starting at equilibrium point A, the decline in autonomous investment expenditure shifts the $I + G$ schedule downward, from $I_0 + G_0$ to $I_1 + G_0$, moving to equilibrium point B, decreasing income from $\overline{Y}_P$ to $\overline{Y}_L$. A compensating increase in discretionary government spending from G_0 to G_1 shifts the $I + G$ schedule upward, to $I_1 + G_1$, moving back to equilibrium point A, and increasing income back to $\overline{Y}_P$.

9.7 percent in 2003. Overall, the U.S. economy has become much more closely linked to those of other nations over the past 40 years. This section focuses on the roles of imports and exports in determining equilibrium income in the simple Keynesian model. Recall from Chapter 2 that GDP (*Y*) consists of consumption, investment, and government spending *plus* net exports. Net exports are exports minus imports. The condition for equilibrium output in the *open* economy (including exports and imports) is

$$Y = E = C + I + G + X - Z \tag{6.23}$$

PERSPECTIVES 6.2
Fiscal Policy in Practice

An example of fiscal stabilization policy within the Keynesian framework is the Kennedy–Johnson tax cut of 1964. There had been a serious recession in 1958, during which the unemployment rate rose to 6.8 percent. Recovery from this recession was short-lived. The economy sank back into a recession in 1960. The Kennedy administration came into office in 1961 with a program to "get the economy moving again"—a program called "the new economics"—which meant the application of Keynesian theory to macroeconomic policy. The Kennedy administration proposed a large cut in both personal and business taxes.

Kennedy's economic advisers believed that aggregate demand was too low for the economy to operate at the full-employment or potential level. The unemployment rate in 1961, for example, was 6.7 percent, compared with the 4.0 percent then considered to be "full" employment. In terms of Figure 6.8, the economy in the early 1960s was at a point such as $\overline{Y}_L$. The tax cut was intended to shift the aggregate demand schedule upward to move the economy to potential output ($\overline{Y}_P$ in Figure 6.8).

The Kennedy administration could not move the tax cut through Congress, mainly because congressional leaders worried about the budget deficit it would create. After Kennedy's assassination, President Lyndon Johnson persuaded Congress to enact the tax cut of 20 percent for persons and 10 percent for businesses early in 1964. Output and employment then grew rapidly, with the unemployment rate falling to 4.8 percent by the first half of 1965 and to 3.8 percent in 1966. This was the high point of influence for the Keynesian theory of fiscal policy.

As U.S. involvement in the Vietnam War grew in the 1966–68 period, government spending on defense increased rapidly. This increase in aggregate demand, with the economy already at potential output, generated inflationary pressures. In terms of Figure 6.8, the aggregate demand schedule was being pushed above the level consistent with potential output (Y_p). The 1960s demonstrated that, in practice, fiscal policy could destabilize as well as stabilize the economy.

Compared with equation (6.2), the condition for equilibrium in the *closed* economy, we have added exports (X) to aggregate demand and subtracted imports (Z). Exports are the foreign demand for domestic output and therefore part of aggregate demand. Also, because imports are included in C, I, and G but are *not* demands for domestic goods, we must subtract them out of aggregate demand.

To find an expression for equilibrium GDP in the open economy model, we follow the same procedure as for the closed-economy case; we take investment and government spending as exogenous—that is, as autonomous expenditure components. Consumption is given by the consumption function

$$C = a + bY \tag{6.24}$$

where, because they play no essential role in our discussion here, we have left out taxes, and therefore do not need to distinguish between GDP (Y) and disposable income ($Y_D = Y - T$). To compute equilibrium output for the open-economy case, we need to specify the determinants of imports and exports.

To simplify our analysis, we assume that imports consist solely of consumption goods. The demand for imports is assumed to depend on income and to have an autonomous component.

$$Z = u + vY \qquad u > 0, \qquad 0 < v < 1 \tag{6.25}$$

The parameter u represents the autonomous component of imports. The parameter v is the marginal propensity to import, the increase in import demand per unit increase in GDP, a concept analogous to the marginal propensity to consume (b) in (6.24).[16]

The demand for U.S. exports is a part of the *foreign* demand for imports. The foreign demand for imports depends on the level of *foreign* income, being determined by an import demand function analogous to equation (6.25). From the U.S. point of view, foreign income and, hence, the demand for our exports are exogenous.

Additional variables that we would expect to influence both U.S. demand for imports and foreign demand for U.S. exports are the relative price levels in the two countries and the level of the exchange rate. These variables determine the relative costs of the two countries' products to residents of either country. Note that for now we are assuming that price levels and the exchange rate are fixed. The effects on imports and exports of changes in the domestic price level or exchange rate are examined in Part IV.

With imports given by equation (6.25) and exports assumed to be exogenous, we can compute equilibrium income from equation (6.23) as follows:

$$Y = C + I + G + X - Z \tag{6.23}$$

$$= \overbrace{a + bY}^{C} + I + G + X \overbrace{- u - vY}^{-Z}$$
$$Y - bY + vY = a + I + G + X - u$$
$$(1 - b + v)Y = a + I + G + X - u \tag{6.26}$$
$$\overline{Y} = \frac{1}{1 - b + v}(a + I + G + X - u)$$

To examine the effects of foreign trade in the model we compare equation (6.26) with the equivalent expression for equilibrium income from the closed economy model, equation (6.14). This expression, omitting the tax variable (T), can be written as

$$\overline{Y} = \frac{1}{1 - b}(a + I + G) \tag{6.27}$$

In both equations (6.26) and (6.27), equilibrium income is expressed as the product of two terms: the autonomous expenditure multiplier and the level of autonomous expenditures. Consider how each of these is changed by adding imports and exports to the model.

---

[16]Note that, because consumption includes imports, b is the marginal propensity to consume both domestic and imported goods. Because v is the marginal propensity to import (consumption goods), $b - v$ is the marginal propensity to consume domestic goods.

Take first the autonomous expenditure multiplier, $1/(1 - b + v)$ in equation (6.26) as opposed to $1/(1 - b)$ in equation (6.27) for the closed-economy model. Because v, the marginal propensity to import, is greater than zero, the multiplier in (6.26), $1/(1 - b + v)$, will be *smaller* than the multiplier in (6.27), $1/(1 - b)$. For example, if $b = 0.8$ and $v = 0.3$, we would then have

$$\frac{1}{1 - b} = \frac{1}{1 - .08} = \frac{1}{0.2} = 5$$

and

$$\frac{1}{1 - b + v} = \frac{1}{1 - 0.8 + 0.3} = \frac{1}{0.5} = 2$$

From these expressions it can be seen that the more open an economy is to foreign trade (the higher v is), the lower will be the autonomous expenditure multiplier.

The autonomous expenditure multiplier gives the change in equilibrium income per unit change in autonomous expenditures. It follows, therefore, that the more open an economy is (the higher v is), the smaller will be the response of income to aggregate demand shocks, such as changes in government spending or autonomous changes in investment demand. The decline in the value of the autonomous expenditure multiplier with a rise in v can be explained with reference to the multiplier process (section 6.5). A change in autonomous expenditures—a change in government spending, for example—will have a direct effect on income and an induced effect on consumption with a further effect on income. The higher the value of v, the larger the proportion of this induced effect that will be a change in demand for *foreign*, not domestic, consumer goods. Consequently, the induced effect on demand for domestic goods and, hence, on domestic income will be smaller.[17] The increase in imports per unit of income constitutes an additional *leakage* from the circular flow of (domestic) income at each round of the multiplier process and reduces the value of the autonomous expenditure multiplier.

Now consider the second term in the expression for equilibrium income in the open economy case [equation (6.26)], the level of autonomous expenditures. In addition to the elements for a closed economy ($a + I + G$), autonomous expenditures for the open economy include exports and the autonomous component of imports. Recall that the autonomous components of aggregate demand are not directly determined by income. Rather, shifts in the components of autonomous expenditures affect the level of aggregate demand *for a given level of income* and result in changes in equilibrium income. Thus, changes in exports and autonomous changes in import demand are additional shocks that will change equilibrium income.

From equation (6.26) we can compute the multiplier effects of changes in X and u.

$$\frac{\Delta \bar{Y}}{\Delta X} = \frac{1}{1 - b + v} \tag{6.28}$$

$$\frac{\Delta \bar{Y}}{\Delta u} = \frac{-1}{1 - b + v} \tag{6.29}$$

---

[17]Recall from footnote 16 that $b - v$ is the marginal propensity to consume domestic goods. A higher v (given b) therefore means a lower MPC for domestic goods and a lower value for the multiplier.

An increase in the demand for our exports is an increase in aggregate demand for domestically produced output and will increase equilibrium income just as would an increase in government spending or an autonomous increase in investment.[18]

In contrast, an autonomous increase in import demand, an increase in u, will cause a decline in equilibrium income. An autonomous increase in import demand represents a shift from demand for domestic goods to demand for foreign goods. For example, because of the large rise in gasoline prices in the 1970s, U.S. consumers shifted demand from domestic to (smaller) foreign automobiles. As such, the autonomous increase in import demand is a *decline* in demand for domestic output and causes equilibrium income to decline.

In summary, an increase in the demand for our exports has an expansionary effect on equilibrium income, whereas an autonomous increase in imports has a contractionary effect on equilibrium income. This outcome should not be interpreted to mean that exports are good and imports harmful in their economic effects. Countries import goods that can be more efficiently produced abroad, and trade increases the overall efficiency of the worldwide allocation of resources. However, the expansionary effect of increases in exports and the contractionary effect of increases in imports do explain why at times nations have tried to stimulate the domestic economy by promoting exports and restricting imports.

6.8 CONCLUSION

The model in this chapter is incomplete. We need to consider money and interest rates and to explain the behavior of prices and wages before we complete our analysis of the Keynesian system. However, this simple model highlights several features of the Keynesian system.

The simple model clearly illustrates the role of aggregate demand in determining income in the Keynesian system. As we will see later, it *overstates* the role of aggregate demand. Still, a key feature of all Keynesian models is that demand plays a crucial role in income determination. In the Keynesian view, changes in the autonomous elements of aggregate demand, especially investment demand, are key factors causing changes in the equilibrium level of income. By means of the multiplier process, such changes in autonomous expenditures also induce changes in consumption spending. Inadequate investment, and a consequent low level of aggregate demand, was the Keynesian explanation for massive unemployment in the Depression of the 1930s.

The model also illustrates the role of fiscal stabilization policy in managing aggregate demand to cushion equilibrium output from shifts in the unstable investment demand. Although the simple expressions we derive for the government expenditure and tax multipliers require modification, the principles behind them remain intact.

---

[18]Note that from equation (6.26) we can also compute $\dfrac{\Delta \overline{Y}}{\Delta G} = \dfrac{\Delta \overline{Y}}{\Delta I} = \dfrac{1}{1 - b + v}$.

In addition, this chapter has considered the role of imports and exports within the simple Keynesian model. Exogenous changes in these components of aggregate demand are additional factors that alter equilibrium income. Moreover, we have seen that the openness of the economy affects the value of the autonomous expenditure multiplier and thus the vulnerability of the economy to both foreign and domestic changes in autonomous expenditures.

KEY TERMS

- consumption function 102
- marginal propensity to consume (MPC) 102
- marginal propensity to save (MPS) 103
- autonomous expenditure multiplier 108
- autonomous expenditures 108
- balanced-budget multiplier 114

REVIEW QUESTIONS AND PROBLEMS

1. Explain how the origins of the Keynesian revolution can be found in the problem of unemployment.
2. Interpret each of the three ways of writing the condition for equilibrium income in the simple Keynesian model [equations (6.2), (6.5.), and (6.6)]. Explain why the three ways are equivalent.
3. Explain the difference between realized and desired investment. In which component of investment does the discrepancy between the two totals occur?
4. Explain Keynes's theory of how expectations affect investment demand. How is this theory related to Keynes's view that aggregate demand would be unstable in the absence of government stabilization policies?
5. Consider the numbers in Table 6.1 giving consumption as a percentage of income in prosperous years (1929, 1955, 1973, 1979, 1989) compared with recession years (1933, 1958, 1975, 1982, 1991). Notice that in each case consumption is higher as a percentage of income in the recession years. Is this outcome what you would predict on the basis of Keynes's consumption function given by equation (6.9)? Explain.
6. In the simple Keynesian model, an increase of one dollar in autonomous expenditure will cause equilibrium income to increase by a multiple of this one-dollar increase. Explain the process by which this happens.
7. Explain carefully why the tax multiplier $[\Delta Y/\Delta T = -b/(1 - b)]$ is negative and why it is smaller in absolute value than the government expenditure multiplier $[\Delta Y/\Delta G = 1/(1 - b)]$.
8. Suppose that for a particular economy and period, investment was equal to 100, government expenditure was equal to 75, net taxes were fixed at 100, and consumption (C) was given by the consumption function

$$C = 25 + 0.8Y_D$$

where Y_D is disposable income and Y is GDP.
   a. What is the level of equilibrium income (Y)?
   b. What is the value of the government expenditure multiplier ($\Delta Y/\Delta G$)? Of the tax multiplier ($\Delta Y/\Delta T$)?

c. Suppose that investment declined by 40 units to a level of 60. What will be the new level of equilibrium income?

9. Suppose that initially equilibrium income was 200 units and that this was also the full-employment level of income. Assume that the consumption function is

$$C = 25 + 0.8Y_D$$

and that, from this initial equilibrium level, we now have a decline in investment of 8 units. What will be the new equilibrium level of income? What increase in government spending would be required to restore income to the initial level of 200? Alternatively, what reduction in tax collections would be sufficient to restore an income level of 200?

10. Suppose that government spending was increased by 10 units and that this increase was financed by a 10-unit increase in taxes. Would equilibrium income change or remain the same as a result of these two policy actions? If equilibrium income changed, in which direction would it move, and by how much? Explain.

11. Suppose that, instead of a fixed level of taxes, we had an income tax so that

$$T = t_1 Y$$

where t_1 was the income tax rate. Following the procedure of section 6.4, derive an expression for equilibrium income ($\overline{Y}$) analogous to equation (6.14) for this case in which the level of tax collections depends on income. What is the expression equivalent to the autonomous expenditure multiplier $[1/(1 - b)]$ for this case of an income tax?

12. In question 8, assume that, beginning from the initial equilibrium position (investment equal to 100, government expenditure equal to 75, and net taxes fixed at 100), there was an autonomous fall in consumption and an increase in saving such that the consumption function shifted from

$$C = 25 + 0.8Y_D$$

to

$$C = 5 + 0.8Y_D$$

a. Find the change in equilibrium income resulting from this autonomous increase in saving.

b. Calculate the level of saving before and after the shift in the consumption and, therefore, the saving function. How do you explain this result?

13. Suppose that within the open-economy version of the Keynesian model in section 6.7, we now include taxes. Disposable income ($Y_D = Y - T$) therefore replaces GDP (Y) in the consumption function (6.24). Compute the expression for equilibrium income for this version of the open-economy model. Compute an expression for the tax multiplier ($\Delta Y / \Delta T$) in the model.

14. Within the open-economy version of the Keynesian model, including taxes (see question 13), suppose there is an autonomous increase in imports of 20 units [u in equation (6.25) rises by 20]. To counteract the effects of this contraction in domestic aggregate demand, assume the government cuts taxes by 20 units. Will equilibrium income rise or fall? By how much? Explain.

Chapter 7

The Keynesian System (II): Money, Interest, and Income

*I*n Chapter 6, we ignored the interest rate and monetary policy. Here we explain the role of the interest rate and money in the Keynesian system and construct a model that shows how the interest rate and income are jointly determined. In Chapter 8, we use this model to provide a more realistic view of how income depends on aggregate demand and to make clear how monetary policy can affect income by having an effect on aggregate demand. We also see how the results in Chapter 6 concerning fiscal policy are modified by including a money market in the model.

7.1 MONEY IN THE KEYNESIAN SYSTEM

Fundamental to Keynes's theory of money was the view that money affects income via the interest rate. An increase in the money supply, for example, lowers the interest rate, and the lower interest rate, in turn, increases aggregate demand and income. We need to examine two links in the chain of events connecting changes in the money supply and changes in income. The first is the relationship between money and the interest rate. The second is the effect of the interest rate on aggregate demand. We begin with the latter one.

Interest Rates and Aggregate Demand

We have already considered the reasons why business investment demand depends on the interest rate. Briefly, an investment project will be pursued only if its expected profitability exceeds the cost of borrowing to finance the project by an amount sufficient to justify the risks of the project. At a high interest rate (borrowing cost), fewer projects satisfy this criterion.

When considering the possible influences of the interest rate, we also need to consider components of aggregate demand other than business investment. The first of these is residential construction investment. Residential construction is a component of investment in the national income accounts, but the reason such investment is affected by the interest-rate level requires further explanation. The value of newly constructed houses enters the gross domestic product (GDP) accounts as the houses are built. One element of building cost is the cost of short-term borrowing to finance construction of a house. Higher interest rates mean higher costs to the builder and, other things equal, these higher costs discourage housing starts. Moreover, an important factor determining the rate of new housing construction is the overall state of demand for houses, existing and newly constructed. Most home purchases are financed by long-term borrowing in the mortgage market, and high interest rates include high rates of mortgage interest. High mortgage rates increase the cost of buying a house and reduce the demand for new and existing homes. This reduced demand in the housing market lowers the volume of new residential construction.

Additional components of aggregate demand are not counted as investment by the national income accounts but would be included in a broader definition of investment and may be affected by interest-rate changes. The first of these is consumer expenditures on durable goods. Such expenditures are counted as current-quarter consumption in the national income accounts, but to the consumer the purchase of a car or an appliance such as a personal computer or television set is a form of investment. Such purchases are often financed by borrowing, especially car purchases. Higher interest rates raise the cost of such purchases and should lower this component of aggregate demand.

A final component of aggregate demand that may be affected by interest rates is a subcomponent of government spending. Government spending in the national income accounts includes state and local government spending for services, consumption goods, and investment goods. In the models constructed here, we take government spending to be exogenously fixed by the policymaker. The actual policymaker would be the federal government, and the appropriate policy variable is federal government expenditures. State and local government spending can more properly be considered with private consumption and investment spending. Much of state and local government investment spending is financed by borrowing through bond issues. High interest rates should, in theory, increase such borrowing costs and discourage this part of state and local government expenditures. There are, however, many determinants of the level and timing of such state and local government spending projects, and the importance of interest rates in practice remains uncertain.

Within the simple model of Chapter 6, the effects on aggregate demand and equilibrium income as a result of a change in the interest rate are illustrated in Figure 7.1. Initially, we assume that the economy is in equilibrium at Y_0 with aggregate demand at E_0 equal to $(C + I_0 + G_0)$, corresponding to an interest rate of r_0. A decline in the interest rate to r_1 shifts the aggregate demand curve up to E_1, equal to $(C + I_1 + G_0)$. This shift represents the combined effects of the interest rate on business investment, residential construction investment, consumer expenditures on durable goods, and state and local government investment spending. Equilibrium income rises to Y_1.

One important factor determining the change in equilibrium income $(Y_1 - Y_0)$ that will occur for a given change in the interest rate is the size of the shift in aggregate

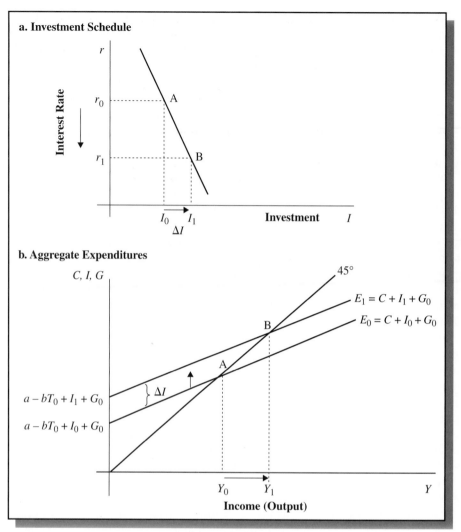

a. Investment Schedule

r

Interest Rate

r_0 ------- A

r_1 ------- B

I_0 I_1 **Investment** I

ΔI

b. Aggregate Expenditures

C, I, G

45°

$E_1 = C + I_1 + G_0$

$E_0 = C + I_0 + G_0$

B

A

$a - bT_0 + I_1 + G_0$

$\left\}\Delta I\right.$

$a - bT_0 + I_0 + G_0$

Y_0 Y_1 Y

Income (Output)

Figure 7.1 Effect of a Decrease in the Interest Rate on Investment
and Equilibrium Income

In part a, as the interest rate decreases from r_0 to r_1, investment increases from I_0 to I_1. In part b, this increase in investment, ΔI, shifts the aggregate expenditure schedule up since the intercept is larger, from $E_0 = C + I_0 + G_0$ to $E_1 = C + I_1 + G_0$. Output increases from Y_0 to Y_1.

demand caused by the change in the interest rate. The more sensitive the components of aggregate demand are to interest-rate changes, the larger will be the shift in the aggregate demand function in Figure 7.1 and the greater the effect on equilibrium income. The interest sensitivity of aggregate demand will therefore be important in determining how effective monetary policy will be in affecting equilibrium income.

Figure 7.1a illustrates the idea that investment is negatively related to the interest rate. At interest rate r_0, investment is I_0 at point A on the investment schedule. If the interest rate decreases to r_1, investment increases to I_1 at point B. Looking at

The negative relationship between residential construction investment and the level of interest rates is illustrated in Figure 7.2. Housing starts (new residential construction) in thousands of units at an annual rate (e.g., 1,200 = 1.2 million per year) are measured along the left axis, and the interest rate (long-term bond rate) is measured as a percent on the right axis. The fact that housing starts decline when the interest rate rises is evident from the graph. Especially notable is the collapse in the housing market as interest rates rose to record levels in the early 1980s. The strong rise in housing starts in recent years as interest rates fell to historically low levels is also apparent in the figure.

Figure 7.1b , since investment is a component of aggregate expenditures, the expenditure schedule shifts up, from equilibrium point A to equilibrium point B, and equilibrium income increases from Y_0 to Y_1.

In our models, we represent the effect of interest rates on aggregate expenditures as simply an effect on I, the investment component of aggregate expenditures. The discussion in this section should, however, be kept in mind. To account fully for the effects of interest rates on aggregate expenditures, we must define investment broadly as including the other components of aggregate expenditure discussed here.

Read Perspectives 7.1.

The Keynesian Theory of the Interest Rate

The next relationship we consider is that between the quantity of money and the rate of interest. Keynes believed that the quantity of money played a key role in determining the rate of interest, and he structured his theory of interest-rate determination to highlight that role.

The Keynesian analysis begins with some simplifying assumptions. First, Keynes assumed that all financial assets can be divided into two groups: (1) money and (2) all nonmoney assets, which we term bonds.

Money can be thought of as the narrowly defined money supply that in the official U.S. monetary statistics is called M1. M1 consists of currency plus bank accounts on which a person can write checks. The "bond" category includes actual bonds plus other long-term financial assets, primarily corporate equities (stock). The *long-term* (bonds) versus *short-term* (money) distinction is the crucial one. In addition, for a long time bonds were the interest-earning asset, and money paid no interest. It is still true that part of the money supply, currency and some checkable accounts, pay no interest, but interest is paid on some components of M1. We first explain the Keynesian theory of interest-rate determination *under the assumption that all money pays no interest*. We then explore the implications of having interest paid on some parts of the money stock.

Also, to keep things simple, we consider bonds in the model to be homogeneous in all respects. As in our discussion of the classical system, we assume that bonds are perpetuities, promises to pay fixed amounts at fixed intervals in the future (e.g., one dollar per year), with no repayment of principal.

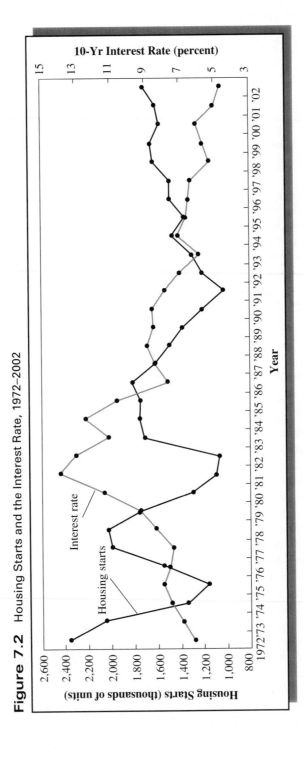

Figure 7.2 Housing Starts and the Interest Rate, 1972–2002

Within this simplified framework, Keynes considers the way in which individuals decide how to allocate their financial wealth between the two assets, money (M) and bonds (B). At a point in time, wealth (Wh) is fixed at some level, and because bonds and money are the only stores of wealth, we have

$$Wh \equiv B + M \qquad \qquad (7.1)$$

The equilibrium interest rate on bonds is that rate at which the demand for bonds is equal to the existing stock of bonds. It might seem most natural to develop a theory of the equilibrium interest rate by studying the factors that directly determine the supply of and demand for bonds. Keynes did not proceed in this manner. Note that given equation (7.1), there is only one independent portfolio decision, the split between money and bonds. If, for an individual, wealth is equal to $50,000, the decision to hold $10,000 in the form of money implicitly determines that bond holdings will be the remainder, $40,000. In terms of equilibrium positions, this means that a person who is satisfied with the level of money holdings relative to total wealth is, by definition [equation (7.1)], satisfied with the bond holdings; this person is at the optimal split of wealth between the two stores of value. To say, for example, that the demand for money exceeds the supply is to say, in the aggregate, that the public is trying to increase the proportion of wealth held in the form of money. This is definitionally the same as saying that the supply of bonds exceeds the demand; the public is trying to reduce the proportion of wealth held as bonds.

Consequently, there are two equivalent ways to describe the equilibrium interest rate: as the rate that equates the supply of and demand for bonds or, alternatively, as the rate that equates the supply of money with the demand for money. Equilibrium in one market implies equilibrium in the other. Keynes chose the latter of these perspectives because he wished to emphasize the relationship between money and the interest rate.

This Keynesian view of interest rate determination is illustrated in Figure 7.3. The money supply is assumed to be fixed exogenously by the central bank at M_0^s. The equilibrium interest rate is r_0, the rate at which money demand, given by the money demand schedule M^d in the graph, is just equal to the fixed money supply.

In a more fundamental sense, the equilibrium rate of interest is determined by factors affecting the supply of money and money demand. In the case of supply, the major factor will be the policies of the central bank. We turn now to the factors that Keynes believed determined money demand, the factors determining the position and slope of the M^d schedule in Figure 7.3.

The Keynesian Theory of Money Demand

Keynes considered three motives for holding money.

Transactions Demand

The first motive Keynes considered is the transactions motive. Money is a medium of exchange, and individuals hold money for use in transactions. Money bridges the gap between the receipt of income and eventual expenditures. The amount of money held for transactions would vary positively with the volume of transactions in which the individual engaged. Income is assumed to be a good measure of this volume of

Figure 7.3
Determination of the Equilibrium Interest Rate

In the Keynesian system, the equilibrium interest rate (r_0) is the interest rate that equates money supply and money demand.

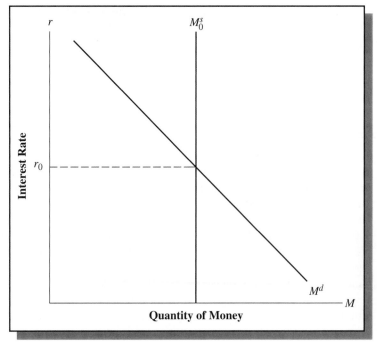

transactions, and thus the transactions demand for money is assumed to depend positively on the level of income.

Money received in one transaction can be used to buy bonds, which could then be sold to get money again when the time came for an expenditure. The gain from doing so is the interest earned for the time the bonds were held. Brokerage fees involved in buying bonds and the inconveniences of a great number of such transactions would make it unprofitable to purchase bonds for small amounts to be held for short periods. Some money would be held for transactions. Still, there is room to *economize* on transaction balances by such bond purchases. Because the return to be gained is interest earnings on bonds, we would expect the incentive to economize on transaction balances to increase as the interest rate increases. Consequently, in addition to depending positively on income, the transactions demand for money would be expected to be negatively related to the rate of interest.

Keynes did not emphasize the interest rate when discussing the transactions motive for holding money, but it has proved to be important, especially for the business sector. Firms with a high volume of transactions can, by cash management practices, reduce considerably their average money holdings. The incentive to make the expenditures required for such cash management depends on the rate of interest.

Precautionary Demand

Keynes believed that, beyond money held for planned transactions, additional money balances were held in case of unexpected expenditures such as medical or repair bills. Keynes termed money held for this motive the precautionary demand for money. He believed that the amount held for this purpose depends positively on income. Again, the interest rate might be a factor if people tended to economize on the amount of money held for the precautionary motive as interest rates rose. Because the motives for holding precautionary balances are similar to those for transactions demand, we simplify our discussion here by subsuming the precautionary demand under the transactions demand category, transactions being expected or unexpected ones.

Speculative Demand

The final motive for holding money that Keynes considered was the speculative motive. This is the novel part of Keynes's analysis of money demand. Keynes began by asking why an individual would hold any money above that needed for the transactions and precautionary motives when bonds pay interest and money does not. Such an additional demand for money did exist, Keynes believed, because of the uncertainty about future interest rates and the relationship between changes in the interest rate and the price of bonds. If interest rates were expected to move in such a way as to cause capital losses on bonds, it was possible that these expected losses would outweigh the interest earnings on the bonds and cause an investor to hold money instead. Such money would be held by those "speculating" on future changes in the interest rate. To see how such speculation works, we analyze the relationship between the interest rate and bond prices.

Consider the case of a perpetuity, which is what we have been assuming the bonds in our model to be. Suppose that at some point in the past you paid the then prevailing market price of $1,000 to buy a government bond that entitles you to payment of $50 per year, termed the coupon payment. You bought a perpetual bond at a price of $1,000, at a market interest rate of 5 percent (50/1,000 = 0.05, or 5 percent). How much would this bond be worth if you tried to sell it today? The value of a financial asset that entitles the owner to a coupon payment of $50 per year depends on the *current* market rate of interest. First, suppose the current market rate of interest is 5 percent, the same as the interest rate that prevailed when you bought the bond. In this case, the bond would still sell for $1,000; at that price, it would yield the current interest rate of 5 percent.

Next consider the case in which the market interest rate has risen to 10 percent over the time since you purchased the bond. The going price today for a bond with a coupon payment of $50 per year is $500 (50/500 = 0.10, or 10 percent). Your bond has no feature that will enable you to sell it for more. Even though you paid $1,000, given the rise in interest rates, you will be able to sell it only at a *capital loss* for $500, the price that makes it competitive at *current* market rates. *A rise in the market interest rate results in a capital loss on previously existing bonds.*

If, instead, from the time you purchased the bond, the market interest rate had fallen, then the value of your bond would have increased. If the interest rate had declined from 5 percent to 2 percent, the bond price would have increased from the $1,000 you paid to $2,500. At that price, your bond, which has a coupon of $50 per year, will pay 2 percent (50/2,500 = 0.02, or 2 percent). Thus, *a decline in interest rates results in a capital gain on previously existing bonds.* With this relationship between bond prices and interest-rate changes in mind, we return to the question of the relative desirability of money and bonds.

The expected returns on the two assets can be expressed as follows:

$$\text{return on money} = 0$$

$$\text{expected return on bonds} = \begin{matrix} \text{interest} \\ \text{earnings} \\ (= r) \end{matrix} \left.\begin{matrix} \\ \\ \end{matrix}\right\} \begin{matrix} (+) \text{ expected capital gain} \\ \text{or} \\ (-) \text{ expected capital loss} \end{matrix}$$

The return on money is zero, because it earns no interest (our assumption so far) and because its value is not subject to capital gains or losses as the interest rate changes.[1] Money has a fixed price. The bond will pay an interest rate of r. The *expected* return on bonds will equal this interest return plus or minus any expected capital gain or loss. For reasons just discussed, an investor who expected interest rates to fall would expect a capital gain, and one who expected interest rates to rise would expect a capital loss. This uncertainty about the future course of interest rates is crucial to Keynes's analysis.

Suppose that an investor believes interest rates will fall. Bonds then have the higher expected return. They pay interest and are expected to yield a capital gain. If interest rates are expected to rise, however, it is possible that the expected capital loss on bonds will outweigh the interest earnings. The expected return on bonds would be negative in such a case, and money would be the preferred asset. Money held in anticipation of a fall in bond prices (a rise in interest rates) is Keynes's speculative demand for money.

To this point, we have a relationship between the amount of money demanded and expected future *changes* in interest rates. Keynes converts this to a relationship between money demand and the *level* of the interest rate by an assumption about how people form expectations about future interest-rate changes. He assumes that investors have a relatively fixed conception of the "normal" interest rate. When the actual interest rate is above the normal rate, investors expect the interest rate to fall. When the interest rate is below the normal rate, they expect it to rise. Given this assumption about how expectations about interest rates are formed, we can develop a relationship between the level of the speculative demand for money and the interest rate. We do so first for an individual investor and then consider the corresponding aggregate relationship.

For the individual investor, the demand curve for speculative balances is shown in Figure 7.4a. Here M_i^2 represents the speculative demand for money by the ith individual, and M_i^1 is the person's transactions demand. We have then

$$M_i^1 + M_i^2 \equiv M_i$$

and

$$M_i + B_i \equiv Wh_i \tag{7.2}$$

---

[1]Notice that so far we are not allowing for the effect of commodity price changes. The *real* value of money declines proportionately with increases in the aggregate price level. However, so does the real value of bonds; therefore, the relative returns are not directly affected by allowing for commodity price changes.

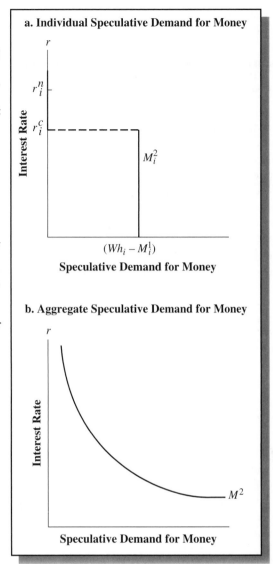

Figure 7.4
Individual and Aggregate Speculative Demand Curves for Money

The individual's speculative demand for money is shown in part *a*. At any interest rate above the critical rate (r_i^c), the speculative demand for money is zero. Below the critical interest rate, the individual shifts into money. Part *b* shows the aggregate speculative demand for money schedule (M^2). As the interest rate becomes lower, it falls below the critical rate for more individuals, and the speculative demand for money rises.

a. Individual Speculative Demand for Money

Interest Rate

r_i^n

r_i^c

M_i^2

$(Wh_i - M_i^1)$

Speculative Demand for Money

b. Aggregate Speculative Demand for Money

Interest Rate

M^2

Speculative Demand for Money

where M_i, B_i, and Wh_i are the individual's total money holdings, bond holdings, and wealth, respectively.

Following Keynes's theory, the individual is assumed to have a preconceived view of the normal interest rate. This rate is shown as r_i^n in Figure 7.4a. Because at rates of interest above r_i^n, interest rates are expected to fall, at those rates bonds will be preferred to money as an asset. The speculative demand for money will be zero, and bond holdings will equal $(Wh_i - M_i^1)$. The speculative demand for money will also be zero for interest rates over a certain range below r_i^n. If the interest rate is not too far below r_i^n, the interest earnings on the bond will be greater than the small expected capital loss. The expected capital loss will be small because only a small rise in r will be expected as r returns to r_i^n.

There is a level of the interest rate below r_i^n, however, at which the expected capital loss on bonds, which increases as the interest rate declines below r_i^n, will come to just equal the interest earnings on the bond. We term this value of the interest rate the individual's critical interest rate (r_i^c). Below this rate, money will be preferred. The individual will sell bonds and hold speculative balances of ($Wh_i - M_i^1$), which means that all of this person's wealth will be held in money.

Keynes assumed that different individuals had different views as to what was a "normal" interest rate. As the interest rate fell, beginning, for example, at a very high rate where there was very little speculative demand, the rate would move successively below the critical rates of different investors. The lower the interest rate, the more investors would find that, given their view of the normal rate, money was the preferred asset. At a very low interest rate, almost all investors would come to expect the interest rate to rise substantially in the future ($r < r_i^c$), and money would be almost universally preferred as an asset. Proceeding in this manner, we construct the aggregate demand for speculative balances shown in Figure 7.4*b*.

The curve is smooth, reflecting the gradual increase in the speculative demand for money at successively lower interest rates. The curve flattens out at a very low rate of interest, reflecting that at this low rate, there is a general expectation of capital losses on bonds that outweigh interest earnings. At this rate, increments to wealth would be held in the form of money, with no further drop in the interest rate. Keynes termed this situation the **liquidity trap**. For the most part, however, we assume that we are on the downward-sloping portion of the speculative demand for money curve.

The Total Demand for Money

We have looked at the three motives for holding money in the Keynesian system and can now put these together to construct the total money demand function. The transactions demand and the precautionary demand vary positively with income and negatively with the interest rate. The speculative demand for money is negatively related to the interest rate. Taking those factors together, we can write total money demand as

$$M^d = L(Y, r) \qquad (7.3)$$

where Y is income and r is the interest rate. A rise in income increases money demand; a rise in the interest rate decreases money demand. In the following analysis, we at times make the simplifying assumption that the money demand function is linear:

$$M^d = c_0 + c_1 Y - c_2 r \qquad c_1 > 0; \qquad c_2 > 0 \qquad (7.4)$$

Equation (7.4) assumes that we can plot the money demand function as a straight line on our graphs. The parameter c_1 is the increase in money demand per unit increase in income, and c_2 gives the amount by which money demand declines per unit increase in the interest rate.

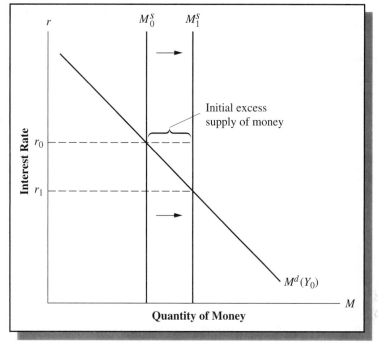

Figure 7.5
Equilibrium in the Money Market

An increase in the money stock from M_0^s to M_1^s causes an initial excess supply of money. The interest rate falls from r_0 to r_1 to restore equilibrium in the money market.

The Effects of an Increase in the Money Supply

In Figure 7.5, we plot this linear Keynesian money demand schedule [equation (7.4)] as a function of the interest rate and illustrate the effect of an increase in the money supply on the money market. The money demand function, M^d, is downward-sloping; a decline in the interest rate, for example, increases the demand for money. To fix the position of the money demand function, we must fix the level of income. The curve in Figure 7.5 is drawn for a level of income Y_0. An increase in income shifts the curve to the right, reflecting the fact that, for a given interest rate, money demand increases with income. The money supply is assumed to be an exogenously con-trolled policy variable set initially at M_0^s.

Now consider the effects of an increase in the money supply to the level shown by the M_1^s schedule in Figure 7.5. At the initial equilibrium interest rate r_0, after the money supply increases, there is an excess supply of money. At r_0 people are not content to hold the new money. They attempt to decrease their money holdings by buying bonds. The increase in the demand for bonds decreases the rate of interest suppliers of bonds (borrowers) offer to sell their bonds. The fall in the interest rate causes the demand for money to rise, and a new equilibrium is reached at interest rate r_1.

Some Implications of Interest on Money

In recent years some components of the money supply have begun to pay market-determined interest rates. This development is contrary to our assumption that bonds are the only interest-bearing asset. What implications does interest-bearing money have for the Keynesian theory?

In Chapter 17, we discuss different definitions of money. Here we consider only one: M1. In the official U.S. monetary statistics, M1 consists of currency, travelers checks (a relatively minor item), demand deposits (regular checking accounts), and a category called "other checkable deposits." Currency, travelers checks, and demand deposits, which together accounted for approximately three-quarters of M1 in 2004, do not pay interest; the "other checkable deposits" do. Moreover, following a period of deregulation of deposit interest rates in the 1980s, banks and other depository institutions can pay whatever interest rate they wish on these deposits.[2]

The question of interest-bearing money comes into our analysis when we consider the Keynesian theory of money demand and the relationship of money demand to the interest rate. Suppose the interest rate on bonds rises. From equation (7.4) or Figure 7.5, the Keynesian theory predicts a decline in money demand as individuals shift into bonds. But this analysis was based on the assumption that money earned no interest.

From the previous discussion, we see that for the majority of the assets in M1, this assumption is valid. For "other checkable deposits" accounts, we would expect the rate paid on deposits to rise as the rate of interest on bonds rises. But we would not expect the rate paid on those deposits to increase by as much as the rise in the interest rate paid on bonds. Banks have costs associated with providing checkable deposits; an important cost results from the requirement that banks set aside a certain percentage of such deposits (currently 10 percent) as reserves, on which the bank itself will not be able to earn any interest. Therefore, if the interest rate on bonds rises by 1 percent, the interest rate on "other checkable deposits" will rise by *less* than 1 percent. The *relative* interest rate on bonds will be higher, and there will still be an incentive for individuals to shift from money to bonds.

Thus, some components of M1 pay no interest, and even for those that do pay interest, the rate adjusts only partially to changes in the interest rate on bonds. Therefore, we continue to assume that the Keynesian money demand function will be downward-sloping, as drawn in Figure 7.5. Money demand depends negatively on the rate of interest, which in our discussion always means the interest rate on bonds. None of this means that the emergence of interest-paying money, one of several financial-sector innovations in recent years, does not have important implications, especially for monetary policy. These implications are discussed in Chapter 18.

Summary

It may seem that we are now ready to analyze the effects of monetary policy in the Keynesian system. We have seen how changes in the money supply affect the interest rate. We have also seen how a change in the interest rate affects aggregate demand. Can we not combine Figure 7.5 with Figure 7.1 to examine sequentially the effect on income of a change in the money supply? Unfortunately, we cannot.

In Figure 7.5, we analyzed the effects of a change in the money supply in the money market not allowing effects in other markets. Specifically, we held income

---

[2]The types of "other checkable deposits" have varied over time. Currently, most of these deposits are NOW (negotiated order of withdrawal) accounts.

constant (at Y_0) to fix the position of the money demand function. Now, as the interest rate drops from r_0 to r_1, we can see from Figure 7.1 (assuming the subscripts have the same meaning in the two diagrams) that income increases from Y_0 to Y_1. This rise in income will shift the money demand schedule in Figure 7.5 to the right. There will be a further change in the interest rate back toward r_0 and consequently a further change in income. What we need to find is the effect of changes in the money supply on the equilibrium values of the interest rate and income, equilibrium values for *both* the money and commodity markets. We have all the relationships required, but we need a new framework in which to fit them together. This new framework is the *IS–LM* model.

7.2 THE *IS–LM* MODEL

Our task in this section is to find the values of the interest rate and income that simultaneously equilibrate both the commodity market and the money market. Note that, because equilibrium in the money market implies equilibrium in the bond market, such a combination will equilibrate all three markets (commodities, money, and bonds). First we identify combinations of income and the interest rate that equilibrate the money market, neglecting the commodity market. Next we identify combinations of income and the interest rate that are equilibrium values for the commodity market. These two sets of equilibrium combinations of interest rate and income levels are then shown to contain one combination that equilibrates both markets. To find a unique point of equilibrium, we have to assume that policy variables, including the money supply, government spending, and taxes, are fixed at some levels. Other autonomous influences on income and interest rates (e.g., the state of business expectations that affects investment) must also be assumed to be fixed. We see that these policy variables and other exogenous influences determine the positions of the equilibrium schedules for the money and product markets, termed below the *LM* and *IS* schedules. In Chapter 8, we see how changes in these policy variables and other exogenous influences affect the equilibrium values of income and the interest rate.

Money Market Equilibrium: The *LM* Curve

Construction of the LM *Curve*
Money demand in the Keynesian model is assumed to depend positively on income because of the transactions demand. Money demand also varies inversely with the rate of interest, owing to the speculative demand for money and because the amount of transaction balances held at any income level declines as the interest rate (the opportunity cost of holding such balances) increases. We expressed this relationship as

$$M^d = L(Y, r) \tag{7.3}$$

or in linear form

$$M^d = c_0 + c_1 Y - c_2 r \qquad c_1 > 0, \qquad c_2 > 0 \tag{7.4}$$

Now we wish to find all the combinations of r and Y that equilibrate money demand with a fixed money supply, denoted M_0^s. The schedule of such points is termed the *LM schedule* because along this schedule, money demand, for which we use the symbol L [equation (7.3)], is equal to the money supply (M). For simplicity, we discuss the case in which money demand is given by the linear form (7.4). For this case, the condition that must be satisfied for money market equilibrium, the *LM* schedule equation, can be written as

$$M_0^s = M^d = c_0 + c_1 Y - c_2 r \qquad (7.5)$$

We have already considered the nature of equilibrium in the money market. In Figure 7.6a, for example, three separate demand-for-money schedules are drawn, corresponding to three successively higher levels of income, Y_0, Y_1, and Y_2. As income increases from Y_0 to Y_1 and then from Y_1 to Y_2, the money demand schedule shifts to the right when plotted against the interest rate. The points where these money demand schedules intersect the vertical line, giving the value of the fixed money supply, are points of equilibrium for the money market. Income–interest-rate

Figure 7.6 Equilibrium Positions in the Money Market and the *LM* Schedule

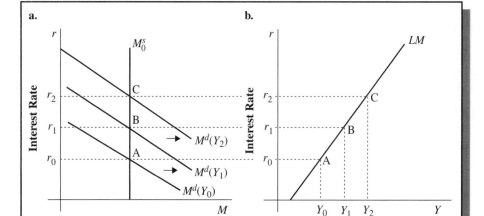

(a) Increases in income from Y_0 to Y_1 to Y_2 shift the money demand schedule from $M^d(Y_0)$ to $M^d(Y_1)$, then to $M^d(Y_2)$. Equilibrium in the money market requires successively higher interest rates r_0, r_1, r_2 at higher levels of income Y_0, Y_1, Y_2. (b) The *LM* schedule shows combinations of income (Y) and the interest rate (r) that equilibrate the money market. Equilibrium combinations such as (r_0, Y_0), (r_1, Y_1), and (r_2, Y_2) from part a are points along the *LM* schedule. As we see in part a, at higher levels of income, higher interest rates are required for money market equilibrium; the *LM* schedule slopes upward to the right.

Note that in part a, at equilibrium point A in the money market, money demand equals money supply at the equilibrium interest rate, r_0. This corresponds with point A on the *LM* schedule in part b, indicating equilibrium in the money market, given Y_0 and r_0. Starting at equilibrium point A in the money market, holding M_0^s constant, increases in income from Y_0 to Y_1 to Y_2 increase interest rates from r_0 to r_1 to r_2, moving from equilibrium points A to B to C. These points of equilibrium correspond with points A to B to C on the *LM* schedule.

combinations at which equilibrium occurs, (Y_0, r_0), (Y_1, r_1), and (Y_2, r_2), are points along the *LM*, or money market equilibrium, schedule. These points are plotted in Figure 7.6b. Proceeding in this manner, we can find the equilibrium value of the interest rate for each level of income and construct the complete *LM* schedule shown in Figure 7.6b.

The *LM* schedule slopes upward to the right. At higher levels of income, equilibrium in the money market occurs at higher interest rates. The reason for the positive slope for the *LM* curve is the following. An increase in income (e.g., from Y_0 to Y_1 in Figures 7.6a and b) increases money demand at a given interest rate, because the transactions demand for money varies positively with income. Restoring demand to a level equal to the fixed money supply requires that the interest rate be higher (r_1 instead of r_0 in Figures 7.6a and b). The higher interest rate results in a lower speculative demand for money and lowers the transactions component *corresponding to any level of income*. The interest rate must rise until this decline in money demand is just equal to the initial income-induced increase in transactions demand.

To complete our discussion of the *LM* schedule, we consider two questions. First, we want to know what determines the value of the slope of the *LM* schedule. We know that the curve is upward-sloping, but is it steep or relatively flat? The slope of the *LM* schedule is important for our later discussion of policy effects. The second question concerns the position of the *LM* schedule: What factors shift the schedule?

Factors That Determine the Slope of the LM Schedule

To see which factors determine the slope of the *LM* schedule, we begin by considering the effect on money market equilibrium of an increase in income, ΔY, for example, from Y_0 to Y_1 in Figures 7.6a and b. The income-induced increase in money demand as a result of this change will equal $c_1 \Delta Y$, where c_1 is the parameter giving the increase in money demand per unit increase in income from equation (7.4). The interest rate will have to rise by enough to offset this income-induced increase in money demand. The higher the value of c_1, the larger the increase in money demand per unit increase in income, and hence, the larger upward adjustment in the interest rate required to restore total money demand to the level of the fixed money supply. The higher the value of c_1, the steeper will be the *LM* curve. The value of c_1 is, however, not a subject of much debate. Controversy on this subject centers on the second factor that determines the slope of the *LM* curve.

For a given income-induced increase in money demand (a given c_1), the amount by which the interest rate has to rise to restore total money demand to the value of the fixed money supply depends on how *elastic* (sensitive) money demand is with respect to changes in the rate of interest.[3] In equation (7.4), the interest elasticity of money demand depends on the value of c_2, which determines the change in money

---

[3]The concept of elasticity refers to the percentage change in one variable that results from a 1-percent change in another variable. In the case of the interest elasticity of money demand, the elasticity is negative. A 1-percent increase in the interest rate will cause money demand to decline. In the text, the term *high elasticity* refers to the absolute value of the elasticity. If money demand is very responsive to changes in the interest rate, we say that money demand is highly elastic. If money demand is not very responsive to interest rate changes, we term this a *low interest elasticity* or *low interest sensitivity* of money demand.

demand for a given change in the interest rate ($-c_2 = \Delta M^d / \Delta r$). The relationship between the interest elasticity of money demand and the slope of the LM curve is illustrated in Figure 7.7.

Part *a* of the figure shows the case of a low interest elasticity of money demand. The money demand curve is steep, reflecting that large changes in the interest rate will not change the level of money demand by very much. To see how the slope of the LM schedule is related to the interest elasticity of money demand, consider how money market equilibrium changes at progressively higher income levels. Increases in income from Y_0 to Y_1 and then to Y_2 will shift the money demand schedule to the right in Figure 7.7a, from $M^d(Y_0)$ to $M^d(Y_1)$, then to $M^d(Y_2)$. These increases in income raise the transactions demand for money by c_1 $(Y_1 - Y_0)$ and c_1 $(Y_2 - Y_1)$, respectively. Because a given increase in the interest rate will not reduce money demand by much (c_2 is small), the interest rate will have to rise by a large amount to reduce money demand back to the fixed M_0^s level. This fact is reflected in the LM curve in Figure 7.7a, which is quite steep.

The case in which money demand is highly interest-elastic is shown in Figure 7.7b. Here the money demand curve is quite flat. A small drop in the interest rate, for example, increases money demand significantly. Here again the money demand curve shifts to the right as income increases from Y_0 to Y_1, then to Y_2. The graph is constructed such that the increase in income and the value of c_1 from equation (7.4) are the same as in Figure 7.7a. Thus, the income-induced increases in money demand are the same in Figure 7.7a and b. Notice that in Figure 7.7b the interest rate must rise by a relatively small amount to restore equilibrium in the money market. As a consequence, the LM curve in Figure 7.7b is relatively flat. If money demand is highly responsive to changes in the interest rate (c_2 is large), a relatively small rise in the interest rate will offset the income-induced increases in transactions balances as income rises from Y_0 to Y_1, then to Y_2.

Two special cases for the slope of the LM curve result from the interest elasticity of money demand taking on the value of zero or, alternatively, becoming extremely high.

First consider the case in which money demand is completely interest-insensitive [c_2 equals zero in equation (7.4)]. Beginning at some initial equilibrium, consider the rise in the interest rate required to reequilibrate the money market if income were to increase. To have income at a higher level would mean increased transactions demand for money. With money demand completely unresponsive to changes in the interest rate, there is *no* possible rise in the interest rate that would reduce money demand back to the level of the fixed money supply. In this case, a rise in the interest rate is assumed not to cause people either to reduce the speculative demand for money or to economize on transactions balances. Consequently, only one level of income can be an equilibrium level. To see this, notice that with c_2 equal to zero, equation (7.4) becomes

$$M^d = c_0 + c_1 Y$$

and the LM curve equation (7.5) is given by

$$M_0^s = c_0 + c_1 Y$$

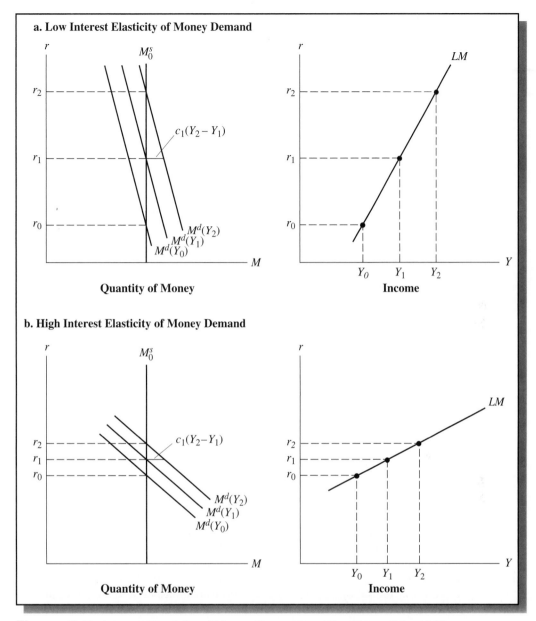

Figure 7.7 Interest Elasticity of Money Demand and the Slope of the *LM* Curve

The steep money demand schedule in part *a* reflects the assumption that the interest elasticity of money demand is low (in absolute value). With a low interest elasticity of money demand, the *LM* schedule is relatively steep. In part *b*, money demand is assumed to be highly interest-elastic and, as a result, the money demand schedule is relatively flat. The *LM* schedule in this case is also relatively flat.

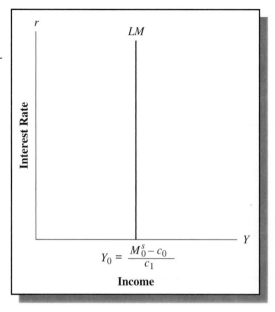

Figure 7.8
LM Schedule, the Classical Case

The *LM* schedule is vertical if money demand is completely interest-insensitive.

Consequently, with M fixed at M_0^s for equilibrium, we must have

$$Y = \frac{M_0^s - c_0}{c_1} \tag{7.6}$$

Only one level of income can be an equilibrium level for the money market.

The *LM* curve for this case is shown in Figure 7.8. We refer to this case as the *classical case* because the Keynesian money demand function *when c_2 equals zero* does not differ substantively from the classical money demand function. As in the classical theory (see section 4.1), money demand depends only on income. The distinguishing feature of the Keynesian theory of money demand is the negative relationship between money demand and the interest rate.

The alternative extreme case occurs when the interest elasticity of money demand becomes extremely large, approaching infinity. What causes this? We saw from our discussion of Keynes's theory of the speculative demand for money that as the interest rate becomes very low, relative to what is considered normal, a consensus develops viewing future interest-rate increases as likely. In this situation, with expected future capital losses outweighing the small interest earnings on bonds, the public would hold any increase in money balances with only a negligible fall in the interest rate. In this range of the money demand schedule, the interest elasticity of money demand becomes extremely high. This case, which Keynes termed the liquidity trap, is illustrated in Figure 7.9. Notice that here we have to abandon the linear form of the Keynesian money demand function. In the liquidity trap case, we are considering a change in the slope of the money demand function. The function becomes very flat at low interest rates.

Figure 7.9
Keynesian Liquidity
Trap

At very low levels of
income, Y_0 and Y_1,
equilibrium in the
money market in part *a*
occurs at points along
the flat portion of the
money demand sched-
ule where the elasticity
of money demand is
extremely high.
Consequently, the *LM*
schedule in part *b* is
nearly horizontal over
this range of low
income levels. At
higher income levels,
such as Y_2 and Y_3,
money market equilib-
rium is at steeper
points along the money
demand curves M^d
(Y_2), $M^d(Y_3)$, and the
LM curve becomes
steeper.

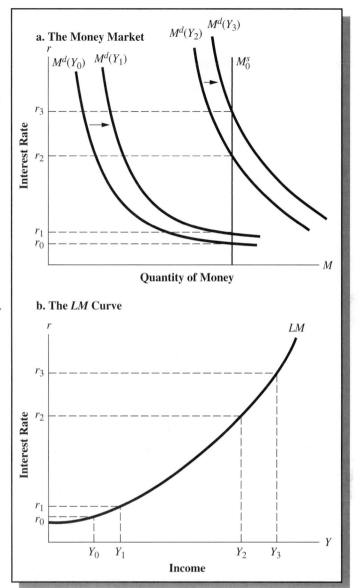

a. The Money Market

Quantity of Money

b. The *LM* Curve

Income

In Figure 7.9*a*, consider first the money demand schedules $M^d(Y_0)$ and $M^d(Y_1)$
corresponding to the income levels Y_0 and Y_1 shown in Figure 7.9*b*. Relative to
income levels Y_2 and Y_3, these are low levels of income. Consequently, $M^d(Y_0)$ and
$M^d(Y_1)$ are to the left of $M^d(Y_2)$ and $M^d(Y_3)$ in Figure 7.9*a*.

At such low income levels, with the money supply at M_0^s, the equilibrium interest rate is so low that we are on the flat portion of the money demand schedule.
Within this range, a rise in income, from Y_0 to Y_1, for example, requires only a very
slight rise in the interest rate to restore equilibrium in the money market; money

demand is highly responsive to changes in the interest rate. In this range, the *LM* curve in Figure 7.9 is nearly horizontal.

At higher levels of income, between Y_2 and Y_3, for example, an increase in income would require a larger increase in the interest rate to restore equilibrium in the money market. Here the equilibrium interest rates are such that we are not in the liquidity trap. The interest elasticity of money demand is lower over this portion of the money demand schedule.

Factors That Shift the LM Schedule

Two factors that shift the *LM* curve are changes in the exogenously fixed money supply and shifts in the money demand function. We set these two factors at given levels to determine the position of the *LM* curve. The money supply is assumed to be a policy variable, and when we consider an increase in the money supply, for example, we mean a policy action setting this policy instrument to a new level.

We have considered shifts in the money demand *schedule* drawn against the interest rate *as the level of income changes*. This is *not* what is meant here by a shift in the money demand *function*. A shift in the money demand function means a change in the amount of money demanded for given levels of the *interest rate and income*, what Keynes called a shift in *liquidity preference*. For example, if very unsettled economic conditions increased the probability of firms' going bankrupt and, hence, the default risk on bonds, the demand for money might increase. This situation would be a shift in individuals' portfolios away from bonds and toward money for given levels of the interest rate and income.

Changes in the Money Supply   The *LM* curve is plotted with the interest rate on the vertical axis and income on the horizontal axis. Solving equation (7.5) for the interest rate identifies the intercept and slope of the *LM* curve.

$$M_0^s = c_0 + c_1 Y - c_2 r$$

Solving for the interest rate:

$$LM: \quad r = \underbrace{\frac{c_0}{c_2} - \frac{1}{c_2}(M_0^s)}_{\text{intercept}} + \underbrace{\frac{c_1 Y}{c_2}}_{\text{slope}} \qquad (7.5a)$$

When the *LM* is plotted, the intercept contains the money supply (M_0^s). Any time the money supply changes, the intercept will change and the *LM* curve will shift. If the money supply increases, the *LM* will shift down. If the money supply decreases, the *LM* will shift up.

Figure 7.10 illustrates the effects of an increase in the money supply from M_0^s to M_1^s. With the initial money supply M_0^s, the *LM* curve is given by LM_0 in Figure 7.10*b*. Along this initial *LM* curve, an income level of Y_0, for example, would be a point of money market equilibrium for an interest rate value of r_0, as shown at point A on the graph. Equilibrium in the money market for income level Y_0 is also shown in Figure 7.10*a* at the intersection of the M_0^s and $M^d(Y_0)$ schedules.

An increase in the money supply from M_0^s to M_1^s can be seen in Figure 7.10*a* to reduce the equilibrium interest rate to r_1 for a given level of income Y_0. With income

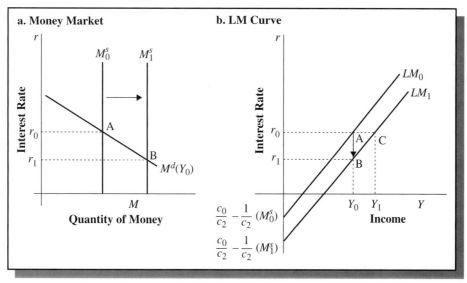

Figure 7.10 Shift in the *LM* Curve with an Increase in the Quantity of Money

Beginning at point A in the money market, with money supply (M_0^s), the equilibrium interest rate is r_0. This is combination Y_0, r_0, at point (A) on the *LM* curve. When the money supply increases, from (M_0^s) to (M_1^s), *given money demand at income level, Y_0*, the money supply curve shifts to the right. Equilibrium in the money market changes from point A to point B, and the interest rate decreases from r_0 to r_1.

fixed, in order for the new higher money supply to be equal to money demand, the interest rate must be lower to increase the speculative demand for money and transactions demand for a given income level. In terms of the *LM* curve in Figure 7.10*b*, the point on the new *LM* schedule (for money supply M_1^s) that gives the equilibrium interest rate for income level Y_0 will be at interest rate r_1. This income–interest-rate combination (Y_0, r_1) is a point on the new *LM* curve, LM_1, as shown at point B on the graph.

In general, with a higher money supply for a given level of income, the interest rate that equilibrates the money market will be lower. The new *LM* curve, LM_1, will lie below the initial curve LM_0, as shown in Figure 7.10*b*.

Alternatively, consider the point on the new *LM* curve that gives the equilibrium level of income corresponding to interest rate r_0. At M_0^s the income level Y_0 was an equilibrium level for interest rate r_0 (point A). With the money supply M_1^s, in order for r_0 to be an equilibrium value in the money market, income would have to be higher at Y_1. With a higher money supply and a given interest rate, in order for there to be equilibrium in the money market, income must be at a higher level. The point on the new *LM* schedule LM_1, corresponding to r_0, must lie to the right of point A. This point is shown as point C in Figure 7.10*b*. The new *LM* curve, LM_1, with the higher money supply M_1^s will lie to the right of the original *LM* schedule in Figure 7.10*b*.

In sum, *an increase in the money supply shifts the LM schedule downward and to the right*. By reversing the foregoing analysis, a decline in the money supply shifts the *LM* schedule upward and to the left.

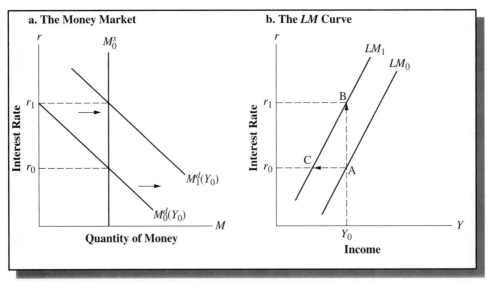

Figure 7.11 Shift in the *LM* Curve with a Shift in the Money Demand Function

A shift in the money demand function upward from $M_0^d(Y_0)$ to $M_1^d(Y_0)$ in part *a* raises the equilibrium interest rate for a given income level. The *LM* schedule in part *b* shifts upward to the left from LM_0 to LM_1.

Shifts in the Money Demand Function   Consider next the effect on the *LM* curve of a shift in the money demand function. Assume that there is an increase in money demand for a given level of income and the interest rate. A possible reason for such a shift, as suggested previously, is a loss of confidence in bonds.

Figure 7.11*a* shows an initial equilibrium in the money market corresponding to income level Y_0. Initially, money demand is given by $M_0^d(Y_0)$. The equilibrium interest rate is r_0, as shown at point A on the initial *LM* curve, LM_0 in Figure 7.11*b*. Now assume that the money demand function shifts to $M_1^d(Y_0)$, an increase in money demand for a given level of income. Note here that it is the *function* that shifts, from $M_0^d(Y_0)$ to $M_1^d(Y_0)$. At the unchanged level of income, Y_0, equilibrium in the money market requires an interest rate of r_1. The point on the new *LM* curve, LM_1 in Figure 7.11*b*, for a given level of income Y_0 will be above the old *LM* schedule. This point is shown as point B in Figure 7.11*b*.

Similarly, maintaining equilibrium in the money market at r_0 after the shift in the money demand curve would require a fall in income to a level below Y_0, which would shift the schedule in Figure 7.11*a* down to the level of the original $M_0^d(Y_0)$ line. Thus the point on LM_1 at r_0 is to the left of LM_0. This is shown as point C in Figure 7.11*b*.

A shift in the money demand function that increases the demand for money at a given level of both the interest rate and income shifts the *LM* schedule upward and to the left. A reverse change in money demand (lowering the amount of money demanded at given levels of income and the interest rate) shifts the *LM* curve downward to the right.

The LM *Schedule: Summary*

We now know the essentials about the *LM* curve:

1. The *LM* curve is the schedule giving the combinations of values of income and the interest rate that produce equilibrium in the money market.
2. The *LM* curve slopes upward to the right.
3. The *LM* curve will be relatively flat (steep) if the interest elasticity of money demand is relatively high (low).
4. The *LM* curve will shift downward (upward) to the right (left) with an increase (decrease) in the quantity of money.
5. The *LM* curve will shift upward (downward) to the left (right) with a shift in the money demand function that increases (decreases) the amount of money demanded at given levels of income and the interest rate.

Product Market Equilibrium: The *IS* Curve

Construction of the IS *Schedule*

The condition for equilibrium in the product market is

$$Y = C + I + G \tag{7.7}$$

An equivalent statement of this equilibrium condition is

$$I + G = S + T \tag{7.8}$$

We construct the product market equilibrium schedule, termed the *IS curve*, from this second form of the equilibrium condition, although the same results could be derived from equation (7.7).

We proceed by finding the set of interest-rate and income combinations that produces equilibrium for the product market. Next we examine the factors that determine the slope and position of this product market equilibrium schedule.

To begin, we consider a simplified case that omits the government sector (i.e., G and T equal zero). The more general case is considered subsequently. For this simple case, we can rewrite (7.8) as[4]

$$I(r) = S(Y) \tag{7.9}$$

Equation (7.9) also indicates that investment depends on the interest rate and saving depends on income. Our task is to find combinations of the interest rate and income that equate investment with saving.

Figure 7.12 illustrates the construction of the *IS* curve for this case. In Figure 7.12*a* investment is plotted as a negatively sloped function of the interest rate; a decline in the interest rate will increase investment expenditures. Saving is depicted as a positively sloped function of income, the slope being the positive marginal propensity to save.

---

[4]The label *IS* comes from this simple version of the product market equilibrium curve, an equality between investment (*I*) and saving (*S*).

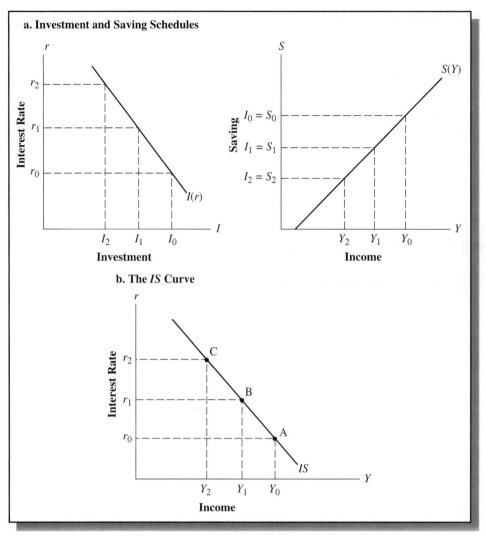

Figure 7.12 Construction of the *IS* Curve (*T = G = O*)

At interest rates r_0, r_1, r_2, investment levels will be I_0, I_1, and I_2 in part *a*. To generate levels of saving S_0, S_1, S_2 equal to these levels of investment, income must be at Y_0, Y_1, and Y_2, respectively. Therefore, interest-rate–income combinations (r_0, Y_0), (r_1, Y_1), and (r_2, Y_2) are points (A, B, C) along the *IS* schedule in part *b*.

Consider an interest rate of r_0. For this level of the interest rate, investment is the amount I_0, as shown along the investment schedule. An amount of saving just equal to I_0 is shown as S_0 along the saving function. This level of saving results if income is at Y_0. Thus, for the interest rate r_0, a point of product market equilibrium will be at Y_0. This interest-rate–income combination (r_0, Y_0) is one point on the *IS* curve, shown as point A in Figure 7.12*b*.

Now consider a higher value of the interest rate, such as r_1. At interest rate r_1, investment will be I_1, a smaller amount than at r_0. For equilibrium, saving must be at

S_1, lower than S_0. This saving level is generated by income level Y_1, which is lower than Y_0. Thus a second point on the IS curve will be at r_1 and Y_1, point B on Figure 7.12b. Notice that for the higher interest rate, the corresponding equilibrium income level is lower. *The IS curve has a negative slope.* By choosing additional interest rate values such as r_2 in Figure 7.12a and finding the corresponding income level for equilibrium Y_2, where $I_2 = S_2$, we can find additional points on the IS curve in Figure 7.12b, such as point C. In this way we trace the complete set of combinations of income and interest-rate levels that equilibrate the product market.

Factors That Determine the Slope of the IS Schedule

Next we consider the factors that determine the degree of the slope of the IS curve. We know that the curve will be negatively sloped, but will it be steep or flat? As with the LM curve, the question is of interest because we will see that the steepness of the IS curve is a factor determining the relative effectiveness of monetary and fiscal stabilization policies.

In constructing the IS curve, we have looked at how investment changes as we vary the interest rate and then at the required change in income to move saving to equal the new investment level. In considering the steepness of the IS curve, we are asking whether, at progressively lower interest rates, for example, equilibrium in the product market requires *much* higher income levels (the curve is relatively flat) or only *slightly* increased income levels (the curve is steep). The answer will depend on the slopes of the investment and saving functions. Figure 7.13 illustrates how the slope of the IS curve is related to the slope of the investment function. Two investment schedules are depicted. The schedule I is very steep, indicating that investment is not very sensitive to changes in the interest rate; the interest elasticity of investment demand is low.[5] The schedule I' is drawn for the case in which investment is more sensitive to movements in the interest rate. For either investment schedule, the graph is constructed so that an interest rate of r_1 corresponds to investment of I_1 (the curves have different intercepts on the interest-rate axis). Equilibrium in the product market for this interest rate will be at Y_1, as can be seen from Figure 7.13b (at that point, $I_1 = S_1$). This will be one point along the product market equilibrium schedules that we construct corresponding to each of these investment schedules. These product market equilibrium schedules, IS for investment schedule I and IS' for investment schedule I', are shown in Figure 7.13c. They have a common point at (Y_1, r_1), point A.

Now consider the point along each of these equilibrium schedules corresponding to a lower interest rate r_2. If investment is given by schedule I in Figure 7.13a, at the lower interest rate r_2 investment will increase to I_2. Equilibrium in the product market requires an equal increase in saving to S_2, which requires that income be at Y_2 in Figure 7.13b. Along the IS schedule, we move to point B in Figure 7.13c. Notice that, because investment was assumed to be relatively insensitive to changes in the interest rate, the increase in investment when the interest rate falls to r_2 is small. Consequently, the required increase in saving, and therefore income, in Figure 7.13b

---

[5]The concept of elasticity is defined in footnote 3. Here, as in the case of money demand, the interest elasticity is negative; an increase in the interest rate lowers investment. By saying that elasticity is low, we refer to the absolute value of the elasticity.

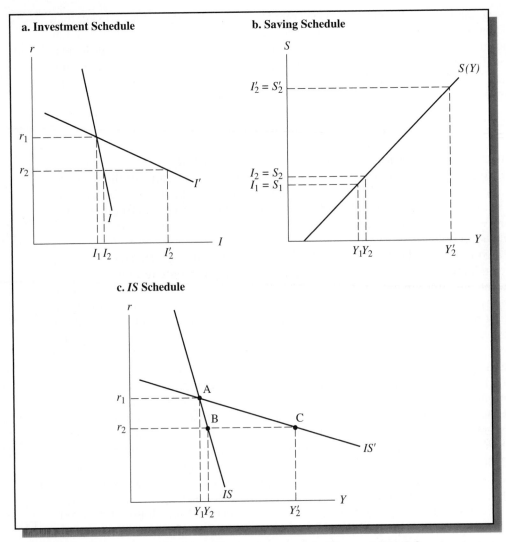

Figure 7.13 Interest Elasticity of Investment and the Slope of the *IS* Curve

Where the investment schedule is steep (*I*) in part *a*, a fall in the interest rate will increase investment by only a small amount. In part *b*, therefore, only a small increase in saving and, hence, income is required to restore product market equilibrium. Therefore, the *IS* schedule in part *c* (*IS* in this case) will be steep. Where the investment schedule is relatively flat (*I'*), investment will increase by more with a fall in the interest rate. Saving, and therefore income, must then increase by more; the *IS* schedule for this case (*IS'*) will be relatively flat.

is small. The *IS* curve is steep in this case; lower levels of the interest rate correspond to only slightly higher levels of income along the product market equilibrium curve.

Next consider the case in which investment is given by the flatter schedule *I'* in Figure 7.13*a*. At the lower interest rate r_2, investment will be at I'_2. The level of income corresponding to r_2 along the investment-equals-saving curve for this case, *IS'* in Figure 7.13*c*, would be Y'_2 at point C. Saving must increase to S'_2, and this requires income Y_2'. In this case, investment is more highly interest-elastic and increases by a greater amount as the interest rate falls to r_2. Consequently, saving must increase by a greater amount than when investment is interest-inelastic, and for this larger saving increase, income must increase by more. The product market equilibrium schedule (IS') is flatter when investment is more sensitive to the interest rate.

This, then, is the first of the factors determining the slope of the IS curve. The curve will be relatively steep if the interest elasticity of investment is low. The curve will be flatter for higher (absolute) values of investment interest elasticity.

One extreme case for the slope of the IS curve is when the interest elasticity of investment demand is zero; investment is completely insensitive to the interest rate. In this case, the investment schedule in Figure 7.13a will be vertical and the IS curve will also be vertical. For this case, a fall in the interest rate from r_1 to r_2 would not increase investment at all. Consequently, equilibrium in the product market requires the same level of saving, and hence income, at r_2 as at r_1. This means that the IS curve will be vertical.

The second factor affecting the slope of the IS curve is the saving function. Until we consider more elaborate theories of consumption, we do not encounter controversy over the slope of the saving function in Figure 7.13b, which is equal to the marginal propensity to save (MPS). Consequently, in this section the value of the MPS does not play much of a role in our discussion of the factors determining the slope of the IS curve. It can be shown, however, that the IS curve will be relatively steeper the higher the MPS.

To see this relationship, first note that the higher the value of the MPS, the steeper is the saving function in Figure 7.13b (saving increases by more per unit of income). Once we have determined the slope of the investment schedule, we fix the change in investment for a given change in the interest rate. A given decline in the interest rate, for example, then leads to a given increase in investment, and for product market equilibrium along the IS curve, saving must be higher by the same amount. If the MPS is relatively high, then a smaller increase in income will generate this new saving than if the MPS were low. Thus, for a given fall in the interest rate, the amount by which income would have to be increased for a new point of equilibrium in the product market is smaller (larger) the higher (lower) the value of the MPS. This means that the IS curve is relatively steeper, other factors as given, the higher the MPS.

Factors That Shift the IS Schedule

Next consider the factors that determine the position of the IS curve and changes that shift the schedule. Here we drop the assumption that government expenditures and taxes are zero; we bring the government sector back into the model. The IS curve will shift when any or all of the components of autonomous expenditures change: a, T, I, and G. With the government sector in the model, the condition for product market equilibrium is given by (7.8), which we rewrite as

$$I(r) + G = S(Y - T) + T \qquad (7.10)$$

Notice that saving must now be written as a function of *disposable income* ($Y_D = Y - T$), which differs from income by the amount of tax collections.

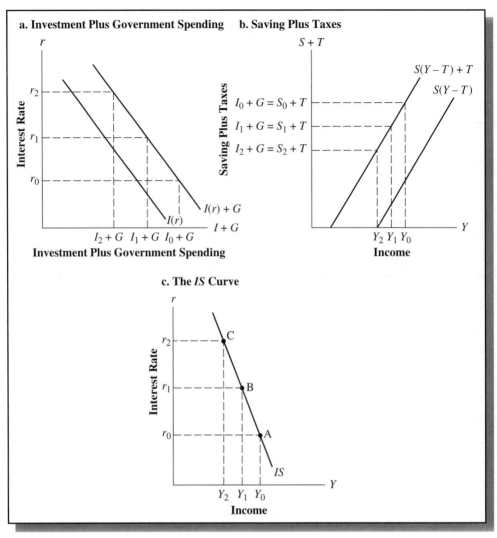

Figure 7.14 *IS* Curve with the Addition of a Government Sector

With the inclusion of the government sector, the condition for equilibrium in the goods market becomes $I + G = S + T$. At an interest rate of r_1 in part *a*, investment plus government spending will be equal to $I_1 + G$. Therefore, equilibrium in the goods market requires that saving plus taxes, as shown in part *b*, equal $S_1 + T$ ($= I_1 + G$), which will be the case at an income level Y_1. Thus, the combination r_1, Y_1 is one point (B) along the *IS* schedule in part *c*.

Construction of the *IS* curve for this more general case is illustrated in Figure 7.14. In part *a*, we plot both the investment function and the level of investment plus government spending. Note that the $I + G$ schedule is downward-sloping only because investment depends on the rate of interest. The $I + G$ schedule lies to the right of the *I* schedule by the fixed amount of government spending. In Figure 7.14*b*, the saving schedule is plotted against the level of income. Saving plus taxes $[S(Y - T) + T]$ is also plotted. We are assuming that tax collections are fixed exogenously, so the saving-plus-taxes schedule lies above the saving schedule by a fixed distance (equal to T).

Consider an interest rate such as r_0 in Figure 7.14. At this interest rate, the level of investment [which can be read from the $I(r)$ curve] plus the fixed level of government spending equals $I_0 + G$. For equilibrium, this must be balanced by an equal total of saving plus tax collections, given by $S_0 + T$ in Figure 7.14b. The level of income that generates this level of saving plus tax collections is given by Y_0. Thus, one point along the IS curve is point A in Figure 7.14c, corresponding to interest rate r_0 and income level Y_0. If we considered a higher interest rate, such as r_1, investment would be less; hence, with government spending unchanged, investment plus government spending would be at the lower level $I_1 + G$. For equilibrium, a lower level of saving plus taxes is required. This level is shown as $S_1 + T$ in Figure 7.14b, where it should be noted that the change is only in the saving component, because taxes are fixed. For this lower level of saving, income must be at Y_1, below Y_0 in Figure 7.14b. The corresponding point on the IS curve is point B in Figure 7.14c.

By similar reasoning, we can establish that an interest rate of r_2 will require an income level of Y_2 for equilibrium in the product market (point C in Figure 7.14c). The complete IS schedule is constructed by proceeding in this manner.

We can now look at factors that would cause a shift in the IS curve. The equilibrium condition given by (7.10) shows that a change in either the level of government spending (G) or the level of taxes (T) will disturb an initial product market equilibrium position—this will be a shift in the IS curve. In addition, an autonomous investment change that shifts the investment function will shift the IS curve. Note that, in general, the factors that shift the IS curve are those that determined autonomous expenditures in the simple Keynesian model of Chapter 6.

Changes in Government Spending   Consider first the effects of a change in government spending. The shift in the IS curve when government spending increases from an initial level G_0 to a higher level G_1 is illustrated in Figure 7.15. For the initial level of government spending, the IS schedule is given by IS_0 in Figure 7.15c. An interest rate of r_0, for example, will be an equilibrium level for the product market if income is at Y_0, as shown at point A on IS_0. At interest rate r_0, investment plus government spending will be $I_0 + G_0$, as shown in Figure 7.15a. As shown in Figure 7.15b, an income level of Y_0 generates saving plus taxes just equal to this amount of government spending plus investment ($S_0 + T_0 = I_0 + G_0$).

Now let government spending increase to G_1 Figure 7.15a shows that this increase shifts the investment plus government spending schedule out to the right. At a given interest rate, investment will be unchanged, and the sum of investment plus government spending will be higher by the increase in government spending ($\Delta G = G_1 - G_0$).

Equilibrium in the product market requires an equally higher level of saving plus taxes, shown as $S_1 + T_0$ in Figure 7.15b. This level of saving plus taxes will be forthcoming at income level Y_1 above Y_0. Thus, a given interest rate r_0, for equilibrium in the product market, requires a higher level of income when government spending is increased. The increase in government spending will shift the IS curve to the right to IS_1 in Figure 7.15c, where at r_0 the point of equilibrium is at point B, corresponding to the higher income level Y_1.

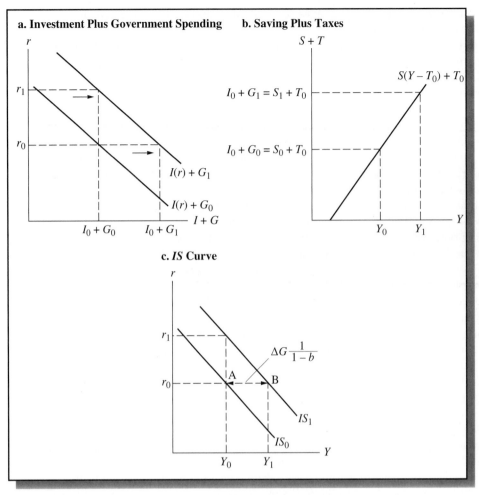

Figure 7.15 Shift in the *IS* Curve with an Increase in Government Spending

At interest rate r_0, an increase in government spending increases the total of investment plus government spending from $I_0 + G_0$ to $I_0 + G_1$ in part *a*. To maintain the condition $I + G = S + T$, with a fixed level of taxes, saving must rise from S_0 to S_1, which requires income to be Y_1 instead of Y_0 in part *b*. At interest rate r_0, the equilibrium point in the product market is point B instead of point A. An increase in government spending shifts the *IS* schedule to the right from IS_0 to IS_1 in part *c*.

It will be useful to establish the amount by which the *IS* curve shifts to the right, the horizontal distance from A to B in Figure 7.15*c*. For each one-unit increase in government spending, with taxes assumed unchanged, to restore equilibrium *at a given interest rate* in the product market, saving must be higher by one unit. This relation can be seen by looking at equation (7.10). So the distance of the horizontal shift in the *IS* curve (e.g., distance AB) is that of the amount of the increase in income required to generate new saving equal to the increase in government spending. Because the increase in saving per unit increase in income is given by the MPS equal to $(1 - b)$, the required increase in income (the horizontal shift in the IS curve) will be $\Delta G [1/(1 - b)]$,

$$\Delta G = \Delta S = (1 - b)\Delta Y\big|_{r_0}$$

$$\Delta G \frac{1}{1 - b} = \Delta Y\big|_{r_0} \qquad\qquad (7.11)$$

where the subscript r_0 on the ΔY term indicates we are computing the increase in the value of Y that will be required to maintain equilibrium in the product market *at interest rate r_0*. This is the amount of the horizontal shift in the IS schedule.

Notice that the amount of the horizontal shift in the IS curve per unit increase in G is $[1/(1 - b)]$, the autonomous expenditure multiplier from Chapter 6. In looking at the horizontal distance that the curve shifts, we are holding the interest rate constant and therefore fixing investment. Once investment is assumed given, our model is identical to that in Chapter 6. We are looking for the increase in income that will come with investment fixed, government spending rising, and a consequent induced increase in consumption. This is the same question analyzed in Chapter 6 and we get the same answer.

Changes in Taxes   Next consider the shift in the IS curve with a change in taxes. The effect on the position of the IS curve of a tax increase from T_0 to T_1 is depicted in Figure 7.16. For each one-dollar increase in taxes *at a given income level*, taxes are higher by one dollar and saving is less by $(1 - b)$ dollars. The latter effect follows because an increase of one dollar in taxes lowers disposable income by one dollar and reduces saving by the MPS $(1 - b)$. For a given income level, the decline in saving is less than the increase in taxes, so an increase in taxes will shift the $S + T$ schedule upward. In Figure 7.16b, an increase in taxes from T_0 to T_1 shifts the schedule from $[S(Y - T_0) + T_0]$ to $[S(Y - T_1) + T_1]$.

At an interest rate such as r_0 in Figure 7.16a, we can find the level of government expenditures plus investment along the $I(r) + G$ schedule at $I_0 + G_0$. Equilibrium in the product market requires an equal amount of saving plus taxes. Initially, with taxes at T_0, the equilibrium level of saving plus taxes is $S_0 + T_0$, and this requires income to be at Y_0. This combination of (r_0, Y_0) is a point on the initial IS curve IS_0, point A in Figure 7.16c.

After the tax increase, for equilibrium in the product market at r_0, we must still have the same total of saving plus taxes. This is because there has been no change in investment plus government spending. With the higher level of taxes, in order for saving plus taxes to be unchanged, saving and therefore income must be lower. The new level of income required for product market equilibrium is given by Y_1 in Figure 7.16b. The corresponding point on the new IS curve is point B in Figure 7.16c. The increase in taxes shifts the IS curve to the left.

As with the change in government spending, we can calculate the magnitude of the horizontal shift in the IS curve as a result of an increase in taxes. *For a given rate of interest*, a tax change does not affect the left-hand side of the equilibrium condition for the product market [equation (7.10)]; investment and government spending are unchanged. So for equilibrium at the same interest rate, the right-hand side must be

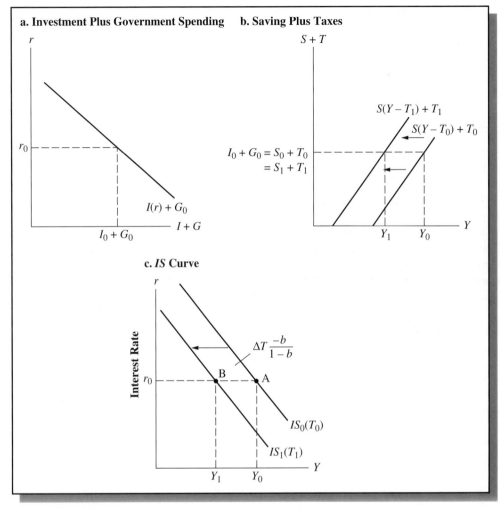

Figure 7.16 Shift in the *IS* Curve with an Increase in Taxes

An increase in taxes shifts the $S + T$ schedule to the left in part *b*. At interest rate r_0, which fixes $I_0 + G_0$, with higher taxes, saving and therefore income must be lower to maintain the condition $I + G = S + T$. After the tax increase, an income level of Y_1 (point B) rather than Y_0 (point A) clears the product market for interest rate r_0. The *IS* curve shifts leftward from IS_0 to IS_1 in part *c*.

unchanged; saving plus taxes must be unchanged. This condition requires that the increase in taxes be exactly balanced by a decline in saving,

$$0 = \Delta S + \Delta T$$

We can express the change in saving as

$$\Delta S = (1 - b)\Delta(Y - T) = (1 - b)\Delta Y - (1 - b)\,\Delta T$$

So for (7.10) to hold requires that

$$\Delta S + \Delta T = 0$$
$$(1 - b)\Delta Y - (1 - b)\Delta T + \Delta T = 0$$
$$(1 - b)\Delta Y - \Delta T + b\Delta T + \Delta T = 0$$
$$(1 - b)\Delta Y + b\Delta T = 0$$
$$(1 - b)\Delta Y = -b\Delta T$$
$$\Delta Y\big|_{r_0} = \frac{-b}{1 - b}\Delta T \tag{7.12}$$

where again in equation (7.12) the subscript r_0 is used on the ΔY term to indicate that this is the change in income that at interest rate r_0 will be an equilibrium value for the product market. From (7.12) we see that, as demonstrated previously, income must be lower for product market equilibrium at r_0 with a higher level of taxes. Also, the amount by which the *IS* curve shifts to the left for a one-unit increase in taxes, $-b/(1 - b)$, is just the tax multiplier from the simple Keynesian model of Chapter 6. When we consider the horizontal shift in the *IS* curve per unit change in taxes, we are fixing the interest rate, and thus investment. So we are calculating the change in equilibrium income per unit change in taxes for a given level of investment. This was given in Chapter 6 by the tax multiplier $-b/(1 - b)$.

Autonomous Changes in Investment   The last factor we consider that shifts the *IS* curve is an autonomous change in investment. By this we mean a shift in the investment schedule as drawn against the interest rate. For example, a favorable shift in expectations about the future profitability of investment projects increases investment demand *corresponding to each interest rate*, shifting the *I(r)* schedule and hence the investment plus government spending schedule to the right in Figure 7.15a. This rightward shift in the *I(r)* schedule, by the amount of the autonomous increase in investment, has exactly the same effect on the *IS* curve as an equal increase in government spending, analyzed in Figure 7.15. Both changes shift the investment plus government spending schedule and, as was seen in the previous discussion, this shift, in turn, shifts the *IS* curve to the right by $1/(1 - b)$ units per unit increase in government spending, or in this case, autonomous investment expenditures.

In this section we have considered the various factors that shift the *IS* schedule. We have also generalized the analysis to allow for a government sector and hence to enable us to see how fiscal policy variables affect the position of the *IS* schedule. Because the new variables, government spending and taxes, were exogenous, the slopes of the investment-plus-government-spending schedule and of the saving-plus-taxes schedule were the same as those for the investment and saving schedules considered in the preceding section. Because the slopes of these functions were shown to determine the slope of the *IS* curve and because they are unchanged, adding the government sector to the model requires no revision of the previous discussion of the slope of the *IS* curve.

The IS *Schedule: Summary*

We have derived the following results concerning the *IS* curve, the equilibrium schedule for the product market:

1. The *IS* curve slopes downward to the right.
2. The *IS* curve will be relatively flat (steep) if the interest elasticity of investment is relatively high (low).
3. The *IS* curve will shift to the right (left) when there is an increase (decrease) in government expenditures.
4. The *IS* curve will shift to the left (right) when taxes increase (decline).
5. An autonomous increase (decrease) in investment expenditures will shift the *IS* curve to the right (left).

The *IS* and *LM* Curves Combined

In Figure 7.17, we combine the *LM* and *IS* schedules. The upward-sloping *LM* schedule shows the points of equilibrium for the money market. The downward-sloping *IS* schedule shows the points of equilibrium for the product market. The point of intersection between the two curves, point E in the figure, is the (only) point of general equilibrium for the two markets. As pointed out at the beginning of our discussion, if the money market is in equilibrium, the bond market must also be in equilibrium. Thus, the interest rate and income level at the intersection of the *IS* and *LM* schedules in Figure 7.17, denoted r_0 and Y_0, are values that produce a simultaneous equilibrium for the money market, product market, and bond market. The nature of equilibrium in the *IS*–*LM* curve model can be better understood by considering why points other than the point of intersection of the two curves are not points of equilibrium. Figure 7.18 shows four points off the *IS* and *LM* curves (A, B, C, and D).

Figure 7.17
IS and *LM* Curves Combined

The point of intersection of the *IS* and *LM* curves gives the combination of the interest rate and income (r_0, Y_0) that produces equilibrium for the money and product markets.

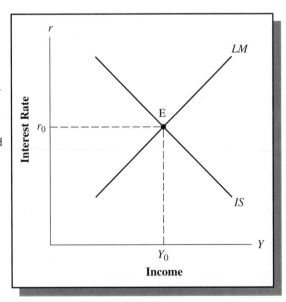

Figure 7.18
Adjustment to
Equilibrium in the
IS–LM Curve Model

At points such as A, B, C, and D, there are either excess supplies or demands in the money and product markets and therefore pressures for the interest rate and output to change. At point F, the product market is out of equilibrium, and there is pressure for output to change. Only at point E are both the money and product markets in equilibrium with no pressure for change in either the interest rate or output.

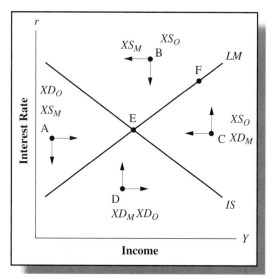

First consider points above the *LM* schedule such as points A and B. At all points above the *LM* schedule, there will be an excess supply of money (XS_M). At the level of income for either point A or B, the corresponding interest rate is too high for money market equilibrium. With an excess supply of money, there is downward pressure on the interest rate, as indicated by the downward-direction arrow. There is a tendency to move toward the *LM* schedule. Conversely, at points below the *LM* schedule, such as points C and D, there will be an excess *demand* for money (XD_M), and consequently upward pressure on the interest rate.

Now consider the same points in relation to the *IS* curve. At points such as B and C, to the right of the *IS* schedule, output will exceed aggregate demand or, analogously, saving plus taxes will exceed investment plus government spending. At the level of the interest rate for either point B or C, the corresponding output level that will equate investment plus government spending to saving plus taxes, given by the point along the *IS* curve, is below the actual output level. There is an excess supply of output (XS_O), and therefore a downward pressure on output, as indicated by the arrows pointing to the left. Conversely, at points to the left of this *IS* schedule, such as points A and D, actual output is below the level that will clear the product market. There is an excess demand for output (XD_O), and there will be upward pressure on output, as indicated by the rightward-directed arrows at these points.

Finally, note that points on one schedule but not on the other are also *disequilibrium* points relative to one of the two markets. A point such as F, for example, is a point of equilibrium for the money market but a point of excess supply for the product market. Similarly, any point along the *IS* curve other than point E would result in disequilibrium in the money market. Only at point E are both the money and product markets in equilibrium. There is no excess demand or supply in either the money or product market, and therefore there are no pressures for the interest rate or output to change.

7.3 CONCLUSION

In this chapter, we have brought the money market into our Keynesian model. The role of money and monetary policy in the Keynesian system was considered. We then analyzed how the equilibrium level of income and the interest rate are simultaneously determined in the *IS–LM* curve model. The next task is to see how these equilibrium values are affected by monetary and fiscal policy variables as well as by other shocks to the model.

KEY TERMS

• liquidity trap 132

REVIEW QUESTIONS AND PROBLEMS

1. Explain the Keynesian theory of interest-rate determination. What differences do you see between this theory and the classical theory of the interest rate?
2. How would the level of aggregate demand be affected by a rise in the interest rate in the Keynesian theory? Which components would be affected most strongly?
3. What are the three motives for holding money according to Keynes's theory of money demand? Explain each motive.
4. What property is shared by all points along the *LM* schedule? Along the *IS* schedule?
5. Explain why the *IS* curve in the *IS–LM* curve model is negatively sloped and the *LM* curve is positively sloped.
6. What factors determine the magnitude of the slope of the *IS* schedule; that is, what factors determine whether the curve is steep or flat?
7. What variables will shift the position of the *IS* schedule? Explain how a change in each variable will shift the schedule (to the left or to the right).
8. What factors determine the magnitude of the slope of the *LM* schedule; that is, what factors determine whether the curve is steep or flat?
9. Trace the procedure for deriving the *IS* schedule, as was done in Figure 7.14, for the case in which, rather than a fixed level of taxes (*T*), we have taxes depending on income

$$T = t_1 Y$$

where t_1 is the marginal income tax rate. Will the *IS* curve for this case be steeper or flatter than when the level of taxes is fixed?
10. Suppose that the interest elasticity of investment demand is zero. What will be the resulting slope of the *IS* curve. Explain.
11. If the level of government spending were to increase by 50 units in the *IS–LM* curve model, how would this affect the position of the *IS* curve? In which direction would the curve shift and by how many units?
12. What variables will shift the position of the *LM* schedule? Explain how a change in each variable will shift the schedule (to the left or to the right).

13. What condition is required for the *LM* schedule to be vertical? What condition is required for the alternative extreme case, in which the *LM* schedule becomes nearly horizontal over a range?
14. Why are we assured that when the money and product markets are in equilibrium, the bond market will also be in equilibrium?
15. Explain why at a point such as B in Figure 7.18, there is downward pressure on both the level of output and the interest rate.

Appendix 1

The Algebra of the IS–LM *Model*

In this appendix, the *IS–LM* curve model is presented in algebraic form; no new material is covered. This algebraic presentation is simply a supplement to the verbal and graphical explanation given in the chapter.

For simplicity, we deal with a linear form of the *IS* and *LM* equations. We have already written out a linear form of the *LM* equation

$$M^s = M^d = c_0 + c_1 Y - c_2 r \qquad c_1; c_2 > 0 \quad \textbf{(7.5)}$$

Equation (7.5) states that the fixed money supply (M^s) is equal to the demand for money (M^d), which depends positively on the level of income (Y) and negatively on the interest rate (r).

The condition met for each point on the *IS* curve is

$$I + G = S + T \qquad \textbf{(7.8)}$$

Investment (I) plus government spending (G) is equal to saving (S) plus taxes (T). Let us derive a linear form of this condition.

In Chapter 6, saving was represented by the saving function

$$\begin{aligned} S &= -a + (1 - b)Y_D \\ &= -a + (1 - b)(Y - T) \end{aligned} \qquad \textbf{(6.12)}$$

Investment is assumed to have an autonomous component and to depend negatively on the

interest rate. In linear form, we can write an *investment function* as follows:

$$I = \bar{I} - i_1 r \qquad i_1 > 0 \qquad \textbf{(A.1)}$$

where $\bar{I}$ is the autonomous component of investment and i_1 is a parameter that measures the interest sensitivity of investment (i.e., $-i_1 = \Delta I / \Delta r$).[1] The levels of government spending (G) and taxes (T) are assumed to be fixed exogenously by policymakers.

Substituting equation (6.12) for S and equation (A.1) for I into the *IS* equation (7.8), we can write a linear *IS* curve equation

$$\bar{I} - i_1 r + G = -a + (1 - b)(Y - T) + T \qquad \textbf{(A.2)}$$

If we rearrange terms so that income appears alone on the left-hand side, we have

$$Y = \frac{1}{1 - b}\left[a + \bar{I} + G - bT\right] - \frac{i_1 r}{1 - b} \qquad \textbf{(A.3)}$$

We can also rearrange the terms in our *LM* equation (7.5) so that the interest rate (r) is alone on the left-hand side, as follows:

$$r = \frac{c_0}{c_2} - \frac{M^s}{c_2} + \frac{c_1 Y}{c_2} \qquad \textbf{(A.4)}$$

---

[1]A parameter is a given or known value. An example of a parameter in our previous analysis is the marginal propensity to save $(1 - b)$ in (6.12).

Equations (A.3) and (A.4) are linear *IS* and *LM* curves. These two equations determine the two endogenous variables in the model, income (Y) and the interest rate (r). From here we consider the properties of the *LM* and then the *IS* curve, deriving in algebraic form the graphical results in section 7.2. We then examine the solution of these two equations for the equilibrium levels of income and the interest rate, the analog to the graphical representation of equilibrium in Figure 7.17.

A.1 THE *LM* CURVE
The Slope of the *LM* Curve

The slope of the *LM* curve is the change in r (movement up the vertical axis in the *IS–LM* curve graph) per unit change in Y (movement along the horizontal axis), holding constant the factors that fix the position of the curve. From equation (A.4) we compute this slope as $\Delta r / \Delta Y$ for fixed values of (c_0/c_2) and $(-M^s/c_2)$, which gives

$$\Delta r = \frac{c_1}{c_2} \Delta Y$$

$$\text{Slope of } LM = \left. \frac{\Delta r}{\Delta Y} \right|_{LM} = \frac{c_1}{c_2} \tag{A.5}$$

The *LM* curve has a positive slope. If the expression for the slope of the curve is large (small), then the curve will be steep (flat). From equation (A.5) it can be seen that the curve will be steeper the higher the value of c_1 and the lower the value of c_2. This means that the more money demand increases per unit increase in income (the higher c_1) and the *less* sensitive money demand is to the interest rate (the lower c_2), the steeper will be the *LM* schedule.[2]

---

[2]Notice also from equation (A.5) that, as c_2 approaches zero, the expression becomes extremely large, indicating that the *LM* curve becomes vertical. This is the so-called classical case illustrated in Figure 7.8. Alternatively, as c_2 becomes extremely large, the expression for the slope of the *LM* curve approaches zero, indicating that the *LM* curve becomes flat. This is the liquidity trap illustrated in Figure 7.9.

Factors That Shift the *LM* Curve

Now consider factors that shift the *LM* curve. One way to look at such shifts mathematically is the change in r for one right-hand-side variable in the *LM* curve equation (A.4), *holding income and the other right-hand-side variables constant*. This is the vertical displacement of the curve. For example, if the money supply changes, all other variables remaining the same, then

$$\Delta r = \frac{-1}{c_2} \Delta M^s \tag{A.6}$$

$$\left. \frac{\Delta r}{\Delta M^s} \right|_{LM} = \frac{-1}{c_2} < 0$$

An increase in the money supply (M^s) causes a downward shift in the *LM* schedule; $\Delta r / \Delta M^s$ is negative. This is what we found in Figure 7.10; the curve shifts downward and out to the right.

The other factor we considered that would shift the *LM* curve was a shift in the money demand *function*, a change in the level of money demand for given levels of income and the interest rate. In our linear version of the *IS–LM* curve model, such a shift in the money demand function is represented as a change in the c_0 term in equation (7.5) and therefore in (c_0/c_2) in equation (A.4). For example, an increase in c_0 would mean that more money was demanded for given levels of income and the interest rate. From equation (A.4) we can see that if c_0 rises, then holding constant the other terms on the right-hand side of the equation, the interest rate will rise. This means that, as illustrated in Figure 7.11, an upward shift in the money demand function will shift the *LM* schedule upward to the left.

A.2 THE *IS* CURVE
The Slope of the *IS* Curve

To compute an expression for the slope of the *IS* curve, we again consider the relationship between r and Y given the values of the terms that fix the position of the curve [the terms in brackets in equation (A.3)]. From equation (A.3), holding these terms constant, we can write

$$\Delta Y = \frac{-i_1}{1-b} \Delta r$$

or, after rearranging terms

$$\text{slope of } IS = \left. \frac{\Delta r}{\Delta Y} \right|_{IS} = -\frac{(1-b)}{i_1} < 0 \quad \textbf{(A.7)}$$

As discussed in section 7.2, the IS slope is negative. The larger the absolute value of the slope of the IS schedule, the steeper the curve will be. From equation (A.7), it follows that the IS curve will be steeper the larger is $(1-b)$, the higher the marginal propensity to save, and the smaller the value i_1, the parameter measuring the interest sensitivity of investment.[3]

Factors That Shift the *IS* Schedule

When we use equation (A.3), it is most convenient to examine the horizontal shift in the IS schedule as the result of changes in the factors that determine the position of the curve. To do this, we examine how Y changes in equation (A.3) as one of the right-hand-side variables changes, *holding constant the interest rate and the other right-hand-side variables*. If, these other things being equal, an increase in a variable raises (lowers) Y, this represents a shift to the right (left) in the IS curve.

For example, if the level of government expenditure changes, from Equation (A.3) we compute

$$\Delta Y = \frac{1}{1-b} \Delta G \quad \textbf{(A.8)}$$

$$\left. \frac{\Delta Y}{\Delta G} \right|_{IS} = \frac{1}{1-b} > 0$$

[3]A special case for the IS curve is where i_1 approaches zero; investment is almost completely interest-insensitive. Here the slope of the IS curve, given by equation (A.7), becomes extremely large; the curve becomes nearly vertical.

This is the same result we found in equation (7.11); an increase in government spending shifts the IS curve to the right. From equation (A.3) we can see that the analogous expression for the horizontal shift in the IS schedule as the result of a change in autonomous expenditure ($\bar{I}$) or in the intercept of the consumption function (a) would be identical to equation (A.8). An increase of one unit in each of these would be an increase in autonomous expenditure of one unit, and the two would have identical effects in the IS–LM curve model.

Finally, consider the effect on the IS curve of a change in taxes (T). From equation (A.3) we compute

$$\Delta Y = \frac{1}{1-b}(-b\Delta T)$$

or

$$\left. \frac{\Delta Y}{\Delta T} \right|_{IS} = \frac{-b}{1-b} < 0 \quad \textbf{(A.9)}$$

As in the chapter [see equation (7.12)], we see that an increase in taxes lowers income (other things being equal), shifting the IS curve to the left.

A.3 EQUILIBRIUM IN THE *IS–LM* CURVE MODEL

An equilibrium point in the IS–LM curve model is a combination of income and the interest rate that satisfies both the IS and LM curve conditions. In terms of our linear IS and LM curves, the equilibrium values of Y and r are the values that satisfy both equations (A.3) and (A.4).

To find these values, we solve the two equations. First, substitute the value of r from equation (A.4) into equation (A.3). Solving the resulting equation for Y yields the equilibrium value for income (Y_0):

$$Y_0 = \left[\frac{1}{(1-b) + i_1 c_1 / c_2} \right]$$
$$\times \left[a + \bar{I} + G - bT + \frac{i_1}{c_2}(M^s - c_0) \right]$$

$$\textbf{(A.10)}$$

We can then find the equilibrium value of the interest rate (r_0) by substituting equation (A.10) or alternatively equation (A.3) into the LM curve equation (A.4). The resulting expression is

$$r_0 = \left[\frac{1}{(1-b) + i_1 c_1 / c_2} \right]$$
$$\times \left[\frac{(1-b)}{c_2} (c_0 - M^s) + \frac{c_1}{c_2} (a + \bar{I} + G - bT) \right]$$

(A.11)

Notice the difference between the IS and LM curve equations (A.3 and A.4) and the solutions

for the equilibrium values of Y and r (equations A.10 and A.11). The former equations are relationships that must hold between the two variables, with both Y and r appearing in each equation. The solution for equilibrium Y and r expresses these endogenous variables as depending on the exogenous variables of the model. In Chapter 8, we examine how these equilibrium values of Y and r change with changes in the exogenous variables. The appendix to Chapter 8 extends this analysis to the linear model considered here.

REVIEW PROBLEMS

1. Suppose that

$$C = 60 + 0.8Y_D$$
$$I = 150 - 10r$$
$$G = 250$$
$$T = 200$$
$$M^s = 100$$
$$M^d = 40 + .1Y - 10r$$

   a. Write the equations for the IS and LM schedules.
   b. Find the equilibrium values for income (Y_0) and the interest rate (r_0).
2. Suppose we change the model in problem 1 such that investment is assumed to be completely interest inelastic; investment does not depend on the rate of interest and we have $I = 150$.
   a. Write the new equations for the IS and LM schedules. Show the schedules graphically.
   b. Find the new equilibrium values for income and the interest rate.

Chapter 8

The Keynesian System (III): Policy Effects in the IS–LM Model

In this chapter, we use the *IS–LM* curve model to analyze the effects of policy actions on income and the interest rate. We also consider other factors that affect income and the interest rate. The groundwork for this analysis was established in Chapter 7. Equilibrium levels of income and the interest rate are given by the intersection of the *IS* and *LM* curves. The factors that change these equilibrium levels are those that shift either the *IS* or the *LM* curve. In section 8.1, we see how such shifts affect income and the interest rate when we consider the two schedules jointly. In section 8.2, we see how the magnitude of the effects of different policies depends on the slopes of the *IS* and *LM* curves. The slopes of the *IS–LM* curves were shown in Chapter 7 to depend on various features of the economic system, the most important being the interest sensitivity of investment and of money demand. Section 8.2 shows how policy effectiveness depends on these factors.

8.1 FACTORS THAT AFFECT EQUILIBRIUM INCOME AND THE INTEREST RATE

Monetary Influences: Shifts in the *LM* Schedule

Consider the effects on income and the interest rate of changes in the money supply. Figure 8.1 illustrates the effects of an increase in the money supply from M_0 to M_1. Initially, assume that the *IS* and *LM* schedules are IS_0 and $LM(M_0)$. Income and the

Figure 8.1

Effects of an Increase in the Quantity of Money

The initial equilibrium is at interest rate r_0 and income level Y_0. An increase in the money supply from M_0 to M_1 shifts the LM schedule to the right from $LM(M_0)$ to $LM(M_1)$. The interest rate falls from r_0 to r_1, and income rises from Y_0 to Y_1.

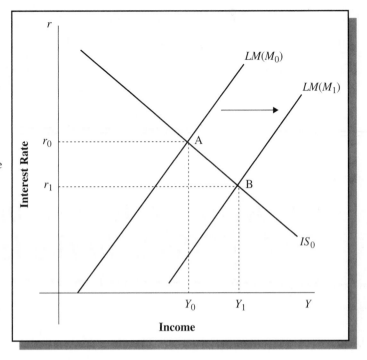

interest rate are at Y_0 and r_0, respectively. As we saw in Chapter 7, an increase in the money supply shifts the LM schedule to the right to a position such as $LM(M_1)$ in Figure 8.1. Consequently, the interest rate falls from r_0 to r_1 and income rises from Y_0 to Y_1.

The economic process producing these results is straightforward. The increase in the money supply creates an excess of money, which causes the interest rate to fall. As the interest rate falls, investment is increased, and this increase causes income to rise, with a further income-induced increase in consumption. A new equilibrium is achieved when the fall in the interest rate and the rise in income jointly increase money demand by an amount equal to the increase in the money supply. This equivalence occurs at the point where the new LM curve intersects the IS curve.

A decline in the money supply has the opposite effects. The LM curve shifts to the left; equilibrium income falls; and the equilibrium interest rate rises.

The other factor that shifts the LM schedule is a shift in the money demand function. Consider, for example, an increase in money demand *for given levels of income and the interest rate*. Such a portfolio shift away from bonds into money will shift the LM schedule to the left. As people try to reduce their bond holdings in order to increase their money holdings, the interest rate will rise. The higher interest rate will cause income to decline. An increase in money demand, in the sense of a shift in the function such that more money is demanded at a given level of income and interest rate, has the same effect as a decline in the money supply. Equilibrium income falls and the interest rate rises. A reverse portfolio shift toward holding more bonds and less money has the opposite effects.

Real Influences: Shifts in the *IS* Schedule

Fiscal policy variables are one set of factors that shift the *IS* schedule and hence affect equilibrium income and the interest rate. Figure 8.2 illustrates the effects of one fiscal policy shift, an increase in government spending from G_0 to G_1. The initial positions of the *IS* and *LM* schedules are given by $IS(G_0)$ and LM_0. The increase in government spending to G_1, as shown in Chapter 7, shifts the *IS* schedule to the right to a position such as $IS(G_1)$ in Figure 8.2. The equilibrium level of income rises, as does the equilibrium interest rate.

The force pushing up the level of income is the increase in aggregate demand both directly as government demand rises and then indirectly as a result of an income-induced increase in consumer expenditures. The forces pushing up the interest rate require some explanation. Notice that the *LM* schedule does not shift. At a given level of income, equilibrium in the money market, and therefore in the bond market, is undisturbed by the government spending change. It is the rise in income in response to the fiscal policy shift that necessitates the interest-rate adjustment. As income increases, the transactions demand for money rises. The attempt to increase transactions balances requires a decline in the demand for bonds. This income-induced increase in money demand and decline in bond demand causes the interest rate to rise.

In the aggregate, the public cannot increase money holdings; the money supply is fixed. The attempt to do so, however, will push up the interest rate, reducing the speculative demand for money and causing individuals to economize on the amount of transactions balances held for any level of income. At the new equilibrium, the

Figure 8.2
Effects of an Increase in Government Spending

An increase in government spending shifts the *IS* schedule to the right from $IS(G_0)$ to $IS(G_1)$. Income rises from Y_0 to Y_1; the interest rate rises from r_0 to r_1.

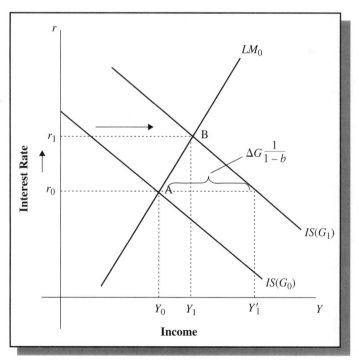

interest rate must rise sufficiently that net money demand is unchanged even though income is higher.

As shown in Chapter 7, the horizontal distance by which the IS curve shifts when government spending increases is equal to $\Delta G [1/(1 - b)]$ where ΔG equals $(G_1 - G_0)$. The distance of the shift in the IS curve is the increase in government spending times the autonomous expenditure multiplier from the simple (no money market) Keynesian model. This distance equals the amount by which income would have increased in that simple model. In Figure 8.2, this increase in equilibrium income would have been to Y_1'. When we take into account the required adjustment in the money market, it can be seen that income rises by less than this amount, to Y_1 in Figure 8.2. Why?

The difference between the simple Keynesian model and the IS–LM curve model is that the latter includes a money market. When government spending increases, as we have just seen, the rate of interest must rise to maintain equilibrium in the money market. The increase in the interest rate will cause a decline in investment spending. The decline in investment spending will partially offset the increase in aggregate demand resulting from the increase in government spending. Consequently, the increase in income will be less than that in the simple Keynesian model, where investment was taken as completely autonomous.

Next, consider the effects of an increase in tax collections (T) as illustrated in Figure 8.3. An increase in tax collections from T_0 to T_1 will, as shown in Chapter 7, shift the IS curve to the left. In the figure, this situation is shown as a shift in the IS curve from its initial position, $IS(T_0)$ to $IS(T_1)$. As can be seen, income declines from Y_0 to Y_1. The interest rate declines, from r_0 to r_1.

Income falls as taxes rise because the tax increase lowers disposable income $(Y - T)$ and causes consumption to decline. The reason for the drop in the interest rate parallels that for the income-induced interest-rate increase when government spending was increased. As income declines due to the tax increase, money demand declines and bond demand increases. This shift causes the interest rate to fall.

Figure 8.3
Effects of an Increase in Taxes

An increase in taxes shifts the IS schedule to the left from $IS(T_0)$ to $IS(T_1)$. Income falls from Y_0 to Y_1, and the interest rate falls from r_0 to r_1.

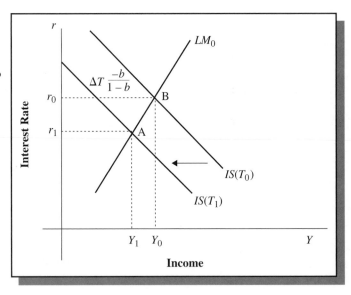

Figure 8.3 indicates that, as was the case with a change in government spending, income falls by less than the horizontal distance of the shift in the IS curve. As explained in Chapter 7, the horizontal distance by which the IS curve shifts with a change in taxes is equal to $\Delta T[-b/(1-b)]$, the tax multiplier from the simple Keynesian model times the change in taxes. Thus it is again true that in the IS–LM curve model, fiscal policy multipliers are reduced relative to our results for the simple Keynesian model. For a tax increase, the reason is that the decline in the interest rate discussed previously will cause investment to rise, partially offsetting the decline in consumption caused by the tax increase.

A decrease in taxes has the opposite effects of a tax increase. The IS curve shifts to the right, and both income and the interest rate rise. Similarly, a decline in government spending has effects just opposite those for an increase in government spending.

Fiscal policy variables are not the only factors that shift the IS schedule. Any autonomous change in aggregate demand will have this effect. One such change is an autonomous change in investment demand, meaning a shift in the function giving the level of investment for each level of the interest rate. For example, such a change would occur if, as a result of some exogenous event, the expected profitability of investment projects changed.

Figure 8.4 illustrates the effects of an autonomous decline in investment. In part a, the investment schedule is plotted. The initial schedule is $I_0(r)$. The autonomous decline in investment of $\Delta \bar{I}$ shifts the schedule to the left to $I_1(r)$, reducing the level of investment at each rate of interest. In Figure 8.4b, this autonomous decline in investment shifts the IS schedule to the left, from $IS(I_0)$ to $IS(I_1)$. Income falls from Y_0 to Y_1. The interest rate declines from r_0 to r_1. Income declines because investment at the initial interest rate has fallen (from I_0 to I_1' in Figure 8.4a). As income falls, an income-induced decline in consumption also occurs. The interest-rate decline is also income-induced, as was the case when we considered the effects of fiscal policy changes. The decline in income causes money demand to fall and bond demand to rise; consequently, the interest rate falls.

Notice that the decline in the interest rate causes investment to return somewhat toward its initial level. At the new equilibrium, investment is at I_1 in Figure 8.4a, having increased from I_1' to I_1 as a result of the decline in the interest rate.

It is interesting to compare the effects of an autonomous decline in investment in the IS–LM curve version of the Keynesian model with the effect of the same shift within the classical model analyzed in section 4.2. There, the interest rate played a stabilizing role such that a change in investment did not affect aggregate demand. The interest rate fell sufficiently to restore aggregate demand to its initial level. In the IS–LM model, the interest-rate adjustment is stabilizing but incomplete. For income to be unchanged with an autonomous decline in investment, the interest rate would have to fall to the level r_2 in Figure 8.4b. At that level of the interest rate, income would be at the original level Y_0 along the new IS schedule, $IS(I_1)$. Figure 8.4a shows that, at level r_2, the interest rate has fallen sufficiently to return investment to its initial level, I_0. The interest rate falls only to r_1, however; the offset to the initial autonomous drop in investment is incomplete.

In one case, the offset is complete. This is where the LM schedule is vertical. In that case, when the IS schedule shifts from $IS(I_0)$ to $IS(I_1)$, we simply move down the vertical LM schedule to a new equilibrium at the initial income level Y_0 and with the interest

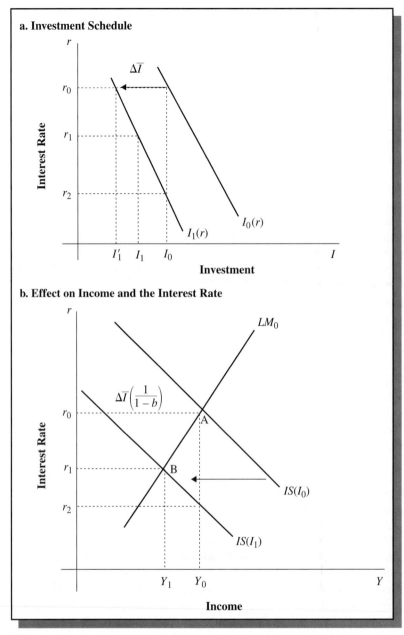

Figure 8.4 Effects of an Autonomous Decline in Investment Demand

An autonomous decline in investment shifts the investment schedule to the left in part *a*. At the initial interest rate r_0 investment falls from I_0 to I_1'. The shift in the investment function causes the *IS* schedule in part *b* to shift to the left from IS_0 to IS_1. Equilibrium income falls from Y_0 to Y_1, and the equilibrium interest rate falls from r_0 to r_1. As a result of the fall in the interest rate, investment is revived somewhat to I_1 in part *a*.

rate declining to r_2. The vertical *LM* schedule was termed a classical case, so it should not be surprising that classical conclusions result from that assumption. An explanation of these results for the vertical *LM* curve case is provided in the next section.

Read Perspectives 8.1.

PERSPECTIVES 8.1
The Monetary–Fiscal Policy Mix: Some Historical Examples

We have seen that in normal cases either monetary or fiscal policy can affect income in the Keynesian view. But the effects of the two on the interest rate, and therefore on investment, are quite different. In the case of expansionary monetary policy, the interest rate declines and investment increases. With an expansionary fiscal policy action—an income tax cut, for example—the interest rate rises and investment declines. This is a significant difference because the level of investment determines the rate of capital formation and is important to long-term growth of the economy.

Our analysis, then, suggests that within a Keynesian framework there is a preference for a policy *mix* of relatively "tight" fiscal policy and "easy" monetary policy in order to keep the interest rate low and to encourage investment. Moreover, whenever fiscal policy actions such as income tax cuts are used to expand the economy, the Keynesians would like to see an *accommodating* monetary policy—an accompanying increase in the money supply that will prevent the interest rate from rising and thus prevent the crowding out of investment. Such a monetary–fiscal policy combination is illustrated in Figure 8.5. At the same time the *IS* curve is shifted to the right by a tax cut, the money stock is increased sufficiently so that the *LM* curve shifts far enough to the right to prevent a rise in the interest rate.

As an example of a coordinated expansion, Keynesians point to the tax cut of 1964 and the accompanying increase in money supply. As explained in Perspectives 6.1, the tax cut was 20 percent for individuals and 10 percent for businesses. Growth in the money supply increased to 4.7 percent over the 1964–65 period, compared

with 3.7 percent in 1963. The result was a GNP growth of 5.4 percent in 1964 and 5.5 percent in 1965 (rates well above growth in potential output). As a result of the accommodating monetary policy, the interest rate (corporate bond rate) rose only slightly, from 4.0 percent in 1963 to 4.3 percent in 1965. The business tax reductions included in the 1964 tax cut were also aimed at preventing any decline in investment. In fact, fixed business investment increased from 9.0 to 10.5 percent of GNP between 1963 and 1965.

Later, Keynesian economists were critical of the monetary–fiscal policy mix in the first Reagan administration. They interpreted this mix as one of tight monetary policy, as growth in the money supply slowed, and easy fiscal policy, primarily the large cuts in personal and business taxes. The Keynesians saw the two policy moves as canceling each other out in terms of their effects on GNP. Keynesian economist James Tobin compared the Reagan policy to putting a train in New Haven, Connecticut, with an engine on the front headed for Boston and one in the back headed for New York. In graphical terms, the Keynesians saw the Reagan administration's monetary policy shifting the *LM* curve to the left to lower income while fiscal policy shifted the *IS* curve to the right to increase income. They believed that both policies would increase the interest rate (both curves shift upward), with unfavorable effects on investment.

More recently, during the Clinton administration, efforts to eliminate the federal deficit (and, in fact generate budget surpluses) were aimed in part at permitting monetary policy to be more expansionary than would otherwise be the case.

Figure 8.5
Monetary–Fiscal
Policy Combination

A tax cut from T_0 to T_1 shifts the IS schedule from $IS(T_0)$ to $IS(T_1)$. Of itself, this fiscal policy shift would push the interest rate upward to r_1'. If the tax cut were accompanied by an increase in the money supply from M_0 to M_1, the LM schedule would shift to the right from $LM(M_0)$ to $LM(M_1)$. Together, the two policy actions would increase output to Y_1, with the interest rate remaining at r_0.

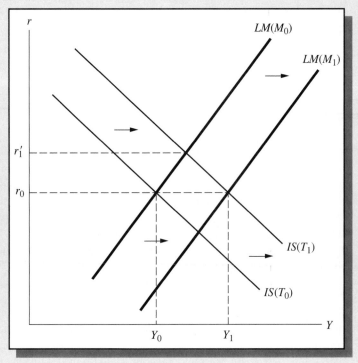

8.2 THE RELATIVE EFFECTIVENESS OF MONETARY AND FISCAL POLICY

In section 8.1, we examined the qualitative effects of monetary and fiscal policy actions within the *IS–LM* curve model, as summarized in Table 8.1. As can be seen from the table, both monetary and fiscal policy instruments can affect the level of income. In this section, we examine the relative effectiveness of the two types of policy actions. By *effectiveness* we mean the size of the effect on income of a given change in the policy variable. The effectiveness of each type of policy (monetary and fiscal)

Table 8.1
Effects of Monetary and Fiscal Policy Variables

EFFECT OF:	M	G	T
on Y	+	+	−
r	−	+	−

Note: M, money stock; G, level of government spending; T, taxes. A + sign indicates that a change in the policy instrument causes the variable in that row (Y, income, or r, the interest rate) to move in the same direction. A (−) sign indicates the reverse.

will be shown to depend on the slopes of the *IS* and *LM* curves, which in turn are determined by certain behavioral parameters of our model.

Policy Effectiveness and the Slope of the *IS* Schedule

First we examine how the slope of the *IS* curve influences the effectiveness of monetary and fiscal policy. As we saw earlier, the crucial parameter determining the slope of the *IS* schedule is the (absolute value of the) interest elasticity of investment. If investment demand is highly interest-elastic, meaning that a given rise in the interest rate will reduce investment by a large amount, the *IS* curve will be relatively flat. The lower the value of the interest elasticity of investment demand, the steeper will be the *IS* curve.

Here, and when we consider the influence on policy effectiveness of the slope of the *LM* curve later, we proceed as follows. First, we compare the effects of monetary and fiscal policy on income when the schedule is steep and when it is flat. The monetary policy action is an increase in the money supply. The fiscal policy action is an increase in government spending. Because both tax and spending changes work by shifting the *IS* schedule, tax and government spending changes are effective or ineffective in the same circumstances. No separate evaluation of tax policy effectiveness is required.

To measure whether fiscal policy actions are effective, we compare the effect of the policy action on income with the effect predicted by the simple Keynesian model. In moving to the *IS–LM* curve model, we add a money market to the Keynesian system. By comparing the effect of fiscal policy in the *IS–LM* model with the effect in the simple Keynesian system, we see how the addition of the money market modifies our previous results. The distance of the horizontal shift in the *IS* curve for a given fiscal policy action equals the effect on income in the simple Keynesian model: for example, $\Delta Y = \Delta G [1/(1 - b)]$, for a government spending change. Consequently, to evaluate the effectiveness of fiscal policy on the following graphs, we compare the change in income with the horizontal shift in the *IS* curve.

To evaluate the effectiveness of monetary policy, we compare the effect on income of the change in the money supply with the horizontal distance of the shift in the *LM* schedule. The horizontal shift in the *LM* schedule when the money supply changes is equal to $\Delta M(1/c_1)$ where c_1 is the coefficient on income in the money demand function [equation (7.4)]. The coefficient c_1 gives the amount of the increase in money demand per unit of income; therefore, $\Delta M(1/c_1)$ gives the increase in income that could occur for an increase in the money supply if *all* new money balances went to support increased transactions demand for money due to increased income. This is the amount of the increase in income for a given level of the interest rate, and thus the amount of the horizontal shift in the *LM* schedule. This distance measures the maximum possible increase in income for a given increase in the money supply.

Monetary Policy Effectiveness and the Slope of the IS *Schedule*

Parts *a* and *b* of Figure 8.6 show the effects of an increase in the money supply for two differently sloped *IS* schedules. In each case, the increase in the money supply shifts the *LM* schedule from LM_0 to LM_1. In Figure 8.6*a*, the *IS* schedule is steep, reflecting a low interest elasticity of investment. As can be seen from the graph, monetary

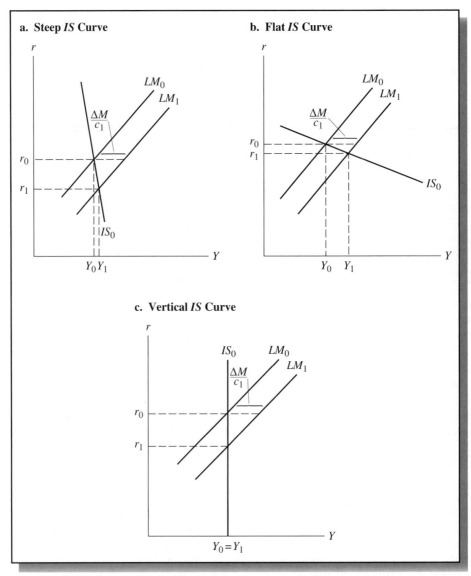

Figure 8.6 Monetary Policy Effects and the Slope of the *IS* Schedule

An increase in the money supply shifts the *LM* schedule to the right from LM_0 to LM_1. This expansionary monetary policy action has only a small effect on output in part *a*, where the *IS* curve is steep. It has a much larger effect in part *b*, where the *IS* curve is relatively flat. In part *c*, where the *IS* curve is vertical, the increase in the money supply has no effect on equilibrium income.

policy is relatively ineffective in this case. Income rises very little as a result of the increase in the money supply.

In Figure 8.6*b*, the slope of the *LM* schedule has been kept the same as in Figure 8.6*a*. The size of the horizontal shift in the *LM* schedule, $\Delta M(1/c_1)$, which fixes the size of the policy action, has also been kept the same. The only difference is in the slope of the IS schedule. In Figure 8.6b, that schedule is drawn much flatter, reflecting a higher interest elasticity of investment. As can be seen, monetary policy becomes more effective when the IS schedule is flatter.

Within the IS–LM curve model, monetary policy affects income by lowering the interest rate and stimulating investment. If investment is little affected by interest-rate changes, which is the assumption in Figure 8.6a, monetary policy will be ineffective. In Figure 8.6b, where the interest sensitivity of investment is assumed to be substantially greater, monetary policy has correspondingly greater effects. Therefore, our first result in this section is that monetary policy is ineffective when the IS schedule is steep—that is, when investment is interest-inelastic. Monetary policy is more effective the higher the interest elasticity of investment, and thus the flatter the IS schedule.

Here and subsequently, we consider several extreme cases for the slope of the IS or LM schedule. Consideration of extreme cases is helpful in understanding our results in the "normal" cases.

The first extreme case is that of the vertical IS schedule. The IS curve will be vertical if investment is completely insensitive to changes in the interest rate (interest elasticity equals zero). The effects of an increase in the money supply for this case are shown in Figure 8.6c. If the IS curve is vertical, increasing the money supply simply shifts the LM schedule down along the IS schedule. The interest rate falls until money demand increases by enough to restore equilibrium in the money market, but income is unchanged. To increase income, the increase in the money supply and resulting fall in the interest rate must stimulate investment. When the IS curve is vertical, investment is not affected by monetary policy because, by assumption, investment does not depend on the interest rate. The steeper the IS curve, the closer we come to this extreme case and the less effective is monetary policy.

Fiscal Policy Effectiveness and the Slope of the IS Schedule

Parts a and b of Figure 8.7 show the effects of an increase in government spending in the case of a steep IS schedule (8.7a) and a relatively flat IS schedule (8.7b). In both cases, the increase in government spending shifts the IS schedule from IS_0 to IS_1. The horizontal distance of the shift in the curve $\Delta G [1/(1 - b)]$ is the same in both cases, meaning that the size of the policy action as well as the autonomous expenditure multiplier from the simple Keynesian model are equal. As these graphs show, fiscal policy is much more effective where the IS schedule is steep (Figure 8.7a).

The steep IS curve occurs when investment is relatively interest-inelastic. We have found that the less sensitive investment is to the interest rate, the greater the effect of a given fiscal policy action is. To see why, consider the role of the interest-rate change in the adjustment to a new equilibrium after an increase in government spending. As income increases, the interest rate must rise to keep the money market in equilibrium. This rise in the interest rate causes investment to decline, partially offsetting the expansionary effect of the government spending increase. This interest-rate–induced decline in investment causes the income response in the IS–LM curve model to fall short of the response given by the multiplier from the simple Keynesian system; that is, income rises by less than the horizontal shift in the IS schedule.

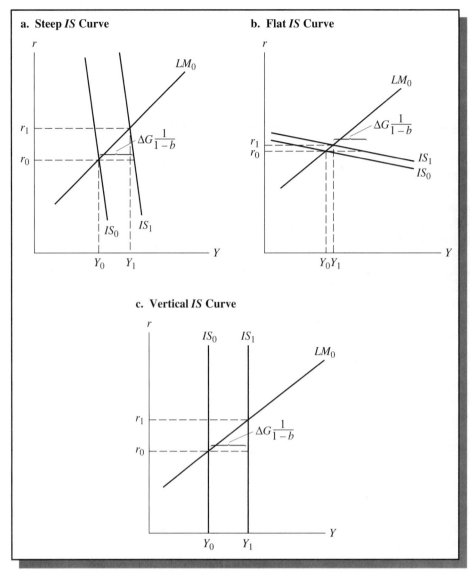

Figure 8.7 Fiscal Policy Effects and the Slope of the *IS* Schedule

In each part of the figure, an increase in government spending shifts the *IS* curve to the right from IS_0 to IS_1. In part *a*, where the *IS* curve is steep, this expansionary fiscal policy action results in a relatively large increase in income. This fiscal policy action is much less effective in part *b*, where the *IS* curve is relatively flat. Fiscal policy is most effective in part *c*, where the *IS* curve is vertical.

How important is this effect on investment, which is often referred to as "crowding out"? One factor determining the importance of such crowding out of private investment is the slope of the *IS* curve. If investment is not very sensitive to changes in the interest rate, the assumption in Figure 8.7*a*, then the interest-rate increase will cause only a slight drop in investment, and income will rise by almost the full amount of the horizontal shift in the *IS* curve. Alternatively, if investment is highly interest-sensitive, the assumption in Figure 8.7b, then the rise in the interest rate will reduce investment substantially, and the increase in income will be reduced significantly relative to the prediction of the simple Keynesian model.

The case of the vertical *IS* curve is shown in Figure 8.7c. Here investment is completely interest-insensitive. The increase in government spending causes the interest rate to rise, but this rise does not result in any decline in investment. Income increases by the full amount of the distance of the horizontal shift in the *IS* curve. In this case, there is no crowding out of private investment.

A comparison of the results in this subsection with those in the preceding subsection shows that fiscal policy is most effective when the *IS* curve is steep (low interest elasticity of investment), whereas monetary policy is most effective when the *IS* curve is flat (high interest elasticity of investment). This is a result of the different role that the interest rate plays in transmitting the effects of these policy actions. Monetary policy affects income by affecting interest rates. Consequently, the greater the effect of interest rates on aggregate demand, *ceteris paribus*, the greater will be the effects of a given monetary policy action. In the case of fiscal policy, the interest-rate change offsets the fiscal policy effects. A larger interest elasticity of investment will mean that more of the expansionary effect of an increase in government spending will be offset by an interest-rate–induced decline in investment, and thus the greater will be the crowding-out effect. Fiscal policy will be more effective, again *ceteris paribus*, the lower the interest elasticity of investment.

Policy Effectiveness and the Slope of the *LM* Schedule

The slope of the *LM* schedule depends most crucially on the interest elasticity of money demand. A high interest elasticity of money demand causes the *LM* schedule to be relatively flat. At progressively lower values of the interest elasticity of money demand, the *LM* curve becomes steeper. If money demand is completely insensitive to the interest rate (interest elasticity is zero), the *LM* schedule is vertical. In this subsection, we see how fiscal and monetary policy effectiveness depend on the slope of the *LM* schedule and, hence, on the interest elasticity of money demand.

Fiscal Policy Effectiveness and the Slope of the *LM* Schedule

Figure 8.8 illustrates the effects of an increase in government spending for three assumptions concerning the slope of the *LM* schedule. In Figure 8.8a the *LM* schedule is rather flat, in 8.8b the schedule is steep, and in 8.8c the schedule is vertical. In each case the increase in government spending is assumed to shift the *IS* curve from IS_0 to IS_1. The slope of the *IS* curve is the same in all three graphs. The size of the increase in government expenditure is also the same. As the graphs show, the effect on income of this expansionary fiscal policy action is largest when the *LM* schedule is relatively flat (Figure 8.8a) and less when the curve is relatively steep (Figure 8.8b). In the extreme case in which the *LM* schedule is vertical, the increase in government spending has no effect on equilibrium income.

Fiscal policy is most effective when the interest elasticity of money demand is high, making the *LM* schedule relatively flat. The reason for this concerns the effect

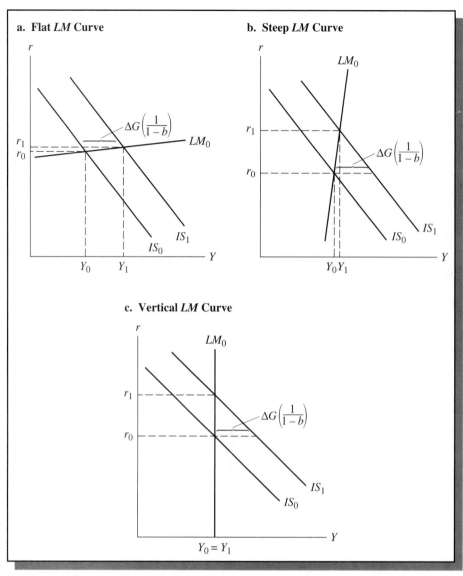

Figure 8.8 Fiscal Policy Effects and the Slope of the *LM* Schedule

In each part of the figure an increase in government spending shifts the *IS* schedule to the right from IS_0 to IS_1. Fiscal policy is most effective in part *a*, where the *LM* schedule is relatively flat; less effective in part *b*, where the *LM* curve is steeper; and completely ineffective in part *c*, where the *LM* curve is vertical.

of the interest-rate adjustment on investment after the fiscal policy shift. The increase in government spending causes income to rise. As income rises, the demand for transactions balances increases, and to reequilibrate the money market with an unchanged supply of money requires a rise in the interest rate. The rise in the interest rate must lower the speculative demand for money and cause individuals and corporations to economize on the use of transactions balances. If money demand is highly sensitive to changes in the interest rate, only a small rise in the interest rate is required to restore equilibrium in the money market. This is the case in Figure 8.8a, where the interest rate rises by only a small amount, from r_0 to r_1.

Because in this case there is only a small increase in the interest rate, other things being equal, the decline in investment because of the interest-rate increase will be small.[1] With little crowding out of private investment, income rises by nearly the full amount of the horizontal shift in the *IS* curve.

When money demand is relatively interest-inelastic (Figure 8.8b), a greater increase in the interest rate (from r_0 to r_1 in Figure 8.8b) is required to reequilibrate the money market as income rises. The larger increase in the interest rate leads to a larger decline in investment, offsetting more of the expansionary effect of the increase in government spending. Consequently, the increase in income for the steeper *LM* curve (Figure 8.8b) is a smaller proportion of the horizontal shift in the *IS* curve.

If money demand is completely insensitive to changes in the interest rate (Figure 8.8c), only one level of income can be an equilibrium level—the level that generates transactions demand just equal to the fixed money supply. An increase in aggregate demand, caused by an increase in government spending, creates an upward pressure on income at a given interest rate. There is an excess demand for goods (G is higher, C and I are unchanged). However, the attempt to increase income (or a temporary rise in income) leads to an increased demand for transactions balances and causes the interest rate to rise. *Equilibrium* income cannot, in fact, be higher than Y_0, because no possible increase in the interest rate will reequilibrate the money market at a higher level of income. A new equilibrium will be achieved when, in the attempt to acquire transactions balances to support a higher income level, an attempt that must fail in the aggregate, individuals bid the interest rate up by enough to return aggregate demand to its initial level. In Figure 8.8c, this occurs at interest rate r_1. At that point, private investment has declined by an amount just equal to the increase in government spending. Crowding out is complete.

The vertical *LM* case was referred to previously as "classical" because the classical economists failed to take account systematically of the dependence of money demand on the interest rate. Implicitly, they assumed that money demand was completely interest-inelastic. Notice that in this classical case our fiscal policy results are classical in nature. An increase in government expenditures affects the interest rate but not income.

At the end of section 8.1, we saw that, for this case of a vertical *LM* curve, an autonomous change in investment demand would also leave income unchanged. The interest-rate adjustment would completely offset the initial drop in investment demand. Again, for changes in the government component of autonomous expenditures, the interest rate adjusts fully, so that total aggregate demand ($C + I + G$) is not affected by the shift.

A necessary element, then, in the Keynesian view that changes in autonomous expenditure resulting from fiscal policy actions do affect income is the belief that

---

[1] The primary "other thing" being held equal in this case is the amount by which a given increase in the interest rate will cause investment to decline—the interest elasticity of investment.

money demand does depend on the rate of interest. This belief follows from considering the role money plays as an asset, an alternative store of wealth to bonds. The classical view of money focused simply on its role in transactions, and thus the classical economists neglected the role of the interest rate in determining money demand.

Monetary Policy Effectiveness and the Slope of the LM Schedule

Figure 8.9 shows the effects of an increase in the money supply for the same three assumptions about the LM schedule as those considered previously. In part a, the LM schedule is relatively flat. In part b, the LM curve is steeper; and in part c, the schedule is vertical. In each case, the increase in the money stock shifts the LM schedule by an equal amount from LM_0 to LM_1.

As can be seen from the figure, monetary policy is least effective in Figure 8.9a, where the LM schedule is relatively flat (the interest elasticity of money demand is high). The effect on income of the increase in the money supply is successively greater as we consider Figure 8.9b, where the interest elasticity of money demand is lower, and then Figure 8.9c, where the interest elasticity of money demand is zero and the LM curve is vertical.

The reason can be seen by comparing the fall in the interest rate that results from the money supply increase in each case. At the initial level of income and interest rate, the increase in the money supply will create an excess amount of money, causing the interest rate to fall. This fall will stimulate investment and, hence, income. The interest rate must decline to a point where the lower interest rate and higher income level have increased money demand by an amount equal to the increase in the money supply. In Figure 8.9a, where money demand is very interest-sensitive, a small drop in the interest rate is all that is required for this purpose. Consequently, the increase in investment, and hence income, will be small in this case. With a highly interest-elastic demand for money, as the interest rate falls, individuals substantially increase their speculative balances and economize less on transactions balances. Most of the newly created money is used for these purposes, and relatively little ends up as transactions balances required by a higher level of income.

In Figure 8.9b, the interest elasticity of money demand is lower, and a larger fall in the interest rate is required to reequilibrate the money market after the money supply increases. As a consequence, investment, and therefore income, increase by a greater amount. In Figure 8.9c, where money demand is completely interest-inelastic, the interest rate again falls after an increase in the money supply. Here the fall in the interest rate itself does nothing to increase the demand for money and to restore equilibrium in the money market, because in this case money demand does not depend on the interest rate. The fall in the interest rate, however, causes investment and income to rise. The rise in income will continue until all the new money is absorbed into additional transactions balances. This is the maximum possible increase in income for a given increase in the money supply, because all of the new money balances end up as transactions balances required by the higher income level. None of the new money is siphoned off as an increase in speculative demand as the interest rate falls. There is also no tendency for the amount of transactions balances held for a given income level to rise as the interest rate falls. In sum, the effect on the level of income of a given increase in the money supply is greater the lower the interest elasticity of money demand.

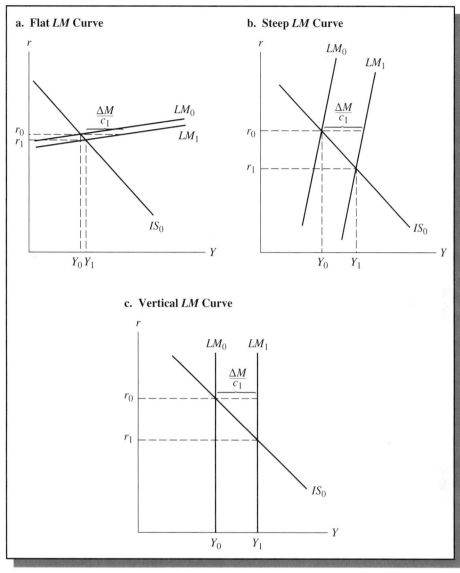

Figure 8.9 Monetary Policy Effects and the Slope of the *LM* Schedule

In each part of the figure an increase in the money supply shifts the *LM* schedule to the right from LM_0 to LM_1. Monetary policy is least effective in part *a*, where the *LM* curve is relatively flat; more effective in part *b*, where the *LM* curve is steeper; and most effective in part *c*, where the *LM* curve is vertical.

As in our discussion of the *IS* schedule, we find here that the condition that makes monetary policy most effective makes fiscal policy least effective. Monetary policy effectiveness increases as the interest elasticity of money demand is reduced. Fiscal policy is more effective the higher the interest elasticity of money demand. The reason for this difference is again the differing role of interest-rate adjustment in transmitting monetary and fiscal policy effects. For the case of monetary policy, which affects income by having an effect on the interest rate, the *greater* the interest-rate response, the more effective the policy action will be. As we have just seen, the interest-rate response is greatest when the interest elasticity of money demand is low (i.e., the *LM* schedule is steep).

For the case of fiscal policy where the interest-rate response, with the resulting crowding out of investment, offsets part of the effect of the policy action, the income response is greater the *smaller* the interest rate response. A high interest elasticity of money demand reduces the effects of a fiscal policy action on the interest rate (compare parts *a* and *b* of Figure 8.8). Therefore, fiscal policy is most effective when the interest elasticity of money demand is high (i.e., the *LM* schedule is flat).

8.3 CONCLUSION

In section 8.1, we examined the effects of monetary and fiscal policy actions on income and the interest rate assuming that the *IS–LM* curves had normal slopes; that is, the slopes of both the *IS* and *LM* schedules were in an intermediate range—neither so steep nor so flat as to make either monetary or fiscal policy impotent. In section 8.2, the relationships between the slopes of the *IS* and *LM* schedules and the relative effectiveness of monetary and fiscal policies were examined. The results of that analysis are summarized in Table 8.2.

A relevant question at this point is, Which of the cases in Table 8.2 actually characterizes the economy? What are the actual slopes of the relationships in our economy that correspond to the model's *IS* and *LM* curves?

Issues concerning the slopes of the *IS* and *LM* schedules form a part of the controversy between the Keynesians and the next group of macroeconomists we will analyze, the monetarists. There is also some divergence between the positions of some of the earlier Keynesians and current-day Keynesians concerning the slopes of these schedules. These differences are analyzed later. Here we confine ourselves to the position of the modern-day Keynesians, who state that both the *IS* and *LM* curve slopes are in the intermediate or normal range, where both monetary and fiscal

Table 8.2
Monetary and Fiscal Policy Effectiveness and the Slopes of the *IS* and *LM* Curves

	MONETARY POLICY	
	IS CURVE	*LM* CURVE
Steep	Ineffective	Effective
Flat	Effective	Ineffective
	FISCAL POLICY	
	IS CURVE	*LM* CURVE
Steep	Effective	Ineffective
Flat	Ineffective	Effective

policies are effective. Our results in section 8.1—summarized in Table 8.1—characterize this modern Keynesian position.

Read Perspectives 8.2.

PERSPECTIVES 8.2
A Liquidity Trap in Japan?

One qualification to the Keynesian view that both monetary and fiscal policy will be effective concerns monetary policy in periods when the interest rate becomes very low. In such situations the economy may approach the liquidity trap discussed in Chapter 7 and illustrated in Figure 7.9.

Some economists believed that the U.S. economy was in a liquidity trap during the Great Depression of the 1930s when short-term interest rates fell to below 1 percent. Interest in the liquidity trap case almost disappeared in the 1970s and early 1980s when interest rates in most industrialized countries were very high, often in double digits. There has been a revived interest in the

liquidity trap as interest rates have fallen to lower levels in recent years. The experience of Japan has been especially important in this revival.

The Japanese economy was in recession during much of the 1990s. Figure 8.10 plots the short-term Japanese interest rate (the rate on 3-month government securities) from 1982 to 2002. It can be seen from the figure that during the 1990s the interest rate fell from around the 7 percent level to approximately zero. While longer-term interest rates are not quite this low, many economists believe that Japan is currently in a liquidity trap and that monetary policy is therefore likely to be ineffective in further stimulating the Japanese economy.

Figure 8.10 Short-Term Japanese Interest Rate

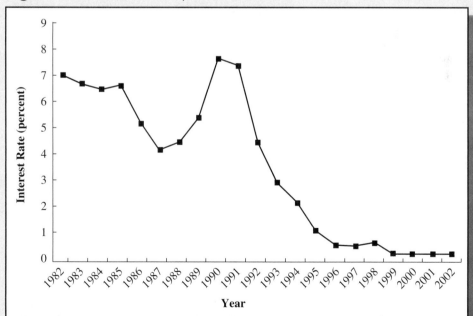

Figure 8.11 illustrates the ineffectiveness of monetary policy in a liquidity trap. At the current low level of interest rates in Japan, the *LM* schedule would be very flat, reflecting a high interest elasticity of money demand. This follows because at such a low level of the interest rate, the speculative demand curve for money would become very flat; a consensus would develop that future increases in interest rates were likely with expected capital losses on bonds. An increase in the money supply would be absorbed with only a very slight fall in the interest rate and therefore little stimulus to investment. In the current Japanese case, where the short-term interest rate has hit zero, we would expect no further decline to be possible.

In later chapters, we will consider some additional channels through which monetary policy may affect the economy even without a change in the interest rate, but in the liquidity trap the main Keynesian channel for monetary policy is effectively foreclosed.

Figure 8.11
Monetary Policy
Ineffectiveness in a
Liquidity Trap

At the low levels of the interest rate that would prevail in liquidity trap conditions, Keynesians expect the economy to be on the nearly horizontal range of the *LM* curve. Monetary policy is ineffective in this situation.

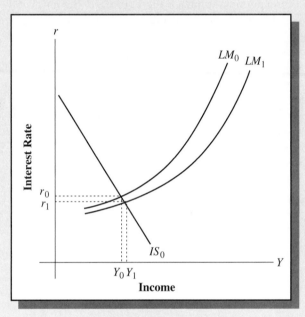

REVIEW QUESTIONS AND PROBLEMS

1. Within the *IS–LM* curve model, show how income and the interest rate are affected by each of the following.
   a. An increase in government spending.
   b. An autonomous decline in investment spending.
   c. An increase in taxes.
   d. An increase in the money supply.
   In each case, explain why the changes in income and the interest rate occur.
2. Within the *IS–LM* curve model, analyze the effects of an increase in government spending financed by an equal increase in taxes. First consider the net horizontal

shift in the *IS* curve as a result of this balanced budget increase. Then consider the effects on income and the interest rate. Finally, compare your result with the balanced-budget multiplier in section 6.5.

3. Within the *IS–LM* curve model, what would be the effect of an autonomous increase in saving that was matched by a drop in consumption—that is, a fall in *a* in the consumption function?

$$C = a + b(Y - T)$$

Which curve would shift? How would income and the interest rate be affected?

4. Explain the relationship between the effectiveness of monetary policy and the interest elasticity of investment. Will monetary policy be more or less effective the higher the interest elasticity of investment demand? Now explain the relationship between the effectiveness of fiscal policy and the interest elasticity of investment demand. Why do the two relationships differ?

5. Explain the relationship between the effectiveness of monetary policy and the interest elasticity of money demand. Will monetary policy be more or less effective the higher the interest elasticity of money demand? Explain. Now explain the relationship between fiscal policy and the interest elasticity of money demand. Why do the two relationships differ?

6. Suppose we had a case in which the interest elasticity of *both* money demand and investment were quite low. Would either monetary or fiscal policy be very effective? How would you interpret such a situation?

7. We saw that the interest rate played a stabilizing role in the classical system, adjusting so that a shock to one component of demand, a decline in autonomous investment, for example, would not affect aggregate demand. Does the interest rate perform a similar stabilizing function in the Keynesian model?

8. In what sense is a vertical *LM* schedule a classical case?

9. Why might Keynesians be pessimistic about the ability of monetary policy to stimulate output in situations such as the 1930s Depression in the United States or the severe recession in Japan in the late 1990s? What type of policy would Keynesian economists expect to be effective in such situations?

10. Consider the case in which the *LM* schedule is vertical. Suppose there is a shock that increases the demand for money for given levels of income and the interest rate. Illustrate the effect of the shock graphically and explain how income and the interest rate are affected.

Appendix 1

Monetary and Fiscal Policy Multipliers in the IS–LM Curve Model

Here we extend the algebraic treatment of the *IS–LM* model given in the appendix to Chapter 7. We examine how the equilibrium value of income, which was derived there, changes as monetary and fiscal policy variables are changed. In doing so, we establish algebraically the graphical results in section 8.1. We then consider the same question taken up in section 8.2, the relative effectiveness of monetary and fiscal policy, within the linear version of the *IS–LM* model.

A.1 THE EFFECTS OF MONETARY AND FISCAL POLICY ON INCOME

In the appendix to Chapter 7, we derived the following expressions[1] for the equilibrium values of income (Y_0) and the interest rate (r_0) in the *IS–LM* curve model:

$$Y_0 = \left[\frac{1}{(1-b) + i_1 c_1/c_2} \right]$$
$$\times \left[a + \bar{I} + G - bT + \frac{i_1}{c_2}(M^s - c_0) \right]$$

(A.10)

$$r_0 = \left[\frac{1}{(1-b) + i_1 c_1/c_2} \right]$$
$$\times \left[\frac{(1-b)}{c_2}(c_0 - M^s) + \frac{c_1}{c_2}(a + \bar{I} + G - bT) \right]$$

(A.11)

We can use these two equations to see how the interest rate and income change when any of the exogenous variables in the model change. This is the mathematical equivalent to seeing how these equilibrium values changed on the graphs in section 8.1 with a shift in the *IS* or *LM* curves. In this section, we compute expressions that show how income changes with changes in policy variables using equation (A.10). Finding the effects on the interest rate of changes in these variables is left as an exercise (see review problem 1).

Fiscal Policy

Consider first how equilibrium income changes with a change in government spending. From equation (A.10), letting G vary but holding constant all other exogenous variables, and for given values of the parameters, we compute

$$\Delta Y = \frac{1}{(1-b) + i_1 c_1/c_2} \Delta G \quad \textbf{(A.12)}$$
$$\frac{\Delta Y}{\Delta G} = \frac{1}{(1-b) + i_1 c_1/c_2} > 0$$

Equation (A.12) indicates that, as we saw graphically (Figure 8.2), an increase in government spending will lead to an increase in equilibrium income within the *IS–LM* curve model. Moreover, the increase in equilibrium income per unit increase in government spending, as given by equation (A.12), is *smaller* than in the simple Keynesian model. Within the simple Keynesian model analyzed in Chapter 6, the increase in equilibrium income per unit increase in government spending was given by the

---

[1]Because we return to equations in the appendix to Chapter 7, to avoid confusion, we number equations here consecutively with those equations.

autonomous expenditure multiplier $1/(1 - b)$. The *multiplier* in equation (A.12) contains an additional positive term in the denominator $(i_1 c_1/c_2)$ and is therefore smaller.

Notice also, looking back at equation (A.10), that the change in equilibrium income per unit change in autonomous investment $(\Delta Y/\Delta \bar{I})$ would be exactly the same as with a change in government spending.

The effect on income from a change in taxes is

$$\Delta Y = \frac{1}{(1 - b) + i_1 c_1/c_2}(-b\Delta T) \quad \textbf{(A.13)}$$

$$\frac{\Delta Y}{\Delta T} = \frac{-b}{(1 - b) + i_1 c_1/c_2} < 0$$

This *tax multiplier* is opposite in sign to the government spending multiplier and smaller in absolute value, because $-b$ rather than 1 appears in the numerator.

Monetary Policy

From equation (A.10) we compute the effects on income from a change in the money supply as

$$\Delta Y = \left(\frac{1}{(1 - b) + i_1 c_1/c_2}\right)\frac{i_1}{c_2}\Delta M^s$$

or

$$\frac{\Delta Y}{\Delta M^s} = \left(\frac{1}{(1 - b) + i_1 c_1/c_2}\right)\frac{i_1}{c_2} > 0$$

which simplifies to

$$\frac{\Delta Y}{\Delta M^s} = \frac{i_1}{(1 - b)c_2 + i_1 c_1} \quad \textbf{(A.14)}$$

An increase in the money supply causes equilibrium income to rise, as was illustrated in Figure 8.1.

A.2 POLICY EFFECTIVENESS AND THE SLOPES OF THE *IS* AND *LM* CURVES

The expressions given by equations (A.12) and (A.14) are, respectively, fiscal and monetary policy *multipliers*. They give the change in equilibrium income per unit change in the policy variables G and M^s. In this section, we examine the relationship between the magnitude of these multipliers and the slopes of the *IS* and *LM* curves. Our results parallel those of section 8.2.[2]

The *IS* Curve and Policy Effectiveness

In the appendix to Chapter 7, we found that the slope of the *IS* schedule was given by

$$\left.\frac{\Delta r}{\Delta Y}\right|_{IS} = -\frac{(1 - b)}{i_1} \quad \textbf{(A.7)}$$

The crucial parameter, over which there is dispute, is i_1, which measures the interest sensitivity of investment demand. If i_1 is large (small), investment demand is interest-sensitive (-insensitive), and the *IS* curve is flat (steep).

Now examine the role i_1 plays in the two multiplier expressions. We see from equation (A.12) that as i_1 becomes smaller, $\Delta Y/\Delta G$ becomes larger. That is, as investment becomes less sensitive to the interest rate and the *IS* curve becomes steeper, fiscal policy becomes more effective (see Figure 8.7). If i_1 goes to zero, equation (A.12) reduces to $1/(1 - b)$, the multiplier from the simple Keynesian model in Chapter 6.

We next consider equation (A.14), the monetary policy multiplier. As i_1 gets smaller (the *IS* curve becomes steeper), the numerator in equation (A.14) becomes proportionately smaller, whereas only one term in the denominator falls. Therefore, the value of the expression declines.[3] The lower the interest elasticity of investment,

[2] As in the chapter, we do not need to consider separately the effectiveness of tax policy. The same factors that influence the effectiveness of changes in G determine the effectiveness of changes in T.

[3] To see this clearly, rewrite the right-hand side of equation (A.14) as $1/[(1 - b)c_2/i_1 + c_1]$. As i_1 falls, the denominator increases in value and the size of the multiplier declines.

the steeper the *IS* curve, and the less effective is monetary policy (see Figure 8.6). In the extreme case, where i_1 is zero (vertical *IS* schedule), the value of equation (A.14) goes to zero, and monetary policy becomes completely ineffective.

The *LM* Curve and Policy Effectiveness

The expression in the appendix to Chapter 7 for the slope of the *LM* curve was

$$\left.\frac{\Delta r}{\Delta Y}\right|_{LM} = \frac{c_1}{c_2} \qquad \textbf{(A.5)}$$

The crucial parameter (the one subject to dispute) determining whether the curve is steep or flat is c_2, which measures the interest sensitivity of money demand. If c_2 is large (small), meaning that money demand is interest-sensitive (insensitive), the *LM* curve will be relatively flat (steep). This outcome follows because the expression in equation (A.5) decreases in value as c_2 becomes larger.

Now examine the way c_2 affects the fiscal policy multiplier given by equation (A.12). As c_2 becomes smaller, the second term in the denominator of equation (A.12) becomes larger. No other terms are affected, so the whole expression becomes smaller. The lower the interest sensitivity of money demand, the steeper is the *LM* schedule and the less effective is fiscal policy (see Figure 8.8). In the extreme case in which c_2 approaches zero, the denominator of equation (A.12) becomes extremely large, and the whole expression goes toward zero. As the *LM* curve becomes vertical, fiscal policy becomes completely ineffective.

Finally, consider the relationship between c_2 and the effectiveness of monetary policy as measured by equation (A.14). As c_2 becomes smaller, the denominator of equation (A.14) becomes smaller, and the expression becomes larger. The less sensitive money demand is to the interest rate, the steeper is the *LM* curve and the more effective is monetary policy (see Figure 8.9). If c_2 is zero, equation (A.14) reduces to $1/c_1$. The *LM* schedule is vertical, and equilibrium income will increase by the full amount of the horizontal shift in the *LM* schedule as the money supply increases (Figure 8.9c).

REVIEW PROBLEMS

1. Using equation (A.11), show how the equilibrium value of the interest rate (*r*) will be affected by
   a. An increase in the money supply (M^s).
   b. An increase in government spending (*G*).
   c. An increase in taxes (*T*).
2. Start with the solution for the equilibrium values of *Y* and *r* from review question 1 in the appendix to Chapter 7. Show how these values would change if government spending rose from 250 to 310.

Chapter 9

The Keynesian System (IV): Aggregate Supply and Demand

C hapters 6, 7, and 8 analyzed income determination assuming that the price level and money wage were fixed. The fixed price–fixed wage version of the Keynesian system highlights the role of aggregate demand. The demand-determined nature of output in this fixed price–fixed wage Keynesian model stands in sharp contrast to the supply-determined nature of output in the classical system. In this chapter, we examine the Keynesian system when prices and wages are not held constant and see that demand factors as well as supply factors play a role in determining output. In this sense the models considered in this chapter are a synthesis of the classical and Keynesian systems. We see, however, that the key feature in the Keynesian system continues to be the fact that aggregate demand is a factor determining aggregate output.

In section 9.1, we illustrate the demand-determined nature of output (income) in the Keynesian system. Here we construct a Keynesian aggregate demand curve. In section 9.2, this Keynesian aggregate demand curve is put together with the classical supply side. It will be seen that as long as we retain the classical assumptions of perfect information in the labor market and perfect price and wage flexibility, the substitution of the Keynesian aggregate demand curve does not change the classical nature of the model. As long as the supply curve remains vertical, as it does if the foregoing labor market assumptions are made, aggregate output will be determined independently of demand. For aggregate demand to play a role in output determination, the classical labor market assumptions must be modified.

Alternative Keynesian assumptions about the supply side of the economy are analyzed in sections 9.3 and 9.4. In these sections, we develop the Keynesian aggregate supply function. In section 9.5, we see how shifts in this aggregate supply function play a role in determining price and output in the Keynesian model. The final section of the chapter compares the classical and Keynesian systems.

9.1 THE KEYNESIAN AGGREGATE DEMAND CURVE

The simple model of Chapter 6 presented Keynes's theory of the aggregate demand for output. The essential notion embodied in the simple Keynesian model was that for output to be at an equilibrium level, aggregate demand must equal output. In Chapters 7 and 8, the effect of the interest rate on investment, and hence on aggregate demand, was considered. It was shown that in order for an output (Y) and interest-rate (r) combination to be an equilibrium point, output must equal aggregate demand, and money demand must equal money supply.

What guarantees that this level of output will also be equal to aggregate supply—equal to the amount the business sector will choose to produce? No supply considerations were included in these versions of the Keynesian model. Our implicit assumption about the aggregate supply curve is depicted in Figure 9.1. We assumed that any level of output demanded would be forthcoming at the given price level. Supply was assumed to be no constraint on output.

Such an assumption could be plausible when the levels of output are far below the capacity of the economy. In these conditions—for example, during the Depression of the 1930s—increases in output might not put upward pressure on the level of the money wage, given the high level of unemployment. Also, the marginal product of

Figure 9.1
Aggregate Supply Curve in the Fixed-Price Keynesian Model

In previous chapters on the Keynesian model, where the price level was fixed and output was determined by aggregate demand, we were assuming that the aggregate supply curve was horizontal. Supply was no constraint on output.

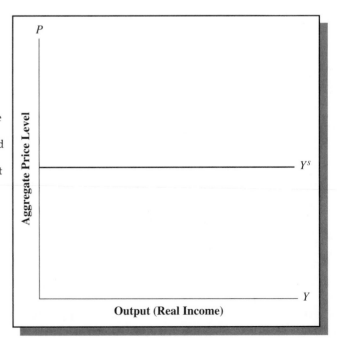

labor (MPN) might not fall as more labor is employed when we begin at a low level of employment (see Figure 3.1). As a consequence, the cost of producing additional units of output W/MPN might remain constant even with increases in output. In more normal conditions, an increase in output would put upward pressure on both the wage and price levels. We would expect the supply curve to be upward-sloping.

In this more general case of the upward-sloping aggregate supply curve, we cannot assume that price is given (supply is no constraint) and determine output simply by determining aggregate demand. Output and price will be jointly determined by supply and demand factors. The Keynesian aggregate supply curve is discussed in sections 9.3 and 9.4. First we construct the Keynesian aggregate demand curve, the relationship between aggregate demand and the price level in the Keynesian model. This aggregate demand curve will later be put together with the Keynesian aggregate supply curve to jointly determine price and output.

The factors that determine aggregate demand in the Keynesian system have been analyzed in detail. These factors determine the positions of the *IS* and *LM* curves and, therefore, the income–interest-rate combination that equilibrates the money market and causes output to equal aggregate demand. In constructing an aggregate demand schedule, we want to find output demanded for each price level. To do this, we examine how the position of the *IS* and *LM* schedules, and consequently the levels of the interest rate and output at which the curves intersect, are affected by price changes. The level of output at which the *IS* and *LM* schedules intersect for a given price level is a point on the Keynesian aggregate demand curve. Consider, first, how a change in the price level affects the position of the *IS* curve. The condition for equilibrium along the *IS* schedule is

$$I(r) + G = S(Y) + T \tag{9.1}$$

where I = investment
       G = government spending
       S = saving
       T = taxes
       Y = output

To see how the price level influences the position of the *IS* schedule, consider how each variable in (9.1) is affected by price changes.

Two variables, government spending (*G*) and taxes (*T*), are assumed to be fixed by the government in *real terms*; that is, we have assumed and will continue to assume that their real levels are unaffected by price changes. The level of investment is also assumed to be determined in real terms; a given interest rate determines a level of real investment. Changes in the price level do not *directly* affect investment.

Similarly, *real* saving is assumed to depend on real income and is not directly affected by changes in the price level. None of the four terms in (9.1), the *IS* curve equilibrium condition, depends directly on the price level, so a change in the price level does not shift the *IS* curve.

What about the *LM* schedule? The equilibrium condition for the money market, the *LM* schedule equation, is

$$\frac{M}{P} = L(Y, r) \tag{9.2}$$

The condition equates the real supply of money (M/P) with the demand for money in real terms (demand for real money balances). The real money supply is equal to the exogenously fixed *nominal* money supply (M) divided by the price level (P).

The Keynesian theory of the demand for money considered in Chapter 7 related the demand for money in *real* terms to the level of *real* income and to the interest rate, although as long as prices were held constant, there was no need to distinguish between changes in real and nominal values. People wish to hold a certain amount of real money balances for a given volume of transactions measured in real (constant-dollar) terms, where real income is a proxy for the real volume of transactions. Consequently, equilibrium in the money market occurs when the demand for real money balances is just equal to the real money supply. It is the nominal money supply—not the real money supply—that can be exogenously fixed by the monetary authority. Any change in the price level will affect the real money supply and consequently will shift the *LM* schedule.

Figure 9.2a illustrates the effect of changes in the price level on the real money supply and, therefore, on the position of the *LM* schedule. Holding the nominal money supply fixed at M_0, three price levels are considered, where $P_2 > P_1 > P_0$. Notice that as we consider the effect of a price increase from P_0 to P_1, then from P_1 to P_2, at the higher price level the *LM* schedule is shifted to the left. The effect of a higher price level reduces the real money supply,

$$\left(\frac{M_0}{P_2}\right) < \left(\frac{M_0}{P_1}\right) < \left(\frac{M_0}{P_0}\right).$$

Overall, the effect of a higher price level is the same as that of a fall in the nominal supply of money; both reduce the real money supply (M/P). The *LM* schedule shifts to the left, raising the interest rate and lowering investment and aggregate demand.

In Figure 9.2b, we plot the level of the aggregate demand corresponding to each of the three price levels considered. This schedule, labeled Y^d, is the aggregate demand schedule. As can be seen from the construction of the curve, this level of output demanded is the equilibrium output level from the *IS–LM* curve model, the output level that for a given price level just equates output and aggregate demand while simultaneously clearing the money market.

The aggregate demand curve reflects monetary influences (factors that affect the *LM* schedule) as well as direct influences on aggregate demand (factors affecting the *IS* schedule). Factors that increase the level of equilibrium income in the *IS–LM* curve model (increase the level of output demanded at a given price level) will shift the aggregate demand curve to the right. Factors that cause equilibrium income to decline in the *IS–LM* curve framework will shift the aggregate demand schedule to the left.

Consider, for example, the effect of an increase in the money supply, from M_0 to M_1, as shown in Figure 9.3. From equilibrium point A,

$$LM\left(\frac{M_0}{P_0}\right),$$

Figure 9.2

Construction of the Aggregate Demand Schedule

At successively higher price levels, P_0, P_1, P_2, the LM schedule in part *a* is shifted farther to the left. This shift results in successively lower levels of aggregate demand Y_0, Y_1, Y_2. These combinations of price and aggregate demand are plotted to give the negatively sloped aggregate demand schedule in part *b*.

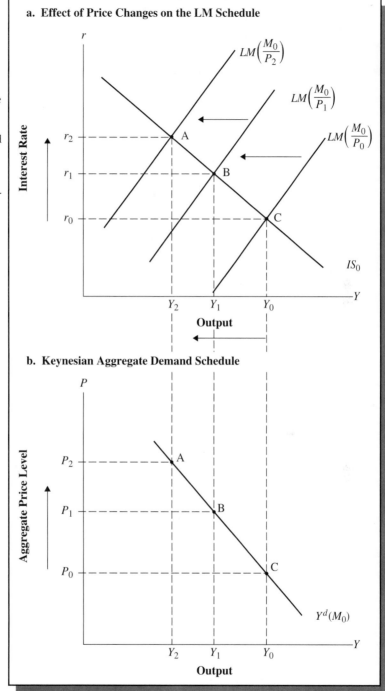

a. **Effect of Price Changes on the LM Schedule**

b. **Keynesian Aggregate Demand Schedule**

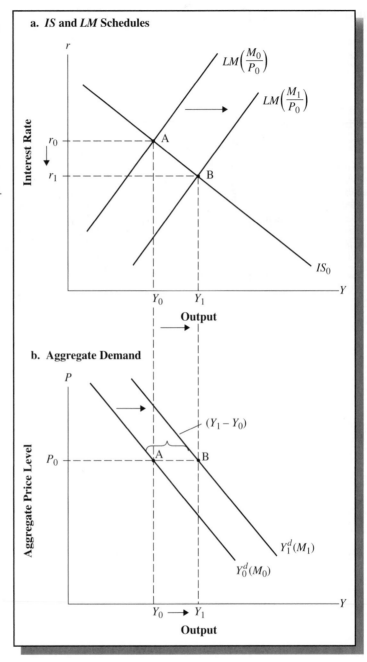

Figure 9.3
Effect on Aggregate Demand of an Increase in the Money Supply

An increase in the money supply shifts the *LM* schedule in part *a* to the right, $LM(M_0/P_0)$ to $LM(M_1/P_0)$ and shifts the aggregate demand schedule to the right from Y_0^d to Y_1^d in part *b*.

the increase in the money supply shifts the LM schedule to

$$LM\left(\frac{M_1}{P_0}\right).$$

The new equilibrium point is at B, as shown in Figure 9.3a. Equilibrium income for a given price level P_0 in the figure increases from Y_0 to Y_1. The aggregate demand curve shown in Figure 9.3b shifts to the right, from Y_0^d to Y_1^d.[1] Notice that the distance of horizontal shift in the aggregate demand curve is $(Y_1 - Y_0)$, the amount of the increase in equilibrium income in the IS–LM curve model. This is the increase in income and aggregate demand that results *at a given price level*. Similarly, changes in government expenditures or taxes that shift the IS schedule shift the aggregate demand schedule such that the distance of the horizontal shift in the schedule equals the amount of the change in equilibrium income from the IS–LM curve model—the amount of the change in aggregate demand for a given price level.

9.2 THE KEYNESIAN AGGREGATE DEMAND SCHEDULE COMBINED WITH THE CLASSICAL THEORY OF AGGREGATE SUPPLY

When prices and wages are not assumed constant, knowing the effects of policy actions on demand is not enough to determine their effects on income. The effect on income will depend on the assumptions we make about aggregate supply. This concept is illustrated in Figure 9.4, where the effect of an increase in government spending is compared for three different assumptions about the aggregate supply schedule.

In each case, the increase in government expenditures shifts the aggregate demand schedule to the right, from Y_0^d to Y_1^d. If the supply schedule is given by Y_2^s, a horizontal schedule, then output increases by the full amount of the horizontal shift in the aggregate demand schedule. Recall from section 9.1 that this is the increase in equilibrium income from the IS–LM curve model, which implicitly assumed that the supply schedule was horizontal. If the supply schedule is upward-sloping (Y_1^s), prices will rise and the increase in income will be less, $Y_1 - Y_0$ compared with $Y_2 - Y_0$ in Figure 9.4. If the supply schedule were vertical (Y_0^s in Figure 9.4), there would be no increase in income even though aggregate demand increased. Clearly, then, the effects of policy changes on income depend on the assumption made concerning aggregate supply. In this section, we consider the implications of making the "classical" assumptions about supply while maintaining the Keynesian apparatus behind the aggregate demand schedule.

---

[1] For simplicity, the Keynesian aggregate demand curve here and in later graphs is drawn as a straight line. The exact curvature of the aggregate demand curve is not important for our analysis.

Figure 9.4
Role of Aggregate Supply in Determining the Output Response to a Policy Shock

An increase in government spending shifts the aggregate demand schedule from Y_0^d to Y_1^d. If the aggregate supply schedule is horizontal (Y_2^s), output increases from Y_0 to Y_2. If the aggregate supply schedule slopes upward (Y_1^s), output increases only to Y_1. If the supply schedule is vertical (Y_0^s), output is unchanged at Y_0.

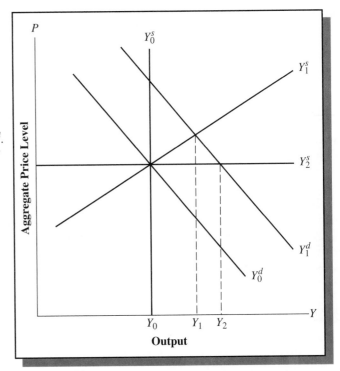

The classical analysis of aggregate supply was explained in Chapter 3. The central elements of this analysis are illustrated in Figure 9.5. In the labor market, both supply and demand depend solely on the real wage (W/P), which is assumed to be known to all. Further, the labor market is assumed always to be in equilibrium with the perfectly flexible money wage, adjusting to equate supply and demand. The labor market has the characteristics of an "auction" market. The equilibrium in the labor market is graphed in Figure 9.5a. As shown in Figure 9.5b, for a given level of employment, output will be determined along the production function, the relationship giving the output produced by each amount of labor, given the fixed capital stock.

As explained in Chapter 3, the classical assumptions result in a vertical aggregate supply curve (see section 3.5). With the classical assumptions concerning the supply side, the aggregate supply curve would be given Y_0^s by in Figure 9.4; output would be completely supply-determined. Factors such as changes in government spending, taxes, and the money supply, which shift the demand schedule, would not affect the equilibrium output.[2]

This analysis shows that *the classical theory of aggregate supply based on the classical auction market characterization of the labor market is fundamentally incompatible with the*

---

[2]Some fiscal policy changes, such as a change in the marginal tax rate, have supply-side effects in the classical system, as explained in section 4.3. These are being ignored here.

Figure 9.5

Classical Supply Assumptions

In the classical model, employment (N_0) is determined at the point where labor supply and demand, both as functions of the real wage, are equated (part *a*). Equilibrium output (Y_0) is then determined using the production function (part *b*).

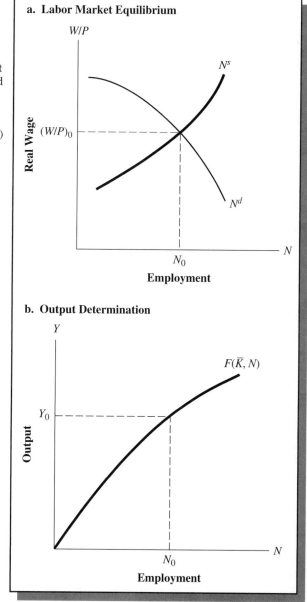

a. **Labor Market Equilibrium**

b. **Output Determination**

Keynesian system. The central feature of Keynesian analysis is the theory of aggregate demand and the influence of aggregate demand on output and employment. With the classical assumptions about aggregate supply, leading to the vertical supply schedule, there is *no* role for aggregate demand in determining output and employment. It was therefore necessary for Keynes and his followers to attack the classical supply assumptions and to develop a Keynesian theory of the supply side.

9.3 THE KEYNESIAN CONTRACTUAL VIEW OF THE LABOR MARKET

Keynes believed that the money wage would not adjust sufficiently in the short run to keep the economy at full employment. In the classical system, both labor supply and demand are functions of the real wage, and the intersection of the labor supply and demand curves determines an equilibrium real wage and level of employment. Wage bargains are, however, set in terms of money wages, and one assumption crucial to the classical model is that the money wage is perfectly flexible. Adjustments in the money wage are required to keep the economy at full employment.

Sources of Wage Rigidity

The Keynesian theory offers a number of reasons why the money wage will *not* quickly adjust, especially in the downward direction, to maintain equilibrium in the labor market. The most important of these explanations for the *rigidity* of money wages are as follows.

1. Keynes argued that workers are interested in their relative as well as their absolute wage. There exists in any labor market a set of wage differentials between workers with different trades and skills. Much of the work of wage bargaining is to arrive at a relative wage structure that is acceptable to both labor and management. Wage differentials can be measured by relative money wages, because price-level changes affect all wages symmetrically.

Keynes believed that workers would resist money wage cuts even as the demand for labor fell. They would see the wage cuts as "unfair" changes in the structure of relative wages. Workers in one firm or industry would have no assurance that if they accepted a cut in money wages, workers in other sectors of the labor market would do the same. A decline in the real wage as a result of a rise in prices would not be seen by labor as affecting the structure of relative wages. For this reason, Keynes believed that declines in real wages caused by price-level increases would meet much less resistance from labor than an equivalent fall in the real wage from a money wage cut.

2. The next factor leading to stickiness in the money wage level is an institutional one. In the unionized sector of the labor market, wages are set by labor contracts, most often of two or three years' duration. Such contracts typically fix money wage levels for the life of the contract. The money wage will not respond to events, such as a decline in labor demand, over the life of the contract. Indexation of the money wage set in the contract (i.e., provisions that tie changes in the money wage to changes in the price level) provides some flexibility in the money wage over the length of the contract. In the United States, however, when any indexation of labor contracts exists, it is generally incomplete. Thus fixed-money-wage contracts impart stickiness to the money wage.

Once such a labor contract is signed, the decision of how much labor to hire is left to the employer. A labor supply curve such as the classical labor supply function in Figure 9.5 no longer plays any role in determining employment. The firm hires the profit-maximizing amount of labor at the fixed money wage.

3. Even in segments of the labor market in which no explicit contract fixes the money wage, there is often an implicit agreement between employer and employee that fixes the money wage over some time period. In particular, such implicit contracts keep employers from cutting money wages in the face of a fall in the demand for their products and consequent decline in labor demand. The incentive for employers to refrain from attempting to achieve such wage cuts, or alternatively from hiring workers from among the pool of the unemployed who might be willing to work for a lower wage, is their desire to maintain a reputation as a "good employer." Firms might achieve a temporary gain by forcing a money wage cut to reduce labor costs, but this gain could be more than counterbalanced by the effect of poor labor relations with existing employees and difficulties in recruiting new employees. Keynesians believe that the "conventions" of labor markets are such that firms find it in their interest to cut the length of the work week or to have layoffs in response to falls in demand rather than to seek money wage cuts.

Keynesians believe that contractual arrangements are central to understanding how modern labor markets function. The *contractual* view of the labor market stands in sharp contrast to the frictionless *auction* market view of the classical economists. In the Keynesian view, as expressed by Arthur Okun,

> Wages are not set to clear markets in the short run, but rather are strongly conditioned by longer-term considerations involving . . . employer worker relations. These factors insulate wages . . . to a significant degree from the impact of shifts in demand so that the adjustment must be made in employment and output.[3]

Read Perspectives 9.1.

PERSPECTIVES 9.1
Price and Quantity Adjustment in Great Britain, 1929–36

Keynes's view that the money wage would not adjust quickly to clear the labor market was in part a result of his observation of events in Great Britain. Table 9.1 provides data for the money wage, price level, real wage, and unemployment rate in Britain for the years 1929–36.

The money wage fell over the first part of the period, but only 5 percent by 1933. After 1933, the money wage rose slowly despite the exceptionally high unemployment rate. Data for the price level, real wage, and unemployment rate clearly indicate that no downward adjustment in the real wage to clear the labor market—the classical labor market adjustment—occurred.

---

[3]Arthur Okun, *Prices and Quantities* (Washington, D.C.: The Brookings Institution, 1981), p. 233.

Table 9.1 Wages, Prices, and Unemployment in Great Britain, 1929–36

Year	Money Wage (W) (Index 1914 = 100)	Price Level (P) (Index 1914 = 100)	Real Wage ($W/P \times 100$)	Unemployment Rate (Percent)
1929	193	164	118	11.0
1930	191	157	122	14.6
1931	189	147	129	21.5
1932	185	143	129	22.5
1933	183	140	129	21.3
1934	183	141	130	17.7
1935	185	143	130	16.4
1936	190	147	129	14.3

Source: B. P. Mitchell and P. Deane, Abstract of British Historical Statistics (Cambridge: Cambridge University Press, 1962), pp. 67, 345.

A Flexible Price–Fixed Money Wage Model

To model this contractual view of the labor market, we assume that, although prices are free to vary, the money wage is *fixed*.[4] A fixed money wage is an extreme version of a sticky wage, and Keynesian economists certainly do not believe that the money wage is completely rigid. Still, if the response of the money wage to labor market conditions is slow to materialize, as the contractual approach to the labor market suggests, results based on the assumption of a fixed money wage will be approximately correct for the short run.

Finally, before we analyze this flexible price–fixed money wage model, we should point out that Keynes's concern was with the downward rigidity of the money wage—the failure of the money wage to fall sufficiently to restore full employment. The main situations to which we would want to apply the fixed-wage model are those in which there is an excess supply of labor.

With the money wage fixed and labor supply greater than labor demand, actual employment will be determined by demand. Firms will be able to hire the amount of labor they demand at the going wage. Keynes did not object to the classical theory of labor demand. According to this theory, as explained in Chapter 3, the profit-maximizing firm demands labor up to the point at which the real wage (W/P) is equal to the marginal productivity of labor (MPN) or, equivalently, to the point at which

$$W = \text{MPN} \cdot P \tag{9.3}$$

The money wage paid to labor is equal to the money value of the marginal product (the marginal revenue product) of labor. Because, with an excess supply of labor and

---

[4]The models in this chapter focus on the traditional Keynesian view that money wage rigidity is the key explanation of why output and employment must respond to changes in aggregate demand. In section 13.2, we consider some *new Keynesian models* in which the key rigidities are, instead, in product prices and real wage rates.

Figure 9.6
Employment with a Fixed Money Wage

With the money wage fixed at $\overline{W}$, employment will be at N_0, the amount of labor demanded.

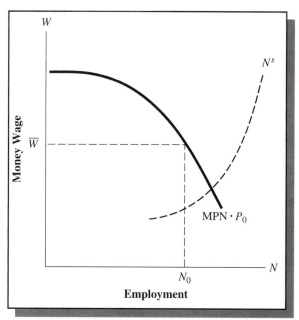

a fixed money wage, employment depends only on labor demand, the determination of employment is as depicted in Figure 9.6. At a fixed money wage $\overline{W}$, labor demand, and therefore employment, will be N_0.

The labor supply schedule is shown in Figure 9.6, as a dashed line. Notice that at the fixed money wage ($\overline{W}$), the labor supply curve is to the right of N_0, indicating an excess supply of labor. Demand, not supply, is the factor constraining employment. The labor supply curve plays *no* role and is not shown in the subsequent figures in this section. The properties of the Keynesian labor supply function are explained in the next section, where we analyze a Keynesian model in which the money wage is allowed to vary.

The position of the labor demand schedule, the schedule giving the money value of the marginal product of labor corresponding to each level of employment (the MPN · P_0 schedule in Figure 9.6), depends on the price level. The number of workers firms will hire, and as a consequence the amount of output they will supply, depends on the price level. This relationship between output supplied and the price level is developed in Figure 9.7.

Figure 9.7*a* shows the level of employment that will result at three successively higher price levels, P_0, P_1, and P_2, with the money wage fixed at $\overline{W}$. An increase in the price level (from P_0 to P_1, then from P_1 to P_2) will increase the money value of the marginal product of labor corresponding to any level of employment and therefore will increase labor demand for a given money wage. The labor demand (MPN · P) schedule shifts to the right, and employment increases. As employment increases, output is shown to rise in Figure 9.7*b*, where we have plotted the aggregate production function giving the level of output for each level of employment.

Figure 9.7*c* combines the information from Figures 9.7*a* and 9.7*b* to show output supplied for each price level. Higher prices result in higher supply; the aggregate supply function is upward-sloping. At some level of output (Y_f in Figure 9.7*c*), full

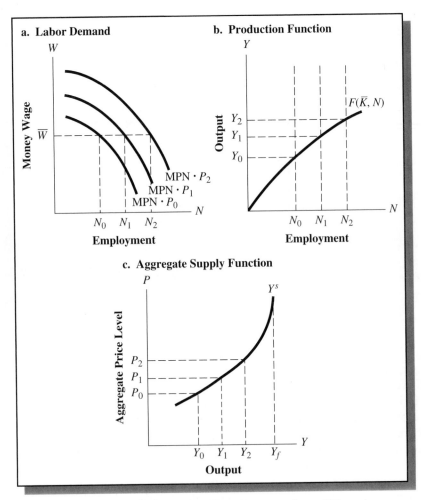

Figure 9.7 The Keynesian Aggregate Supply Curve When the Money Wage Is Fixed

Part a shows the levels of employment N_0, N_1, N_2 for three successively higher price levels, P_0, P_1, P_2. Part b shows the levels of output, Y_0, Y_1, Y_2 that will be produced at these three levels of employment. In part c, we put together the information in a and b to show output supplied at each of the three price levels. Notice that at higher price levels, employment, and hence output supplied, increase; *the aggregate supply curve* (Y^s) *is upward-sloping.*

employment would be reached and further increases in price would have no effect on output. The aggregate supply curve becomes vertical at this level.

Below full employment, the supply curve will not be vertical; shifts in the aggregate demand curve will change the level of output. The effects of an increase in the money supply and the effects of an increase in government spending are illustrated in Figures 9.8 and 9.9, respectively.

In Figure 9.8a, an increase in the money supply shifts the LM schedule from $LM(M_0/P_0)$ to $LM(M_1/P_0)$. This shift in the LM curve is a direct result of the change

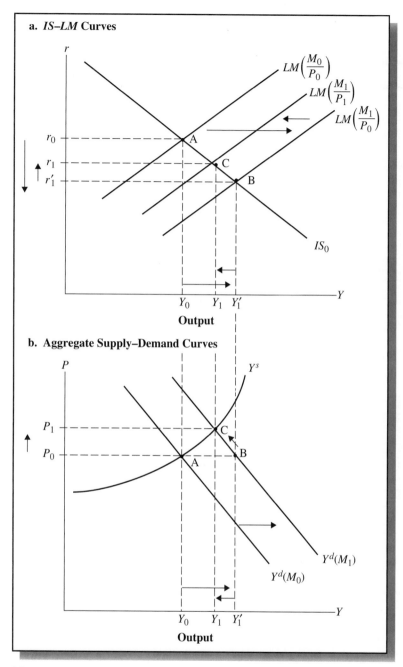

Figure 9.8 Effects of an Increase in the Money Supply When the Price Level Is Flexible

An increase in the money supply shifts the LM schedule from $LM(M_0/P_0)$ to $LM(M_1/P_0)$ (part a) and shifts the aggregate demand curve from $Y^d(M_0)$ to $Y^d(M_1)$ (part b). The increase in agregate demand causes output to rise from Y_0 to Y_1 and the price level to rise from P_0 to P_1. The increase in the price level shifs the LM schedule from $LM(M_1/P_0)$ to $LM(M_1/P_1)$.

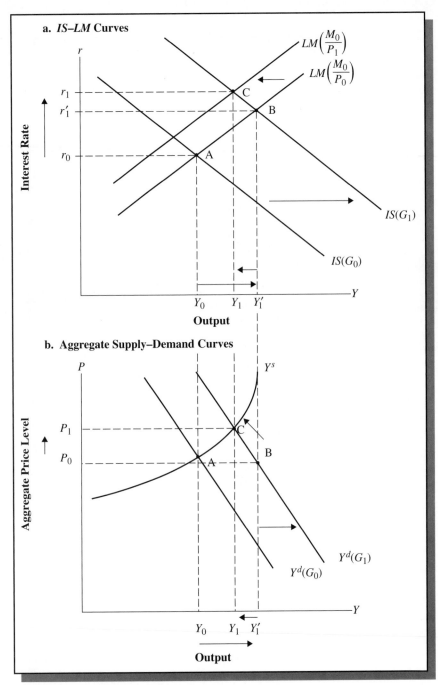

Figure 9.9 Effects of an Increase in Government Spending When the Price Level Is Flexible

An increase in government spending shifts the *IS* curve from $IS(G_0)$ to $IS(G_1)$ (part *a*) and shifts the aggregate demand curve from $Y^d(G_0)$ to $Y^d(G_1)$ (part *b*). The increase in aggregate demand causes output to rise from Y_0 to Y_1 and the price level to rise from P_0 to P_1. The increase in the price level shifts the *LM* schedule from $LM(M_0/P_0)$ to $LM(M_0/P_1)$.

in the money supply. The increase in the money supply shifts the aggregate demand schedule to the right in Figure 9.8b, from $Y^d(M_0)$ to $Y^d(M_1)$. At the initial price level P_0, output would increase to Y_1' as shown in Figure 9.8. But for output to increase, the price level must rise and the new equilibrium is reached not at Y_1' but at Y_1, where the price level has risen to P_1. The rise in price shifts the LM schedule in Figure 9.8a to $LM(M_1/P_1)$.

Thus we find the same type of Keynesian results from an increase in the money supply as we did for the fixed-price IS–LM curve model in Chapter 8. Output and employment will rise, and the interest rate will fall, from r_0 to r_1 in Figure 9.8a. When the price level is allowed to vary, the increase in output will be less than when the price level is fixed. Output rises to Y_1 instead of to Y_1'. The reason is that the increase in the price level reduces the real money supply (M/P), and this reduction *partially* offsets the effects of the increase in the nominal money supply. The interest rate falls only to r_1, not to r_1'. As a consequence, this expansionary monetary policy action has a smaller effect on investment and, hence, on output.

The situation is much the same with fiscal policy. The results are Keynesian in that fiscal policy does affect output, but again the effect of a given policy action is smaller in magnitude when the price level is variable than when the price level is fixed. The effects of an increase in government spending are illustrated in Figure 9.9.

An increase in government spending shifts the IS curve from $IS(G_0)$ to $IS(G_1)$ in Figure 9.9a. The increase in government spending has no direct effect on the LM schedule, which is initially given by $LM(M_0/P_0)$. The increase in aggregate demand as the IS curve shifts right is reflected in Figure 9.9b in the shift of the aggregate demand curve from $Y^d(G_0)$ to $Y^d(G_1)$. Output increases to Y_1, and the price level rises to P_1. The increase in the price level decreases the real money supply (M/P), causing the LM schedule to shift from $LM(M_0/P_0)$ to $LM(M_0/P_1)$ in Figure 9.9a. Output rises only to Y_1, not to Y_1', the increase in output that would have occurred had the price level remained fixed.

9.4 LABOR SUPPLY AND VARIABILITY IN THE MONEY WAGE

In this section, we bring the supply side of the labor market into the picture. We discuss the differences in the Keynesian and classical views of labor supply and then examine a version of the Keynesian model in which both the aggregate price level and the money wage are allowed to vary.

Classical and Keynesian Theories of Labor Supply

Classical economists believed that the supply of labor depended positively on the real wage,

$$N^s = g\left(\frac{W}{P}\right) \qquad (9.4)$$

The reasoning behind this formulation is that individuals maximize utility, which depends positively on real income and leisure. A rise in the real wage increases the income that can be gained from an hour's labor or, looked at in reverse, increases the opportunity cost of taking one hour of leisure. Consequently, an increase in the real wage increases labor supply.

The Keynesian theory of labor supply begins with the observation that the wage bargain is struck in terms of the *money* wage, not the real wage. The classical theory assumes that suppliers of labor (workers) know the price level (P) and money wage (W), and therefore know the real wage (W/P). Keynesians argue that, because the labor bargain is in terms of the money wage, we can assume that workers know the money wage but not the price level. As explained previously, through implicit or explicit contracts, workers agree to provide labor services over some period, let us say for a year. They have no way of knowing the value that the aggregate price level will take on over the coming year. It is this aggregate price level that will determine the purchasing power of any money wage they agree to in a current wage bargain. As a consequence, the Keynesians believe that decisions about labor supply depend on the current money wage and the *expectation* of the aggregate price level. Further, the Keynesian view has been that workers' expectations about the price level depend for the most part on the past behavior of prices.

To see the implications of the Keynesian view of workers' bargaining for a known money wage with only imperfect information about prices, we construct a Keynesian labor supply curve, which we compare with the classical labor supply curve [equation (9.4)]. We then consider a model in which the money wage is perfectly flexible but labor supply is given by the Keynesian labor supply function. In this analysis, we neglect the factors enumerated previously, which Keynesians believe cause the money wage to be sticky. One purpose of this analysis is to show that *even if the money wage were perfectly flexible*, with the Keynesian labor supply curve, the aggregate supply curve would not be vertical. Output and employment would not be completely supply-determined; aggregate demand would also play a role. In reality, the Keynesians believe that the money wage *is* sticky in the downward direction and that much of unemployment is the result of the failure of the money wage to clear the labor market. Imperfect information about prices is, however, an additional factor that the Keynesians believe explains fluctuations in output and employment.

The Keynesian labor supply function can be written as

$$N^s = t(W/P^e) \tag{9.5}$$

An increase in the money wage (W) for a given value of the expected price level (P^e) would increase labor supply, because it would be viewed by workers as an increase in the real wage. An increase in the expected price level would cause labor supply to decline. Fundamentally, workers are interested in the real wage, not the money wage, and they reduce their supply of labor when they perceive that the real wage has declined. The difference between the Keynesian and classical labor supply functions is that in the Keynesian version workers must form an expectation of the price level. Labor supply therefore depends on the *expected* real wage. In the classical system, workers know the real wage; labor supply depends on the *actual* real wage.

The Keynesian theory of labor supply is incomplete without an assumption about how workers form an expectation of the price level (P^e). The Keynesian assumption is that such price expectations are based primarily on the past behavior of the price level. Thus

$$P^e = a_1 P_{-1} + a_2 P_{-2} + a_3 P_{-3} + \cdots + a_n P_{-n} \tag{9.6}$$

where P_{-i} ($i = 1, 2, 3, \ldots$) is the price level from i periods back and $a_1, a_2, \ldots, a_n$ are the weights given to a number of past observations on the price level in forming the expectation of the current price level. Clearly, there is additional information that might prove useful in accurately predicting the behavior of prices. The Keynesian assumption is that the cost of gathering and processing such additional information is high enough that the price expectations of labor suppliers are reasonably accurately represented by a simple formulation such as equation (9.6). As we will see later, this assumption has not gone unchallenged.

According to equation (9.6), price expectations are essentially *backward-looking*, adjusting to the past behavior of the price level. Moreover, in the Keynesian view there is considerable inertia in this adjustment process; price expectations adjust only *slowly* to the past behavior of the price level. If this is the case, then price expectations do not change as a result of current economic conditions. In analyzing the effects of various policy changes, for example, we can take P^e as constant. In the longer run (after many short periods have passed), we need to take account of how stabilization policies affect P^e, because such policies will have affected price levels from past periods.

The Keynesian Aggregate Supply Curve with a Variable Money Wage

Figure 9.10 illustrates the construction of the aggregate supply curve, where labor supply is given by equation (9.5) and the money wage is assumed to adjust to equate labor supply and labor demand. In Figure 9.10a, labor supply (N^s) and labor demand are plotted as functions of the money wage. As in the previous analysis, labor demand depends on the real wage; firms are assumed to know the price level at which they will be able to sell their products. The labor demand curve will shift to the right with an increase in the price level. Figure 9.10a shows labor demand curves for three successively higher price levels, P_0, P_1, and P_2, respectively.

The labor supply curve is drawn for a given value of the *expected* aggregate price level. As just explained, this expected price level is assumed to be fixed in the short run. With the fixed labor supply curve, increases in the price level shift the labor demand curve along the supply curve, so that for a higher price level the equilibrium levels of employment and the money wage are increased. The process at work here is as follows. The increase in price (from P_0 to P_1, for example) causes an excess demand for labor at the old money wage (W_0). The money wage is bid up, and for a given value of P^e, an increase in the money wage causes more workers to accept jobs (or to increase hours worked in existing jobs); employment rises.

At the higher levels of employment N_1 and N_2, corresponding to the higher price levels P_1 and P_2, output is higher at the levels shown by Y_1 and Y_2 in Figure 9.10b.

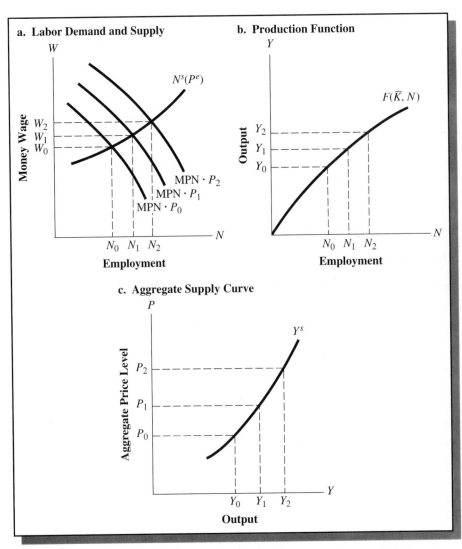

Figure 9.10 The Keynesian Aggregate Supply Curve When the Money Wage Is Variable

Part *a* shows equilibrium levels of employment N_0, N_1, N_2, corresponding to successively higher values of the price level, P_0, P_1, P_2. Part *b* gives the level of output, Y_0, Y_1, Y_2 that will be produced at each of these employment levels. Part *c* combines the information in parts *a* and *b* to show the relationship between the price level and output supplied. At higher values of the price level, output supplied increases; as in the fixed-wage case, *the aggregate supply curve (Y^s) is upward-sloping.*

Thus, a higher price level corresponds to a higher level of output supplied. This information is reflected in the upward-sloping aggregate supply curve in Figure 9.10c, plotting output supplied for each price level (points such as P_0, Y_0; P_1, Y_1; and P_2, Y_2).

Policy Effects in the Variable-Wage Keynesian Model

Because the variable-wage Keynesian aggregate supply curve is still upward-sloping (nonvertical), changes in aggregate demand that shift the aggregate demand curve will affect the level of output. Increases in the money supply or level of government expenditures will shift the aggregate demand curve to the right, increasing both output and the aggregate price level. Graphical illustrations of such policy shifts are *qualitatively* the same as Figures 9.8 and 9.9.

Suppose that we compare the effects on price and output from a given change in aggregate demand when the money wage is variable with the effects for the case in which the money wage is fixed. Is there a predictable *quantitative* difference? The answer is yes. When the money wage is variable, a given increase in aggregate demand will cause output to increase by less than when the money wage is fixed. When the money wage is variable, an increase in aggregate demand will cause the price level to rise by more than when the money wage is fixed. The reason for these results is that the aggregate supply curve when the money wage varies is steeper than when the money wage is fixed. As the aggregate demand curve is shifted to the right along the steeper aggregate supply curve, the increased demand results less in increased output and more in increased price.

The reason the aggregate supply curve is steeper in the variable-money-wage case is illustrated in Figure 9.11. In Figure 9.11a, the labor market response to an increase in the price level is illustrated for the fixed- and variable-money-wage cases. If the money wage is fixed at $\overline{W} = W_0$, an increase in the price level from P_0 to P_1 shifts the labor demand curve from MPN $\cdot$ P_0 to MPN $\cdot$ P_1, and employment rises from N_0 to N_1. Recall from the previous section that in the fixed-money-wage case, we assume there is an excess supply of labor. The labor supply curve in this case, N^s ($W = \overline{W}$), is to the right of N_0 at $\overline{W}$ (as in Figure 9.6). Labor supply is no constraint on employment, which is determined solely by labor demand. For this case of $W = \overline{W}$, output supplied can be seen from Figure 9.11b to rise from Y_0 to Y_1. The aggregate supply curve is given by $Y^s(W = \overline{W})$ in Figure 9.11c.

With a variable money wage, when the labor demand curve shifts from MPN $\cdot$ P_0 to MPN $\cdot$ P_1, as a result of the increase in price, employment rises only to N_1'. Here we are assuming that there is no initial excess supply of labor. At W_0, labor demand just equals supply along the labor supply curve N^s (W variable). The money wage must rise from W_0 to W_1 to get workers to increase labor supply. This increase in the money wage dampens the effect of the increase in labor demand. Because employment increases by less than in the fixed-wage case, output supplied also increases by less, rising only to Y_1', as shown in Figure 9.11b. The increase in the price level leads to a smaller rise in output supplied, and this relationship is reflected in the steeper aggregate supply curve for the variable-money-wage case, as shown in Figure 9.11c, the Y^s (W variable) curve.

At this point it is useful to draw some conclusions from the preceding two sections concerning how allowing price and wage flexibility affects the policy implications of the Keynesian system. In section 9.3, we saw that when the price level was assumed to vary (the money wage still fixed), policy multipliers were reduced relative to their values in the simple *IS–LM* curve model of Chapter 8, where both the price level and the money wage had been fixed. In that simple *IS–LM* curve model, the assumption was that the aggregate supply curve was horizontal. Supply was no

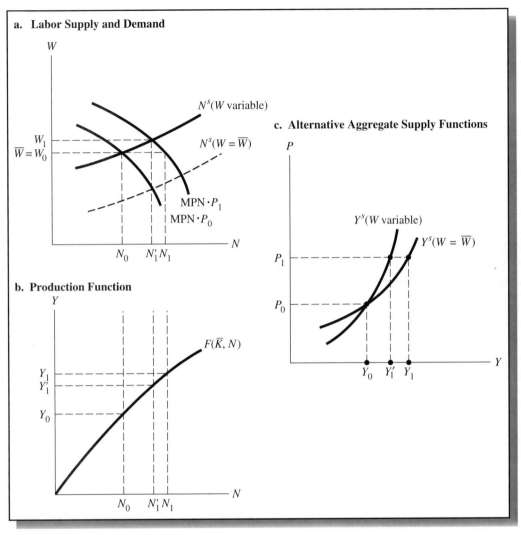

a. Labor Supply and Demand

W

$N^s(W \text{ variable})$

W_1
$\overline{W} = W_0$

$N^s(W = \overline{W})$

$MPN \cdot P_1$
$MPN \cdot P_0$

N

$N_0 \quad N_1' N_1$

b. Production Function

Y

$F(\overline{K}, N)$

Y_1
Y_1'

Y_0

N

$N_0 \quad N_1' N_1$

c. Alternative Aggregate Supply Functions

P

$Y^s(W \text{ variable})$
$Y^s(W = \overline{W})$

P_1

P_0

Y

$Y_0 \quad Y_1' \quad Y_1$

Figure 9.11 Keynesian Aggregate Supply Curves for the Fixed- and Variable-Money-Wage Cases

The aggregate supply schedule in part *c* for the case when the money wage is variable [$Y^s(W \text{ variable})$] is steeper than when the money wage is fixed [$Y^s(W = \overline{W})$] because the increase in employment (part *a*) with a rise in price and therefore the increase in output (part *b*) are smaller when the money wage is variable than when it is fixed. In essence, this outcome follows because the rise in the money wage in the variable-wage case dampens the effect on employment and output from an increase in the price level.

barrier to an increase in output. In the model in section 9.3, we were taking account of the fact that in normal circumstances, as output increases, the marginal product of labor declines. Because the unit cost of producing additional units of output is the money wage divided by the marginal product of labor, firms will supply a greater output only at a higher price—even if the money wage is fixed. The aggregate supply curve was upward-sloping, and increases in aggregate demand consequently had smaller output effects than with the horizontal aggregate supply curve.

When the money wage is also assumed to be variable, the implied aggregate supply curve becomes steeper. Now as output is increased, not only does the marginal product of labor decline, causing an increase in unit costs (W/MPN), but the rise in the money wage required to induce workers to supply more labor will also push up unit cost. As a result, any increase in output supplied requires a larger increase in price; the aggregate supply curve is steeper. Aggregate demand changes have still smaller output effects.

In the classical system, the aggregate supply curve was vertical; output was completely supply-determined. The price and wage were perfectly flexible. In the simple *IS–LM* curve model, output was completely demand-determined. Prices and wages were completely rigid. The models in these two sections, by introducing price and wage flexibility in the Keynesian system, have brought the Keynesian results closer to those of the classical model. Still, the models in these sections remain "Keynesian" in that aggregate demand continues to play a role in determining output.

9.5 THE EFFECTS OF SHIFTS IN THE AGGREGATE SUPPLY SCHEDULE

So far in our development of the Keynesian theory of aggregate supply we have focused on how taking account of supply factors changes the role of aggregate demand in determining output. The output and employment effects of changes in aggregate demand—shifts in the aggregate demand schedule—depend on the slope of the aggregate supply schedule. In addition, supply factors have an independent role in determining output and employment. Shifts can occur in the aggregate supply schedule, and such shifts will affect output, employment, and the price level.

Shifts in the aggregate supply schedule have at times played an important part in the Keynesian explanation of movements in price, output, and employment. In fact, if shifts in the aggregate supply schedule are not taken into account, the behavior of price, output, and unemployment over the decade of the 1970s cannot be explained within a Keynesian framework. To see why, consider the data in Table 9.2. Notice that while the GNP deflator increased substantially in each year between 1973 and 1981, real output fell in three of those years. In fact, output fell in three of the four most inflationary years.

Table 9.2
Percentage Growth Rates in Real GNP and the GNP Price Deflator, 1973–81

YEAR	GROWTH IN REAL GNP	INCREASE IN GNP DEFLATOR
1973	5.8	5.8
1974	−0.6	8.8
1975	−1.2	9.3
1976	5.4	5.2
1977	5.5	5.8
1978	5.0	7.4
1979	2.8	8.6
1980	−0.3	9.2
1981	2.5	9.6

This pattern of price and output changes is inconsistent with the Keynesian model unless shifts in the aggregate supply schedule are taken into account. Consider Figure 9.12. In part a, movements in output and price are caused by shifts in the aggregate demand schedule (from Y_0^d to Y_1^d, then to Y_2^d). In this case, increases in price (from P_0 to P_1, then to P_2) would be accompanied by increases in output (from Y_0 to Y_1, then to Y_2). The demand schedule shifts to the right along the fixed upward-sloping supply schedule, increasing both price and output. Shifts to the left in the aggregate demand schedule cause *both* output and price to fall. Therefore, shifts in the aggregate demand schedule do not explain the behavior of price and output in years such as 1974, 1975, and 1980, when output fell but price rose.

In Figure 9.12b, we can see that shifts to the left in the aggregate supply schedule (from Y_0^s to Y_1^s and to Y_2^s) would result in price increases (from P_0 to P_1, then to P_2) associated with declines in output (from Y_0 to Y_1, then to Y_2). Such "supply shocks" could explain the U.S. economy's inflationary recessions over the 1970s—periods when output declined and prices increased.

Figure 9.12
Price and Output Variations with Shifts in Aggregate Demand and Supply

If changes in output were the result of shifts in the aggregate demand schedule along a fixed supply schedule, as in part a, we would expect a positive relationship between price and output changes. On the other hand, if output changes resulted from shifts in the aggregate supply schedule along a fixed demand schedule, as in part b, we would expect a negative association between price and output changes.

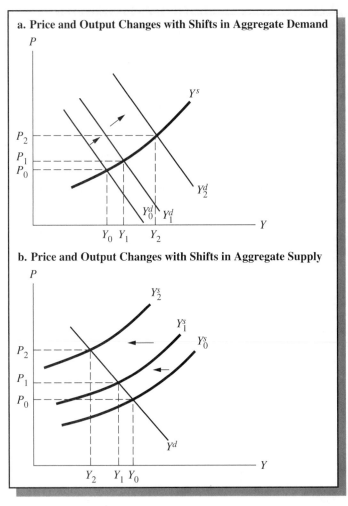

a. Price and Output Changes with Shifts in Aggregate Demand

b. Price and Output Changes with Shifts in Aggregate Supply

Factors That Shift the Aggregate Supply Schedule

The question remains of the causes of shifts in the aggregate supply schedule—the nature of supply shocks. Recall that points on the aggregate supply schedule give the desired output of the firms for each aggregate price level. Each firm, and therefore firms in the aggregate, will choose the level of output that maximizes profits. This implies, as discussed in Chapter 3, that firms produce up to the point where P is equal to marginal cost (MC):

$$P = \text{MC} \tag{9.7}$$

Marginal cost is the addition to total cost as a result of increasing the use of variable factors of production to increase output. In our previous analysis, we assumed that labor was the only variable factor of production. In this case, the marginal cost of producing an additional unit of output was the money wage (W), the amount paid for an additional unit of labor, divided by the marginal product of labor (MPN). Marginal cost (W/MPN) increased as output increased because as more labor was hired, the marginal product of labor (MPN) declined. In addition, in the variable-wage model of the preceding section, in order for workers to supply additional labor, the money wage had to be increased, a further factor causing marginal cost to rise as output increased. These two factors, the declining marginal product of labor and increasing upward pressure on money wages as output and employment increase, explain why the aggregate supply schedule is upward-sloping.

A shift in the aggregate supply schedule—for example, a shift upward to the left, as in Figure 9.12b—means that after the shift, firms will produce less for a given price or, put differently, firms will find it optimal to continue to produce the same output, only at a higher price. From condition (9.7) it can be seen that any factor that causes marginal cost to increase *for a given output level* will cause such a shift upward and to the left in the aggregate supply schedule. If marginal cost increases for a given output, then to continue to meet condition (9.7) *at a given price*, the firm must decrease output. As output declines, marginal cost will decline (MPN will rise and W will fall) and equality (9.7) can be restored. Alternatively, price would have to rise by the amount of the increase in marginal cost for the firm to find it optimal to continue to produce the same level of output.

This is only half the story; the next task is to determine the factors that will change marginal cost for a given output level. Such factors are often termed *cost push factors* because they affect price independently of the level of demand, acting by shifting the supply curve. One set of cost push factors affects the money wage demands on the part of labor at a given level of employment; these are factors that shift the labor supply curve as drawn, for example, in Figure 9.10. So far we have considered one factor that shifts the labor supply schedule, a change in workers' expectation about the aggregate level of price (P^e).

In the preceding section, we assumed that workers' expected price level depended on the past behavior of prices and, hence, was given in the short run. Over time, however, as new information is received, workers will adjust their price expectation. Figure 9.13 shows the effect on labor supply and on the aggregate supply curve of an increase in workers' expectations concerning the aggregate price level.

Figure 9.13 Shift in the Aggregate Supply Schedule with an Increase in the Expected Price Level

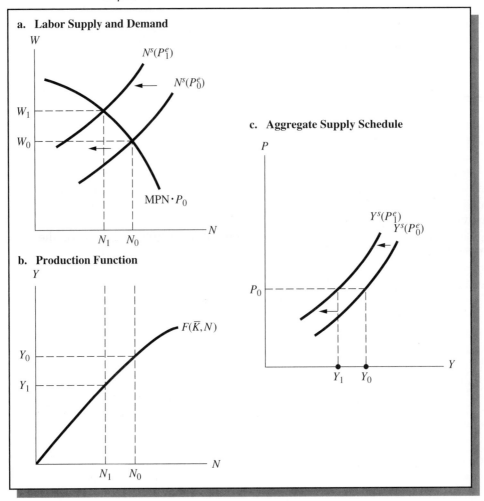

a. **Labor Supply and Demand**

b. **Production Function**

c. **Aggregate Supply Schedule**

An increase in the expected price level shifts the labor supply schedule to the left from $N^s(P_0^e)$ to $N^s(P_1^e)$ in part a. At a given price level, P_0, employment declines from N_0 to N_1, and output falls from Y_0 to Y_1 (part b). This decline in output for a given price level is reflected in a shift to the left in the aggregate supply schedule from $Y^s(P_0^e)$ to $Y^s(P_1^e)$ in part c.

Suppose that as a result of observed past increases in the aggregate price level, workers' expectation of the current price level rose from P_0^e to P_1^e. The labor supply schedule would then shift to the left in Figure 9.13a, from $N^s(P_0^e)$ to $N^s(P_1^e)$. Less labor would be supplied at each money wage because with the higher expectation about the aggregate price level, a given money wage would correspond to a lower real wage. At the initial price level P_0, the shift in the labor supply schedule would reduce employment (from N_0 to N_1). Consequently, output at price level P_0 would fall (from Y_0 to Y_1), as can be seen in Figure 9.13b. The aggregate supply schedule would shift to the left in Figure 9.13c [from $Y^s(P_0^e)$ to $Y^s(P_1^e)$].

Thus, any factor that shifts the labor supply curve upward to the left, lowering labor supply for a given money wage or, what amounts to the same thing, increasing the money wage at which a given amount of labor will be supplied, shifts the aggregate supply schedule to the left. Such shifts in the labor supply function play an important part in our analysis of the longer-run adjustment of output and employment to policy changes.

If we broaden our analysis to allow for variable factors of production other than labor, it follows that an autonomous increase in the price of *any* variable factor of production will increase marginal cost for a given output level and shift the aggregate supply schedule to the left.

In particular, autonomous increases in the price of raw materials have this type of cost push effect. Keynesians believe that increases during the 1970s in the world price of raw materials for production, primarily energy inputs, caused large increases in production cost for a given level of output and resulted in significant shifts to the left in the aggregate supply schedule, increasing the domestic aggregate price level and reducing real output.

In addition to the direct effects that increases in raw material prices have on the aggregate supply schedule, such supply shocks have indirect effects that come through an effect on labor supply. Increases in raw material prices—for example, the price of imported oil and other energy products—push up the domestic price level. As domestic prices rise and enough time passes for these price increases to be perceived by the suppliers of labor, the workers' expectation about the aggregate price level (P^e) will increase. As was just explained, such an increase in the expected price level will cause a shift to the left in the aggregate supply curve, further increasing the price level and causing an additional decline in real output.

The Keynesian explanation of the large price increases and output declines in the 1973–75 period and again in 1979–80 relies on such direct and indirect effects of supply shocks. The key supply shock in each case was a massive increase in the price of crude oil on the world market. Figure 9.14 shows the price of crude oil for the period 1965–2003. The spikes in the series in 1974 and 1979–80 are evident. (The later spikes in 1990 and 2000 are discussed in the next subsection.) In 1974–75, there was a fourfold increase in the price of oil caused by the firming up of the OPEC (Organization of Petroleum Exporting Countries) pricing cartel. The 1979 disruption of the world oil market following the Iranian revolution again precipitated a huge increase in crude oil prices. The Keynesian view of the effects of such supply shocks is represented graphically in Figure 9.15. The initial increase in oil prices and the increase in the price of other energy sources (coal, natural gas, etc.), which results from the attempt of energy users to substitute other fuels for the higher-priced oil, cause a shift in the aggregate supply schedule from $Y_0^s(P_0^e)$ to $Y_1^s(P_0^e)$. Output declines from Y_0 to Y_1, and price rises from P_0 to P_1. This is the direct effect of the supply shock. As prices of energy-related products and of all products that use such energy in the production process—a virtually all-inclusive category—rise, labor suppliers in time perceive the increase in price; the expected price level rises (from P_0^e to P_1^e). There is a further shift to the left in the aggregate supply schedule, from $Y_1^s(P_0^e)$ to $Y_1^s(P_1^e)$. Price increases further to P_2, and output declines to Y_2.

Read Perspectives 9.2.

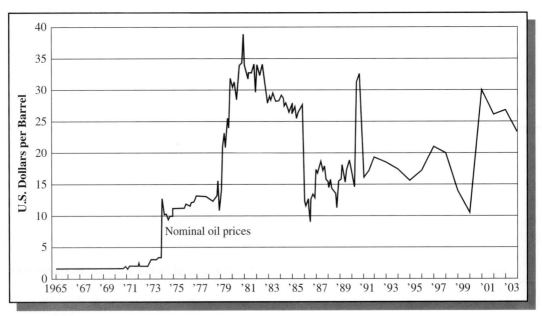

Figure 9.14 Oil Prices, 1965–2003

Source: IMF Survey.

Figure 9.15
Effects of an
Autonomous
Increase in the
World Price of
Energy Inputs

An autonomous
increase in the price of
energy inputs shifts the
aggregate supply
schedule to the left
from $Y_0^s(P_0^e)$ to $Y_1^s(P_0^e)$;
output falls from Y_0 to
Y_1 and the price level
rises from P_0 to P_1. As
labor suppliers perceive
the rise in the price
level, the expected price
level rises from P_0^e to P_1^e.
The aggregate supply
schedule shifts farther
to the left to $Y_1^s(P_1^e)$.
Output falls to Y_2,
and the price level
rises to P_2.

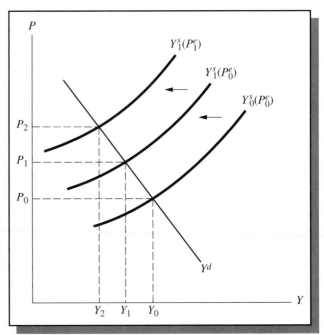

PERSPECTIVES 9.2
Severe Supply Disruption: The Case of the Former Soviet Republics

When the United States and other industrialized countries experienced rising inflation accompanied by recession in the 1970s, the term *stagflation* was coined to describe the phenomenon. Table 9.3 shows that, after the breakup of the Soviet Union, the former Soviet republics experienced stagflation with a vengeance. The cause of the large output declines in these countries can be seen as an extreme form of supply shock, here a massive disruption of the whole organization of industry. The old Soviet system of central planning was gone, and new capitalistic institutions were in their infancy. Making the situation worse is the fact that the old Soviet economic system was explicitly designed to be highly integrated. After the breakup, each republic had to function as a separate economic unit.

Among the institutions that suffered disruption was the revenue-raising system. As tax revenues fell and expenditures have rose to try to maintain some form of social safety net, the republics resorted to printing money to pay their bills. The result was very high inflation. In some countries (e.g., Georgia), price increases reached the hyperinflation stage. But as can be seen from the data, for some republics, especially the Baltic countries, the worst of the adjustment was past by 1995. Still, by the end of the decade, several former Soviet Republics had failed to regain their 1990 output levels.

Table 9.3 Growth in Real GDP and Consumer Price Inflation in the Former Soviet Republics (percent)

	REAL GDP				INFLATION[a]			
	1992	1993	1994	1995	1992	1993	1994	1995
Estonia	−17	−2	6	4	1,069	89	47	29
Latvia	−35	−15	0	1	951	109	36	25
Lithuania	−38	−17	2	3	1,021	410	72	35
Belarus	−9	−10	−22	−12	969	1,188	2,127	800
Moldova	−21	−15	−13	−4	1,276	837	327	30
Ukraine	−17	−14	−23	−12	1,210	4,735	842	375
Russia	−19	−12	−12	−4	1,353	896	303	190
Armenia	−52	−15	3	7	825	3,732	5,459	175
Azerbaijan	−23	−13	−25	−17	616	833	1,456	412
Georgia	−43	−35	−35	−5	913	3,126	20,000	160
Kazakhstan	−14	−12	−25	−9	1,381	1,570	1,681	180
Kyrgyz Republic	−19	−16	−26	−6	855	1,209	283	45
Tajikistan	−30	−28	−15	−12	1,157	2,195	1,500	635
Turkmenistan	−5	−8	−5	−5	493	3,102	2,001	1,800
Uzbekistan	−10	−2	−45	−2	528	851	746	315

[a]*Average year-on-year percentage increase.*
Source: IMF staff estimates.

More Recent Supply Shocks

Figure 9.14 shows that the price of oil remained volatile during the post-1980 period. Oil prices fell sharply in the years from 1981 to 1986 as new sources became available and the OPEC cartel weakened. This was in effect a favorable supply shock. By simply reversing the graphical analysis in Figure 9.15, we can see that such a favorable shock would, in the absence of other changes, reduce the aggregate price level and increase output. In fact, during the first half of this period, there was a severe recession, which in the Keynesian view was caused by demand-side factors. The decline in the price of oil did contribute to the dramatic fall in the inflation rate during these years.

The next large change in oil prices came in August 1990, following Iraq's invasion of Kuwait. The price of oil shot up as Kuwaiti oil production was halted and the United Nations placed an embargo on Iraqi oil exports. The price of oil declined as rapidly as it had risen once a swift victory of U.N. forces was evident in early 1991. The effects of both the rise and fall of oil prices can be seen in the behavior of the producer price index. The index rose by more than 15 percent (at an annual rate) between August and October 1990 and then fell by 5 percent (again at an annual rate) between December 1990 and March 1991.

The price of oil fell sharply in the latter part of the 1990s, bottoming out at $10 per barrel in 1999. This fall contributed to the benign inflation performance in Europe and the United States during these years. Then, in 2000, the price of oil tripled to $30 per barrel in what has been called the "fourth oil price shock." The price of oil remained above $25 per barrel through the period of the U.S. invasion of Iraq. This latest spike in the price of oil has had only modest effects on the industrialized economies. One reason is that these economies have reduced their dependence on oil. Oil input per dollar of GDP in industrialized countries has fallen by approximately 50 percent over the years since 1972. In addition, even at $30 per barrel, the real (inflation-adjusted) oil price is still only back up to the level of the mid-1970s.

9.6 CONCLUSION: KEYNES VERSUS THE CLASSICS

Chapters 6–9 have analyzed the Keynesian view of macroeconomics. What are the major differences between the Keynesian view and the classical macroeconomic theory that Keynes attacked? In this chapter, we have seen how the Keynesian system can be summarized by the aggregate supply and aggregate demand relationships. The classical model was expressed in the same manner in Chapter 4. A convenient way to summarize the differences between the Keynesian and classical theories is to examine the differences between the respective aggregate demand and aggregate supply relationship in the two models.

Keynesian Versus Classical Theories of Aggregate Demand

The classical model did not contain an explicit theory of aggregate demand. The *quantity theory of money* provided an implicit classical theory of aggregate demand. Using the quantity theory relationship

$$MV = PY \tag{9.8}$$

Figure 9.16

Classical and Keynesian Aggregate Supply and Demand Curves

The classical aggregate supply schedule is vertical, whereas the Keynesian aggregate supply schedule slopes upward to the right. The classical aggregate demand schedule depends only on the level of the money supply (M_0); in the Keynesian system, aggregate demand depends also on the levels of fiscal variables (G_0, T_0), the level of autonomous investment ($\bar{I}_0$), and other variables.

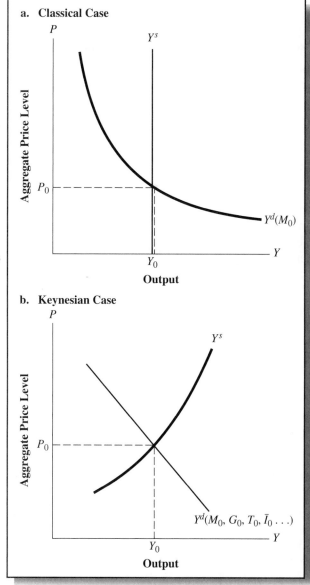

a. **Classical Case**

b. **Keynesian Case**

with the assumption that V is constant, we can determine PY for a given value of M. This relationship gives the rectangular hyperbola $Y^d(M_0)$ plotted in Figure 9.16*a* for M equals M_0. This was the classical aggregate demand curve.

The logic behind this relationship was clearest for the Cambridge form of the quantity theory:

$$M = M^d = kPY \tag{9.9}$$

Because k is equal to $1/V$, (9.8) and (9.9) are equivalent. From (9.9) it can be seen that an increase in M will, for a given value of PY and an assumed constant k, cause an excess supply of money. The classical theory assumed that this excess money would be reflected in an excess demand for goods.

Increases in demand by one sector of the economy—government demand or autonomous investment demand, for example—would not affect aggregate demand in the classical system. Changes in sectoral demands would cause adjustments in the interest rate. The interest rate played a stabilizing role in the classical system and ensured that such changes in sectoral demands could not change aggregate demand. For example, in the classical model an increase in government spending financed by selling bonds to the public would cause the interest rate to rise until private spending had declined by just the amount of the increase in government spending. Aggregate demand would be unchanged. *Only monetary factors shift the classical aggregate demand curve.*

The Keynesian aggregate demand curve is shown in Figure 9.16b. Although both the classical and Keynesian aggregate demand curves are downward-sloping, there is an important difference between them. Whereas the classical aggregate demand schedule shifts only when the supply of money changes, the position of the Keynesian aggregate demand schedule depends on variables such as the level of government spending (G_0), the level of tax collections (T_0), and the level of autonomous investment expenditures ($\bar{I}_0$) in addition to the quantity of money (M_0). As we have seen, the Keynesian aggregate demand schedule will shift when any of these other factors vary. The interest rate does not completely insulate aggregate demand from changes in sectoral demands in the Keynesian system. This difference in the determinants of aggregate demand in the Keynesian and classical models produces important differences in their respective explanations of instability in the economy.

Keynes believed that the instability of investment demand was the major cause of cyclical fluctuations in income. Autonomous changes in investment demand caused by changes in expectations cause shifts in the aggregate demand schedule and consequently instability in price and output.

Keynesian Versus Classical Theories of Aggregate Supply

The key difference between the classical and Keynesian aggregate supply schedules is their slope. The classical aggregate supply schedule, shown in Figure 9.16a, is vertical, resulting from the classical assumptions about the labor market. Labor supply and demand are assumed to depend only on the real wage, which is known to all. The money wage is assumed to be perfectly flexible, adjusting quickly to equate supply and demand. Because the aggregate supply schedule is vertical, output and employment are completely supply-determined. Aggregate demand plays no systematic role in determining output.

In the short run the Keynesian aggregate supply schedule slopes upward to the right. We would expect the curve to be quite flat at levels of output well below full capacity and to become steeper as full-capacity output is approached. The Keynesian view of aggregate supply (sections 9.3 and 9.4) emphasizes the stickiness of the money wage and the failure of market participants to perceive the real wage correctly. As a consequence, the labor market will not be in continual equilibrium at full employment. Actual output and employment will not be completely determined by the supply factors that determine *full employment* output. Shifts in the aggregate demand function will move the economy along the upward-sloping supply schedule, causing output to change. In the Keynesian system, the level of aggregate demand is important in determining the level of output and employment.

The Keynesian aggregate supply schedule in Figure 9.16b was termed a short-run supply schedule, to emphasize that it pertained to a short period of time, not to a long-run equilibrium situation. Factors such as explicit long-term labor contracts, implicit contracts, and resistance to wage cuts seen as cuts in the relative wage would slow but not permanently prevent the necessary wage adjustment to return the economy to a full-employment level. Imperfect information about the real wage on the part of labor suppliers would also be a short-run phenomenon. Eventually, expectations would approach the actual value of the price level and, hence, of the real wage. The Keynesians do not deny that eventually the economy would approach full employment. But to the Keynesians such long-run "classical" properties of the economy are unimportant. They agree with Keynes that "this *long run* is a misleading guide to current affairs. *In the long run* we are all dead. Economists set themselves too easy, too useless a task if in tempestuous seasons they can only tell us that when the storm is long past the ocean is flat again."[5]

Keynesian Versus Classical Policy Conclusions

Classical economists stressed the self-adjusting tendencies of the economy. If left free from destabilizing government policies, the economy would achieve full employment. Classical economists were noninterventionist in that they did not favor active monetary and fiscal policies to stabilize the economy. Such policies, to affect aggregate demand, would have no effects on output or employment given the supply-determined nature of those variables in the classical system.

Keynesians view the economy as unstable as a result of the instability of aggregate demand, primarily its private-investment component. Aggregate demand does affect output and employment in the Keynesian view. Consequently, swings in aggregate demand will cause undesirable fluctuations in output and employment in the short run. These fluctuations can be prevented by using monetary and fiscal policies to offset undesirable changes in aggregate demand. Keynesians are interventionists, favoring active policies to manage aggregate demand.

REVIEW QUESTIONS AND PROBLEMS

1. Explain why the Keynesian aggregate demand curve is downward-sloping when plotted against the price level.
2. Derive the Keynesian aggregate demand curve for the case in which investment is completely interest-inelastic and therefore the *IS* schedule is vertical (follow the procedure in Figure 9.2). Explain the resulting slope of the aggregate demand curve for this case.
3. In what sense is the classical theory of aggregate supply "fundamentally incompatible" with the Keynesian system?

---

[5]John M. Keynes, *A Tract on Monetary Reform* (London: Macmillan, 1923), p. 80.

4. Why are fiscal policy multipliers smaller in magnitude in the variable price–fixed wage version of the Keynesian model than in the fixed-price *IS–LM* model? Why are these multipliers still smaller when we allow the money wage as well as the price level to be variable?

5. Return to the case considered in question 2 where investment is completely interest-inelastic and the *IS* schedule is vertical. Analyze the effects of an increase in government spending in this case within the variable price–fixed wage version of the Keynesian model. Compare the effects with those in the fixed price version of the model.

6. Analyze the effects of an increase in the money supply within the Keynesian model where both the price level and money wage are assumed to be variable. Include in your answer the effects on the level of real income, the price level, the interest rate, and the money wage.

7. In the Keynesian system, increases in aggregate demand lead to increases in output because the money wage rises less than proportionately with the price level in response to such increases in demand. This condition is necessary because firms will hire more workers only if the real wage (W/P) falls. Explain the possible reasons why the money wage does not adjust proportionately with the price level in the short-run Keynesian model.

8. Assume that there is an exogenous decline in the price of imported oil. Using the graphical analysis in this chapter, explain how such a shock would affect output and the price level. Explain the role inflationary expectations play in this adjustment.

9. "Money is more important in the Keynesian system than in the classical system." Do you agree? Or would you maintain that the opposite is true?

10. What do you see as the essential differences between the classical and Keynesian theories of aggregate supply?

11. What do you see as the essential differences between the classical and Keynesian theories of aggregate demand?

12. Compare the effects of an expansionary fiscal policy action—an increase in government spending financed by government bond sales to the public, for example—in the Keynesian and classical models. Include in your answer the effects of this policy shift on the level of real income, employment, the price level, and the rate of interest.

13. Within the variable price–variable wage version of the Keynesian model, analyze the effects that an unfavorable supply shock, such as a rise in the price of oil, would have on the rate of interest. Would the equilibrium rate of interest rise or fall?

Part III

Macroeconomic Theory After Keynes

*T*he Keynesian revolution succeeded in creating a new framework in which macroeconomic questions were addressed. Little time passed, however, before there were challenges to the new orthodoxy, challenges which had roots in the earlier classical model. In this Part we consider these challenges and the Keynesian responses to them.

Chapter 10

The Monetarist Counterrevolution

10.1 INTRODUCTION

The British news magazine *The Economist* defined a monetarist as someone "who thinks it more important to regulate the supply of money in an economy than to influence other economic instruments. This is thought very wicked by those who can't be bothered to find out what it means." In this chapter we examine the monetarist position. First, we look at the historical background against which monetarism developed.

The Keynesian attack on the classical orthodoxy was successful. After Keynes died in 1946, his successors took up the task of refining his theories and applying them to the policy questions facing Western nations as they converted to peacetime economies in the aftermath of World War II. As we have seen, one aspect of the Keynesian revolution was an attack on the classical quantity theory of money. In fact, *early* Keynesian economists attached very little importance to the money supply. Monetarism began as an attempt to reassert the importance of money and therefore of monetary policy.

Rather than attempt to give a definition of monetarism, we instead list four propositions that characterize the monetarist position:

1. The supply of money is the dominant influence on nominal income.
2. In the long run, the influence of money is primarily on the price level and other *nominal* magnitudes. In the long run, *real* variables, such as output and employment, are determined by real, not monetary, factors.
3. In the short run, the supply of money does influence real variables. Money is the dominant factor causing cyclical movements in output and employment.
4. The private sector is inherently stable. Instability in the economy is primarily the result of government policies.

From these propositions, two policy conclusions follow:

1. Stability in the growth of the money supply is crucial for a stable economy. Monetarists believe that such stability is best achieved by adopting a rule for the

growth rate in the money supply. Milton Friedman has long proposed a constant money growth rate rule. Other monetarists favor less inflexible rules, but monetarists generally favor rules rather than discretion in policymaking.

2. Fiscal policy, by itself, has little systematic effect on either real or nominal income. Fiscal policy is not an effective stabilization tool.

The first monetarist proposition is that the level of economic activity in current dollars is determined primarily by the supply of money. An important element in this proposition is that causation is assumed to be from money to income. For the most part, changes in the money supply are assumed to *cause* changes in nominal income. The level and rate of growth of the money supply are assumed to be determined primarily by the actions of the central bank.

The second monetarist proposition asserts that, in the long run, economic activity measured in real dollars does not depend on the quantity of money. In the long run, real output is determined by real factors such as the stock of capital goods, the size and quality of the labor force, and the state of technology. If, in the long run, the level of real economic activity is not affected by the quantity of money while the level of economic activity in nominal terms is almost completely determined by the supply of money, it follows that the long-run effect of money is on the price level.

The third proposition states that, in the short run, output and employment *are* strongly influenced by changes in the supply of money. Prices are influenced as well, but in the short run, prices, including wage rates (the price of labor), are not perfectly flexible. Thus, when the quantity of money changes, in the short run, prices do not make the full adjustment. Output and employment are also affected.

The fourth monetarist proposition asserts that the private sector (businesses and households) is not the source of instability in the economy. As one monetarist, Karl Brunner, put it, the private sector is "essentially a shock-absorbing, stabilizing and self-adjusting process. Instability is produced dominantly by the operation of the government sector." The government causes instability in the economy primarily by allowing instability in the growth of the money supply, the major determinant of economic activity. In the monetarist view, the government can also destabilize the economy by interfering with the normal adjustment mechanisms in the private economy. Mandatory controls on prices and wages are an obvious example of government interference with such adjustment properties. Other examples are usury ceilings on interest rates, rent controls, and minimum wage laws.

Two policy conclusions follow from the four monetarist propositions. Given propositions 1 and 3, the importance of stable money growth for a stable economy is evident. The monetarists believe that adopting a rule is the best way to achieve stable money growth.

If monetary factors dominate the determination of nominal income and short-run real income, only a secondary role is left for other systematic influences. The term *dominate* does, however, allow for ambiguity. Does it mean that movements in the money supply explain 55 percent of the systematic movement in income, or 95 percent? This question is important in assessing the role of fiscal policy in determining economic activity. As stated, our second policy conclusion allows little independent role for fiscal policy. This conclusion is consistent with the position of monetarists such as Milton Friedman. Other monetarists do not accept such a strong form of this policy proposition, but the general monetarist position has been that fiscal policy is not an effective stabilization tool.

In considering these monetarist propositions and policy conclusions, it is convenient to divide the analysis into two parts. First we examine the reasons why the monetarists ascribe such predominance to money (i.e., the basis of propositions 1 and 3). We postpone until Chapter 11 the question of what monetary policy cannot do, the basis for proposition 2. Although proposition 4 is not given separate consideration, it will be important in our discussion.

10.2 THE REFORMULATION OF THE QUANTITY THEORY OF MONEY

The early development of monetarism centered on redefining the quantity theory of money in light of Keynes's attack. The central monetarist in this period was Milton Friedman, a professor of economics at the University of Chicago from 1946 until his retirement in 1977, and since that time a senior research fellow at the Hoover Institution.

Friedman described the classical quantity theory as follows:

> In monetary theory, that analysis was taken to mean that in the quantity equation $MV = PT$ the term for velocity could be regarded as highly stable, that it could be taken as determined independently of the other terms in the equation, and that as a result changes in the quantity of money would be reflected either in prices or in output.[1]

This is proposition 1 of monetarism, as stated previously. (Notice that stable velocity means not only that changes in M will cause changes in PT but also that *only* changes in M can change PT.)

The quantity theory had come into disrepute, together with the rest of classical economics, as a result of the Great Depression of the 1930s. Friedman believed that the events of the 1930s had been improperly assessed and did not, in fact, offer evidence against the quantity theory of money. He did, however, see the need to restate the quantity theory in terms that took account of Keynes's contribution. His purpose was to reassert the importance of money. The reasons he felt this reassertion was needed can be seen best by first considering the role (or lack of a role) that some early Keynesians attributed to money as a determinant of economic activity.

Money and the Early Keynesians

Our analysis of the Keynesian system made clear that within that framework money was one important determinant of economic activity. But velocity was not constant or independently determined; it was systematically determined within the system. Factors other than money could also affect the level of economic activity. Consider,

---

[1]Milton Friedman, *The Counter-revolution in Monetary Theory* (London: Institute of Economic Affairs, 1970).

Figure 10.1

Effects of an Increase in Government Spending: The Keynesian View

An increase in government spending shifts the *IS* schedule to the right. Both the interest rate and equilibrium level of income rise. Because the money supply is unchanged and income has risen, the velocity of money, the ratio of income to money, has increased.

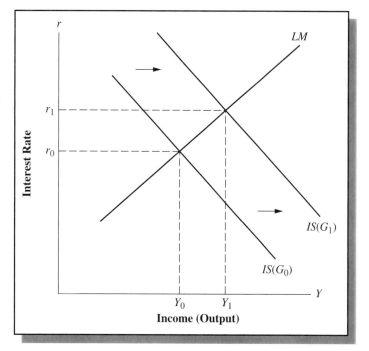

for example, the response of the system to an increase in government spending, as depicted in Figure 10.1.

The increase in government spending from G_0 to G_1 shifts the *IS* curve from *IS* (G_0) to $IS(G_1)$. Income rises from Y_0 to Y_1, and the interest rate increases from r_0 to r_1. The money supply is held constant here, with the increased government spending assumed to be financed by selling bonds to the public. The higher level of income causes a higher transactions demand for money. Bringing money demand back into equality with the unchanged money supply requires a rise in the interest rate. At the higher interest rate the speculative demand for money will have declined, and the demand for transactions balances *at a given level of income* will also have fallen. Thus, the same money supply can support a higher income level. Another way to express this finding is to say that velocity varies positively with the interest rate.

Because velocity is variable in the Keynesian system, there is no one level of income corresponding to a given money supply. It is not even an approximately accurate statement of the Keynesian view that in the short run nominal or real income is determined solely by the level of the money supply. This is not to say that the Keynesians believe that money is unimportant; they do not. The quantity of money is *one* key determinant of income in the Keynesian system.

Many *early* Keynesian economists (circa 1945–50) did, however, believe that money was of little importance and monetary policy of little use as a stabilization tool. Their view was based on empirical judgments about the slopes of the *IS–LM* curves, which, as we saw in our analysis of the Keynesian system, are important in determining the relative effectiveness of monetary and fiscal policy. Influenced by the Depression, they believed that the *LM* schedule was quite flat and the *IS* schedule quite steep—the configuration that would be characteristic of depression conditions such as those of the 1930s. The Depression was characterized by low levels of income and the interest rate. At such a low level of the interest rate, the elasticity of money demand would be high, for reasons discussed in Chapter 7. Such a situation approaches the liquidity trap case; the *LM* curve becomes very flat. Further, in depression conditions, the early Keynesian economists believed that investment would be relatively interest-inelastic, making the *IS* curve quite steep. The Depression was a period with a very low utilization rate of existing plant and equipment. Early Keynesian economists thought that, with massive excess capacity, investment would be unlikely to respond much to changes in the interest rate.

Figure 10.2 shows this configuration of the *IS* and *LM* curves and illustrates the ineffectiveness of an increase in the quantity of money that shifts the *LM* curve from LM_0 to LM_1. With the *LM* curve flat around the point of equilibrium, a given change in the money supply does very little to lower the interest rate, the first link in the chain connecting money and income in the Keynesian model. (See, for example, the discussion of current conditions in Japan in Perspective 8.2) Further, with a steep *IS* curve, a drop in the interest rate would not increase investment very much. This combination of an assumed high interest elasticity of money demand and low interest elasticity of investment led early Keynesian economists to conclude that the quantity of money was unimportant.

What role was there for monetary policy? During World War II much of the war expenditure had been financed by selling bonds to the public at relatively low interest rates. Keeping the interest rate on bonds low and stable would have the desirable effects of keeping the cost of interest payments on the debt low and protecting the

Figure 10.2
Early Keynesian View of Monetary Policy Ineffectiveness

With the *IS* curve quite steep and over the range where the *LM* schedule is nearly horizontal, an increase in the quantity of money, which shifts the *LM* schedule from LM_0 to LM_1, has little effect on income.

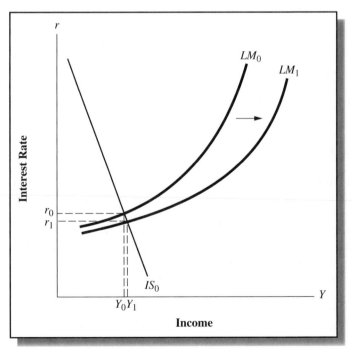

capital value of the bonds for the investors (recall that bond prices and interest rates vary inversely). Low interest rates also meant that monetary policy would make whatever limited contribution it could to strengthening aggregate demand. Because early Keynesian economists feared a return to the depression conditions of the 1930s, this was another desirable feature of low interest rates. Thus low and stable interest rates became the goal of monetary policy. To achieve this goal, the monetary authority cooperated with the U.S. Treasury to "peg," or fix the level of interest rates.

A further element in the view of the early Keynesians made pegging the interest rate desirable. Following Keynes, they felt that the demand for money was highly unstable. The *LM* curve was not only flat (in the relevant range) but shifted around in an unpredictable way. These shifts would lead to instability in financial markets that could be avoided by pegging the interest rate.

In Chapter 18, we will consider the process by which the monetary authority can "peg" or fix the interest rate for a certain period of time. For our purposes here, the key point is that, in doing so, the monetary authority loses control of the money supply. The monetary authority must supply whatever quantity of money it takes to produce equilibrium in the money (and therefore bond) market at the desired interest rate. To the early Keynesians, this loss of control of the money supply was not important because the quantity of money was not important.

Read Perspectives 10.1.

Friedman's Restatement of the Quantity Theory

Contrary to the view of early Keynesians, Friedman argued that the demand for money was stable. Contrary to the near-liquidity-trap characterization, Friedman maintained that the interest elasticity of money demand was certainly not infinite and was in fact "rather small." The quantity of money, far from being unimportant, was the dominant influence on the level of economic activity.

Friedman's conclusions rest on a restatement of the classical quantity theory of money. Friedman's version of the quantity theory is closest to the Cambridge approach we considered previously. That approach focused on the demand for money. The central relationship was

$$M^d = \bar{k}PY \tag{10.1}$$

expressing a proportional relationship between money demand (M^d) and the level of nominal income [price (P) times real income (Y)]. The factor of proportionality (k) was taken as constant in the short run.

Friedman emphasizes that the quantity theory was, as can be seen from equation (10.1), a theory of money demand. Because k was treated as a constant by the Cambridge economists and the *nominal* supply of money (M) was treated as being set exogenously by the monetary authority, the Cambridge equation can be transformed into a theory of nominal income,

$$M = M^d = \bar{k}PY$$
$$M\frac{1}{\bar{k}} = PY \tag{10.2}$$

PERSPECTIVES 10.1
The Monetarist View of the Great Depression

Both Friedman and the Keynesians agree that the Great Depression of the 1930s put the classical theories, including the quantity theory of money, in disrepute. Friedman, however, believes that the Keynesians misread the evidence from the Depression.

Friedman does not deny that the experience of the United States and other industrialized countries in the 1930s contradicts the classical view of the labor market, where the money wage adjusts quickly to maintain full employment. Friedman does believe that Keynesians wrongly concluded that the Depression disproved the quantity theory of money.

Table 10.1 shows the level of several macroeconomic aggregates in 1929, at the start of the Depression, compared with their level in 1933, at the low point of the slump. From the table we see that nominal GNP fell 46.0 percent, and real GNP fell 29.6 percent. The rest of the drop in nominal GNP is accounted for by a fall in the aggregate price level. Column 3 shows that the narrowly defined money supply, M1 (currency plus checkable deposits), fell by 26.5 percent between 1929 and 1933. The M2 measure of the money supply, a broader measure that includes other bank deposits, fell by 33.3 percent.

We see that there *was* a large decline in the money supply as we fell into the Great Depression, which is consistent with the quantity theory. Velocity also fell, as evidenced by the larger percentage decline in nominal income relative to the fall in either money supply measure. But quantity theorists would expect this outcome, because, during the deflation of the Depression, the value of money (in terms of purchasing power) was rising. This rise would be likely to increase the demand for money for a given nominal income and therefore to lower velocity.

Keynesians dispute the monetary explanation of the Depression. They do believe that if the Federal Reserve had been able to prevent a decline in the money supply during the 1929–33 period, the Depression would have been less severe than it was. They believe, however, that the primary causes of the Depression were autonomous declines in several components of aggregate demand: consumption, investment, and exports, caused in turn by factors such as the stock market crash in 1929, overbuilding in the construction sector by the late 1920s, and the breakdown of the international monetary system. This has been called the "spending hypothesis," in contrast to the "money hypothesis" advanced by Friedman and other monetarists.[a]

Table 10.1 Selected Macroeconomic Aggregates (1929, 1933)

	Nominal GNP($P \times Y$)	Real GNP(Y) (1982 Dollars)	M1	M2
1929	$103.9 billion	$708.6 billion	$26.4 billion	$46.2 billion
1933	$56.0 billion	$498.5 billion	$19.4 billion	$30.8 billion
Percentage decline	46.0%	29.6%	26.5%	33.3%

[a]For Friedman's analysis, see Milton Friedman and Anna J. Schwartz, *The Great Contraction* (Princeton, N.J.: Princeton University Press, 1965). Also on the subject of the causes of the Great Depression, see Peter Temin, *Did Monetary Forces Cause the Great Depression?* (New York: Norton, 1976), and *Lessons from the Great Depression* (Cambridge, Mass.: MIT Press, 1990).

or the alternative form (where V, the velocity of money, equals $1/k$).

$$M\overline{V} = PY \qquad \text{(10.3)}$$

where the bar over k or V indicates that these magnitudes do not vary. Friedman examined the changes in the Cambridge theory of money demand that must be made in the light of Keynes's theory of money demand.

Keynes's theory of money demand stressed the role of money as an asset in addition to its role in transactions. In studying the factors that determined how much money people would hold, Keynes considered factors that determined the desirability of money relative to other assets. He made the simplifying assumption that other assets were a homogeneous enough group that he could lump them together under the category "bonds." He then considered how an individual allocated wealth between money and bonds. The key factors that he thought determined the split were the level of income and the level of the interest rate. Put in terms of the Cambridge equation, Keynes focused on the interest rate as the primary determinant of k, the amount of money balances a person would hold for a given level of income. A rise in the interest rate led to a fall in k or, equivalently, a rise in velocity, as we saw in the preceding subsection. Because k was a variable, not a constant, the Cambridge equation could not by itself provide a theory of nominal income.

Friedman accepted Keynes's emphasis on the role of money as an asset. With this as a basis, he sets out his own theory of the demand for money. Again income is one determinant of money demand and, as with Keynes's analysis, we can view Friedman's analysis as providing a theory of what determines the Cambridge k, money holdings as a proportion of nominal income. Friedman's money demand function can be written as follows:

$$M^d = L(P, Y, r_B, r_E, r_D) \qquad \text{(10.4)}$$

where P = price level
Y = real income
r_B = nominal interest rate on bonds
r_E = nominal return on equities
r_D = nominal return on durable goods

Money demand is assumed to depend on nominal income, the product of the first two arguments in the demand function. An increase in nominal income would increase money demand. For a given level of nominal income, Friedman assumes, as did Keynes, that the amount of money demanded depends on the rate of return offered on alternative assets. The money demand function given by equation (10.4) is a simplification of Friedman's equation and includes the rates of return on major alternatives to money as an asset. These are bonds (the asset Keynes focused on), equities (shares of stock in corporations), and durable goods such as consumer durables, land, and houses. Durable goods do not pay an explicit interest rate. Their return is the expected increase in the price of the good over the period for which it is held. Thus, the expected rate of inflation is also a determinant of money demand. An increase in the rate of return on any of these alternative assets causes the demand for money to decline.

Friedman's theory differs from Keynes's in several respects. First, Friedman views the money demand function as stable. Keynes's view was that the demand-for-money function was unstable, shifting with changes in the public confidence in the economy.

Second, Friedman does not segment money demand into components representing transaction balances, speculative demand, and a precautionary demand. Money, like other "goods," has attributes that make it useful, but Friedman does not find it helpful to specify separate demands based on each of the uses of money.

The third difference between Keynes's and Friedman's money demand theories is that Friedman includes separate yields for bonds, equities, and durable goods. Keynes focused on the choice of money versus bonds. It is not clear how substantive this difference is, since what Keynes termed "bonds" can be considered more broadly as at least including equities. Often this has not been done, however, and Keynesian analysis has focused narrowly on the choice between money and bonds. Friedman makes explicit the possibility of other substitutions and also allows for a shift from money directly into commodities (durable goods) as rates of return change.

Friedman's money demand theory can be used to restate the Cambridge equation as follows:

$$M^d = k(r_B, r_E, r_D)PY \tag{10.1}$$

where instead of a constant k we now have k expressed as a function of the rates of return on the assets that are alternatives to holding money. A rise in the rate of return on any one of these alternative assets would cause k to fall, reflecting the increased desirability of the alternative asset. In these terms, we see that Friedman restated the quantity theory, providing a systematic explanation of k, that takes into account the Keynesian analysis of money's role as an asset.

If this is the restated quantity theory, how would we characterize a modern quantity theorist? How would this person differ from a Keynesian? In Friedman's view, a quantity theorist believes the following:

1. The money demand function is stable.
2. This demand function plays an important role in determining the level of economic activity.
3. The quantity of money is strongly affected by money supply factors.

In Friedman's version of the Cambridge equation, the equilibrium condition in the money market is

$$M = M^d = k(r_B, r_E, r_D)PY \tag{10.5}$$

With a stable money demand function, an exogenous increase in the money supply must either lead to a rise in PY or cause declines in $r_B, r_E,$ and r_D *(which will cause k to rise), with indirect effects on PY.*[2] A quantity theorist believes that the money demand function is in fact stable; that changes in the money supply come mostly from the supply side as a result of central bank policies; and finally, that changes in the

---

[2]Notice that a fall in the rates of return on the alternative assets to money (r_B, r_E, r_D) *will increase money demand for a given income level and therefore will raise k.*

quantity of money are important in determining nominal income (that much of the effect of a change in M comes in the form of a change in PY).

In what way does a quantity theorist differ from a Keynesian? The answer depends on whether the term *Keynesian* refers to the position of the *early* Keynesians or, more generally, to the *modern* Keynesian theory. Friedman's theory, as outlined so far, is clearly antithetical to the early Keynesian position. The early Keynesians believed that the money demand function was unstable; that the interest elasticity of money demand was extremely high; and that, as a consequence, changes in the quantity of money did not have important predictable effects on the level of economic activity. In Friedman's view, the quantity theorist believes that the money demand function is stable and that the quantity of money is an important determinant of the level of economic activity. Further, Friedman believes, as we will see shortly, that the interest elasticity of money demand is low.

What about the differences between the quantity theory as outlined so far and the modern Keynesian position? Keynesians today believe that money is important. They believe that innovations in the financial sector during recent years have cast doubt on the stability of the money demand function. The problem is partly a matter of how to define money as new types of deposits become available. The monetarists recognize these definitional problems as well. On the interest elasticity of money demand, recent estimates by Keynesians are higher than suggested by Friedman's own research, but certainly not so high as to indicate the presence of a liquidity trap in most countries. Overall, if a quantity theorist or monetarist need only subscribe to the three propositions listed by Friedman, the modern Keynesian and modern quantity theory positions would differ but not be extremely far apart.

Friedman's Monetarist Position

Friedman, however, used his restatement of the quantity theory to develop a strong monetarist position that did produce sharp differences with the Keynesian positions.

Friedman's monetarist position extends the quantity theory from a theory of money demand to one of nominal income. We have seen how the Cambridge quantity theorists extended the quantity theory with the assumption of a constant k [see equation (10.1) or (10.3)]. Friedman points out that his version of the quantity theory can also be turned into a theory of nominal income if the variables in his money demand function [equation (10.4)] other than nominal income (r_B, r_E, r_D) have little effect on money demand. This being the case, these variables will have little effect on k. Money holdings as a proportion of income (k) will be nearly constant. Friedman does not believe that money demand is completely independent of these rates of return, so the theory of nominal income that results from assuming that k is a constant will only be an approximation. But *any* theory will hold only approximately. Friedman and others have done empirical work that convinces them that such a strong monetarist position, which can be written as

$$PY = \frac{1}{k}M \qquad (10.6)$$

is a better approximation than that given by simple representations of the Keynesian view. This monetarist position is required for statements by Friedman such as, "I regard the description of our position as 'money is all that matters for changes in *nominal* income and for *short-run* changes in real income' as an exaggeration but one that gives the right flavor to our conclusions"; or "appreciable changes in the rate of growth of the stock of money are a necessary and sufficient condition for appreciable changes in the rate of growth of money income."[3]

It is useful to represent the monetarist position in terms of the *IS–LM* diagram and the aggregate supply–aggregate demand framework used to explain the Keynesian position. In Figure 10.3, we have drawn *IS–LM* curves as monetarists would. The *LM* curve is nearly, but not quite, vertical, reflecting Friedman's view that the interest elasticity of money demand is low.

Another divergence from the Keynesian position concerns the slope of the *IS* curve. Here a flatter *IS* curve is consistent with the monetarist position that aggregate demand is quite sensitive to changes in the interest rate. Modern Keynesians also believe that the interest rate affects aggregate demand and would not argue that the *IS* curve should be as nearly vertical as we drew it for the model of the early Keynesians (Figure 10.2). The difference between modern Keynesians and monetarists on this point is one of degree. Monetarists argue that Keynesians restrict the channels by which the interest rate affects aggregate demand to an effect on investment by means of a change in the cost of borrowing funds. Monetarists argue that this is too narrow an interpretation of the effects of interest rates, resulting from the

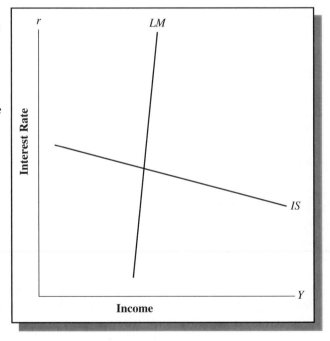

Figure 10.3
IS–LM: A Monetarist Version

In the monetarist view, the *IS* schedule is quite flat, reflecting a high interest elasticity of aggregate demand. The *LM* schedule is nearly vertical, reflecting a very low interest elasticity of money demand.

---

[3]These two quotations are from Milton Friedman, "A Theoretical Framework for Monetary Analysis," in Robert Gordon, ed., *Milton Friedman's Monetary Framework* (Chicago: University of Chicago Press, 1974), p. 27; and Milton Friedman and Anna Schwartz, "Money and Business Cycles," *Review of Economics and Statistics*, 45, Suppl. (February 1963), pp. 32–64, respectively.

tendency of Keynesians to think of "bonds" as just one class of financial assets rather than as all assets other than money.

In his theory of money demand, Friedman did not lump all nonmoney assets into one category. He separately considered bonds, equities, and durable goods, avoiding Keynes's simplification of aggregating to just "bonds" and money. Monetarists believe that if a change in *the* interest rate is really a change in all these yields, its effects go beyond the effects of a change in borrowing cost to firms that buy investment goods. In addition, a change in *the* interest rate means a change in the prices of corporate stock, the prospective return on real estate, and holding durable goods as well. Monetarists believe that the interest rate plays a more important role in determining aggregate demand than the Keynesian model allowed.

Figure 10.3 brings out several of the features of the monetarist view, but it is deficient in one respect. We have generally used the *IS–LM* curves by themselves to show how real GNP and the interest rate were determined, with the price level held constant. A constant price level is *not* an assumption made by the monetarists. Figure 10.4 shows the monetarist view within the aggregate supply–aggregate demand framework of previous chapters.

Three positions for the aggregate demand curve are shown in the graph, $Y^d(M_0)$, $Y^d(M_1)$, and $Y^d(M_2)$, corresponding to three values of the money supply, M_0, M_1, and M_2. Recalling the monetarist formula, giving nominal income

$$PY = \frac{1}{k} M \qquad (10.6)$$

Figure 10.4
Aggregate Supply and Demand: The Monetarist View

In the monetarist view, the position of the aggregate demand schedule is determined by the money supply. Increases in the money supply from M_0 to M_1, then to M_2, shift the aggregate demand schedule from $Y^d(M_0)$ to $Y^d(M_1)$, then $Y^d(M_2)$.

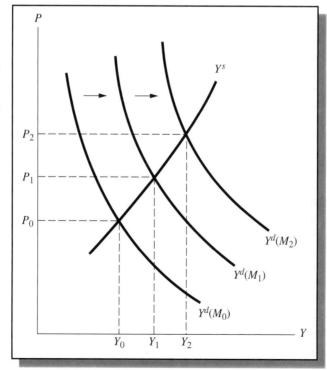

the monetarist position can be represented as asserting that changes in M are *required* for significant shifts in the aggregate demand curve. Money is the only important systematic influence on aggregate demand.

Left unanswered is the question of what determines aggregate supply. The real variables that determine the position of the aggregate supply curve will, in the monetarist view, determine the level of real output *in the long run* (see proposition 2). There is also the question of the slope of the aggregate supply curve and, consequently, the proportions of a money-induced rise in nominal income that go to increase output and price, respectively. This is the central question of the next chapter. In the following section, we analyze the differing views of monetarists and Keynesians on the relative effectiveness of fiscal and monetary policies. Here the issue is the effect of these policies on aggregate demand. Whether the change in aggregate demand primarily affects prices or output is not crucial to this analysis, and we revert to the use of the *IS–LM* curve graph to illustrate these policy differences.

10.3 FISCAL AND MONETARY POLICY: MONETARISTS VERSUS KEYNESIANS

Fiscal Policy

The monetarist and Keynesian frameworks produce quite different views about the effectiveness of fiscal policy changes. The monetarist view on the effectiveness of fiscal policy has been expressed by Milton Friedman as follows: "I come to the main point—in my opinion, the state of the budget by itself has no significant effect on the course of nominal income, on deflation, or on cyclical fluctuations."[4] In reference to the Keynesian proposition that fiscal policy was effective, Friedman wrote: "The 'monetarists' rejected this proposition and maintained that fiscal policy by itself is largely ineffective, that what matters is what happens to the quantity of money."[5]

When Friedman discusses the independent effects of fiscal policy, the question at issue, he means the effects of changes in the government budget *holding constant the quantity of money.* Consider an increase in government spending. If tax rates are not changed, which has been our usual assumption when we consider one policy change at a time, the new spending must be financed by printing money or by selling bonds. Similarly for a tax cut, if spending is to be unchanged, lost tax revenues must be replaced by sales of bonds to the public or by printing new money.

If a tax cut or spending increase is financed by printing new money, we have both a monetary policy action (M increases) and a fiscal policy action (G increases or T falls). In terms of the *IS–LM* framework, both the *IS* and *LM* curves shift. Monetarists *do not* argue that this type of policy change will be ineffective. They do argue that the policy effect will come mainly because the supply of money changes. The controversy is over what Friedman refers to as the effect of a change in the federal budget *by itself*, meaning without an accompanying change in the quantity of

---

[4]Milton Friedman and Walter Heller, *Monetary Versus Fiscal Policy* (New York: Norton, 1969), p. 51.
[5]Friedman, *The Counter-revolution in Monetary Theory*, p. 18.

Figure 10.5

Effects of an Increase in Government Spending: The Monetarist Case

An increase in government spending shifts the IS schedule from IS_0 to IS_1. With the relatively flat IS schedule and nearly vertical LM schedule, this fiscal policy action has little effect on income (Y rises only from Y_0 to Y_1).

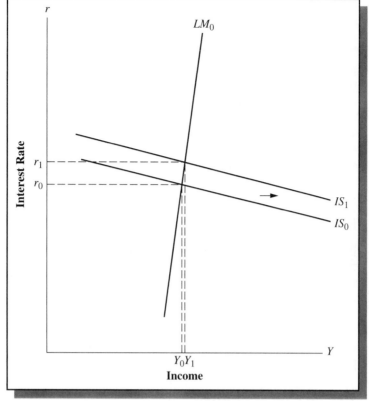

money. This means, in the case of a tax cut or spending increase, that the deficit created by these actions would be financed completely by sales of bonds to the public. The monetarist position is that such policy actions will have little systematic effect on nominal income (prices or real output) over short-run periods of perhaps one to three years.

The reasons monetarists reach this conclusion can be seen from Figure 10.5. There we consider the effects of an increase in government spending when we accept the monetarist assumptions about the slopes of the IS and LM curves. An increase in government spending from G_0 to G_1 shifts the IS curve to the right, from IS_0 to IS_1. The effect of the increase in government spending in the monetarist case is to cause the interest rate to rise (from r_0 to r_1). Income is changed only slightly (from Y_0 to Y_1). Why?

In essence, the explanation has already been supplied in the discussion about the dependence of the relative effectiveness of monetary and fiscal policy on the slopes of the IS and LM curves, in particular on the assumed magnitudes of the interest elasticities of money demand and of investment demand. Monetarists assume that the interest elasticity of money demand is small; the LM curve is steep. The increase in government spending increases aggregate demand initially. As income begins to rise, the demand for transactions balances increases. With the money supply fixed, this increase puts upward pressure on the interest rate, which rises until money supply and demand are again equal. If money demand is interest-inelastic, a large increase in the interest rate is required to reequilibrate money demand with the fixed money supply.

The *IS* curve is relatively flat in the monetarist view. Investment demand is highly sensitive to changes in the interest rate. Therefore, the rise in the interest rate required to keep the money market in equilibrium will cause private-sector aggregate demand to decline substantially as government spending begins to stimulate income. This reduction in private-sector aggregate demand is what we referred to in Chapter 4 as "crowding out." In the monetarist model, crowding out occurs almost dollar for dollar with an increase in government spending. On net, aggregate demand and, hence, income are increased very little by an increase in government spending.

Monetary Policy

Both monetarists and modern Keynesians believe that monetary policy actions have substantial and sustained effects on nominal income. The early Keynesians did, as we have seen, doubt the effectiveness of monetary policy. At one stage in the debate over monetarism (perhaps circa 1945–50), it might have been correct to refer to Keynesians as "fiscalists" relying solely on fiscal policy, in contrast to the monetarist reliance on monetary policy. This is not the case today. The difference today between Keynesians and monetarists over monetary policy concerns not *whether* monetary policy can affect income but *how* monetary policy should be used to stabilize income.

The Monetarist Position

Monetarists believe that changes in the quantity of money are the dominant influence on changes in nominal income and, for the short run, on changes in real income as well. It follows that stability in the behavior of the money supply would go a long way toward producing stability in income growth. Friedman traces most past instability in income growth to unstable money growth. Because of the importance of money and because of what Friedman regards as past mistakes in money management, his position on monetary policy is as follows:

> My own prescription is still that the monetary authority go all the way in avoiding such swings by adopting publicly the policy of achieving a specified rate of growth in a specified monetary total. The precise rate of growth, like the precise monetary total, is less important than the adoption of some stated and known rate.[6]

To give an example, the monetary authority might announce and achieve a target rate of growth in M1 (currency plus checkable deposits) of 5 percent per year. Friedman believes that nominal income growth would then be approximately 5 percent per year. If the trend growth in real income were 3 percent per year, the price level would

---

[6]Milton Friedman, "The Role of Monetary Policy," *American Economic Review*, 58 (March 1968), p. 16.

rise by about 2 percent per year. The 5 percent level is not crucial, but whatever level is picked, Friedman wants a constant growth rate in the money stock.

Today most monetarists propose alternative rules for money growth that are less inflexible than Friedman's constant money growth rate rule. Reasons for these alternatives are considered in section 10.4. The common element in the monetarist proposals, however, is that monetary policy should be determined by a rule, not left to the discretion of policymakers.

If we accept the reasoning that one will do pretty well with such a monetary rule, the question still remains: Why not the best? Why not use monetary policy to offset even minor shocks that affect income? Why not "fine-tune" the economy? Friedman's answer is, "We simply do not know enough to be able to recognize minor disturbances when they occur or to be able to predict either what their effects will be with any precision or what monetary policy is required to offset their effects."[7] Friedman and other monetarists believe that changes in the money supply will have a strong effect on income, but that there is a lag, with the bulk of the effect occurring only after 6 to 18 months. Thus, to offset a minor shock, we must be able to predict its size and when it will affect the economy several quarters in advance. Friedman and other monetarists do not think we know enough to do this.

Monetarist economist Allan Meltzer, on the basis of a study of the accuracy of economic forecasts, concluded that "forecasts of main economic aggregates are so inaccurate—so wide of the mark on average—that discretionary policies based on forecasts are unlikely to stabilize the economy."[8] To again quote Milton Friedman: "There is a saying that the best is often the enemy of the good, which seems highly relevant. The goal of an extremely high degree of economic stability is certainly a splendid one; our ability to attain it, however, is limited."[9]

Contrast with the Keynesians

Keynesians believe that both monetary and fiscal policy should be *actively* adjusted to offset shocks to the economy. Franco Modigliani, a leading Keynesian, expressed this view (which he characterized as nonmonetarist) as follows:

> Nonmonetarists accept what I regard to be the fundamental practical message of *The General Theory*: that a private enterprise economy using an intangible money *needs* to be stabilized, *can* be stabilized, and, therefore, *should* be stabilized by appropriate monetary and fiscal policies.[10]

Keynesians favor active discretionary monetary as well as fiscal policy actions. They oppose money growth rate rules espoused by Friedman and other monetarists.

The first explanation for these differing views is the disagreement between monetarists and Keynesians concerning the need for active stabilization policies. Whereas monetarists view the private sector as stable and "shock-absorbing,"

---

[7]Ibid., p. 14.

[8]Allan Meltzer, "Limits of Short-Run Stabilization Policy," *Economic Inquiry*, 25 (January 1987), p. 1.

[9]Milton Friedman, *The Optimum Quantity of Money and Other Essays* (Chicago: Aldine, 1969), p. 187.

[10]*The General Theory* was Keynes's major work. Franco Modigliani, "The Monetarist Controversy, or Should We Forsake Stabilization Policies?" *American Economic Review*, 67 (March 1977), p. 1.

Keynesians see the private sector as shock-producing and unstable. This is not to say that Keynesians believe that without government stabilization policies we would constantly experience depressions and hyperinflations, but rather that shocks would result in substantial prolonged deviations from conditions of full employment and price stability.

A second source of the differing views of monetarists and Keynesians is also evident from Modigliani's statement. He believes that we *can* stabilize the economy. We can predict shocks that will hit the economy and design policies to combat them. To be sure, there will be errors, but overall such policies will result in more stable economic performance than we would have with simple policy rules.

10.4 UNSTABLE VELOCITY AND THE DECLINING POLICY INFLUENCE OF MONETARISM

The peak in monetarist influence on policy came at the end of the 1970s. In October of 1979, the U.S. Federal Reserve began what has been called its *monetarist experiment*—an attempt to get control of the money supply to rein in an accelerating inflation rate. Also in 1979, the Thatcher government came to power in the United Kingdom and adopted a monetary policy along monetarist lines. In the post-1980 period, however, the influence of the monetarists eroded as the money–income relationship showed increasing instability.

Recent Instability in the Money–Income Relationship

Figure 10.6 shows the velocity of the M1 measure of the money supply for each year from 1979 through 2003. In the monetarist view, changes in velocity should be only a minor factor in explaining the cyclical behavior of nominal GDP. If the money supply and nominal GDP move closely together, then velocity, which is the ratio of the two (PY/M), should be stable. Figure 10.6 indicates, however, that velocity was subject to considerable instability after 1980. Especially notable are the sharp declines in velocity during 1983–86, 1989–93, and then a sharp rise in velocity post-1993.

Monetarist Reaction

Because of the instability in the money–income relationship, *The Economist* was led to ask in 1986, "Is this the year monetarism vanishes?" The data from the post-1980 period have led monetarists to reconsider their position in some areas but not to change their fundamental views.

Friedman and other monetarists have a number of explanations for the instability of velocity in the post-1980 period. They believe that lower interest rates and lower inflation rates in the 1980s reduced the opportunity cost of holding money. This led to a general increase in the demand for money relative to income (fall in velocity) for much of that decade. There was also substantial deregulation of deposit markets

Figure 10.6
M1 Velocity,
1979–2003

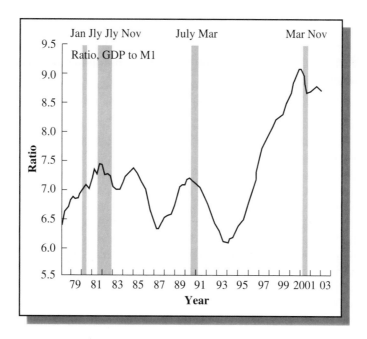

in the 1980s, leading to innovations in deposit markets that caused instability in money demand and therefore velocity. These innovations, which will be discussed in Chapter 22, continued in the 1990s.

Still, as noted previously, the instability in velocity has led many monetarists to favor more flexible rules for money growth than Friedman's constant money growth rate rule. Some have moved away from support of money growth rate rules to rules that directly target the inflation rate. Such rules will be discussed in Chapter 18. Monetarists, however, continue to support Friedman, who concludes that "the long and the short of it is that I remain convinced of a fundamental tenet of monetarism: Money is too important to be left to the central bankers."[11] Thus, monetarists continue to support rules over discretion for monetary policy.

10.5 CONCLUSION

This chapter examined the monetarist belief in the importance of money. According to the monetarist position, money is the dominant determinant of nominal income. This position contrasts with the modern Keynesian view that money is one of several variables having important effects on income. These different positions on the importance of money lead monetarists and Keynesians to different conclusions about monetary and fiscal policy.

---

[11]Milton Friedman, "M1's Hot Streak Gave Keynesians a Bad Idea," in Peter McClelland, ed., *Readings in Introductory Macroeconomics* (New York: McGraw-Hill, 1988), p. 78, reprinted from the *Wall Street Journal*.

The monetarist view is that fiscal policy actions have little independent effect on the level of economic activity. Keynesians believe that fiscal policy actions exert significant and sustained influence on the level of economic activity. Fiscal policy variables are among the important nonmonetary factors that they believe affect income.

On monetary policy, the difference between monetarists and modern Keynesians is not about the potential of monetary policy to significantly affect economic activity; both believe monetary policy has strong effects. They differ on what they view as the proper role for monetary policy. Monetarists are *noninterventionists*. They favor a rule for monetary policy that creates an environment in which a stable private sector of the economy can function effectively. Keynesians are *interventionists*. They see the need for active discretionary monetary and fiscal policies to keep an unstable private economy on track.

Given the erosion in the policy influence of monetarism, it might be surprising that a nonmonetarist economist, Bradford De Long, would in 2000 entitle an article "The Triumph of Monetarism." Also surprising would be that Ben Bernanke, another nonmonetarist and a member of the Board of Governors of the Federal Reserve, would write in 2003, "Friedman's monetary framework has been so influential that, in its broad outlines at least, it has nearly become identical with modern monetary theory and practice."[12]

But central features of Milton Friedman's framework *have* become part of the common wisdom concerning monetary policy even as specific policy recommendations of the monetarists have lost influence. Rule-based monetary policies have gained popularity among academic economists and central bankers. The dominant role of monetary policy in determining inflation has been widely accepted. Friedman's views on the limitations of stabilization policy also remain highly influential. It is to one of these limitations to which we now turn our attention.

REVIEW QUESTIONS AND PROBLEMS

1. Compare Keynesian and monetarist views on how the velocity of money is determined. How do their differing views on velocity affect their respective policy conclusions?
2. Why were early Keynesian economists so pessimistic about the effectiveness of monetary policy?
3. Compare Milton Friedman's formulation of the money demand function with the Keynesian specification in previous chapters.
4. Show how the *IS* and *LM* curves look in the monetarist view. Use these *IS* and *LM* curves to illustrate the monetarist conclusions about the relative effectiveness of monetary and fiscal policy.
5. Compare monetarist and Keynesian views on the proper conduct of fiscal policy. For both monetarists and Keynesians, explain not only their conclusions con-

---

[12]References here are to Bradford De Long, "The Triumph of Monetarism," *Journal of Economic Perspectives*, 14 (Winter 2000), pp. 83–94; and Ben Bernanke, "Remarks," Federal Reserve Bank of Dallas Conference (October 2003).

cerning fiscal policy but also how those conclusions are related to their respective theories.

6. Compare monetarist and modern Keynesian views on the proper conduct of monetary policy. For both monetarists and Keynesians, explain not only their conclusions concerning monetary policy but also how those conclusions are related to their respective theories.

7. Analyze the effects of a decrease in taxes from T_0 to T_1 in the monetarist framework. In your answer be sure to take account of the financing of the deficit that results from the tax cut. How are the equilibrium levels of income and the interest rate affected by the tax cut?

Chapter 11

Output, Inflation, and Unemployment: Alternative Views

*T*his chapter examines alternative views of the relationship between the levels of output and unemployment and the rate of inflation. In Chapter 1, we saw that for the 1953–69 period there was a negative relationship between unemployment and inflation (see Figure 1.5*a*), but the post-1970 relationship between these two variables was much less clear (Figure 1.5*b*). Some explanations for the shift in this relationship are provided in this chapter, beginning with Milton Friedman's theory of the natural rate of unemployment. We also examine Keynesian views on the output-inflation trade-off, including Friedman's natural rate concept. Finally, we consider how thinking about the natural rate of unemployment has varied over the 35 years since Friedman introduced the concept and evaluate the current relevance of the concept.

11.1 THE NATURAL RATE THEORY

In Chapter 10, we analyzed the monetarist proposition that *short-run* changes in the money supply are the primary determinant of fluctuations in output and employment. However, the monetarists place a limitation on the real effects of changes in the money supply, as expressed in the second of the monetarist propositions given in Chapter 10.

> In the long run the influence of money is primarily on the price level and other *nominal* magnitudes. In the long run, *real* variables, such as real output and employment, are determined by real, not monetary, factors.

The basis of this proposition is the theory of the **natural rates of unemployment and output** developed by Milton Friedman.[1]

According to the natural rate theory, there exists an equilibrium level of output and an accompanying rate of unemployment determined by the supply of factors of production, technology, and institutions of the economy (i.e., determined by real factors). This is Friedman's natural rate. Changes in aggregate demand, which Friedman believes are dominated by changes in the supply of money, cause temporary movements of the economy away from the natural rate. Expansionary monetary policies, for example, move output above the natural rate and move the unemployment rate below the natural rate for a time. The increased demand resulting from such an expansionary policy would also cause prices to rise. In the short run, the price adjustment would not be complete, as in the classical theory where increases in demand cause prices to rise but do not affect output. *The monetarists do not agree with the classical position that output is completely supply-determined even in the short run.*

Friedman does believe that equilibrating forces cause output and employment to return to their natural rate over a longer period. It is not possible, in Friedman's view, for the government to use monetary policy to maintain the economy permanently at a level of output that holds the unemployment rate below the natural rate. At least it is not possible for the policymakers to do so unless they are willing to accept an ever-accelerating rate of inflation. The natural rate of unemployment is defined by Friedman as the rate "which has the property that it is consistent with equilibrium in the structure of *real* wage rates."[2] Thus the natural rate of unemployment, or the corresponding natural rate of employment, will be such that labor demand equals labor supply at an equilibrium real wage, as depicted in Figure 11.1a.

The labor demand schedule in part *a* of the figure is the familiar marginal product of labor schedule (MPN). At N^*, the natural rate of employment, labor demand is equated with labor supply, where in drawing the labor supply schedule, $N^s[W/(P^e = P)]$, we stipulate that the price level expected by labor suppliers is equal to the actual price level ($P^e = P$). Only at this level of employment is there no tendency for the real wage to change. Labor demand and supply are equated. Moreover, labor suppliers have a correct expectation of the price level. If such were not the case, labor supply would tend to change as workers perceived that their expectations were in error.

The natural rate of unemployment can be found simply by subtracting those employed from the total labor force to find the number unemployed and then expressing this number as a percentage of the total labor force. Using the production function in Figure 11.1b, we can find the level of output that will result from an employment level N^*. This is the natural level of output, Y^*.

Figure 11.1 shows that the natural rates of output and employment depend on the supply of factors of production and the technology of the economy—supply-side

> **natural rates of unemployment and output** in the monetarist model are determined by *real* supply-side factors: the capital stock, the size of the labor force, and the level of technology.

---

[1]The theory of the natural rate of unemployment was also developed independently by Edmund Phelps. See, for example, the contributions by Phelps and others in Edmund Phelps, ed., *Employment and Inflation Theory* (New York: Norton, 1970).

[2]Milton Friedman, "The Role of Monetary Policy," *American Economic Review*, 58 (March 1968), p. 8.

Figure 11.1
Natural Rates of Employment and Output

In part *a*, the natural rate of employment (N^*) is determined at the point where labor supply is equated with labor demand *and* with labor suppliers' correct evaluation of the price level ($P^e = P$). The natural rate of output (Y^*) is determined in part *b* along the production function.

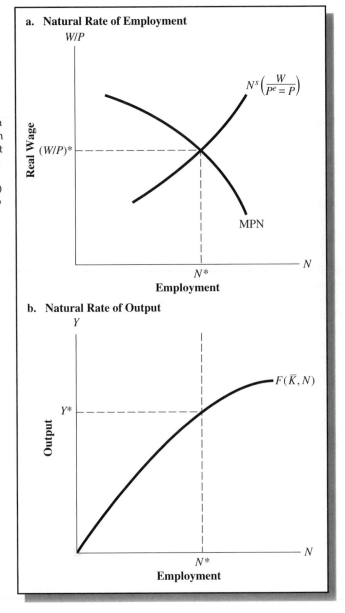

a. Natural Rate of Employment

W/P

Real Wage

$(W/P)^*$

$N^s\left(\dfrac{W}{P^e = P}\right)$

MPN

N^*

Employment

N

b. Natural Rate of Output

Y

Output

Y^*

$F(\bar{K}, N)$

N^*

Employment

N

factors. The natural rates of output and employment do *not* depend on aggregate demand. All this is much the same as in the classical system; the difference between the monetarists and the classical economists is that the monetarists do not assume that the economy is necessarily at these natural levels of employment and output in the short run.

As do the Keynesians, the monetarists assume that labor suppliers do not have perfect information about the real wage. They must base their labor supply decisions on the expected real wage (W/P^e). Therefore, in the short run, labor supply may not be given by the supply schedule in Figure 11.1a; P^e may not equal P. In this case, employment and hence output will not be at their natural rates.

11.2 MONETARY POLICY, OUTPUT, AND INFLATION: A MONETARIST VIEW

To see why Friedman and other monetarists believe that output and employment diverge from their natural rates temporarily, but will eventually be drawn to these rates, we examine Friedman's analysis of the short-run and long-run consequences of an increase in the rate of growth in the money supply.

Monetary Policy in the Short Run

Let us begin with a situation in which the economy is in equilibrium at the natural rate of unemployment and output. Also suppose that the money supply (and hence nominal income) has been growing at a rate equal to the rate of growth of real output. Thus the price level is assumed to have been stable for some time. Suppose now that the rate of growth in the money supply is increased above the rate consistent with price stability. For concreteness, assume that the rate of growth in the money supply rises from 3 percent to 5 percent.

The increase in the growth rate of the money supply will stimulate aggregate demand and, as a consequence, nominal income. The *short-run* consequences of this increase in aggregate demand are described by Friedman as follows:

> To begin with, much or most of the rise in income will take the form of an increase in output and employment rather than in prices. People have been expecting prices to be stable, and prices and wages have been set for some time in the future on that basis. It takes time for people to adjust to a new state of demand. Producers will tend to react to the initial expansion in aggregate demand by increasing output, employees by working longer hours, and the unemployed by taking jobs now offered at former nominal wages. This much is pretty standard doctrine.[3]

The *standard doctrine* to which Friedman refers is the **Phillips curve**. The Phillips curve (PC) is a negative relationship between the unemployment rate (U) and the inflation rate ($\dot{P}$), such as that plotted in Figure 11.2. High rates of growth in aggregate demand stimulate output and hence lower the unemployment rate. Such high rates of growth in demand also cause an increase in the rate at which prices rise (i.e., raise the inflation rate). Thus the Phillips curve postulates a trade-off between inflation and unemployment; lower rates of unemployment can be achieved, but only at the cost of higher inflation rates.[4] Friedman is agreeing with this notion of a trade-off between inflation and unemployment *in the short run*.

Phillips curve
is the schedule showing the relationship between the unemployment and inflation rates

---

[3]Ibid., p. 10.
[4]The Phillips curve derives its name from the British economist A. W. H. Phillips, who studied the trade-off between unemployment and wage inflation (a key element in price inflation) in the British economy.

Figure 11.2
The Phillips Curve

In the short run, an increase in the rate of growth in the money supply moves the economy from point A to point B along the short-run Phillips curve (PC). Unemployment declines, and inflation rises.

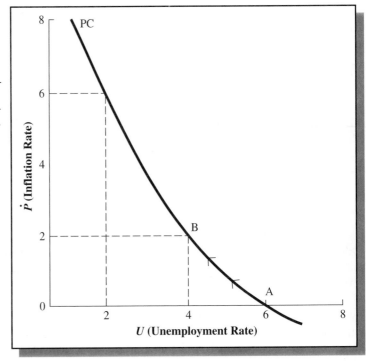

Monetary Policy in the Long Run

The distinctive element in Friedman's analysis is his view of the long-run effects of monetary policy. Here the notion of the natural rate of unemployment comes into play. We have just considered the short-run effects of an increase in the rate of growth of the money supply from 3 percent to 5 percent. In terms of Figure 11.2, the original equilibrium was with stable prices ($\dot{P} = 0$) and unemployment equal to the natural rate assumed to be 6 percent (point A in Figure 11.2). We assume that, as a result of the increase in the rate of growth in the money supply, the economy moves to a new *short-run* equilibrium, with unemployment reduced to 4 percent and an inflation rate at 2 percent (point B in Figure 11.2). The expansionary aggregate demand policy lowers the unemployment rate below the natural rate.

Friedman accepts this outcome:

> But it describes only the initial effects. Because selling prices of products typically respond to an unanticipated rise in nominal demand faster than prices of factors of production, real wages received have gone down—though real wages anticipated by employees went up, since employees implicitly evaluated the wages offered at the earlier price level. Indeed, the simultaneous fall *ex post* in real wages to employers and rise *ex ante* to employees is what enabled employment to increase. But the decline *ex post* in real wages will soon come to affect anticipations. Employees will start to reckon on rising prices of the things they buy and to demand higher nominal wages for the

future. "Market" unemployment is below the natural level. There is an excess demand for labor so real wages will tend to rise toward their initial level.[5]

Consider this explanation. Friedman points out that in the short run, product prices increase faster than factor prices, the crucial factor price being the money wage. Thus the real wage (W/P) falls. This is necessary for output to increase, because firms must be on the labor demand curve shown in Figure 11.1. Firms expand employment and output only with a decline in the real wage.

Friedman does not argue that workers are always on the labor supply curve shown in Figure 11.1. That curve expresses labor supply as a function of the *actual* real wage, and Friedman does not assume that workers know the real wage. In the short run, after a period of stable prices, workers are assumed to evaluate nominal wage offers "at the earlier price level." Prices have risen, but workers have not yet seen this rise, and they will increase labor supply if offered a higher money wage *even if this increase in the money wage is less than the increase in the price level, even if the real wage is lower*. In the short run, labor supply increases because the *ex ante* (or expected) real wage is higher as a result of the higher nominal wage and unchanged view about the behavior of prices. Labor demand increases because of the fall in the *ex post* (actual) real wage paid by the employer. Consequently, unemployment can be pushed below the natural rate.

This situation is temporary, for workers eventually observe the higher price level and demand higher money wages. In terms of Figure 11.1, the real wage has been pushed below $(W/P)^*$, the wage that clears the labor market once labor suppliers correctly perceive the price level and, hence, the real wage. At a lower real wage, an excess demand for labor pushes the real wage back up to its equilibrium level, and this rise in the real wage causes employment to return to the natural rate shown in Figure 11.1.

The implications for the Phillips curve of this long-run adjustment back to the natural rate are illustrated in Figure 11.3. The schedule labeled $PC(\dot{P}^e = 0)$ is the short-run Phillips curve from Figure 11.2. Here the curve is explicitly drawn for a given expected rate of inflation on the part of the suppliers of labor, in this case stable prices ($\dot{P}^e = 0$, where $\dot{P}^e$ is the expected rate of inflation). We have already analyzed the process whereby an increased rate of growth of the money supply from 3 percent to 5 percent moves the economy in the short run from point A to point B.

As suppliers of labor anticipate that prices are rising, the Phillips curve will shift upward to the right. Suppliers of labor will demand a higher rate of increase in money wages and, as a consequence, a higher rate of inflation will now correspond to any given unemployment rate. If money growth is continued at 5 percent, the economy will return to the natural 6 percent rate of unemployment, but now with an inflation rate of 2 percent instead of the initial stable price level. In terms of Figure 11.3, this longer-run adjustment moves the economy from point B to point C.

A policymaker who is not content with this return to 6 percent unemployment (the natural rate) may still pursue a target unemployment rate below the natural rate by again increasing the rate of growth in the money supply. Let us suppose that this time the policymaker increases money supply growth from 5 percent to 7 percent. The

---

[5]Friedman, "The Role of Monetary Policy," p. 10.

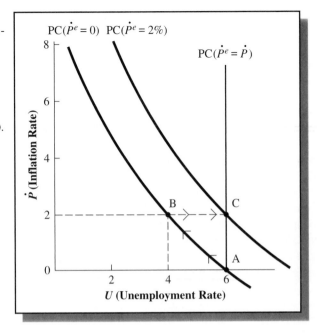

Figure 11.3
Short-Run and Long-Run Phillips Curves

As labor suppliers come to anticipate the higher inflation rate, the short-run Phillips curve shifts from PC ($\dot{P}^e = 0$) to PC($\dot{P}^e = 2\%$). The unemployment rate returns to the natural rate of 6 percent; the inflation rate remains higher at 2 percent (we move from point B to point C).

effects of this further expansion of aggregate demand are illustrated in Figure 11.4. Until the suppliers of labor come to anticipate the further increase in the inflation rate, employment will expand. The economy will move to a point, such as D in Figure 11.4, with unemployment below the natural rate of unemployment.

Suppliers of labor, after a time, will come to anticipate the higher inflation that corresponds to a 7 percent growth in the money supply. The short-run Phillips curve will shift to the schedule labeled PC($\dot{P}^e = 4\%$), and the economy will return to the natural rate of unemployment, with the inflation rate increased to 4 percent (7 percent money growth minus 3 percent growth in real income). In terms of Figure 11.4, we move from point D to point E. If the policymaker persists in attempting to "peg" the unemployment rate, money supply growth will again increase, for example, to 9 percent. This increase will move the economy in the short run to point F, but in the long run to point G, with a still higher rate of inflation.

Eventually, the policymaker will conclude that inflation has become a more serious problem than unemployment (or will be replaced by a policymaker who has this view), and the acceleration of inflation will stop. Notice, however, that when inflation has persisted for a long time, inflationary expectations become built into the system. At a point such as point G in Figure 11.4, expansionary aggregate demand policies have increased the expected (and actual) inflation rate to 6 percent (9 percent money growth minus 3 percent growth in real income). An attempt to lower inflation by slowing the rate of growth in the money supply, let us suppose all the way back to the initial noninflationary 3 percent, will *not* immediately move the economy back to a point such as the initial point A. In the short run, we would move along the short-run Phillips curve that corresponds to an expected inflation rate of 6 percent, to a point such as H in Figure 11.4, with high inflation and unemployment above the natural rate. Just as it took time for suppliers of labor to recognize that the rate of

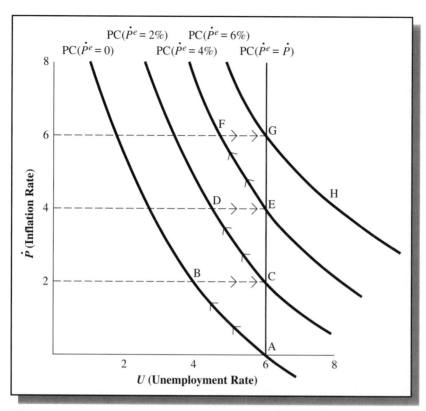

Figure 11.4 Effect of an Attempt to "Peg" the Unemployment Rate

Increases in money growth, to 5 percent, then 7 percent, then 9 percent, result in temporary reductions in unemployment (movements from C to D and from E to F, for example). But in the longer run we simply move up the vertical Phillips curve (to points E and G, for example).

inflation had increased and, hence, to demand a faster rate of growth in money wages, it will take time for them to recognize that the inflation rate has slowed and to modify their money wage demands to a level compatible with price stability. In the meantime, in the monetarist view, the economy must suffer from high inflation and high unemployment.

Monetarists believe that expansionary monetary policy can only temporarily move the unemployment rate below the natural rate. There is a trade-off between unemployment and inflation only in the short run. In terms of Figures 11.3 and 11.4, the downward-sloping short-run Phillips curves *that are drawn for given expected inflation rates* illustrate the short-run trade-off between unemployment and inflation. The long-run Phillips curve showing the relationship between inflation and unemployment *when expected inflation has time to adjust to the actual inflation rate* ($\dot{P} = \dot{P}^e$)—*when inflation is fully anticipated*—is vertical, as shown in Figures 11.3 and 11.4.

Friedman's theory of the natural rate of unemployment and output is the theoretical foundation for the monetarist belief that in the long run the influence of the money supply is primarily on the price level and other nominal variables. Real variables such as output and employment have time to adjust to their natural rates in the long run. Those natural rates of output and employment depend on real variables such as factor supplies (labor and capital) and technology.

Policy Implications

The theory of the natural rate of unemployment implies that the policymaker cannot peg the unemployment rate at some arbitrarily determined target rate. Attempts to lower the unemployment rate below the natural level by increasing the growth in aggregate demand will be successful only in the short run. The unemployment rate will gradually return to the natural rate, and the lasting effect of the expansionary policy will be a higher inflation rate.

Monetarists believe that the natural rate theory strengthens the case for non-interventionist policies. They believe that the record of the U.S. economy in the post–World War II years provides evidence that interventionist policies to affect unemployment resulted in only short-run gains and were responsible for increased inflation rates. Consider, for example, the behavior of unemployment, inflation, and money growth rates for the United States for the years 1961 to 1971, a time-period where Keynesian influence on policy was at a highpoint, as shown in Table 11.1.

According to the monetarist interpretation, expansionary policies in the mid-1960s temporarily lowered unemployment from an average rate of 5.8 percent for 1961–64 to an average rate of 3.8 percent for the 1965–69 period. In the monetarist view, this decline in unemployment resulted from the increased rate of growth in the money supply beginning in 1964, which is evident in the table. The natural rate

Table 11.1 Unemployment, Inflation, and Money Growth Rates for the United States, 1961–71

Year	Unemployment Rate[a]	Inflation Rate[b]	Money Growth Rate[c]
1961	6.7	0.7	2.1
1962	5.5	1.2	2.2
1963	5.7	1.6	2.9
1964	5.2	1.2	4.0
1965	4.5	1.9	4.2
1966	3.8	3.4	4.7
1967	3.8	3.0	3.9
1968	3.6	4.7	7.2
1969	3.5	6.1	6.1
1970	4.9	5.5	3.8
1971	5.9	3.4	6.7

[a]Civilian unemployment rate (percent).
[b]Annual percentage rate of change in the consumer price index.
[c]Annual percentage rate of growth in M1 (currency held by the public plus checkable deposits).

theory suggests that at first the increased money growth would stimulate output and employment, the effect on prices coming with a longer lag. Consequently, the theory would have predicted the higher inflation rates observed in the table for the later 1960s. The natural rate theory would also have predicted the reversal of the downward movement in the unemployment rate, the average unemployment rate for 1970–71 being 5.4 percent, even though the inflation rate remained high relative to the early 1960s.[6]

Friedman's analysis of the Phillips curve can also be used to explain the simultaneously high inflation and high unemployment later in the 1970s. Excessive monetary growth had eventually resulted in entrenched expectations of high inflation. These raised the average inflation rate corresponding to a given unemployment rate; the Phillips curve was shifted upward. When the Federal Reserve sometimes shifted toward a more anti-inflationary policy, the economy operated at points like H in Figure 11.4, with high inflation and unemployment.

In the 1980s, the monetarists saw the high unemployment early in the decade as again the result of previous excessive monetary growth that had created high inflationary expectations. As the Federal Reserve shifted to a more prolonged restrictive policy, at first we moved along a very unfavorable short-run Phillips curve. Only after the actual inflation rate fell did the expected inflation rate gradually fall, causing the short-run Phillips curve to shift downward. In the monetarist view, this eventual downward shift enabled unemployment to decline in the late 1980s and in the 1990s as the inflation rate remained low.

11.3 A KEYNESIAN VIEW OF THE OUTPUT–INFLATION TRADE-OFF

Friedman's theory of the natural rate of unemployment explains both the short-run and long-run relationship between inflation and unemployment. What is the Keynesian view of the Phillips curve, and how does it differ from the natural rate view? How can Keynesians defend activist policies to affect output and employment if the natural rate theory is correct and such policies have only a temporary effect on output and employment? These questions are considered in this section.

To anticipate our conclusions, we find the following:

1. Traditional Keynesian models, such as those considered in Chapter 9, also imply that once the economy has fully adjusted to a change in inflation (caused, for example, by a change in money supply growth), output and employment will be unaffected. These Keynesian models also imply a vertical long-run Phillips curve.
2. Keynesians, however, draw different policy conclusions from this absence of a long-run trade-off between inflation and unemployment.

---

[6]The inflation rate did fall from 5.5 percent in 1970 to 3.4 percent in 1971, but this drop was in part because of mandatory price and wage controls instituted on August 15, 1971. The inflation rate before controls were imposed was still in excess of 5 percent.

The Phillips Curve: A Keynesian Interpretation

Keynesians' view of the relationship between the rate of inflation and the levels of employment and output follows directly from their theory of how price and output are determined. Here we relate that theory to the Phillips curve.

The Short-Run Phillips Curve

Figure 11.5 shows the effect on price, output, and employment of a sequence of expansionary policy actions increasing aggregate demand. The version of the Keynesian model here is the same as in section 9.4. The money wage is flexible, and labor supply is assumed to depend on the expected real wage (W/P^e), the money wage divided by the expected price level.

In the Keynesian system, an expansionary aggregate demand policy might be a monetary policy action, such as the increase in the rate of growth in the money supply analyzed in the preceding section, or it might be a fiscal policy action, such as a series of increases in government spending. In either case, policy will produce a series of shifts in the aggregate demand schedule, as shown in Figure 11.5a. As can be seen, the effects of these increases in aggregate demand will be to increase output (from Y_0 to Y_1, to Y_2, then to Y_3) and employment (from N_0 to N_1, to N_2, then to N_3), as well as the price level (from P_0 to P_1, to P_2, then to P_3). As employment increases, the unemployment rate will decline. The level of the money wage will increase.

Figure 11.5 Short-Run Effects of Increases in Aggregate Demand in the Keynesian Model

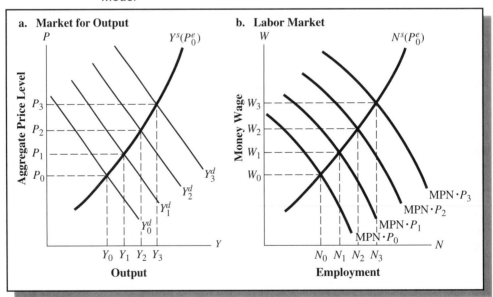

An expansionary aggregate demand policy, such as an increase in the rate of growth in the money supply will cause a series of shifts to the right in the aggregate demand schedule (from Y_0^d to Y_1^d, to Y_2^d, to Y_3^d). In the short run, output, the price level, and employment all rise.

These results can be interpreted in terms of a Phillips curve relationship. The more quickly aggregate demand grows, the larger will be the rightward shifts in the aggregate demand schedule, and, other things being equal, the faster will be the rate of growth in output and employment. For a given growth in the labor force, this means that the unemployment rate will be lower the faster the rate of growth in aggregate demand. As can also be seen from the example in Figure 11.5a, increases in aggregate demand cause the price level to rise, so again, other things being equal, the faster the growth of aggregate demand is, the higher the rate of inflation will be.

The Keynesian model, then, implies a trade-off between inflation and unemployment. High rates of growth in demand correspond to low levels of unemployment and high rates of inflation. Slower growth in aggregate demand means a lower inflation rate but a higher rate of unemployment. The Phillips curve implied by the Keynesian model is downward-sloping.

But is this a short-run or a long-run relationship? Notice that so far we are holding the expected price level constant. We are considering the effects of increases in demand in the short run. As explained in Chapter 9, Keynesians view the expected price level as depending primarily on the past behavior of prices. Thus, as successive periods go by with increases in the actual price level, the expected price level will rise. In the long run, we must take account of the effects of such increases in the expected price level. Because we did not do so in Figure 11.5, our results there, and the Phillips curve relationship derived from them, pertain to the short run. To emphasize their short-run relevance, we have labeled the labor supply curve $N^s(P_0^e)$ and the aggregate supply curve $Y^s(P_0^e)$ to indicate that these curves are drawn for the initial value of the expected price level. In Figure 11.6, we

Figure 11.6
The Phillips Curve:
The Keynesian
Perspective

In the short run, the Phillips curve implied by the Keynesian model is downward-sloping. In the long run in the Keynesian model, as in Friedman's analysis, the Phillips curve is vertical.

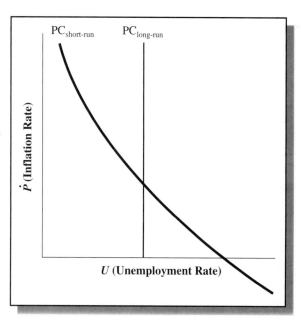

label the Phillips curve implied by the example in Figure 11.5 as the short-run Phillips curve, $PC_{\text{short-run}}$.[7]

The Long-Run Phillips Curve

In the long run, the expected price adjusts to the actual price. Suppliers of labor perceive the inflation that has resulted from the expansionary aggregate demand policy.

The longer-run adjustment of output and employment following an increase in aggregate demand is illustrated in Figure 11.7. Recall that, in the Keynesian system, labor supply depends on the expected real wage:

$$N^s = t\left(\frac{W}{P^e}\right) \tag{11.1}$$

Figure 11.7 Long-Run Effects of Increases in Aggregate Demand in the Keynesian Model

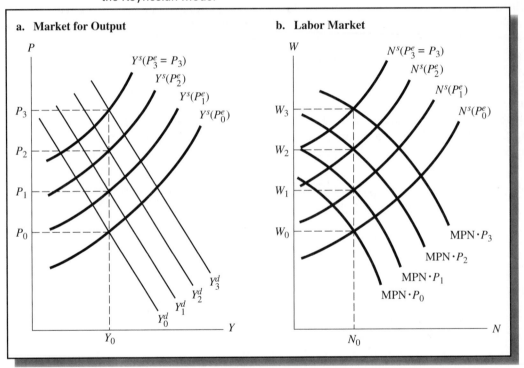

In the long run, leftward shifts in the labor supply and the aggregate supply schedules reverse the increases in output and employment that result from the expansionary aggregate demand policy. Output and employment return to their initial levels, Y_0 and N_0.

---

[7]The short-run nature of the downward-sloping Phillips curve was recognized before Friedman's work. Paul Samuelson and Robert Solow wrote in this context:

> All of our discussions has been phrased in short-run terms, dealing with what might happen in the next few years. . . . What we do in a policy way during the next few years might cause it [the Phillips curve] to shift in a definite way. [Paul Samuelson and Robert Solow, "Analytical Aspects of Anti-Inflation Policy," *American Economic Review*, 50 (May 1960), pp. 177–94.]

where the effect of the money wage on labor supply is positive and the effect of an increase in expected price is negative. As the expected price rises, the labor supply curve in Figure 11.5b shifts to the left. Less labor will be supplied at any money wage (W) because a given money wage corresponds to a lower expected real wage (W/P^e) after an increase in the expected price level. This shift in the labor supply curve is shown in Figure 11.7b. As the expected price level rises to P_1^e, to P_2^e, and then to P_3^e, the labor supply curve shifts to $N^s(P_1^e)$, to $N^s(P_2^e)$, then to $N^s(P_3^e = P_3)$.

As the labor supply curve shifts to the left, the level of employment for any given price level declines. We move back up on a given labor demand curve (which is drawn for a given price level). The increase in expected price lowers employment for any price level and, therefore, lowers output supplied at any price level. The aggregate supply curve also shifts upward to the left with each increase in expected price, reflecting this decline in output supplied at a given price level. These shifts in the supply curve are illustrated in Figure 11.7a.

The labor supply and aggregate supply curves continue to shift to the left until expected price and actual price are equal. The *long-run* equilibrium position is shown in Figure 11.7, where the labor supply curve is $N^s(P_3^e = P_3)$ and the aggregate supply curve is $Y^s(P_3^e = P_3)$. Notice that at this point income and employment have returned to their initial levels Y_0 and N_0. This must be the case, because output and employment can be maintained above Y_0 and N_0 only as long as the expected price is below the actual price—that is, only as long as labor suppliers underestimate inflation. Once the suppliers of labor correctly perceive the increases in the price level, they will demand increases in the money wage proportionate to the increase in the price level. At this point, the real wage will have returned to its initial level ($W_3/P_3 = W_0/P_0$). Both labor supply and labor demand will have returned to their initial levels. Consequently, employment and output will be at their initial levels of N_0 and Y_0.[8] An increase in aggregate demand increases output and employment and, as a consequence, lowers the unemployment rate only in the short run. As shown in Figure 11.6, the long-run Phillips curve is vertical in the Keynesian as well as the monetarist view.

Stabilization Policies for Output and Employment: The Keynesian View

Why does the absence of a long-run effect of aggregate demand on output and employment not lead the Keynesians to accept the monetarist noninterventionist policy position? The reason is that in the Keynesian view, aggregate demand policies are aimed at stabilizing output and employment in the *short run*.

The goal of such stabilization policies is to keep the economy at its equilibrium level in the face of shocks to aggregate demand or supply. In other words, the aim of *stabilization* policies is, as the name implies, to offset what would otherwise be

---

[8]In this discussion, we are ignoring elements of the Keynesian theory of labor supply that explain why the money wage is sticky in the *short run* (see section 9.3). We are not, for example, allowing for the effects of implicit or explicit labor contracts that prevent the money wage from adjusting to changes in demand conditions. Such factors are important in explaining the short-run behavior of the labor market. They are, however, factors that can slow but not ultimately prevent adjustment to the long-run equilibrium position.

destabilizing influences on output and employment. The focus of such policies is on the short run.

The monetarist noninterventionist policy conclusion is based, to a large extent, on the propositions discussed in Chapter 10. The private sector is basically stable if left to itself. Thus we would not expect large destabilizing shocks to private-sector demand for output. Even if such shifts in private-sector demand (undesired shifts in the *IS* schedule) occurred, they would have little effect on output if the money supply were held constant, because of the steepness of the *LM* schedule (see Figure 10.6). Small shocks may cause output and employment to deviate somewhat from the natural rate, but Friedman and other monetarists do not believe that our knowledge of the economy allows us to predict such shocks and design policies with sufficient precision to offset them.

We could still argue that, left to itself, the private sector produces equilibrium levels of output and employment that are "undesirable." Unemployment might be "too high." It could then be proposed that the role of monetary policy would be to ensure that unemployment and output were at "desirable" levels. The theory of the natural rate of unemployment shows that monetary policy cannot fulfill this role and indicates that attempts to achieve such arbitrary unemployment targets will have destabilizing effects on the price level in the long run.

If we do not accept the other propositions of the monetarists—and Keynesians do not—there is a short-run role for stabilization policies, whether monetary or fiscal. Keynesians believe that private-sector aggregate demand is unstable, primarily because of the instability of investment demand. Keynesians believe that *even for a given money supply*, such changes in private-sector aggregate demand can cause large and prolonged fluctuations in income. Consequently, they believe that monetary and fiscal policies should be used to offset such undesirable changes in aggregate demand and to stabilize income.

11.4 EVOLUTION OF THE NATURAL RATE CONCEPT

Milton Friedman's purpose in advancing the concept of natural rates of output and unemployment was to illustrate a limitation on monetary policy. Monetary policy could not permanently lower unemployment below the natural rate, not without causing an ever-accelerating inflation rate. Over the three decades since Friedman introduced the concept, however, much attention has also been focused on what determines the natural rate and what that value is for different countries.[9] If, for example, it is important for policymakers to avoid driving the unemployment rate below the natural rate and thereby setting off inflationary pressures, how do they know how much they can safely reduce the unemployment rate by? In the late 1990s this became a crucial question in the United States as the unemployment rate fell to a 30-year low.

---

[9]In this subsequent literature, the term *nonaccelerating inflation rate of unemployment* (*NAIRU*) is often used in place of *natural rate of unemployment*.

Determinants of the Natural Rate of Unemployment

Friedman did address the question of what determines the natural rate of unemployment. As we have seen, the natural rate is the rate that is consistent with an equilibrium real wage. Within our model of the labor market, this is simply an equilibrium between labor supply and demand subject to the condition that labor suppliers correctly estimate the price level. Friedman argued that, in the real world, the natural rate would be the rate "ground out" by an equilibrating process that would also be affected by "the actual structural characteristics of labor and commodity markets, including market imperfections, stochastic variability in demands and supplies, the cost of gathering information about job vacancies and labor availabilities, the cost of mobility, and so on."[10] These additional characteristics are ones we think of as determining the levels of *frictional* and *structural* unemployment. Low labor mobility in a country, for example, might be expected to lead to a higher natural rate of unemployment because, as demand shifted from one region of the country to another, workers would not be quick to follow. Poor information about job vacancies might also lead to a higher natural rate of unemployment, as workers take longer to find initial jobs or to move between jobs. In Friedman's view, then, the natural rate in each country will be determined by the structural characteristics of that country's commodity and labor markets.

Time-Varying Natural Rates of Unemployment

One observer commented that "when Milton Friedman first proposed the natural rate hypothesis . . . in 1968, it sounded like a royal edict had established the natural rate as another one of the universe's invariant constants."[11] If, as Friedman argued, the natural rate of unemployment depends on the structural characteristics of a country's commodity and labor markets, there is no reason why it need be constant over time, though we would expect changes to be gradual rather than abrupt. In fact, the behavior of unemployment over the past three decades indicates that if the natural rate of unemployment is a useful concept, it *must* be time-varying.

To see why, consider the unemployment figures for selected European countries in Table 11.2. Shown are average unemployment rates in eight countries for five periods ranging in length from 6 to 10 years. Averages over periods of this length should give reasonable approximations of the natural rate. If there is a tendency for unemployment to move to one rate, as suggested by the natural rate hypothesis, then actual unemployment should fluctuate around that rate—sometimes above it, sometimes below it. If averaging the unemployment rate over these periods does provide an estimate of the natural rate, then the natural rate of unemployment in the countries in the table has been rising over the past three decades. Almost all reached extremely high levels in the 1990s.[12]

---

[10]Friedman, "The Role of Monetary Policy," p. 11.

[11]Joseph Stiglitz, "Reflections on the Natural Rate Hypothesis," *Journal of Economic Perspectives*, 11 (Winter 1997), p. 3.

[12]There are other more sophisticated methods of estimating the natural rate of unemployment. These other estimates also indicate sharp increases in the natural rate for the countries in the table, as well as for some other European nations.

Table 11.2 European Unemployment Rates, Selected Periods (percent)

	1960–67	1968–73	1974–79	1980–89	1990–98
Belgium	2.1	2.3	5.7	11.1	11.5
Germany	0.8	0.8	3.5	6.8	8.8
Spain	2.3	2.7	5.3	17.5	20.5
France	1.5	2.6	4.5	9.0	11.2
Ireland	4.9	5.6	7.6	14.0	13.6
United Kingdom	1.5	2.4	4.2	9.5	7.9
Italy	4.9	5.7	6.6	9.9	11.7
Denmark	1.6	1.0	5.8	9.0	9.6

Sources: *Historical Statistics, 1960–89 (Paris: Organization for Economic Cooperation and Development)* and *Economic Outlook (December 1998)*.

In the United States, there is also evidence of a time-varying natural rate of unemployment. As in Europe, the unemployment rate trended upward in the United States in the 1970s and 1980s, though less sharply. In the 1990s, however, the behavior of the U.S. unemployment rate was quite different from unemployment rates in most European economies. The U.S. unemployment rate fell steadily throughout the 1990s to below 4 percent in 2000, before rising as a recession began in 2001.

Explaining Changing Natural Rates of Unemployment

If the natural rate of unemployment changes over time, is it still a useful concept? To use a changing natural rate as a guide for monetary policy, for example, policymakers would need to know what it was and where it was going. Policymakers would want to understand the factors that cause changes in the natural rate.

There is a large amount of literature on the apparent increase in the natural rate of unemployment in European countries.[13] One possible cause researchers have pointed to is rigidity in European labor markets, especially among nations that are members of the European Union. Labor market regulations in European Union countries include limitations on plant closings and provisions for mandatory severance pay that may discourage firms from expanding employment. European countries also have high degrees of unionization, which may result in wage rigidity. Moreover, European countries typically have generous unemployment compensation and other social benefits that make unemployment less painful.

Rising European unemployment may not be the result of *increases* in rigidities and the generosity of the social "safety net," but may be the result of growing competition from lower-wage countries, in particular the rapidly growing Asian economies, given the existing rigidity of labor markets and benefit levels. In other

---

[13]Two useful surveys of this literature are Olivier Blanchard and Lawrence F. Katz, "What We Know and Do Not Know About the Natural Rate of Unemployment," *Journal of Economic Perspectives*, 11 (Winter 1997), pp. 51–72; and Charles Bean, "European Unemployment: A Survey," *Journal of Economic Literature*, 32 (June 1994), pp. 573–619.

words, growing competition, instead of pulling down European real wages, raises European unemployment.

An alternative explanation for high European unemployment focuses on the idea that the current value of the unemployment rate may be strongly influenced by its past values, a property called **hysteresis**. From this perspective, high unemployment in the recessions of the 1970s and 1980s, which was *cyclical* in nature, had long-lasting effects on unemployment in later years. The economic processes that result in unemployment having the hysteresis property are considered in Chapter 13, which examines recent directions in Keynesian research.

hysteresis
is the property that, when a variable is shocked away from an initial value, it shows no tendency to return even when the shock is over. Persistently high unemployment rates in many European countries have led economists to argue that unemployment exhibits hysteresis

The divergent behavior of unemployment in the United States and Europe, especially in the 1990s, has been attributed to different structural characteristics of labor markets in the two regions. According to this view, greater flexibility in the U.S. labor market, due to less regulation and lower unionization, has meant that increased global competition and skill-biased technological change have caused stagnant real wages in the United States (especially for low-skilled workers) instead of slower job growth and higher unemployment. Moreover, in the post-1990 years any hysteresis effects have been favorable in the United States, as a low-unemployment environment has been maintained for a long period.

Writing in the late 1990s it would have been possible to be optimistic about European unemployment. In each of the countries in Table 11.2, unemployment was falling, in some such as Denmark and Ireland the fall was dramatic. But then as output growth slowed in 2001, unemployment in most of these countries began to rise again. By early 2004 the unemployment rate in the twelve countries that form the Euro (European common currency) area was 8.8 percent, 10 percent in the largest economies, France and Germany. High unemployment remains a major economic problem in Europe.

11.5 CONCLUSION

Friedman's theory of the natural rates of unemployment and output has been highly influential. It demonstrates the limits of the trade-off between inflation and unemployment. However, the apparent large variations of the natural rate of unemployment in Europe have caused some to doubt the usefulness of the concept to the conduct of macroeconomic policy. Robert Solow, for example, argues that "a natural rate that hops around . . . under the influence of unspecified forces, *including past unemployment rates*, is not 'natural' at all."[14] In contrast, Joseph Stiglitz, chairman of the Counsel of Economic Advisors in the Clinton administration, defends the concept, believing that "the natural rate provides a useful framework for thinking about policy questions even if there is considerable uncertainty about its exact magnitude."[15]

---

[14]Robert Solow, "Unemployment: Getting the Questions Right," *Economica*, 33, Suppl. (1986), p. S.33. See also James K. Galbraith, "Time to Ditch the NAIRU," *Journal of Economic Perspectives*, 11 (Winter 1997), pp. 93–108.
[15]Stiglitz, "Reflections on the Natural Rate Hypothesis," p. 10.

KEY TERMS

- natural rates of unemployment and output 243
- Phillips curve 245
- hysteresis 259

REVIEW QUESTIONS AND PROBLEMS

1. Explain the concept of the natural rate of unemployment. What are the implications of Milton Friedman's theory of the natural rate of unemployment for the effectiveness of economic stabilization policies?
2. Explain why monetarists believe that monetary policy affects output and employment in the short run but not in the long run. What is the crucial difference between the short run and the long run?
3. Contrast monetarist and Keynesian views of the relationship between real output (or employment) and aggregate demand in both the short run and the long run. Contrast the conclusions that monetarists and Keynesians draw from this analysis of the aggregate demand–output relationship for the usefulness of activist policies to stabilize output and employment. To what degree do differences in the theoretical analysis explain the differences in policy conclusions?
4. Explain the concept of the Phillips curve. Is there any difference between monetarist and Keynesian views of the Phillips curve?
5. Within the monetarist framework, would an expansionary fiscal policy action have short-run and long-run effects similar to those of the expansionary monetary policy analyzed in section 11.1?
6. At the end of the inflationary decade of the 1970s, the Federal Reserve is widely perceived to have moved to a much more restrictive monetary policy. Use the Phillips curve framework of Figures 11.2 and 11.3 to provide a monetarist analysis of the effects this policy shift would have on inflation and unemployment.
7. Summarize what you believe to be the essential differences between the monetarist and Keynesian positions.
8. "A supply shock such as the exogenous increase in the price of oil analyzed in section 9.5 would have no effect on real or nominal income within the monetarist model. This follows because such a supply shock would not affect the quantity of money, which is the dominant factor determining nominal income and, in the short run, real income." Do you agree or disagree with this statement? Explain.
9. Contrast monetarist and classical views on the short-run effects of an increase in the quantity of money.
10. Beginning in the late 1960s, the number of entrants to the labor market increased as the baby boom generation came to working age. In addition, labor force participation rates for women began to increase in the mid-1960s. What effect do you think these demographic factors had on the U.S. natural rate of unemployment at the time? What effect did they have on the natural rate of output?
11. Is the data in Table 11.2 for European unemployment consistent with the existence of a natural rate of unemployment in these countries? Explain why or why not.

Chapter 12

New Classical Economics

The next theoretical system we consider, the *new classical economics*, developed against the background of the high inflation and unemployment of the 1970s and the accompanying dissatisfaction with the prevailing Keynesian orthodoxy. Both monetarism and the new classical economics have their origins in aspects of classical economics, and the two schools of economists reach similar noninterventionist policy conclusions. Robert Lucas, the central figure in the development of the new classical economics, basically agrees with Milton Friedman's proposal for noninterventionist policy rules.[1] Much in the spirit of Friedman, Lucas says, "As an advice giving profession we are in way over our heads."[2] In fact, new classical economists are even more skeptical than monetarists about the usefulness of activist stabilization policies.

The new classical economics, however, is a more fundamental attack on the Keynesian *theoretical* system than is monetarism. Monetarists and Keynesians reach different policy conclusions and differ on a number of empirical questions,[3] but in Chapters 10 and 11 we presented no distinct monetarist theoretical model. New classical economists have attacked the Keynesian theoretical structure as "fundamentally flawed."

This chapter first presents the new classical economists' critique of Keynesian macroeconomics, focusing especially on the differences in the policy conclusions of the two groups (section 12.1). Next, we take a broader look at the new classical economics (section 12.2). We then consider the Keynesian response to the new classical economics (section 12.3). The final section (12.4) contains concluding comments on the current state of the controversy between Keynesian and new classical economists.

---

[1]Robert Lucas, "Rules, Discretion, and the Role of the Economic Advisor," in Stanley Fischer, ed., *Rational Expectations and Economic Policy* (Chicago: University of Chicago Press, 1980), p. 259.
[2]Ibid., p. 259.
[3]The stability of the private sector, the interest elasticity of money demand, and the importance of fiscal policy crowding out are a few.

12.1 THE NEW CLASSICAL POSITION

We have already quoted Franco Modigliani's Keynesian view that a private-enterprise economy needs to be, can be, and should be stabilized by active government aggregate demand management. The central policy tenet of the new classical economics is that stabilization of *real* variables, such as output and employment, cannot be achieved by aggregate demand management. The values of such variables *in both the short run and the long run* are insensitive to *systematic* aggregate demand management policies. In other words, in the new classical view, systematic monetary and fiscal policy actions that change aggregate demand will not affect output and employment, even in the short run. This has been termed the **new classical policy ineffectiveness proposition**.

Although monetarists question the necessity and desirability of activist policies to affect output and employment as well as the effectiveness of *fiscal* policy actions, they believe that systematic *monetary* policy actions have real effects in the short run. The new classical objection to activist stabilization policies is thus more far-reaching than that of monetarists.

new classical policy ineffectiveness proposition asserts that systematic monetary and fiscal policy actions that change aggregate demand will *not* affect output and employment even in the short run

A Review of the Keynesian Position

To see the basis for this new classical policy position, we first consider the new classical economists' critique of Keynesian macroeconomics. A good starting place is a review of the Keynesian analysis of the relationships among output, employment, and aggregate demand, as discussed in section 11.3. Consider the effects in the Keynesian model of an expansionary policy action—for example, an increase in the money supply. In the short run, such a policy action would increase aggregate demand. The aggregate demand curve would shift to the right along the upward-sloping aggregate supply schedule (as illustrated, for example, in Figure 11.5a). The price level and level of output would rise. Parallel to the increase in output is a rise in employment as labor demand increases, with the rise in prices shifting the labor demand schedule to the right along the upward-sloping (drawn against the money wage) labor supply schedule (as illustrated, for example, in Figure 11.5b).

Crucial to these results is the fact that the positions of both the aggregate supply schedule and labor supply schedule are fixed in the short run. The position of both these schedules depends on the value of the expected price level (P^e), which is assumed to depend primarily on past prices and not to change with current policy actions.

In the long run, the expected price level converges to the actual price level, and both the aggregate supply schedule and the labor supply schedule shift to the left. The initial levels of employment and output are restored, with only the price level and the money wage left permanently higher as a result of the increase in the money supply (see Figure 11.7). Output and employment remain above their long-run equilibrium levels only for as long as it takes labor suppliers to perceive correctly the change in the price level that results from the expansionary policy action. As long as our attention is confined to monetary policy actions, monetarists would agree with the foregoing analysis of an increase in aggregate demand.

The Rational Expectations Concept and Its Implications

The new classical economists do not agree. In particular, they do not accept the difference between the short-run and long-run results in the Keynesian or monetarist analysis of the effects of aggregate demand on output and employment. The focal point of their criticism is the Keynesian (and monetarist) assumption concerning price expectations. This formulation assumes that labor suppliers form an expectation of the current aggregate price level (or inflation rate) on the basis of the past behavior of prices. In practice, Keynesians and monetarists have assumed that such price expectations adjust slowly and can be fixed for the analysis of policy effects over short periods.

New classical economists criticize such formulations of expectations as "naive in the extreme." Why, they ask, would rational economic agents forming an expectation of the price level rely only on past values of the price level? Why especially would they do so when in general such behavior results in their being *systematically* wrong when aggregate demand shifts? We have been assuming that after changes in aggregate demand—for example, the increase in the money supply considered in the preceding subsection—labor suppliers fail to perceive that the demand shift will affect price. New classical economists argue that economic agents will not persist in making such systematic errors.

New classical economists propose that economic agents will form **rational expectations,** rational in that they will not make systematic errors. According to the hypothesis of rational expectations, *expectations are formed on the basis of all available relevant information concerning the variable being predicted.* Furthermore, the hypothesis maintains that individuals use available information intelligently; that is, they understand the way in which the variables they observe will affect the variable they are trying to predict. Thus, according to the rational expectations hypothesis, expectations are, as the originator of the concept, John Muth, suggested, "essentially the same as the predictions of the relevant economic theory,"[4] based on available information.

If expectations are rational, then in forming a prediction of the value of the aggregate price level for the current period, labor suppliers will use all relevant past information, not just information about the past behavior of prices. In addition, they will use any information they have about the current values of variables that play a role in the price level. Most important from the standpoint of aggregate demand management policy, labor suppliers will take account of any anticipated (expected) policy actions. Further, they are assumed to understand the relationship between such policies and the price level.

A useful contrast can be made between the *backward-looking* nature of expectations in the Keynesian model and the *forward-looking* nature of rational expectations. In the Keynesian model, expectations are backward-looking. The expectation of a variable such as the price level adjusts (slowly) to the past behavior of the variable. According to the rational expectations hypothesis, economic agents instead use all

rational expectations
expectations formed on the basis of all available relevant information concerning the variable being predicted. Moreover, economic agents are assumed to use available information intelligently; that is, they understand the relationships between the variables they observe and the variables they are trying to predict

---

[4]John Muth, "Rational Expectations and the Theory of Price Movements," *Econometrica,* 29 (July 1961), p. 316.

available relevant information and intelligently assess the implication of that information for the future behavior of a variable.

If labor suppliers make forward-looking rational forecasts of the price level, then the preceding analysis must be modified in an important way. To see this modification, we analyze the effects of an expansionary policy action previously considered, a one-time increase in the money supply. To analyze this change with the assumption that expectations are rational, we must begin by specifying whether the policy change was anticipated.[5] Anticipated and unanticipated policy changes have very different effects when expectations are assumed to be rational. First, we assume that the policy change is anticipated, perhaps because the policymaker announced the policy change. Alternatively, the public may anticipate the change because the policymaker is known to act in certain ways. For example, if the policymaker systematically responds to an increase in unemployment in one period by increasing the money supply in the next period (to counteract unemployment), the public will come to anticipate an increase in the money supply for period t when they observe an increase in the unemployment rate of period $t - 1$.

To begin, consider the characterization of equilibrium output and employment in the new classical analysis, as illustrated in Figure 12.1. The crucial difference

Figure 12.1 Output and Employment in the New Classical Model

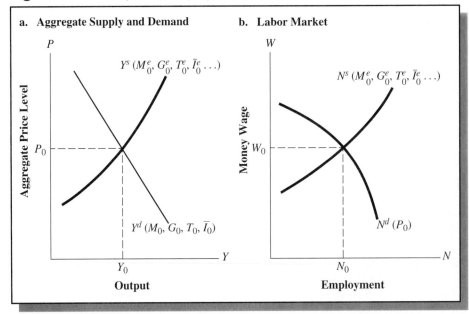

a. **Aggregate Supply and Demand**

P

$Y^s \, (M_0^e, G_0^e, T_0^e, \bar{I}_0^e \dots)$

Aggregate Price Level

P_0

$Y^d \, (M_0, G_0, T_0, \bar{I}_0)$

Y_0

Y

Output

b. **Labor Market**

W

$N^s \, (M_0^e, G_0^e, T_0^e, \bar{I}_0^e \dots)$

Money Wage

W_0

$N^d \, (P_0)$

N_0

N

Employment

The distinctive feature of the new classical model is that the aggregate supply and labor supply schedules depend on the rationally formed expectations of current variables, including monetary and fiscal policy variables (M_0^e, G_0^e, T_0^e).

[5]The terms *expected* and *anticipated* or *unexpected* and *unanticipated* are used interchangeably here. Policy shifts are referred to as either *anticipated* or *unanticipated*, whereas we refer to *expected* levels of variables, including policy variables.

between the new classical case and the Keynesian case concerns the variables that determine the positions of the labor supply and the aggregate supply schedules. As in the Keynesian theory, we assume here that labor supply depends on the expected real wage, the known money wage divided by the expected price level:

$$N^s = t\left(\frac{W}{P^e}\right) \tag{12.1}$$

Consequently, the position of the labor supply schedule, and therefore the aggregate supply schedule, depends on the expected price level. Increases in the expected price level will shift both schedules to the left.

In the new classical model, with the assumption of rational expectations, the expected price level depends on the expected levels of the variables in the model that actually determine the price level. These include the *expected* levels of the money supply (M^e), government spending (G^e) and tax collections (T^e), autonomous investment ($\bar{I}^e$), and possibly other variables.[6] The dependence of the expected price level, and hence the positions of the labor supply and aggregate supply schedules on these variables, is indicated by the labeling of these curves in Figure 12.1. Especially important is the fact that the positions of the labor supply and aggregate supply schedules depend on the expected levels of the policy variables (M^e, G^e, T^e).

Consider the effect of a fully anticipated increase in the money supply from M_0 to M_1, as depicted in Figure 12.2.[7] Initially, assume that the aggregate demand, aggregate supply, and labor supply and demand schedules are at the same positions as in Figure 12.1, with actual and expected variables subscripted zero (0). The increase in the money supply will shift the aggregate demand schedule out to $Y^d(M_1, \dots)$. If the supply schedule did not shift, output would rise from Y_0 to Y_1', and the price level would increase from P_0 to P_1'. With the rise in the price level, the labor demand curve shifts to the right [to the dashed schedule $N^d(P_1')$ in Figure 12.2b]. *If the labor supply curve did not also shift,* employment would rise (from N_0 to N_1'). In the Keynesian or monetarist frameworks, with the expected price level unrelated to the current level of policy variables, the positions of the aggregate supply curve and labor supply schedules *would* be fixed in the short run and our analysis would be complete.

But as Figure 12.2 shows, in the new classical case the positions of the labor supply and aggregate supply schedules are *not* fixed in the short run. The expansionary policy action is fully anticipated. Therefore, the level of the *expected* money supply also increases. This increase will raise the *expected* price level because, with rational expectations, labor suppliers will understand the inflationary effect of the increase in the money supply. The labor supply schedule and, as a consequence, the aggregate supply schedule will shift to the left to the positions given by $N^s(M_1^e, \dots)$ and $Y^s(M_1^e, \dots)$, as shown in Figure 12.2. As the decline in aggregate supply puts further upward pressure on the price level, the labor demand schedule shifts out to $N^d(P_1)$. The new equilibrium is where output and employment have returned to their initial levels, Y_0,

---

[6]Expected changes in oil prices or other supply-side factors, for example, would affect the expected price level.

[7]The positions for the aggregate demand schedule and other schedules continue to depend on all the variables discussed previously, including policy variables, but for notational simplicity the labels on the schedules in the graph contain only the variables that are assumed to change.

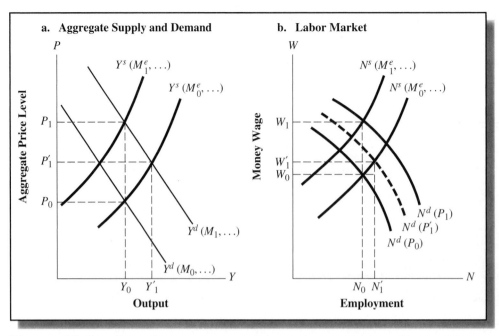

a. Aggregate Supply and Demand

P

Aggregate Price Level

$Y^s(M_1^e, \ldots)$

$Y^s(M_0^e, \ldots)$

P_1

P_1'

P_0

$Y^d(M_1, \ldots)$

$Y^d(M_0, \ldots)$

Y

$Y_0 \quad Y_1'$

Output

b. Labor Market

W

Money Wage

$N^s(M_1^e, \ldots)$

$N^s(M_0^e, \ldots)$

W_1

W_1'
W_0

$N^d(P_1)$
$N^d(P_1')$
$N^d(P_0)$

N

$N_0 \ N_1'$

Employment

Figure 12.2 Effects of an Increase in the Money Supply: The New Classical View
The increase in the money supply shifts the aggregate demand curve from $Y^d(M_0, \ldots)$ to $Y^d(M_1, \ldots)$. By itself, this change would increase output to Y_1' and the price level to P_1'. The increase in the price level would shift the labor demand schedule from $N^d(P_0)$ to $N^d(P_1')$, and employment would rise to N_1'. However, because the increase in the money supply was anticipated, there is also an increase in the *expected* money supply. This increase shifts the aggregate supply schedule to the left from $Y^s(M_0^e, \ldots)$ to $Y^s(M_1^e, \ldots)$ and shifts the labor supply schedule to the left from $N^s(M_0^e, \ldots)$ to $N^s(M_1^e, \ldots)$. These shifts cause employment and output to fall back to their initial levels N_0 and Y_0.

N_0, while the price level and the money wage are permanently higher at P_1 and W_1, respectively. Notice that the return to the initial levels of output and employment takes place in the short run when expectations are rational.

The new classical analysis differs from either a Keynesian or monetarist analysis in that labor suppliers are assumed to perceive correctly the price increase that will result from the increase in the money supply. They will demand proportionately higher money wages. The labor market will return to equilibrium only after the money wage and price level have increased in the same proportion, the real wage is unchanged, and consequently employment and output are back at their initial levels. Put differently, in the Keynesian or monetarist analysis, the increase in the money supply leads to an increase in employment and output in the short run—that is, until labor suppliers correctly perceive the increase in the price level that results from the expansionary monetary policy action. In the Keynesian or monetarist view, because expectations about prices are backward-looking, depending on the past behavior of prices and adjusting only slowly to current conditions, this short-run period in which the increase in the money supply affects output and employment can be of considerable length. If expectations are rational, forward-looking labor suppliers thus cannot be systematically "fooled" by anticipated changes in aggregate demand policy.

If expectations are formed rationally, anticipated aggregate demand policy actions will not affect real output or employment, even in the short run. Notice that, because the public will learn any systematic "rules" of policy action, such as the hypothetical response of the money supply to unemployment mentioned previously, any such set of systematic policy actions will be anticipated and will not affect the behavior of output or employment.[8] The values of real variables such as output and employment will be insensitive to systematic changes in aggregate demand management policies.

Thus far we have been assuming that the increase in the money supply was anticipated either because it was announced or because it was a systematic policy response that could be predicted. Now consider the effects of an *unanticipated* increase in aggregate demand. We again consider the effects of an increase in the money supply from M_0 to M_1, but the analysis would be similar for an unanticipated increase in aggregate demand from another source. The short-run effects of this unanticipated increase in the money supply—what can be termed a *monetary surprise*—can also be explained with reference to Figure 12.2. As before, the increase in the money supply shifts the aggregate demand schedule from $Y^d(M_0, \ldots)$ to $Y^d(M_1, \ldots)$. As the price level rises to P_1', the labor demand schedule also shifts out to the right, to $N^d(P_1')$. If the increase in the money supply is unanticipated, these are the only curves that shift in the short run. The additional shift to the left in the labor supply curve and consequently the shift to the left in the aggregate supply curve shown in Figure 12.2, where the increase in the money supply was anticipated, does *not* occur for an unanticipated increase in the money supply. When the increase in the money supply is not anticipated, it does not affect the labor suppliers' expectation of the value the aggregate price level will take on over the current period, so the labor supply curve does not shift.

When the increase in the money supply is unanticipated, the new classical model indicates that output and employment will be affected. In Figure 12.2, output will rise from Y_0 to Y_1', and employment will increase from N_0 to N_1', results identical to those of the Keynesian or monetarist analysis of such an increase in aggregate demand. For the short run, even assuming rational expectations, labor suppliers do not perceive the inflationary effect of the increase in aggregate demand. This was the assumption in both the Keynesian and monetarist views for any change in aggregate demand. New classical economists deny that anticipated changes in aggregate demand can affect output and employment, but their view of the effects of unanticipated changes in aggregate demand does not differ from that of Keynesians and monetarists.

This analysis of the effects of an unanticipated monetary policy action illustrates an important difference between the new classical theory and the classical theory explained in Chapters 3 and 4. In the new classical model, economic agents form rational expectations but they do not have perfect information; they make mistakes in predicting the price level, and such mistakes cause short-run deviations of output

---

[8]That the public would learn systematic policy rules follows from the assumption of rational expectations. Estimates of such rules could be based on past policy behavior. Such estimates would be helpful in predicting policy actions and consequently in predicting the behavior of prices and other variables, so the rational economic agent would use the information.

and employment from their long-run equilibrium rates. In the classical model, economic agents were assumed to have perfect information. Labor suppliers knew the real wage; there were no monetary (or other) surprises and no deviations from the supply-determined rates of output and employment.

New Classical Policy Conclusions

The new classical view that unanticipated aggregate demand changes affect output and employment still does not provide a meaningful role for macroeconomic stabilization policy. To see this, consider the new classical economists' view of the proper policy response to a decline in private-sector demand—for example, an autonomous decline in investment. We have already analyzed the Keynesian view of the proper policy response to shocks of this type. Keynesians argue that a decline in private-sector demand should be offset by an expansionary monetary or fiscal policy action to stabilize aggregate demand, output, and employment.

The effects of the decline in investment are depicted in Figure 12.3. The decline in investment demand shifts the aggregate demand schedule from $Y^d(\bar{I}_0)$ to $Y^d(\bar{I}_1)$ in Figure 12.3a. This shift causes output to decline from Y_0 to Y_1'. The price level will fall

Figure 12.3 Effects of an Autonomous Decline in Investment: A New Classical View

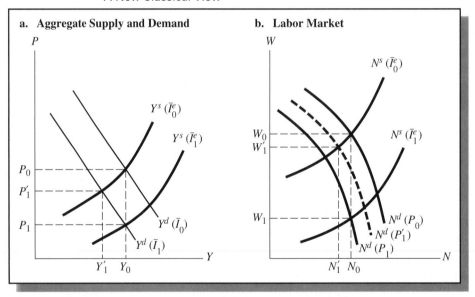

An autonomous decline in investment shifts the aggregate demand schedule from $Y^d(\bar{I}_0)$ to $Y^d(\bar{I}_1)$. This shift would reduce output from Y_0 to Y_1' and lower the price level from P_0 to P_1'. The fall in the price level shifts the labor demand schedule from $N^d(P_0)$ to $N^d(P_1')$, and as a result employment falls from N_0 to N_1'. These are the only effects if the decline in investment was not anticipated. If the decline in investment was anticipated, the expected level of autonomous investment ($\bar{I}^e$) will also fall (from $\bar{I}_0^e$ to $\bar{I}_1^e$). The aggregate supply schedule will shift from $Y^s(\bar{I}_0^e)$ to $Y^s(\bar{I}_1^e)$, and the labor supply schedule will shift from $N^s(\bar{I}_0^e)$ to $N^s(\bar{I}_1^e)$. Those shifts cause output and employment to return to their initial levels.

from P_0 to P_1' and as a result, the labor demand curve in Figure 12.3b will shift downward from $N^d(P_0)$ to $N^d(P_1')$. Whether there are additional effects from the decline in investment depends, in the new classical view, on whether the decline was or was not anticipated. To begin, we assume that it was anticipated.

In that case, labor suppliers will anticipate the decline in the price level that will result from the decline in aggregate demand. Labor suppliers, now expecting the price level to be lower, will supply more labor at a given money wage, because with the lower expected price level, a given money wage corresponds to a higher expected real wage. This fall in the expected price level shifts the labor supply curve to the right in Figure 12.3b [from $N^s(\bar{I}_0^e)$ to $N^s(\bar{I}_1^e)$]. As a consequence, the aggregate supply schedule shifts to the right in Figure 12.3a [from $Y^s(\bar{I}_0^e)$ to $Y^s(\bar{I}_1^e)$.] There is a further decline in the price level to P_1, and therefore a further downward shift in the labor demand schedule to $N^d(P_1)$. At the new *short-run* equilibrium, the money wage and price level have fallen sufficiently to restore employment and output to their initial levels, N_0 and Y_0.

This analysis is just the reverse of our analysis of an anticipated increase in aggregate demand resulting from an increase in the money supply. In the new classical system, output and employment are not affected by anticipated changes in aggregate demand, even in the short run. Consequently, there is no need for a stabilization policy response to an anticipated demand change such as a decline in investment.

But what if the decline in investment had not been anticipated? In that case, the labor suppliers would not have foreseen the price decline that resulted from the decline in aggregate demand. The labor supply curve (Figure 12.3b) and the aggregate supply curve (Figure 12.3a) would have remained at $N^s(\bar{I}_0^e)$ and $Y^s(\bar{I}_0^e)$, respectively. The decline in investment would have caused output and employment to decline to the levels given by Y_1' and N_1'. Would not an offsetting policy action to raise aggregate demand back to its initial level be called for?

The answer is that such a policy response would be desirable but not feasible. The decline in investment was by definition unanticipated. That is, assuming rational expectations, the decline could not have been predicted on the basis of *any* available information. Policymakers, like any other economic agent, would have been unable to foresee the investment decline in advance. They could not have acted to raise aggregate demand to offset the decline. Once the investment decline has occurred and had its effect on output, policymakers could act to raise aggregate demand if the low investment level was expected to be repeated in future periods. If low investment was *expected* to continue, however, there would be no need for a policy response because private agents would also hold this expectation. At this point, the shift in the labor supply and aggregate supply schedules would take place. In other words, as long as the shock is unanticipated, policymakers lack the knowledge needed to offset the shock. Once the shock is anticipated by policymakers, it is also anticipated by other economic agents, including labor suppliers, and there is no need to offset the shock.

The foregoing analysis indicates that the new classical view includes no useful role for aggregate demand policies aimed at stabilizing output and employment. New classical economists' policy conclusions are strongly noninterventionist, just as were those of classical economists. In this respect, new classical economists agree with the monetarists. Concerning monetary policy, many new classical economists arrive at the same position as monetarists, favoring a policy rule. A policy rule targeting money growth or inflation would reduce unanticipated changes in the money supply, which have no stabilization value and move the economy away from the natural rate of output and employment by causing economic agents to make price forecast errors.

In the case of fiscal policy, new classical economists favor stability and the avoidance of excessive and inflationary stimuli. New classical economists Thomas Sargent and Neil Wallace, for example, were critical of the large deficits that resulted from the Reagan administration's fiscal policy of the 1980s.[9]

Instability in fiscal policy causes uncertainty, making it difficult for agents forming rational expectations to correctly anticipate the course of the economy. Moreover, Sargent and others believe that a *credible* noninflationary monetary policy cannot coexist with a fiscal policy that generates large deficits. Huge deficits put great pressure on the monetary authority to increase money growth in order to help finance the deficit. Sargent and other new classical economists believe that control of the government budget deficit is necessary for a credible, noninflationary monetary policy.

Read Perspectives 12.1.

PERSPECTIVES 12.1
U.S. Stock Prices: Rational Expectations or Irrational Exuberance?

We have been considering the implications of the rational expectations assumption for macroeconomic stabilization policies. The assumption of rational expectations also has implications for other economic questions, an important one being determining the prices of financial assets. Here we consider the rational expectations assumption applied to the theory of stock price determination.

If agents form rational expectations, then in deciding how much a given stock (e.g., General Electric) is worth, they will use all information and use it intelligently. The relevant information in this context would be anything known about the future earnings prospects of the corporation, what are called market fundamentals. In a market populated by such agents, stock prices will move very quickly in response to new information about a corporation's earning prospects. In fact, prices will move so quickly that the current price of a corporation's stock is assumed to already reflect all currently available information. Such a market is termed an *efficient market*.[a]

Just as in the case of stabilization policy, the application of the rational expectations assumption to prices in the stock market is controversial. Many doubt that investors in the stock market are so rational. These doubters believe that decisions to buy and sell stock are in large part made independently of new information about market fundamentals. Among the early doubters was John Maynard Keynes. Keynes described the stock market as "a game of Snap, of Old Maid, of Musical Chairs—a pastime in which he is victor who says Snap neither too soon nor too late, who passes the Old Maid to his neighbor before the game is over, who secures a chair for himself when the music stops." Keynes and later doubters believe that "herd instincts," "momentum investing," and "feedback trading" are better descriptions of the motives for buying and selling stock than decisions motivated by rational expectations. According to these doubters, investors are strongly conditioned by what other investors are doing.

[9]Thomas Sargent and Neil Wallace, "Some Unpleasant Monetarist Arithmetic," Federal Reserve Bank of Minneapolis *Review* (Fall 1981).

As opposed to the behavior of stock prices in an efficient market, stock prices in a market driven by the type of investors described by Keynes might be excessively volatile as investors feed off one another's actions and drive prices either up or down. In 1996, Federal Reserve Board Chairman Alan Greenspan questioned whether the rapid rise in stock prices at that time was not being driven by "irrational exuberance," rather than rational expectations.[b]

Figure 12.4 plots the values of two stock price indices, the broad Standard and Poors 500 and the NASDAQ, which contains many high-tech companies, for the period 1984–2003. The sharp run-up in stock prices in the late 1990s and the subsequent sharp decline in 2000–2002 lent support to believers in irrational exuberance. The boom and collapse in NASDAQ seemed especially to be more consistent with the idea of a speculative bubble as opposed to an efficient stock market.

Defenders of the efficient market were not convinced. Burton Malkiel in an article in 2003 argued that while market pricing was not always "perfect" deviations from market efficiency were more the "exception than the rule."[c] Malkiel argues that any serious market inefficiency should present an exploitable profit opportunity. If information is not efficiently incorporated into stock prices, there should be potential profit in its use. On this point he quotes Richard Roll, a finance theorist and also a portfolio manager, as follows, "I have personally tried to invest money, my clients' money and my own, in every single anomaly and predictive device that academics have dreamed up. . . . And I have yet to make a nickel on any of these supposed market inefficiencies."[d]

Whether the stock market is driven by rational expectations or irrational exuberance has important implications for the economy. Excessive volatility is costly in that it may drive investors

Figure 12.4   The NASDAQ & S&P 500 (10/10/84–11/21/03)

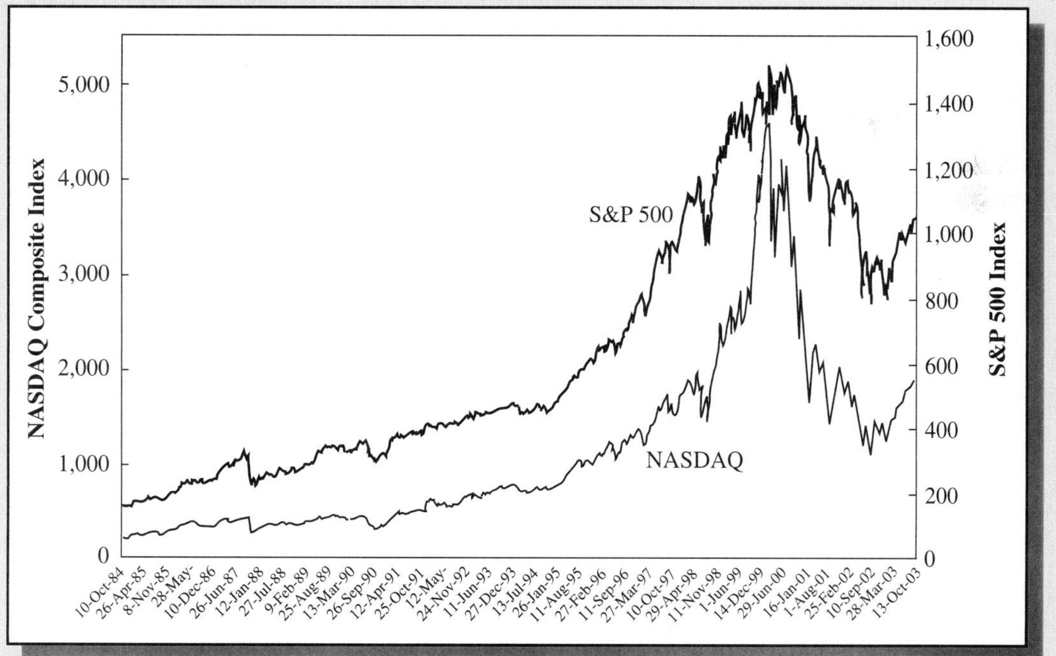

Source: Yahoo Finance.

away from the market and increase firms' costs of obtaining funds. A market made up of mainly irrational investors would be a more likely target for regulation than one in which prices were determined by investors with rational expectations responding to market fundamentals.

---

[a]A classic statement of the efficient markets hypothesis is in Eugene F. Fama, "Efficient Capital Markets: A Review of Theory and Empirical Work," *Journal of Finance* (1970), pp. 383–416.

[b]Robert Shiller has used Greenspan's phrase as the title of his book *Irrational Exuberance* (Princeton, N.J.: Princeton University Press, 2000), which questions the validity of the efficient markets hypothesis.

[c]Burton Malkiel, "The Efficient Market Hypothesis and Its Critics," *Journal of Economic Perspectives*, 17(Winter 2003), pp. 59–82.

[d]Ibid., p. 72.

12.2 A BROADER VIEW OF THE NEW CLASSICAL POSITION

New classical economists are critical of Keynesian economics as a whole. New classical economists Robert Lucas and Thomas Sargent use terms such as "fundamentally flawed," "wreckage," "failure on a grand scale," and "of no value" to describe major aspects of the Keynesian theoretical and policy analysis.[10] Lucas, Sargent, and other new classical economists are critical of the theoretical foundations of the Keynesian system. They argue that Keynes's rules of thumb such as the consumption function and Keynesian money demand function replaced classical functions based on individual optimizing behavior. The Keynesian model is, in their view, made up of *ad hoc* elements, which were failed attempts at explaining the observed behavior of the economy in the aggregate. A good example of this failing of the Keynesian system is the handling of expectations. The Keynesian system uses a rule of thumb whereby the expected current price is expressed as a function of the past behavior of prices. Such an assumption is not based on individuals' making optimal use of information and implies, in general, that economic agents choose to ignore useful information in making their price forecasts. New classical economists make the alternative assumption that expectations are rational, which they argue to be consistent with optimal use of information by the economic agents in the model.

New classical economists are also critical of Keynes's assumption that wages are "sticky," meaning, as they interpret this assumption, that wages "are set at a level or by a process that could be taken as uninfluenced by the macroeconomic forces he proposed to analyze." We have already considered the arguments that Keynesians advance to support the assumption of wage rigidity. New classical economists do not find these arguments convincing. They favor the classical view that markets, including the labor market, "clear"; that is, prices, including the money wage rate, move to equate supply and demand.

---

[10]Robert Lucas and Thomas Sargent, "After Keynesian Macroeconomics," in *After the Phillips Curve: Persistence of High Inflation and High Unemployment* (Boston: Federal Reserve Bank of Boston, 1978).

New classical economists argue that fruitful macroeconomic models should rectify the failures of Keynesian economics by consistently adhering to the following assumptions:

1. Agents optimize; that is, they act in their own self-interest.
2. Markets clear.

Why, then, did Keynes dispense with those assumptions? Keynesian economics was a response to the failure of classical economics to explain the problem of unemployment and the relationship between unemployment and aggregate demand. Recall that the classical aggregate supply schedule was vertical. With such a vertical supply schedule, aggregate output was totally dependent on supply factors. The classical model was abandoned by Keynes because it did not explain prolonged deviations of output and employment from full-employment levels.

New classical economists argue that a model in the classical tradition can explain the deviations from full employment if the assumption of rational expectations is incorporated into the classical system. Recall that the classical theory of the labor market, which was the basis for the classical vertical aggregate supply function, assumed that labor suppliers knew the real wage, implying that labor suppliers had *perfect information* about the value that the aggregate price level would take on over the short run. New classical economists substitute the assumption that labor suppliers make a rational forecast of the aggregate price level. In this case, as we have seen, systematic, and hence anticipated, changes in aggregate demand will not affect output and employment, but unanticipated changes in aggregate demand will. Such unanticipated changes in aggregate demand can explain deviations from full employment.

This substitution of the assumption of rational expectations for the classical assumption of perfect information does not require substantive changes in the non-interventionist classical policy conclusions, for as we saw earlier in this chapter, meaningful aggregate demand management policies involve *systematic* variations in aggregate demand, and these have no effect on output and employment in the new classical view.

12.3 THE KEYNESIAN COUNTERCRITIQUE

The theme that runs through the Keynesian response to the new classical criticisms is that, although they raise valid points, especially concerning the weakness of the Keynesian treatment of expectations formation, it is still, as the Keynesian Robert Solow puts it, "much too early to tear up the *IS–LM* chapters in the textbooks of your possibly misspent youth."[11] Keynesians continue to believe that Keynes provided the basis for a useful framework in which to analyze the determinants of output and employment. They continue to believe in the usefulness of activist policies to

---

[11]Robert Solow, "Alternative Approaches to Macroeconomic Theory: A Partial View," *The Canadian Journal of Economics* (August 1979).

stabilize output and employment. The major areas in which the Keynesians have raised objections to the new classical view are as follows.

The Question of Persistence

In the preceding section, we saw that the new classical model, with the concept of rational expectations, could explain deviations from potential output. Unanticipated declines in aggregate demand would move output and employment below the potential levels. Keynesians argue that although such an explanation might be plausible for brief departures from potential output and employment, it is not adequate to explain the persistent and substantial deviations that we have experienced. An unanticipated decline in investment, such as we considered previously (Figure 12.3), might well cause output and employment to decline over a short period, let us say one year. By the next year, however, this decline in aggregate demand would be apparent; it would no longer be unanticipated. Labor suppliers would recognize that the price level had declined. Consequently, the shifts to the right in the labor supply curve and the aggregate supply curve discussed previously (see Figure 12.3) would restore employment and output to their initial levels.

This being the case, how can the new classical model explain unemployment rates of 10 percent or more in Great Britain for the entire period 1923–39 or during the Great Depression of the 1930s in the United States, when the unemployment rate exceeded 14 percent for 10 consecutive years? In the more recent past, how can the model explain the movement of the unemployment rate during the deep and prolonged recessions of the mid-1970s and early 1980s?

New classical economists respond that although the source of the unemployment, the unanticipated change in aggregate demand, will be of short duration, the effects of the shock will persist. Consider, for example, the response to an unanticipated decline in demand. Assume that after one year or so, everyone recognizes that demand has fallen, so the change is no longer unanticipated. Declines in output and employment will have occurred. New classical economists argue that it will take time before such declines are reversed. Firms that have already cut output will not find it optimal to restore production immediately to preshock levels because of the cost of adjusting output. Moreover, firms will have accumulated excess inventory stocks over the period during which output was in decline. It will take time to run off such stocks; in the meantime, production and employment will remain depressed. On the labor supply side, workers who have become unemployed will not find it optimal to take the first job offer that comes along but will search for the best opportunity. New classical economists argue that, as a consequence of these adjustment lags, lengthy deviations from full employment, such as the United States experienced during the mid-1970s and early 1980s, can be explained even though the shocks that cause such deviations are short-lived.

What about the depression in Great Britain and the United States in the 1930s? One proponent of the new classical position, Robert Barro, has explained the severity of the U.S. experience by the extent of the largely unanticipated monetary collapse during the early years of the Depression, when the money supply fell by one-third. The slow recovery is viewed as a result of the massive government intervention during the New Deal period that subverted the normal adjustment mechanisms of the private sector.[12] Other new classical economists, such as Sargent and Lucas, agree with Keynesians that the Great Depression is not well explained by their theory, but do not find the Keynesian explanation convincing.

On this question of persistence, Keynesians remain unconvinced that adjustment lags sufficiently explain prolonged and severe unemployment. They believe that accepting the classical or new classical framework can explain episodes such as the Great Depression only as a result of factors on the supply side, which in their view are the only factors in these models that could cause prolonged unemployment. If markets clear and there is no involuntary unemployment, then, as Modigliani puts it, to the classical or new classical economists "what happened to the United States in the 1930s was a severe attack of contagious laziness."[13]

The Extreme Informational Assumptions of Rational Expectations

Keynesians accept the new classical economists' criticism of price expectations formulations based only on information about past prices. Such rules are naive because they assume that economic agents neglect available and potentially useful information in making their forecasts. Such naive assumptions about expectations came into use in the 1950s and early 1960s when the inflation rate was both low and stable. In these circumstances, such rules might have been reasonable approximations of the way people made forecasts, because good forecasts could, in fact, have been based on the past behavior of prices. With the volatile and, at times, high inflation of the post-1970 period, it is harder to believe that economic agents did not find it worthwhile to make more sophisticated forecasts.

Still, many Keynesians argue that the rational expectations assumption errs in assuming that economic agents are unrealistically sophisticated forecasters, especially when rational expectations are assumed for individual suppliers of labor. Keynesians criticize the assumption that individuals use *all* available relevant information in making their forecasts. Such an assumption ignores the costs of gathering information.

The rational expectations theory also presumes that individuals use available information intelligently. They know the relationships that link observed variables with variables they are trying to predict. They are also able to understand the systematic response pattern of policymakers. For example, if the monetary policymaker typically responds to rising unemployment by increasing the money supply, the public will come to anticipate such policy actions. Moreover, they will be able to predict the price effects of such anticipated monetary policy actions. Many

---

[12]See Robert Barro, "Second Thoughts on Keynesian Economics," *American Economic Review*, 69 (May 1979), p. 57. Examples of such New Deal interventions include NRA codes to fix prices and wages, agricultural policies to restrict output and raise prices, and increased regulation of the banking and securities industry, which might have hindered the raising of funds for investment. (See Perspectives 12.2.)

[13]Franco Modigliani, "The Monetarist Controversy, or Should We Forsake Stabilization Policies?" *American Economic Review*, 67 (March 1977), p. 6.

Keynesians deny that individual labor suppliers possess knowledge of both the working of the economy and the behavior patterns of policymakers.

If the economy, including the behavior of policymakers, had been stable and subject to little change for a long period of time, it is perhaps reasonable to believe that economic agents would come to know the underlying relationships that govern policy variables and economic aggregates. The rational expectations assumption might be realistic in a long-run equilibrium model, but Keynesians argue that it is not realistic in the short run. In the short run, the cost of gathering and processing information may be high enough that labor suppliers making forecasts of the aggregate price level or inflation rate do not find it worthwhile to use much information over and above the past behavior of prices.

If expectations are not rational, there is a role for aggregate demand management aimed at stabilizing output and employment. Even systematic changes in aggregate demand will affect output and employment because they will not be predicted by economic agents. If private-sector aggregate demand is unstable, as Keynesians believe it is, a stabilization policy is needed. Further, the monetary and fiscal policymaking authorities should be able to forecast systematic changes in private-sector aggregate demand. These policymaking authorities *do* gather what they consider to be all the available and important information on variables they wish to forecast and control. They also invest considerable resources in trying to estimate the relationships that characterize the economy. Keynesians regard the rational expectations assumption as reasonably correct when applied to the policymakers. The policymakers can design policy changes to offset what to the public are unanticipated changes in private-sector aggregate demand. In essence, this role for stabilization policy stems from an *information advantage* on the part of the policymaker.

Keynesians conclude:

> Macroeconomic models based on the assumptions of the rational expectations hypothesis do not demonstrate the short-run ineffectiveness of policy, therefore, because they are not really short-run models. The information availability assumption of the rational expectations hypothesis implicitly places such models in a long-run equilibrium context in which their classical properties . . . are not surprising.[14]

New classical economists defend the rational expectations assumptions. They admit that the rational expectations hypothesis is "unrealistic," but as Bennett McCallum argues, "All theories or models are 'unrealistic' in the sense of being extremely simplified descriptions of reality. . . . So the true issue is: of all the simple expectational assumptions conceivable, which one should be embodied in a macroeconomic model to be used for stabilization analysis?"[15] New classical economists favor the rational expectations assumption over the assumption that individuals

---

[14]Benjamin Friedman, "Optimal Expectations and the Extreme Informational Assumptions of 'Rational Expectations' Macromodels," *Journal of Monetary Economics* (January 1979), pp. 39–40.

[15]Bennett McCallum, "The Significance of Rational Expectations Theory," *Challenge Magazine* (January–February 1980), p. 39.

form price expectations based on the past history of prices because the rational expectations hypothesis is consistent with individual optimizing behavior.

Auction Market Versus Contractual Views of the Labor Market

In the new classical view, as in the original classical theory, the money wage is assumed to adjust quickly to clear the labor market—to equate labor supply and demand. This is an *auction market* characterization. In contrast, in the Keynesian *contractual* view of the labor market, "wages are not set to clear markets in the short run, but rather are strongly conditioned by longer-term considerations involving . . . employer–worker relations."[16] The money wage is sticky in the downward direction. In Arthur Okun's phrase, the labor market functions more by the *invisible handshake* than by the *invisible hand* of a competitive market mechanism. Most of the response to a decline in aggregate demand and, consequently, the demand for labor comes in the form of a reduction in employment rather than in a fall in the money wage.

Keynesians view the labor market as one in which long-term arrangements are made between buyers and sellers. In general, such relationships fix the money wage while leaving the employer free to adjust hours worked over the course of the explicit or implicit contract. Layoffs or reduced hours are considered an "acceptable" response on the part of the employer to a fall in demand. Applying pressure for wage cuts or replacing current workers with unemployed workers who will work for lower wages is not acceptable. This contractual Keynesian view explains wage stickiness on the basis of the institutional mechanisms that characterize the labor market. Much work is under way to investigate the theoretical reasons such labor market institutions have developed. Even without such theoretical foundations, the Keynesians argue that institutional mechanisms of this nature *do exist*, and they criticize new classical economists for ignoring these elements of reality that their model cannot explain.

New classical economists agree that the labor market is, at least in part, characterized by long-term contracts. They deny, however, that the existence of such contracts has, of itself, any implication for whether the labor market will clear—that is, for whether there will be involuntary unemployment. They deny that the terms of labor contracts are so rigid that employers and employees cannot effect changes desirable to both parties. For example, if the money wage specified is too high to maintain the market-clearing level of employment, workers could give up other provisions in the contract, increase the work done per hour, or in extreme cases allow revision of the wage in some fashion. New classical economists do not deny that labor contracts cause some deviation of employment from the market-clearing levels, but they do not believe this deviation is significant.

Read Perspectives 12.2.

---

[16]Arthur Okun, *Price and Quantities* (Washington, D.C.: The Brookings Institution, 1981), extends this contractual view to product markets, with resulting price stickiness. New Keynesian models of this type are examined in Chapter 13.

The world depression of the 1930s was a pivotal event in the development of our thinking about macroeconomic questions. Consequently, it is of interest to examine how each of the theories we consider explains this phenomenon. As we have seen, Keynesian economists do not believe that new classical economists can convincingly account for the Great Depression.

Let us examine what several leading proponents of the new classical view have had to say about the Depression. First, Robert Lucas:

If you look back at the '29 to '33 episode, there were a lot of decisions made that, after the fact, people wished that they had not made. There were a lot of jobs people quit that they wished they had hung onto; there were job offers that people turned down because they thought the wage offer was crappy. Then three months later they wished they had grabbed [them]. Accountants who lost their accounting jobs passed over a cab driver job, and now they're sitting on the street while their pal's driving a cab. So they wish they'd taken the cab driver job. People are making this kind of mistake all the time. Anybody can look back over the '30's and think of decisions he could have taken to make a million. Stocks I would have bought. All kinds of things. I don't see what's *hard* about this question of people making mistakes in the business cycle.[a]

Lucas points to misperceptions—unanticipated changes in prices—having real effects. Lucas sees unanticipated declines in the price level as the result of the sharp decline in the money supply, as Milton Friedman suggests (see Perspectives 10.1).[b]

Robert Barro also sees monetary and other government policies as key factors in the 1929–33 experience: "The unprecedented monetary collapse over this period accords quantitatively with the drastic decline in economic activity."[c] In addition to the effects that the rapid decline in the money supply may have had, Barro points to a real (or supply-side) effect from the collapse of much of the banking system during this period. (Nine thousand banks failed between 1923 and 1933.) As banks failed, for example, crops might not be produced because farmers could not get loans to buy farm machinery. In general, a decline in the availability of financial services may have reduced overall output supply in the 1929–33 period.[d]

As a further alternative to Keynesian explanations of the Depression, Barro suggests that "the government interventions associated with the New Deal, including the volume of public expenditures and direct price regulations, retarded the recovery of the economy, which was nevertheless rapid after 1933."[e]

But both Barro and Lucas still find parts of the Depression phenomenon puzzling and would, at least in some respects, agree with new classical economist Thomas Sargent that

I do not have a theory, nor do I know somebody else's theory that constitutes a satisfactory explanation of the Great Depression. It's really a very important, unexplained event and process, which I would be very interested in and would like to see explained.[f]

---

[a]Arjo Klamer, *The New Classical Macroeconomics: Conversations with the New Classical Economists and Their Opponents* (Totowa, N.J.: Rowman and Allanheld, 1983), p. 41.

[b]Ibid., p. 42.

[c]Robert J. Barro, "Second Thoughts on Keynesian Economics," *American Economic Review*, 69 (May 1979), p. 58.

[d]Robert J. Barro, "Rational Expectations and Macroeconomics in 1984," *American Economic Review*, 74 (May 1984), p. 180.

[e]Barro, "Second Thoughts on Keynesian Economics," p. 57.

[f]Klamer, *The New Classical Macroeconomics*, p. 69.

12.4 CONCLUSION

The new classical economics presents a fundamental challenge to Keynesian ortho-doxy. On the theoretical level, new classical economists question the soundness of the Keynesian model, arguing that many of its relationships are not firmly based on individual optimizing behavior. New classical economists point to the naive treat-ment of price expectations in the Keynesian model as an example. Further, they criticize what they consider Keynesians' arbitrary assumptions concerning wage stickiness and consequent involuntary unemployment.

On policy questions, new classical economists maintain that output and employ-ment are independent of systematic and, therefore, anticipated changes in aggregate demand. This is the new classical policy ineffectiveness postulate. Because meaning-ful aggregate demand management policies to stabilize output and employment consist of systematic changes in aggregate demand, new classical economists see no role for these policies. They arrive at noninterventionist policy conclusions similar to those of the classical economists.

Keynesians criticize the new classical theory on several grounds. They argue that the new classical model cannot explain the prolonged and severe unemployment experienced by the United States and other industrialized countries. They claim that the rational expectations assumption ascribes an extreme and unrealistic availability of information to market participants. Finally, and most important, they criticize the auction market characterization of the labor market in the new classical model. Keynesians believe that the labor market is a contractual market and that the nature of these contractual arrangements leads to wage rigidities and consequent involun-tary unemployment.

The new classical critique has, however, stimulated new avenues of Keynesian research on the causes of unemployment. The new Keynesian models emerging from this research are considered in Chapter 13, in which we also examine the develop-ment of a second generation of new classical models—the so-called real business cycle models.

KEY TERMS

- new classical policy ineffectiveness proposition 262
- rational expectations 263

REVIEW QUESTIONS AND PROBLEMS

1. Explain the concept of *rational expectations*. How does this view of how expecta-tions are formed differ from the assumption made in previous chapters that workers form expectations of current and future price levels based on past infor-mation about prices?
2. Explain the implications of the rational expectations assumption for the effec-tiveness of economic stabilization policy.
3. Contrast the new classical and Keynesian views of the way labor markets function.

4. Within the new classical framework, how could you explain a sustained departure from potential output such as that experienced by the United States beginning in 2001?

5. Compare the new classical and monetarist positions concerning the effectiveness of aggregate demand management policies to stabilize output.

6. Even within the new classical model, anticipated policy actions such as an increase in the money supply will affect *nominal* income. Explain why the adjustment of economic agents' expectations, which offsets the real effects of such a policy change, does not offset the nominal effects as well.

7. Why attach the adjective *new* to *classical* to describe the model in this chapter? How does this analysis differ from the classical model presented in Chapters 3 and 4?

8. Comment on the following statement. Do you agree or disagree with this view concerning the effectiveness of systematic or anticipated fiscal policy actions within a new classical economic framework? Explain.

> The new classical economics or rational expectations theory provides a convincing explanation of the inability of systematic monetary policy to affect real income or employment. The situation is quite different, however, with fiscal policy actions such as increases in government spending, which will affect real output and employment whether they are anticipated or not—the difference between monetary and fiscal policy being that monetary policy affects aggregate demand and, hence, output by *inducing* private economic agents to change their demands for output. With rational expectations this effect will be offset. An increase in government spending affects aggregate demand directly, and there is no way for the private sector to offset its effects on income and employment.

9. How would a supply shock, such as the exogenous increase in the price of oil analyzed in section 9.5, affect the aggregate price level and the level of real output in the new classical model?

10. During the administration of George W. Bush, reductions in the tax rates on labor income, dividends and capital gains were the centerpiece of fiscal policy. Analyze the macroeconomic effects of such tax cuts within the new classical model.

Chapter 13

Real Business Cycles and New Keynesian Economics

*C*oncerning the debate between Keynesians and new classical economists, one observer commented that the most impressive feature of the position of each side was its criticism of the other. Whether this is the case or not, the debate did leave some in each camp feeling that further research was needed to bolster their fundamental position. These feelings spawned two new directions in macroeconomic research. One, strongly rooted in the classical tradition, is the *real business cycle theory*. The second, the *new Keynesian theory*, as its name suggests, follows in the Keynesian tradition. The real business cycle theory is discussed in section 13.1. We then turn to the new Keynesian theory in section 13.2.

13.1 REAL BUSINESS CYCLE MODELS

Real business cycle theory is an outgrowth of the new classical theory, which in turn built on the original classical economics. In fact, real business cycle models are sometimes referred to as the second generation of new classical models. Real business cycle models share several important features with new classical models.

Central Features of Real Business Cycle Models

Recall that new classical economists believe useful macroeconomic models should have two characteristics:

1. Agents optimize.
2. Markets clear.

Real business cycle theorists agree. A hallmark of real business cycle models is their careful attention to microeconomic foundations—the individuals' optimizing decisions. Real business cycle theorists also believe that the business cycle is an *equilibrium* phenomenon, in the sense that all markets clear. This belief contrasts with the Keynesian view that the labor market does not clear. The Keynesian model includes involuntary unemployment. In real business cycle models, as in new classical models, all unemployment is voluntary.

Where real business cycle theorists part company with new classical economists is on the causes of fluctuations in output and employment. Real business cycle theorists see these fluctuations as "arising from variations in the real opportunities of the private economy."[1] Factors that cause such changes include shocks to technology, variations in environmental conditions, changes in the real (relative) prices of imported raw materials (e.g., crude oil), and changes in tax rates. Fluctuations in output also occur with changes in individuals' preferences—for example, a change in the preference for goods relative to leisure. These are the same factors that determined output in the classical model presented in Chapter 3. But classical economists believed that for the most part these factors changed only slowly over time. In the short run, they were taken as given.[2] They were the factors that would determine long-run growth. The real business cycle theorists argue that these supply-side variables are also the source of short-run fluctuations in output and employment.

This view distinguishes the real business cycle theorists from new classical economists, who regarded unanticipated changes in aggregate demand, resulting, for instance, from "monetary surprises," as the main source of fluctuations in output and employment. Nothing in the new classical framework precludes an important role for supply-side variables, such as the oil price shocks of the 1970s or changes in tax rates, in the short run. Still, unanticipated changes in demand were viewed as the major source of cyclical fluctuations in output. Factors such as technology shocks or changes in individual preferences received less attention.

The view that changes in real supply-side factors determine short-run fluctuations in output and employment also differentiates real business cycle models from Keynesian models. As we saw in Chapter 9, Keynesian models can incorporate the effects of supply-side shocks, but a central tenet of the Keynesian theory is the importance of aggregate demand in determining output and employment in the short run.

Before we consider a real business cycle model, there are two more general points to make. First is the question of why real business cycle theorists reject the new classical explanation of the source of short-run fluctuations in output, while in other respects the two approaches are so similar. One reason is that the empirical evidence on the role of unanticipated changes in aggregate demand in determining output is mixed. Probably more importantly, real business cycle theorists believe that the view that errors in predicting aggregate demand can explain large and costly fluctuations in output ultimately violates the postulate that agents optimize. As

---

[1]Robert G. King and Charles Plosser, "Money, Credit and Prices in a Real Business Cycle Model," *American Economic Review*, 74 (June 1984), p. 363.

[2]Tax rates could, of course, change in the short run, with effects that we considered in section 4.3. As noted there, however, classical economists gave little attention to the effect of changes in tax rates because of the low level of tax rates at the time they wrote.

Robert Barro expresses this view, "If information about money and the general price level mattered much for economic decisions, people could expend relatively few resources to find out quickly about money and prices."[3] If they do not, they are not optimizing.

Finally, note that there are two possible interpretations of the real business cycle theory. One views it as proposing that real supply-side factors are simply more important than nominal demand-side influences. In this interpretation, however, real business cycle models are just versions of the new classical model which, as explained previously, can also incorporate supply-side shocks. When real business cycle theorists differentiate their models from new classical models, such as the one considered in Chapter 12, they assert a much stronger position—that is, that monetary and other nominal demand-side shocks have *no* significant effect on output and employment.

A Simple Real Business Cycle Model

Real business cycle models, in the words of one of their developers,

> . . . view aggregate economic variables as the outcomes of the decisions made by many individual agents acting to maximize their utility subject to production possibilities and resource constraints. As such the models have an explicit and firm foundation in microeconomics.[4]

In this section, we construct a simple real business cycle model. Having constructed the model, we consider how optimizing economic agents respond to changes in economic conditions and the implications of their responses for aggregate economic variables.

A usual assumption in real business cycle models is that the economy is populated by a group of identical individuals. The behavior of the group can then be explained in terms of the behavior of one individual, called a *representative agent*. We will call the agent Robinson Crusoe.

Robinson's goal is to maximize his utility in each period of his life. He gets utility from two sources: consumption and leisure. We assume that he has the following utility function (U):

$$U_t = U(C_t, le_t) \tag{13.1}$$

where C is consumption and le is leisure. To consume, Robinson must first produce output. In doing so, he forgoes leisure. Thus, as in the earlier models, there is a labor–leisure trade-off. Output in the model is generated by the production function

$$Y_t = z_t F(K_t, N_t) \tag{13.2}$$

Equation (13.2) is similar to the aggregate production function in the classical model in Chapter 3. The production function specifies the amount of output (Y) that will result from employing given amounts of capital (K) and labor (N) in time period t.

---

[3]Robert J. Barro, *Modern Business Cycle Theory* (Cambridge, Mass.: Harvard University Press, 1989), p. 2.
[4]Charles Plosser, "Understanding Real Business Cycles," *Journal of Economic Perspectives*, 3 (Summer 1989), p. 53.

There are two differences between equation (13.2) and our earlier production function. Equation (13.2) contains the additional term z_t, which represents "shocks" to the production process. By such shocks we mean events that change the level of output forthcoming for given levels of labor and capital. Real business cycle theorists include a number of factors in this category. Among the important ones are shocks to technology, environmental factors, changes in government regulations that affect productivity, and changes in the availability of raw materials.

The second difference between equation (13.2) and our earlier version of the production function is the absence of a bar over the K in (13.2). In the real business cycle, the capital stock is not taken as given but rather is chosen for each period by the representative agent, in a manner discussed presently.

Robinson does not have to consume all the output he produces each period. The young Robinson might want to save for when he is an old Robinson or for a future generation of Crusoe Jrs. What is required is that

$$Y_t = C_t + S_t \qquad (13.3)$$

Saving (S) plus consumption (C) must equal income, ignoring the existence of taxes. Equation (13.3) indicates that, in addition to a labor–leisure trade-off, the representative agent faces a trade-off between consumption today and saving for future consumption. Saving today will increase consumption in the future because saving is assumed to be invested to increase the capital stock in the next period:

$$K_{t+1} = S_t + (1 - \delta)K_t \qquad (13.4)$$

The capital stock in period $t + 1$ is equal to saving in period t plus the portion of the capital stock $(1 - \delta)$ left over from period t, where δ is the depreciation rate for capital (the fraction of the capital stock that wears out in each period).

In this representative agent framework, the behavior of aggregate output, employment, consumption, and saving is described in terms of the choices made by Robinson Crusoe. We now consider how those choices are affected by a change in the economic environment Robinson confronts.

Effects of a Positive Shock to Technology

Let us suppose that in a given time period there is a favorable shock to technology. For now we will assume that the shock is temporary, lasting only one period; later we will consider shocks that are more long-lived. This shock is assumed to occur exogenously and is represented in our model by a rise in the z_t term in equation (13.2), let us say from an initial level z_{0t}, to a higher value z_{1t}. Given K_t and N_t, there is an exogenous rise in Y_t.

The effect of this shock is illustrated in Figure 13.1. Initially, with z_t equal to z_{0t}, the production function is given by $z_{0t}F(K_t, N_t)$. Let us suppose that, faced with this set of production possibilities, Robinson chooses N_0 as the optimal amount of work to perform, and as a result, output is at Y_0. The positive technology shock shifts the production function upward to $z_{1t}F(K_t, N_t)$. In addition to this upward shift, the nature of the shock is assumed to be such that the production function becomes steeper for any level of the labor input. Recall from Chapter 3 that the slope of the

Figure 13.1

The Effect of a Positive Technology Shock in a Real Business Cycle Model

A positive technology shock shifts the production function up from $z_{0t}F(K_t, N_t)$ to $z_{1t}F(K_t, N_t)$. Robinson responds to this rise in his productivity by increasing his labor input from N_0 to N_1. Because of the increase in productivity and increase in the labor input, output rises from Y_0 to Y_1.

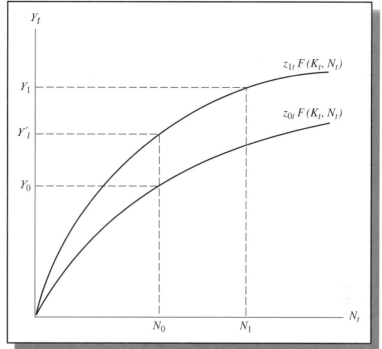

production function is the marginal product of labor. So we are assuming that the shock increases Robinson's marginal productivity.

Even at the same level of labor input (N_0), this increase in productivity would cause a rise in output, to Y_1' in Figure 13.1. The favorable shock has, however, changed the production possibilities facing Robinson. If he observes the change, which we will assume to be the case, he will react. In the figure we assume that he reacts to the increase in his productivity by working more. The level of the labor input rises to N_1 in Figure 13.1, and output rises to Y_1.

Now Robinson must decide what to do with the increased output. Equation (13.3) tells us that the increase in output will go to consumption or saving. He could just consume it all. But, particularly in the case of a temporary shock, it is likely that he will save a portion of the increase in output to allow consumption to also be higher throughout the future. If this is the case, then equation (13.4) tells us that the higher saving, which in turn means higher investment, will cause the capital stock to be higher in the next period than it otherwise would be. Because of a higher capital stock, output in the next period as well as other future periods will also be higher than it would have been in the absence of the technology shock. This is true even though the *direct* effect of the shock lasted for only one period.

Had the shock lasted for several periods or caused permanent effects, Robinson's responses would have been somewhat different. He would know that output would be high for a longer period, so his incentive to save would be reduced and his incentive to consume increased. Also, because he would know that his productivity would be higher for several periods, because of the direct effect of the shock, he might increase his work effort in each period by less. Long-lived productivity shocks will, however, also result in changes in output, the capital stock, and employment that persist for many periods.

It is important that the effects of technology shocks last for many periods. A key Keynesian criticism of the new classical model, which shares the equilibrium approach taken by the real business cycle theorists, is that it cannot explain the *persistence* of real-world business cycles. Real business cycle theorists argue that the dynamic responses of optimizing agents to changes in economic conditions will, as just explained, have long-lasting effects. These responses can explain periods of persistently high or low economic activity.

We have focused on shocks to technology because they are central to real business cycle theorists' explanation of economic fluctuations. As noted earlier, however, other factors considered in real business cycle models include changes in environmental conditions, relative prices of raw materials, variations in tax rates, and changes in preferences. All these shocks are additional potential causes of cyclical movements in output and employment.

Macroeconomic Policy in a Real Business Cycle Model

In a real business cycle model, fluctuations arise from individuals' responses to changes in the economic environment. These responses are the result of optimizing behavior. In these models, it would be suboptimal for policymakers to eliminate the business cycle if they could actually do so. What role is there, then, for macroeconomic policy in a real business cycle model? Let us start with monetary policy and then turn to fiscal policy.

Monetary Policy

The defining feature of real business cycle models is that real, not monetary, factors are responsible for fluctuations in output and employment. In real business cycle models, the role of money is to determine the price level, much the same as in the original classical model. Changes in the quantity of money result in proportionate changes in the price level with no change in output or employment.[5]

It follows, then, that monetary policy should focus on controlling the price level. A desirable monetary policy would result in slow, steady growth in the money supply and thus stable prices, or at least a low rate of inflation. When we consider fiscal policy, however, we will see that an alternative view of the optimal conduct of monetary policy emerges from the real business cycle theory. In any case, there is certainly no role for activist monetary stabilization policy of a Keynesian type. Monetary policy

---

[5]Here we are considering a model in which all money is issued by the government: a world of only currency. Were we to consider bank deposits as well, the role of money in a real business cycle model would become considerably more complex because banks that issue deposits also provide credit and other services to firms. These services can affect the productivity of firms. Thus, changes in the banking industry—bank failures, for example—have real effects in a real business cycle model. It remains true, however, that changes in the quantity of money do not cause changes in output and employment. For a real business cycle model that includes both currency and bank deposits, see King and Plosser, "Money, Credit and Prices in a Real Business Cycle Model."

cannot affect output and employment, and even if it could, it would be suboptimal to try to eliminate the business cycle.

Fiscal Policy

Many fiscal policy actions *will* affect output and employment in a real business cycle model. The effect will not be by means of an effect on nominal aggregate demand, as in the Keynesian model, but via supply-side effects. Changes in tax rates on labor income or the return to capital will affect the choices of optimizing agents. Moreover, these effects will be distortionary. A tax on labor income, for example, will cause an individual to choose too much leisure in relation to employment (with resulting lower consumption). Even a lump-sum tax will affect individual behavior by affecting wealth over the planning horizon.

The task of fiscal policy in the real business cycle framework is to minimize these tax distortions subject to providing needed government services (e.g., defense). This is where an alternative role for monetary policy emerges (alternative to simply keeping inflation low through slow, steady money growth). Recall from our previous discussion of the government budget constraint (section 4.3) that an alternative to financing government spending by taxation is to finance it by printing money.[6] Policymakers can reduce the distortion due to taxation by financing a portion of government spending with newly created money. The term economists use for this practice in which the government gets real resources through money creation is **seigniorage**. However, seigniorage also has costs because the faster the money supply grows, the higher will be the inflation rate. In the real business cycle model, it follows that the optimal use of monetary and fiscal policy is to combine them so as to minimize the total costs from inflation and tax distortion. This is far different from the Keynesian view of optimal monetary and fiscal *stabilization* policy.

seigniorage
is the amount of real resources bought by the government with newly created money

Read Perspectives 13.1.

Questions About Real Business Cycle Models

Real business cycles have been an active research area in recent years, but the approach is not without its critics. These critics argue that "real business cycle theory does not provide an empirically plausible explanation of economic fluctuations."[7] Critics have raised several issues concerning the realism of the theory's explanation of economic fluctuations. We consider two that appear to be central: the question of

---

[6]Borrowing from the public by selling government bonds is another way to pay for government spending. In real business cycle models, however, the government is constrained to repay all borrowing at some point. Thus bond sales can affect only the timing of taxation or money financing, not their amount.

[7]N. Gregory Mankiw, "Real Business Cycles: A New Keynesian Perspective," *Journal of Economic Perspectives*, 3 (Summer 1989), p. 79. Additional surveys of the real business cycle literature, from several viewpoints, include Bennett T. McCallum, "Real Business Cycle Models," in Barro, ed., *Modern Business Cycle Theory*; Lawrence H. Summers, "Some Skeptical Observations on Real Business Cycle Theory," Federal Reserve Bank of Minneapolis *Quarterly Review*, 10 (Fall 1986), pp. 23–27; George Stadler, "Real Business Cycles," *Journal of Economic Literature*, 32 (December 1994), pp. 1750–83; Robert G. King and Sergio T. Rebelo, "Resuscitating Real Business Cycles" in John B. Taylor and Michael Woodford, *Handbook of Macroeconomics* (Amsterdam: North Holland, 1999), pp. 927–1007.

PERSPECTIVES 13.1
Robert Lucas and Real Business Cycle Theory

As noted at beginning of the chapter, real business cycle models and the new classical models in the previous chapter share important features. Moreover, one interpretation of the real business cycle theory is simply that real supply-side factors are quantitatively much more important than nominal demand-side influences. With that interpretation real business cycle theories are simply extensions of new classical models that focus attention on these real supply-side variables. In a recent paper, Robert Lucas, the central figure in the development of the new classical models, concludes that this type of model is characteristic of the United States economy.

Lucas therefore argues that "Taking U.S. performance over the past 50 years as a benchmark, the potential for welfare gains from better long-run, supply-side policies exceeds *by far* the potential from further improvements in short-run demand management."[a] Lucas accepts that "the stability of monetary aggregates and nominal spending in the postwar United States is a major reason for the stability of aggregate production and consumption during these years, relative to the experience of the inter-war period and the contemporary experience of other economies."[b] But, he argues that important welfare gains from further improvement in such demand-side policies are unrealistic. His estimate of such potential gains is about one-half of one-tenth of 1 percent of aggregate consumption.

This estimate is based on consideration of optimizing agents functioning in an environment such as the Robinson Crusoe economy of section 12.1 and subject to uncertainty about their consumption streams. Within such an economy, Lucas estimates the welfare gain that could be generated by reducing consumption risk via improved aggregate demand stabilization.

While the estimated gain from this source is tiny, Lucas cites other studies indicating that much larger welfare gains would result from fiscal policy changes that improved incentives to work and save—*supply-side* policies that will be analyzed in Chapter 20.

---

[a]Robert Lucas, "Macroeconomic Priorities," *American Economic Review*, 93 (March 2003), p. 1.
[b]Ibid., p. 11.

---

whether technology shocks are of sufficient magnitude to explain observed business cycles and the related question of whether observed changes in employment can actually be explained as the voluntary choices of economic agents facing changing production possibilities (or changing tastes).

The Importance of Technology Shocks

Critics of the real business cycle approach question whether shocks to technology are large enough to cause economic fluctuations of the type and size we observe. These critics point out that many technology shocks are likely to be specific to individual industries. In any given year, while some industries might be experiencing negative shocks, others will have positive shocks. But in a real-world recession, for example, the decline in output is widespread across industries of very diverse structure. Although the critics do not deny that some technology shocks affect many industries (e.g., the information transmission revolution), they do not believe there are enough of these to explain recessions in which output falls to as much as 10 percent below potential output.

Technology shocks are, of course, only one type of shock considered in the real business cycle theory, though they have received the most emphasis. Concerning the other shocks (and technology shocks as well) included in real business cycle models, critics allow that real supply side shocks are important, but argue that they are not all-important. Many economists who do not accept the real business cycle explanation of economic fluctuations do believe that the sharp rise in the relative price of imported oil was the central cause of the deep recession in the United States and other industrialized nations in the mid-1970s. Other recessions, such as the one in the United States in the early 1980s, the critics believe are better explained by changes in aggregate demand—in this case, by a restrictive Federal Reserve monetary policy.

Voluntary Employment Changes

In real business cycle models, changes in employment come as economic agents respond to changes in economic conditions. In our discussion of the effects of a positive shock to technology, we saw that Robinson Crusoe became more productive and responded by working more. Output rose because of both the direct effect of the shock and the increase in Crusoe's labor input. A negative technology shock would have the opposite effect; both output and employment would decline. In each case, the changes in employment would be voluntary and desirable (agents are optimizing).

Another way of putting this concept is that individuals are moving along their labor supply curves in response to changes in their marginal productivity and, therefore, their real wage. This was the analysis of employment changes in the classical model presented in Chapter 3. Critics of the real business cycle approach argue that to explain real-world fluctuations in this manner requires an implausibly high response of labor supply to changes in the real wage—a very flat labor supply curve. This outcome follows because, although swings in employment over the business cycle are large, changes in the real wage are small. Critics argue that studies show only small responses of hours worked to changes in the real wage (a steep labor supply curve).[8] They argue that the data are more consistent with the Keynesian explanation in which workers are assumed to be thrown off of their labor supply curves; unemployment is involuntary.

Read Perspectives 13.2.

Concluding Comment

Real business cycle theorists are convinced that the business cycle can be explained as an equilibrium phenomenon. Fluctuations in output come as optimizing economic agents respond to real shocks that affect production possibilities. Policies which try to prevent these fluctuations are unnecessary and misguided. Critics of the real business cycle approach, many of whom view the business cycle from a Keynesian perspective, find this explanation implausible. They see business cycles as the result

---

[8]See, for example, Joseph G. Altongi, "Intertemporal Substitution in Labor Supply: Evidence from Micro Data," *Journal of Political Economy*, 94 (June 1986), part 2, pp. S176–S215.

Critics of the real business cycle approach argue that the nature of labor market flows is inconsistent with a theory in which cyclical unemployment is voluntary. Figure 13.2 shows the share of total unemployment accounted for by job leavers and job losers for the years 1984–96. Job leavers are those who quit their jobs; these workers would be classified as voluntarily unemployed. Job losers are those who were laid off or fired.

Notice that during the long recovery following the 1981–82 recession the proportion of job losers fell and that of job leavers rose. This trend is consistent with a pattern: As economic activity picked up, layoffs fell, and as other job opportunities were created, the number of job leavers rose. Then, in the recession that began in 1990, the proportion of job losers rose sharply while fewer workers quit their jobs. Later in the 1990s, with improving conditions in the labor market, the proportion of job losers fell and that of job leavers rose.

The pattern of labor market flows in Figure 13.2 is not, however, easily explained from a real business cycle perspective. If cyclical unemployment is voluntary, then job leavers should rise, not fall, during a recession. Moreover, a real business cycle explanation of Figure 13.2 must somehow account for job losers. Did they voluntarily lose their jobs? On the face of it, these data seem more consistent with an explanation of cyclical unemployment as involuntary.

Figure 13.2 Job Losers and Job Leavers, Shares of Total Unemployment, 1984–96

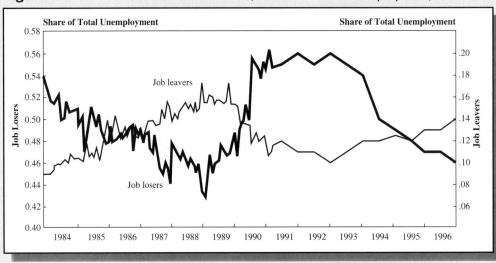

of changes in nominal aggregate demand as well as changes in real supply-side variables. Economists who view the business cycle from this Keynesian perspective believe that the policy prescription of the real business cycle theory wrongfully calls for inaction in the face of costly deviations from potential output.

13.2 NEW KEYNESIAN ECONOMICS

Keynes wanted to explain involuntary unemployment—at times, mass involuntary unemployment. He set out to show how aggregate demand affected output and employment. The Keynesian models can explain unemployment and a role for aggregate demand in determining output and employment. A key element in these models is money wage rigidity. A fall in aggregate commodity demand, for example, leads to a fall in labor demand. As a result of fixed-wage labor contracts and workers' backward-looking price expectations, the money wage will not fall sufficiently in the short run to maintain the initial employment level. Employment and output will fall. Unemployment will rise.

In recent years, economists working within the Keynesian tradition have pursued additional explanations of involuntary unemployment. The models emerging from this research effort are called *new Keynesian models*. In part, this new research is a response to the new classical critique of the older Keynesian models. N. Gregory Mankiw and David Romer, both of whom have made important contributions to the new Keynesian economics, state that "the new classical economists argued persuasively that Keynesian economics was theoretically inadequate, that macroeconomics must be built on a firm microeconomic foundation."[9] Not all new Keynesians are this critical of the earlier Keynesian models, but their main task has been to improve the microeconomic foundations of the Keynesian system. Because they see wage and price rigidities as central to Keynes's explanation of involuntary unemployment, much effort has gone to show that these rigidities can arise from the behavior of optimizing agents; that is, they can be given a solid microeconomic basis.

New Keynesian economists have not tried to develop one rationale for all price and wage rigidities. Rather, they believe that a number of features of the wage- and price-setting process explain such rigidities. In fact, the new Keynesian literature is characterized by what has been called a "dizzying diversity" of approaches. These approaches have, however, the following common elements:

1. In new Keynesian models, some form of imperfect competition is assumed for the product market. This assumption contrasts with the earlier Keynesian models that assumed perfect competition.
2. Whereas the key nominal rigidity in earlier Keynesian models was the money wage, new Keynesian models also focus on product price rigidity.
3. In addition to factors that cause nominal variables (e.g., the money wage) to be rigid, new Keynesian models introduce real rigidities—factors that make the real wage or firm's relative price rigid in the face of changes in aggregate demand.

---

[9]N. Gregory Mankiw and David Romer, eds., *New Keynesian Economics* (Cambridge, Mass.: MIT Press, 1991), p. 1. This two-volume collection of articles is a good sample of the new Keynesian research effort. Surveys of new Keynesian literature are Robert J. Gordon, "What Is New Keynesian Economics?" *Journal of Economic Literature*, 28 (September 1990), pp. 1115–71; David Romer, "The New Keynesian Synthesis," *Journal of Economic Perspectives*, 7 (Winter 1993), pp. 5–22; and John B. Taylor, "Staggered Price and Wage Setting in Macroeconomics," in John B. Taylor and Michael Woodford, *Handbook of Macroeconomics* (Amsterdam: North Holland, 1999), pp. 1009–1050.

We consider three types of new Keynesian models: sticky price (menu cost) models, efficiency wage models, and insider–outsider models.

Sticky Price (Menu Cost) Models

Early Keynesian models viewed the money wage as the variable that failed to adjust to changes in aggregate demand; output and employment had to adjust. The product market in those models was characterized by perfect competition. Keynesian economists did not necessarily believe that most real-world product markets were perfectly competitive. The assumption of perfect competition was made for simplicity and reflected the view that money wage rigidity was the real culprit in explaining unemployment.

sticky price models (or menu cost models) are those in which costs of changing prices prevent price adjustments when demand changes. Consequently, output falls when, for example, there is a decline in demand

A crucial element in new Keynesian **sticky price models** is that the firm must *not* be a perfect competitor.[10] With perfect competition, prices are set by the forces of supply and demand. Individual firms have no power over their product price; they face horizontal demand schedules. The perfectly competitive firm, a dairy farm, for example, can sell all the milk it wants to at the going market price of, say, one dollar per gallon. If, owing to a drop in aggregate demand, the market price declines to 80 cents per gallon, the firm can sell all it wants at this new price. If in the face of the fall in demand the perfectly competitive firm maintained its original product price, it would sell no output. There is no room for sticky prices in this market.

However, in the case of a monopolistic competitor or oligopolistic firm, the situation is different.[11] If La Residence, a Chapel Hill restaurant, did not lower prices in the face of a general fall in the demand for restaurant meals, it would lose some, but not all, of its customers. Similarly, during a recession, when the demand for automobiles declines, Ford Motor Company can continue to sell cars even if its prices remain unchanged. Monopolistic competitors and oligopolies have some control over the price of their products. In fact, the incentive to lower prices may be fairly weak for these types of firms. If they hold to their initial price when demand falls, they will lose sales, but the sales they retain will still be at the relatively high initial price. Also, if all firms hold to the initial price, no individual firm will lose sales to its competitors.

menu costs refer to any type of cost that a firm incurs if it changes its product price

Still, in the face of a fall in demand, the profit-maximizing price will decline even for a firm in a setting of imperfect competition. Though the gain in profits from lowering price may be small, there is some gain. Why, then, might firms still not lower prices? Firms would hold product prices constant even as demand fell if there was a perceived cost to changing prices that outweighed the benefit of the price cut. Such costs of price changes are called **menu costs**.

---

[10]Examples of sticky price models are N. Gregory Mankiw, "Small Menu Costs and Large Business Cycles: A Macroeconomic Model of Monopoly," *Quarterly Journal of Economics*, 100 (May 1985), pp. 529–38; and George Akerlof and Janet Yellin, "A Near Rational Model of the Business Cycle with Wage and Price Inertia," *Quarterly Journal of Economics*, 100, Suppl. (1985), pp. 823–38.

[11]Recall from microeconomics that monopolistic competition is a situation in which many firms provide differentiated products, for example, different types of food at different restaurants. Oligopoly refers to situations in which, owing to substantial costs to enter the market, there are only a few firms. The product may be standardized or differentiated (e.g., aluminum or automobiles).

The name stems from the fact that if restaurants change prices, they must print new menus. More generally when firms change prices they incur direct and indirect cost of several types.

One type is called managerial costs. These include the costs of gathering the information required to decide on the optimal price change, the cost of communicating to customers the logic for the change, and perhaps negotiating with customers who resist the change. Each of these activities take management time away from other activities.

A second cost is potential loss of consumer goodwill. Consumer goodwill would be lost only through price increases, but firms that cut prices in recessions must raise them in recoveries. Firms may instead find it optimal to change prices when their costs change, the necessity of which customers will understand, but not to vary prices with changes in demand. They will thus not be considered "price gougers" in periods of high demand and will not lower prices when demand falls off.

A second possible perceived cost of a price reduction in a recession is that it may set off competitive rounds of price cuts or even lead to a price war as other firms respond. This potential cost is most relevant for oligopolistic markets, where firms are cognizant of other firms' reactions to their pricing decisions.

If these perceived costs of price changes are high enough, price stickiness will exist. Declines in aggregate demand will result in falls in output and employment, not price reductions. Of course, not all prices need to be sticky. As long as the number of industries in which prices are rigid constitutes a significant segment of the economy, the declines in output and employment will be substantial.

Read Perspectives 13.3.

Efficiency Wage Models

In 1914, Henry Ford instituted the five-dollar day for his workers. At the time, the going competitive wage rate was between two and three dollars a day. Ford decided to pay this above-market wage because he thought it would discourage absenteeism, reduce turnover in Ford's labor force, and improve worker morale; productivity would therefore increase. Modern **efficiency wage models** have the same premise: The efficiency of workers depends positively on the real wage they are paid.[12]

The efficiency wage idea can be formalized by defining an index of worker efficiency, or productivity (*e*), such that

efficiency wage models are models where labor productivity depends on the real wage workers are paid. In such models, the real wage is set to maximize the efficiency units of labor per dollar of expenditure, not to clear the labor market

$$e = e\left(\frac{W}{P}\right)$$

(13.5)

---

[12]Ford's experiment with the five-dollar day is analyzed from the viewpoint of the modern efficiency wage theory in Daniel M. G. Ruff and Lawrence H. Summers, "Did Henry Ford Pay Efficiency Wages?" *Journal of Labor Economics*, 5 (October 1987), part 2, pp. S57–S86. Examples of efficiency wage models are Akerlof and Yellin, "A Near Rational Model of the Business Cycle with Wage and Price Inertia"; and Lawrence Katz, "Efficiency Wage Theories: A Partial Evaluation," *NBER Macroeconomics Annual*, (Cambridge, Mass.: MIT Press, 1986), pp. 235–76.

PERSPECTIVES 13.3
Are Prices Sticky?

New Keynesian economists have examined whether real-world prices are in fact sticky. In one study, Stephen Cecchetti found considerable rigidity in the newsstand prices of magazines.[a] *Readers Digest*, for example, changed its newsstand price only six times between 1950 and 1980. In many years, only a few of the 38 magazines in the study had price changes.

In a broader study, Alan Blinder supervised interviews of corporate executives on the frequency with which their firms change prices.[b] A summary of some of his findings is given in Table 13.1. The survey data indicate that 49.5 percent of firms change prices once a year or less. This finding indicates a considerable departure from auction-market behavior.

Table 13.1
Frequency of Price Changes

NUMBER OF PRICE CHANGES PER YEAR	PERCENT OF COMPANIES
More than 12	14.5
4 to 12	7.5
2 to 4	12.9
1 to 2	15.6
1	39.3
Less than 1	10.2

[a]Stephen Cecchetti, "The Frequency of Price Adjustment: A Study of the Newsstand Prices of Magazines," *Journal of Econometrics*, 31 (April 1986) pp. 255–74.

[b]Alan Blinder, "On Sticky Prices," in N. Gregory Mankiw, ed., *Monetary Policy* (Chicago: University of Chicago Press, 1994), pp. 117–50.

Worker efficiency is a positive function of the real wage. This being the case, we now write the aggregate production function as

$$Y = F[\overline{K}, eN]$$

(13.6)

As before, output (Y) depends on the amount of capital (K).[13] Output also depends on the amount of the labor input, which we now measure in efficiency units. The number of efficiency units of labor equals the number of physical units (N), measured in man-hours per period, for example, multiplied by the index of efficiency (e). Output increases either when more units of labor are hired (N increases) or when the efficiency of the existing labor force improves (e is increased by a rise in W/P).

[13]Here we have gone back to the specification of the aggregate production function in earlier chapters, where the stock of capital is fixed, as indicated by the bar over K. We also ignore the technology shock introduced in the previous section on real business cycle models and for simplicity omit the time (t) subscripts used earlier in the chapter.

With the production function as given by equation (13.6), the goal of the firm is to set the real wage so that the cost of an efficiency unit of labor is minimized, or to say the same thing in reverse, to maximize the number of efficiency units of labor bought with each dollar of the wage bill. This goal is accomplished by increasing the real wage to the point where the elasticity of the efficiency index $[e(W/P)]$ with respect to the real wage is equal to 1.

Let's use an example to see why this is the case. First, recall that elasticity is the percentage change in one variable (here the efficiency of labor) per 1 percent change in another (here the real wage). So we are saying that the condition that determines the optimal level of the real wage, which in the literature is called the efficiency wage, $(W/P)^*$, is

$$\frac{\text{percentage change in } e\left(\dfrac{W}{P}\right)}{\text{percentage change in }\left(\dfrac{W}{P}\right)} = 1 \tag{13.7}$$

Suppose that, beginning at a low level, a 1 percent increase in the real wage leads to a 2 percent increase in the efficiency of labor. The firm will benefit from this increase because each dollar of the wage bill will buy more efficiency units of labor (wage bill up 1 percent, number of efficiency units up 2 percent). With further increases in the wage bill, efficiency gains begin to decline. At the point where a 1 percent increase in the real wage produces only a 1 percent increase in efficiency, the firm will not find it optimal to increase the real wage any further; the efficiency wage has been reached.[14]

Proponents of the efficiency wage theory argue that in many industries real wages are set on efficiency grounds. Real wages do not adjust to clear labor markets. In fact, the rationales that underlie efficiency wage models imply that firms will set the real wage *above* the market-clearing level. Persistent, involuntary unemployment will result. Our next task is to examine these rationales for efficiency wages, some of which were anticipated by Henry Ford.

Several rationales have been offered for the payment of efficiency wages:

1. **The shirking model.** By setting the real wage above going market levels (i.e., a worker's next best opportunity), a firm gives a worker an incentive not to shirk or loaf on the job. If he does, he may be fired, and he knows it would be hard to get another job at such a high wage. If firms can monitor job performance only imperfectly and with some cost, such a high-wage strategy may be profitable.
2. **Turnover cost models.** By paying an above-market wage, firms can reduce quit rates and, thus, recruiting and training costs. The high wage also allows them to develop a more experienced, and therefore more productive, workforce.
3. **Gift exchange models.** Another explanation of why efficiency depends on the real wage centers on the morale of a firm's workers. According to this argument, if the

---

[14]If, for example, the firm had increased the real wage further to the point at which a 1 percent increase in the real wage resulted in a 1/2 percent increase in efficiency, the number of efficiency units per dollar of the wage bill would have fallen.

firm pays a real wage above the market-clearing wage, this higher wage improves morale, and workers put forth more effort. The firm pays the workers a *gift* of the above-market wage, and the workers reciprocate with higher efficiency.[15]

None of these rationales is intended to apply to all parts of the labor market. If, however, efficiency wage considerations are important and therefore real wage rates are set above market-clearing levels in many sectors, substantial involuntary unemployment may result. Workers will continue to seek jobs in the high-wage sector, working, for example, when demand is high, rather than take low-paying jobs.

Notice that the real wage is fixed on efficiency grounds [to meet condition (13.7)]. Efficiency wage models explain a *real* rigidity. We have just seen how this real rigidity can explain involuntary unemployment. By itself, however, the rigidity of the *real* wage due to the payment of efficiency wages does not explain why changes in aggregate demand affect output and employment and therefore the level of involuntary unemployment. If there was a fall in nominal aggregate demand, resulting, for example, from a decline in the money supply, firms could lower their prices sufficiently to keep output (sales) unchanged and lower the *money* wage by the same amount to keep the real wage at the efficiency wage, $(W/P)^*$. If, however, firms do not lower prices because of menu costs, as explained in the previous section, then to keep the real wage at the efficiency wage requires the money wage also to be fixed. In this case, when aggregate demand declines, output and employment will fall and involuntary unemployment will rise. Thus, a nominal rigidity, the menu cost, and the real wage rigidity due to efficiency wages combine to explain changes in involuntary unemployment.

Insider–Outsider Models and Hysteresis

The last direction in new Keynesian research that we consider is the one most closely related to persistent high unemployment rates in Europe since 1980 (see Table 11.2). Such persistent high unemployment contrasts sharply with the low unemployment for the same countries from the late 1950s to the early 1970s. These patterns have led to the hypothesis that present unemployment is strongly influenced by past unemployment. Economies can, as it were, get stuck in *unemployment traps*. The term for this condition that we used in Chapter 11 is **hysteresis**. A variable exhibits hysteresis if, when shocked away from an initial value, it shows no tendency to return even when the shock is over. In terms of unemployment, hysteresis models try to explain why high unemployment persists even after its initial cause is long past.

There are a number of explanations for hysteresis in the unemployment process. This discussion is limited to one model that has received

hysteresis
is the property that, when a variable is shocked away from an initial value, it shows no tendency to return even when the shock is over

---

[15]A different argument for the positive relationship between worker efficiency and the real wage is applicable to developing countries. A higher real wage allows for a higher consumption level, which provides better nutrition and health. These in turn reduce absenteeism and make workers more energetic and productive. An early model of this relationship is given by Harvey Leibenstein, "The Theory of Underemployment in Densely Populated Backward Areas," in *Economic Backwardness and Economic Growth* (New York: Wiley, 1963), though a similar argument can be found in the work of Alfred Marshall in the nineteenth century.

considerable attention—the **insider–outsider model**.[16] Rather than present the model formally, we will explain it with an example.

As with the sticky price models, versions of the insider–outsider model require imperfect competition. In the case of the insider–outsider model, it is assumed that both the product and the labor market are imperfectly competitive. So we will consider a situation with a labor union on the employee side and a few firms as employers—for example, the German steel industry. The union members, whom we will call *insiders*, are assumed to have bargaining power with employers because it is costly to replace them with *outsiders* (nonunion members). The cost of replacing them is a recruiting and training cost for new workers. Union members may also impose costs on outsiders who attempt to underbid them for jobs, for example, by setting up picket lines.

The insiders are assumed to use their bargaining power to push the real wage above the market-clearing level, resulting in an unemployed group of outsiders. Insiders will push the real wage only up to a certain point, however, because the higher the real wage, the fewer insiders will be employed. This relationship follows because employment is equal to the firms' demand for labor, which depends negatively on the real wage. If in our example the insiders number 200,000, we will assume they bargain for a real wage that they *believe* will result in all (or almost all) of them being employed. They may not, however, end up being employed, because if economywide aggregate demand slackens unexpectedly, output and employment will fall. A portion of the insiders will be laid off.

Thus, in the insider–outsider model, unemployment results from a real wage set above the market-clearing level (outsider unemployment) as well as from a cyclical response to changes in aggregate demand. A novel feature of these models is the interrelationship of these two types of unemployment.

To see this interrelationship, consider the effect of several prolonged recessions such as those in the 1970s, early 1980s, and then 1990s. During the recessions, some layoffs are permanent, and some workers drift out of the union. *Some insiders become outsiders.* How quickly this happens depends on union rules. With the pool of insiders reduced, let us say to 160,000 workers, when an economic recovery takes place, the union will bargain for a higher real wage than previously (before the recessions when there were 200,000 insiders). There are now fewer insiders whose employment prospects matter. (Notice here the assumption that insiders are unconcerned about outsiders.) With a higher real wage, employment will remain lower than in the pre-recession period.

Past unemployment, then, causes current unemployment by turning insiders into outsiders; this is the hysteresis phenomenon. Once insiders have become outsiders, a sort of unemployment trap occurs. The outsiders do not exert downward

insider–outsider models

provide one explanation of hysteresis in unemployment. Insiders (e.g., union members) are the only group that affects the real wage bargain. Outsiders (e.g., those who want jobs) do not. Recessions cause insiders to become outsiders. After the recession, with fewer insiders, the real wage rises and unemployment persists

---

[16]An early version of the insider–outsider model is provided by Olivier J. Blanchard and Lawrence Summers, "Hysteresis and the European Unemployment Problem," in Stanley Fischer, ed., *NBER Macroeconomics Annual* (Cambridge, Mass.: MIT Press, 1986). See also Assar Lindbeck and Dennis Snower, "Wage Setting Unemployment and Insider–Outsider Relations," *American Economic Review*, 76 (May 1986), pp. 235–39; and Robert M. Solow, "Insiders and Outsiders in Wage Determination," *Scandinavian Journal of Economics*, 87 (1985), pp. 411–28.

pressure on real wages because they are irrelevant to the wage-bargaining process.[17] Insider–outsider models thus explain why high unemployment has persisted in some European countries for such long periods—periods too long to be the result of fixed money wage contracts or backward-looking price expectations.

13.3 CONCLUSION

Real business cycle theory and the new Keynesian economics are extensions of two conflicting traditions in macroeconomics. The real business cycle theory is a modern version of classical economics. The business cycle is an equilibrium phenomenon. It is the result of the actions of optimizing agents in the face of changes in the economic environment (e.g., productivity shocks) or in preferences. Macroeconomic stabilization policies are counterproductive. The real business cycle theorists therefore reach noninterventionist policy conclusions, as did the original classical economists.

The new Keynesian economics is set firmly in the tradition of John Maynard Keynes. New Keynesian economists believe that much unemployment is involuntary. They believe that the deviations of output below potential output during recessions are socially costly. There is a potential role for stabilization policy in preventing such output shortfalls and alleviating the personal costs of involuntary unemployment. New Keynesian economics is an attempt to improve the microeconomic foundations of the traditional Keynesian models, not to challenge their major premises.

We have looked at criticisms of the real business cycle explanation of economic fluctuations. New Keynesian economics also has its critics. Some doubt that menu costs, efficiency wage considerations, or bargaining models are of much substantive importance. The challenge to the new Keynesian economists is to provide empirical support for their theoretical models.

KEY TERMS

- seigniorage 287
- sticky price models 292
- menu costs 292
- efficiency wage models 293
- hysteresis 296
- insider–outsider models 297

---

[17]There are extensions of the basic insider–outsider model, in which the unemployed outsiders do have some influence on the wage bargain. In these extended models, the higher the rate of unemployment, the less bargaining power the insiders are able to exert. Their fear of becoming unemployed is greater, because they know that their prospect of finding another job is poorer, and the employers' threat to replace them with unemployed workers is more credible. In these extended models, however, there is still persistent unemployment. See the discussion in Olivier J. Blanchard, "Wage Bargaining and Unemployment Persistence," *Journal of Money, Credit, and Banking*, 23 (August 1991), pp. 278–92.

REVIEW QUESTIONS AND PROBLEMS

1. Compare the real business cycle theorists' view of the causes of fluctuations of output and employment with the view of new classical economists.
2. Within the simple real business cycle model presented in section 13.1, analyze the effect of a negative shock to technology (a negative shock to z_t) that lasts for one period.
3. Explain the real business cycle theorists' views on the proper conduct of monetary and fiscal policy.
4. Suppose there was a change in preferences in a real business cycle model such that the representative agent valued leisure more and consumption goods less. How would output and employment be affected by the change?
5. Explain why the assumption of imperfect competition is important within each of the new Keynesian models considered in section 13.2.
6. Suppose that you observe in wage data that workers with identical skills are paid very different wage rates in different industries. Is this difference consistent with the assumption that the labor market is competitive? Is it consistent with the efficiency wage model?
7. Explain how the insider–outsider model accounts for the persistent high unemployment in European countries during the post-1980 period.
8. New classical economists believe that in useful macroeconomic models (1) agents optimize and (2) markets clear. Do the models that emerge from the new Keynesian research effort have either or both of these properties? Explain.
9. Explain the relationship of the new Keynesian models to the Keynesian models considered in Chapters 6 through 9.
10. During the administration of George W. Bush, reductions in the tax rates on labor income, dividends, and capital gains were the centerpiece of fiscal policy. Analyze the effects of these tax cuts within the real business cycle theory.

Chapter 14

Macroeconomic Models:
A Summary

*T*his chapter summarizes the theories considered in earlier chapters
and clarifies areas of agreement and controversy among the various
schools.

14.1 THEORETICAL ISSUES

It is convenient to center our discussion on the aggregate supply–aggregate demand
framework used previously to characterize the various economic models. The first
model we considered, the classical model, views output as completely determined
by supply factors. This view is embodied in the *vertical aggregate supply schedule*
shown in Figure 14.1*a*.

Central to the classical theory of output and employment are the classical labor
market assumptions. Both labor supply and demand depend only on the real wage,
which is known to all market participants. The money wage is perfectly flexible and
moves to equate demand and supply in the labor market. Increases in aggregate
demand cause the price level to rise. The price rise, other things being equal, spurs
production. To clear the labor market, however, the money wage has to rise proportionately with the price level. The real wage is then unchanged, and consequently
employment and output are unchanged in the new equilibrium.

In the classical system, the role of aggregate demand is to determine the price
level. The classical theory of aggregate demand is an implicit theory based on the
quantity theory of money. The quantity theory provides a proportional relationship
between the exogenous quantity of money and nominal income. In the Cambridge
form, this relationship is

$$M = kPY \qquad \qquad (14.1)$$

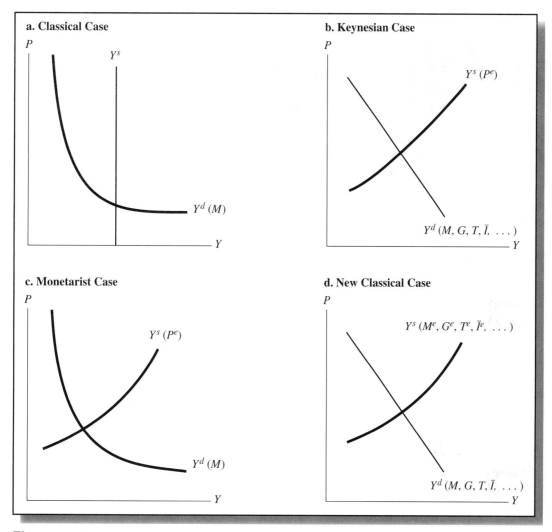

Figure 14.1 Theories of Aggregate Demand and Supply

With k treated as a constant, changes in the quantity of money result in proportional changes in nominal income (PY). With real income (Y) fixed, the full adjustment comes in prices.

This relationship provides the classical aggregate demand schedule in Figure 14.1a. The economic process behind this theory is that if, for example, there is an excess supply of money ($M > kPY$), a corresponding excess demand for commodities will drive up the aggregate price level. Equilibrium between money demand and supply implies that there is no spillover to the commodity market causing a change in the price level. The classical model has a *monetary theory of aggregate demand*.

The real business cycle theory is a modern version of the classical theory. As in the classical model, output and employment in the real business cycle model are determined by supply-side variables. The labor market is always in equilibrium; all unemployment is voluntary. The role of money in the real business cycle model, as in the classical model, is solely to determine the price level.

In its simplest form, the Keynesian model is the antithesis of both the classical and real business cycle theories. In a simple Keynesian model, such as that discussed in Chapter 6, supply plays no role in output determination. The aggregate supply curve implied by such simple Keynesian models is horizontal, indicating that supply is no constraint on the level of production, an assumption appropriate, if ever, only to situations in which production is well below capacity levels. On the demand side, the simple Keynesian model concentrates on the determinants of autonomous expenditures: government spending, taxes, and autonomous investment demand. Monetary factors are neglected. This simple model highlights a central notion in Keynesian economics—the importance of aggregate demand in determining output and employment.

But this simple Keynesian model is an incomplete representation of Keynes's work. The Keynesian theory has been modified and refined over the period since Keynes wrote. The modern Keynesian model allows for the influence of both supply factors on output and monetary factors on aggregate demand. Still, the model remains "Keynesian" in that aggregate demand is important in determining output.

On the supply side, the Keynesian view is illustrated by the aggregate supply schedule shown in Figure 14.1b. In contrast to the vertical classical supply schedule, the Keynesian aggregate supply schedule slopes upward to the right. Increases in aggregate demand that shift the aggregate demand schedule out to the right will increase both price and output. In the short run, an increase in the price level will cause firms to supply a higher level of output because the money wage will not rise proportionately with price.

The money wage is assumed to adjust only incompletely as a result of institutional factors in the labor market, the most important being fixed money wage contracts, as well as labor suppliers' imperfect information about the aggregate price level and, hence, about the real wage. Much of the research of the new Keynesian economists is directed toward providing additional rationales for wage and price stickiness—toward improving the microeconomic foundation of the Keynesian aggregate supply schedule in Figure 14.1b .

On the demand side (the Y^d schedule in Figure 14.1b), the modern Keynesian model provides a role for monetary factors (M) as well as fiscal policy variables (G and T) and other autonomous elements of aggregate demand (e.g., autonomous investment, $\bar{I}$). The Keynesian theory of aggregate demand is an *explicit* theory, in contrast to the *implicit* theory of classical economists, in that the level of aggregate demand is found by first determining the level of the components of aggregate demand: consumption, investment, and government spending. Then we sum these to find aggregate demand. Money affects aggregate demand, primarily its investment component, by influencing the interest rate. There is no reason to believe that such monetary effects on aggregate demand are small. Neither is there reason to believe that monetary influences are dominant. Money is one of several important influences on aggregate demand in the Keynesian system.

There are, thus, two important differences between the Keynesian and classical frameworks:

1. In the classical model, output and employment are completely supply-determined, whereas in the Keynesian theory in the short run, output and employment are determined jointly by aggregate supply and demand. In the Keynesian system, aggregate demand is an important determinant of output and employment.
2. Aggregate demand in the classical model is determined solely by the quantity of money. In the Keynesian system, money is only one of several factors that determine aggregate demand.

These two issues, the role of aggregate demand in determining output and employment and the relative importance of monetary and other factors as determinants of aggregate demand, are also the ones that divide the Keynesians from monetarists and new classical economists.

The major controversy between monetarists, whose view of aggregate supply and demand is represented in Figure 14.1c, and Keynesians has centered on point 2, the degree to which monetary forces dominate the determination of aggregate demand. Monetarists have taken the Cambridge version of the quantity equation [equation (14.1)] as the basis for their own quantity theory view that money is the dominant influence on aggregate demand and, therefore, on nominal income.

On the supply side, there is no fundamental difference between the monetarist and Keynesian theories. In both monetarist and Keynesian models, the aggregate supply schedule slopes upward to the right in the short run and approaches the vertical classical formulation only in the long run. In both models, changes in aggregate demand affect output in the short run. But agreement on this issue has not kept monetarists and Keynesians from reaching substantially different conclusions about the usefulness of aggregate demand management policies to stabilize output and employment in the short run.

The new classical view of aggregate supply and demand is illustrated in Figure 14.1d. The issue dividing new classical economists and Keynesians concerns point 1, the degree to which aggregate demand plays a role in determining real output. New classical economists believe that systematic, and therefore predictable, changes in aggregate demand will not affect real output. Such changes will be anticipated by rational economic agents. The aggregate demand schedule and the aggregate supply schedule will shift symmetrically, changing the price level but leaving real output unchanged. To reflect this dependence of the aggregate supply schedule on expected changes in the determinants of aggregate demand and consequently in the rational expectation of the price level, the aggregate supply schedule in Figure 14.1d is shown as depending on the expected level of the money supply (M^e) as well as expected values of fiscal policy variables and other possible determinants of aggregate demand ($G^e, T^e, \bar{I}^e, \dots$).

Unanticipated changes in aggregate demand—for example, an increase in the money supply (M) that could not have been predicted (M^e is unchanged)—will shift the aggregate demand schedule without shifting the aggregate supply schedule. Such unanticipated changes in aggregate demand will cause labor suppliers to make price forecast errors and will therefore affect output and employment. In this respect the new classical model is a modification of the original classical model in which aggregate demand had *no* role in determining output and employment. The modification is the substitution of the rational expectations assumption in the new classical analysis for the classical assumption of perfect information. In the classical analysis, there were no price forecast errors on the part of labor suppliers. Labor suppliers had perfect information about the price level. No unanticipated changes in aggregate demand were assumed. On the demand side, there are no obvious differences between the new classical and Keynesian positions. (Compare the Y^d schedules in Figure 14.1b and d.) This is not to say, however, that new classical economists agree with all aspects of the Keynesian theory of aggregate demand. In fact, they do not believe that much of the Keynesian theory rests on strong microeconomic foundations.

From the foregoing it should be clear that the monetarist–Keynesian dispute and the Keynesian–new classical dispute revolve around the same issues that separate Keynesians from classical economists and real business cycle theorists. The Keynesian revolution attacked the classical supply-determined, full-employment theory of output and employment, as well as the quantity theory of money. New classical economists and monetarists have modified these two aspects of classical economics and used the modified versions to attack the Keynesian system. Points 1 and 2, which in terms of Figure 14.1 concern the slope of the short-run aggregate supply function and the determinants of the aggregate demand function, have been the central issues in macroeconomic controversies for over 60 years.

14.2 POLICY ISSUES

Given the classical roots of the real business cycle, monetarist, and new classical theories, it is not surprising that these modern theories share the noninterventionist policy conclusions of the original classical model. In contrast, Keynesians are policy interventionists who favor managing aggregate demand to stabilize output and employment.

In the classical system, output and employment are self-adjusting to the supply-determined level of full employment. There is clearly no role for aggregate demand stabilization policies. This is also the case in real business cycle models, where fluctuations in output and employment result from optimal responses of economic agents to changes in the economic environment. In the new classical model, unanticipated shifts in aggregate demand do affect output and employment. Sensible stabilization policies, however, would have to consist of systematic reaction patterns to the state of the economy. Such systematic shifts in aggregate demand would be anticipated by the public and, therefore, would not affect output or employment. Consequently, new classical economists also view aggregate demand stabilization policies as ineffective.

Monetarists believe that *monetary* policy actions, whether anticipated or not, affect output and employment in the short run. Still, they arrive at the same noninterventionist policy conclusions as classical and new classical economists. As do classical economists, monetarists believe that the private sector is stable if left free from destabilizing government policy actions. Further, because monetarists view aggregate demand as determined predominantly by the money supply, the best way to stabilize aggregate demand is to provide stable growth in the money supply.

Against this noninterventionist view is the Keynesian position that a private-enterprise monetary economy is unstable without government policies to regulate aggregate demand. Keynesians favor activist monetary and fiscal policies to offset shocks to private aggregate demand.

Thus, although we have considered several schools of macroeconomic theory, the major policy controversy is between two positions—the noninterventionist position, with roots in the original classical system, and the Keynesian interventionist position. On this issue, as with the theoretical issues discussed previously, the controversy is long-standing. In modern form, it extends back to the Keynesian attack on the classical orthodoxy. But there were heretics before Keynes, and the origins of the policy and theoretical controversies discussed here date back to the early 1800s.

How can such controversies proceed for so long without resolution? In economics, we have no way to conduct controlled laboratory experiments aimed at settling controversies. We cannot, for example, construct an economy, let the money supply grow for 10 years at a constant rate, and then see if the monetarist predictions are verified. As Milton Friedman has written on this issue,

> Controlled experiments permitting near isolation of one or a few forces are virtually impossible. We must test our propositions by observing uncontrolled experience that involves a large number of people, numerous economic variables, frequent changes in other circumstances, and, at that, is imperfectly recorded. The interpretation of the experience is further complicated because the experience affects directly many of the observers, often giving them reasons, irrelevant from a scientific view, to prefer one rather than another interpretation of the complex and ever-changing course of events.[1]

Or as Keynes wrote earlier, "In economics you cannot *convict* your opponent of error—you can only convince him of it."[2]

Failure to resolve the continuing controversies in macroeconomics is unsettling even if it is not surprising. This and preceding chapters in Part II present areas of agreement as well as controversy. We have attempted to show that the controversies center on well-defined issues based on theoretical differences in the underlying models.

REVIEW QUESTIONS AND PROBLEMS

1. Suppose that investment demand in a given economy is predicted to be weak next year, let us say 10 percent below this year's level, because of an exogenous shock. All other components of aggregate demand are predicted to be at levels comparable to this year's. These levels were consistent with high employment and relatively stable prices. For each of the following macroeconomic systems, explain the effects of this exogenous fall in aggregate demand and explain the

---

[1]Milton Friedman, "Why Economists Disagree," in Milton Friedman, *Dollars and Deficits* (Upper Saddle River, N.J.: Prentice Hall, 1968), pp. 15–16.
[2]Quoted from Paul Davidson, *Money and the Real World* (New York: Wiley, 1978), p. ix.

proper policy response implied by the model; that is, what action should the policymaker take?

   a. Classical model.
   b. Keynesian model.
   c. Monetarist model.
   d. New classical model.

2. The question of what information market participants possess at any point in time and how quickly they learn—in other words, the information structure of the model—is a distinguishing feature of the different macroeconomic systems discussed. With reference to the classical, Keynesian, monetarist, and new classical models, explain the differing assumptions about the information that market participants possess and the degree to which these differing assumptions account for the different policy conclusions derived from these models.

3. Within the classical, real business cycle, Keynesian, monetarist, and new classical models, analyze the effect of an autonomous fall in the price of imported oil. Explain the effect of this change on output, employment, and the aggregate price level within each framework.

4. One rule that has been proposed for fiscal policy is that the government budget should be balanced each year—no budget deficits. What position do you think each of the following groups of economists would take on this proposal?

   a. Monetarists.
   b. Keynesians.
   c. Real business cycle theorists.

5. Which of the frameworks that we have considered do you view as the most useful in explaining the behavior of the economy and in providing proper policy prescriptions? Defend your choice.

Part IV

Open Economy Macroeconomics

CHAPTER 15

Exchange Rates and the International Monetary System

CHAPTER 16

Monetary and Fiscal Policy in the Open Economy

*P*art IV examines U.S. international economic relations, including both trade flows and capital movements. Chapter 15 analyzes how exchange rates are determined in different international monetary systems and considers the relative merits of these systems. In Chapter 16, we develop an open economy version of the *IS–LM* curve model. We then use this model to study the effects of monetary and fiscal policy in the open economy under both fixed and flexible exchange rates.

Chapter 15

Exchange Rates and the International Monetary System

*I*n 1960, U.S. imports of goods and services totaled 4.4 percent of GDP; by 2003, this figure was 13.8 percent. Exports rose from 4.9 percent of GDP in 1960 to 9.7 percent in 2003. Financial markets in the United States and other nations have also become much more closely linked over the past three decades. Overall, the U.S. economy has become much more *open* in the sense of having more extensive trade and financial dealings with other economies.

In other chapters, examples and Perspectives emphasize the interrelations of the U.S. economy and the economies of other nations. The chapters in this part focus explicitly on the macroeconomics of open economies, which brings these interrelations to center stage. This chapter considers the determination of exchange rates, the current international monetary system as well as the system it replaced, and the interactions between the domestic economy and our international economic transactions.

We begin by examining the U.S. **balance of payments accounts**, which summarize our foreign economic transactions (section 15.1). Next, we explain how exchange rates are determined in currency markets under differing exchange rate systems (section 15.2). The actual exchange rate arrangements that make up the current international monetary system are then examined (section 15.3). The relative merits of pegged versus flexible exchange rate systems are assessed (section 15.4). Finally, we review the U.S. experience with a system of at least partially flexible exchange rates over the years since 1973 (section 15.5).

balance of payments accounts
the Balance of Payments Accounts record economic transactions between U.S. and foreign residents both in goods and assets

Exchange rates are central to the focus of this chapter. An exchange rate between two currencies is the price of one currency in terms of the other. The price of the British pound in terms of the U.S. dollar on February 4, 2004 was $1.83 ($1.83 = 1 pound); the price of a Canadian dollar was 75 U.S. cents; the price of a euro (the common currency of 12 European countries) was $1.25. Exchanges between the U.S. dollar and other currencies take place when U.S. residents want to purchase foreign goods or assets as well as when foreign residents want to purchase U.S. goods and assets. A look at the nature of these transactions between the United States and other countries will be the starting point for our study of how exchange rates are determined.

15.1 THE U.S. BALANCE OF PAYMENTS ACCOUNTS

The U.S. Department of Commerce records foreign economic transactions in the balance of payments accounts. On one side of the accounts, all earnings from the foreign activities of U.S. residents and the U.S. government are recorded as credits; on the other side, expenditures abroad are reported as debits. A point to notice is that, by the usual principles of double-entry bookkeeping, each credit must be matched by an equal debit, and vice versa. Each expenditure on foreign goods, for example, must be financed somehow; the source of financing is recorded as a credit. A first conclusion, then, before we even look at the numbers, is that if *all* transactions are counted, the balance of payments always balances.

We will, however, want to consider subcategories of our foreign transactions, and for such subcategories there is no reason to believe that receipts from abroad will equal earnings from abroad. In recent years, for example, expenditures on our merchandise exports by foreign residents (a credit in our balance of payments) have fallen far short of our expenditures on imported goods (a debit in our balance of payments). This *deficit* in our **merchandise trade balance** has been a matter of concern, for reasons to be discussed.

Table 15.1 summarizes the U.S. balance of payments accounts for 2002.

merchandise trade balance
measures exports minus imports in the U.S. balance of payments

The Current Account

The first group of items in the table are **current account** transactions. Among these, the first items listed are *merchandise exports and imports*, to which we have just referred. Examples of merchandise exports are the sale of a U.S. computer system to a British firm or the sale of U.S. grain to Russia. Purchases of Japanese cars, German cameras, or Honduran bananas by U.S. residents are examples of U.S. imports. In 2002, U.S. merchandise imports exceeded exports by $482.9 billion. We had a merchandise trade deficit of that amount.

The next category in the table is imports and exports of *services*, entered only in terms of their net value. Examples of transactions in the service category are financial, insurance, and shipping services. Also in this category are dividends and interest

current account
in the U.S. balance of payments is a record of U.S. merchandise exports and imports as well as trade in services and foreign transfer payments

Table 15.1 U.S. Balance of Payments, 2002 (billions of dollars)

	CREDIT (+)	DEBIT (−)	BALANCE (−) DEFICIT (+) SURPLUS
Current account			
Merchandise exports (+) and imports (−)	681.8	−1,164.7	−482.9
Service transactions (net)	65.0		
Transfers (net)		−63.0	
Current account balance			−480.9
Capital account			
Capital inflows (+) and outflows (−)[a]	612.1	−184.0	
Capital account subbalance			428.1
Statistical discrepancy			−45.8
Official Reserve Transactions			
Reduction in U.S. official reserve assets			3.7
Increase in foreign official assets in the United States			94.9
Total official reserve transactions			98.6

[a]Includes increases in U.S. government foreign assets other than official reserve assets.

Source: *Survey of Current Business*, October 2003. Data are on a slightly different basis (coverage and timing) from U.S. census data shown elsewhere in the book.

earned by U.S. residents from their assets abroad (a credit) and interest and dividends paid to foreign residents who hold U.S. assets (a debit). The net item in the table, $65 billion, indicates that in 2002 we exported more of such services than we imported. The last transactions in the current account are *net transfers*. Recorded here are private and government transfer payments made between the United States and other countries. Such payments include U.S. foreign aid payments (a debit) and private or government pension payments to persons living abroad (a debit). Any such transfer to a U.S. resident from abroad would be a credit on this line.

If we stop or draw the line at this point, we can compute the *current account balance*. The table indicates that in 2002 the current account was in deficit by $480.9 billion. Overall, just considering current account transactions, U.S. residents spent over $480.9 billion more abroad than was earned.

capital account
in the balance of payments is a record of purchases of U.S. assets by foreign residents (capital inflows) and purchases of foreign assets by U.S. residents (capital outflows)

The Capital Account

The next entries in the table record **capital account** transactions.[1] Capital inflows (credits) are purchases of U.S. assets by foreign residents. Capital inflows include purchases by foreigners of U.S. private or government

---

[1]In previous chapters, the term *investment* has been used exclusively to refer to purchases of physical capital goods. The term *capital* referred to those physical goods themselves. In the discussion of international economic relations, the term *capital flows* refers to exchanges of financial assets involving individuals in different countries as well as direct investment such as the purchase of a plant in another country.

bonds, stocks, and bank deposits. In addition, foreign direct investments in the United States, such as Honda's building of a plant in Ohio, are capital inflows in the balance of payments. Purchases by U.S. residents of financial assets or direct investments in foreign countries are capital outflows (debits) in the balance of payments. During the 1980s, the United States began to run large surpluses in the capital account that partly balanced out large deficits in the current account. In 2002, this surplus was $428.1 billion.

An important point concerning the U.S. capital account is that foreign purchases of our assets largely represent U.S. borrowing from foreign residents. The large capital inflows of 1982–2002 included $1,000 billion of foreign purchases of U.S. government securities and an even larger amount of foreign loans or purchases of private U.S. securities. During this period, large excesses of merchandise imports over exports (trade deficits) were, in effect, financed by borrowing from abroad. Between 1983 and 2002, as a result of this borrowing, the United States went from being a net creditor nation to a nation with a net foreign debt in excess of $2,600 billion.

Statistical Discrepancy

The next item in the table is the *statistical discrepancy*. Because not all international economic transactions are properly recorded, the statistical discrepancy (or errors and omissions term) is the amount that must be added to make the total balance of payments balance. As can be seen from the table, the statistical discrepancy for 2002 was a negative $45.8 billion. This means that on net the expenditures of U.S. residents abroad were undercounted by that amount.

Official Reserve Transactions

Let us stop and examine the point we have now reached in considering U.S. foreign economic transactions. Suppose we draw a line below the statistical discrepancy. All the items above the line represent international economic transactions undertaken by private U.S. residents or the U.S. government for some independent motive. By this we mean a motive other than the effect the transaction will have on the balance of payments, or, as we will see presently, on the value of the U.S. dollar relative to other currencies. A U.S. resident buys a Japanese car or a share of stock in a German company because of a preference for it over its domestic counterpart. The U.S. government may give foreign aid to another government to stabilize the political situation in that country. All the items above the line are what, from the point of view of the balance of payments accounts, can be termed *autonomous*, or independently motivated, transactions.

In contrast, the official reserve transactions below this line are carried out by central banks, either the U.S. Federal Reserve System or foreign central banks (e.g., the Bank of England or the Bank of Japan) in pursuit of international economic policy objectives. Here we simply explain the nature of these transactions. The motivation for them is explained later in the chapter.

The first item below the statistical discrepancy in Table 15.1 is the *reduction in U.S. official reserve assets*. Official reserve assets are holdings of gold, special drawing rights (a reserve asset created by the International Monetary Fund),[2] and foreign currency holdings. From Table 15.1 we see that, in 2002, U.S. official reserve assets declined by $3.7 billion. That amount of our reserve assets was used to finance expenditures abroad. Reductions in official reserve assets are a credit in the balance of payments.

The next and last item in the balance of payments table is the *increase in foreign official assets in the United States*. Foreign central banks hold a portion of their reserve assets in the form of dollars. Dollars are an important reserve asset because the dollar is commonly used in international transactions. If foreign central banks buy dollars, that is a credit in our balance of payments (a capital inflow), because they are investing in the United States.[3] In 2002, foreign central banks increased the amount of official reserve assets held in the United States by $94.9 billion, hence the positive item in this line of our balance of payments accounts.

Read Perspectives 15.1.

15.2 EXCHANGE RATES AND THE MARKET FOR FOREIGN EXCHANGE

foreign exchange
a general term to refer to an aggregate of foreign currencies

The demand for foreign currencies by domestic residents is called the demand for **foreign exchange**. The foreign exchange market is the market in which national currencies are traded for one another. It is in this market, for example, that U.S. residents sell dollars to purchase foreign exchange (foreign currencies). In the United States, the central market for foreign exchange is composed of brokers and bank foreign exchange departments in New York City.

To see the link between the balance of payments accounts and transactions in the foreign exchange market, we begin by recognizing that all expenditures by U.S. residents on foreign goods, services, or assets and all foreign transfer payments (debits in the balance of payments accounts) also represent demands for foreign currencies—that is, demands for *foreign exchange*. The U.S. resident buying a Japanese car pays for it in dollars, but the Japanese exporter will expect to be paid in yen. So dollars must be exchanged for yen in the foreign exchange market. Take another example: If a U.S. resident wants to buy a share of stock on the London stock exchange, a broker must convert the buyer's dollars into British pounds before actually making the purchase. *Thus, the total U.S. residents' expenditure abroad represents a demand for foreign exchange.* Looked at from the point of view of the dollar, we can also state that the *total foreign expenditure of U.S. residents represents an equal supply of dollars in the foreign exchange market.*

Conversely, all foreign earnings of U.S. residents reflect equal earnings of foreign exchange. American exporters, for example, will expect to be paid in dollars, and to

---

[2]The International Monetary Fund (IMF) is an agency that was set up near the end of World War II to administer the international monetary agreements signed at that time. These agreements, the Bretton Woods agreements, are discussed in sections 15.3 and 15.4. Special drawing rights (SDRs) are sometimes referred to as "paper gold." They are a type of deposit at the IMF that can be exchanged between nations to settle payment imbalances.

[3]They need not hold U.S. currency. After buying dollars, they can use them to purchase U.S. government or private securities.

PERSPECTIVES 15.1
U.S. Current Account Deficits—Are They Sustainable?

From Table 15.1 it can be seen that the U.S. current account deficit was nearly $500 billion in 2002, approximately 5 percent of GDP. As of mid-2004 the current account deficit continued to run at nearly $50 billion per month. Are current account deficits of this magnitude something we should be concerned about? How concerned?

Many argue that we should worry about these deficits. In early 2004 the International Monetary Fund (IMF) warned that the U.S. current account deficit posed serious risks for both the U.S. and the world economy. Domestically, many have warned that, at least eventually, such current account deficits will result in a crisis where the value of the U.S. dollar will fall precipitously, the demand for U.S. financial assets will fall, and U.S. interest rates will shoot upwards.

Other observers, including as of 2004, Alan Greenspan, chairman of the Federal Reserve Board, see no impending crisis. They believe that the current account deficit is likely to be reversed by market forces in a benign fashion. Let's look at the issues.

Table 15.1 shows that the U.S. deficit on the current account is balanced for the most part by a surplus in the capital account and an increase in foreign official assets in the United States. The United States finances its current account deficit by borrowing abroad: from private investors (the capital account surplus) and from foreign central banks (the increase in foreign official assets). As the United States has run repeated large current account deficits, our foreign debt has grown to approximately $3 trillion by 2004.

Those who are worried about current account deficits believe that at a not too distant point foreign investors, including foreign central banks, will no longer be willing to buy such large amounts of U.S. financial assets. At this point, the dollar will fall sharply and U.S. interest rates will rise. In particular, these observers point to the huge purchases of dollars by Asian central banks over the past few years, an unsustainable flow of capital to the United States. Moreover, as the IMF has pointed out, the U.S. borrowing to finance the current account deficit has, by increasing overall borrowing, led to an increase in world interest rates making it harder for other countries, including emerging economies, to borrow to finance their investment needs.

Those who do not see the current account deficit as an immediate serious problem point to increasing globalization of the world capital markets. As other countries have liberalized their capital markets, investors in those countries have increased their demand for foreign assets, in large part U.S. assets. Even in countries that had for a long time allowed capital mobility, investors have made more cross-border investments in recent years. Economists have referred to this tendency as a decline in "home bias." These observers see the increased demand for dollar-denominated assets by Asian central banks as due to the particular policies of these countries. China, for example, whose central bank has in recent years been the largest purchaser of dollars, does so to keep the value of their currency, the remimbi, fixed in terms of the dollar. The factors that have led to the increased demand for U.S. assets and forces in the United States that contribute to the current account deficit will, in their view, be reversed in a gradual manner.

When we consider policy questions in Part V, we will look at the U.S. policies that have contributed to large current account deficits over the past 20 years and return to the question of the implications of these deficits.

buy our goods, foreigners must sell their currency and buy dollars. *Total credits in the balance of payments accounts are then equal to the supply of foreign exchange or, what is the same thing, the demand for dollars.*

Demand and Supply in the Foreign Exchange Market

Exchange rates among national currencies are determined in the foreign exchange market. In our discussion of this process, we make the following simplifying assumptions. Initially, we exclude official reserve transactions by central banks. In the jargon of international economics, we assume that central banks do not *intervene* in the foreign exchange market. We relax this assumption later in this section. Also for simplicity, we assume that there are only two countries, the United States, whose domestic currency is the dollar, and "Europe," whose domestic currency is the euro.[4] The *exchange rate* in this simple situation is the relative price of the two currencies, which we express as *the price of the euro in terms of dollars*. For example, if the price of the euro is 0.80 dollar (80 cents), then 1.25 euros trade for 1 dollar; at 1.00 dollar, the exchange rate (price of the euro) is higher, and 1 euro equals 1 dollar. It is important to remember that with the exchange rate expressed in this manner, a higher exchange rate means that the price of foreign currency (or foreign exchange) has risen. When the exchange rate rises, we say that the foreign currency has *appreciated* or the dollar has *depreciated*. Alternatively, a fall in the exchange rate means that the price of foreign exchange (price of the euro) has declined. The euro has *depreciated* while the dollar has *appreciated*.

Figure 15.1 shows the supply and demand curves for foreign exchange plotted against the exchange rate (π). As was explained, foreign expenditures by U.S. residents (imports, purchases of foreign assets, and foreign transfers) are demands for foreign exchange. How will this demand for foreign exchange vary with the price of foreign exchange? In Figure 15.1, the demand curve (D_{fe}) is downward-sloping, indicating that as the price of foreign exchange (price of euros) rises, the demand for foreign exchange falls. The reason is that a rise in the price of foreign exchange will increase the cost *in terms of dollars* of purchasing foreign goods. Imports will therefore decline, and less foreign exchange will be demanded. Note that here we are holding all prices other than the exchange rate constant. Suppose that you are considering the purchase of a German camera that costs 250 euros. If the exchange rate, the price of the euro in terms of dollars, is 0.80, the camera will cost $200 (250 euros = $200 at 1.25 euros to the dollar). If the exchange rate rises to 1.00, the camera will cost $250 (250 euros = $250 at 1 euro to the dollar). The higher the exchange rate, the higher the dollar cost of imported goods and the lower the demand for foreign exchange.

What about the demand for foreign exchange for the purchase of foreign assets and for foreign transfers? With respect to the latter, there is no reason for a definite relationship between the amount of foreign transfers and the exchange rate. It is not clear what effect the change in the exchange rate would have on foreign aid programs,

---

[4]Europe is, of course, not one country. We refer here to the set of European countries that have the euro as a common currency. Details are discussed in Perspectives 15.3. The fiction of a two-country world is employed to avoid the details of how the individual exchange rate with each foreign currency is determined.

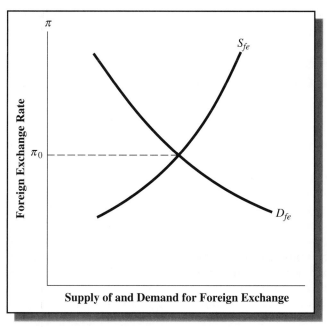

Figure 15.1 Foreign Exchange Market

The demand schedule for foreign exchange is downward-sloping plotted against the exchange rate (π), because the demand for foreign exchange to finance imports falls as the exchange rate rises, making foreign goods more expensive. The supply schedule for foreign exchange is upward-sloping, reflecting the assumption that the foreign exchange proceeds from export sales rise as the exchange rate rises, making domestic goods less expensive to foreign buyers. The equilibrium value of the exchange rate is π_0, the rate that equates demand and supply.

pension payments to persons living abroad, or gifts to foreign nationals. In the case of purchases of foreign assets, an increase in the exchange rate will, as in the case of imported goods, push up the price in dollars of the foreign stocks or bonds. The rise in the exchange rate will, however, also result in a proportional increase in the interest or dividend payment on the foreign bond or stock, again as measured in dollars. For example, a French bond costing 1,000 euros and paying interest of 100 euros per year will cost $800 and pay interest of $80 per year at an exchange rate of 0.80 (1.25 euros = 1 dollar). At an exchange rate of 1.0 (1 euro = 1 dollar), the bond will cost $1000 and pay interest of $100 per year. In either case, the bond represents an asset that pays a return of 10 percent per year. Consequently, we would not necessarily expect any effect on the demand for foreign assets as a result of a change in the exchange rate.[5] The downward slope of the demand for foreign exchange schedule results only from the fact that imports decline as the exchange rate rises.

---

[5]It is the expectation of a change in the exchange rate that would trigger changes in the demand for foreign versus domestic assets. If, for example, you expected the price of the euro to rise from 0.80 dollar today to 1.00 dollar next week, you could buy the French bond discussed in the text now for $800 and sell it next week for $1,000. For now, we are not allowing for *expected* changes in exchange rates.

The supply schedule for foreign exchange is drawn with a positive slope in Figure 15.1, which reflects the assumption that the supply of foreign exchange increases as the exchange rate rises. As the exchange rate (price of euros) rises, U.S. export goods become less expensive to Europeans in terms of euros. Again we are holding all other prices, including the dollar price of U.S. exports, fixed. For example, U.S. wheat that sells for $4 a bushel would cost a European 5 euros per bushel at an exchange rate of 0.80 but only 4 euros at an exchange rate of 1.00.

The demand for U.S. exports should therefore increase as the exchange rate rises. Notice, however, that a given *dollar* volume of exports earns less foreign exchange (fewer euros) at the higher exchange rate. For example, if the exchange rate rose by 10 percent and as a result the *dollar* volume of exports rose 10 percent, earnings of foreign exchange would be unchanged. The United States would be selling 10 percent more but earning 10 percent fewer euros on each sale.

For the supply of foreign exchange to increase as the exchange rate rises, the foreign demand for our exports must be more than *unit elastic*, meaning that a 1 percent increase in the exchange rate (which results in a 1 percent decline in the price of the export good to Europeans) must result in an increase in demand of more than 1 percent. If this condition is met, the dollar volume of our exports will rise more than in proportion to the rise in the exchange rate, and earnings of euros (the supply of foreign exchange) will increase as the exchange rate rises. This is the assumption we make in Figure 15.1.[6]

Exchange Rate Determination: Flexible Exchange Rates

So far we have excluded intervention (official reserve transactions) by central banks. The supply and demand schedules in Figure 15.1 are for only autonomous transactions in the balance of payments accounts. Let us continue with this assumption and see how the exchange rate is determined in the absence of intervention. In this case we would expect the exchange rate to move to clear the market, to equate the demand for and supply of foreign exchange. In Figure 15.1, this equilibrium exchange rate is π_0. The autonomous elements in the balance of payments account, those above the lines where the official reserve transactions are recorded, are equated by the adjustment of the exchange rate. Such a system of exchange rate determination, in which there is no central bank intervention, is a *flexible exchange rate system* or, as it is sometimes called, a *floating rate system*. An exchange rate system or regime is a set of international rules governing the setting of exchange rates. A completely flexible or floating rate system is a particularly simple set of rules for the central banks to follow; they do nothing to directly affect the level of their exchange rate. The exchange rate is market-determined.

To better understand the workings of a flexible exchange rate system, we examine the effect of a shock that increases the demand for foreign exchange. Suppose the

---

[6]Empirical support for this assumption is provided by Hendrik Houthakker and Stephen Magee, "Income and Price Elasticities in World Trade," *Review of Economics and Statistics*, 5 (May 1969), pp. 111–25. A later estimate by Jaime Marquez, "Bilateral Trade Elasticities," *Review of Economics and Statistics*, 72 (February 1990) pp. 75–76, indicates a just unit-elastic foreign demand for U.S. exports. This implies a vertical supply of foreign exchange. To assume a vertical supply curve would not change our analysis.

U.S. demand for imported goods increases. For example, assume that an increase in energy prices causes an increased demand for small, fuel-efficient foreign cars. The effect of this increase in import demand would show up in the foreign exchange market as a shift to the right in the demand schedule for foreign exchange—for example, from D_{fe}^0 to D_{fe}^1 as illustrated in Figure 15.2. At a given exchange rate, there is a greater demand for imports in the United States and correspondingly a greater demand for foreign exchange to finance imports. At the initial equilibrium exchange rate π_0, there is now an excess demand for foreign exchange (shown as XD_{fe} in Figure 15.2). To clear the market, the exchange rate must rise to the new equilibrium value, π_1. The rise in the exchange rate will cause the quantity of imports demanded to decline, because the dollar price of imported goods rises with the exchange rate. Also, the quantity of exports demanded will increase because the rise in the exchange rate makes U.S. exports less expensive to foreigners. At the new equilibrium with the higher exchange rate (π_1), the supply and demand for foreign exchange are again equal. The increase in import demand leads to a depreciation of the dollar.

In 1973, the United States moved toward greater flexibility in the exchange rate, as did other industrialized countries. Over the post-1970 period, however, the United States has not had a *completely* flexible exchange rate system. To varying degrees over this period, central banks, including the U.S. central bank, have intervened in the foreign exchange market to influence the values of their currency. The features of the current international monetary system are discussed later. Before we begin this discussion, it is useful to examine the working of the foreign exchange market under the polar opposite of a completely flexible rate system, a system of *fixed*, or *pegged*, exchange rates.

Figure 15.2
Effect in the Foreign
Exchange Market of
an Increase in the
Demand for Imports

An autonomous
increase in import
demand shifts the
demand schedule for
foreign exchange from
D_{fe}^0 to D_{fe}^1. At the initial
equilibrium exchange
rate, there is an excess
demand for foreign
exchange (XD_{fe}). The
exchange rate rises to π_1
to reequilibrate supply
and demand in the for-
eign exchange market.

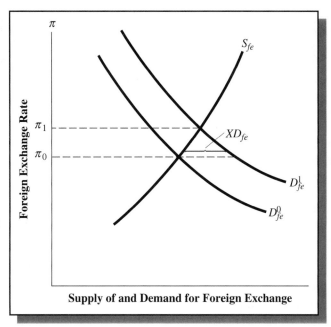

Exchange Rate Determination: Fixed Exchange Rates

An international monetary system is a set of rules organizing exchange rate determination and agreeing on which assets will be official reserve assets. An example of a fixed exchange rate system is the post–World War II **Bretton Woods system**. The international monetary agreements that made up this system were negotiated near the end of the war (at Bretton Woods, New Hampshire). The International Monetary Fund (IMF) was set up to administer the Bretton Woods system. According to IMF rules, the United States was to set a parity, or *par value*, for its currency in terms of gold. Other nations would set parities for their currencies in terms of dollars, which with the dollar tied to gold also fixed the gold value of these other currencies. The United States agreed to maintain convertibility between the dollar and gold at the fixed price (originally $35 per ounce). Other countries agreed to maintain convertibility (after a period of postwar adjustment) with the dollar and other currencies but not with gold. The other countries agreed to maintain their exchange rates vis-à-vis the dollar within a 1 percent range on either side of the parity level. The differential responsibility of the United States compared to other IMF members concerning convertibility into gold seemed sensible because, at the time, the United States had approximately two-thirds of the official world gold reserves.

Bretton Woods system
was a pegged exchange
rate system set up at the
end of World War II

Pegging the Exchange Rate

To see how a system of fixed exchange rates functions, we examine the way a country can "peg," or fix, the level of its exchange rate. To do so we return to our two-country example and assume that the United States wants to fix its exchange rate against the euro, which we are using to represent the currencies of the rest of the world. We ignore the 1 percent margin just mentioned and assume that the U.S. central bank wishes to fix an exact par value for the dollar, let us say at an exchange rate of 1 euro equals 0.8 dollar (1.25 euros = 1 dollar). The working of the foreign exchange market with this fixed exchange rate system is illustrated in Figure 15.3.

We assume that this official fixed exchange rate, 0.8, is below the equilibrium exchange rate in a flexible rate system, the equilibrium rate in Figure 15.3 being 1.0 (1 euro = 1 dollar). At the fixed exchange rate in such a situation, the dollar would be said to be *overvalued* and the euro *undervalued*. This terminology means that, if the exchange rate were market-determined, the price of the euro relative to the dollar (the exchange rate) would have to rise to clear the market. What prevents this from happening?

Recall that the demand and supply schedules we constructed for the foreign exchange market measure only *autonomous* transactions; they do not take account of accommodating transactions undertaken by central banks to finance payments imbalances. It is precisely such *intervention* by central banks that is required to peg the exchange rate at a nonequilibrium value such as 0.8 dollar in Figure 15.3. To keep the rate at 0.8, the United States must stand ready to buy and sell dollars at that exchange rate. If the U.S. central bank will buy euros for 0.8 dollar, the exchange rate cannot fall below that point because no one would sell elsewhere for less. Similarly, the exchange rate cannot rise above 0.8 because the central bank will be willing to sell euros at that price.

Figure 15.3
Foreign Exchange
Market with Fixed
Exchange Rate

In a fixed exchange rate system if the official exchange rate ($\pi = 0.8$) is below the market equilibrium rate ($\pi = 1.0$), there will be an excess demand for foreign exchange, XD_{fe}. To keep the exchange rate from rising, domestic or foreign central banks must supply an amount of foreign exchange equal to XD_{fe}.

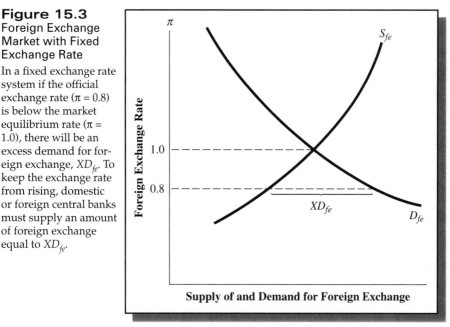

In the situation depicted in Figure 15.3, with the exchange rate below the equilibrium rate, there is an excess demand for foreign exchange (euros), shown as XD_{fe} in the figure. To keep the exchange rate from rising, the U.S. central bank must supply foreign exchange; that is, it must exchange euros for dollars in the foreign exchange market.

Alternatively, the European central bank might be the one to intervene. This bank would supply euros (sell euros and buy dollars) to satisfy the excess demand for euros and to keep the price of the euro at the official exchange rate.

Implications of Intervention

There are two points to note concerning central bank intervention. The first concerns the effect on the U.S. balance of payments as a result of intervention in the foreign exchange market. Suppose the U.S. central bank intervenes. Where does it get the euros that it sells to keep the exchange rate from rising? Our central bank must use up its international reserve assets to buy euros from the European Central Bank in order to sell them in the foreign exchange market. This action would show up in Table 15.1 as a reduction in U.S. official reserve assets.

Alternatively, if the European Central Bank supplied the euros directly in the foreign exchange market to satisfy the U.S. excess demand for foreign exchange, it would end up with increased holdings of dollars. In the U.S. balance of payments (Table 15.1), this action would show up as an increase in foreign official assets in the United States. The sum of these two items (a reduction in U.S. official reserve assets and an increase in foreign official assets in the United States) equals the U.S. balance of payments *deficit*. This is a deficit because it is the amount by which our spending abroad (demand for foreign exchange) exceeds our earnings from abroad (supply of foreign exchange), taking account of only autonomous transactions (those reflected in the D_{fe} and S_{fe} curves). This deficit must be financed by central bank intervention if the official exchange rate is to be maintained.

Conversely, if, at the official exchange rate, the supply of foreign exchange exceeds the demand (there is an excess supply of foreign exchange), a country will have a surplus in the balance of payments. In this case, earnings from sales to foreign residents that produce the supply of foreign exchange exceed domestic residents' expenditures abroad. When this occurs in the United States, our official reserve assets increase, or foreign official reserve assets in the United States decrease.

The second point to note about central bank intervention is that countries that must intervene continually to finance deficits will run out of official reserve assets. In our example, it is clear that if the United States financed its deficits by reducing U.S. official assets, it would eventually exhaust its reserve holdings. But what if the deficit were financed by the European Central Bank (or other central banks), increasing reserve assets in the United States by buying dollars? If foreign central banks continued to hold dollars, our reserves would not be affected. Under the Bretton Woods agreement, however, if they wished, the foreign central banks could request that the U.S. buy back dollars, using reserve assets (gold and SDRs). If they did, our reserves would then fall.

To an extent, the United States was able to run continual balance of payments deficits during the Bretton Woods period because foreign central banks did not ask us to buy back dollars they had acquired in foreign exchange market interventions. At first, they did not do so because they wanted the dollars, which served as a reserve asset for them. (Remember, they were committed to maintaining the convertibility between their currency and the dollar.) Later on, they did not ask us to redeem our dollars because they knew we could not do it; foreign dollar holdings far exceeded our reserves. This situation contributed to the collapse of the system, as we will see.

Countries other than the United States—Denmark, for example—could not run persistent deficits without losing their reserves quickly. Their currency, Danish krone, was not used as a reserve asset, so other central banks would expect the Danish central bank to buy back the Danish krone they had obtained in foreign exchange market intervention. To do so, Denmark would have had to use up its official reserves (gold, SDRs, and U.S. dollars).

15.3 THE CURRENT EXCHANGE RATE SYSTEM

The Bretton Woods system collapsed in 1971. The current world system of exchange rate determination is best described as a *managed float* for major industrialized countries (or in the case of Europe for a group of countries). Developing nations often have fixed exchange rate systems, although some allow exchange rate flexibility of varying degrees. A managed, or dirty, float contains elements of a flexible exchange rate system (the float part) and a fixed rate system (the managed part). For a country with a managed float, the exchange rate is allowed to move in response to market forces. However, the central bank can intervene to prevent *undesirable* or *disruptive*

Table 15.2
Exchange Rate
Arrangement of IMF
Member Countries

Exchange Rate Arrangement	Number
Fixed peg arrangements	44
Pegged arrangements within bands	14
Crawling pegs	5
Participate in an exchange rate mechanism	11
Managed floating and float independently	77
Other	34

Source: IMF, *International Financial Statistics*, March 2000.

movements in the exchange rate. The question of how an undesirable or disruptive movement in the exchange rate has been defined in practice, and therefore when central banks have chosen to intervene in foreign exchange markets, will be considered presently. The factors that led to the breakdown of the Bretton Woods system are also discussed.

Current Exchange Rate Arrangements

Table 15.2 summarizes the exchange rate arrangements of the countries that are members of the IMF. As can be seen from the table, there is no one system of exchange rate determination. Some countries peg their exchange rate to one currency or a composite of currencies within a narrow margin of 1 percent or less. This is the group of 44 countries labeled "fixed peg arrangements" in the table. The group labeled "pegged arrangements within bands" also follow a fixed exchange rate policy but with a wider band. The currency group labeled "crawling pegs" adjusts the value of their currency relative to a central rate in response to a set of economic indicators (e.g., domestic versus foreign inflation rates) and thus fall partway between fixed and flexible rates. The group labeled "participate in an exchange rate mechanism" comprise the European nations that have adopted a common currency, the euro, but float as a group relative to other currencies. This exchange rate setup is described in more detail later in the chapter. The next group in the table, 77 countries, have floating rate systems, though some are managed floats. The final group, called "other," have exchange rate systems that we will describe in Perspectives 15.2.

Japan, Canada, the United Kingdom, and the United States are among the countries having floating exchange rates.

Read Perspectives 15.2.

How Much Managing? How Much Floating?

In a managed float, central banks intervene in foreign exchange markets to prevent undesirable or disruptive movements in their exchange rates. Otherwise, their exchange rates float. During the post-1973 period, the degree to which the major industrialized countries intervened in the foreign exchange market varied significantly.

PERSPECTIVES 15.2
Currency Boards and Dollarization

Without a unified international monetary system such as the Bretton Woods system, individual countries have been left to choose their exchange rate arrangement as part of their overall macroeconomic policy setup. A number of emerging market countries have followed pegged exchange rate systems. Such a system aims at providing exchange rate stability to foster growth of trade and investment. In some cases the commitment to a exchange rate peg is part of a anti-inflation package.

In a world of high capital mobility, however, some countries have found they are unable to maintain the pegs they set for their currencies. Capital outflows threaten to exhaust their reserves and they are forced to devalue the currency. Two ways to bolster a fixed rate system are: Currency Boards and Dollarization.

With a currency board a country commits to fixing the value of its currency to some strong currency such as the dollar and being ready to convert its currency into that foreign currency on demand. It further commits itself to print more of its own currency only as it accumulates the foreign currency. This effectively takes monetary policy out of

the hands of the domestic country and alleviates fear of foreign investors that inflation will destroy the value of their holdings of the domestic currency. Currency boards therefore create credibility for the fixed exchange rate. Argentina, long plagued by high inflation, adopted a currency board in 1991 with the dollar as the foreign currency. The currency board enabled Argentina to halt inflation for a decade but collapsed in 2001. The cause of the collapse is widely believed to be continued and growing government budget deficits that eventually undermined the credibility of the fixed exchange rate.

Dollarization goes a step beyond a currency board in that a country simply adopts a strong foreign currency again often the dollar, and eliminates its own domestic currency. Because the country's currency is for example, the dollar, this is an extreme form of a fixed exchange rate (relative to the dollar). Again here the country gives up its ability to conduct an independent monetary policy. In the midst of high inflation and other economic difficulties, Ecuador dollarized in 2000. Panama has used the dollar as its currency since its independence in 1903.

In the United States during the 1970s, the U.S. central bank frequently intervened in the foreign exchange market. For example, in November 1978, a massive support program for the price of the dollar was coordinated by the U.S. government. In 1981, the Reagan administration announced that central bank intervention would occur only when necessary to prevent disorder in the foreign exchange market initiated by crisis situations. Following this shift in the interpretation of what constituted a disruptive movement in the exchange rate, U.S. intervention in the foreign exchange market declined markedly. During the first Reagan administration, there were periods of several quarters in which *no* intervention took place.

Even in the absence of U.S. central bank intervention, the price of the dollar does not float freely with the current exchange rate system because other central banks buy or sell dollars to influence the price of their currencies relative to the dollar. For example, in 1981 and again in 1984, European central banks sold dollars from their reserve holdings to slow the rise in the price of the dollar, which would have meant a fall in the price of their currencies (a rise in their exchange rate relative to the dollar). Then, with the Plaza Accord in September 1985, central banks of the large industrialized countries began concerted intervention aimed at lowering the value of the dollar (raising the U.S. exchange rate). In 1987, for reasons that will be explained later, these central banks reversed course and intervened, again in concert, to prop up the dollar. During some years in the 1990s, there was also heavy intervention by foreign central banks in support of the dollar. In 1993, for example, foreign official assets in the United States rose by $70 billion because of such intervention.

In 2003–2004, foreign central banks predominantly in Japan, China, and other Asian countries engaged in massive intervention to support the dollar relative to their currencies. By early 2004, Japan and China alone had accumulated over $600 billion in dollar-denominated foreign exchange reserves.

The Breakdown of the Bretton Woods System

We see from Table 15.2 that the current international monetary system is quite disorganized. How did such a disorganized system come about? In other words, what process led to the breakdown of the Bretton Woods fixed exchange rate system?

Central to the Bretton Woods system was the set of fixed exchange rates and the key currency role of the dollar. Par values set for currencies were not assumed to be fixed for all time; the Bretton Woods system was to be one of adjustable pegs. A country was to be able to change its exchange rate if it found a "fundamental disequilibrium" in its balance of payments. Such changes were to be made in consultation with the IMF. Countries with chronic deficits would *devalue* their currencies, which means to lower the par value of the currency in terms of the dollar, and because the dollar's value in terms of gold was fixed, to also lower the currency's value in terms of gold. Countries with persistent surpluses would *revalue* their currencies at higher par values in terms of the dollar and gold.

In fact, adjustments proved extremely difficult. Countries with persistent surpluses were under no pressure to revalue their currencies. Governments of countries with persistent deficits found it politically difficult to devalue, because a decline in the value of the currency was taken as a sign of failed government economic policy. Moreover, rumors that a currency was to be devalued led to waves of speculation against the currency, as speculators sold the currency with an eye to buying it back after it had been devalued. Because of these difficulties in adjusting the par values of currencies, over the Bretton Woods period, some countries (e.g., Great Britain) developed chronic balance of payments deficits, and others (e.g., Germany) developed chronic surpluses.

Most damaging to the system was the fact that the United States developed into a chronic deficit country, an indication that the dollar was overvalued. Devaluing the dollar meant a rise in the price of gold because the dollar was convertible into gold at the fixed par value. This presented special difficulties because of the key currency role played by the dollar within the system. But the growing deficits in the U.S. balance of payments were creating a glut of dollars on the market. The problem became acute in the late 1960s and especially in 1971.

In the late 1960s, the U.S. balance of payments position worsened. Severe inflationary pressure developed in the United States as a result of government spending on the Vietnam War, which was not adequately financed by increased taxes. This increased inflation worsened the U.S. balance of payments in the following way. Prices in the United States rose faster than prices in other industrial countries. With the exchange rate fixed, U.S. export goods became more expensive to foreigners, while the price of foreign imports fell relative to domestic goods prices in the United States. As a consequence, the demand for U.S. exports fell and U.S. demand for imports rose; the U.S. balance of payments deficit increased. In 1971, the deficit on the official reserve transaction balance was $29.8 billion.

Foreign central banks could not continue to absorb so many dollar reserves. The glut of dollars and the presumption that eventually the dollar would have to be devalued led to a lack of confidence in the dollar as a reserve asset.

In 1972, the dollar was devalued, and the price of gold increased to $38 per ounce. A new set of par values for other IMF member currencies was established. However, attempts to defend the new set of par values had collapsed by 1973. Again an upward surge of inflation in the United States and loss of confidence in the dollar were proximate causes of the problems in maintaining a set of fixed currency values. Also, beginning in 1973–74, huge increases in oil prices led to large balance of payments deficits for the industrialized oil-consuming nations and surpluses for the oil-producing countries. Exchange rate adjustments were required to restore equilibrium. The system of a managed float that emerged in the 1970s was the mechanism by which exchange rate adjustments necessitated by the declining strength of the dollar and rising oil prices were achieved.

15.4 ADVANTAGES OF ALTERNATIVE EXCHANGE RATE REGIMES

Within the current framework of exchange rate determination, each country or group of countries chooses an exchange rate regime. A key element in this decision is choosing the degree of exchange rate flexibility. A country chooses along a spectrum that at one end specifies complete flexibility of the exchange rate and at the other a rigid peg. There are other aspects of the choice of an exchange rate regime such as which currency to choose for a "peg" if a currency is pegged to another currency and the level and type of reserve assets to hold. Still the choice of the degree of flexibility is central to the exchange rate regime.

The relative merits of pegged (fixed) versus flexible exchange rates have long been debated by economists and central bankers. In this section we review the major arguments that have been advanced for and against each system.

Advantages of Exchange Rate Flexibility

We begin by discussing the arguments advanced in favor of exchange rate flexibility. Two advantages cited for greater flexibility of exchange rates are:[7]

1. Flexibility of exchange rates would allow policymakers to concentrate on domestic goals, free of worries about balance of payments deficits. Exchange rate flexibility would remove potential conflicts that arise between *internal balance* (domestic goals) and *external balance* (balance of payments equilibrium).

---

[7]A classic statement of the advantages of flexible exchange rates is Milton Friedman, "The Case for Flexible Exchange Rates," in *Essays in Positive Economics* (Chicago: University of Chicago Press, 1957).

2. Flexible exchange rates would insulate the domestic economy from economic shocks that originate abroad.

Policy Independence and Exchange Rate Flexibility

Our earlier analysis indicated that if a nation's central bank intervened in the foreign exchange market to finance a balance of payments deficit, it would lose official reserve assets. Continuing deficits would then lead, eventually, to the central bank's running out of reserves. Before the central bank ran out of reserves, it would have to take policy actions aimed at eliminating the balance of payments deficit. This is where the possible conflict comes between domestic goals and balance of payments equilibrium.

To see the nature of the conflict more clearly, we examine how the main balance of payments items are related to the level of domestic economic activity.

The Trade Balance and the Level of Economic Activity. Figure 15.4 plots imports (Z) and exports (X) on the vertical axis and domestic national income on the horizontal axis. The import schedule is drawn sloping upward because the demand for imports depends positively on income. This relationship follows because consumption depends positively on income. As income rises, consumption of both imported and domestic goods increases. Also, as domestic national income increases, more imported inputs will be needed (e.g., imported crude oil).

In contrast, the export schedule is horizontal. The demand for U.S. exports is a part of the foreign demand for imports. The foreign demand for imports depends on *foreign* income. From the U.S. point of view, foreign income, and hence the demand for exports, are exogenous.

Additional variables that influence both U.S. demand for imports and foreign demand for U.S. exports are the relative price levels in the two countries and the level of the exchange rate. These variables determine the relative costs of the two

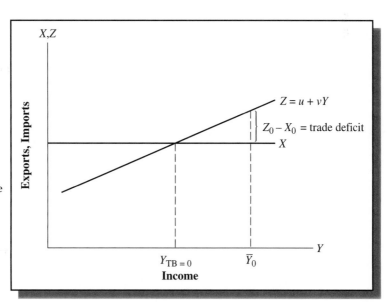

Figure 15.4
Trade Balance (TB) and the Level of Economic Activity

The level of income that equates imports (Z) with the exogenous level of exports (X) is $Y_{TB=0}$. There is no reason that the equilibrium level of income is equal to $Y_{TB=0}$. For example, if $\bar{Y}_0$ is the equilibrium level of income, imports will exceed exports, and there will be a deficit in the trade balance $(Z_0 - X_0)$.

X, Z

$Z = u + vY$

$Z_0 - X_0 = \text{trade deficit}$

X

Exports, Imports

$Y_{TB=0}$ $\bar{Y}_0$ Y

Income

countries' products to citizens of either country. Note that, for now, we are assuming that price levels and the exchange rate are fixed.

As shown in Figure 15.4, exports and imports will be equal if income is at $Y_{TB=0}$ (where TB, the trade balance, equals zero). This level of income generates import demand just equal to the exogenous level of exports. But there is no reason to expect that $Y_{TB=0}$ will be an equilibrium level of income. Equilibrium income will be determined by aggregate demand and supply in the overall economy, not by the foreign sector alone. For example, in Figure 15.4, assume that equilibrium income is at $\overline{Y}_0$, above $Y_{TB=0}$. At $\overline{Y}_0$, imports exceed exports and there is a trade deficit.

We have seen in earlier chapters how aggregate demand management can, at least in the Keynesian view, affect equilibrium income. Such policies could then be used to move equilibrium income to the level $Y_{TB=0}$, where exports equal imports. If the other current account items and the capital account were in balance, this would be a position of *external balance* for the economy, which in a fixed exchange rate system, means balance of payments equilibrium (official reserve transactions deficit equals zero). In terms of Figure 15.4, the policymaker could, for example, use a restrictive fiscal policy such as a tax increase to reduce income from $\overline{Y}_0$ to $Y_{TB=0}$.

But policymakers also have domestic goals. Within the Keynesian framework, aggregate demand management policies are to be used to pursue unemployment and inflation goals—that is, to achieve *internal balance*. The problem is that there is no reason to believe that the level of income that produces external balance is the optimal level with regard to domestic goals. Suppose, for example, that in Figure 15.4 the optimal level from the point of view of domestic goals is $\overline{Y}_0$. If a restrictive fiscal policy were used to lower income $Y_{TB=0}$, an undesirably high unemployment rate would result, and internal balance would be disturbed. But if income is maintained at $\overline{Y}_0$, there will be a trade deficit; the economy will not have external balance.

We see then that *under a fixed exchange rate system, potential conflicts arise between the goals of internal balance and external balance.*

Capital Flows and the Level of Economic Activity. The primary determinants of the level of capital flows between nations are expected rates of return on assets in each of the countries. With a fixed exchange rate system, the effects of expected exchange rate movements on asset returns can be ignored (except at times when there is speculation that the official exchange rate is to change). Interest rates in the various countries will be measures of relative rates of return. If we take the rate of return in other countries as given, the level of the capital flow into a particular country will depend positively on the level of its interest rate (r); that is,

$$F = F(r) \tag{15.1}$$

where F is the net capital inflow (a negative value of F represents a net outflow or deficit on capital account).[8] How changes in economic activity affect the balance on

---

[8]Capital flows include purchases of shares of stock in other countries and direct investments as well as purchases of bonds, the asset that earns the interest rate (r). Thus, other variables that influence the expected returns on stocks and direct investments might be included in a more complex specification of the capital flow function.

the capital account will therefore depend on how the interest rate varies with the change in economic activity.

First, consider increases in economic activity caused by expansionary monetary policies. An expansionary monetary policy will stimulate aggregate demand by *lowering* the rate of interest. The effect of the lower interest rate will be unfavorable to the balance on the capital account. The amount of investment in the United States by foreigners will decline, and U.S. investment abroad will increase as foreign assets become relatively more attractive. (Remember here that the foreign interest rate is assumed to be unchanged.) In the preceding section, we saw that increases in income for any reason increase imports while leaving exports unchanged and therefore worsen the trade balance. If the increased income results from an expansionary monetary policy, it follows that both the trade balance and the capital account will deteriorate.

Now suppose, alternatively, that the increase in economic activity is the result of an expansionary fiscal policy. As income rises, there is a consequent increase in the demand for money, and with a fixed money supply, the interest rate will rise. In this case, the increase in income is accompanied by an increase in the interest rate. Consequently, while the balance of trade worsens, the rise in the interest rate will stimulate a capital inflow. Whether the overall effect on the balance of payments is favorable or unfavorable depends on the relative strength of these two effects of the fiscal policy–induced expansion: the favorable effect on the capital account or the unfavorable effect on the trade balance.

We therefore find that in a fixed exchange rate system, conflicts may arise between domestic goals such as low unemployment and the goal of external balance as measured by balance of payments equilibrium. The conflict is especially severe with respect to monetary policy, in which expansionary policy actions have unfavorable effects on both the trade balance and the capital account.

A final linkage between the balance of payments and economic activity is through the price level. Unless the economy is far from full employment, expansionary aggregate demand policies, whether monetary or fiscal, will cause the price level to rise. With a fixed exchange rate, an increase in the domestic price level will, for a constant foreign price level, increase imports and cause exports to decline. Foreign goods will be relatively cheaper to U.S. citizens, and U.S. exports will be more expensive to foreign buyers. This *price effect* on the balance of trade reinforces the directly unfavorable effect that an economic expansion has on the trade balance for *both* monetary and fiscal policies.

Exchange Rate Flexibility and Insulation from Foreign Shocks

A second advantage for a flexible exchange rate system is that it will insulate an economy from certain shocks. To see the reasoning behind this claim, consider a country that is initially in a state of macroeconomic equilibrium, with an optimal level of unemployment, an optimal price level, and equilibrium in the balance of payments. Now suppose there is a recession abroad and foreign income declines. Because import demand by foreigners, which is the demand for this country's exports, depends on foreign income, it will fall with the foreign recession. In the foreign exchange market, this decline in export demand will show up as a shift to the

Figure 15.5

Insulation of the Domestic Economy in a Flexible Exchange Rate System

A foreign recession results in a fall in exports and a shift to the left in the supply of the foreign exchange schedule from S_{fe}^0 to S_{fe}^1. With a fixed exchange rate system, there will be a balance of payment deficit (distance AB). In a flexible exchange rate system, the exchange rate will rise to π_1 to clear the foreign exchange market.

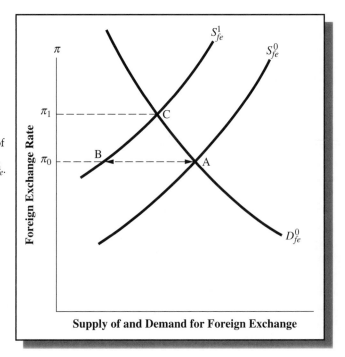

Supply of and Demand for Foreign Exchange

left in the supply of foreign exchange schedule. As shown in Figure 15.5, the supply curve will shift from S_{fe}^0 to S_{fe}^1 as a result of the foreign recession.

In a fixed exchange rate system, the country would find itself with a balance of payments deficit equal to distance AB in Figure 15.5. Also, because export demand is a portion of aggregate demand (the foreign demand for domestic output), the recession abroad will have contractionary effects on the domestic economy; aggregate demand will fall and income will decline.

In a system of flexible exchange rates, the excess demand for foreign exchange (equal to the balance of payments deficit AB), which resulted from the foreign recession, will cause the exchange rate to rise. The new equilibrium will be at point C, with the higher exchange rate π_1. The increase in the exchange rate will eliminate the balance of payments deficit. Notice another aspect of the adjustment to a new equilibrium. As we go to point C, the increase in the exchange rate stimulates export demand and lowers import demand. This increase in exports induced by the rise in the exchange rate will have an expansionary effect on aggregate demand. The reduction in imports caused by the rise in the exchange rate will also be expansionary; domestic aggregate demand will increase as residents switch from buying imports to buying domestic goods.

In the flexible exchange rate case, we see that adjusting the exchange rate offsets the contractionary effect on the domestic economy that results from a foreign recession. In this sense, a system of flexible exchange rates works to insulate an economy from certain external shocks.

Arguments in Favor of Fixed Exchange Rates

Not all economists and central bankers favor flexibility of exchange rates, though more have come to appreciate the advantages of such a system in recent years. Still, there have been calls for a new Bretton Woods type system or for a somewhat less formal system that would limit exchange rate fluctuations. What case can be made for a system of fixed exchange rates?

Advocates of fixed exchange rates believe that such a system will provide a more stable environment for growth in world trade and international investment. They also argue that the combination of a fixed exchange rate system and increased policy coordination among industrialized economies will lead to increased macroeconomic stability.

After the breakdown of a previous fixed exchange rate system early in the 1930s, the world economy went through a period of freely fluctuating exchange rates. On the basis of that experience, Norwegian economist Ragnar Nurkse made the case against flexible exchange rates as follows:

> Freely fluctuating exchange rates involve three serious disadvantages. In the first place they create an element of risk which tends to discourage international trade. The risk may be covered by "hedging" operations where a forward exchange market exists; but such insurance, if obtainable at all, is obtainable only at a price. . . .
>
> Secondly, as a means of adjusting the balance of payments, exchange fluctuations involve constant shifts of labor and other resources between production for the home market and production for export. Such shifts may be costly and disturbing; they tend to create frictional unemployment, and are obviously wasteful if exchange-market conditions that call for them are temporary. . . .
>
> Thirdly, experience has shown that fluctuating exchanges cannot always be relied upon to promote adjustment. A considerable if continuous movement of the exchange rate is liable to generate anticipations of a further movement in the same direction, thus giving rise to speculative capital transfers of a disequilibrating kind.[9]

Consider each of these purported flaws of a system of fluctuating exchange rates.

Exchange Rate Risk and Trade

Exchange rates have been volatile both in the short and long-run during the post Bretton Woods period. This volatility poses a risk, for example, to a domestic exporter or an investor who plans a foreign investment, such as a plant, in another country. Some such risks can be hedged in the *forward market* for foreign exchange. A U.S. exporter who is to receive Japanese yen in 3 months can contract to trade those yen for dollars at a price that is set today.

---

[9]Quoted in Peter Kenen, "Macroeconomic Theory and Policy: How the Closed Economy Was Opened," in Ronald Jones and Peter Kenen, eds., *Handbook of International Economics*, vol. 2 (Amsterdam: North Holland, 1985), pp. 625–77.

But not all exchange risk in foreign trade and investment can be easily hedged. If a U.S. firm is deciding whether to enter the export market, which involves costs such as establishing foreign business contacts and foreign advertising, it must consider the future prospects of the dollar. For example, a future rise in the value of the dollar may make the firm's product noncompetitive in the export market. Fluctuations in the exchange rate are then an additional risk. Similarly, a U.S. firm planning to build a plant in a foreign country to produce for the foreign market would want to know the exchange rate to determine what the plant would earn in terms of dollars. Exchange rate risk would again be a factor.

Fluctuating exchange rates do add risks to foreign trade and investment, not all of which can be easily hedged. Whether these risks seriously discourage such activities is a question that has not yet been definitely answered.

Exchange Rate Swings and Adjustment Costs

Nurkse's second argument was that exchange rate fluctuations would cause resources to be shifted into and out of export industries, with consequent adjustment costs, including frictional unemployment. As the value of the U.S. dollar rose in the early 1980s, our export performance did suffer. Then as the value of the dollar fell and our export performance improved, problems arose for German and Japanese exporters. The adjustment costs that accompanied the wide swings in the value of the U.S. dollar in the 1980s were probably the most important source of the growing discontent with flexible exchange rates.

Speculation and Exchange Rate Instability

Nurkse's last argument was that freely fluctuating exchange rates would lead to destabilizing speculation in foreign exchange markets. Many economists believe that this type of speculation may have been a factor in the height to which the dollar rose in 1985. Investors in financial assets saw the dollar rising, and believing it would rise even more, they demanded dollar-denominated assets. This demand put further upward pressure on the value of the dollar. To the degree that such speculation magnifies exchange rate movements, it exacerbates the problems discussed in the previous two subsections.

15.5 EXPERIENCE WITH FLOATING EXCHANGE RATES

How has the system of floating exchange rates worked during the post-1973 period? What light does evidence from this period shed on the issue of the merits of fixed versus floating rates? To consider these questions, let us look at the behavior of the U.S. exchange rate over the years of floating rates.

Figure 15.6 plots the price of the German mark measured in U.S. cents over the 1973–2000 period. The mark was the German currency unit prior to the adoption of the euro in 1999. Thus, for much of the period of floating rates the mark is an analogue to π in previous graphs where π, the price of foreign exchange, was measured

Figure 15.6 Price of the German Mark, 1973–2000 (in U.S. cents)

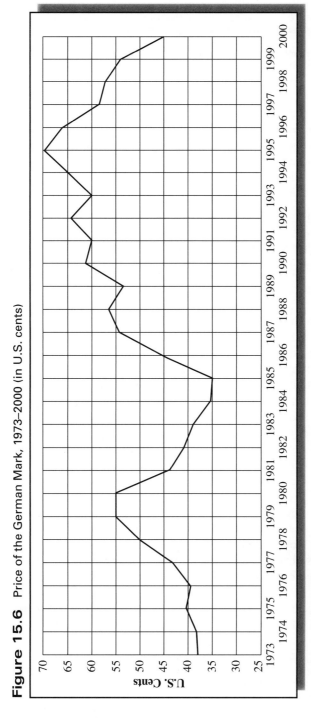

Source: Federal Reserve Bulletin.

by the euro.[10] Figure 15.7 shows a more comprehensive measure of the relative price of the U.S. currency, the *effective exchange rate*, which measures the value of the U.S. dollar relative to a weighted average of other currencies. The weights given to the other currencies depend on their importance in U.S. foreign trade. Note here that what we are measuring in Figure 15.7 is the *value of the dollar*, which is the inverse of the price of foreign exchange; for example, when the value of the dollar rises, π (the price of foreign exchange) falls.

From Figures 15.6 and 15.7, we can see that the U.S. exchange rate has been quite volatile during the floating rate period. Were we to look at weekly values of the exchange rate, we would see that short-term volatility of the exchange rate was also large. This short and medium-run volatility of exchange rates has been one cause of concern about the system of flexible exchange rates.

We can also see from either figure that there have been several sharp swings in the U.S. exchange rate over the floating rate period. Examining the causes of these is useful to an understanding of the functioning of the current exchange rate regime.

The Dollar in Decline, 1976–80

An important factor determining the behavior of exchange rates among the industrialized countries in the mid to late 1970s was their different responses to the oil price shocks of the period. Countries confronted with an unfavorable supply shock, such as the fourfold increase in the price of oil in 1973–74, had to choose the degree to which their aggregate demand policy would *accommodate* the shock. To accommodate, in this context, means to expand aggregate demand to try to offset the unfavorable output and employment effects of the supply shocks. The cost of such accommodation is higher inflation.

Although other factors were at work during 1976–80, the currencies of countries that chose more accommodation, especially through expansionary monetary policy, tended to depreciate relative to those that had little or no accommodation. To see why, let us examine the effects of an expansionary monetary policy the foreign exchange market in a flexible exchange rate system, as illustrated in Figure 15.8.[11]

In the figure, we assume that the initial positions of the supply and demand curves for foreign exchange are given by S_{fe}^0 and D_{fe}^0, respectively. The initial equilibrium exchange rate is therefore at π_0, where these curves intersect.

Now consider the effects of an expansionary monetary policy. Such a policy will reduce the domestic interest rate and increase domestic income and the price level. As discussed previously, the demand for imports will rise as a result of both the increase in income and the increase in the domestic price level. Further, the decline in the domestic interest rate will make domestic assets less attractive, and domestic investors will shift to foreign assets. The increase in the demand for both imported goods and foreign assets represents increased demand for foreign exchange. In terms

---

[10]The exchange rate between the euro and the dollar is discussed in Perspectives 15.3.

[11]The U.S. exchange rate was not completely flexible during these years. There was a managed float and, as discussed previously, the U.S. central bank did intervene frequently in the foreign exchange market in the 1970s. Still, during the 1970s and afterward, although intervention by the U.S. and foreign central banks may have affected the exchange rate over short periods, over periods of several years such as those that we are considering, market forces determined the movements of exchange rates.

Figure 15.7 Value of the U.S. Dollar, 1973–2004

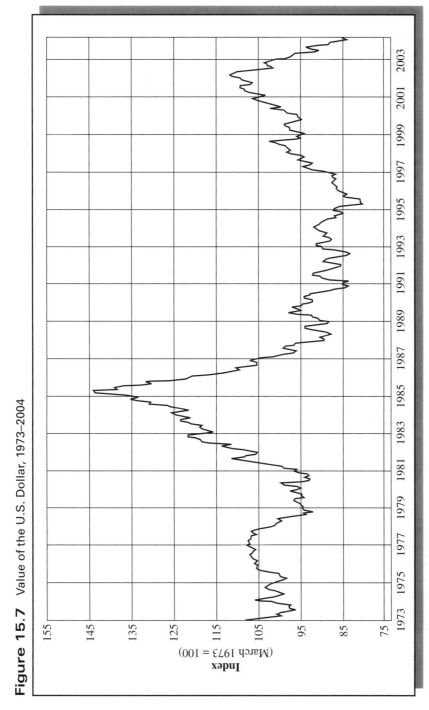

Source: Federal Reserve Board of Governors.

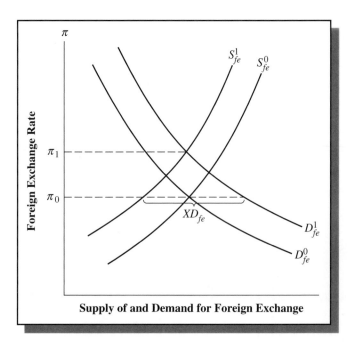

Figure 15.8
Effect of an Expansionary Monetary Policy in the Foreign Exchange Market: Flexible Exchange Rates

Supply of and Demand for Foreign Exchange

of Figure 15.8, the demand schedule for foreign exchange will shift from D_{fe}^0 to D_{fe}^1 as a result of the expansionary monetary policy. The expansionary monetary policy will also affect the supply of foreign exchange. The monetary policy–induced decline in the interest rate will cause foreign investors to buy fewer of the country's assets, and the rise in the domestic price level will reduce export demand. The supply of foreign exchange schedule in Figure 15.8 will shift from S_{fe}^0 to S_{fe}^1.

With a flexible exchange rate, the increase in demand and decline in supply will cause the exchange rate to rise. As the exchange rate rises, the quantity of foreign exchange demanded will fall, and the quantity of foreign exchange supplied will increase. A new equilibrium will be reached at exchange rate π_1, where the demand and supply for foreign exchange are again equal.

Thus, we see that in a flexible exchange rate system, an expansionary monetary policy causes the exchange rate to rise (the value of the domestic currency to fall). Figure 15.8 considers the action of one country in isolation. Applied to the behavior of the major industrialized countries in the late 1970s, this analysis suggests that countries that followed more accommodative, and therefore more expansionary, monetary policies would have caused their exchange rates to rise (their currencies to depreciate). Those that accommodated less would have seen their exchange rates fall (their currencies appreciate).

The rise in the U.S. exchange rate over the 1976–80 period, measured as the price of the German mark (see Figure 15.6), can be attributed to a higher degree of accommodative aggregate demand policy in the United States relative to Germany. The fall in the value of the dollar measured more generally against the currencies of other trading partners during this period indicates that U.S. policy was among the more expansionary ones. Switzerland, for example, showed no indication of accommodating the supply shocks of the 1970s by an expansion in demand, and the Swiss franc appreciated by 54 percent relative to the dollar between 1975 and 1980. At the opposite end of the spectrum, Italy followed a more expansionary monetary policy than the United States, and the Italian lira depreciated by 24 percent relative to the dollar during this period.

The Rising Dollar, 1981–85

Beginning in 1981, the dollar reversed course and began to rise sharply in value relative to other major currencies, as can be seen in Figure 15.7. This meant that our exchange rate *fell* over this period, as can be seen from Figure 15.6. Between 1980 and the peak in the dollar's value in early 1985, the mark fell from a price of 55 cents (fewer than 2 per dollar) to 31 cents (more than 3 per dollar), a drop of 44 percent. Against the trade-weighted average of foreign currencies (see Figure 15.7), the dollar rose by 64 percent.

If a relatively expansionary aggregate demand policy was important to the declining value of the dollar in the late 1970s, what explains the reversal in the early 1980s? Did aggregate demand policy in the United States become restrictive relative to the policies of Germany and its other trading partners?

Although there is considerable disagreement about the factors causing the rise in the value of the dollar, one explanation does see restrictive *monetary* policy, and the resulting high interest rates, as the primary cause of the dollar's rise in value. However, especially beginning with the recovery from the 1981–82 recession in 1983, aggregate demand policy in the United States was not, on the whole, less expansionary than in the other industrialized countries because U.S. *fiscal* policy was very expansionary. This policy *mix*, a combination of tight monetary policy and easy fiscal policy, is seen as the cause of the rising dollar at a time when the recovery in the United States was more rapid than in other major industrialized countries. How might a tight monetary–easy fiscal policy mix lead to a rising dollar even with strong U.S. expansion? The restrictive monetary policy would cause a rise in the value of the dollar (fall in the U.S. exchange rate). The analysis here is just the reverse of the case depicted in Figure 15.8. High U.S. interest rates increase the net capital inflow. Moreover, the restrictive monetary policy lowers income, thereby lowering imports. Finally, other things being equal, a more restrictive monetary policy would lead to a lower domestic inflation rate, further discouraging imports and encouraging exports.

Clearly these changes indicate that the demand for foreign exchange would fall and the supply rise; therefore, the exchange rate should fall and the value of the dollar rise. But just as clearly, other things being equal, a country with a more restrictive monetary policy than its trading partners would have less robust rates of economic expansion.

The other factor not equal is fiscal policy. An expansionary fiscal policy will, because of positive effects on income and the domestic price level, encourage imports and discourage exports (through the price level effect). The expansionary fiscal policy will, however, result in higher interest rates and therefore increase the net *inflow* of capital. Consequently, whether an expansionary fiscal policy will, on balance, cause an excess demand for foreign exchange (through the import and export effects) or a net excess supply (through the increase in the capital inflow) is uncertain. Of itself, an expansionary fiscal policy may raise or lower the exchange rate (with the opposite effect on the value of the dollar).

The U.S. experience over the first half of the 1980s is consistent with a pattern in which either the expansionary fiscal policy contributed to the rise in the value of the dollar or, if it would by itself have lowered the value of the dollar, this effect was overwhelmed by the restrictive monetary policy. Although monetary policy effects are assumed to have been predominant in pushing up the price of the dollar, fiscal policy effects were sufficiently strong domestically to have generated a robust recovery.

One additional factor that may be important in explaining the rise in the dollar's value, especially near its peak in early 1985, is *speculative buying* of U.S. financial assets. In section 15.2, we pointed out that the demand for foreign assets does not depend on the *level* of the exchange rate. For example, if the exchange rate rose from one level to a higher level, say 10 percent higher, then the foreign asset would cost 10 percent more in domestic currency, but the interest payment on the asset would be 10 percent higher, again expressed in the domestic currency. The percentage return on the asset would be the same at either level of the exchange rate.

What would matter for asset demands, however, are *expected changes* in the exchange rate. If the U.S. exchange rate were expected to fall (the value of the dollar were expected to rise), foreign investors would want to buy U.S. financial assets now. German investors, for example, would buy U.S. financial assets because they would expect the dollar to rise relative to the mark, enabling them to sell the assets later and receive more marks. In buying dollars with which to purchase the U.S. assets, the German investors would be *speculating* on a future rise in the dollar's value. Some believe that, near its peak in early 1985, such speculative buying was the only factor explaining the dollar's continued rise.

The Dollar's Slide, 1985–88

In October 1985, the finance ministers of five of the largest market economies (the G5, or Group of Five) met at the Plaza Hotel in New York.[12] They agreed jointly to intervene in the foreign exchange market to bring down the value of the dollar. The central banks in these countries would do so by selling dollars from their reserve supplies (buying their own currencies) in the foreign exchange market, thereby increasing the supply of dollars (reducing the supply of foreign currencies) and driving the price of the dollar down.

Other factors were driving down the value of the dollar as well. Just as speculative buying of dollars had contributed to the rise of the dollar, with fear of central bank intervention and other signs of weakness, speculative selling began in 1986 to contribute to the dollar's fall. The dollar had risen so high that few believed its value was sustainable. In addition, as the economic expansion in the United States slowed, U.S. monetary policy became less restrictive, and the U.S. interest rate fell. Relative to those of some European countries, U.S. financial assets were no longer so attractive.

---

[12]The G5 countries are the United States, Japan, Germany, France, and the United Kingdom.

By 1987, relative to the weighted average of foreign currencies (see Figure 15.7), the value of the dollar had fallen 32 percent from its peak in 1985. In February, the finance ministers met again, this time in Paris, and reached what has been called the Louvre Accord. They decided that the dollar had fallen far enough. They agreed to use foreign exchange market intervention to try to maintain their exchange rates within ranges around their then-current values. At first these efforts were not successful, and the value of the dollar continued to fall throughout 1987. In 1988, however, as central bank intervention continued, the value of the dollar stabilized.

The Dollar Since 1988

As can be seen from Figure 15.7, the years from 1988–98, did not bring another dramatic swing in the value of the dollar. Perhaps it is not surprising that during this period there was less pressure for change in the system of exchange rate determination.

The value of the dollar generally rose in the late 1990s and then began a sharp fall in 2002. As we will see presently (Figure 15.9), the swing in the exchange rate between the dollar and the euro was especially large. This most recent swing in the value of the dollar has led to a call not so much for change in the system of exchange rate determination but for change in U.S. policies that have been deemed responsible for the recent fall in the value of the dollar. These are the policies that have produced the large U.S. current account deficits and large current and projected government budget deficits.

Read Perspectives 15.3.

PERSPECTIVES 15.3
The Euro

A number of European countries have, among themselves, participated in some type of fixed exchange rate system since 1979. The details of the system and the number of countries participating have varied over time.

In the 1980s and until January of 1999, as was the case with the Bretton Woods system, exchange rates were not set permanently within the European exchange rate mechanisms. There were periodic realignments of currency values when economic conditions warranted. As with the Bretton Woods system, this practice caused problems. When speculators expected a currency's value to be lowered, they would stage a speculative attack on the currency, selling it in massive volumes. Such attacks knocked Italy and the United Kingdom out of the then-current exchange rate mechanism in 1992.

The exchange rate mechanism, with all its problems, was one step in the plan of the European Union (EU) to form a complete monetary union. In the Maastricht Treaty of 1991, the countries in the EU agreed to move, in stages, to a system with a single currency and a common European central bank. Before these steps would be taken, countries had to meet a set of guidelines concerning levels of interest rates, inflation rates, government budget deficits, and amounts of outstanding government debt. The purpose of these guidelines was to achieve a convergence of the countries' macroeconomic policies prior to irrevocably fixing the relative values of their

Figure 15.9 Euro Against the Dollar

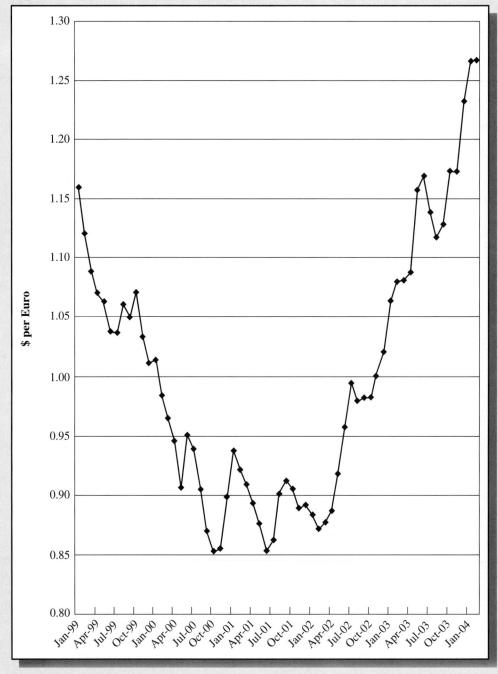

currencies, which is what adopting a common currency means.

In May of 1998, the countries decided to go ahead with a single currency, the **euro**. The currency was launched in January 1999. Initially, 11 EU members adopted the euro (Germany, the Netherlands, Luxembourg, Belgium, Finland, Spain, Portugal, France, Ireland, Italy, and Austria). Having later met the Maastricht guidelines, Greece joined the system in 2001. The United Kingdom, Denmark, and Sweden, while they are members of the EU, have not adopted the euro.

As put in effect in 1999, interbank transactions were conducted in euros and customers could set up accounts in euros. Beginning in January 2002, euro notes and coins replaced those of previous national currencies. The European Central Bank now sets monetary policy for all 12 countries.

How has the euro fared in the 5 years since its introduction? Technically, the euro was introduced without major glitches. The exchange rate of the euro against the U.S. dollar is plotted in Figure 15.9. For the first 3 years of its existence the euro was "weak" compared to the dollar. The value of the euro fell from 1.17 dollars per euro to a low of 0.85 euros per dollar. But beginning in early 2002, the euro reversed course and rose sharply in value against the dollar. By mid-2004, the euro traded above 1.25 dollars per euro.

15.6 CONCLUSION

This chapter has dealt with the determination of exchange rates and the related question of the setup of the International Monetary system. A critical question in the area is the optimal degree of flexibility in exchange rate determination. The collapse of the Bretton Woods system led to a period of a managed float for most major currencies.

The value of the U.S. dollar has been quite volatile during the period of floating exchange rates. There have been several sharp swings in the value of the dollar. During periods of sharply changing currency values there have been calls for changes in the International Monetary system to provide more stability of exchange rates.

As we have seen, however, swings in the value of the dollar relative to other national currencies are in large part due to divergences in the domestic monetary and fiscal policies that countries pursue. Greater exchange rate stability would most likely require greater coordination of national macroeconomic policies. There are many obstacles to effective international policy coordination, not the least of which are different preferences of policymakers and different industrial structures in major world economies. Floating exchange rates free countries from the need to coordinate policies but at the cost of highly volatile exchange rates.

KEY TERMS

- balance of payments accounts 308
- merchandise trade balance 309
- current account 309
- capital account 310
- foreign exchange 312
- Bretton Woods system 318

REVIEW QUESTIONS AND PROBLEMS

1. Why do the balance of payments accounts always balance?
2. Explain how the exchange rate for a country is determined under:
   a. A fixed exchange rate system.
   b. A flexible exchange rate.
   c. A managed, or dirty, float.
3. Analyze the effects of an autonomous fall in the demand for a country's exports under fixed and flexible exchange rate systems. In each case, indicate the effects on the country's balance of payments and on the exchange rate.
4. If central banks never intervened in foreign exchange markets, could there be deficits or surpluses in a country's balance of payments? Explain.
5. Describe the Bretton Woods system of exchange rate determination that was set up at the end of World War II and lasted until 1973.
6. Explain the relationship between the trade balance and the level of economic activity in a fixed exchange rate system. Why does this relationship create a potential conflict between the goals of internal and external balance?
7. Taking account of the effect on both the trade balance and the capital account, explain the relationships between balance of payments equilibrium and both expansionary monetary and fiscal policies within a fixed exchange rate system.
8. "Adoption of a system of flexible exchange rates would free monetary and fiscal policy for use in attaining domestic goals of full employment and price stability." Do you agree or disagree with this statement? Explain.
9. What are some of the relative advantages and disadvantages of fixed versus flexible exchange rates?
10. Illustrate graphically the effects in the foreign exchange market of an expansionary monetary policy carried out by the *foreign* country in our two-country framework. Consider the cases of both a fixed and a flexible exchange rate.

Chapter 16

Monetary and Fiscal Policy in the Open Economy

*E*conomies that are *open*, as all economies are to some extent, have trade and capital flows with other economies. In this chapter, we consider monetary and fiscal policy in an open economy model. How do the effects of policy actions differ in the open economy relative to the closed economy? How do they differ depending on whether exchange rates are fixed or flexible? We consider conflicts that arise between internal and external balance in a system of fixed exchange rates as discussed in Chapter 15. We illustrate why those conflicts do not arise when exchange rates are flexible.

There are several open economy macroeconomic frameworks. The one used here is the Mundell–Fleming model, often called the *workhorse model* for open economy macroeconomics.[1] The model is explained in section 16.1. Then, in sections 16.2 and 16.3, we consider the effects of changes in policy and other variables under two different assumptions about the mobility of capital between countries.

16.1 THE MUNDELL–FLEMING MODEL

The Mundell–Fleming model is an open economy version of the *IS–LM* model considered in Chapters 7 and 8. The closed economy *IS–LM* model consists of the following two equations:

$$M = L(Y, r) \tag{16.1}$$
$$S(Y) + T = I(r) + G \tag{16.2}$$

---

[1] The model is named for its developers, Robert Mundell and Marcus Fleming. See Robert Mundell, "Capital Mobility and Stabilization Policy Under Fixed and Flexible Exchange Rates," *Canadian Journal of Economics and Political Science*, 29 (November 1963), pp. 475–85; and Marcus Fleming, "Domestic Financial Policies Under Fixed and Under Floating Exchange Rates," International Monetary Fund *Staff Papers*, 9 (November 1962), pp. 369–79.

Equation (16.1) is the money market equilibrium (*LM* schedule), and equation (16.2) is the goods market equilibrium (*IS* schedule). The model simultaneously determines the nominal interest rate (*r*) and the level of *real* income (*Y*), with the aggregate price level held constant. What changes will be required to analyze an open economy?

When we consider an open economy, the *LM* schedule will not be changed. Equation (16.1) states that the *real* money supply, which we assume to be controlled by the domestic policymaker, must in equilibrium equal the real demand for money. It is the nominal supply of money that the policymaker controls, but with the assumption of a fixed price level, changes in the nominal money supply are changes in the real money supply as well.

The equation for the *IS* schedule (16.2) is derived from the goods market equilibrium condition for a closed economy:

$$C + S + T \equiv Y = C + I + G \tag{16.3}$$

which, when *C* is subtracted from both sides, reduces to

$$S + T = I + G \tag{16.4}$$

If we add imports (*Z*) and exports (*X*) to the model, (16.3) is replaced by[2]

$$C + S + T \equiv Y = C + I + G + X - Z \tag{16.5}$$

and the *IS* equation becomes

$$S + T = I + G + X - Z \tag{16.6}$$

where $(X - Z)$, net exports, is the foreign sector's contribution to aggregate demand. If we bring imports over to the left-hand side and indicate the variables upon which each element in the equation depends, the open economy *IS* equation can be written as

$$S(Y) + T + Z(Y, \pi) = I(r) + G + X(Y^f, \pi) \tag{16.7}$$

Saving and investment are the same as in the closed economy model. Imports, as discussed in Chapter 15, depend positively on income. Imports also depend negatively on the exchange rate (π). And, as in Chapter 15, we are defining the exchange rate as the price of foreign currency—for example, U.S. dollars per euro. A rise in the exchange rate will, therefore, make foreign goods more expensive and cause imports to fall. U.S. exports are other countries' imports and thus depend positively on foreign income and the exchange rate. The latter relationship follows because a rise in the exchange rate lowers the cost of dollars measured in terms of the foreign currency and makes U.S. goods cheaper to foreign residents.

By a derivation analogous to that in Chapter 7, the open economy *IS* schedule can be shown to be downward-sloping, as drawn in Figure 16.1. High values of the interest rate will result in low levels of investment. To satisfy equation (16.7), at such high levels of the interest rate, income must be low so that the levels of imports and

---

[2]Private transfer payments to foreigners should also appear on the left-hand side of equation (16.5), but we will ignore this minor item.

Figure 16.1
Open Economy
IS–LM Model

The *LM* schedule shows combinations of *r* and *Y* that are points of equilibrium for the money market, and the *IS* schedule shows combinations of *r* and *Y* that clear the goods market. The *BP* schedule shows the combinations of *r* and *Y* that will equate supply and demand in the foreign exchange market at a given exchange rate.

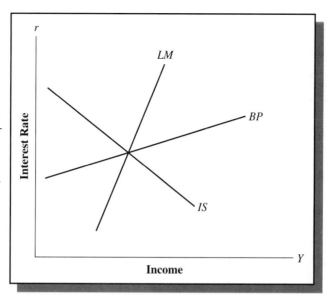

saving will be low. Alternatively, at low levels of the interest rate, which result in high levels of investment, goods market equilibrium requires that saving and imports must be high; therefore, *Y* must be high.

In constructing the open economy *IS* schedule in Figure 16.1, we hold four variables constant: taxes, government spending, foreign income, and the exchange rate. These are variables that shift the schedule. Expansionary shocks, such as an increase in government spending, a cut in taxes, an increase in foreign income, or a rise in the exchange rate, shift the schedule to the right. A rise in foreign income is expansionary because it increases demand for our exports. A rise in the exchange rate is expansionary both because it increases exports and because it reduces imports for a given level of income; it shifts demand from foreign to domestic products. An autonomous fall in import demand is expansionary for the same reason. Changes in the opposite direction in these variables shift the *IS* schedule to the left.

In addition to the *IS* and *LM* schedules, our open economy model contains a balance of payments equilibrium schedule, the *BP* schedule in Figure 16.1. This schedule plots all interest rate–income combinations that result in balance of payments equilibrium at a given exchange rate. Balance of payments equilibrium means that the official reserve transaction balance is zero. The equation for the *BP* schedule can be written as

$$X(Y^f, \pi) - Z(Y, \pi) + F(r - r^f) = 0 \qquad \text{(16.8)}$$

The first two terms in equation (16.8) constitute the trade balance (net exports). The third item (*F*) is the net capital inflow (the surplus or deficit in the capital account in the balance of payments as shown in Table 15.1). The net capital inflow depends positively on the domestic interest rate minus the foreign interest rate $(r - r^f)$, as discussed in Chapter 15. A rise in the U.S. interest rate relative to the foreign interest rate leads to an increased demand for U.S. financial assets (e.g., bonds) at the expense of foreign assets; the net capital inflow increases. A rise in the foreign interest rate has the opposite effect. The foreign interest rate is assumed to be exogenous.[3]

The BP schedule is positively sloped, as shown in Figure 16.1. As income rises, import demand increases whereas export demand does not. To maintain balance of payments equilibrium, the capital inflow must increase, which will happen if the interest rate is higher. Now consider factors that shift the BP schedule. An increase in π will shift the schedule horizontally to the right. For a given level of the interest rate, which fixes the capital flow, at a higher exchange rate, a higher level of income will be required for balance of payments equilibrium. The reason is that the higher exchange rate encourages exports and discourages imports; thus a higher level of income that will stimulate import demand is needed for balance of payments equilibrium. Similarly, an exogenous rise in export demand (due to a rise in Y^f) or a fall in import demand will shift the BP schedule to the right. If exports rise—for example, at a given interest rate that again fixes the capital flow—a higher level of income and therefore of imports is required to restore balance of payments equilibrium. The BP schedule shifts to the right. A fall in the foreign interest rate would also shift the BP schedule to the right; at a given domestic interest rate (r), the fall in the foreign interest rate increases the capital inflow. For equilibrium in the balance of payments, imports and therefore income must be higher.

Before we consider the effects of various policy changes, there is one point to note about the BP schedule. The BP schedule will be upward-sloping in the case of *imperfect capital mobility*. For this case, domestic and foreign assets (e.g., bonds) are substitutes, but they are not perfect ones. If domestic and foreign assets were perfect substitutes, a situation called *perfect capital mobility*, investors would move to equalize interest rates among countries. If one type of asset had a slightly higher interest rate temporarily, investors would switch to that asset until its rate was driven down to restore equality.

In the context of our model, perfect capital mobility implies $r = r^f$. We will see later that this equality implies a horizontal BP schedule. If assets are less than perfect substitutes, their interest rates need not be equal. Factors that might make assets in foreign countries less than perfect substitutes for U.S. assets include differential risk on the assets of different countries, risks due to exchange rate changes, transaction costs, and lack of information on properties of foreign assets. In section 16.2, we assume that such factors are sufficient to make foreign and domestic assets less than perfect substitutes. Perfect capital mobility is examined in section 16.3.

16.2 IMPERFECT CAPITAL MOBILITY

To consider monetary and fiscal policy under the assumption of imperfect capital mobility, we begin with the case of fixed exchange rates.

---

[3]Notice also that we did not include the foreign interest rate in the money demand function. We assume that, although investors substitute between foreign and domestic bonds on the basis of their respective yields, the demand for money depends only on the domestic interest rate.

Policy Under Fixed Exchange Rates

Monetary Policy

Consider the effects of an expansionary monetary policy action, an increase in the money supply from M_0 to M_1, as illustrated in Figure 16.2. The increase in the money supply shifts the LM schedule to the right, from $LM(M_0)$ to $LM(M_1)$. The equilibrium point shifts from E_0 to E_1, with a fall in the interest rate from r_0 to r_1 and an increase in income from Y_0 to Y_1. What has happened to the balance of payments? First, note that all points below the BP schedule are points of balance of payments deficit, whereas all points above the schedule are points of surplus. As we move from an equilibrium point on the BP schedule to points below the schedule—for example, increasing income or reducing the interest rate, or both—we are causing a deficit in the balance of payments. Consequently, as we move from point E_0 to point E_1 after the increase in the money supply, the balance of payments also moves into deficit. As discussed in section 15.4, the expansionary monetary policy increases income, stimulating imports and lowering the interest rate and thereby causing a capital outflow (F declines).

The fact that, beginning from a point of equilibrium, an expansionary monetary policy leads to a balance of payments deficit raises potential conflicts between domestic policy goals and external balance. If at point E_0 in Figure 16.2 the level of income, Y_0, is low relative to full employment, then the move to point E_1 and income level Y_1 may well be preferable on domestic grounds. But at point E_1 there will be a deficit in the balance of payments, and with limited foreign exchange reserves, such a situation cannot be maintained indefinitely.

Figure 16.2
Monetary Policy with a Fixed Exchange Rate

An increase in the quantity of money shifts the LM schedule from $LM(M_0)$ to $LM(M_1)$. The equilibrium point shifts from E_0 to E_1. The rate of interest falls, and the level of income rises. The new equilibrium point is below the BP schedule, indicating a deficit in the balance of payments.

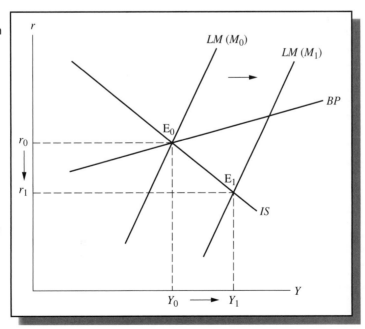

Fiscal Policy

The effects of an increase in government spending from G_0 to G_1 for the fixed exchange rates case are illustrated in Figure 16.3. The increase in government spending shifts the *IS* schedule to the right from $IS(G_0)$ to $IS(G_1)$, moving the equilibrium point from E_0 to E_1. Income rises from Y_0 to Y_1, and the interest rate rises from r_0 to r_1. As shown in Figure 16.3, at the new equilibrium point we are above the *BP* schedule; there is a balance of payments surplus. We get this result because in Figure 16.3 the *BP* schedule is flatter than the *LM* schedule. Alternatively, if the *BP* schedule were steeper than the *LM* schedule, an expansionary fiscal policy action would lead to a balance of payments deficit, as can be seen in Figure 16.4.

The *BP* schedule will be steeper the less responsive capital flows are to the rate of interest. The smaller the increase in the capital inflow for a given increase in the interest rate (given the fixed value of r^f), the larger will be the rise in the interest rate required to maintain balance of payments equilibrium as we go to a higher income (and hence import) level; that is, the steeper will be the *BP* schedule. The *BP* schedule will also be steeper the larger the marginal propensity to import. With a higher marginal propensity to import, a given increase in income will produce a larger increase in imports. For equilibrium in the balance of payments, a larger compensatory increase in the capital inflow and consequently a larger rise in the interest rate will be required.

The expansionary fiscal policy action depicted in Figures 16.3 and 16.4 causes income to increase. Increased income leads to a deterioration in the trade balance and causes the interest rate to rise, resulting in an improvement in the capital account. The foregoing discussion indicates that the steeper the *BP* schedule, the larger the unfavorable effect on imports and the trade balance and the smaller the favorable

Figure 16.3
Fiscal Policy with a Fixed Exchange Rate

An increase in government spending shifts the *IS* schedule from $IS(G_0)$ to $IS(G_1)$. The equilibrium point shifts from E_0 to E_1. Income and the interest rate rise. The new equilibrium point is above the *BP* schedule, indicating that, with a fixed exchange rate for the case in which the *BP* schedule is flatter than the *LM* schedule, the expansionary fiscal policy results in a surplus in the balance of payments.

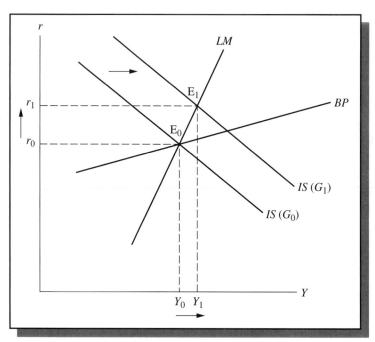

Figure 16.4

Fiscal Policy with a Fixed Exchange Rate: An Alternative Outcome

As in Figure 16.3, an increase in government spending shifts the *IS* schedule to the right, increasing both income and the rate of interest. In this case, where the *BP* schedule is steeper than the *LM* schedule, the new equilibrium point (E_1) is below the *BP* schedule. The expansionary fiscal policy results in a balance of payments deficit.

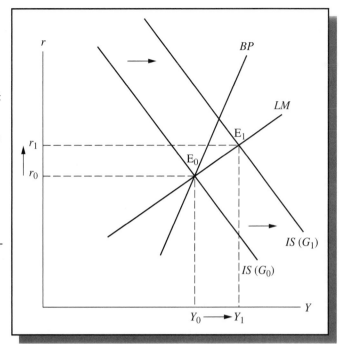

effect on capital flows. Therefore, the steeper the *BP* schedule, the more likely it becomes that an expansionary fiscal policy action will lead to a balance of payments deficit.

Finally, notice that the slope of the *BP* schedule relative to the slope of the *LM* schedule determines whether an expansionary fiscal policy action will result in a balance of payments surplus or deficit. Given the slope of the *BP* schedule, the steeper the *LM* schedule, the more likely it is that the *LM* schedule will be steeper than the *BP* schedule, the condition required for a surplus to result from an expansionary fiscal policy action. This result follows because, other things being equal, the steeper the *LM* schedule, the larger the increase in the interest rate (which produces the favorable capital inflow) and the smaller the increase in income (which produces the unfavorable effect on the trade balance).

Policy Under Flexible Exchange Rates

Monetary Policy

We turn now to the case in which the exchange rate is completely flexible; there is no central bank intervention. The exchange rate adjusts to equate supply and demand in the foreign exchange market. First consider the same monetary policy action analyzed previously, an increase in the quantity of money from M_0 to M_1. The effects of this expansionary monetary policy action in the flexible exchange rate case are illustrated in Figure 16.5.

The initial effect of the increase in the money supply—the effect before an adjustment in the exchange rate—is to move the economy from point E_0 to point E_1. The

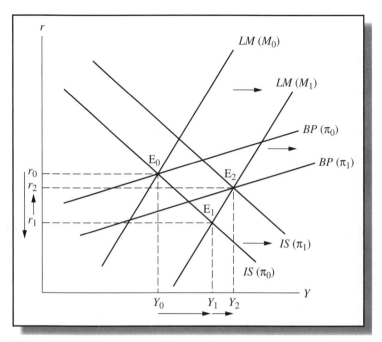

Figure 16.5 Monetary Policy with a Flexible Exchange Rate
An increase in the money supply shifts the *LM* schedule to the right, moving the equilibrium point from E_0 to E_1. The point E_1 is below the *BP* schedule, where there is an incipient balance of payments deficit. In the flexible exchange rate case, the exchange rate rises, causing the *BP* schedule to shift to the right from $BP(\pi_0)$ to $BP(\pi_1)$ and the *IS* curve to shift right from $IS(\pi_0)$ to $IS(\pi_1)$. The final equilibrium point is at E_2 with an income level Y_2, above Y_1, the new equilibrium for a fixed exchange rate.

interest rate falls from r_0 to r_1. Income rises from Y_0 to Y_1, and we move to a point below the *BP* schedule where there is an *incipient* balance of payments deficit. In a flexible exchange rate system, the exchange rate will rise (from π_0 to π_1) to clear the foreign exchange market. (This is the adjustment shown previously in Figure 15.8.) The rise in the exchange rate will shift the *BP* schedule to the right; in Figure 16.5, the schedule shifts from $BP(\pi_0)$ to $BP(\pi_1)$. The rise in the exchange rate also causes the *IS* schedule to shift to the right, from $IS(\pi_0)$ to $IS(\pi_1)$ in Figure 16.5, because exports rise and imports fall with an increase in the exchange rate. The new equilibrium is shown at point E_2, with the interest rate at r_2 and income at Y_2. The exchange rate adjustment reequilibrates the balance of payments after the expansionary monetary policy and eliminates the potential conflict between internal and external balance.

Notice that the rise in income as a result of the expansionary monetary policy action is greater in the flexible rate case than in the fixed rate case. With a fixed exchange rate, income would rise only to Y_1 in Figure 16.5 or Figure 16.2. With a flexible exchange rate, the rise in the exchange rate would further stimulate income by increasing exports and reducing import demand (for a given income level). Monetary policy is therefore a more potent stabilization tool in a flexible exchange rate regime than in a fixed rate regime.

Fiscal Policy

Figure 16.6 illustrates the effects of an increase in government spending from G_0 to G_1 with a flexible exchange rate. The initial effect—meaning again the effect before the adjustment in the exchange rate—is to shift the *IS* schedule from $IS(G_0, \pi_0)$ to $IS(G_1, \pi_0)$ and move the economy from E_0 to E_1. The interest rate rises (from r_0 to r_1), and income increases (from Y_0 to Y_1). With the slopes of the *BP* and *LM* schedules as drawn in Figure 16.6 (with the *BP* schedule flatter than the *LM* schedule), an incipient balance of payments surplus results from this expansionary policy action. In this case, the exchange rate must *fall* (from π_0 to π_1) to clear the foreign exchange market. A fall in the exchange rate will shift the *BP* schedule to the left in Figure 16.6, from $BP(\pi_0)$ to $BP(\pi_1)$. The *IS* schedule will also shift left, from $IS(G_1, \pi_0)$ to $IS(G_1, \pi_1)$, because the fall in the exchange rate will lower exports and stimulate imports. The exchange rate adjustment will partially offset the expansionary effect of the fiscal policy action. The new equilibrium point will be at Y_2, which is above Y_0 but below Y_1, the level that would have resulted with the fixed exchange rate.

There is not, however, a definite relationship between the potency of fiscal policy and the type of exchange rate regime, as there is with monetary policy. If the *BP*

Figure 16.6 Fiscal Policy with a Flexible Exchange Rate

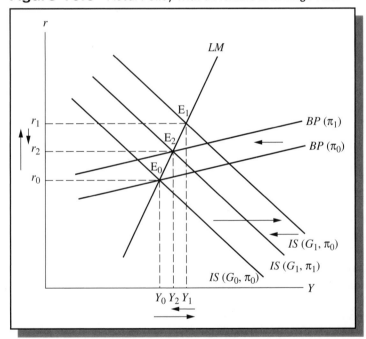

An increase in government spending shifts the *IS* schedule to the right from $IS(G_0, \pi_0)$ to $IS(G_1, \pi_0)$, moving the equilibrium point from E_0 to E_1. With the *BP* schedule flatter than the *LM* schedule, E_1 is above the initial *BP* schedule, $BP(\pi_0)$. There is an incipient balance of payments surplus, and the exchange rate will fall, shifting the *BP* schedule to the left to $BP(\pi_1)$ and shifting the *IS* schedule to the left from $IS(G_1, \pi_0)$ to $IS(G_1, \pi_1)$. The final equilibrium is at E_2 with income level Y_2, below Y_1, the new equilibrium for a fixed exchange rate.

schedule is steeper than the *LM* schedule, as in Figure 16.4, an expansionary fiscal policy will, for a given exchange rate, cause a balance of payments deficit. With an incipient balance of payments deficit in the flexible exchange rate regime, the exchange rate must *rise* to restore equilibrium in the foreign exchange market. The *BP* schedule and the *IS* schedule will shift to the right and reinforce the initial expansionary effect of the increase in government spending. In this case, the expansionary fiscal policy action would have a *larger* effect on income than it would in the fixed exchange rate case.

Although this alternative outcome is possible in theory, most economists think the outcome in Figure 16.6 is more likely. They believe an expansionary fiscal policy will lower the exchange rate (raise the value of the domestic currency). This belief follows from the view that there is a relatively high degree of international capital mobility, so the *BP* schedule is relatively flat and therefore likely to be flatter than the *LM* schedule, as in Figure 16.6.

16.3 PERFECT CAPITAL MOBILITY

So far we have been assuming that, although foreign and domestic assets are substitutes, they are not perfect substitutes. In this section, we consider monetary and fiscal policy for the case in which assets are perfect substitutes, the case of perfect capital mobility. In this case, capital moves freely between countries, differential risk in assets among countries is not important, and transactions costs are negligible.

In such a world, flows of capital bring the domestic and foreign interest rates into equality.[4] For example, if the interest rate on domestic bonds was 4.1 percent, and the interest rate on foreign bonds was 4.0 percent, in a world of perfect capital mobility, the domestic country would experience a massive inflow of capital until the domestic rate was driven down to equal the foreign rate.

In the Mundell–Fleming model, the assumption of perfect capital mobility means that the *BP* equation (16.8) is replaced with the condition

$$r = r^f \tag{16.9}$$

Graphically, the assumption of perfect capital mobility makes the *BP* schedule horizontal. Because massive capital flows result from any interest-rate differential, balance of payments equilibrium can occur only when the domestic interest rate is equal to the exogenously given foreign (world) interest rate.

Before looking at policy effects in the case of perfect capital mobility, consider the assumption that the domestic interest rate must in equilibrium equal the exogenously given foreign rate. In section 16.2, we also assumed that the foreign interest rate was exogenous, but in the case of imperfect capital mobility, the domestic interest rate could deviate from the foreign interest rate. In that case, there are two possibilities. One is that we are considering a country so small that its actions have no effect on the world economy. An expansionary monetary policy that lowers the

---

[4]It should be noted here that we are not taking into account possible expectations of future movements in exchange rates. As explained in Chapter 15, expected changes in exchange rates are another factor, in addition to interest-rate differentials, that influence the choice between domestic and foreign assets.

domestic interest rate has no effect on world interest rates or income in foreign countries, which was also assumed to be exogenous. A second possible assumption is that the country is large, such as the United States, but that we were simply ignoring the effects of its actions on foreign economies and therefore ignoring possible repercussive effects. We were assuming that these were of second-order importance.

In the perfect capital mobility case, only the first assumption is plausible: The domestic country is so small that its actions cannot affect world financial market conditions, and capital is so mobile that the country's interest rate must move into line with world rates. To consider the United States in the perfect capital mobility case, we would have to model the effect of U.S. policies on the world interest rate. It is unrealistic to view the U.S. interest rate as pinned down by a world interest rate completely outside its influence.

Policy Effects Under Fixed Exchange Rates

Monetary Policy

We will see that, with perfect capital mobility, monetary policy is completely ineffective when exchange rates are fixed. To understand this result, we need to consider further the relationship between intervention in the foreign exchange market and the money supply.

In section 16.2, we found that with a fixed exchange rate, an expansionary monetary policy led to a balance of payments deficit. Suppose, for example, that at point E_1 in Figure 16.2, the balance of payments deficit is \$5 billion; there is an excess demand for foreign exchange equal to \$5 billion. As explained in Chapter 15, either the domestic or the foreign central bank must intervene to provide this amount of foreign exchange if the fixed exchange rate is to be maintained. Here we consider only the case in which intervention is by the domestic central bank.

The U.S. central bank, the Federal Reserve, then sells \$5 billion worth of foreign reserve assets (foreign currencies, SDRs, or gold). It buys \$5 billion. The direct effect of this is to reduce the U.S. money supply by \$5 billion. The money supply in circulation falls because the Federal Reserve has now increased its holdings of dollars by 5 billion and the public has reduced theirs by that amount. What we implicitly assumed in section 16.2 was that the Federal Reserve offset this effect on the money supply by putting the dollars it purchased back into circulation. They do this by buying existing U.S. government bonds from the public. This action, called *sterilization*, prevents intervention in the foreign exchange market from affecting the domestic money supply.

With this as background, consider the effect of an expansionary monetary policy action in the case of perfect capital mobility. In line with the previous discussion, assume that a small country, such as New Zealand, increases its money supply. As illustrated in Figure 16.7, the increased money supply shifts the LM schedule to the right from $LM(M_0)$ to $LM(M_1)$. The New Zealand interest rate temporarily falls from r_0 toward r_1. The New Zealand interest rate is temporarily below the foreign (world) interest rate.

With the domestic interest rate below the foreign interest rate in the case of perfect capital mobility, there will be a massive outflow of capital. Investors will be selling off New Zealand assets and therefore sell New Zealand dollars. In this case the

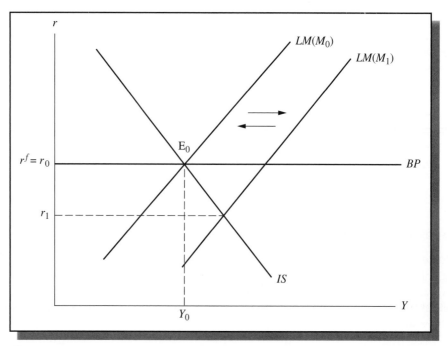

Figure 16.7 Monetary Policy with a Fixed Exchange Rate

An increase in the money supply shifts the *LM* schedule from $LM(M_0)$ to $LM(M_1)$. The domestic interest rate falls below the foreign interest rate, triggering a massive capital outflow. Central bank intervention to maintain the fixed exchange rate causes the money supply to fall back to the initial level, M_0. The domestic interest rate is restored to equality with the foreign interest rate, and income is back at its initial level.

New Zealand central bank cannot restore equilibrium through sterilized intervention in the foreign exchange market. The massive capital outflow would continue as long as the New Zealand interest rate remained below the foreign rate. Sterilized intervention would just mean that the New Zealand central bank would soon exhaust its holdings of foreign reserve assets.

To restore equilibrium, the central bank must let its intervention reduce the money supply via the process explained at the beginning of this section. The money supply will fall until the *LM* schedule shifts back to the initial position, $LM(M_0)$. At this point (E_0), the New Zealand interest rate will be restored to equality with the foreign interest rate. The capital outflow, and therefore the downward movement in the money supply, will stop. But also at this point the money supply and level of income will be back at their initial levels. The monetary policy action will have been completely ineffective.

Fiscal Policy

The situation is quite different for fiscal policy. Figure 16.8 illustrates the effects of an increase in government spending in the perfect capital mobility case. The direct effect of the increased spending is the shift of the *IS* schedule to the right from $IS(G_0)$ to $IS(G_1)$. The increase in spending pushes the domestic interest rate above the

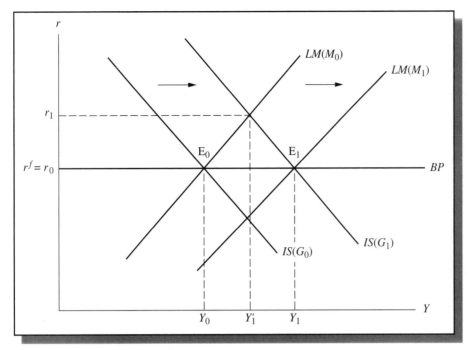

Figure 16.8 Fiscal Policy with a Fixed Exchange Rate

An increase in government spending shifts the *IS* schedule from $IS(G_0)$ to $IS(G_1)$. The domestic interest rate is pushed above the foreign interest rate, resulting in a massive capital inflow. Central bank intervention to maintain the fixed exchange rate causes the money supply to rise. The *LM* schedule shifts from $LM(M_0)$ to $LM(M_1)$. The domestic interest rate is brought back into equality with the foreign rate, and the increase in the money supply reinforces the expansionary effect of the increase in government spending.

foreign interest rate and sets in motion a massive capital inflow. The domestic central bank, again assume it is New Zealand's, must intervene and in this case buy foreign exchange with New Zealand dollars. This action will cause the New Zealand money supply to expand. The New Zealand central bank will have to keep buying foreign exchange until the money supply has increased enough to shift the *LM* schedule to $LM(M_1)$ and to restore equality between the domestic and foreign interest rates at point E_1. This endogenous increase in the money supply strengthens the expansionary effect of the increase in government spending. Output rises to Y_1 instead of to Y_1'.

In a system of fixed exchange rates, with perfect capital mobility, this expansionary fiscal policy is highly effective because there is no rise in the domestic interest rate and therefore no crowding out of private-sector spending.

Policy Effects Under Flexible Exchange Rates

In a system of flexible exchange rates, the situation is reversed. Here we find that monetary policy is highly effective and fiscal policy is completely ineffective.

Monetary Policy

Again we consider an increase in the money supply from M_0 to M_1. As shown in Figure 16.9, this increased money supply shifts the *LM* schedule from $LM(M_0)$ to $LM(M_1)$. As in the fixed exchange rate case, the increase in the money supply temporarily causes the New Zealand interest rate to fall below the foreign interest rate, triggering a massive capital outflow. But in a flexible exchange rate system, there is no resulting foreign exchange market intervention by the New Zealand central bank.

Instead, as investors sell off New Zealand assets and therefore sell New Zealand dollars, the New Zealand exchange rate rises and the value of the New Zealand dollar falls. This rise in the exchange rate increases New Zealand exports, decreases New Zealand imports, and shifts the *IS* schedule to the right. The selling of New Zealand dollars continues until the exchange rate rises sufficiently, from π_0 to π_1, and shifts the *IS* schedule from $IS(\pi_0)$ to $IS(\pi_i)$. At this point (E_1), the New Zealand interest rate has been restored to equality with the foreign interest rate. Income has risen to Y_1.

Monetary policy is highly effective with perfect capital mobility and flexible exchange rates. Income rises by the full amount of the horizontal shift in the *LM* schedule. Notice that the mechanism by which monetary policy works is no longer

Figure 16.9   Monetary Policy with a Flexible Exchange Rate

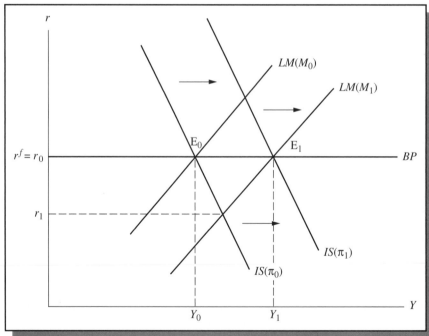

An increase in the money supply causes the *LM* schedule to shift from $LM(M_0)$ to $LM(M_1)$. The domestic interest rate falls below the foreign interest rate, triggering a massive outflow of capital. The capital outflow causes the exchange rate to rise, shifting the *IS* schedule from $IS(\pi_0)$ to *IS* (π_1). The domestic interest rate is brought back into equality with the foreign interest rate, and income rises to Y_1.

through the interest rate, which is fixed at the foreign rate. It is instead through the exchange rate and therefore net exports.

Fiscal Policy

The effects of an increase in government spending with flexible exchange rates and perfect capital mobility are illustrated in Figure 16.10. The direct effect of increased government spending is to shift the IS schedule from $IS(G_0, \pi_0)$ to $IS(G_1, \pi_0)$. As a result, the domestic interest rate rises (toward r_1 in the figure) above the foreign interest rate. This movement triggers a massive capital inflow, which with a flexible exchange rate causes the exchange rate to fall (the domestic currency to appreciate). As a result, exports fall and imports rise. The IS schedule shifts to the left.

Equilibrium is restored only when the IS schedule has shifted all the way back to $IS(G_0, \pi_0) = IS(G_1, \pi_1)$ and the domestic interest rate is again equal to the foreign interest rate. At this point, the capital inflow and downward pressure on the exchange rate end. Also at this point, income is back to its initial level. Fiscal policy is completely ineffective.

Read Perspectives 16.1.

Figure 16.10 Fiscal Policy with a Flexible Exchange Rate

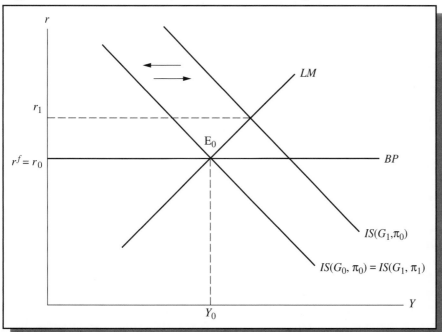

An increase in government spending causes the IS schedule to shift from $IS(G_0, \pi_0)$ to $IS(G_1, \pi_0)$. The domestic interest rate rises above the foreign interest rate with a resulting massive inflow of capital. The capital inflow causes the exchange rate to fall. The fall in the exchange rate shifts the IS schedule back to $IS(G_0, \pi_0) = IS(G_1, \pi_1)$. The domestic interest rate is reequated with the foreign interest rate, and income returns to its initial level.

PERSPECTIVES 16.1
The Saving–Investment Correlation Puzzle

In a closed economy, we would expect saving to have a strong positive relationship to investment. From the equation for the closed economy *IS* schedule given by (16.4), we see that

$$S + T = I + G \qquad \text{(16.4)}$$

or

$$S + (T - G) = I \qquad \text{(16.10)}$$

Private domestic saving (*S*) plus government saving (*T* − *G*) (or dissaving if there is a deficit) must equal domestic investment (*I*).

In an open economy, equation (16.10) is modified to include imports and exports and becomes

$$S + (T - G) + (Z - X) = I \qquad \text{(16.11)}$$

Domestic saving (again adjusted for government saving or dissaving) plus the trade deficit (*Z* − *X*) must equal domestic investment. Countries could therefore have large deviations of saving from investment if there were large current account surpluses or deficits. A country could, for example, have a large current account deficit (*Z* − *X*), which in the balance of payments accounts was financed by a surplus in the capital account, which in turn financed investment in excess of domestic saving. This was the case for the United States over much of the 1980s and 1990s.

In a world of high capital mobility, we would not expect saving and investment in a particular country to be closely related. Saving would flow to the country where the return to investment was greatest. If residents of one country saved a great deal, but the return to investment was low, that country would invest abroad and would have a capital account deficit and a trade surplus.

In fact, however, as can be seen from Figure 16.11, saving and investment in a sample of developed countries are closely associated (have a high positive correlation). Countries with a high ratio of saving to income, such as Japan and Norway, also have high ratios of investment to income. Conversely, countries with relatively low saving-to-income ratios, such as the United Kingdom and United States, have relatively low investment-to-income ratios. This relationship was pointed out in a study by Martin Feldstein and Charles Horioka and is thus referred to as the Feldstein–Horioka saving investment puzzle.[a]

What explains the puzzle? Perhaps overall capital mobility is not actually so high. But there are other possibilities. If we go back to equation (16.11), we see that a large divergence of domestic saving (adjusted for government saving or dissaving) requires a large current account surplus or deficit. If governments initiate policies to limit the extent of such current account imbalances, they force a convergence of domestic saving and investment. Certainly some countries do have substantial current account imbalances at times. The United States in recent years is an example, but limits on such imbalances could still be great enough to explain the relationship in Figure 16.11, which covers 10 countries over two decades.

A second explanation for the positive saving–investment correlation is related to limits on many firms' access to capital markets in general. If firms have limited access to capital markets, they must finance investment out of retained earnings, which are part of domestic saving.

Although these explanations of the positive saving–investment correlation are consistent with a high degree of international capital mobility, there is little empirical evidence on their importance. The puzzle remains.

Before leaving the puzzle of the high saving–investment correlation, it should be noted that, while still high, this correlation has declined somewhat over the past decade. This is partly due to the record high U.S. current account deficit, which

---

[a]Martin Feldstein and Charles Horioka, "Domestic Saving and International Capital Flows," *Economic Journal*, 90 (June 1980), pp. 314–29.

has been accompanied by relatively high domestic investment and low domestic saving. But even leaving the United States out, the correlation has declined. The most likely cause for the decline is the increasing globalization of capital markets, which has raised capital mobility. Another way this shows up is that in their portfolios investors are including more foreign assets. This has been a decline in what economists call "home bias," the preference of investors to hold domestic financial assets. As we saw in Perspectives 15.1, this increasing capital mobility is one factor that has made financing the U.S. current account deficit easier.

Figure 16.11
Saving (*S*) and Investment (*I*): Ratio to GNP (*Y*), 1965–86

Source: Tamin Bayoumi, "Saving Investment Correlations," International Monetary Fund *Staff Papers*, 37 (June 1990), p. 364.

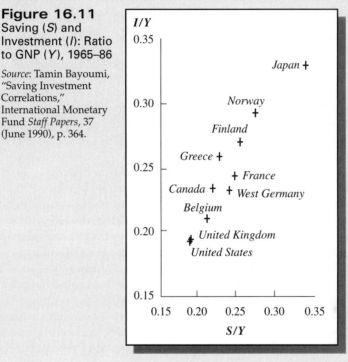

16.4 CONCLUSION

In this chapter we have analyzed monetary and fiscal policy within an open economy version of the *IS–LM* model for the cases of both imperfect and perfect capital mobility. We have seen significant differences between the two cases. In particular, the assumption of perfect capital mobility produces some striking results: Monetary policy is completely ineffective if the exchange rate is fixed, and fiscal policy is completely ineffective if the exchange rate is flexible. With imperfect capital mobility, our results are more in line with those for the closed economy *IS–LM* model, as summarized in Table 8.1, though there are some quantitative differences.

Given these differences, which case is relevant to the real world? Few things are perfect in the world, and capital mobility is not one of them. But is the degree of capital mobility high enough that perfect capital mobility is not a bad approximation?

On the basis of the mid-1980s, one study concluded that world capital markets were probably "two-thirds or three-fourths of the way but no further than that" toward perfect capital mobility.[5] Capital markets have moved further in that direction over the past 20 years. This trend might lead to a preference for the model with imperfect capital mobility but a relatively flat *BP* schedule.

It is hard, however, to make a blanket statement that is relevant for all countries. Some countries, though the number is diminishing, have government controls on capital movements that severely restrict capital mobility. For other countries whose capital markets are closely integrated with those of a large neighbor, such as Canada and Austria, the assumption of perfect capital mobility is most likely preferable.

REVIEW QUESTIONS AND PROBLEMS

1. Explain why the *BP* schedule in Figure 16.1 is upward-sloping. What factors cause a shift in the *BP* schedule? Explain.
2. Within the Mundell–Fleming model assuming *imperfect* capital mobility, analyze the effects of the following policy actions for both the fixed and flexible exchange rate cases.
   a. A decline in the money supply from M_0 to M_1.
   b. A decrease in government spending from G_0 to G_1.
   Include in your answer the effects of the policy action on both income and the interest rate as well as on the balance of payments and the exchange rate.
3. Explain what it means to say that we have perfect capital mobility. Why is the *BP* schedule horizontal in the case of perfect capital mobility?
4. Consider the effects of a lump-sum tax cut, from T_0 to T_1, in a fixed exchange rate system. Consider both imperfect and perfect capital mobility. In which case will the tax cut have a larger effect on income?
5. What is meant by *sterilization* of the effects of foreign exchange market intervention? Explain how sterilization works in the case of imperfect capital mobility.
6. Within the Mundell–Fleming model assuming perfect capital mobility, analyze the effects of a positive shock to money demand (i.e., an increase in the demand for money for given levels of income and the interest rate). Consider the effect of the shock on income when the exchange rate is fixed and when it is flexible.
7. Within the Mundell–Fleming model assuming perfect capital mobility, analyze the effect of a lump-sum tax increase for the case of a flexible exchange rate. Will the tax cut be effective? Explain.

[5]Ralph Bryant, *International Financial Intermediation* (Washington, D.C.: The Brookings Institution, 1987), p. 86.

Part V

Economic Policy

*T*he chapters in this Part extend the discussion of macroeconomic policy. Although monetary and fiscal policies were analyzed in previous chapters, the policy actions we considered were simple policy shifts such as a "lump-sum" change in tax collections or an exogenous change in the money supply. Consideration of such simple policy shifts was useful to an understanding of the properties of the models we considered. In the next four chapters we take a more detailed and realistic look at macroeconomic policymaking.

Chapters 17 and 18 deal with monetary policy. Chapter 19 considers fiscal policies aimed at stabilizing the economy. Chapter 20 looks at policies to promote economic growth many of which are also fiscal policies. It is in Chapter 20 that we consider issues concerning what is called "supply-side economics."

Chapter 17

The Money Supply and the Banking System

*S*o far we have assumed that the supply of money is exogenously determined by the central bank. In this chapter, we consider the money supply process in more detail. We discuss the structure of the central bank in the United States, the **Federal Reserve System**, which has a pivotal role in determining the supply of money. The banking system and the nonbank public also play a part in determining the money supply. We will see that the realism of our previous assumption that the money supply is exogenous depends on the behavior of the Federal Reserve. Because the Federal Reserve has the power to offset in large part the actions of the other participants in the money supply process (the banking system and the nonbank public), the money supply is *potentially* an exogenous policy variable. For reasons explained in this chapter, the Federal Reserve has often chosen not to offset such private-sector actions, and the actual determination of the money supply has resulted from both private-sector and Federal Reserve actions. In this chapter, we consider only the way the money supply is determined under different assumptions about the way the Federal Reserve behaves. In Chapter 18, we turn to the question of how the Federal Reserve *should* behave—the question of *optimal* monetary policy.

Federal Reserve System (Federal Reserve, or the Fed, for short) is composed of 12 regional Federal Reserve banks and the Board of Governors located in Washington

We begin in section 17.1 with a definition of money. Section 17.2 discusses the structure of the Federal Reserve System and the tools the Federal Reserve uses for monetary control. In section 17.3, we explain the relationship between bank reserves and deposits, a vital link in the process of Federal Reserve control over the money supply and the level of interest rates. In section 17.4, we return to the question raised previously concerning the relative roles of the nonbank public, the banking system, and the Federal Reserve in determining the money supply.

Section 17.5 concludes our analysis of the money supply process and its relationship to interest-rate determination.

17.1 THE DEFINITION OF MONEY

The Functions of Money

The standard definition of *money* is whatever performs monetary functions. The three widely accepted functions of money are (1) a means of exchange, (2) a store of value, and (3) a unit of account.

Means of Exchange

Money serves as a means of exchange. You buy goods or services with money. You receive money for selling goods or services. We do not often think about it, but this function of money contributes greatly to economic efficiency. Exchange without money would require swaps of goods for goods—what is called *barter*. Some barter transactions exist even in a monetary economy.

But barter as the predominant means of trade is inefficient because barter transactions require a *double coincidence of wants*. Suppose that Ms. Jones wants to buy shoes and sell jewelry, while Ms. Smith wants to sell shoes but buy a computer. No trade takes place, and both must take time to look for trading partners whose buying *and* selling desires coincide with theirs. In a monetary economy, Ms. Jones buys the shoes from Ms. Smith with money. Ms. Smith can then use the money to buy a computer from *anyone* selling one. Ms. Jones needs only to find someone who wants to buy jewelry (without necessarily wanting to sell shoes).

Store of Value

Money functions as a store for wealth, a way to save for future spending. Money is one type of financial asset. Other stores of value (e.g., a corporate or government bond) are not money because they do not perform the other monetary functions. They cannot be used as a means of exchange or as a unit of account, the third central function of money.

Unit of Account

Prices are measured in terms of money. In Albania, prices (and debts) are measured in terms of the lek, in Poland the zloty, in Britain the pound. In the United States, as you already know, prices and debts are measured in dollars and cents. As with the means-of-exchange function, money provides conveniences as a unit of account. Merchants simply post one price in dollars, not in terms of each commodity that might be traded for their goods.

Components of the Money Supply

The money supply is composed of financial assets that serve the preceding functions. Which assets are these in the United States? This question is harder to answer than it might at first appear. There are several different measures of the money supply. All are composed of currency and deposits at commercial banks and other depository institutions (e.g., savings and loan associations).

One measure, called **M1**, is the narrowest of the money measures in the United States. It consists of currency plus *checkable* deposits. Checkable deposits are those on which you can write checks—that is, those on which you can direct the bank in writing to make payments to another party.[1] Currency fulfills the three monetary functions previously discussed. So do bank deposits, as long as you can write checks on them.[2] Checks on deposits can be used to buy things (means-of-exchange function), deposits are a store of value, and currency or deposits are a unit of account.

Two other measures, **M2** and **M3**, are broader. They include the components of M1 plus additional bank deposits that have no or only limited provisions for checks. M2 includes money market mutual fund accounts, which often allow only checks for amounts above some minimum, and regular savings and time deposits on which no checks can be written.[3] M3 is an even broader measure of money, which includes large deposits, termed *certificates of deposit* (CDs), on which no checks can be written. Details of the composition of each of these measures of money, as well as figures for the level of these measures for February 2004, are given in Table 17.1.

The rationale for the broader money measures is that the additional deposit categories included in them relative to M1 are very similar to checkable deposits or are

Table 17.1   Money Supply Measures, February 2004 (billions of dollars)

M1	$1,311.4	Averages of daily figures for (1) currency outside the Treasury, Federal Reserve banks, and the vaults of commercial banks; (2) travelers checks on nonbank issuers; (3) demand deposits at all commercial banks other than those due to domestic banks, the U.S. government, and foreign banks and official institutions less cash items in the process of collection and Federal Reserve float; and (4) negotiable order of withdrawal (NOW) and automatic transfer service (ATS) accounts at banks and thrift institutions, credit union share draft (CUSD) accounts, and demand deposits at mutual savings banks
M2	6,127.6	M1 plus savings and small-denomination time deposits at all depository institutions, overnight repurchase agreements at commercial banks, overnight Eurodollars held by U.S. residents other than banks at Caribbean branches of member banks, money market mutual fund shares, and money market deposit accounts (MMDAs)
M3	8,928.4	M2 plus large-denomination time deposits at all depository institutions and term repurchase agreements at commercial banks and savings and loan associations

Source: Board of Governors of the Federal Reserve.

---

[1]Another small item included in M1 is travelers checks. Our discussion here ignores a number of small items in the different definitions of money. For detailed definitions, see Table 17.1.

[2]It is convenient to refer to deposits as *bank* deposits, but keep in mind that other institutions such as savings and loans and credit unions, which are not strictly banks, provide some of these deposit accounts.

[3]Balances in savings accounts are, in practice, available on demand. Time deposits, however, are for a specified time period (e.g., 1 year), and there may be penalties for early withdrawal.

easily converted to checkable deposits. Balances in savings accounts, for example, can be converted into checkable deposits (or currency) simply by going to the bank (or using an ATM machine). If these additional deposit types are sufficiently close substitutes for checkable deposits and currency, we may want to consider them as money.

17.2 THE FEDERAL RESERVE SYSTEM

The Structure of the Central Bank

The U.S. system of central banking was established by the Federal Reserve Act of 1913. Unlike many other countries, which have a single central bank, the United States has a system of Federal Reserve banks, one for each of 12 Federal Reserve districts. Each Federal Reserve bank is named for the city in which it is located: the Federal Reserve Bank of New York, the Federal Reserve Bank of Chicago, the Federal Reserve Bank of San Francisco, and so forth. For some of the functions of central banking the regional character of our system is important, but the making of macroeconomic policy has become centralized in Washington in two policymaking groups.

The first group is the **Board of Governors of the Federal Reserve**. The board is composed of seven members (governors) appointed by the president of the United States with the advice and consent of the Senate for a term of 14 years. One member of the board is appointed by the president as chairman for a four-year term. When this post has been held by forceful individuals, the chairman has been the dominant figure in monetary policy formation.

The second monetary policymaking group is the **Federal Open Market Committee**. The most important method by which the Federal Reserve controls the money supply is the purchase and sale of government securities in the open market—that is, in the market of dealers in government securities located in New York City. We will see how the Federal Reserve uses open-market purchases or sales of securities to increase or decrease the *legal reserves* of the banking system. Because banks are required to hold fixed proportions of their deposits in the form of legal reserves, such **open-market operations** can control the deposit component of the money supply. The Open Market Committee controls open-market operations. This committee is composed of 12 voting members: the 7 members of the Board of Governors and 5 of the presidents of the regional Federal Reserve banks. The presidents of the regional banks serve on a rotating basis, except for the president of the New York Bank, the bank charged with carrying out open-market operations, who is always a voting member of the Open Market Committee.

Board of Governors of the Federal Reserve is composed of seven members (governors) appointed by the president of the United States with the advice and consent of the Senate for a term of 14 years. One member of the board is appointed chairman

Federal Open Market Committee is composed of 12 voting members: the 7 members of the Board of Governors and 5 of the presidents of regional Federal Reserve banks. Presidents of the regional banks serve on a rotating basis, with the exception of the president of the Federal Reserve Bank of New York, who is vice chairman and a permanent voting member of the committee

open-market operations are purchases and sales of government securities in the open market by the Federal Reserve

Federal Reserve Control of the Money Supply

Recall that the monetary aggregates discussed in section 17.1 consist of currency held by the public plus various classes of bank deposits. To simplify our discussion, let us assume that only one type of deposit represents all the different types of deposits on which checks can be written—what we will refer to as *checkable deposits*. These include demand deposits, NOW accounts, and credit union share drafts. Savings and time deposits are brought into our discussion at a later point. For now, the term *deposits* refers to one type of checkable deposit. Currency in the United States consists primarily of Federal Reserve notes, paper money issued by the Federal Reserve.

To control the deposit component of the money supply, the Federal Reserve sets legal reserve requirements on deposits. These requirements specify that banks must hold a certain percentage of their deposit liabilities either in the form of vault cash (currency) or as deposits at regional Federal Reserve banks. Given the existence of legal reserve requirements, the Federal Reserve can control the money supply by regulating the supply of legal reserves. Technically, setting reserve requirements and fixing the level of reserves sets a ceiling only on the level of deposits. For example, if the required reserve ratio was 10 percent and reserves were set at $60 billion, the maximum amount of deposits would be $600 billion. In fact, because legal reserves (currency or deposits at regional Federal Reserve banks) do not pay interest, banks hold few reserves beyond those required by Federal Reserve regulations. Thus the actual level of deposits remains close to the maximum value supportable by a given reserve level.

A convenient starting point for analyzing Federal Reserve control of bank deposits is the balance sheet summarizing the assets and liabilities of the Federal Reserve System. This balance sheet is shown in Table 17.2. The primary assets held by the Federal Reserve are U.S. government securities. A much smaller item on the asset side of the balance sheet, but one that we return to later in the discussion, is the amount of loans to banks; these are the *borrowed reserves* of the banking system. On the liability side, the two important items are Federal Reserve notes outstanding, which make up the bulk of U.S. paper currency, and bank reserve deposits. This latter item consists of the deposits held at the Federal Reserve banks by the banking system to satisfy legal reserve requirements.[4]

monetary base
is equal to currency plus bank reserve deposits

These two items on the liability side of the Federal Reserve balance sheet (currency plus bank reserve deposits) form what is termed the **monetary base**, because together they provide the foundation for the money supply. Currency is directly included in the money supply if held by the nonbank public. The portion of currency held as bank reserves plus bank reserve deposits

Table 17.2 Balance Sheet of Federal Reserve Banks, March 2004 (billions of dollars)

ASSETS		LIABILITIES	
U.S. government securities	673.0	Federal Reserve notes	714.1
Loans to banks	0.1	Bank reserve deposits	9.3
Other assets	107.1	Other liabilities and capital	56.8
Total assets	780.2	Total liabilities and capital	780.2

Source: Board of Governors of the Federal Reserve.

---

[4]Hereafter we drop the adjective *legal* when referring to bank reserve assets that satisfy reserve requirements.

provides the reserves supporting the deposit component of the money supply. The Federal Reserve controls the quantity of its liabilities, which means that it can control the monetary base and therefore control bank reserves and the money supply.

The Tools of Federal Reserve Control

The Federal Reserve uses several tools to control bank reserves. In section 17.3, we explain the process by which changes in bank reserves affect the level of bank deposits. One point should be noted before proceeding. When the Federal Reserve takes some action changing the monetary base—an action increasing the base, for example—the net effect on bank reserves depends on how much of the increase in the base goes into increased currency holding by the (nonbank) public. The behavior of the public's currency holdings, then, influences the ultimate effect of Federal Reserve actions on the level of bank reserves and, hence, deposits. This influence is explained in the next section, but for now we assume that the public's holding of currency is fixed. With this assumption, changes in the monetary base produce dollar-for-dollar changes in the quantity of bank reserves. The Federal Reserve can use three tools to control the reserve position of banks: open-market operations, the discount rate, and the required reserve ratio. In practice open-market operations are the dominant means by which the Federal Reserve controls bank reserves. We discuss the other two tools because they are used by other central banks and have been used by the Federal Reserve in the past.

Open-Market Operations

The first tool, open-market operations, was referred to previously. For an example of how an open-market action by the Federal Reserve affects bank reserves, consider an open-market purchase of a government security worth $1,000.

Government securities constitute the major part of Federal Reserve assets, as can be seen from Table 17.2. The purchase of the additional security increases the government security item on the asset side of the Federal Reserve's balance sheet by $1,000. To pay for this security, the Federal Reserve writes a check on itself, drawn on the New York Federal Reserve Bank. A key point to note here is that the Federal Reserve, by writing this check, does not reduce the balance in *any* account. The Federal Reserve simply creates a new liability against itself. What happens to the check? Let us suppose that an individual investor sold the security to the Federal Reserve. That individual will take the check received and deposit it at a bank, Citibank in New York, for example.

Citibank will then present the check to the New York Federal Reserve Bank for payment. The Federal Reserve will credit the Citibank account balance at the New York Federal Reserve Bank by $1,000. The open-market purchase results in an increase of an equal amount in bank reserve deposits with the Federal Reserve. The effects of the open-market purchase on the balance sheet of the Federal Reserve are summarized in Table 17.3.

In a similar manner, a sale of government securities in the open market will reduce bank reserve deposits by an equal amount. In this case, the Federal Reserve receives a check drawn on a bank by the individual who purchased the security. The Federal Reserve lowers that bank's deposit balance at a regional Federal Reserve

Table 17.3 Effect on the Federal Reserve's Balance Sheet of a $1,000 Open-Market Purchase

ASSETS		LIABILITIES	
Government securities	+1,000	Bank reserve deposits	+1,000

bank by the amount of the check. Such open-market purchases and sales of securities provide a flexible means of controlling bank reserves. Open-market operations are the most important of the Federal Reserve's tools of monetary control.

The Discount Rate

discount rate
the interest rate charged by the Federal Reserve on its loans to banks

The Federal Reserve Open Market Committee oversees open-market operations. The remaining tools of monetary control are administered by the Board of Governors of the Federal Reserve System. One of these is the Federal Reserve **discount rate**, the interest rate charged by the Federal Reserve on its loans to banks. The Federal Reserve can raise or lower this rate to regulate the volume of such loans to banks. To see the effect on bank reserve deposits of changes in the volume of loans from the Federal Reserve, consider a loan of $1,000 from the Federal Reserve to a bank. The effects on the Federal Reserve's balance sheet are shown in Table 17.4.

The asset item "loans to banks" increases by $1,000. The proceeds from the loan are credited to the account of the borrowing bank at the Federal Reserve. At this point, bank reserve deposits increase by $1,000. By lowering the discount rate, the Federal Reserve encourages banks to borrow and increase the borrowed component of bank reserve deposits. Raising the discount rate has the reverse effect.

From Table 17.2 it can be seen that loans to banks by the Federal Reserve were a very small balance sheet item in 2004. These discount loans declined dramatically in the 1990s for a variety of reasons. One was that if it was found that a bank had borrowed from the Federal Reserve, it would be interpreted as a sign of possible financial problems at the bank with adverse consequences for the bank's stock price.

While in some countries manipulation of the discount rate and of borrowed reserves is an important tool for monetary control, at present this is not the case in the United States. Still such lending does have a role in monetary policy. The Federal Reserve plays the role of "lender of last resort" to banks, an important role for a central bank. The Federal Reserve will lend to a bank and provide liquidity at times of crisis when other lending channels have been shut down. To keep the discount

Table 17.4 Effect on the Federal Reserve's Balance Sheet of a $1,000 Loan to a Bank

ASSETS		LIABILITIES	
Loans to banks	+1,000	Bank reserve deposits	+1,000

channel operative and continue to act as lender of last resort, the Federal Reserve has recently made a number of changes in the way in which it makes loans to banks. It now, for example, charges different rates to institutions based on their financial status. Thus, institutions that can borrow at a low rate because they are financially stable should not be hesitant do so for fear that such borrowing would signal otherwise. If the discount "window" is active and rates at which banks borrow is not public information, the stigma to borrowing from the central bank will decrease.

The Required Reserve Ratio

A potential third tool that the Federal Reserve can use to control banks' reserve positions is the **required reserve ratio**, the percentage of deposits banks must hold as reserves. Changes in this policy instrument do not change total bank reserves, but by changing the required reserve ratio on deposits, the Federal Reserve changes the quantity of deposits that can be supported by a given level of reserves. Increases in the required reserve ratio reduce the quantity of deposits that can be supported by a given amount of reserves. Consider our previous example, where reserves were set at $60 billion, so that with a 10 percent reserve requirement, the maximum level for checkable deposits was $600 billion. If the required reserve ratio were increased to 15 percent, the maximum level of deposits, with reserves unchanged at $60 billion, would be $400 billion. The increase in the required reserve ratio from 10 to 15 percent would have the same effect as a reduction in reserves (e.g., through an open-market sale of securities) from $60 billion to $40 billion ($40 = 0.10 \times 400$).

required reserve ratio is the percentage of deposits banks must hold as reserves

Although we have included them in our discussion, changes in reserve requirements are not often used to affect banks' reserve positions. One reason is that increases in reserve requirements are very unpopular with banks; being forced to hold more non-interest-paying reserves lowers bank profits.

17.3 BANK RESERVES AND BANK DEPOSITS

Thus far we have seen how the Federal Reserve can use open-market operations, changes in discount rate, and changes in the required reserve ratio on deposits to affect the reserve position of banks. In this section we examine the process whereby changes in reserves affect the level of deposits in the banking system. Again a convenient starting point is a balance sheet, in this case one for the commercial banking system.

A simplified consolidated balance sheet for all commercial banks is shown in Table 17.5. On the asset side, the first item is cash assets of commercial banks. Reserves (vault cash plus deposits at the Federal Reserve) come under this category, but other items are included as well (e.g., bank deposits at other banks). Reserves as of the time period for which the table was compiled (October 2003) totaled $40.8 billion, of which all but $1.6 billion were required reserves. As explained previously, banks hold few excess reserves, because reserve assets do not pay interest. The other major items on the asset side of the ledger are loans by the commercial banks, which include loans to consumers and businesses and the banks' holdings of both

Table 17.5 Consolidated Balance Sheet for the Commercial Banking System, March 2004 (billions of dollars)

ASSETS		LIABILITIES	
Cash assets, including reserves	313.5	Checkable deposits	639.3
Loans	4,363.0	Time and savings deposits	4,083.3
U.S. Treasury securities	1,081.8	Other liabilities and capital	2,571.0
Other securities	733.1		
Other assets	802.2		
Total assets	7,293.6	Total liabilities and capital	7,293.6

Source: Board of Governors of the Federal Reserve.

government and private securities. The major liabilities of the commercial banks are deposits, both checkable and savings plus time deposits.[5]

A Model of Deposit Creation

Now consider the effects on the bank of an increase in reserves. Let us return to our example of Citibank. Recall our assumption that the Federal Reserve has purchased a $1,000 security from an individual, using a check drawn on the New York Federal Reserve Bank. The individual had deposited the check at Citibank. When the check is presented for payment at the New York Federal Reserve Bank, Citibank's reserve deposits at the New York Federal Reserve increase by $1,000. To this point, the effects on Citibank's balance sheet as a result of this open-market purchase by the Federal Reserve are as shown in Table 17.6. Checkable deposits and reserves have both increased by $1,000. For simplicity, we continue to assume that there is a uniform reserve requirement of 10 percent. In that case, the increase in reserves will consist of an increase of $100 in required reserves ($0.10 \times 1,000$) and an increase of $900 in excess reserves, as shown in Table 17.6.

Table 17.6, however, gives only the initial effects of the open-market purchase on Citibank's balance sheet. The position described in Table 17.6 will *not* be an equilibrium

Table 17.6 Initial Effect on Citibank's Balance Sheet from a $1,000 Open-Market Purchase

ASSETS			LIABILITIES	
Reserves		+1,000	Checkable deposits	+1,000
Required reserves	+100			
Excess reserves	+900			
Total assets		+1,000	Total liabilities	+1,000

---

[5]There is a significant "other liabilities and capital" category. This contains funds borrowed by banking corporations. Also, bank capital was $542.6 billion.

for Citibank because the bank will not, in general, wish to increase *excess* reserves. Because reserves do not pay interest, the bank will convert the excess reserves, which are in the form of deposits at the New York Federal Reserve, into interest-earning assets. This conversion sets in motion a process of deposit creation whereby the initial increase in reserves of $1,000 causes deposits to increase by a multiple of that increase.

In describing this process, it is convenient to make some simplifying assumptions. First, we continue to assume that the public's holdings of currency remain unchanged. None of the initial increase in the monetary base, which was in the form of bank reserves, is siphoned off into increased currency holdings by the public. Second, we assume that the quantities of time and savings deposits are fixed. We continue to focus only on checkable deposits. Finally, we assume that the banking system's *desired* level of excess reserves is constant. The effect of altering these assumptions is examined later.

Having made these assumptions, we are ready to describe the process of deposit creation. Citibank has $900 in excess reserves, which it wants to convert into interest-earning assets. The bank can make this conversion by either increasing loans or purchasing additional securities. Neither of these actions will produce any lasting effect on the liability side of the ledger; there is no effect on the *equilibrium* level of Citibank's deposits. Citibank's purchase of a security does not change deposits. If the bank makes a loan, temporarily it may credit the amount of the loan to the checking account of the customer, and this action would increase deposits. But customers do not borrow just to increase their checking account balance. Suppose that the loan was to a consumer who used the proceeds to buy a new boat. The consumer pays for the boat with a check drawn on Citibank, and when this transaction is completed, deposits at Citibank will have returned to their initial level (before the loan).

The consumer's check will be deposited in the account of the firm that sold the boat. This firm's checking account balance, let us suppose at Bank of America, increases by $900. Bank of America presents the check to Citibank for payment—the check clears through the Federal Reserve System—and the result is a transfer of funds from Citibank's account at the New York Federal Reserve Bank to the account of Bank of America at that Federal Reserve Bank. At this point, the $900 in excess reserves is eliminated from Citibank's balance sheet; the bank's reserve deposits have declined by $900. Citibank's balance sheet is now at its final position, where the effects of the open-market operation are shown in Table 17.7. On the liability side, deposits are higher by the $1,000 deposit of the original individual who sold a government security to the Federal Reserve. Required reserves are higher by $100 ($0.10 \times 1,000$). Earning assets of the bank, loans in our example, have risen by $900.

Table 17.7 Final Effects on Citibank's Balance Sheet from a $1,000 Open-Market Purchase

ASSETS		LIABILITIES	
Reserves	+100	Checkable deposits	+1,000
Required reserves	+100		
Loans	+900		
Total assets	+1,000	Total liabilities	+1,000

Table 17.8 Initial Effects on Bank of America's Balance Sheet

ASSETS			LIABILITIES	
Reserves		+900	Checkable deposits	+900
Required reserves	+90			
Excess reserves	+810			
Total assets		+900	Total liabilities	+900

Table 17.9 Final Effects on Bank of America's Balance Sheet

ASSETS			LIABILITIES	
Reserves		+90	Checkable deposits	+900
Required reserves	+90			
Securities		+810		
Total assets		+900	Total liabilities	+900

Although we are now finished with Citibank's balance sheet, the process of deposit creation is not complete. Table 17.8 shows the effects on Bank of America's balance sheet to this point. Because of the deposit by the boat manufacturer, checkable deposits are up by $900. After the check has cleared through the Federal Reserve System, $900 has been transferred to Bank of America's reserve account. Thus reserves are increased by $900, of which only $90 ($0.10 \times 900$) is required to back the increase in deposits. Bank of America, finding itself with $810 of excess reserves, will convert them into interest-earning assets by proceeding in the same manner as did Citibank. The bank will increase loans or buy additional securities.

Suppose that the bank uses the $810 of excess reserves to purchase a security, a corporate bond, for example. The final position of Bank of America will be as shown in Table 17.9. Deposits remain up by $900, increasing required reserves by $90. As soon as Bank of America pays for the security with a check drawn upon itself and that check clears the Federal Reserve System, the bank's excess reserves are zero. Earning assets have increased by $810, and the bank is in equilibrium.

The process of deposit creation continues beyond this point, however, because the individual who sold the corporate bond to Bank of America deposits the proceeds of the check for $810 into an account at some other commercial bank. That bank now has excess reserves of $729, the $810 minus the $81 of reserves required to back the deposit. Another round of deposit creation will ensue.

The initial increase of $1,000 in reserves began a process of deposit creation whereby deposits of $1,000, then $900, then $810, then $729 resulted from the banking system's attempts to convert what were initially excess reserves into earning assets. The individual bank's attempt to rid itself of excess reserves, under the assumptions made to this point, simply transfers the reserves to another bank, together with creating a deposit at that bank. The newly created deposits increase required reserves by 10 percent of the increase in deposits; thus at each round in the process, the newly created deposit is 10 percent smaller than the previous round. The process will stop when all the new reserves have been absorbed in required reserves. With a $1,000 increase in reserves and a required reserve ratio of 10 percent, the new equilibrium will be reached when the quantity of deposits has increased by $10,000 ($1,000 = 0.10 × $10,000). At this point, required reserves have increased by $1,000. There are no longer any excess reserves in the system. The expansion of bank credit and the resulting creation of new bank deposits will come to an end.

More generally, an increase in reserves (R) of ΔR causes deposits to increase until required reserves have increased by an equal amount. The increase in required reserves is equal to the increase in checkable deposits times the required reserve ratio on checkable deposits; that is,

$$\text{increase in required reserves} = rr_d \Delta D \qquad \text{(17.1)}$$

where rr_d is the required reserve ratio and ΔD is the increase in deposits. Thus, for equilibrium,

$$\text{increase in reserves} = \text{increase in required reserves} \qquad \text{(17.2)}$$

$$\Delta R = rr_d \Delta D \qquad \text{(17.3)}$$

Therefore,

$$\Delta D = \frac{1}{rr_d} \Delta R \qquad \text{(17.4)}$$

The increase in deposits will be a multiple $(1/rr_d)$ of the increase in reserves. In our previous example, with ΔR equal to 1,000 and rr_d equal to 0.1 (a 10 percent reserve requirement), we have, from equation (17.4),

$$\Delta D = \frac{1}{0.1}(1,000) = 10,000 \qquad \text{(17.5)}$$

the result reached previously.

From equation (17.4) we can also define a *deposit multiplier*, giving the increase in deposits per unit increase in bank reserves:

$$\frac{\Delta D}{\Delta R} = \frac{1}{rr_d} \qquad \text{(17.6)}$$

The deposit multiplier for the simple case considered so far is equal to the reciprocal of the required reserve ratio on checkable deposits. For rr_d equal to 0.1 in our example, the deposit multiplier would be 10. Deposits increase by ten dollars for each one-dollar increase in reserves.

This form of the deposit multiplier results from the simplifying assumptions made previously and will have to be modified when we relax those assumptions. What follows generally is that, given the system of fractional legal reserve requirements, an increase in reserves causes deposits to increase by a multiple of the reserve increase. All of our analysis can be reversed to consider the effects of an open-market sale of securities, which lowers bank reserves and begins a process of deposit contraction. Also note that a similar process of deposit creation results from a reduction in the Federal Reserve discount rate, which would increase borrowed reserves, or from a lowering of reserve requirements, which, although it would not change total reserves, would create excess reserves in the banking system at the initial level of deposits. The balance sheet changes for such policy actions would be somewhat different from those shown in Tables 17.6 to 17.9, but the general effect would be the same. Both of these alternative expansionary policies would cause both bank credit and bank deposits to increase.

The relationship just derived between reserves and deposits can be restated as a relationship between the monetary base (MB) and the money supply (M^s). The monetary base is equal to currency held by the public plus bank reserves. Thus far we are assuming that the public's currency holdings are constant so that the change in the monetary base equals the change in reserves (ΔMB = ΔR). In this case, the change in the *money supply* will be equal to the change in bank deposits, again because currency held by the public is held constant ($\Delta D = \Delta M^s$). As a consequence, we can write a

money multiplier
gives the increase in the money supply per unit increase in the monetary base

money multiplier, giving the increase in the money supply per unit increase in the monetary base:

$$\frac{\Delta M^s}{\Delta MB} = \frac{\Delta D}{\Delta R} = \frac{1}{rr_d} \qquad (17.7)$$

which in this simple case is just equal to the deposit multiplier. This expression will also require modification when we relax our simplifying assumptions, and the money multiplier will usually not be equal in value to the deposit multiplier. In general, however, a given increase in the monetary base will cause the money supply to rise by a multiple of the increase in the base.

As described so far, the process of deposit or money creation must seem mechanical. New doses of reserves are converted by simple multipliers into new deposits, and the money supply increases. Such simple models are helpful in explaining the relationship between bank deposits and bank reserves, but they tell us little about the economic processes behind deposit and money creation. Before we go on to more complex models of deposit creation, it is worthwhile to stop and consider these processes.

When banks find themselves with excess reserves after a Federal Reserve open-market purchase of securities, they attempt to convert those excess reserves into interest-earning assets. They expand bank credit by making more loans and purchasing securities. To increase its lending, a bank offers lower interest rates on loans and perhaps adopts lower standards of creditworthiness. In buying securities, banks bid up the prices of such securities; they bid down the interest rate on securities. Among the earning assets banks buy are mortgages; thus in times of credit expansion, mortgage interest rates fall. Federal Reserve open-market purchases, as well as other expansionary policy actions that increase bank reserves, therefore lead to credit expansion and a general decline in interest rates. This is the other side of the process of deposit and money creation.

Deposit Creation: More General Cases

In addition to obscuring the economic process involved, simple models such as the one just discussed overstate the degree of precision in the relationship between

Federal Reserve actions and resulting changes in the supply of deposits or money. In this subsection, we note some of the complexities involved in this relationship.

First, consider the effect of modifying the assumption that the public's currency holdings are constant throughout the process of deposit creation. Instead assume, as seems likely, that as the quantity of deposits grows, the public also chooses to hold an increased amount of currency. In this case, some of the increase that occurs in the monetary base as a result of an open-market purchase ends up, not as increased bank reserves, but as an increase in the public's holding of currency.

Suppose for simplicity that the public holds a fixed ratio of currency to checkable deposits—for example, one dollar in currency per four dollars in checkable deposits ($CU/D = 0.25$, where CU denotes currency). Now, the individual who in our previous example sold the $1,000 bond to the Federal Reserve will not deposit the full $1,000 in a checking account but only $800, keeping the remaining $200 as currency ($200/800 = 0.25 = CU/D$). Bank reserves will increase by only $800 as a result of the $1,000 open-market operation. Further, at each stage in the deposit creation, as checkable deposits rise, the public's demand for currency increases in order to maintain a constant currency/checkable deposit ratio. At each stage, there will be a further leakage from bank reserves into currency.

As a consequence of the fact that reserves will increase by less, the increase in deposits for a given increase in the monetary base will be lower when the public's holding of currency rises than when it is fixed. The increase in the money supply will also be lower. This effect follows because each dollar of the base that is part of bank reserves backs a multiple number of dollars in deposits—ten in our example of a 10 percent reserve requirement—whereas each dollar of the monetary base that ends up as currency held by the public is simply *one* dollar of the money supply. The more of the increase in the base that goes into bank reserves, the higher is the money multiplier.

Relaxing the assumption that banks do not change their desired holdings of excess reserves provides an additional reason that the expression derived in the preceding subsection ($1/rr_d$) is an overstatement of the true money multiplier. It appears likely that as deposits rise, banks increase their excess reserves. Excess reserves are held as a buffer against unexpected deposit flows, and as deposits increase, so does the potential volume of deposit flows. In addition, as we have discussed, the process of deposit expansion leads to a drop in the level of interest rates. The cost of holding excess reserves is the interest forgone by not using these funds to purchase interest-bearing assets. As the interest rate falls, this cost becomes lower. Banks are likely to respond by holding more excess reserves.

If some of the increase in bank reserves ends up as new excess reserves, the quantity of deposits created by a given increase in reserves is smaller than when excess reserves are constant. In general, the higher the bank's desired excess reserve/checkable deposit ratio (ER/D), the lower is the money multiplier.

Next, consider the effect of modifying the assumption that the public's holdings of time and savings deposits are fixed. A more realistic assumption would be that the public increases its time and savings deposits together with its holdings of checkable deposits. How the increase in time and savings deposits affects the money multiplier depends on whether there are legal reserve requirements on these deposits and which of the monetary aggregates we are considering.

In the United States, legal reserve requirements on time and savings deposits were in effect during most of the post–World War II period. In this case, the money multiplier for the M1 definition was smaller when time and savings deposits increased than when they were assumed to be fixed. With some reserves going to satisfy reserve requirements on new time and savings deposits, fewer were available to support an increase in checking deposits—the only deposits included in the M1 aggregate. Thus the larger the increase in time and savings deposits, the smaller is the M1 multiplier.

Reserve requirements on time and savings deposits were phased out in the early 1990s. Currently, because these deposits absorb no required reserves, the M1 money multiplier is unaffected by increases in time and savings deposits. The amount of the increase does affect the size of the money multiplier for M2, which includes these deposits, but here we confine our attention to M1.

This discussion leads to the conclusion that the expression for the money multiplier will be more complex than the one derived in the preceding subsection. We would instead expect the money multiplier (m) *for the narrowly defined money supply* (M1) to be a function of the following form:

$$m = \frac{\Delta M^s}{\Delta (MB)} = m\left(rr_d, \frac{CU}{D}, \frac{ER}{D}\right) \tag{17.8}$$

The money multiplier (m) depends on:

1. The required reserve ratio on checkable deposits (rr_d); the higher the required reserve ratio, the lower the money multiplier.
2. The public's desired currency/checkable deposit ratio (CU/D); the higher the currency/checkable deposit ratio, the lower the money multiplier.
3. The excess reserve/checkable deposit ratio (ER/D); the higher the bank's desired excess reserve/checkable deposit ratio, the lower the money multiplier.

If the value of the money multiplier (m) in (17.8) were known, the Federal Reserve could predict the change in the money supply that would result from a given change in the monetary base:

$$\Delta M^s = m\Delta MB \tag{17.9}$$

The same information can be expressed slightly differently by defining a *money supply function* giving the supply of money corresponding to a given level of the monetary base:

$$M^s = m \cdot MB \tag{17.10}$$

Equation (17.10) replaces our previous assumption that the money supply was given exogenously. Before the complications discussed in this subsection are introduced, a money supply function in the form of equation (17.10) would still imply that the money supply was exogenously set by the Federal Reserve as long as the monetary base was controlled by the Federal Reserve; the money multiplier (m) depended only on the required reserve ratio on checkable deposits, which was set exogenously by the Federal Reserve. With both the monetary base and money multiplier set by the

Federal Reserve, the public or the banking system would have no role in determining the money supply. The more complicated expression for the money multiplier given by equation (17.8) contains variables determined by the nonbank public (CU/D) and by the banking system (ER/D), implying that even if the Federal Reserve set the monetary base exogenously, the level of the money supply would not be exogenous; it depends to a degree on the behavior of the public and the banking system.

17.4 WHO CONTROLS THE MONEY SUPPLY?

What, then, can be said about the relative importance of the Federal Reserve, the banking system, and the nonbank public in determining the money supply? To begin with, let us continue to assume that the monetary base is set exogenously by the Federal Reserve. In that case, the reason the Federal Reserve would not have perfect control over the money supply is that, as just explained, the value of the money multiplier depends to some extent on the behavior of the banking system and the public. How great is the loss of control resulting from these sources?

If we are considering a short period of time, such as one to two months, uncertainty about the money multiplier results in a serious loss of money supply control for the Federal Reserve. The variables that affect the money supply and are outside the direct control of the Federal Reserve—the currency/deposit ratio and the excess reserve/deposit ratio—cannot be predicted with precision in the short run. Notice that, although we made simplifying assumptions in our discussion, such as a fixed currency/deposit ratio, in fact the currency/deposit and excess reserve/deposit ratios are *variables* that depend on the decisions of the banking system and the public. These decisions depend in turn on the behavior of other economic variables. For example, the excess reserve/deposit ratio depends on the cost of holding such reserves—the interest rate that could be earned on loans and securities. The introduction in the 1980s of accounts that pay a market-determined interest rate created the added complication that the currency/checkable deposit ratio will fluctuate with movement in this rate. Precise control of the money supply would require highly accurate predictions of those variables, among others. Although no one would deny that movements in the monetary base are an important determinant of money growth from month to month, uncertainty concerning short-run variations in the money multiplier makes precise monetary control difficult over such a time horizon.

For a longer period, such as six months to one year, difficulties in monetary control caused by uncertainty about the money multiplier are less serious. Although the Federal Reserve may not be able to predict in a given month the response of the money supply to a given change in the monetary base, policymakers can monitor the month-to-month behavior of the money supply and make the adjustments in the monetary base required to achieve the desired *average* rate of growth in the money supply over a period of several months. To see how this averaging might be done, consider the following example.

Suppose that the Federal Reserve wished to achieve a growth rate for the money supply (M1) of 5 percent for a given calendar year. If no change in the money multiplier was expected, the Federal Reserve could attempt to achieve this target by increasing the monetary base at an annual rate of 5 percent. Assume that in February of that year, the data show that for January, with a 5 percent growth (all growth rates expressed at annual rates) in the monetary base, the money supply grew by only 1 percent. There was a fall in the money multiplier. The Federal Reserve could then, in February and the following months, cause the monetary base to grow by more than 5 percent to offset this fall in the money multiplier. If the action taken in one month was insufficient to get the money supply back on the 5 percent growth path, a further adjustment to the growth rate in the monetary base could be made. P. T. Barnum once said that the trick to keeping a lamb in a cage with a lion is to have a large reserve supply of lambs. Federal Reserve control over the money supply rests on a supply of actions that can be taken to offset undesired movements stemming from other sources. Even over periods as long as six months or one year, such control is not perfect. If the Federal Reserve set a target growth rate for the money supply of 5 percent and concentrated all its policy actions on achieving that target, we might end up with growth of 4.8 percent or 5.2 percent. We would not, however, end up with 2 percent or 8 percent.

In actual historical experience, the Federal Reserve has announced growth-rate targets for 6- to 12-month periods and has ended up wide of the mark. If the Federal Reserve *can* control the money supply with a reasonable degree of precision over periods of this length, what explains its failure to hit its own preannounced money growth targets? Why in practice has the Federal Reserve often not closely controlled the money supply?

We previously assumed that the Federal Reserve controlled the monetary base and *concentrated its policy actions* on achieving a money supply target. The reason monetary growth targets are not achieved in practice is that the Federal Reserve is unwilling to concentrate all its efforts on this one policy goal. The Federal Reserve has also been interested in controlling the behavior of other financial market variables, the most important being interest rates. Conflicts arise between hitting target levels of money supply growth and achieving desirable behavior of these other variables. When such conflicts arise, the Federal Reserve has sometimes chosen to miss the money growth target rather than accept what is viewed as the cost of hitting such targets, the resulting undesirable behavior of interest rates. We consider this choice between money supply targets and interest-rate targets at greater length in Chapter 18, but the essence of the conflict can be explained at this point.

Figure 17.1*a* reproduces an earlier graph showing the money demand and supply schedules (M^d and M^s) intersecting to determine the equilibrium interest rate r^*. We assume, as we did earlier, that the money supply is exogenous. In terms of this chapter's analysis, we assume that the Federal Reserve uses control of the monetary base to achieve its money supply target (M^*). Also suppose that the equilibrium interest rate r^* shown in Figure 17.1*a* is regarded by the Federal Reserve as the desired level of the interest rate.

Now consider the effects of shifts in the money demand schedule, as shown in Figure 17.1*b*. Such shifts could result from changes in income, which change money demand for a given interest rate. Alternatively, such shifts could represent the effects of actual shifts in the money demand *function*—changes in the amount of money demanded at given levels of both income and the interest rate. Changes in the demand for money might shift the money demand schedule to positions such as M_1^d (an increase in money demand) and M_2^d (a decline in money demand) in Figure 17.1*b*.

Figure 17.1
Interest Rate Versus Money Supply Control

Part *a* shows money market equilibrium with interest rate *r** and money supply *M**. If, however, as shown in part *b*, the money demand function shifts from M_0^d to either M_1^d or M_2^d, then if the Federal Reserve keeps the money supply at M_0^s, the interest rate must diverge from the target level *r**. Alternatively, the Federal Reserve could accommodate the shift in money demand, to M_1^d, for example, by raising the money supply to M_1^s. In this case the money supply target, *M** will not be achieved.

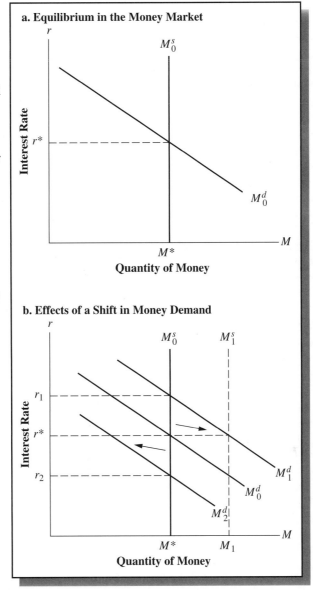

a. Equilibrium in the Money Market

b. Effects of a Shift in Money Demand

What will the Federal Reserve do in response to such shifts? If it sticks to its money supply target and maintains the money supply at *M**, the interest rate will move away from *r**, the Federal Reserve's desired level for the interest rate. A decline in money demand (a shift in the money demand schedule from M_0^d to M_2^d) would cause the interest rate to fall to r_2; an increase in money demand (a shift in the money demand schedule from M_0^d to M_1^d) would cause an undesirable rise in the interest rate to r_1.

The Federal Reserve can prevent or mitigate these movements in the interest rate only by changing the monetary base, and hence the money supply. In the case of an increase in money demand, the Federal Reserve could, by increasing the monetary base, move the money supply to the level given by the M_1^s schedule in Figure 17.1b. This increase in the money supply would produce equilibrium in the money market at the desired interest rate r^*. The Federal Reserve would, however, miss the money supply target; the money supply would be M_1, which is above M^*. This is a case in which the Federal Reserve is *accommodating* the public's increased demand for money. The Federal Reserve supplies new money balances in order to keep the increased demand for money from pushing up the interest rate. Notice that with such accommodation, neither the money supply nor the monetary base is any longer being set exogenously. Both are responding to the behavior of the public.

To the degree that the Federal Reserve engages in such accommodation, the public will have a large role in determining the value of the money supply even over periods of six months to a year. In the extreme case in which the Federal Reserve pegs the interest rate at a fixed level for a long period of time, as was done in the United States in the early post–World War II period, the monetary authority plays a completely passive role in the money supply process, having to supply whatever amount of money is required to maintain the desired interest rate.

Read Perspectives 17.1.

PERSPECTIVES 17.1
The Money Supply During the Great Depression

The monetary collapse during the Great Depression, which demonstrates the potential importance of banks and the nonbank public in the money supply process, is illustrated in Figure 17.2. Part *a* of the figure charts the behavior of two factors that affect the value of the money multiplier (m): the currency/deposit ratio (CU/D) and the excess reserve/deposit ratio (ER/D). The first of these is determined by the public and the second by banks. Both of these ratios rose sharply in

Figure 17.2
Monetary Statistics, 1927–34

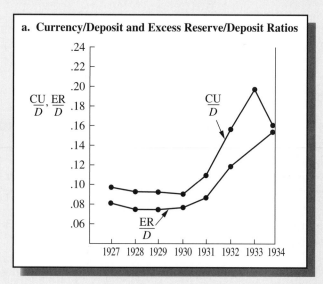

a. **Currency/Deposit and Excess Reserve/Deposit Ratios**

the early 1930s. The cause of the rise in both ratios was the large number of bank failures during the period; more than 9,000 banks failed between 1929 and 1933. The bank failures caused a loss of confidence in bank deposits. As a consequence, the public held more of their money balances in the form of currency. Banks that did not fail held more excess reserves to ward off "runs" by depositors that could result in the banks' insolvency.

As discussed in this chapter, a rise in either the currency/deposit ratio or the excess reserve/deposit ratio causes the money multiplier to fall. This effect can be seen from the plot of the money multiplier (*m*) in part *b* of Figure 17.2. Besides the multiplier, the other factor determining the money supply is the monetary base (MB). Part *b* of the figure shows that the monetary base increased over this period. As can be seen from part *c*, however, the increase in the base was too small to keep

Figure 17.2
Continued

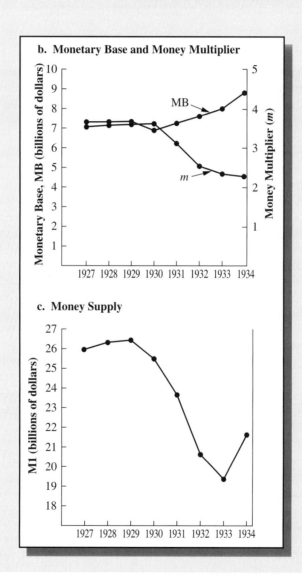

the M1 measure of the money supply from declining sharply. Between 1929 and 1933, M1 fell by 26.5 percent. The decline in M2 was even larger (33.3 percent).

The behavior of the Federal Reserve during this period has been criticized, especially by monetarists who see the decline in the money supply as the cause of the Depression. There is, however, a question of whether the Federal Reserve in the early 1930s had adequate tools to prevent the collapse.[a] In any case, the fall in the money multiplier and consequent fall in monetary aggregates in the early 1930s do indicate that the public and the banks can be major players in the money supply process.

[a]On these issues, see Milton Friedman and Anna Schwartz, *A Monetary History of the United States* (Princeton N.J.: Princeton University Press, 1963); Peter Temin, *Did Monetary Forces Cause the Great Depression?* (New York: Norton, 1976); and Peter Temin, *Lessons from the Great Depression* (Cambridge, Mass.: MIT Press, 1990).

17.5 CONCLUSION

The first sections of this chapter explained how the Federal Reserve, controls the monetary base (currency plus bank reserve deposits) and the link between the monetary base and the money supply. We have seen that, because of uncertainty about the money multiplier, precise Federal Reserve control of the money supply in the very short run (one or two months) is quite difficult. The behavior of the public and the banking system have a substantial influence on such short-term variations in the money supply. Over longer periods (six months to a year, for example), the Federal Reserve can control the money supply with reasonable precision by altering the monetary base to offset any undesirable changes in the money supply as a result of the behavior of the banking system or nonbank public. When the Federal Reserve does not control the money supply over such long periods, the failure to do so is one of will rather than ability.

The reason the Federal Reserve does not always concentrate solely on controlling the money supply is that to do so would result in what the Federal Reserve regards as undesirable fluctuations in the interest rate. To prevent such undesirable interest-rate movements, the Federal Reserve at times accommodates changes in the public's demand for money with the effect that the monetary base and the money supply are no longer exogenous. The reasons for the Federal Reserve's concern over fluctuations in interest rates and the relative desirability of controlling interest rates or the money supply are discussed in Chapter 18, when we analyze the Federal Reserve's operating procedures in more detail.

KEY TERMS

- Federal Reserve System 360
- M1, M2, M3 362
- Board of Governors of the Federal Reserve 363
- Federal Open Market Committee 363
- open-market operations 363
- monetary base 364
- discount rate 366
- required reserve ratio 367
- money multiplier 372

REVIEW QUESTIONS AND PROBLEMS

1. What are the major policymaking bodies within the Federal Reserve System? Explain their composition and functions.
2. Suppose that the Federal Reserve wants to increase bank reserves. Explain the various measures that could be taken to achieve that end. In each case, illustrate the link between the Federal Reserve's policy action and the level of bank reserves.
3. What is the maximum amount of the increase in checkable deposits that can result from a $1,000 increase in legal reserves if the required reserve ratio for checkable deposits is 10 percent? Explain how this increase comes about in the banking system. Give two reasons why the actual increase may fall short of the theoretical maximum.
4. Suppose that the level of the required reserve ratio on checkable deposits was 0.10. Also assume that the public's holdings of currency were constant, as were banks' desired excess reserves. Analyze the effects on the money supply of a $1,000 open-market sale of securities by the Federal Reserve. In your answer, explain the role of the banking system in adjusting to this monetary policy action.
5. Explain the concept of the money multiplier. What factors determine the size of the money multiplier?
6. Within the *IS–LM* curve model used in Chapters 7 and 8, show how income and the interest rate will be affected by each of the following changes.
   a. An increase in the required reserve ratio for checkable deposits.
   b. An open-market sale of securities by the Federal Reserve.
   c. A decrease in the Federal Reserve discount rate.
7. The chapter stated that the Federal Reserve would find it very difficult to exert close control of the rate of growth in the money supply over very short periods but would be able to achieve much greater control over somewhat longer periods. What is the nature of the difficulties in short-run monetary control, on a month-to-month basis? Why are these difficulties less serious over longer periods?
8. Within the *IS–LM* curve model, illustrate the nature of the conflict the Federal Reserve faces between trying to control the money supply and trying to achieve "desirable" interest-rate levels.

Chapter 18

Monetary Policy

*T*he focus of this chapter is on the optimal conduct of monetary policy. What should central banks *do*? The first section discusses the structure of the U.S. central bank, the Federal Reserve System. We then examine the competing monetary policy strategies from which the Federal Reserve can choose and the choices that have been made. The final section of the chapter looks at monetary policy in other countries. Dissatisfaction with the conduct of monetary policy under existing legal frameworks has led to institutional changes in the central banks of a number of countries. These reforms address the question of how we can get central banks to "do the right thing."

18.1 THE MONETARY POLICYMAKING PROCESS

As explained in Chapter 17, the key bodies within the Federal Reserve System are the Board of Governors of the Federal Reserve and the Federal Open Market Committee (FOMC). The Board of Governors is composed of 7 governors, appointed by the president of the United States, with Senate confirmation, to terms of 14 years, with one of the governors designated by the president as chairman for a four-year term. The FOMC has 12 voting members, the 7 governors and 5 of the presidents of the 12 regional Federal Reserve banks. Presidents of regional Federal Reserve banks serve on a rotating basis, with the exception of the president of the Federal Reserve Bank of New York who is a permanent voting member.

Also discussed in Chapter 17, open-market operations are the major tool the Federal Reserve uses to conduct monetary policy, and our discussion in this chapter focuses on the behavior of the FOMC.

An important feature of the Federal Reserve's situation is the considerable degree of independence given to the monetary policymaking authority. The 14-year terms for which the governors are appointed and the fact that they cannot be reappointed provide insulation from the political process. The chairman of the Board of Governors is appointed for a four-year term, but this term is not concurrent with that of the president of the United States. Therefore, an incoming president does not immediately get to appoint his choice of chairman. The other members of the FOMC, the regional bank presidents, are appointed by the directors of the regional banks with the approval of the Board of Governors.

In the 1970s, Congress passed legislation requiring periodic reports from the Federal Reserve on the conduct of policy, but monetary policy decisions, such as the target growth rate in the money supply or the target level for interest rates, are not subjects on which Congress legislates. Those decisions are made by the FOMC. Further, the Federal Reserve has a degree of independence from the budget appropriations process because its expenses are paid by its interest earnings on holdings of government securities.

All this is not to say that the Federal Reserve is completely autonomous or that monetary policy is conducted in an apolitical setting. The chairman of the Board of Governors comes up for reappointment (as chairman) during the course of a president's term. For example, President Carter declined to reappoint Arthur Burns as chairman in 1978, replacing him with G. William Miller. In 1983, President Reagan did reappoint Paul Volcker (who was appointed by Carter in 1979 when Miller became Secretary of the Treasury), but only after much speculation that Reagan would prefer his own nominee. In 1987, when Volcker asked not to be considered for a third term as chairman and was replaced by Alan Greenspan, there was speculation that he did so because President Reagan had failed to signal directly that he wanted Volcker to stay. Greenspan, a Republican, came up for and was granted reappointment by President Clinton in 1996 and 2000. Also, because board members often resign before the end of their terms, a president can sometimes make several appointments to the board and, therefore, change the course of monetary policy. By 1987, for example, President Reagan had appointed all the members of the board. By 1998, four of the members of the board were new Clinton appointees.

Perhaps most important, Federal Reserve independence is itself the result of congressional legislation, and the Federal Reserve recognizes that new legislation could weaken this independence. In fact, at times of severe conflict between the Federal Reserve and the administration or Congress over the proper course of monetary policy, bills to limit Federal Reserve independence are often proposed in Congress. The Federal Reserve recognizes this threat and the fact that there are limits on how far it can go in pursuing goals that deviate from those of Congress and the president.

The FOMC meets approximately eight times a year. At these meetings members review the current domestic and international economic situation. They also consider forecasts of the Federal Reserve staff concerning future economic events. On the basis of this information, they formulate a "directive" to the Open Market Desk at the New York Federal Reserve Bank, explaining how open-market operations should be conducted during the period until the next FOMC meeting. The question of an optimal monetary policy strategy can then be viewed as the choice of a directive by the FOMC.

Read Perspectives 18.1.

Central Bank Independence and Economic Performance

The degree of central bank independence has at times varied greatly among countries. Some central banks have had virtually complete independence; others have been subservient to their country's finance ministry. The horizontal axis of Figure 18.1 measures central bank independence as of the late 1980s using an index constructed by Alberto Alesina and Lawrence Summers for a sample of industrialized countries.[a] The higher the index value, the greater is the independence. The most independent central banks in the sample were those of Switzerland and Germany, followed by the U.S. Federal Reserve. The least independent at that time was the Bank of New Zealand.

The vertical axis of the figure plots the average inflation rate for these countries for the 1955–88 period. Notice the downward slope of the scatter of points; the countries with more independent central banks had lower inflation rates. This better inflation performance has led a number of countries, including New Zealand, the United Kingdom, and Canada, to grant greater independence to their central banks. The European Central Bank set up by the 11 (now 12) countries that have adopted the euro as a common currency was given a high degree of independence. These increases in central bank independence are among the institutional reforms discussed in section 18.7.

Figure 18.1
Central Bank
Independence and
the Rate of Inflation
Ranking is from least
(1) to most (5)
independent

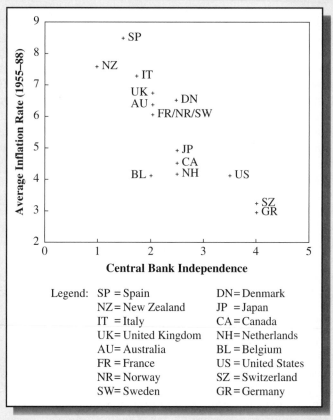

[a]Alberto Alesina and Lawrence Summers, "Central Bank Independence and Macroeconomic Performance," *Journal of Money, Credit and Banking,* 25 (May 1993), pp. 151–62.

18.2 COMPETING STRATEGIES FOR MONETARY POLICY: TARGETING MONETARY AGGREGATES OR INTEREST RATES

In one sense, what the Federal Reserve should do is clear. Monetary policy should be conducted in a way that leads to stable growth in aggregate demand. The Federal Reserve should keep demand from growing too rapidly, with resulting inflation, or too slowly, with resulting high unemployment and slow economic growth. But what procedures are likely to result in desirable outcomes in an uncertain world? What strategy should guide monetary policy? In the next two subsections, we explain two competing monetary policy strategies: intermediate targeting monetary aggregates and targeting interest rates.

Targeting Monetary Aggregates

The ultimate *targets* that the monetary authority would like to control are macroeconomic goal variables such as the unemployment rate, the inflation rate, and growth in real gross domestic product (GDP). Rather than simply adjusting monetary policy instruments, primarily the level of open-market operations, on the basis of past observations on these variables and forecasts of their future behavior, in the short run the Federal Reserve has at times tried to influence these ultimate targets by influencing intermediate target variables.

An intermediate target is a variable that the Federal Reserve controls not because the variable is important in its own right but because by controlling it the policymakers believe they are influencing the ultimate policy targets in a predictable way. With a monetary aggregate as an intermediate target, the implicit assumption in Federal Reserve strategy is that, other things being equal, higher rates of growth in the money supply increase inflation while lowering unemployment (raising the level of economic activity) in the short run. Slower monetary growth rates are, again, other things being equal, associated with lower inflation rates and higher short-run rates of unemployment.

What is the rationale for such intermediate targeting? Even if there is a predictable relationship between money growth rates and ultimate economic targets that the Federal Reserve wants to control, why use an intermediate target rather than control the ultimate targets directly? To understand the possible usefulness of the intermediate targeting approach, we must recognize that monetary policy must be made under conditions of imperfect information and, therefore, uncertainty about the behavior of the economy. If the ultimate targets of policy can be observed at less frequent intervals (e.g., quarterly versus weekly) than financial market variables such as interest rates, bank reserves, and monetary aggregates, then as information about such financial market variables becomes available, it can be used to adjust the previous policy setting. The intermediate targeting approach is one way of employing such financial market information.

As implemented by the Federal Reserve, intermediate targeting on a monetary aggregate proceeds as follows.[1] At the beginning of each calendar quarter, the FOMC chooses the money growth rate target that it views as consistent with its ultimate policy goals for the next year. The committee makes this choice based on past data and staff forecasts of the behavior of the economy for given money growth rates. After this choice has been made, monetary policy during the quarter proceeds *as if the chosen money growth target is the ultimate target of monetary policy*. Policy actions within the quarter are aimed at hitting this money target. At the beginning of the next quarter, the money target is reviewed and adjusted on the basis of new forecasts and the experience within the quarter.

Targeting the Interest Rate

There are a number of alternatives to the strategy of intermediate targeting on a monetary aggregate. In practice, the main alternative has been for the Federal Reserve to focus on the level of an interest rate.

An example will help clarify how a Federal Reserve strategy focused on interest rates would work. Although at times policy has not been so mechanical, the strategy described will be one in which the Federal Reserve sets explicit interest-rate targets. The FOMC could, for example, set a range for the coming month of 5 to 6 percent for the rate on three-month Treasury bills. As with money supply targets, the range for the target interest rate would be chosen to hit the ultimate policy targets (inflation rate, unemployment rate, and growth rate of the economy). The interest rate would replace the money supply as an *intermediate target*.

Once the target range was set, the Open Market Desk would monitor the market where Treasury bills trade, which is part of the open market. If the interest rate on Treasury bills rose above the 6 percent ceiling of the target range, the desk manager would begin open-market purchases. These could involve Treasury bills or other government securities. The effect of open-market purchases, as we have seen, is to expand credit and lower interest rates. The desk would carry out enough open-market purchases to reduce the Treasury bill rate below 6 percent.

Alternatively, if the Treasury bill rate temporarily fell below 5 percent, the Open Market Desk would begin to *sell* securities in the open market—reducing bank reserves, restricting credit, and raising interest rates—until the Treasury bill rate rose back above 5 percent. Thus, the Open Market Desk would keep the average Treasury bill rate between 5 and 6 percent for the month.

Note that in carrying out open-market purchases or sales, the Open Market Desk increases or decreases bank reserves, bank deposits, and therefore the money supply. For example, keeping the interest rate in the target range might require large open-market purchases or sales, and therefore large changes in the money supply. The point is that a focus on the interest rate is in fact *an alternative* to targeting a monetary aggregate. The Federal Reserve cannot, in general, do both. Given this fact, which is the better strategy?

---

[1]The implementation of targeting monetary aggregates has varied in details over time. The description in this section best fits the way the procedure worked in the late 1970s and early 1980s. Later modifications are considered in section 18.6.

18.3 IMPLICATIONS OF TARGETING A MONETARY AGGREGATE

To answer the question just posed, we first consider how a strategy of targeting a monetary aggregate would work in practice. In section 18.4, we do the same for interest-rate targeting. Section 18.5 then evaluates the relative merits of each strategy.

To summarize our conclusion in advance, we find that, rather than one strategy being preferable under all circumstances, there are circumstances in which each is preferred. Recall that the rationale for any strategy of intermediate targeting depends on the fact that the Federal Reserve acts under uncertainty about what is going on in the economy. Whether targeting interest rates or monetary aggregates is the preferable strategy depends on the source of that uncertainty, though there are some other considerations as well.

The Ideal Case for Targeting a Monetary Aggregate

We first consider the ideal case for targeting a monetary aggregate, in which this is clearly the optimal strategy. This case is depicted within the *IS–LM* framework in Figure 18.2. Suppose the Federal Reserve has one ultimate target, the level of real income (Y), the desired level of which is Y^*.[2] Also assume that in a given quarter, on

Figure 18.2
Ideal Case for Targeting a Monetary Aggregate

If the demand for money is totally interest-inelastic and perfectly stable, then by hitting the money supply target M^*, the Federal Reserve fixes the vertical *LM* schedule at $LM(M^*)$. Income will be at the target level Y^* regardless of the *IS* schedule.

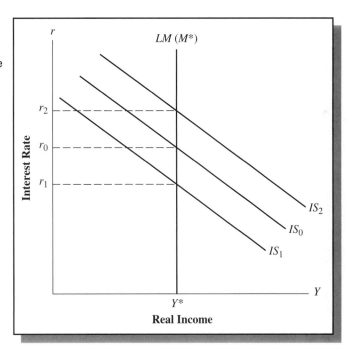

---

[2]We assume that the Federal Reserve does not want income to fall below Y^* because that would cause excessive unemployment. Levels of income above Y^* are undesirable because of their future inflationary consequences.

the basis of forecasts, the monetary policy authority concludes that the target level of income will be achieved if the money supply is set at M^*.[3]

The LM schedule in Figure 18.2 is vertical, reflecting an assumption that the demand for money is totally interest-inelastic. Money demand depends only on income. Further, we assume that the demand-for-money function is perfectly stable. There are no shifts in the function—no changes in the amount of money demanded for a given income level. On the supply side, the Federal Reserve is assumed to offset changes in the money supply that result from the behavior of the public and the banking system. Thus, if the Federal Reserve achieves its target level of the money supply (M^*), the LM schedule will be perfectly stable at $LM(M^*)$ in Figure 18.2. This means that successfully hitting the intermediate target for the money supply will in fact mean successfully hitting the ultimate income target (Y^*).

To see this outcome, consider the situation depicted in the figure. We assume that the Federal Reserve cannot predict with certainty the position of the IS schedule. Assume that the predicted position for the curve is IS_0. Real-sector demand factors such as exports, autonomous investment, and government spending may turn out to be weaker than predicted, causing the IS schedule to be to the left of IS_0, at IS_1. Alternatively, such real-sector demand factors may be stronger than predicted, causing the IS schedule to be at IS_2, to the right of IS_0. By targeting the money supply, the Federal Reserve ensures that the vertical LM schedule will be fixed at $LM(M^*)$, and consequently income will be at Y^*, regardless of the position of the IS schedule. When the Federal Reserve uses a money aggregate as an intermediate target, within the quarter, policy proceeds as if the chosen money supply target *were* the ultimate target of monetary policy. In the case depicted in Figure 18.2, hitting the money supply target guarantees hitting the income target. This is the optimal case for targeting money.

Notice that, although hitting the money supply target guarantees that we will hit the income target, unpredicted shocks that shift the IS schedule will cause volatility in the interest rate. If the position of the IS schedule is IS_1 or IS_2 instead of the Federal Reserve's predicted position, IS_0, the interest rate will be r_1 or r_2 instead of the predicted level, r_0. If the Federal Reserve also had a desired level for the interest rate, for example r_0, the Federal Reserve would miss this interest-rate target. The interest-rate must be free to adjust depending on the position of the IS curve. This situation illustrates the point made earlier that the Federal Reserve cannot generally hit both interest-rate and money supply targets.

A final point to note about this case for targeting a monetary aggregate is that it approximates the *monetarist* case. Monetarists believe that the LM curve is steep and that, at least in most circumstances, money demand is stable—the conditions in Figure 18.2. It is then not surprising that the monetarists favor targeting monetary aggregates.

---

[3]An important early analysis of the relative merits of an interest rate versus a monetary aggregate as a target under conditions of uncertainty is William Poole, "Optimal Choice of Monetary Policy Instruments in a Simple Stochastic Macro Model," *Quarterly Journal of Economics*, 84 (May 1970), pp. 197–216.

Less Than Ideal Cases for Intermediate Targeting a Monetary Aggregate

Figure 18.3 illustrates cases in which achieving the money supply target does not generally mean that the income target will be achieved. In Figure 18.3a, we still assume that if the Federal Reserve hits its money supply target, it will fix the position of the *LM* curve. For this to be the case, we must assume that the money demand function is perfectly stable. There are no unpredictable shifts in money demand that will shift the *LM* schedule for a given value of the money supply. In Figure 18.3a, we

Figure 18.3
Less Than Ideal Cases for Targeting Money

Part *a* shows that, if money demand is not totally interest-inelastic and the *LM* schedule is upward-sloping, hitting the money supply target will cause income to be at the target level Y^* only if the *IS* schedule is at the predicted position IS_0. If, because of unpredicted shocks, the *IS* schedule is instead at IS_1 or IS_2, income will be away from Y^*, at Y_1 or Y_2, even though M is at M^*. In part *b*, we assume that the Federal Reserve hits the money supply target M^*, which, on the basis of its forecast of money demand, should set the *LM* schedule at LM_0 (M^*) and hit the income target Y^*. If, because of an unpredicted shock to the money demand function, the *LM* curve shifts to either $LM_1(M^*)$ or $LM_2(M^*)$, income will be at Y_1 or Y_2 and the income target will be missed even if the money supply is at the target level M^*.

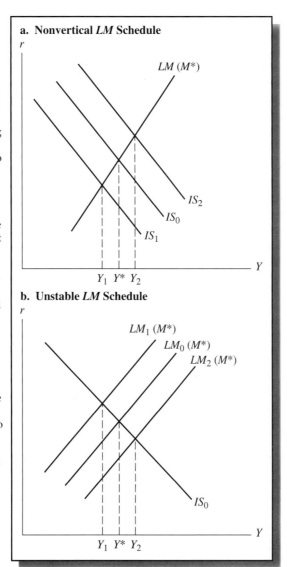

a. Nonvertical *LM* Schedule

b. Unstable *LM* Schedule

do not assume that money demand is totally interest-inelastic; the *LM* schedule is therefore not vertical.

In this case, notice that even though the Federal Reserve achieves its target level of the money supply, it will hit the ultimate income target only if the *IS* curve is at the predicted position, IS_0—only if the Federal Reserve's real-sector forecast, on which the choice of the money supply target was predicated, was correct. If real-sector demand was weaker than predicted and the *IS* schedule was at IS_1 in Figure 18.3*a* instead of IS_0, income would be at Y_1, below Y^*. If real-sector demand was stronger than predicted and the *IS* schedule was at IS_2, income would exceed the target level. In both cases, the income target is missed even though the Federal Reserve hits the money supply target M^*. With a nonvertical *LM* schedule, fixing the money supply does not fix the level of income.

In Figure 18.3*b*, we consider a case in which the money demand function is not perfectly stable. There are unpredicted shifts in money demand for given levels of income and the interest rate. Such shocks to money demand shift the *LM* schedule. In this case, even if the Federal Reserve hits its money supply target, the *LM* schedule will not be fixed. In Figure 18.3*b*, assume that, on the basis of a forecast of money demand, the Federal Reserve predicts that the *LM* schedule will be at $LM_0(M^*)$. To isolate the effects of uncertainty about money demand clearly, let us assume that the Federal Reserve's forecast about the real sector is correct: The predicted and actual position of the *IS* curve is IS_0.

If the Federal Reserve is using the money supply as an intermediate target and hits the money supply target (M^*), it will hit the income target (Y^*) only if the prediction of money demand is correct—only if the *LM* schedule is at $LM_0(M^*)$ as predicted. This outcome can be seen in Figure 18.3*b*. If an unpredicted shock increases the demand for money above the predicted level and the *LM* schedule is at $LM_1(M^*)$ instead of $LM_0(M^*)$, income (Y_1) will fall short of the target level.[4] In the reverse case, when an unpredicted shock reduces money demand below the predicted level and the *LM* curve is at a position such as $LM_2(M^*)$, income will be at Y_2, above the target level. Again, hitting the money supply target does not guarantee that the income target will be hit.

18.4 IMPLICATIONS OF TARGETING THE INTEREST RATE

Next consider a strategy of targeting the rate of interest. Here we ignore the range within which the interest rate might be targeted and simply assume that there is a single target level, r^*, for the interest rate. As with a money supply target, the policymaker is assumed to have one ultimate target, that of keeping real income (Y) at a desired level (Y^*).

If the Federal Reserve targets the interest rate, then in the *IS–LM* framework the *LM* schedule becomes horizontal. The *LM* schedule depicts equilibrium in the money

---

[4]A shock that reduces (or increases) money demand is a shift in the money demand function that reduces (or increases) the quantity of money demanded for a given level of income and the rate of interest. The way this shifts the *LM* schedule is explained in section 7.2.

market. To peg the interest rate, the Federal Reserve supplies whatever amount of money is necessary for money market equilibrium at the target interest rate.

To see how a strategy of targeting the interest rate works, we consider the same cases as we did for a money supply target.

Uncertainty About the *IS* Schedule

In the first two cases we assume the only uncertainty is about the *IS* schedule. Figure 18.4 depicts the situation in which, as in Figure 18.2, the predicted position of the *IS* schedule is IS_0. But positions IS_1 and IS_2 might occur, respectively, if demand is weaker or stronger than expected. In addition to the horizontal *LM* schedule, which is relevant when the interest rate is pegged (solid line), we also show (as a dashed line) the position of the *LM* schedule that would have resulted if we had targeted the money supply (at M^*). In Figure 18.4, we assume that money demand is totally interest-inelastic (zero interest elasticity). Therefore, if the money supply were the intermediate target, the *LM* schedule would be vertical.

We see from Figure 18.4 that, with the interest rate targeted at r^*, we will hit the income target, Y^*, only if the *IS* schedule turns out to be in the predicted position IS_0. If, for example, business investment demand were lower than predicted and the *IS* schedule were at IS_1, income would fall below the desired level (to $Y_{r,1}$). In the case depicted in Figure 18.4, we are better off with a money supply target, where we stay at Y^* regardless of the position of the *IS* schedule.

Figure 18.4
Targeting the Interest Rate with *IS* Uncertainty: Zero Interest Elasticity of Money Demand

With an interest rate target, the *LM* schedule is horizontal. If the *IS* schedule is at IS_1 instead of at the predicted position IS_0, income will be at $Y_{r,1}$, below the target level. If the money supply is the intermediate target, the *LM* schedule is vertical and the income target will be hit.

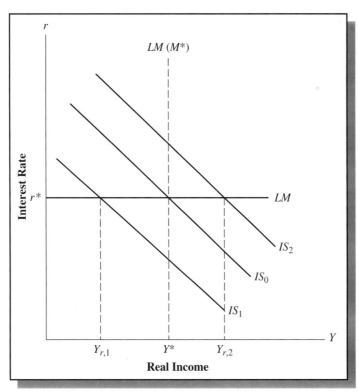

Figure 18.5
Targeting the Interest Rate with *IS* Uncertainty: Non-zero Interest Elasticity of Money Demand

If the interest rate is targeted and the *IS* schedule is at IS_1, income will be at $Y_{r,1}$, below the target level. If the money supply is the intermediate target, with the nonvertical *LM* schedule, income will also fall below the target level, but by less, only to Y_1.

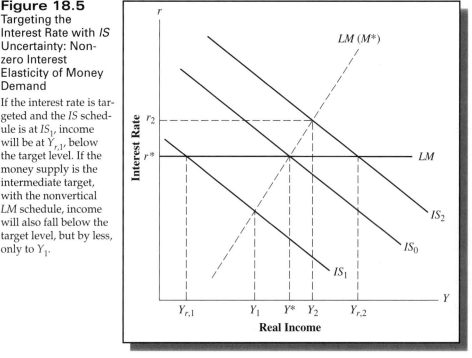

Figure 18.5 depicts the case in which we allow only for uncertainty about the *IS* schedule but will no longer assume that money demand is completely interest-inelastic. (This is the case depicted previously in Figure 18.3*a*.) The assumption about the interest elasticity of money demand has no effect on the *LM* schedule when the interest rate is the (intermediate) target. That *LM* schedule (the solid *LM* line in the figure) is horizontal because the Federal Reserve supplies whatever money is required to keep the interest rate at r^*. The *LM* schedule with a money supply target, shown as a dashed line in Figure 18.5, $LM(M^*)$, will be upward-sloping, not vertical.

Again, the predicted position of the *IS* schedule is IS_0, but the schedule may turn out actually to be at IS_1 or IS_2, respectively, if private-sector demand is weaker or stronger than predicted. As in Figure 18.4, the money supply target is superior to the interest rate in keeping income close to Y^* when the *IS* schedule is not at the predicted level. If the *IS* schedule turns out to be at IS_1 or IS_2, income will be at Y_1 or Y_2, respectively, with a money supply target. With an interest-rate target, income would be at $Y_{r,1}$ or $Y_{r,2}$, respectively, for the same positions of the *IS* schedule; both levels are farther from Y^*.

We see then that, regardless of whether the *LM* curve is vertical or upward-sloping, *a money supply target is superior to an interest-rate target when the uncertainty facing the policymaker concerns the IS schedule*. The reason is that, when the *IS* schedule shifts away from its predicted position, the movement in the interest rate *dampens* the effect of the shift on income. When the interest rate is targeted, this *monetary dampener* is shut off.

Consider the effects of an autonomous rise in investment demand (e.g., a shift from IS_0 to IS_2 in Figure 18.5). If the money supply is the target, as the rise in investment causes income to rise, money demand rises and, with a fixed money supply, the interest rate must rise (to r_2 in Figure 18.5). The rise in the interest rate will work against the autonomous rise in demand and cause investment to rise by less than it otherwise would. If the Federal Reserve is targeting the interest rate, this will not happen. As income increases, to keep the interest rate at r^*, the Federal Reserve must carry out open-market purchases to expand the money supply by enough to satisfy the increased demand for money. The dampening effect on the expansion is lost, and income moves farther from the target level, Y^*.

Uncertainty About Money Demand

Figure 18.6 depicts the case in which money demand is not perfectly stable (the case shown previously in Figure 18.3b). With the interest rate as a target, the LM schedule is horizontal and does *not* shift when there is a shift in the money demand function. For example, if a positive shock (a desirable new type of bank deposit) increases the demand for money at a given level of income and the interest rate, the Federal Reserve increases the money supply. Shocks to money demand, therefore, do *not* affect income with an interest-rate target. Real income remains at the target level Y^*.

With a money supply target, however, a positive shock to money demand *does* shift the position of the LM schedule away from the predicted level, even if the target level of the money supply is achieved. If with the money target, M^*, the expected position of the LM schedule were the dashed line $LM_0(M^*)$, then a positive shock to

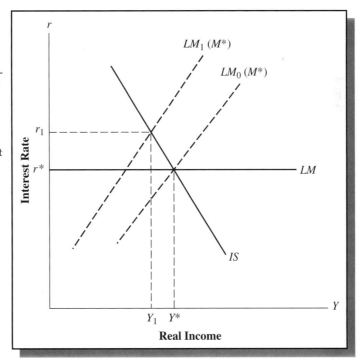

Figure 18.6
Targeting the Interest Rate with *LM* Uncertainty

If the interest rate is targeted, the *LM* schedule is horizontal and does not shift when there is a shock to money demand. The money demand shock does not displace income from the target level. If the money supply is the intermediate target, a positive shock to money demand will shift the *LM* schedule from $LM_0(M^*)$ to $LM_1(M^*)$; income will fall below the target level to Y_1.

money demand would shift the schedule to $LM_1(M *)$. The interest rate would be pushed up to r_1, and real income would fall to Y_1, below Y^*.

We see, then, that *if uncertainty centers on instability in money demand, an interest-rate target is preferable to a money supply target*. If the interest rate is the target, the real sector (output market) is *insulated* from shocks to money demand; the money supply adjusts to maintain the target level of the interest rate. In the case of a money supply target, the shock to money demand *does* affect the interest rate, and therefore real income is displaced.

18.5 MONEY SUPPLY VERSUS INTEREST-RATE TARGETS

We now summarize the relative advantages and disadvantages of a monetary aggregate versus an interest rate as an intermediate target for monetary policy.

The Sources of Uncertainty and the Choice of a Monetary Policy Strategy

The analysis in the previous section indicates that one important consideration in choosing between alternative intermediate targets is the source of the uncertainty faced by the monetary policymaker. If the predominant sources of uncertainty are unpredictable shifts in the *IS* schedule, a money supply target is superior to an interest-rate target. The implication for the actual economy is that, when uncertainty comes from sources such as unpredictable shifts in the business sector's investment spending, residential construction investment, and consumer durable purchases—all private-sector demands for output—the money supply target is preferable.

The interest-rate target was seen to be superior when uncertainty stems from shifts in the *LM* schedule due to unstable money demand. In the *IS–LM* model, assets are split into two groups: one termed *money* and one composite, nonmoney asset termed *bonds*. Any factors that change the relative desirability of the two assets shift the model's *LM* schedule. The implication for the actual economy is that when the predominant source of uncertainty centers on shifts in asset demands (for bonds and money), the interest rate is the superior intermediate target.

When we discuss Federal Reserve policy, we will see that consideration of the type of uncertainty that is greatest has been an important element in the choice of a monetary policy strategy. There are, however, other relative advantages and disadvantages of money supply targets compared with interest-rate targets.

Other Considerations

One additional advantage for a money supply target is that a strong commitment to keeping the money supply growing in a target range ensures control over inflation for medium-term periods (e.g., three to five years). Virtually all economists believe that sustained high inflation requires accommodating money supply growth. Strict adherence to money supply targets severely limits monetary accommodation.

Advocates of targeting monetary aggregates argue that by setting low, noninflationary money supply targets, *and hitting them*, the Federal Reserve can build up anti-inflationary *credibility*; the public starts to believe that the Federal Reserve will carry out announced policies. This strategy has the advantage of keeping inflationary expectations at a low level.

An interest-rate target provides no such anti-inflationary guarantee. If the central bank targets the interest rate, it must increase the money supply to accommodate any increases in money demand. If a potentially inflationary boom begins, money demand will increase (higher transactions demand). The Federal Reserve may then unwittingly be led to fuel inflation by an accommodating increase in the money supply. This outcome is not inevitable; the Federal Reserve may instead observe the potential for inflation and raise the target level of the interest rate. The point here is that simply hitting a particular interest-rate target does not provide the inflation protection that targeting monetary aggregates does.

However, some considerations favor an interest-rate target. For one thing, interest rates are not subject to the measurement problems that have arisen concerning monetary aggregates (e.g., new deposit types). Interest-rate stability, at least in the short run, is another advantage cited for an interest-rate target. To hit a money supply target, the Federal Reserve must let the interest rate fluctuate freely (see Figure 18.3*a*). Some economists and central bankers worry that a freely fluctuating interest rate will cause instability in financial markets. Recall, for example, that sharp rises in interest rates cause significant capital losses on bonds. These losses may, in turn, lead to instability for financial institutions that hold large quantities of bonds.

18.6 THE EVOLUTION OF FEDERAL RESERVE STRATEGY

In the years since 1970, the Federal Reserve's emphasis has varied between controlling the interest rate and targeting monetary aggregates. Twice during this time period, the Federal Reserve dramatically shifted from one strategy to another. Federal Reserve strategy, as well as the reasons for these shifts, can be best explained by looking at three subperiods.

1970–79: Targeting the Federal Funds Rate

During the 1970s, the Federal Reserve targeted a short-term interest rate. The particular rate it chose was the **federal funds rate**, which is the interest rate charged on loans from one bank to another. When one bank lends to another, deposits at a regional Federal Reserve bank are transferred from the lending bank to the borrowing bank. These deposits are bank reserves, so loans in the federal funds market are transfers of reserves.

federal funds rate
is the rate at which banks make loans to one another

On a month-to-month basis during the 1970s, the Federal Reserve targeted the weekly average for the federal funds rate within a narrow range of one-half to three-fourths of a percentage point. This was done through open-market operations, as described in section 18.2 (where we assumed the Treasury bill rate was the target rate). For example, if the rate went above the upper end of the target range, the Open

Market Desk at the Federal Reserve Bank of New York would purchase Treasury securities in the open market, thereby increasing bank reserves. With more reserves in the system, there would be fewer banks trying to borrow reserves from other banks—fewer borrowers in the federal funds market. There would also be more lenders. This situation would cause the federal funds rate to fall. The Open Market Desk would create enough additional reserves to drive the federal funds rate down to within the target range. Conversely, if the federal funds rate fell below the lower boundary of the target range, the Open Market Desk would sell securities and reduce bank reserves.

Federal Reserve strategy in the 1970s was not to peg the interest rate near any one value for a long period of time. The target range of the federal funds rate was moved around from month to month. The target range would be increased to tighten monetary policy and lowered to move to a more expansionary policy.

Monetary aggregates were not neglected in the 1970s. Although on a month-to-month basis the interest-rate target was given precedence, the Federal Reserve attempted to hit annual targets for the growth in several money supply measures. Still, at several points in the 1970s, the Federal Reserve allowed money supply targets to be missed in order to achieve the interest-rate target.

1979–82: Targeting Monetary Aggregates

The first dramatic switch in Federal Reserve policy came on October 6, 1979, when the Federal Reserve abandoned targeting the federal funds rate. It instead adopted a strategy of directly controlling bank reserves to increase its ability to hit target ranges for growth in the monetary aggregates (M1 and M2). Our analysis in this chapter is helpful for understanding the reasons for this shift.

In 1979, the inflation rate was accelerating rapidly. The recession that many had expected during the year had not materialized. There was a great deal of uncertainty about the strength of private-sector demand. In this situation of uncertainty about the *IS* schedule, a monetary aggregate is superior to an interest rate as an intermediate target.

We have also seen that a commitment to achieving low money growth targets virtually guarantees that high inflation rates will not be sustained, whereas a nominal interest-rate target provides no such guarantee. With the inflation rate over 13 percent in 1979, this was a considerable advantage.

1982–2004: Current Federal Reserve Strategy

Although the Federal Reserve was not entirely successful in hitting money supply targets during the 1979–82 period, most observers credit the shift toward a more restrictive monetary policy in 1979 for the decline in inflation to around 4 percent by 1982, albeit with the cost of a serious recession in 1981–82.

The Federal Reserve, however, abandoned the strategy of intermediate targeting on monetary aggregates in the summer of 1982, the second of the policy shifts. Although it later returned to specifying target growth rates for the M2 aggregate, and in some years the M1 aggregate as well, these targets did not assume as much importance in the post-1982 period as during 1979–82.

The reason for the deemphasis of monetary aggregates, was the breakdown of the money–income relationship that occurred in the 1980s. There was substantial instability in money demand during this period. Swings in money demand did not reflect underlying economic conditions but were more heavily influenced by innovations in the deposit market as deregulation took place and banks offered many new types of deposits.

Instability of money demand, and consequent uncertainty about the *LM* schedule, is the condition that favors the interest rate as an intermediate target. The Federal Reserve was reluctant to go all the way back to the strategy of targeting the federal funds rate, partly because of fears that, as in the 1970s, this strategy would provide insufficient protection from accelerated inflation. Therefore, throughout the 1980s, the Federal Reserve continued to closely monitor the behavior of the broader aggregates, especially M2, to be sure that growth in the money supply was not fast enough to generate inflationary pressure. During the recovery from the 1990–91 recession, however, M2 began also to "misbehave." Despite a climate of low interest rates and economic expansion, the demand for the M2 aggregate grew very slowly. Put differently, M2 velocity grew rapidly. The Federal Reserve responded with a further deemphasis of monetary aggregates. By 1995, monetary policy had returned to a strategy of almost complete concentration on the federal funds rate. This reversion to the monetary policy strategy of the 1970s was made explicit in 1997, when the FOMC policy directive was reworded to set a specific target for the federal funds rate.

Read Perspectives 18.2.

PERSPECTIVES 18.2
The Taylor Rule

With a strategy of federal funds rate targeting, monetary policy can be represented by an interest rate *reaction function* that shows the response of the interest rate to the state of the economy. John Taylor, at the time a member of the U.S. Council of Economic Advisors (now Under Secretary of the Treasury for International Affairs), proposed a rule for setting the federal funds rate, which has received a great deal of attention.

The rule Taylor proposed was the following:

$$RF = pdot + 0.5(pdot\text{-}pdot^*) + 0.5(Y\text{-}Y^*) + RF^*$$

$$(18.1)$$

where: RF = the federal funds rate
  $pdot$ = the inflation rate
  Y = real output

and the superscript (*) is the target level for each of these variables.

The rule suggested by Taylor would have the Federal Reserve increase the interest rate automatically by one percentage point for each percentage point increase in the inflation rate (the first term in the rule). The federal funds rate would also rise by an additional 0.5 percentage point for each one percentage point increase in the inflation rate relative to its target level ($pdot^*$) or in output relative to the target output level (Y^* = potential output). Monetary policy would become more restrictive as inflation rose and more expansionary as output fell, both relative to target levels. The last term in equation (18.1) is the equilibrium *real* federal funds rate, the rate, adjusted for inflation, which would be chosen if both output and inflation were at their target levels.[a]

Much of the attention given to the Taylor rule has come from the fact that equation (18.1) did a good job of tracking the actual behavior of monetary policy in the late 1980s and early 1990s. Did the Federal Reserve perhaps follow something like a Taylor rule during those years? In addition Taylor argued that had policy followed a Taylor rule, mistakes would have been avoided in earlier years. Policy he argues would have been more restrictive during the inflationary 1970s. As a consequence policy could have been less restrictive in the early 1980s, thus reducing unemployment during that period.

Discussion of the Taylor rule is one example of the growing interest in monetary policy by rules rather than by the discretion of central bankers. The Taylor rule is not an "optimal rule" but more in the spirit of Milton Friedman's belief that in choosing a course for monetary policy, "The best should not be the enemy of the good."

[a]See John Taylor, "Discretion versus Monetary Policy Rules in Practice," *Carnegie-Rochester Conference Series on Public Policy*, 39(1993), pp. 195–214.

18.7 CHANGES IN CENTRAL BANK INSTITUTIONS: RECENT INTERNATIONAL EXPERIENCE

In the United States, monetary policy strategy has changed as the economic environment has varied. The institutional structure of the Federal Reserve has, however, not changed in any significant manner. Other industrialized countries, beginning in the late 1980s, have made major changes in central bank structure. In response to what governments have believed to be subpar macroeconomic performance, many countries have changed the mandates and accountability of their central banks.

The most common change has been to instruct central banks to target inflation as the sole goal of monetary policy. Countries that have adopted inflation targeting as a mandate to their central banks include Canada, New Zealand, the United Kingdom, and Sweden. In addition, the new European Central Bank has adopted inflation targeting.

In the United States, as in all of those countries, low inflation has always been one monetary policy goal. In the 1990s, these countries decided to make low inflation *the* goal of monetary policy. Why?

time inconsistency
problems arise when a future policy plan is no longer optimal at a later date even when no new information has arrived in the meantime

Here we examine two strands in the argument for the move to inflation targeting in many industrialized countries. The first, which grows out of the new classical macroeconomic perspective, is the recognition of **time inconsistency** problems that arise when monetary policy is conducted under discretion. The second involves more pragmatic considerations. Both bring us back to the arguments for rules versus discretion in macroeconomic policy formation.

The Time Inconsistency Problem

Our analysis so far suggests that monetary policy strategy should change over time as the sources of uncertainty facing policymakers vary. This view argues for flexibility, or policy by discretion. Recognition of time inconsistency problems in policy formation, however, lends support to the argument for policy by rules.

A time (or dynamic) inconsistency problem for policy arises when, as Stanley Fischer explains, a "future policy that forms part of an optimal plan formulated at an initial date is no longer optimal from the viewpoint of a later date, even though no new information has appeared in the meantime."[5] In other words, a policy announcement will be time-inconsistent if economic agents know that the policymaker will want to renege on the decision when it comes time to act.

As applied to monetary policy under discretion, the time inconsistency problem arises in the following way.[6] Suppose that, because of some distortion in the economy, social welfare would be increased if output were pushed above the *natural rate*, the level discussed in Chapter 11 that is consistent with price and wage setters accurately predicting the price level. A possible reason might be that noncompetitive features of labor and product markets lead to a natural rate that is too low (e.g., the outcome in the insider–outsider model in section 13.2). Moreover, suppose that, consistent with the rational expectations hypothesis examined in Chapter 12, the monetary policymaker can push output above the natural rate by generating an unexpectedly high rate of monetary growth. Finally, assume that, as is reasonable, wages and prices are set at less frequent intervals (e.g., annually) than monetary policy actions are implemented (e.g., monthly).

At one point, say the beginning of the year, the policymaker might announce a noninflationary rate of monetary growth of zero. But later in the year, after wages and prices have been set, the policymaker may find it optimal to renege on this commitment and generate "surprise" inflation. Firms and workers, knowing the policymaker's preferences (remember here we assume rational expectations), will anticipate that the policymaker will *cheat*. There will be no output gain. There will be higher inflation than at zero money growth. The time inconsistency problem causes an inflationary bias in monetary policy.

If, instead, a monetary policy rule bound the policymaker to a zero inflation policy, society would be better off than with policy by discretion. The rule would give credibility to the policymaker's announcement.

It is worth noting that time inconsistency problems exist in contexts other than monetary policy. For example, consider the patent system. Before inventions are made, it is optimal to offer patents as an incentive. After the new devices exist, however, it is optimal to invalidate the patents to avoid monopolistic inefficiency.

Other Arguments for Inflation Targeting

Are time inconsistency problems important for monetary policy? Alan Blinder, a Princeton professor and former vice chairman of the Board of Governors of the Federal Reserve, argues that academic economists who have worried about time

---

[5]Stanley Fischer, "Rules Versus Discretion in Monetary Policy," in Benjamin M. Friedman and Frank H. Hahn, eds., *Handbook in Monetary Economics*, vol. 2 (Amsterdam: North Holland, 1990), pp. 1169–70.

[6]Two important papers on the time inconsistency problem are Finn Kydland and Edward Prescott, "Rules Versus Discretion: The Time Inconsistency Problem," *Journal of Political Economy* (June 1977), pp. 473–91; and Robert J. Barro and David B. Gordon, "Rules, Discretion and Reputation in a Model of Monetary Policy," *Journal of Monetary Economics*, 12 (July 1983), pp. 101–21.

inconsistency problems "have been loudly barking up the wrong tree."[7] Or perhaps, as is the problem with dogs, they are barking up what used to be the right tree.

Time inconsistency problems might partly explain inflationary monetary policies during the 1970s. By the late 1980s and into the early 1990s, however, disinflation had been achieved in most industrialized countries. An analogy to the patent system might be useful here. The industrialized countries do not renege on patents even though in the short run doing so may seem optimal. They do not because of reputational considerations, the way their present actions affect the behavior of future generations of inventors. Central banks might have learned a lesson from the 1970s and, though tempted to achieve output gains through surprise inflation, now tell themselves "just don't do it."

If not to solve the time inconsistency problem, what is the motivation behind the move to inflation-targeting rules in many countries? There seem to be more pragmatic considerations. One is to reduce the effect of political pressures on central banks. In general, the move to inflation targeting coincides with a grant of greater independence to central banks. Giving the central bank independent control of its policy instruments and a clear mandate to target inflation greatly limits a government's ability to manipulate monetary policy for political purposes. Even before explicit inflation-targeting rules were common, central bank independence was positively associated with lower inflation (see Perspectives 18.1). Inflation targeting is a way of giving central banks independence for their *instruments* while keeping them accountable for *goals*.

Another pragmatic motivation for the move to inflation targeting in several countries was that they experienced problems similar to those the United States experienced with monetary aggregates as intermediate targets. As the money–income relationship became more unstable, they relied more on short-term interest rates to implement monetary policy. As explained previously, this approach leaves monetary policy without any anchor that serves as an anti-inflation guarantee. Direct targeting on inflation provides such an anchor.

Read Perspectives 18.3.

18.8 CONCLUSION

In this chapter, we have considered alternative strategies that central banks can pursue and, in particular, those that the U.S. Federal Reserve has chosen. The Federal Reserve's choice of a strategy, and the goals toward which the strategy is aimed, have been its own (within limits set by legislation that does not set clear priorities on alternative goals). We have also seen that several other countries, by moving to rules for inflation targeting, have set the goals for central banks. Should the United States follow this route?

Bills have been introduced in Congress to mandate inflation targeting as the Federal Reserve's strategy. So far they have failed to pass. Arguments for such bills

---

[7]Alan S. Blinder, "What Central Bankers Could Learn from Academics and Vice Versa," *Journal of Economic Perspectives,* 11 (Spring 1997), p. 13.

After two decades with inflation rates that exceeded the OECD (Organization for Economic Cooperation and Development) average and growth rates that fell short of that average, the New Zealand government adopted a very strict form of inflation targeting in 1990. The main provisions for monetary policy are contained in the Reserve Bank Act of 1989.[a] The act specifies that the prime function of the Reserve Bank of New Zealand is to "maintain stability in the general level of prices." The act mandates that the Minister of Finance and the Governor of the Reserve Bank agree on monetary policy targets to achieve price stability. For much of the 1990s, price stability was defined as an inflation rate within a range of 0–2 percent. In 1997, this definition was loosened a bit to a range of 0–3 percent.

The Reserve Bank is then free to choose the strategy that it believes will best achieve the policy target. If inflation is not kept within the target range, the Reserve Bank governor is subject to dismissal. Thus the arrangement has been termed a "performance contract" for a central bank.

This type of inflation targeting leaves the Reserve Bank with little leeway to directly pursue goals other than price stability; that constraint was the point of the act. The fact that the inflation target is a range does provide some scope to consider economic growth or unemployment in formulating monetary policy. Also, the policy agreement between the Minister of Finance and the Reserve Bank allows for adjustment of the target inflation range if there are special circumstances such as changes in indirect taxes (sales and excise taxes) or the international terms of trade that cause one-time changes in the price level. Still, the New Zealand plan is a very strict form of inflation targeting.

After an initial adjustment period, the performance of the New Zealand economy under inflation targeting has been reasonably good. Real GDP growth averaged approximately 3 percent and inflation 2 percent over 1992–2003. Both figures are better than OECD averages.

[a]The New Zealand experiment with inflation targeting is described in Andreas Fischer, "New Zealand's Experience with Inflation Targets," in Leonardo Leiderman and Lars E. O. Swensson, eds., *Inflation Targets* (Paris: Center for Economic Policy Research, 1995).

follow along the lines that have led to the adoption of inflation targeting in other countries. Arguments against such bills point to the need for monetary policy to also focus on the goals of high employment and steady economic growth. The recent low inflation and low unemployment in the United States have lent support to the old argument "If it ain't broke, don't fix it." Proponents of inflation targeting counter with another old adage "better to fix the roof while the sun is still shining."

KEY TERMS

- federal funds rate 395
- time inconsistency 398

REVIEW QUESTIONS AND PROBLEMS

1. What is the Federal Open Market Committee (FOMC)? What role does this committee play in formulating monetary policy?

2. Evaluate the arguments for and against intermediate targeting a monetary aggregate.

3. Why is it natural for a monetarist economist to favor the policy strategy of targeting a monetary aggregate?

4. Using the *IS–LM* curve framework, analyze whether an increase in the instability of the money demand function would increase or decrease the desirability of intermediate targeting a monetary aggregate.

5. Describe the shift that took place in Federal Reserve policy in 1979. Explain the reasons for this shift.

6. Why does the Federal Reserve often use intermediate target variables? Why not just focus on the ultimate policy objectives, such as inflation and unemployment?

7. Suppose that the Federal Reserve is using an interest rate as an intermediate target, while real income is the ultimate policy target, and there is an autonomous drop in business investment that the Federal Reserve had not predicted. Use the *IS–LM* model to show the effects of the shock. Would income have been affected less or more if the Federal Reserve had been using a money supply target?

8. Explain the time inconsistency problem as it pertains to monetary policy.

9. What relationship do you see between the problems many countries have experienced with money supply targeting and the move to inflation targeting?

Chapter 19

Fiscal Stabilization Policy

*F*or outside observers, it has been hard to keep track of U.S. fiscal policy debates over recent decades. Debates in the 1980s and 1990s focused on the budget deficit. Large deficits were clearly perceived as a problem, but were they "the Devil at the door" or, as others suggested, more like "termites in the basement"? Before the question had been decided, budget agreements between the Clinton administration and Republican-controlled Congresses, abetted by rapid economic growth, had by the late 1990s replaced the budget deficits with surpluses, and even larger surpluses were projected for the medium-term future. By 2001, however, the budget had again fallen into deficit. By 2004, the deficit had risen to levels not seen since the 1980s. Over a ten-year horizon, projections had shifted from a cumulative surplus of over $3 trillion to a deficit of over $2 trillion, a swing of over $5 trillion. Further complicating the budget picture are long-term projections of huge federal budget deficits due to the demands on Medicare and Social Security that will come as the "baby boomer" generation reaches retirement age.

In Parts II and III, we looked at fiscal policy along with monetary policy as tools to stabilize the economy. How does this stabilization role fit in with the other considerations that have been driving the federal budget? What role, for example, have stabilization considerations played in causing the dramatic swings in budget deficits we have just described? One long-standing question we address is whether fiscal policy is best conducted by rules, such as ones that would mandate balancing the federal budget (in some sense), or whether policy is best left to the discretion of policymakers.

We begin by examining the goals of fiscal policy and the possibility that the goals of the policymakers, who in the case of fiscal policy are the Congress and administration, may diverge from the goals of the public. Some economists use this divergence to argue in favor of constraining the behavior of fiscal policymakers. Next we consider the behavior of the federal budget over the post–World War II period and the relationship between the federal budget and the state of the economy. With this background, we examine the long-standing objections of Keynesian economists to balanced-budget rules, as well as the perhaps confusing positions of different schools of economists over proper budget policies for the first part of the twenty-first century.

19.1 THE GOALS OF MACROECONOMIC POLICY

What are the goals of macroeconomic policy? Low unemployment and price stability are agreed-upon policy goals, although, as we saw in Parts II and III, there is considerable disagreement about the ability of policymakers to achieve those goals by managing aggregate demand. There are also differences of opinion about the relative weights that should be assigned to each goal. Economic growth is a third policy goal and one that is closely related to the low unemployment goal, because creating new jobs requires a growing economy.

Suppose we agree that the goals of macroeconomic policy should be to achieve target levels of inflation, unemployment, and economic growth. The question of optimal conduct of macroeconomic policy would then be how to set the policy *instruments*, variables such as the levels of government spending and various tax rates in the case of fiscal policy, in order to come as close as possible to the target levels. One way of formulating this problem is to assume that the policymaker minimizes a social-loss function of the following form:

$$L = a_1(U - U^*)^2 + a_2(\dot{P} - \dot{P}^*)^2 + a_3(\dot{Y} - \dot{Y}^*)^2 \quad a_1, a_2, a_3 > 0 \tag{19.1}$$

In this equation, L is the social-loss that results when macroeconomic goal variables deviate from target levels—for example, the costs of excessively high unemployment. The goal variables themselves are the level of unemployment (U), the inflation rate ($\dot{P}$), and the rate of growth in real income ($\dot{Y}$). The target levels for these variables are U^*, $\dot{P}^*$, and $\dot{Y}^*$, respectively. In the form given by equation (19.1), the loss in social welfare depends on the squared deviations of the goal variables from the target levels. The social-loss from a given increase in the deviation of a goal variable from the target level increases as we get further from the target level; large deviations from desired levels receive especially heavy weights. The coefficients a_1, a_2, and a_3 in equation (19.1) represent the relative weights attached to the different targets.

Equation (19.1) is only one representation of the social-welfare-loss function that is relevant to macroeconomic policies. The key assumption for formulating this type of optimal policy is simply that the policymaker minimizes some social-welfare-loss function. The problem is, then, to find the setting of the instruments that results in the minimum loss. We can further investigate whether various rules, such as a balanced-budget rule, outperform more activist policy prescriptions.

19.2 THE GOALS OF MACROECONOMIC POLICYMAKERS

There is literature questioning the realism of the preceding formulation of the optimal policy question. We examine two strands in this literature: the **public-choice** view and the **partisan theory**. A common element in both of these criticisms is that politics plays a much more important role in macroeconomic policymaking than was suggested in the previous section.

The Public-Choice View

Proponents of the public-choice view argue that macroeconomic policymakers act to maximize their own welfare or utility rather than to maximize the social good.[1] As Gordon Tullock, a proponent of the public-choice view, puts it: "Bureaucrats are like other men. . . . If bureaucrats are ordinary men, they will make most (not all) their decisions in terms of what benefits them, not society as a whole."[2] Rather than a social-welfare-loss function as given by (19.1), the relevant loss function is one that measures variables of direct importance to policymakers. In the case of elected officials making fiscal policy decisions, this alternative approach emphasizes votes as the central goal motivating policymakers.

Within the public-choice framework, one representation of the appropriate loss function that the policymaker seeks to minimize is

$$L = b_1 \text{VL} \qquad b_1 > 0 \qquad \text{(19.2)}$$

where VL is vote loss and b_1 is the weight given to votes lost. Macroeconomic goal variables enter the picture because the behavior of the economy affects votes.

For example, vote loss might be represented as

$$\text{VL} = c_0 + c_1(U - U^*)^2 + c_2(\dot{P} - \dot{P}^*)^2 + c_3(\dot{Y} - \dot{Y}^*)^2 \qquad \text{(19.3)}$$

The macroeconomic goal variables and their target levels are the same as in equation (19.1). The parameters c_1, c_2, and c_3 represent the loss of votes resulting from deviations of the macroeconomic goal variables from target levels. This particular representation assumes that vote loss depends on the squared deviation from the target level, assuming as before that an especially heavy weight is given to large deviations from desired target levels. The c_0 parameter represents other influences on voter behavior (e.g., foreign policy questions or other domestic issues).

Suppose that vote loss is given by equation (19.3) and the policymaker acts to minimize vote loss; the relevant loss function is equation (19.2). Will policy actions differ from those that would result from the policymaker's acting more altruistically and minimizing the social-loss function given by equation (19.1)? Advocates of the

public choice
is the application to macroeconomic policy-making of the micro-economic theory of how decisions are made

partisan theory
views macroeconomic policy outcomes as the result of ideologically motivated decisions by leaders of different political parties. The parties represent constituencies with different preferences concerning macro-economic variables

---

[1] More generally, the term *public choice* can be defined as the application of choice theoretic economic analysis to political decision making. See, for example, Dennis Mueller, *Public Choice II* (Cambridge: Cambridge University Press, 1989).
[2] Gordon Tullock, *The Vote Motive* (London: Institute of Economic Affairs, 1976).

public-choice view of policymaker behavior argue that they would. To see why, we first examine the condition necessary for behavior in the two cases to be the same and then explain why the advocates of the public-choice view do not believe that this condition will be met in practice.

First, assume that voter behavior is governed by what we may call "collective rationality," meaning that vote loss because of *macroeconomic concerns* is proportional to social-welfare loss. This assumption means that when macroeconomic variables affect voting behavior, voters reward or punish incumbent politicians depending on their performance in minimizing social-welfare loss. In this case, the optimal strategy to minimize vote loss [equation (19.2)] is to minimize social-welfare loss [equation (19.1)]. As has been recognized in the public-choice literature, when this type of collective rationality does not exist, the behavior of the vote-maximizing policymaker will deviate from social-welfare–maximizing behavior.

The following hypotheses about voter behavior have been advanced in the public-choice literature.[3]

1. *Voters are myopic.* Advocates of the public-choice view argue that voting behavior is heavily influenced by the state of the economy over the few quarters before the election and that the level of economic activity, not the inflation rate, is the variable whose recent performance determines votes. "Incumbent politicians desire re-election and they believe that a booming preelection economy will help to achieve it."[4] As a consequence, we have a *political business cycle*, in which aggregate demand is overly stimulative in the preelection period, with inflation following after the election.

2. *Unemployment is more likely to result in vote loss than is inflation.* The inflation process is presumed to be sufficiently complex and ill-understood so that politicians can avoid blame for inflation more easily than they can avoid blame for unemployment: "At any moment of time the inflation is blamed on events which are not under the control of the political party in power, but ideally on the political party previously in power."[5] As a consequence, advocates of the public-choice view argue that elected officials rarely respond to inflation with restrictive policies, but respond to unemployment with expansionary policies. Thus, the fiscal policy process has an inflationary bias.[6]

3. *A deficit bias exists in the budget process.* This inflationary bias is reinforced by the inherent bias toward budget deficits that public-choice writers believe to be characteristic of democratic government fiscal policies. For example, as James Buchanan and Richard Wagner argue:

> Elected politicians enjoy spending public monies on projects that yield some
> demonstrable benefits to their constituents. They do not enjoy imposing
> taxes on these same constituents. The pre-Keynesian norm of budget balance

---

[3]See, for example, James M. Buchanan and Richard E. Wagner, *Democracy in Deficit* (New York: Academic Press, 1977); and Edward R. Tufte, *Political Control of the Economy* (Princeton, N.J.: Princeton University Press, 1978).

[4]Tufte, *Political Control of the Economy*, p. 5.

[5]Morris Perlman, "Party Politics and Bureaucracy in Economic Policy," in Tullock, *The Vote Motive*, p. 69.

[6]In terms of (19.1) and (19.3), these public-choice writers argue that, although inflation does cause significant social-welfare loss [a_2 in (19.1) may be large], inflation does not result in much of a vote loss [c_2 is small in (19.3)]. Therefore, the vote-maximizing policymaker does not respond.

served to constrain spending proclivities so as to keep governmental outlays roughly within the revenue limits generated by taxes. The Keynesian destruction of this norm, without an adequate replacement, effectively removed the constraint. Predictably politicians responded by increasing spending more than tax revenues, by creating budget deficits as a normal course of events.[7]

If we accept the public-choice characterization, how can this deficit bias in the fiscal policy process be corrected? Buchanan and Wagner believe that we must restore the "pre-Keynesian norm of budget balance"; we must avoid *all* deficit spending. They favor an amendment to the U.S. Constitution that would require Congress and the president to balance the budget.

Also, because new or expanded government spending programs would have to be financed by new taxes in a balanced-budget system, the growth of the government sector would be curtailed by such an amendment. In the public-choice view, optimal fiscal policy does not mean designing policies to stabilize the macroeconomy. Rather, it involves imposing rules on the policymakers that eliminate the destabilizing effects of deficit spending.

The Partisan Theory

In the partisan theory, political factors also affect macroeconomic policy. The partisan theory, however, views politicians as *ideologically* motivated leaders of competing parties.[8] The parties, in turn, represent different constituencies with different preferences concerning macroeconomic outcomes. In the most common partisan party model, there is a liberal (or labor) party and a conservative party. The liberal party primarily emphasizes full employment and income redistribution, whereas the conservative party values price stability most highly.

Rather than a political business cycle, the partisan theory predicts *party cycles* as macroeconomic policy varies, depending on which party is in power. In the case of fiscal policy, for example, the partisan model predicts that if the liberal party gains office, government spending will rise as politicians try to stimulate demand and, hence, employment. Government outlays may also rise as transfer payments are increased to redistribute income. In most circumstances, the more expansionary fiscal policy will also increase the rate of inflation. If the liberal party loses office at a later point, fiscal policy will become more restrictive as the conservatives seek to combat inflation. Unemployment will rise, and a recession may result.

As with political business cycles, partisan party cycles would be prevented or at least mitigated by a fiscal policy rule such as a constitutional balanced-budget

---

[7]Buchanan and Wagner, *Democracy in Deficit*, pp. 93–94.

[8]An early contribution to the partisan theory is Douglas Hibbs, "Political Parties and Macroeconomic Policy," *The American Political Science Review*, 71 (December 1977), pp. 1467–87. See also Thomas Havrilesky, "A Partisan Theory of Fiscal and Monetary Regimes," *Journal of Money, Credit and Banking*, 19 (August 1987), pp. 308–25; and Alberto Alesina, "Macroeconomics and Politics," *NBER Macroeconomics Annual* (1988), pp. 13–61.

amendment. A rule for fiscal policy would limit the ability of each party to pursue its goals by manipulating aggregate demand. Also, redistribution efforts by the liberal party would be hampered if any increased transfer payments required new taxes.

Read Perspectives 19.1.

PERSPECTIVES 19.1
Rational Expectations and the Partisan Theory

The original forms of the political business cycle model and the partisan model did not assume that expectations were *rational* and therefore forward-looking. In fact, the myopic behavior of voters in the political business cycle model is clearly inconsistent with rational expectations.

The partisan model of fiscal policy has been modified to assume rational expectations in a paper by Alberto Alesina and Jeffrey Sachs.[a] As before, assume that there are two parties—one liberal, whose constituency is most concerned about unemployment, and one conservative, with a constituency most concerned about inflation.

The economic environment assumed by Alesina and Sachs is consistent with the new classical model in that expectations are rational, but it has the Keynesian element that money wages are set by contracts of several years' duration. In such a framework, elections create uncertainty concerning the future behavior of the inflation rate and therefore the money wage demands workers (or their unions) should make.

Consider the situation in the year before a general election. Workers might presume that if the liberals win, the inflation rate will be high, let's say 7 percent, whereas if the conservatives win, it will be low, say 3 percent. Even if expectations are rational, the best the workers can do is form an expectation of inflation that is a weighted average of the two possible outcomes. If they view the election of each party as equally likely, then in the previous example, the rational expectation of inflation would be 5 percent. Firms and workers would set money wages accordingly.

Now consider what will happen after the election. If the liberals win, the inflation rate (7 percent) will exceed the expected inflation rate (5 percent) on the basis of which money wages were set. This higher rate will cause rapid expansion of output as firms hire additional workers because the real wage will be unexpectedly low for firms. On the other hand, if conservatives win, actual inflation (3 percent) will be below expected inflation (5 percent), and money wages will have been set too high. Unemployment will rise, and a recession may ensue.

Party cycles are then possible in the partisan model even if expectations are rational. The theory predicts that recessions are most likely in the first couple of years following the election of a conservative president—a prediction borne out in 1981–82 and again in 1990–91. The accelerated pace of the recovery from the 1990–91 recession after President George H. W. Bush was defeated by Bill Clinton in 1992 is also consistent with the rational expectations version of the partisan theory.

Later evidence does not entirely support the Alesina and Sachs hypothesis, but there are relatively few observations that provide a test. Administrations have changed party only every 4, 8, or sometimes 12 years during the sample period considered. The replacement of the Clinton administration by the Republican administration of George W. Bush provided a fresh observation to test the hypothesis. A recession did begin in March of 2001. This may be too soon after the election to fit the party cycles hypothesis.

---

[a]Alberto Alesina and Jeffrey Sachs, "Political Parties and the Business Cycle in the United States, 1948–84," *Journal of Money, Credit and Banking*, 20 (February 1988), pp. 63–82.

Public-Choice and Partisan Theories from the Perspective of 2004

By 1999, as previously noted, the U.S. federal budget had moved into surplus. Many European countries had also successfully reduced or eliminated their budget deficits. One might have thought that the public in these countries had become more sophisticated in understanding the inflationary consequences of deficits and other long-run costs of accumulating a large national debt. Perhaps politicians came to believe that large deficits would cause them to lose votes. This view is consistent with polls in the United States before the 1996 and 2000 elections, which showed that voters ranked deficit reduction ahead of tax cuts as an issue.

In Europe, countries that had adopted the euro as a common currency had bound themselves to the Stability Pact, which limited deficits to 3 percent of GDP, except during recessions. In other countries such as New Zealand, rules were legislated for monetary and fiscal policy. Have political factors ceased to influence government budget deficits because of a combination of increased voter sophistication and budget rules?

From the perspective of 2004 things look different—the U.S. federal budget is heavily in deficit. Projected deficits are over $500 billion for 2004–2005. In Europe many countries are exceeding the 3 percent limit set by the stability pact. Part of the problem is cyclical. Slow growth or recession has lowered tax revenue. But, particularly in the United States, this is not the major cause in the budget swing. According to estimates of the Congressional Budget Office, by 2004 all of the deficit was due to policy decisions not cyclical factors. With an election coming, new spending projects such as the prescription drug benefit for Medicare are popular. Tax cuts are also popular. Vice President Richard Cheney is quoted as saying "Reagan proved that deficits don't matter" (politically that is).

Although the public-choice and partisan models we have considered are too simple to explain the swings in budget policy that have taken place, their adherents still have reason to believe that political factors may influence fiscal policy.

19.3 THE FEDERAL BUDGET

Two fiscal policy variables, the levels of government spending and tax collections, were included in the theoretical models in Parts II and III. The government spending variable (G) was the spending component in national income, which includes federal, state, and local government spending on *currently produced goods and services*. The tax variable (T) included federal, state, and local tax collections. Fiscal stabilization policy is conducted by the federal government. States and localities have limited abilities to run budget deficits. The levels for both their expenditures and revenues are determined by local needs and the state of the economy rather than being set to influence macroeconomic goals. Therefore, our discussion here focuses on federal budget policy.

Read Perspectives 19.2.

Figure 19.1 shows figures for total federal government receipts and outlays (expenditures) for 1959–2003. The figures reveal rapid growth in both outlays and

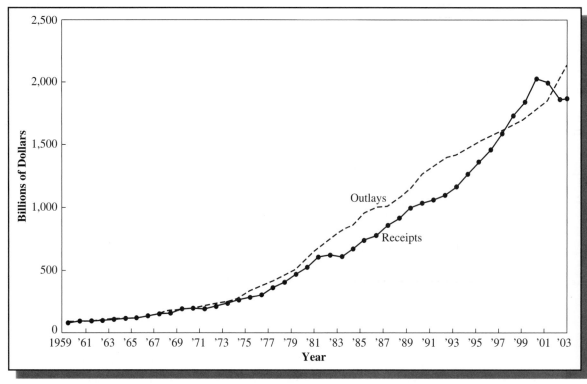

Figure 19.1 Federal Receipts and Federal Outlays, Annual 1959–2003

revenues. But the economy has been growing as well. Figure 19.2 expresses budget items as percentages of gross domestic product (GDP). There we can see more clearly how the government has grown relative to the economy as a whole.

In 1929, the federal government was a very small portion of the economy. Total federal outlays were less than 3 percent of GDP. Fiscal policy changes typically represented minor budget adjustments and were of little significance to the overall economy. Both outlays and revenues rose modestly during the 1930s. Outlays rose more than revenues, with a resulting budget deficit. World War II brought a huge expansion in government military spending that was only partly paid for by increasing tax revenues. Budget deficits in the early 1940s rose as high as 25 percent of GDP, the equivalent of a deficit of over $1,500 billion in terms of GDP today. These huge wartime deficits were financed by massive sales of bonds to the public.

After the war, both expenditures and tax revenues declined as proportions of GDP. Yet federal government outlays did not fall back to the level of the 1920s. By the mid-1950s, both outlays and revenues were about 17 to 18 percent of GDP. The federal government had taken on new domestic functions in the 1930s: regulatory agencies, the Social Security system, price supports for agricultural products, and rural electrification, among others. Also, with the onset of the Cold War in the late 1940s, defense spending remained high even in peacetime.

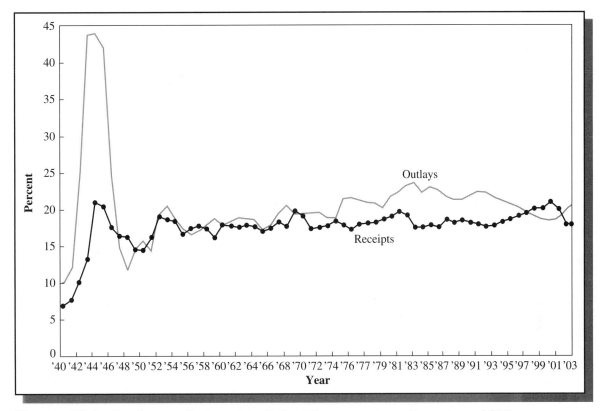

Figure 19.2 Receipts and Outlays of the Federal Government, as a Percentage of GDP, Selected Years

Figure 19.2 shows that in recent decades outlays have grown as a percentage of GDP, from 17 percent in 1955 to 22 percent in 2002. Tax revenues have grown as well, but beginning in the late 1960s, growth in spending outpaced revenue growth, resulting in persistent deficits. The budget deficit grew rapidly during the first half of the 1980s as the upward trend in outlays continued, while revenues declined slightly as a percentage of GDP. By 1986, the budget deficit was roughly 5 percent of GDP. The deficit declined in absolute terms from 1987 to 1989, and then rose sharply with the recession of 1990–91. The deficit began to decline again in 1993 when the Clinton deficit reduction plan was passed. Further spending cuts virtually eliminated the deficit by early 1998, and the budget then moved into surplus. Strong economic growth as well as legislative actions led to the budget turnaround.

After 2001, the budget returned to deficit. As was the case in the late 1990s, both legislative actions, primarily the tax cuts in the Bush administration, and the state of the economy, in this case the recession in 2001, were responsible for the turnaround in the budget. By 2005, however, estimates indicated that the burgeoning deficit would be almost completely the result of tax cuts and policy changes that increased federal outlays, the economy having almost returned to potential output.

Although our discussion of fiscal stabilization policy centers on the federal government, we should not ignore state and local government finances. State and local government spending currently accounts for 8 percent of gross domestic product, up from 6 percent in 1959. State and local governments spend to provide for: education, public welfare, health and hospitals, correction and police protection, and additional services. They raise funds through taxation of income (both corporate and individual), sales, and property. They also levy various fees and specific taxes such as those on alcohol and tobacco.

In recent years (2002–2004), state and local governments, especially states, have faced their most severe budget crisis since World War II. Figure 19.3 shows state and local government revenues and expenditures for the years since 1960. Typically, during recession periods (1974–75, 1981–82, 1990–91) revenues fell short of expenditures. The shortfall was especially sharp following the 2001 recession, and even when an economic recovery began, state finances continued to worsen. Going into fiscal 2004, states faced prospective deficits of approximately $80 billion, forcing spending cuts and increases in taxes and fees, including tuition at state universities. States have limited ability to run deficits. Most have rules that force them to balance their budget, even though some can carry over deficits for a year or resort to other short-run stopgaps.[a] These spending cuts and tax increases acted as a dampener on the recovery of aggregate demand.

What caused this crisis in state and local government finance, and what are likely trends for the future? Figure 19.3 shows that revenues declined sharply after the recession began in 2001. This was part of the problem but, as noted, this is typical in a recession. What was different this time is that as revenues increased during the prosperous 1990s, states responded by cutting both income and sales taxes. Notice that revenues had begun to fall before the recession began. Spending continued to rise. Some components, in particular Medicaid spending, are entitlements that states are largely unable to reduce. The current budget crisis was primarily the result of states financing permanent tax cuts with revenue from the temporarily booming economy and then facing difficult to reduce spending needs.

What about the future? It is hard to be optimistic. The strengthening recovery is likely to improve the states' financial position in the short run. In the longer term, the growth in Medicaid costs and, for some states, spending on underfunded pension liabilities will put renewed pressure on the spending side. On the revenue side, the move to a service economy has eroded the revenue from state and local sales taxes that fall mainly on "goods." Finally, the tendency for state legislatures to increase spending and cut taxes in prosperous times, ignoring the existence of a business cycle, seems to be an endemic feature of our political system.

---

[a]It is the current operating budget that must be balanced. States and localities do issue bonds to fund investment projects such as school or hospital construction. Also there are exceptions to budget balancing; California approved a bond issue of $15 billion to finance a budget deficit in 2004.

Figure 19.3 State and Local Government Revenues and Expenditures

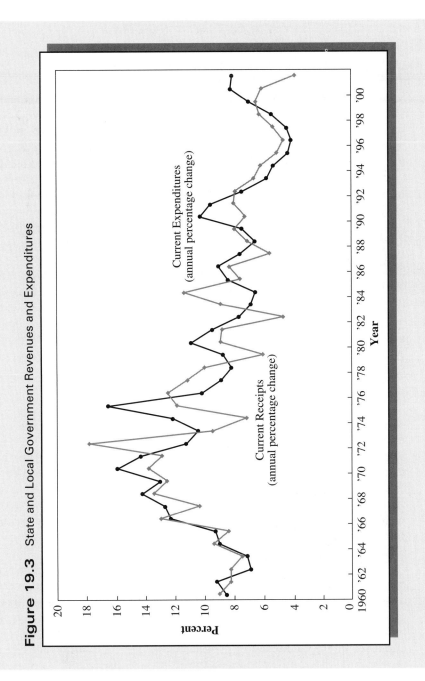

19.4 THE ECONOMY AND THE FEDERAL BUDGET: THE CONCEPT OF AUTOMATIC FISCAL STABILIZERS

automatic stabilizers are changes in taxes and government transfer payments that occur when the level of income changes

Viewed from the standpoint of stabilization policy, the federal budget contains three variables that affect macroeconomic goals: government purchases of goods and services, government transfer payments (including grants to state and local governments), and government tax receipts. In Part II, we analyzed the effects of changes in government spending, specifically spending on goods and services, and changes in tax receipts. In the models in Part II, tax receipts were net of transfers (taxes minus transfer payments); therefore, an increase in transfer payments would have the same effects in those models as a reduction in taxes. In this section, we reverse the question and, instead ask how the level of income affects items in the federal budget. In doing so, we see how changes in the government budget work as an **automatic stabilizer** for economic activity.

To consider how the level of economic activity affects the government budget, we modify our assumption that the level of net tax receipts (gross tax receipts minus government transfer payments) is exogenous. An assumption more in line with reality is that the schedule of tax *rates* is exogenously set, but the level of net tax collections depends on the level of income. With this assumption, we can specify *net* tax collections (T) as determined by the following *net tax function*:

$$T = t_0 + t_1 Y, \qquad t_0 < 0, \qquad t_1 > 0 \qquad \textbf{(19.4)}$$

where t_0 and t_1 are parameters that represent the tax structure. The parameter t_1 is the marginal net tax rate, giving the increase in taxes (net of transfers) per unit increase in income ($t_1 = \Delta T / \Delta Y$). If the tax system were proportional, the other parameter in the tax function, t_0, would be zero; tax collections would be equal to $t_1 Y$. Notice that, in this case, the marginal tax rate $\Delta T / \Delta Y$ would be equal to the average tax rate T/Y, both being given by t_1. The negative term t_0 allows the average tax rate, which from equation (19.4) would be ($t_0/Y + t_1$), to be less than the marginal rate (t_1). The negative term t_0 also allows for transfers, negative net taxes, which are independent of income.

From the net tax function given by equation (19.4), it follows that as income rises, net tax collections increase and the government budget surplus increases (or the deficit declines); at higher levels of economic activity, more tax revenue is collected at any given set of tax rates. The positive relationship between *net* tax revenues and economic activity also results from the fact that transfer payments, especially payments for unemployment compensation, decline as economic activity rises. On the expenditures side of the budget, in the absence of discretionary policy shifts, there is no reason to expect government spending (G) to respond to changes in the level of economic activity.[9] Our previous assumption that government spending was exogenous can be maintained.

---

[9]Here and later, the term *government spending* refers to federal government purchases of goods and services only, with transfer payments included in the net tax variable.

Consequently, the net effect of a rise in income is to increase the federal budget surplus or decrease the size of an existing deficit. An expansion in the level of economic activity therefore causes fiscal policy, as measured by the budget surplus, to become more restrictive. This more restrictive policy dampens the expansion. Similarly, a shock that causes economic activity to fall automatically results in a decline in the federal budget surplus or a rise in the deficit, which cushions the fall in income. This is the essence of the concept of *automatic fiscal stabilizers*.

To examine automatic fiscal stabilizers in more detail, we return to the multiplier analysis of the Keynesian model in Chapter 6. We considered the way in which aggregate demand responded to exogenous shocks such as changes in autonomous investment demand or government spending. In effect, automatic fiscal stabilizers reduce the response of aggregate demand, and hence income, to such exogenous shocks. To show this outcome, we analyze the effects on the multiplier expressions, the expressions giving the aggregate demand response to these shocks, which result from allowing for endogenous changes in net tax revenues.

The equilibrium condition for income from Chapter 6 is

$$Y = C + I + G \tag{19.5}$$

Consumption (C) is assumed to be given by

$$C = a + bY_D \tag{19.6}$$

where Y_D is disposable income, defined as national income minus net tax collections $(Y - T)$. Investment, government spending, and the level of tax collections are all taken to be exogenous in that simple version of the Keynesian system. Similar to the procedure followed in Chapter 6, we substitute equation (19.6) into the equilibrium condition for income given by equation (19.5), and using the definition of Y_D, we compute an expression for equilibrium income ($\overline{Y}$):

$$\overline{Y} = \frac{1}{1 - b}(a - bT + I + G) \tag{19.7}$$

From equation (19.7) we compute the effects on equilibrium income of exogenous changes in investment (I), government spending (G), and *exogenous* tax collections (T) as follows:

$$\frac{\Delta\overline{Y}}{\Delta I} = \frac{1}{1 - b}, \frac{\Delta\overline{Y}}{\Delta G} = \frac{1}{1 - b}, \frac{\Delta\overline{Y}}{\Delta T} = \frac{-b}{1 - b} \tag{19.8}$$

The task here is to see how these expressions are modified when the net tax function given by equation (19.4) is substituted for the assumption that tax collections are exogenous.

To begin, consider the form of the consumption function given by equation (19.6) with our new assumption about taxes. Using the definition of disposable income ($Y_D = Y - T$) and with T defined by equation (19.4), we can write the consumption function as

$$\begin{aligned} C &= a + b(Y - T) \\ &= a + bY - bt_0 - bt_1Y \\ &= a - bt_0 + (b - bt_1)Y \\ &= a - bt_0 + b(1 - t_1)Y \end{aligned} \tag{19.9}$$

Substituting equation (19.9) into the condition for equilibrium income given in equation (19.5), we can derive the revised expression for the equilibrium level of income as follows:

$$Y = \overbrace{a - bt_0 + b(1 - t_1)Y}^{C} + I + G$$

$$Y\left[1 - b(1 - t_1)\right] = a - bt_0 + I + G$$

$$\bar{Y} = \frac{1}{1 - b(1 - t_1)}(a - bt_0 + I + G) \tag{19.10}$$

As with the previous expression (19.7), equation (19.10) specifies equilibrium income as determined by an autonomous expenditure multiplier, in this case $1/[1 - b(1 - t_1)]$, and the autonomous influences on income given by $a - bt_0 + I + G$. As before, we can compute the effects on equilibrium income of a change in investment or in the level of government spending.

$$\frac{\Delta\bar{Y}}{\Delta I} = \frac{\Delta\bar{Y}}{\Delta G} = \frac{1}{1 - b(1 - t_1)} \tag{19.11}$$

Note that the autonomous expenditure multiplier and hence the effect on income from a change in autonomous expenditures (changes in I or G, for example) is *smaller* when tax collections depend on income than when the level of tax collections is exogenous; that is,

$$\frac{1}{1 - b(1 - t_1)} < \frac{1}{1 - b}$$

For example, if b, the marginal propensity to consume, were equal to 0.8, and t_1, the marginal tax rate, were 0.25, we would have

$$\frac{1}{1 - b} = \frac{1}{1 - 0.8} = 5$$

$$\frac{1}{1 - b(1 - t_1)} = \frac{1}{1 - 0.8(1 - 0.25)} = \frac{1}{1 - 0.6} = 2.5$$

In this example, the marginal tax rate of 0.25 cuts the value of the multiplier in half.

A marginal net income tax rate lowers the effect on equilibrium income of shocks to autonomous expenditure, such as an autonomous change in investment demand. In this sense, the income tax functions as an automatic stabilizer. This stabilizing effect of an income tax can be explained with reference to our earlier discussion of the multiplier process (see section 6.5). An initial shock to investment demand, for example, changes income and has an induced effect on consumption spending. This induced effect on consumption demand causes equilibrium income to change by a multiple of the original change in investment demand. With a marginal income tax rate of t_1, each one-dollar reduction in gross domestic product (GDP) reduces an individual's disposable income, the determinant of consumption, by only $(1 - t_1)$ dollars, because the individual's tax liability falls by t_1 dollars. Disposable income is affected less per unit change in GDP, so the induced effects on consumer demand are smaller at each round of the multiplier process. The total effects on income of a change in autonomous investment, which consists of the original shock to investment plus the induced effects on consumption, are therefore smaller when there is a marginal income tax rate than when tax collections are assumed to be exogenous.

The automatic response of taxes and transfers to the level of economic activity has been a substantial stabilizing force in the U.S. economy since World War II, generally moving the budget sharply into deficit during recessions, with falling deficits or at times (in the 1950s and late 1990s) surpluses during expansionary periods. The increased size of the federal budget in the postwar period relative to the prewar period has increased the effectiveness of automatic fiscal stabilizers; in terms of our tax function, the marginal net tax rate is higher now than it was in a period such as the 1920s, and thus the multiplier is lower.

Substituting the net tax function given by equation (19.4) for the assumption that the level of tax collections is exogenous also requires modifying the analysis of the effects of discretionary tax changes in the model. In the revised expression for equilibrium income given by equation (19.10), tax policy is represented by two variables: t_0, the intercept of the tax function, and t_1, the marginal income tax rate.

The analog to a lump-sum change in tax collections in the revised income equation is a change in t_0. Such a change could represent a lump-sum tax rebate to each taxpayer, for example, or a lump-sum change in transfer payments. From equation (19.10), the effects of a change in t_0 can be computed as

$$\frac{\Delta \overline{Y}}{\Delta t_0} = \frac{1}{1 - b(1 - t_1)}(-b) = \frac{-b}{1 - b(1 - t_1)} \tag{19.12}$$

Taking account of the change in the autonomous expenditure multiplier, this expression is the same as the tax multiplier where tax collections were exogenous [see equation (19.8)]. Again, the effect of a tax change, here a change in the intercept of the tax function, is opposite in sign from the effect of a change in government spending or autonomous investment given by equation (19.11). An increase in t_0, for example, causes equilibrium income to fall. Also, the effect of a one-dollar change in t_0 is smaller in absolute value than the effect of a one-dollar change in I or G. As in the earlier case, at a given level of GDP (Y), a one-dollar change in taxes changes autonomous expenditures [the term in parentheses in equation (19.10)] by only b (< 1) dollars, with the remaining ($1 - b$) dollars absorbed by a change in saving. A one-dollar change in government spending or autonomous investment changes autonomous expenditures by one full dollar.

From equation (19.10), equilibrium income can also be seen to depend on the marginal tax rate, t_1. An increase in t_1 lowers the autonomous expenditure multiplier, and therefore lowers equilibrium income, given the values of the autonomous expenditure components. How equilibrium income is affected by a change in the marginal income tax rate can best be seen graphically. Figure 19.4 illustrates the effects of an increase in the marginal tax rate from t_1 to t_1'. Figure 19.4a shows the effect of the increase in the tax rate on the consumption function.

With an income tax, consumption is given by equation (19.9). Before the increase in the marginal tax rate, the consumption line is $C = (a - bt_0) + b(1 - t_1)Y$ in the graph. The increase in the income tax rate rotates the function downward to the schedule $C = (a - bt_0) + b(1 - t_1')Y$. The new consumption line is flatter, indicating that a given increase in Y causes consumption to rise by less with the higher tax rate. This result

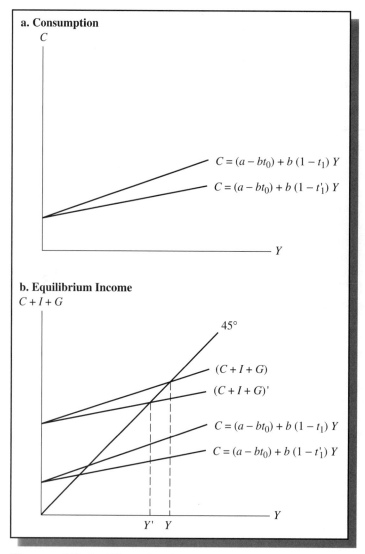

a. Consumption

C

$C = (a - bt_0) + b(1 - t_1)Y$

$C = (a - bt_0) + b(1 - t_1')Y$

Y

b. Equilibrium Income

$C + I + G$

$45°$

$(C + I + G)$

$(C + I + G)'$

$C = (a - bt_0) + b(1 - t_1)Y$

$C = (a - bt_0) + b(1 - t_1')Y$

Y

Y' Y

Figure 19.4 Effect of an Increase in the Marginal Income Tax Rate (t_1)

An increase in the income tax rate from t_1 to t_1' rotates the consumption function downward in part a. Consequently, the $C + I + G$ schedule in part b also rotates downward from $(C + I + G)$ to $(C + I + G)'$. Equilibrium income declines from Y to Y'.

follows, because with a higher tax rate, a given increase in Y, national income, causes a smaller increase in disposable income and hence in consumption. Figure 19.4b shows the effect on equilibrium income from the rise in the tax rate. The consumption function rotates downward, as in Figure 19.4a, so the $C + I + G$ line also rotates downward, from $(C + I + G)$ to $(C + I + G)'$. The equilibrium income falls from Y to Y'. The higher tax rate lowers aggregate demand and causes equilibrium income to fall.

19.5 FISCAL POLICY CONTROVERSIES: FROM THE REAGAN YEARS TO THE PRESENT

In this section we consider controversies over the federal budget for the past several decades. We begin by looking at differing views concerning balanced-budget rules for fiscal policies. If adhered to, such rules would limit or completely eliminate government budget deficits. The reasons why Keynesian economists have opposed balanced-budget rules are explained. The remaining parts of the section review the U.S. experience with budget deficits and deficit projections for the future.

The Pros and Cons of Balanced-Budget Rules

In his final economic report to Congress in 1989, President Reagan renewed his call for a constitutional amendment that would mandate a balanced federal budget. By 1995, with budget deficits still high and both houses in Republican control, Congress came within one vote of passing a balanced-budget amendment. The Maastricht guidelines in Europe are other fiscal policy rules that, although not calling for balanced budgets, set fiscal policy to meet deficit targets.

We have seen that economists who accept the public-choice view of the budget process tend to favor fiscal policy rules. The major opponents of rules that set fiscal policy to balance the budget (or to meet other arbitrary deficit goals) are Keynesians, who argue that such rules impede the stabilization role that fiscal policy should play—a role that at times *requires* budget deficits.

The role of the tax-transfer system as an automatic fiscal stabilizer, which was explained in section 19.4, requires that the budget be allowed to go into deficit (or surplus) at appropriate points in the business cycle. During a recession, as the level of economic activity falls, in the Keynesian view, the budget should sometimes go into deficit. Raising tax rates or cutting expenditures would only exacerbate the recession. Keynesians cite the 1932 tax increase as an example of the misguided fiscal policies that result from pursuing the goal of a balanced budget. The Hoover administration raised tax *rates* substantially in 1932 to try to balance the budget at a time when tax *revenues* were falling because of the Depression. The tax-rate increase came at a time when the unemployment rate was 24 percent. The policy did not succeed in balancing the budget because of the sharp decline in income, which was partly the result of the tax increase. During the 1974–75 recession, the federal budget deficit soared to nearly $70 billion. Keynesians believe that we would have risked a rerun of the Great Depression had we tried to balance the budget or seriously limit the size of the deficit under such conditions.

In addition to impeding the working of automatic stabilizers, a balanced-budget rule would limit the ability of policymakers to take *discretionary* countercyclical fiscal actions. These are changes in government spending and in tax rates aimed at stabilizing private-sector aggregate demand—the real economy equivalents of the fiscal policy shifts discussed in previous chapters. Keynesians do not deny that there are past examples of ill-timed, and at times destabilizing, discretionary fiscal policy actions, as well as stabilizing ones. Moreover, Keynesians agree that some of the failures of discretionary fiscal policy stem from interactions between the political process and macroeconomic policymaking. Keynesians opposed to constitutional budget-balancing amendments or other rules for fiscal policy argue, however, that the record for discretionary policy is not uniformly bad and that the cost of interfering with automatic fiscal stabilizers through such amendments is great.

What About the Deficit?

In 1963, Senator Harry Byrd, Sr., asked Budget Director Kermit Gordon, a Keynesian economist, what balancing the budget would do for the country. Gordon replied, "It probably would add about 2.5 million people to the rolls of the unemployed, delay the recovery about four years, and knock 10 percent off U.S. output."[10] Yet, by the mid-1980s, Keynesian economists were among the harshest critics of the large budget deficits that emerged in the Reagan years. What had changed?

Cyclical Versus Structural Deficits

One useful distinction in understanding the differing Keynesian positions on the deficits of the early 1960s versus those of the 1980s and 1990s is between **cyclical deficits** and **structural deficits**. We have seen that the federal budget deficit depends in part on the level of economic activity. The *cyclical deficit* is the portion of the deficit that results from a low level of economic activity. In the Keynesian view, cyclical deficits that reflect the working of automatic stabilizers are desirable.

cyclical deficits are the portion of the federal deficit that result from the economy's being at a low level of economic activity

The portion of the deficit that would exist even if the economy were at its potential output is called the *structural deficit*. A structural deficit is not directly attributable to the behavior of the economy and is the part of the deficit for which policymakers are directly responsible. In other words, the structural deficit is the result of decisions policymakers have made about tax rates, the level of government spending, and benefit levels for transfer programs.

structural deficits are the part of the federal deficit that would exist even if the economy were at its potential level of output

To break the deficit into cyclical and structural components, we need a measure of potential output—the level of output achieved when both capital and labor are utilized at their highest sustainable rates. We can then compute the changes in tax revenues and transfer payments that would have taken place if the economy had moved from actual to potential output. Using these figures, we can find the structural deficit. For example, suppose the actual deficit is $100 billion, but the economy is below potential output. If the level of economic activity increased to the potential level, tax revenues would rise, let us assume by $30 billion. Transfer payments would fall, say by $10 billion, because unemployment compensation payments would decline as employment rose. The structural deficit—the deficit at potential output—is then $60 billion (100 − 30 − 10).

There is no one agreed-upon definition of potential output, and consequently, there are different measures of the structural deficit. Figure 19.5 shows the measure based on the Congressional Budget Office's estimate of potential output. Notice that

---

[10]Walter Heller, "Kermit Gordon," *Brookings Papers on Economic Activity*, 2 (1976), pp. 283–87.

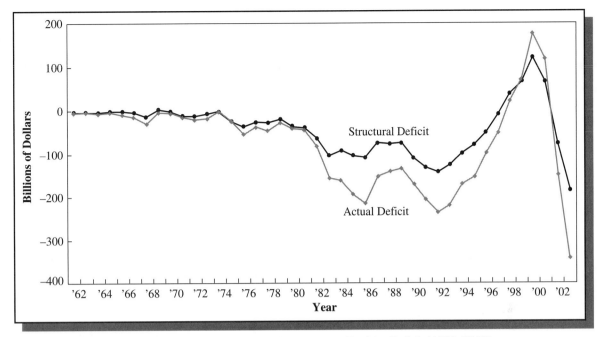

Figure 19.5 Structural and Actual Federal Government Budget Deficit (1962–2003)

Source: Congressional Budget Office, *The Budget and Economic Outlook: Fiscal Years 2005–2014* (January 2004). Adjustments made to the actual budget, in addition to removing the cyclical part of the deficit, remove the effect of one-time factors such as the Savings and Loan crisis, various privatizations, and allied contributions for the first Gulf War.

in recession periods such as 1981–82, and 1990–91, the actual deficit rose sharply above the structural deficit. These were periods of significant cyclical deficits. Notice also, however, that the structural deficit rose rapidly in the post-1982 period and remained high for more than a decade.

Although Figure 19.5 is based on revised data, earlier estimates indicated that the deficits of the early 1960s were cyclical deficits. In 1963, for example, when Kermit Gordon gave his previously quoted response to Senator Byrd, rather than a deficit measured at potential output (as it was estimated at the time), the budget showed a surplus of $13 billion; there was a structural *surplus*.[11] Gordon and other Keynesians opposed balancing the budget in 1963 because the deficit simply reflected the working of beneficial automatic fiscal stabilizers at a time when the economy was apparently operating substantially below potential output.

The Keynesian View of Deficits in the 1980s

In the 1980s, Keynesians were critical of Reagan policy because they believed that the large structural deficits reflected a mistaken *mix* of fiscal and monetary policies. Specifically, they believed that the deficits resulted from an overly expansionary fiscal policy. This fiscal policy was composed of the Reagan administration's large tax

---

[11]Keith Carlson, "Estimates of the High-Employment Budget 1947–67," Federal Reserve Bank of St. Louis *Review*, 49 (June 1967), p. 11.

cuts and increased defense spending that more than counterbalanced cuts in nondefense spending. In the view of Keynesians, the overly expansionary fiscal policies meant that, throughout much of the 1980s, monetary policy had to be especially restrictive to keep the level of aggregate demand from growing too quickly. Keynesians believe that this mix of an easy fiscal and tight monetary policy had unfavorable effects on the *composition* of output in the following ways.

Keynesians believed the tight monetary and easy fiscal policy resulted in high U.S. interest rates during much of the 1980s. They believed this policy mix discouraged investment at the expense of consumption. They also believed that the high U.S. interest rates pushed up the value of the U.S. dollar as foreign investment was attracted; this in turn encouraged imports and discouraged exports, leading to what were at the time record trade deficits.

Keynesians favored a policy mix of tighter fiscal and easier monetary policy that would have led to higher capital formation (more investment) and higher exports (a lower trade deficit).

The Federal Budget in the Late 1990s and into the Twenty-First Century

Beginning in the mid-1990s, a combination of tax increases and spending cuts, aided by rapid economic growth, moved the budget from large deficits to a surplus. Huge future surpluses were forecast for the medium term. There was concern about the effects of erasing the national debt that was forecast to go the zero by 2011. This concern was premature because, as noted in the introduction, by 2004 ten-year budget projections showed a cumulative deficit of over $2 trillion, compared to a surplus of over $3 trillion projected in the beginning of 2001.

Part of this shift was the result of the recession in 2001. This can be seen from Figure 19.5, which shows that in 2001–2003 the actual deficit substantially exceeded the structural deficit. Especially in 2001 and 2002, a large part of the deficit was cyclical. By 2004, almost the whole of the deficit was structural. The current and projected medium-term deficits result from legislated actions, primarily the large tax cuts put through by the Bush administration. This shift in fiscal policy rekindled the debates of the 1980s and 1990s over the economic effects of large structural deficits. Moreover, as in the 1980s, large government budget deficits were accompanied by record foreign trade deficits, raising additional concerns.

A new element in these debates was concern over long-term budget pressures. These long-term budget pressures result from the coming retirement of the large "baby boom" generation and the growing lifespan of the population. Both factors will put a strain on the Social Security and Medicare system. Increases in health care costs at a higher rate than the general price level will, if they continue, further strain the Medicare budget and also increase the cost of the Medicaid program. Projections by the Congressional Budget Office (CBO) shows federal spending on Social Security rising from 4.2 percent of GDP in 2003 to 6.2 percent in 2050. Projecting the increase in Medicare and Medicaid spending is more difficult since future health care costs are difficult to predict. Based on different scenarios for health care costs, the CBO projects the cost of these two programs to rise from 3.9 percent in 2003 to anywhere between 6.4 and 21 percent of GDP by 2050. These figures compare with total federal revenues of 16.7 percent of GDP in 2003.[12] Even with a relatively optimistic view of future health care costs, Social Security, Medicare, and Medicaid would come to absorb almost all federal revenues unless taxes increase.

Critics of Bush administration fiscal policy, especially of the large tax cuts, argue that we should be running budget surpluses now to reduce outstanding debt and prepare for these huge future expenditures. Supporters of the tax cuts counter that lower tax rates will increase economic growth and thus the future tax base to finance higher expenditures. These arguments about the relationships between fiscal policy and economic growth are at the center of the discussion in Chapter 20.

19.6 CONCLUSION

The issue of the deficit dominated the debate over fiscal policy in the 1980s and 1990s. Over the next several decades, the longer-run pressures on the budget discussed in this chapter are likely to be the center of attention. Any potential stabilization role for fiscal policy is complicated by the presence of these alternative concerns. In this environment, the major role for stabilization policy has fallen to monetary policy. This has been true not only in the United States but in most industrialized countries.

KEY TERMS

- public-choice 405
- partisan theory 405
- automatic stabilizers 414

- cyclical deficits 420
- structural deficits 420

REVIEW QUESTIONS AND PROBLEMS

1. Some economists who accept the public-choice view of the fiscal policymaking process have concluded that a constitutional amendment to mandate a balanced federal budget would be desirable. Summarize their arguments in favor of such an amendment.
2. Explain the central element of the *partisan* theory of fiscal policymaking. Contrast the implications of the partisan theory concerning the relationship of fiscal policy to the business cycle with those of the public-choice view.
3. Explain the concept of an automatic fiscal stabilizer. Give examples.
4. Suppose that, within the simple Keynesian model used in section 19.4, the level of government spending (G) was 100, the level of investment spending (I) was 75, and consumption (C) was given by

$$C = 25 + 0.8Y_D$$

Net taxes (T) are initially given by the tax function

$$T = -50 + 0.30Y$$

---
[12]Congressional Budget Office, "The Long-Term Budget Outlook" (December 2003).

Calculate equilibrium income ($\overline{Y}$). Now suppose the tax rate is decreased from 0.30 to 0.25. Find the new level of equilibrium income. Compute the values of the autonomous expenditure multiplier before and after the tax cut.

5. Explain the Keynesians' objections to fixed rules for fiscal policy, such as a constitutional amendment that would mandate a balanced federal budget.

6. Refer to the first equilibrium income you calculated in problem 4. Now suppose that the intercept of the net tax function (t_0) changes from -50 to -40. Find the new level of equilibrium income.

7. Explain the concept of the structural budget deficit. How do structural deficits differ from cyclical deficits?

8. In recent debates over the federal budget, why has the issue of balanced-budget rules become largely irrelevant? What criteria have become relevant in deciding on the optimal surplus or deficit in the budget?

Chapter 20

Policies to Promote Economic Growth

*T*his chapter considers the factors that determine the growth of output over periods longer than the short run but not necessarily periods of long-run equilibrium such as those analyzed in Chapter 5. Our specific focus is on policies that foster sustained economic growth.

The short-run period in our earlier analysis was characterized by the assumptions of a constant capital stock, a fixed labor force, and an unchanged technology. Output changes came as the level of employment varied. When considering changes in output in the intermediate run, perhaps over 10 to 15 years rather than 2 to 4 years, we are not entitled to those assumptions. Variations in the rates of capital formation, growth in the labor force that results from growth in the working-age population as well as changes in labor force participation rates, and variations in the rate of technological change are factors that determine growth rates of output in the intermediate run. What about the importance of demand? Economists who accept the classical, real business cycle, or new classical views see little direct role for aggregate demand as a significant factor in determining the growth path of output over periods of intermediate length. In the classical or real business cycle theories, aggregate demand does not play a role in determining output even in the short run. In the new classical model, only unanticipated demand changes affect output. Therefore, only deviations of demand growth from the average rather than the average rate of growth in demand over a period of 10 to 15 years itself would affect output.

The situation is different with respect to the monetarist and Keynesian (or new Keynesian) views. As we have explained, the long-run equilibrium growth rate is supply-determined, but both monetarists and Keynesians believe that changes in demand affect output over periods of several years. If we look at any 10- to 15-year period, the average rate of growth may be affected by demand-induced recessions or expansions within that period. Demand factors might explain why the growth rate of output was approximately zero for the 1929–39 decade of the Great Depression. Unstable growth in aggregate demand might also be used by a monetarist or a Keynesian to explain why growth in real output averaged 3.1 percent in the decade from 1969 to 1979, a period during which two recessions occurred, compared with an annual growth rate of 4.3 percent in the 1960s, when there was a sustained expansion from February 1961 to December 1969.

Thus, as with analysis of the short run, economists disagree over the relative importance of supply and demand in determining output over intermediate-run periods. We will examine the position of a group called *supply-side* economists. As their name indicates, the supply-side economists ascribe predominance to supply factors as the determinants of the behavior of output. The origins of their views are in the classical economics and consequently their theories share elements with real business cycle theories and the new classical economics. There are, however, additional questions that arise in considering output growth in the intermediate run and different types of policy issues. On these issues real business cycle theorists and new classical economists have in many cases taken positions that differ from *supply-siders*.

Rather than considering a full range of views on policies in the intermediate run, we will confine ourselves to contrasting the supply-side view with the Keynesian view. It has in fact been Keynesian economists who have been the sharpest critics of the supply-side economics. The Keynesian position maintains, as James Tobin has said, that God gave us two eyes so that we could watch both supply and demand (albeit with the danger of becoming a bit walleyed). In addition to the issue of the relative importance of supply and demand, supply-side economists and Keynesians disagree on which policies have favorable (or unfavorable) effects on aggregate supply.

We proceed by laying out the supply-side position as it has evolved over the past three decades and then considering the Keynesian critique. Next we describe the redirection of macroeconomic policy that took place during the Reagan and Bush presidencies—a redirection inspired by supply-side economics. In the 1990s, voters seemed to call for policy to move in another direction by twice electing Bill Clinton to the presidency. But in 1994, the House Republicans "Contract with America," which drew heavily on the precepts of supply-side economics, proved popular. Moreover, in 2000, George W. Bush was elected and followed an economic program of large tax cuts in line with the prescriptions of supply-side economists. We will conclude the chapter with a consideration of these conflicting aspects of the recent policy-making climate.

Before turning to these topics, however, it is useful to review the growth performance of the U.S. economy over the past several decades.

Table 20.1 U.S. Growth Experience 1960–2002

ITEM	AVERAGE ANNUAL PERCENTAGE GROWTH RATE					
	1960–68	1968–73	1973–79	1979–91	1992–97	1998–2002
Gross Domestic Output	4.5	3.2	2.4	2.5	3.4	3.0
Labor Productivity	2.6	1.0	0.0	1.0	1.7	2.3
Total Labor Force	1.6	2.4	2.6	1.7	1.3	1.2
Capital Formation	5.0	3.7	1.9	2.3	4.0	3.9

Sources: Historical Statistics, 1960–89 (Paris: OECD, 1991); *Economic Report of the President*, 1992, 1997, 2004; OECD *Economic Outlook* (December 1997, June 2003).

20.1 U.S. ECONOMIC GROWTH, 1960–2002

The growth experience for the United States for the 1960–2002 period is summarized in Table 20.1. As the table shows, the rates of growth in output and labor productivity slowed down after 1973. The rate of capital formation also declined. Growth in the labor force increased in the late 1960s and into the 1970s as the post–World War II baby boom generation came to adulthood, and then returned to its earlier level in the 1980s.

Then, at some point in the 1990s, a turnaround appears to have occurred. While growth in the labor force continued to decline because of demographic factors, capital formation, and growth in both output and labor productivity increased almost back to pre-1973 levels.

The facts that supply-side and Keynesian economists must explain are, therefore, the following:

1. The growth rate in U.S. output slowed markedly in the 1973–92 period.
2. The growth rate in labor productivity declined sharply in the 1970s.
3. The rate of capital formation also slowed in the 1970s and 1980s relative to pre-1973 years.
4. After 1992, capital formation and growth in output and labor productivity rose back to near pre-1973 levels.

Read Perspectives 20.1.

20.2 THE SUPPLY-SIDE POSITION

The origins of supply-side economics lie in the classical theories examined in Chapters 3 and 4. In particular, for the intermediate run, supply-side economists accept the classical view that output is determined by real variables—growth of factor supplies and changes in technology. They adhere to a classical view of the saving–investment process, in which the interest rate is the crucial variable. Most fundamentally, supply-side economists share the classical economists' faith in the

PERSPECTIVES 20.1
Growth and Productivity Slowdowns in Other Industrialized Economies

Table 20.2 shows growth rates for output and labor productivity for six major industrialized countries. The data are average annual percentage growth rates for time periods similar to those considered for the United States in Table 20.1. The striking feature in the table is a marked slowdown in output growth and productivity growth in the post-1970 period in *all* these countries.

The data in the tables are for large industrialized economies, but data for smaller ones tell the same story. The growth and productivity slowdown of the 1970s, with relatively slow growth continuing into the 1980s and early 1990s, affected virtually every industrialized economy. This trend suggests that, as we seek explanations of the slowdown, we should look for causes that have broad international effects.

The turnaround in the growth picture in the United States was not widely shared across other industrialized economies. Japan, the world's second largest economy, suffered several recessions and slow growth throughout the decade of the 1990s. Germany, the third largest economy, showed signs of more rapid growth in the mid- to late-1990s but has returned to slow growth in more recent years.

Table 20.2 Growth Rate in Output and Labor Productivity, Selected Countries, Annual Averages

COUNTRY	ITEM	1960–68	1968–73	1973–79	1979–89	1990–97	1998–02
Canada	Output	5.5	5.4	4.2	3.1	2.6	3.8
	Labor Productivity	4.0	3.2	1.4	1.2	1.7	1.7
France	Output	5.4	5.9	3.0	2.1	1.9	2.8
	Labor Productivity	4.9	4.7	2.7	2.0	1.5	1.0
Italy	Output	5.7	4.6	2.6	2.5	1.6	1.8
	Labor Productivity	6.3	4.9	1.7	2.1	1.9	0.5
Japan	Output	10.4	8.4	3.6	4.1	1.6	0.5
	Labor Productivity	8.8	7.3	2.9	3.0	1.5	1.1
Germany	Output	4.1	4.9	2.3	1.8	2.0	1.5
	Labor Productivity	4.2	4.1	2.9	1.7	2.1	0.7
United Kingdom	Output	3.1	3.2	1.5	2.3	2.2	2.5
	Labor Productivity	2.7	3.0	1.3	1.7	1.7	1.5

Sources: Historical Statistics, Paris: OECD, 1988, 1992; OECD *Economic Outlook* (December 1997, June 2003).

free-enterprise capitalist system and dislike of government intervention in the economy. To analyze these ideas, we begin by stating some propositions of supply-side economics. We then explain each proposition in terms of its classical roots and show how each applies to current U.S. economic problems and policies.

The following four propositions are important elements of supply-side economics.[1]

1. Output growth in the intermediate run is predominantly supply-determined by rates of growth in factor supplies and the rate of technological change.
2. The rate of growth of the capital input is determined primarily by incentives for saving and investment, the incentives being the *after-tax* returns to saving and investment.
3. Growth in the labor input, although in the long run determined by demographic factors, can also be affected significantly by incentives, in this case, changes in the after-tax real wage.
4. Excessive government regulation of business discouraged capital formation and contributed to the slowdown in the growth of labor productivity in the 1970s and 1980s.

Intermediate-Run Output Growth Is Supply-Determined

We pointed out in the introduction to the chapter that, in the long run, economic growth depends predominantly on supply factors. Supply-side economists believe that this dependency is also true in the intermediate run. It clearly follows in the classical model, where even in the short run output is supply-determined. Intermediate-run growth in the classical model is illustrated in Figure 20.1. Output increases from Y_0 to Y_1 to Y_2 as the supply curve shifts to the right, reflecting growth in factor supplies and changes in technology. If the aggregate demand schedule remains at Y_0^d in Figure 20.1, prices will fall successively to P_1 and then to P_2. Instead, if demand is increased as a result of growth in the money supply proportional to the growth in output, the price level will be maintained at P_0. Whichever is the case, the growth in output is determined solely by shifts in the supply curve.

It is overly restrictive to say that Figure 20.1 represents the supply-side view. Most supply-side economists accept that demand plays a role in the *short-run* determination of income; the very short-run aggregate supply curve is upward-sloping to the right rather than vertical, as classical economists would have drawn it. Consequently, to avoid short-run disruptions, many supply-side economists would favor a policy strategy in which demand was raised sufficiently to avoid the need for deflation (the fall in prices from P_0 to P_2 in Figure 20.1). Still, a central element in the

---

[1]Early expositions of the supply-side position may be found in George Gilder, *Wealth and Poverty* (New York: Basic Books, 1981), especially Chapters 4 and 15–16; Paul Craig Roberts, *The Supply-Side Revolution* (Cambridge, Mass.: Harvard University Press, 1983); Arthur B. Laffer and Jan P. Seymour, eds., *The Economics of the Tax Revolt: A Reader* (New York: Harcourt Brace Jovanovich, 1979); and Laurence Meyer, ed., *The Supply-Side Effects of Economic Policy* (St. Louis: Center for the Study of American Business, 1981). The last two sources also contain critiques of the supply-side positions. Two useful analyses of supply-side economics are James Barth, "The Reagan Program for Economic Recovery: Economic Rationale (A Primer on Supply-Side Economics)," Federal Reserve Bank of Atlanta *Review* (September 1981), pp. 4–14; and John Tatom, "We Are All Supply-Siders Now!" Federal Reserve Bank of St. Louis *Review*, 63 (May 1981), pp. 18–30. Later evaluations are Martin Feldstein, "Supply-Side Economics: Old Truths and New Claims," *American Economic Review*, 76 (May 1986), pp. 26–30; Lawrence Chimerine and Richard Young, "Economic Surprises and Messages of the 1980s," *American Economic Review*, 76 (May 1986), pp. 31–36; and Paul Krugman, *Peddling Prosperity* (New York: Norton, 2000), Chapters 1–3.

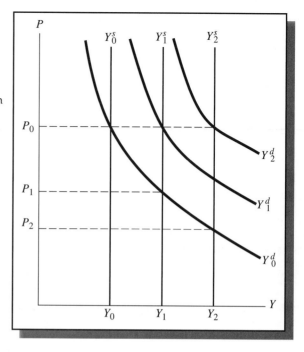

Figure 20.1
Intermediate-Run Growth in the Classical System

Growth in factor supplies shifts the supply curve to the right (from Y_0^s to Y_1^s to Y_2^s). If demand is unchanged, the price level falls (from P_0 to P_1 to P_2). Appropriate increases in the quantity of money would increase demand sufficiently (from Y_0^d to Y_1^d to Y_2^d) to maintain the initial equilibrium price level (P_0).

supply-side position is that for *intermediate-run* periods, growth in output is supply- and not demand-determined.[2]

Saving and Investment Depend on After-Tax Rates of Return

Supply-side economics stresses the after-tax rate of return to investment as a primary determinant of investment and therefore the rate of capital formation. The after-tax rate of return is the pretax profit rate multiplied by 1 minus the rate at which profits are taxed. Similarly, supply-side economists believe the after-tax return for saving is an important influence on the saving rate. Here the relevant rate of return is the after-tax *real* interest rate, which equals the after-tax nominal interest rate (the nominal rate multiplied by 1 minus the rate at which interest payments are taxed) minus the expected inflation rate.

This view of saving and investment is a classical notion. Recall our discussion of the theory of interest in the classical model, as illustrated in Figure 20.2. The equilibrium (real) interest rate is determined by the intersection of the saving and investment schedules. This outcome reflects the assumption we make for the moment that

---

[2]On this issue and those discussed later, we can distinguish between a moderate and an extreme supply-side position. On many issues moderate supply-side economists differ from the Keynesians only in ascribing more importance to supply-side factors. The more extreme supply-side positions virtually ignore the demand side. For example, Martin Feldstein, chairman of the Council of Economic Advisors under President Reagan, whose work on incentives for investment is described later, is an economist who has emphasized the importance of supply-side variables but has been at odds with extreme supply-siders.

Figure 20.2
Classical Theory of Interest

The position of the saving schedule depends on the tax rate for interest and dividend income (t_0^{wh}). The position of the investment schedule depends on the effective tax rate on corporate profits (t_0^{cp}) as well as on the pretax corporate profit rate (cp). These tax rates, t_0^{wh} and t_0^{cp}, therefore, affect the equilibrium real interest rate (r).

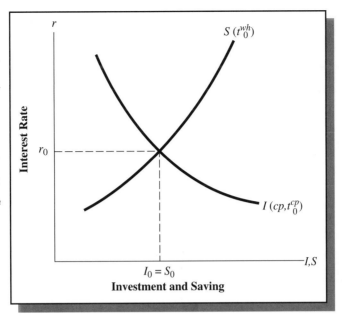

the government deficit ($G - T$) is zero. Otherwise, government deficit bond financing would be an additional demand for loanable funds. The position of the investment schedule is shown to depend on cp, the pretax corporate profit rate, and t^{cp}, the effective tax rate on corporate profits, to be explained later. The position of the saving schedule depends on t^{wh}, the rate of taxation of individual income earned on accumulated savings (wealth). In the classical model, income earned from accumulated savings would simply be interest income on bonds. In the real economy, t^{wh} would also represent tax rates on dividend income and tax rates on capital gains produced by changes in asset prices. In our earlier analysis, we established that the real interest rate (r) was determined by what the classical economists called the forces of productivity and thrift, productivity being reflected in the profit rate and therefore the position of the investment schedule, and thrift reflected in the position of the saving schedule (both for a given structure of taxes). Here the important point is that in the classical view, productivity and thrift, *as well as the structure of taxes*, determine saving and investment, and consequently the rate of capital formation.

Supply-side economists need not accept the particular specification of the saving and investment functions in our simple version of the classical system. For example, in predicting the level of investment spending for the United States in a particular year in the 2000s, supply-side economists would use a much more complex investment function than that plotted in Figure 20.2. They would take account of factors such as lags and adjustment costs. The essentially classical feature in supply-side economists' view of the saving–investment process is their stress on rates of return as influences on the rates of saving, investment, and thus capital formation. Where else might the emphasis be placed? The answer is on income and, hence, on aggregate demand. Keynesians believe that the level of income is the most important determinant of investment. Investment can best be kept high, according to this Keynesian view, by keeping the economy at a high rate of capacity utilization. Keynesians do not ignore rates of return, nor do supply-side economists ignore income as a determinant of saving or investment. The difference between the two views is a matter of emphasis, and supply-side economists emphasize rates of return as incentives for saving and investment.

By stressing the importance of incentives for saving and investment, we are led to seek the source of the decline in the rate of U.S. capital formation in the post-1970 period in factors that weakened these incentives. The solution to slow capital formation may lie in increased incentives for savers and investors. Martin Feldstein and other economists claim that the interaction of inflation and the U.S. tax system weakened these incentives over the course of the 1970s.

First, Feldstein and others have argued that, given existing tax laws, the high inflation of the 1970s raised the effective tax rate on corporate income.[3] They offered several reasons; one important reason concerns the rules for depreciation allowances. Firms can deduct depreciation of capital investments only at *original* cost. In inflationary periods, the true cost of depreciating capital is the replacement cost. This cost is understated by depreciation at original or "historical" cost, so profits are overstated, and the effective corporate tax liability was increased in the inflationary 1970s.

Supply-side economists also argue that the combination of inflation and the U.S. tax system reduced the incentives to save during the 1970s. The income tax an individual pays is based on the *nominal* interest, dividends, or capital gains earned on invested savings. Two examples will illustrate how increased inflation and taxation of nominal interest payments or capital gains lower the real return on saving. Suppose that initially the nominal interest rate is 6 percent and the rate of inflation is 2 percent (a pretax real rate of 4 percent). At a 50 percent marginal tax rate, an investor would have an after-tax *nominal* return of 3 percent [6 percent $\times$ $(1 - t^{wh})$ = 6 percent $\times$ $(1 - 0.5)$] and an after-tax real return of 1 percent (3 percent $-$ 2 percent). Now suppose that the nominal interest rate is 16 percent, with an inflation rate of 12 percent (again a pretax real rate of 4 percent). The after-tax nominal return will be 8 percent [16 percent $\times$ $(1 - 0.5)$], which means that the after-tax real return is now -4 percent (8 percent $-$ 12 percent).

Or consider the taxation of nominal capital gains on corporate equities, for example. Suppose that an individual purchased a share of stock at a price of $100 in 1967 and sold it in 1980 for $200. Because the price level rose by over 150 percent in this period while the price of the stock doubled, or rose 100 percent, the individual's real return is negative even before taxes. Still, the individual must pay a capital gains tax on the nominal capital gain (of $100), increasing the size of the real loss. Supply-side economists argue that taxing nominal capital gains and interest earnings during inflationary periods results in an increased effective tax rate on real returns and will retard saving.

The effects of overtaxing both corporate profits and the return to saving during inflationary periods are illustrated in Figure 20.3. Suppose that we move from a

---

[3]See Martin Feldstein and Lawrence Summers, "Inflation and the Taxation of Capital Income in the Corporate Sector," *National Tax Journal*, 32 (December 1979), pp. 445–70.

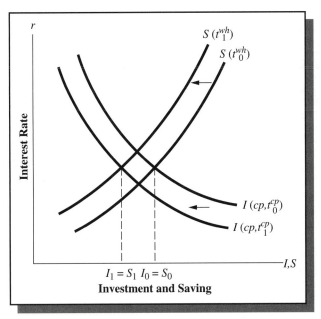

Figure 20.3 Inflation, the Tax System, and the Saving–Investment Process

An increase in the effective corporate tax rate due to increased inflation caused the investment schedule to shift leftward from $I(cp, t_0^{cp})$ to $I(cp, t_1^{cp})$. An inflation-induced increase in the effective tax rate on interest income and capital gains shifts the saving schedule leftward from $S(t_0^{wh})$ to $S(t_1^{wh})$. The equilibrium levels of saving and investment fall from $I_0 = S_0$ to $I_1 = S_1$.

period of relatively low inflation rates such as the 1950s and 1960s to a period of higher inflation rates such as the 1970s. Because of historical cost depreciation, this change results in an increase in the effective tax rate on corporate profits from t_0^{cp} to t_1^{cp} in Figure 20.3. For a given before-tax profit rate cp, this increase in the effective tax rate will shift the investment schedule to the left, as shown in the graph. Further, owing to the taxing of nominal interest payments and capital gains, the effective tax on the return to saving is increased from t_0^{wh} to t_1^{wh}, and the saving schedule shifts to the left in Figure 20.3. After the adjustment to a new equilibrium, saving and investment are reduced from the levels I_0 and S_0 to the levels shown as S_1 and I_1 in Figure 20.3. The rate of capital formation is reduced by the interaction of inflation and the tax system.

Labor Supply Is Responsive to Changes in the After-Tax Real Wage

Supply-side economists argue that labor supply is responsive to changes in *after-tax* real wages. Here again the supply-side view is rooted in classical economics—in this case, building on the classical analysis of the supply-side effects of changes in the marginal

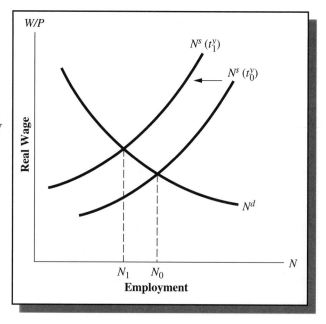

Figure 20.4
Taxes and Labor Supply in the Classical System

An increase in the income tax rate from t_0^y to t_1^y reduces the after-tax real wage and causes the labor supply schedule to shift to the left. Employment declines from N_0 to N_1.

income tax rate (see section 4.3). Figure 20.4 illustrates the determination of equilibrium employment in the classical system and the effect of a change in the after-tax real wage as a result of a change in the marginal income tax rate t^y. Initially assume that the income tax rate is set at t_0^y. The labor supply curve is given by $N^s(t_0^y)$ and intersects the labor demand curve at N_0, the equilibrium level of employment.

Now assume that the income tax rate is raised to a higher level, t_1^y. According to the supply-side view, labor supply depends on the after-tax real wage, which will equal $(1 - t^y) W/P$. For example, with a marginal tax rate of 0.20, the after-tax real wage will be 0.80 times the pretax real wage. The marginal income tax rate thus forms a "wedge" between the wage paid by the employer, W/P, and the wage received by the worker, $(1 - t^y) W/P$. Increasing the tax rate from t_0^y to a higher level, t_1^y, causes the labor supply schedule to shift to the left from $N^s(t_0^y)$ to $N^s(t_1^y)$. Less labor is supplied at each level of the pretax real wage because, with a higher tax rate, a given pretax real wage represents a *lower* after-tax real wage. Employment declines from N_0 to N_1.

Supply-side economists believe that rising marginal tax rates in the United States during the 1970s increased the size of the wedge which the income tax creates between the real wage paid by the employer and the after-tax wage received by the employee (see Perspectives 4.2). They claim that work incentives were reduced, with negative effects on employment and output. Here again inflationary aggregate demand policies and a tax system not well designed to cope with the effects of inflation deserve much of the blame. The U.S. income tax system in the 1970s was progressive, so as *nominal* incomes went up due to inflation, individuals moved into higher marginal tax brackets.

Read Perspectives 20.2.

A "simplified" income tax form circulated as a joke reads

> Form "1040"
>
> This year's income _____.
>
> SEND IT IN.

A tax system represented by this form, that of a 100 percent tax rate, would not collect any revenue. Who would work and report income? At the other end of the tax rate spectrum, a rate of 0 percent would also obviously yield no revenue. Therefore, we know that if we plot a relationship between tax *revenue* and the tax *rate*, with revenue on the vertical axis, the curve will first rise as the tax rate moves up from zero, but at some point, before the tax rate hits one, it will decline. For example, the relationship might be as shown in Figure 20.5.

This curve showing tax revenue collected at each tax rate (or overall level of tax rates) is called the Laffer curve. The curve is named after its popularizer, Arthur B. Laffer. The Laffer curve received much attention because it illustrated the possibility that increases in tax rates may *reduce* tax revenue. Conversely, a cut in tax rates may *increase* revenue. The latter effect will occur if tax rates are initially in the range to the right of point A in Figure 20.5.

A number of supply-side economists, including Laffer, argued that this was the case for the United States in the early 1980s. Tax cuts would expand the economy through the supply side. This expansion would increase the tax base. Moreover, supply-siders argued that tax avoidance (e.g., through the use of tax shelters) and tax evasion (e.g., failure to report taxable income) would decline. Together, it was argued, these effects would lead to increased tax revenues even at lower tax rates.

Economists of other than the supply-side persuasion, and many moderate supply-siders, did not believe the U.S. economy was on the downward-sloping portion of the Laffer curve. They saw the huge deficits that emerged in the 1980s after tax cuts as support for their view.

Figure 20.5
The Laffer Curve

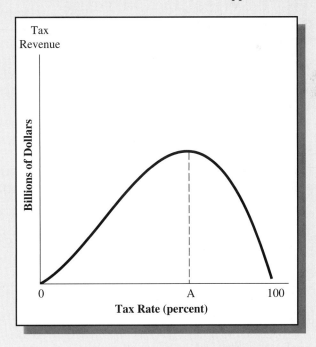

Government Regulation Contributed to the Slowdown in the U.S. Economic Growth Rate

Supply-side economists argue that the proliferation of government regulation of business contributed significantly to the slowdown in U.S. economic growth during the 1970s. A new wave of government regulatory activity began in the 1960s. New agencies were set up, and laws were passed for pollution control, protection of worker safety, consumer product safety, and pension reform. Supply-side economists argue that this increase in government regulatory activity slowed economic growth in two ways.

First, complying with such regulations increases the cost of producing a given output. Increases in government regulation therefore have the same effects as the supply shocks considered in Chapter 9. The aggregate supply curve shifts to the left, reducing output. Note that some of the increase of cost comes from employing workers not directly for production of output—steel, for example—but for cleaning smokestacks to comply with pollution controls, eliminating on-the-job safety hazards, or otherwise to comply with regulations. Thus, increased government regulation is a possible explanation for the decline in the growth of labor productivity.

Second, supply-side economists argue that government regulatory activity retarded capital formation, at least capital formation that contributed to increased productivity in terms of measured output. According to one estimate, expenditures on pollution control absorbed approximately 20 percent of net investment in 1970.[4]

20.3 THE KEYNESIAN CRITIQUE OF SUPPLY-SIDE ECONOMICS

We have stressed the classical roots of supply-side economics. Supply-side economics can be regarded as the intermediate-run counterpart to the monetarist and new classical attacks on the Keynesian orthodoxy that dominated by the mid-1960s; those attacks were also based on classical notions. In this section, we analyze the Keynesian critique of the supply-side position in terms of each of the supply-side propositions discussed in the preceding section.

The Supply-Determined Nature of Intermediate-Run Growth

The Keynesian position is that for periods of a decade or so, both supply and demand factors are important in determining output growth. For example, in explaining the lower growth in the United States in the 1970s, James Tobin sees as the primary causes supply shocks, the most important from the energy sector, and monetary policy "overkill," meaning overly restrictive policy actions imposed to slow the economy when a slowdown was already under way. Tobin blames such mistimed

---

[4]See Lawrence Summers, "Tax Policy and Corporate Investment," in Meyer, ed., *The Supply-Side Effects of Economic Policy.*

monetary actions in part for the severity of the recessions of the 1970s, which resulted in the lower growth rate for the decade.[5]

Saving and Investment and After-Tax Rates of Return

On the question of whether depressed rates of return have lowered saving, investment, and capital formation, there are areas of agreement and disagreement between the supply-side economists and the Keynesians. Keynesian economists do not deny that capital formation is important to growth or that the slowdown in net capital formation was one cause of the growth slowdown of the post-1970 period. Nor do the Keynesians oppose policies to improve investment incentives. Tobin points out, for example, that the first investment tax credit was passed during the Kennedy administration, a high point of Keynesian influence.

Still, in the Keynesian view, the primary explanation for the slowdown in net capital formation in the 1970s lies in the low levels of output growth during that period, which caused investment demand to lag. Keynesians believe that, *for the most part,* causation runs from low output to low investment rather than in the reverse direction. The low output levels are ascribed, as explained previously, to supply shocks and, at times, to overly restrictive monetary policies.

What about the role of incentives for saving and investment? Although not ignoring the effects of changes in after-tax returns on investment demand, Keynesians argue that output is the key variable determining investment. Thus, the best way to encourage investment is to keep the economy near potential output. In the case of saving, the Keynesians would not deny that the rate of return (after taxes) is a determinant of saving. Nor would Keynesians deny that a decline in this rate of return may have caused the saving rate to decline in the late 1970s. They believe, however, as Tobin states, that "an explanation of the slowdown in business capital formation in the 1970s may be sought in investment demand rather than saving supply."

The Effect of Income Tax Cuts on Labor Supply

Keynesian economists do not believe that "vast increases" in labor supply will result from lowering marginal income tax rates. They do not believe that current income tax rates are a serious impediment to labor supply. As evidence, Keynesian economists cite the high labor force participation ratios in Western European countries (Germany, for example), where marginal tax rates are substantially higher than in the United States. Further, they point out that, although inflation due to a progressive income tax will push individuals into higher tax brackets, actual tax rates paid will increase only if the tax schedule is unchanged. If, instead, Congress periodically lowers tax rates to offset the effects of inflation (or for some other reason), actual marginal tax rates may not rise. According to estimates cited by Tobin, the federal marginal rate of personal income tax averaged over all brackets was actually lower in 1975 than in 1960—18.0 percent, compared with 18.8 percent. In 1975–80, there does appear to have been some "bracket creep" because of inflation, with the average

---

[5]See James Tobin, "Stabilization Policy Ten Years After," *Brookings Papers on Economic Activity*, 1 (1980), pp. 19–71.

marginal tax rate increasing to 21.6 percent. But Tobin found no evidence of a weakened "propensity to supply labor."[6]

In rebuttal, supply-side economists point to the large increase in payroll taxes over recent years. Payroll (Social Security) taxes are an additional element in the wedge between the wage paid by the employer and that received by the worker. In addition, the supply-side economists point to empirical studies indicating that, given secular trends that have increased labor force participation rates, income and payroll tax rates have negative effects on labor supply.[7]

The issues, then, appear to be the empirical ones of whether increases in marginal tax rates have been sufficient enough to create an important work disincentive and, further, whether reductions in marginal tax rates affect labor supply strongly enough to increase employment and output substantially.

Regulation As a Source of Inflation and Slow Growth

Regarding the effects of government regulation on inflation and growth, the issues are broad, and it is incorrect to argue that there is a single Keynesian position that contrasts with the supply-side position. As stated previously, there is no doubt that government regulation increased in the period from the late 1960s to 1980. There is also no doubt that complying with many of these regulations was costly to firms and that much of the cost was passed on to consumers. Nor is it doubtful that many of the regulations were cost-ineffective, in that more efficient ways exist to achieve the same benefits.

Economists who would not go as far as the supply-siders in dismantling the regulatory structure that arose since the 1960s believe either that the benefits are greater than the supply-side economists believe or that the costs, in terms of lost growth, are lower. In addition, they may be more optimistic about the possibility of improving regulatory effectiveness. The prospective benefits from these new regulations include cleaner air, cleaner water, safer workplaces, and safer consumer products. These are, of course, desirable to all, but opinions differ as to the degree to which government intervention in the economy is needed to achieve them.

20.4 GROWTH POLICIES FROM RONALD REAGAN TO GEORGE W. BUSH

Economic Redirection in the Reagan Years

After the high inflation and unemployment of the 1970s, voters in the United States were ready in 1980 for an experiment with supply-side economics. To be sure, Ronald Reagan's economic proposals and, to an even greater degree, his policies as enacted, contained elements of theories other than those of the supply-siders.

---

[6]See James Tobin, "The Reagan Economic Plan—Supply-Side, Budget and Inflation," in *The Reagan Economic Plan* (San Francisco: Federal Reserve Bank of San Francisco, 1981).

[7]See, for example, Jerry Hausman, "Income and Payroll Tax Policy and Labor Supply," in Meyer, ed., *The Supply-Side Effects of Economic Policy*; Jerry Hausman, "Labor Supply," in Henry Aaron and Joseph Pechman, eds., *How Taxes Affect Economic Behavior* (Washington, D.C.: The Brookings Institution, 1981); and Jerry A. Hausman and James M. Poterba, "Household Behavior and the Tax Reform Act of 1986," *Journal of Economic Perspectives*, 1 (Summer 1987), pp. 101–20.

Still, the central elements of what became known as Reaganomics were supply-side proposals.

Personal Income Tax Reductions

As enacted by Congress, the Reagan tax cut bill reduced marginal income tax rates, in three stages, by a total of 23 percent. The bill also lowered the top rate on income earned from capital from 70 to 50 percent. Beginning in 1985, the tax bill indexed tax brackets to inflation to prevent "bracket creep." As discussed in section 20.2, in the view of supply-side economists, such income tax cuts should increase labor supply and therefore output (supply-side proposition 3).

Personal income tax cuts should also increase personal saving. The reduction in the maximum tax bracket from 70 to 50 percent was especially aimed at increasing saving. In addition, to encourage saving, the tax act extended the opportunity to use IRA accounts to all households. IRA accounts allow for deposit of $2,000 per year ($4,000 for a two-worker couple) to a retirement account. Contributions to these accounts were made deductible from taxable income, with taxes paid as withdrawals are made after retirement. Accumulated interest on IRA accounts was also made tax-free until withdrawal.[8]

In the second Reagan administration, the centerpiece was *tax reform*—touted by President Reagan as a "second American Revolution." The aims of tax reform were, first, to broaden the tax *base* by eliminating many deductible items and, second, to reduce *marginal tax rates*. The combination of these actions was to be offsetting, so that total revenues would neither rise nor fall. However, lower marginal tax rates would improve incentives for labor supply, saving, and investment.

Congress passed a tax reform act in August 1986 that reflected not only the president's wishes but also the goals of tax reformers in Congress from both political parties. The act lowered the highest tax rate from 50 percent to 28 percent, the lowest top rate since 1931. Moreover, it created only two tax rates, 15 percent (on income up to approximately $30,000 on a joint return) and 28 percent.[9] The act also raised personal exemptions so that approximately 6 million low-income recipients were removed from the tax rolls. To keep tax reform from reducing tax revenues, the act removed many deductions and eliminated a number of tax shelters.

Reductions in Business Taxes

The first Reagan administration's tax act had several features aimed at encouraging capital formation by increasing the after-tax return to investment. The most important of these was the accelerated cost recovery system (ACRS), which was a set of accelerated depreciation allowances for business plant and equipment. For example, a piece of equipment that could have been depreciated over an 8.6-year period under the previous tax law could be depreciated over a 5-year period under the act's provisions. In addition, the investment tax credit for certain types of equipment was increased to encourage capital formation.

---

[8]The Tax Reform Act of 1986 established an income threshold above which IRA contributions were non-deductible from taxable income. Interest was still tax-free until withdrawal, regardless of income. In 1997, further changes were made in IRAs.

[9]The tax rate for high-income taxpayers was raised in 1993 to 39 percent as part of the Clinton deficit reduction plan.

These business tax cuts were aimed at offsetting the inflation-induced increase in the effective tax rate on business profits, which was discussed in section 20.2. Such tax cuts are consistent with the supply-side view (proposition 2) that the way to encourage capital formation is by increasing the after-tax return to investment.

Reductions in Nondefense Government Spending

According to the supply-side view, personal and business tax cuts should increase aggregate supply and, therefore, produce noninflationary real output growth. Also, supply-siders hoped that such growth would increase the tax base and therefore increase tax revenues to offset, in large part (or completely), the revenue lost due to the lower tax rates. However, to ensure that demand was not overly stimulated and to keep the budget deficit as small as possible, the Reagan program proposed cuts in nondefense government spending in areas such as housing, education, and income maintenance programs. Such cuts were also needed, in part, to finance a proposed increase in defense spending.

After some early success, cuts in nondefense spending met more resistance. Given the increase in defense spending, the overall lack of much success in cutting nondefense spending meant that government spending as a percentage of GNP *rose* rather than fell during President Reagan's first term. Failure to cut spending, together with tax reduction, led to high government budget deficits in both the first and second terms of the Reagan administration.

Reductions in Government Regulation

Consistent with the supply-side view that government regulation in areas such as air quality, worker safety, and consumer product safety has been overly costly and has retarded economic growth (proposition 4), the Reagan administration began a regulatory review. The aim was to eliminate "wasteful or outdated regulation and to make necessary regulation more efficient and more flexible." Some specific regulatory initiatives in the first Reagan administration shifted some responsibilities for air pollution control to the states, decontrol of petroleum markets, proposals to abolish the Departments of Energy and Education, and an executive order calling for a cost-benefit analysis before issuing any new federal regulation.

Initiatives in the Bush Administration

President George (H. W.) Bush was at first highly critical of supply-side economics, terming it "voodoo economics." Moreover, when he took office in 1989, both houses of Congress had substantial Democratic majorities that had always been skeptical of supply-side policy prescriptions. Still, some of Bush's proposals were certainly consistent with supply-side positions.

When he ran for president in 1988, a central plank in Bush's economic platform was his pledge of "no new taxes." This pledge conformed to the supply-side view of the disincentive effects of higher taxes. Unfortunately from a supply-sider's view, as the budget deficit ballooned in 1990 and 1991, Bush abandoned this pledge to reach a deficit reduction compromise with Congress. A second Bush proposal was to lower the capital gains tax. The supply-side analysis suggests that such a reduction would have a favorable effect on saving and thus on capital formation. Bush was, however, unable to push a capital gains tax cut through Congress.

Growth Policies During the Clinton Administrations

In 1992, the public appeared to choose a new direction in macroeconomic policy. Clintonomics would replace Reaganomics. President Bill Clinton's program envisioned a more activist role for government, one that "recognizes both the market's efficiencies *and* its imperfections." He proposed a "stimulus package" consisting of public investment in infrastructure, worker retraining, and partnerships between business and government to move resources from "sunset" to "sunrise" industries.

Given concern about the large government budget deficit at the time, Congress was unwilling to pass the stimulus package. Prospects for such an activist approach became even bleaker when voters returned Republican majorities to both houses of Congress in the 1994 election. In that election, the House Republicans' "Contract with America," with its provisions for cuts in taxes and spending, a line item veto, a moratorium on new federal regulation, and a constitutional amendment to balance the budget, was rooted in supply-side economics. But, with the exception of the line item veto, House Republicans were unable to achieve veto-proof margins for the elements of their program; gridlock developed over budget issues, and at one point there was a temporary shutdown of much of the federal government.

After President Clinton was reelected and Republican majorities were returned to the House and Senate in the 1996 election, both sides were ready for compromise. Republicans got tax cuts, including the long-sought reduction in the capital gains tax. Provisions for IRA accounts were liberalized to make them more desirable and so encourage saving. President Clinton limited the extent of tax cuts and targeted some of them toward subsidizing education and worker retraining.

Most importantly, during President Clinton's second term, budget agreements were reached that led to perennial deficits being replaced by surpluses and (at that time) even larger projected future budget surpluses. The role this change in the federal budget played in the stronger performance of the U.S. economy in the late 1990s is still controversial.

U.S. economic growth was strong in the late 1990s, and the rate of growth in labor productivity rose (see Table 20.1). But factors other than fiscal policy were also at work. Many attribute the strong performance of the U.S. economy during these years to the revolution in information technology and to the conduct of monetary policy. Stronger growth in labor productivity, and thus output growth, in the United States relative to other industrialized countries is attributed to faster U.S. implementation of advances in information technology.

Tax Cuts During the Administration of George W. Bush

In 2000, George W. Bush won a very close election. From the start of his administration, tax cuts were the centerpiece of economic policy. At first, during the recession of 2001, tax cuts were offered as a short-run stimulus for recovery. The central motivation for the tax cuts was, however, to stimulate growth over the medium term. Even after the recovery was well underway, new tax cuts were passed and more proposed for the future. The economic rationale offered for these tax cuts draws heavily from the proposition of supply-side economics. In fact, it is often said that on economic policy, George W. Bush is the heir of Ronald Reagan, not his father George W. H. Bush.

The packages of tax cuts passed by 2004 included cuts in the income tax, cuts in the tax on corporate dividends and capital gains, and abolition of inheritance tax. The income tax cuts were expected to have a positive effect on labor supply and therefore aggregate supply (the reverse of the effects of a tax increase in Figure 20.4). The reduction of the capital gains tax and tax on dividends were aimed at increasing saving and investment by raising the after-tax return to these activities (the reverse of the effect of negative changes in these rates of return, illustrated in Figure 20.3). The inheritance tax affected very few estates, so it is hard to see significant supply-side effects from its abolition.

Keynesians, as well as a number of other economists, opposed tax cuts of the size favored by President Bush, especially after the recovery from the 2001 recession became robust. As we saw in Chapter 19, the tax cuts were by 2004 responsible for large current and projected future structural federal budget deficits. Keynesians argued that the deficits would push up interest rates and cancel out any beneficial effects on saving and investment. Keynesians also remained doubtful that income tax cuts have significant effects on labor supply. Another ground on which many criticized the tax cuts was their effect on income distribution. Tax cuts on capital gains, dividends, and inheritances directly benefit the wealthy, who are the main recipients of these forms of income and wealth.

Read Perspectives 20.3.

PERSPECTIVES 20.3
Labor Productivity and the Jobless Recovery

A major issue in the presidential election campaign of 2004 has been the slow job growth during the first two years of the recovery from the 2001 recession—what has been called the "jobless recovery." To see why the recovery has been characterized this way, consider Figure 20.6. The figure shows output and employment growth over the years since 1980. The difference between the two series measures growth in labor productivity (output growth minus employment growth). Notice that during recoveries from the 1982 and 1990 recession employment growth picked up shortly after the turnaround in output growth. The figure also shows the high growth in labor productivity in the last half of the 1990s; output growth is substantially above employment growth during those years.

Now look at the plot for 2001–2003. Output growth picks up, but employment continues to decline. Output growth outpacing employment growth by so much indicates a very rapid increase in labor productivity. Such a large increase in labor productivity would be expected to lead to faster growth in real wages and to stimulate future growth in hiring by firms. Neither of these was happening in 2002 or 2003, thus the term *jobless recovery*.

Especially given the political campaign, there has been no shortage of explanations for the slow job growth over this period. But it is, in fact, too soon to know why the labor market has behaved in this way. Perhaps the lag in the pickup in job creation was just especially long in this recovery, but there may be more important structural changes taking place.

Figure 20.6 Output and Employment Growth (1980–2003)

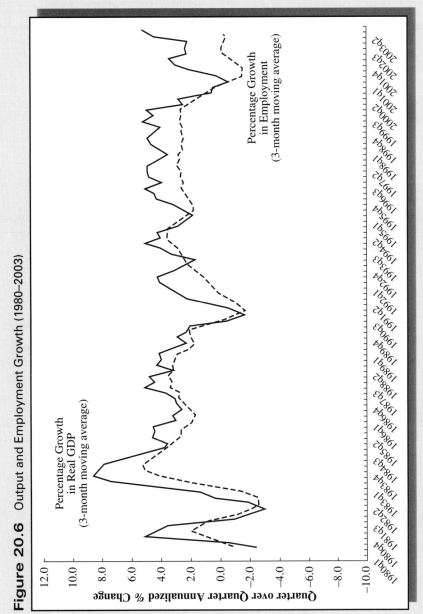

Source: Survey of Current Business.

20.5 CONCLUSION

Even modest changes in the rate of economic growth have large cumulative effects over periods of several decades. Proper policy to help "grow" the economy is an important and controversial subject for economic analysis. Public opinion, and therefore public policy, has shifted several times as to the best approach to fostering economic growth. The proposals of supply-side economics have been central to this debate.

REVIEW QUESTIONS AND PROBLEMS

1. Outline the main features of a supply-sider's prescription for policies to foster noninflationary economic growth. How do these policy prescriptions differ from those of the Keynesians?
2. Compare the Keynesian and supply-siders' positions on the effects of reduction in the income tax rate.
3. Compare the Keynesian and supply-siders' positions on the determinants of saving, investment, and capital formation.
4. Within the supply-side theory, what is the proper role for aggregate demand management policies?
5. An investment tax credit allows firms to deduct a portion of investment spending from their corporate tax liability. Analyze the effect on output of such a tax credit in the Keynesian model and, alternatively, within the supply-side framework.
6. Outline recent (post-1995) trends in U.S. growth rates in GDP and labor productivity. What are the possible factors responsible for these trends?
7. Use the *IS–LM* and aggregate demand–aggregate supply diagrams to present the case in favor of the George W. Bush administration tax cuts as a stimulus to growth. What criticisms would Keynesian economists put forward to refute this case?

Microeconomic Foundations

*T*he two chapters in this part examine microeconomic foundations and extensions for some of the relationships in the models of Parts I and II. Chapter 21 considers consumption and investment. In Chapter 22 we take a more detailed look at money demand.

Chapter 21

Consumption and Investment

*T*his chapter provides a detailed look at the private sector's demand for output. First we consider household consumption (section 21.1), then we turn to investment spending (section 21.2).

21.1 CONSUMPTION

Early Empirical Evidence on the Keynesian Consumption Function

Household consumption expenditures account for approximately two-thirds of gross domestic product (GDP). In Part II, we saw that the consumption-to-income relationship—the consumption function—is a key element in the Keynesian theory of income determination. The starting point for Keynes's theory of consumer behavior is the following:

> The fundamental psychological law, upon which we are entitled to depend with great confidence both *a priori* from our knowledge of human nature and from the detailed facts of experience, is that men are disposed, as a rule and on the average, to increase their consumption as their income increases, but not by as much as the increase in their income.[1]

This psychological law translates into the Keynesian consumption function:

$$C = a + bY_D \qquad a > 0, \qquad 0 < b < 1 \tag{21.1}$$

where C is real consumption and Y_D is real disposable income, which equals real GDP minus taxes (and other adjustments). The parameter b is the marginal propensity to consume (MPC), the increase in consumption per unit increase in disposable

---

[1]John M. Keynes, *The General Theory of Employment, Interest and Money* (New York: Harcourt, Brace and Company, 1936), p. 96.

446

Figure 21.1
Keynesian Consumption Function

The Keynesian consumption function shows consumption as a function of disposable income. The intercept (a) gives the level of consumption corresponding to a zero level of disposable income. The slope of the consumption function (b) is the marginal propensity to consume ($\Delta C / \Delta Y_D$).

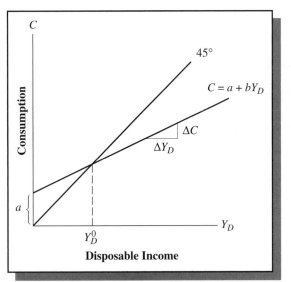

income ($\Delta C / \Delta Y_D$). The intercept, a, measures consumption at a zero level of disposable income. The consumption function (21.1) is shown in Figure 21.1.

Because of the intercept, the Keynesian consumption function is not a proportional relationship between consumption and income; that is, consumption is not a constant fraction of disposable income. The ratio of consumption to income is termed the **average propensity to consume (APC)**, which from equation (21.1) is given by

average propensity to consume (APC)
the ratio of consumption to disposable income

$$APC = \frac{C}{Y_D} = \frac{a}{Y_D} + b \qquad \text{(21.2)}$$

The APC is greater than the MPC by the amount a/Y_D. It also follows from equation (21.2) that the APC declines as income increases. The implication is that, as income rises, households consume a smaller fraction of income, which is to say that they save a larger fraction of income. The ratio of saving to income is termed the **average propensity to save (APS)** and is equal to (1 − APC),

average propensity to save (APS)
the ratio of saving to disposable income

$$APS = 1 - \frac{a}{Y_D} - b = \frac{-a}{Y_D} + (1 - b) \qquad \text{(21.3)}$$

which can be seen to increase as disposable income rises. In Figure 21.1, below the income level Y_D^0, consumption exceeds disposable income. In this range, the APC is greater than 1, and the APS is negative. Above Y_D^0, the APC is less than 1, and the APS is positive. Total consumption increases less than proportionately with Y_D, so the APC declines and the APS rises as we move to higher income levels in the graph.

The version of the consumption function just described is called the *absolute income hypothesis*; consumption reacts mechanically to current income. Keynes advanced this hypothesis about consumption on the basis of "knowledge of human nature" and "detailed facts of experience." His followers attempted to provide a stronger empirical basis for this form of the consumption function, with mixed results.

Using statistical techniques and annual data for a short period, 1929–41, Keynesian economists obtained the following type of estimate for the consumption function:[2]

$$C = 26.5 + 0.75Y_D \qquad (21.4)$$

In equation (21.4), the estimate of the MPC (b) is 0.75, and the estimate of the intercept (a) is \$26.5 billion. The positive value of the intercept (a) confirmed the Keynesian view that the APC ($a/Y_D + b$) exceeded the MPC (b). Equation (21.4) implies that the APC declines as income rises. At a level of disposable income equal to \$100 billion, the APC estimated from equation (21.4) would be 1.015 ($26.5/100 + 0.75$), implying that the APS is negative (-0.015), but at an income level of 200, the APC would be 0.883 ($26.5/200 + 0.75$). An estimated consumption function such as equation (21.4) seemed to predict annual levels of consumer expenditures during this period (1929–41) reasonably well.

Further support for the Keynesian form of the consumption function came from comparative studies of family budgets. In the budgets of families at progressively higher incomes, the absolute amount of consumption increased ($b > 0$), but by less than the increase in income ($b < 1$). Also, families at higher income levels consumed a smaller proportion of income; the APC declined as income rose.

The fact that the proportion of income saved apparently increased as income rose led some early Keynesians to be concerned about secular stagnation in the economy. They worried that, as the ratio of saving to income increased, aggregate demand would fall short of output. Recall that saving is a *leakage* from the circular flow of income and expenditure. Aggregate demand would be inadequate unless the fall in the C/Y_D ratio (rise in the S/Y_D ratio) were balanced by growth in the other components of aggregate demand: government spending and investment. These economists feared that, in the absence of such growth, aggregate demand would fall short of full-employment output, resulting in stagnation.[3] Whether a secular decline in the ratio of consumption to income would have led to chronically deficient levels of aggregate demand is a matter of conjecture. It turns out that, despite continued growth in real income in the United States and other industrialized countries, there has been no tendency for the APC to decline and the APS to rise. The shares of consumption and saving in income have been relatively constant for over a century, as became apparent when estimates of income shares extending back into the nineteenth century became available in the early post-World War II period.

Data from an early study by Simon Kuznets for real national income (Y), real consumption (C), and the ratio of the two (C/Y) are given in Table 21.1. The data are overlapping decade averages of annual figures. As can be seen from the table, there was no downward trend in the ratio of consumption to income even though national income grew from an average of \$9.3 billion in the 1869–78 decade to \$72.0 billion in

---

[2]Gardner Ackley, *Macroeconomic Theory* (New York: Macmillan, 1961), p. 226.
[3]For an example of the stagnationist thesis, see Alvin Hansen, "Economic Progress and Declining Population Growth," *American Economic Review*, 29 (March 1939), pp. 1–15.

Table 21.1
Consumption and National Income, 1869–1938

YEARS	Y	C	C/Y
1869–78	9.3	8.1	0.87
1874–83	13.6	11.6	0.85
1879–88	17.9	15.3	0.85
1884–93	21.0	17.7	0.84
1889–98	24.2	20.2	0.83
1894–1903	29.8	25.4	0.85
1899–1908	37.3	32.3	0.87
1904–13	45.0	39.1	0.87
1909–18	50.6	44.0	0.87
1914–23	57.3	50.7	0.88
1919–28	69.0	62.0	0.90
1924–33	73.3	68.9	0.94
1929–38	72.0	71.0	0.99

Note: Y, national income, billions of dollars; C, consumption expenditure, billions of dollars.

Source: Simon Kuznets, *National Product Since 1869* (New York: National Bureau of Economic Research, 1946), p. 119.

the 1929–38 decade. Nor is there evidence of a downward trend in the APC in more recent years. The APC (C/Y_D) was 0.93 in 1950, 0.89 in 1970, 0.93 in 1990, and 0.94 in 2000. The Kuznets data, as well as later estimates, strongly suggest that the long-run relationship between consumption and income is proportional, as illustrated in Figure 21.2.

In addition, data from the early post-World War II period showed that quarter-to-quarter changes in consumption were not well explained by quarter-to-quarter movements in income. Gardner Ackley, for example, examined 22 quarter-to-quarter changes

Figure 21.2
Long-Run Consumption Function

As indicated by the data going back to the nineteenth century, the long-run consumption function is a proportional relationship, in which MPC = APC, both approximately 0.9.

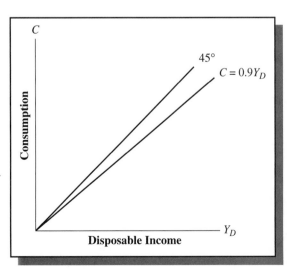

in consumption and income. He found that in five quarters the changes in consumption and income were in opposite directions. In 10 of the cases in which consumption and income did change in the same direction, the change in consumption *exceeded* the change in income. In only 7 of the 22 quarters were the movements in consumption and income consistent with a short-run MPC ($\Delta C/\Delta Y_D$) that was positive and less than 1.[4] This erratic short-run behavior of consumption indicated that either the relationship of consumption to current income in the short run was not as mechanical as predicted by the absolute income hypothesis or that other variables were influencing consumption behavior.

We can summarize the early evidence about the consumption function as follows. Evidence from short-run annual time series data and family budget studies seemed to support the Keynesian hypothesis about consumption—the absolute income hypothesis—as represented by equation (21.1). Time series data for a longer time period (e.g., 1869–1938) suggest that the consumption–income relationship is proportional, rather than nonproportional as given by (21.1). There is, therefore, a need to reconcile long-run evidence on the consumption function with the short-run time series evidence and cross-sectional evidence from family budget studies. Finally, erratic quarter-to-quarter movements of consumption relative to income cast doubt on the closeness of the consumption–income relationship in the short run. Resolving these puzzles posed by the early empirical evidence on consumer behavior has been the task of the modern theory of the consumption function.

To see how post-Keynesian consumption theories have tried to reconcile the disparate implications from different data sources, we consider one theory, the *life cycle hypothesis*, in detail. We then compare the conclusions of this theory with another explanation of the same phenomena, Milton Friedman's *permanent income hypothesis*.

The Life Cycle Hypothesis of Consumption

life cycle hypothesis asserts that saving and consumption decisions of households reflect a plan for an optimal consumption pattern over their lifetime, subject to the constraint of their resources

The **life cycle hypothesis** was developed by Franco Modigliani, Albert Ando, and Richard Brumberg.[5] As stated by Modigliani:

The point of departure of the life cycle model is the hypothesis that consumption and saving decisions of households at each point of time reflect a more or less conscious attempt at achieving the preferred distribution of consumption over the life cycle, subject to the constraint imposed by the resources accruing to the household over its lifetime.[6]

---

[4]See Ackley, *Macroeconomic Theory*, pp. 253–54.

[5]Two early papers on the life cycle hypothesis are Franco Modigliani and Richard Brumberg, "Utility Analysis and the Consumption Function: An Interpretation of Cross Section Data," in K. Kurihara, ed., *Post-Keynesian Economics* (New Brunswick, N.J.: Rutgers University Press, 1954), pp. 388–436; and Albert Ando and Franco Modigliani, "The Life Cycle Hypothesis of Saving: Aggregate Implications and Tests," *American Economic Review*, 53 (March 1963), pp. 55–84. For an evaluation of the performance of the life cycle hypothesis by one of its originators, see Franco Modigliani, "Life Cycle, Individual Thrift and the Wealth of Nations," *American Economic Review*, 76 (June 1986), pp. 297–313.

[6]Franco Modigliani, "The Life Cycle Hypothesis of Saving, the Demand for Wealth and the Supply of Capital," *Social Research*, 33 (June 1966), pp. 160–217, 162.

An individual or household's consumption depends not just on current income but also, and more importantly, on long-term expected income. Individuals are assumed to plan their expenditures based on expected earnings over their lifetime.

To see the implications of this theory, we first look at a simplified example. Consider a worker who has a life expectancy of T years and plans to remain in the labor force for N years. Our representative consumer might, for example, be 30 with a life expectancy of 50 (additional) years, plan to retire after 40 years, and therefore have expected years in retirement equal to $(T - N)$, or 10. To keep the example simple, we make the following assumptions about the individual's plans. We assume the individual desires a constant consumption flow throughout life. Further, we assume that this person intends to consume the total amount of lifetime earnings plus current assets and that he plans no bequests. Finally, we assume that interest paid on assets is zero; current saving results in dollar-for-dollar future consumption.

These assumptions imply that consumption in a given period will be a constant proportion, $1/T$, of expected *lifetime* resources. The individual plans to consume lifetime earnings in T equal installments. The consumption function implied by this simple version of the life cycle hypothesis is

$$C_t = \frac{1}{T}\left[Y_t^1 + (N - 1)\overline{Y}^{1e} + A_t\right] \qquad (21.5)$$

C_t is consumption in time period t. The term in brackets is expected lifetime resources, which consist of

Y_t^1 = the individual's labor income in the current time period (t)
$\overline{Y}^{1e}$ = the average annual labor income expected over the future $(N - 1)$
    years during which the individual plans to work
A = the value of presently held assets

Equation (21.5) indicates that, according to the life cycle hypothesis, consumption depends not only on current income but also on expected future income and current asset holdings (i.e., current wealth). In fact, the life cycle hypothesis suggests that consumption would be quite unresponsive to changes in current income (Y_t^1) that did not also change average expected future income. From equation (21.5), for example, we can compute

$$\frac{\Delta C_t}{\Delta Y_t^1} = \frac{1}{T} = \frac{1}{50} = 0.02$$

An increase in income that was expected to persist throughout the work years would mean that $\overline{Y}^{1e}$ also rose and that the effect on consumption would be much greater:

$$\frac{\Delta C_t}{\Delta Y_t^1} + \frac{\Delta C_t}{\Delta \overline{Y}^{1e}} = \frac{1}{T} + \frac{N-1}{T} = \frac{N}{T} = \frac{40}{50} = 0.8$$

A one-time or transient change in income of, say, $100 will have the same effect as a change in wealth (note that $\Delta C_t / \Delta Y_t^1 = \Delta C_t / \Delta A_t = 1/T$) of the same amount. Lifetime resources will go up by $100, and this will be spread out in a planned consumption

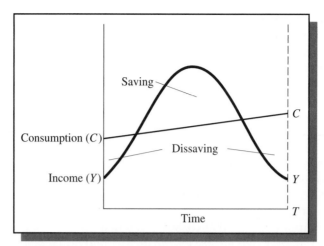

Figure 21.3 Income and Consumption over the Life Cycle

Consumption rises gradually over the life cycle. Income rises sharply over the early working years, peaks, and then declines, especially with retirement. This pattern of consumption and income results in dissaving in the early working years and the late stage of the life cycle, with positive saving over the high-income middle years of the life cycle.

flow of $100/T = 100/50 = 2$ per period in our example of an individual who expects to live for 50 additional years. A permanent increase in income of \$100 will lead to an increase in consumption of \$80 in each of the remaining periods, including the 10 planned periods of retirement. The increase of \$80 in each of these 10 retirement years, a total of \$800, is financed by a saving of \$20 $(100 - 80)$ in each of the 40 remaining working years.

The life cycle hypothesis accounts for the dependence of consumption and saving on the individual's position in the life cycle. Young workers entering the labor force have relatively low incomes and low (possibly negative) saving rates. As income rises in middle-age years, so does the saving rate. Retirement brings a fall in income and a period of *dissaving* (negative saving rates). This time profile of consumption and saving is depicted in Figure 21.3. Here the desired pattern of consumption rises mildly with time instead of maintaining the constant desired consumption pattern assumed in our individual example. The pattern of income rises more sharply, though, and the typical individual smooths out consumption flow by a short period of early dissaving, a period of positive saving, and then a longer period of dissaving in retirement.

The general form of the aggregate consumption function implied by the life cycle hypothesis is

$$C_t = b_1 Y_t^1 + b_2 \overline{Y}^{1e} + b_3 A_t \tag{21.6}$$

where the variables C_t, Y_t^1, $\overline{Y}^{1e}$, and A_t are as defined for equation (21.5) but should now be interpreted as economy-wide averages. If the previous simplifying assumptions of no bequests, zero interest on saving, and a uniform consumption pattern over time are relaxed, the parameters b_1, b_2, and b_3 will no longer be simple functions of N and T as were the coefficients in equation (21.5). Still, in the aggregate consumption function (21.6), as in the case of equation (21.5), consumption depends not just on current labor income (Y_t^1) but also on average future expected labor income $(\overline{Y}^{1e})$ and wealth (A_t). It will also be true in the aggregate, as in the simplified individual example, that the response to a *transient* or one-time increase in labor income (an increase in Y_t^1) will be quite small, much less than the response to a permanent income change (an increase in Y_t^1 and $\overline{Y}^{1e}$).

To study actual consumer behavior using equation (21.6), we must make some assumption about the way individuals form expectations concerning lifetime labor income. In a study for the United States, Ando and Modigliani assume that expected average future labor income is just a multiple of current labor income:

$$\overline{Y}^{1e} = \beta Y_t^1 \qquad \beta > 0 \qquad (21.7)$$

According to this specification, individuals revise their expectation of future expected labor income $\overline{Y}^{1e}$ by some proportion β of a change in current labor income. Substitution of equation (21.7) for $\overline{Y}^{1e}$ in the aggregate consumption function (21.6) yields

$$C_t = (b_1 + b_2\beta)Y_t^1 + b_3 A_t \qquad (21.8)$$

A representative statistical estimate of the equation based on the work of Ando and Modigliani is

$$C_t = 0.72Y_t^1 + 0.06A_t \qquad (21.9)$$

An increase in current labor income of $100 *with the assumed effect on future labor income* will increase consumption by $72. An increase in wealth of $100 will increase consumption by $6. As noted previously, an increase in income that was known to be temporary and therefore would *not* affect future expected labor income would have the same effect as an increase in wealth. Thus, according to this estimate, the MPC out of such a transient income flow is on the order of 0.06, the MPC out of wealth.

The life cycle hypothesis can explain the puzzles that emerged from the early empirical work on consumption functions. According to the life cycle hypothesis, the relationship between consumption and current income would be nonproportional, as seems to be the case in *short-run* time series estimates [see equation (21.4)]. The intercept of the function measures the effect of wealth [$0.06A_t$ in equation (21.9)]. But the intercept is not constant over time; such short-run consumption functions shift upward as wealth grows. These upward shifts in the short-run consumption function (SCF) are illustrated in Figure 21.4. The shifting short-run consumption functions trace out a long-run consumption function (LCF).

If the ratios of wealth and labor income to disposable personal income are relatively constant over time, the life cycle consumption function [equation (21.9)] is also consistent with the evidence from long-run time series data that the long-run consumption–income relationship (LCF in Figure 21.4) is proportional, with the APC (C/Y_D) relatively stable in the neighborhood of 0.9. To see this relationship, first note that the ratio of labor income to disposable personal income has been approximately

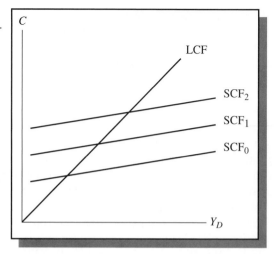

Figure 21.4
Short-Run and Long-Run Consumption Functions

As wealth increases over time, the non-proportional short-run consumption function (SCF) shifts upward (from SCF_0 to SCF_1, then to SCF_2) to trace out the long-run proportional consumption income relationship (LCF).

0.88—that is, $Y_t^1 = 0.88Y_D$. The ratio of wealth to disposable income is approximately 4.75; $A_t = 4.75Y_D$. Substituting these expressions for A_t and Y_t^1 in the estimated aggregate consumption function (21.9) yields

$$C_t = 0.72(0.88Y_D) + 0.06(4.75Y_D)$$
$$= 0.63Y_D + 0.29Y_D$$
$$= 0.92Y_D$$

or

$$\frac{C_t}{Y_D} = 0.92$$

which is approximately the average value of the APC over the post-World War II period.

The life cycle hypothesis also explains evidence from cross-sectional family budget studies showing that higher-income families consume a smaller proportion of their income than do lower-income families. A larger proportion of high-income families might be expected to be in their peak earning years—that is, in the "humped" portion of Figure 21.3. In this range, according to the life cycle hypothesis, income should exceed consumption by the greatest amount, and the APC should be the lowest. Conversely, a sample of low-income families would have a high proportion of new entrants to the labor market and retirees, both groups that tend to dissave. These groups with high APCs would push up the APC for the sample of low-income families.

Finally, the life cycle hypothesis explains why quarter-to-quarter movements in consumption do not closely mirror quarter-to-quarter movements in income, the other anomalous finding of early research on the consumption function. The change in income from any given quarter to the next will be partly the result of one-time factors that will not affect individuals' perceptions of lifetime average income. We have seen that transient income changes have little impact on consumer behavior according to the life cycle hypothesis.

Critics of the Life Cycle Hypothesis

Although the life cycle hypothesis explains several features of the consumption–income relationship, the approach is not without its critics.

One criticism of the life cycle approach is that it fails to recognize the importance of *liquidity constraints*. Even if a household possessed a vision of future income, there may be little opportunity in capital markets for borrowing on the basis of expected future income. As a result, consumption may be more responsive to changes in current income, whether temporary or not, than would be predicted by the life cycle hypothesis. The response of consumption to current income may not be the simple mechanical one predicted by the "absolute income" hypothesis. The consumption pattern of younger households facing liquidity constraints may be very responsive to changes in current income. The consumption of older households with more accumulated wealth may not be responsive to temporary variations in current income. Small, temporary changes in income may be financed out of a buffer of liquid assets, but larger changes may cause liquidity constraints to become binding and begin to affect consumption behavior. Consideration of liquidity constraints on households, therefore, leads us to believe that current income may be a more important influence on consumption than would be predicted on the basis of the life cycle hypothesis, but the consumption-to-current-income relationship may be more complex than that implied by Keynes's absolute income hypothesis. Statistical work does, in fact, suggest the importance of liquidity constraints in explaining the considerable response of consumption to current income.[7]

Other research emphasizes the importance of bequests in determining saving, rather than the life cycle motive, which emphasizes saving to finance consumption in retirement. A study by Laurence Kotlikoff and Lawrence Summers concluded that the desire to make bequests was the most important motive for saving.[8] Franco Modigliani has disputed the Kotlikoff and Summers evidence. To him, the data suggest that only 15 to 20 percent of saving is for bequests; the bulk is life cycle saving.[9]

Read Perspectives 21.1.

Policy Implications of the Life Cycle Hypothesis

The consumption function is an important element in Keynesian macroeconomic theory. Fluctuations in the unstable investment component of aggregate demand are amplified and transmitted throughout the economy by the induced consumption response to the initial income change; this is the multiplier process. A change in government spending would have multiplier effects, again through induced effects on consumption. A change in taxes would affect disposable income and therefore consumption, but this effect was also predicated on the absolute income hypothesis

---

[7]See Marjorie Flavin, "Excess Sensitivity of Consumption to Current Income," *Canadian Journal of Economics*, 18 (February 1985), pp. 117–36, and "The Adjustment of Consumption to Changing Expectations about Future Income," *Journal of Political Economy*, 89 (October 1981), pp. 974–1009.

[8]Laurence J. Kotlikoff and Lawrence H. Summers, "The Role of Integenerational Transfers in Aggregate Capital Accumulation," *Journal of Political Economy*, 89 (August 1981), pp. 706–32.

[9]See Franco Modigliani, "The Role of Intergenerational Transfers and Life Cycle Saving in the Accumulation of Wealth"; and Laurence Kotlikoff, "Intergenerational Transfers and Savings," *Journal of Economic Perspectives*, 2 (Spring 1988), pp. 15–58.

PERSPECTIVES 21.1

Declining U.S. Personal Saving

Whether saving is primarily for life cycle reasons or the bequest motive, the U.S. personal (household) saving rate fell during the post-1985 period. This decrease can be seen from Figure 21.5, which shows U.S. personal saving as a percentage of disposable income for the years 1959–2002. The decline in saving has been a concern, because saving provides funds required to finance investment and consequently capital formation. The decline in saving has also been surprising because Reagan administration tax policies contained several features aimed at strengthening the incentives to save.

Several explanations have been offered for the decline in the saving rate.[a] One consistent with the life cycle hypothesis is that increased Social Security benefits have reduced the need to save for retirement years. Another explanation is that increased access to borrowing (e.g., credit card borrowing, home equity loans) has decreased saving for future purchases of durable goods. A third explanation is that the growing number of two-income families, in which the chance that both wage earners will become unemployed is small, has reduced saving for a "rainy day."

In the 1990s, when the U.S. saving rate really seemed to dive, another factor was at work as a result of the way U.S. income and wealth accounts are structured. The value of U.S. corporate equities rose dramatically in the 1990s. Because of this increase in wealth, households spent more. But capital gains on existing stock holdings are not

Figure 21.5 U.S. Personal Saving Rate, 1959–2002

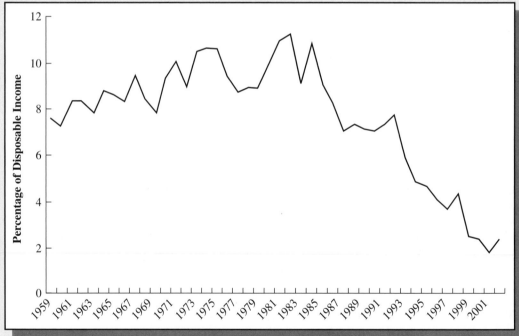

---

[a]See the discussion in Lawrence Summers and Chris Carroll, "Why Is U.S. National Saving So Low?" *Brookings Papers on Economic Activity*, 2 (1987), pp. 607–35.

about consumer expenditures. In this subsection, we examine the changes required in the Keynesian analysis of the multiplier process and the effects of fiscal policy when consumption is assumed to be determined according to the life cycle hypothesis instead of the absolute income hypothesis. We also consider the implications of the life cycle hypothesis for the effectiveness of monetary policy.

Fiscal Policy and the Multiplier Process

The key element in the Keynesian analysis of the multiplier effects of changes in investment or fiscal policy variables is the response of consumption to current income. According to the life cycle hypothesis, consumption is determined primarily by expected lifetime income and wealth. A change in current income, of itself, has little influence on consumer behavior. In the empirical work of Ando and Modigliani discussed previously, expected future income is assumed to be proportional to current income. If this assumption is correct, we would expect a strong response of consumption to current income, because changes in current income cause proportional changes in expected lifetime income as well. Ando and Modigliani's estimate of the consumption function [equation (21.9)] implies that the MPC out of current labor income is 0.72. This value is high enough to imply strong effects for changes in taxes and government spending. In other empirical work by Modigliani, expected lifetime income is assumed instead to depend on a weighted average of the past 12 quarters' income.[10] With this assumption as well, the response of consumption to income was strong enough to produce results consistent with earlier Keynesian analysis. The life cycle hypothesis does not, therefore, imply an essential modification of the Keynesian multiplier or fiscal policy analysis.

One modification is required in the Keynesian view of fiscal policy if the life cycle hypothesis is adopted in place of the absolute income version of the consumption function. According to the life cycle hypothesis, current income has a strong effect on consumption only if changes in current income affect expected average lifetime income. This is not the case when the change in current income is known to be transient, as it would be with a temporary change in tax rates or government transfer payments.

Even temporary tax changes may have strong effects, however, if liquidity constraints are important in determining consumption, as discussed previously. If a household would choose a higher level of consumption if it were not constrained by

---

[10]See Franco Modigliani, "Monetary Policy and Consumption," in *Consumer Spending and Monetary Policy*.

the amount that can be borrowed, then even a one-time tax rebate would increase consumption substantially. The rebate would reduce the liquidity constraint. Regarding the efficacy of temporary tax changes, therefore, the crucial issue is the importance of liquidity constraints.

Monetary Policy and Consumption

In our analysis of monetary policy effects, the main focus was on investment. The life cycle hypothesis implies that monetary policy has important direct effects on consumption as well. According to the life cycle hypothesis, household wealth is one of the main determinants of consumption. Monetary policy affects wealth and therefore consumption. Monetary policy actions affect wealth primarily by affecting interest rates and consequently the market value of assets, such as government and private bonds and corporate equities (stocks). In Chapter 7, we analyzed the relationship between the interest rate and the market value of bonds. An increase in the interest rate resulting from a tight money policy causes bond prices to fall and, hence, households to suffer capital losses on bonds. A decline in interest rates resulting from an expansionary monetary policy causes bond prices to rise, with resulting capital gains on bonds. Equity prices are also expected to move inversely with interest rates. Equities pay streams of dividends, and with higher market interest rates, the price that investors are willing to pay for an equity with a given dividend flow falls.

Tight money policies therefore reduce wealth and consumption, whereas expansionary policies have the opposite effects. Empirical work by Modigliani, mentioned previously, indicates that effects on consumption are a large component of the overall effects of monetary policy.

The hypothesis that liquidity constraints are important provides an additional channel by which monetary policy might affect consumption. Tight money policies result in larger down-payment requirements and stricter credit standards for consumer credit, thus increasing the severity of the liquidity constraint facing many households. Expansionary monetary policies make credit more available and reduce liquidity constraints. An illustration of how consumption may be affected by liquidity constraints, whether real or only perceived, came in the spring of 1980. The Federal Reserve, in an effort to reduce the growth of consumer credit, instituted a number of credit controls. Apparently the public overreacted and feared that credit would simply become unavailable. Owing in part to this expected liquidity constraint, real consumer expenditure fell by 10.5 percent at an annual rate in the second quarter of 1980.

permanent income hypothesis
shares with the life cycle hypothesis the view that consumption depends on a long-term average of income earned from labor and asset holdings

The Permanent Income Hypothesis

An alternative explanation of consumer behavior is the **permanent income hypothesis** suggested by Milton Friedman.[11] This hypothesis shares with the life cycle hypothesis the assumption that long-term income is the primary determinant of consumption.

---

[11]Milton Friedman, *A Theory of the Consumption Function* (Princeton, N.J.: Princeton University Press, 1957).

Friedman's Consumption Function

Friedman postulates that consumption is proportional to permanent income:

$$C = \kappa Y^p \qquad\qquad \textbf{(21.10)}$$

where Y^p is permanent income and κ (Greek kappa) is the factor of proportionality ($\kappa > 0$). Permanent income is expected average long-term income from both "human and nonhuman wealth"—that is, both expected labor income (the return to human wealth or human capital) and expected earnings from asset holdings (nonhuman wealth).[12]

Friedman does not expect this equation to predict consumption perfectly. In addition to the part of consumption determined on the basis of permanent income, in any period there is a random element to consumption that Friedman terms "transitory" consumption. Similarly, in any period, there is a transitory component of income; measured income generally does not equal permanent income for the individual or in the aggregate. We can then write measured income (Y) as

$$Y = Y^p + Y^t$$

where Y^t is transitory income, which may be either positive or negative, causing measured income to exceed or fall short of permanent income. According to the permanent income hypothesis, only the permanent component of income influences consumption. Consumption, even the transitory component of consumption, is independent of transitory income.

As with the life cycle hypothesis, in order to implement the permanent income hypothesis, we must make an assumption about how individuals form long-term expectations about income. Friedman assumed that individuals revise their initial estimate of permanent income from period to period in the following manner:

$$Y_t^p = Y_{t-1}^p + j(Y_t - Y_{t-1}^p), \; 0 < j < 1 \qquad\qquad \textbf{(21.11)}$$

Equation (21.11) states that in each period individuals adjust their estimate of permanent income by a fraction j of the discrepancy between actual income in the current period and the prior period's estimate of permanent income. For example, suppose $j = 0.40$. Then, coming into 2000, assume that an individual estimated her permanent income to be \$30,000 (Y_{t-1}^p), but actual income in 2000 turned out to be \$40,000 (Y_t). From equation (21.11), we compute

$$
\begin{aligned}
Y_t^p &= \$30{,}000 + 0.40\,(\$40{,}000 - \$30{,}000)\\
&= \$34{,}000
\end{aligned}
$$

The individual assumes that 40 percent (\$4,000) of the deviation of actual income from the previous estimate of permanent income represents a change in permanent income, whereas the other 60 percent (\$6,000) is transitory income.

The permanent income hypothesis can explain the puzzles about the consumption–income relationship discussed earlier. The permanent income hypothesis is consistent

---

[12]Although here we drop the D subscript, which indicates disposable income, each of the income concepts discussed is net of taxes.

with the proportional long-run consumption function (APC is constant) and the non-proportional short-run consumption function (APC declines as Y increases) found in time series data. In the long run, income growth is dominated by changes in permanent income, with positive and negative transitory changes in income canceling out. The long-run consumption–income relationship will therefore be approximately the proportional relationship given by equation (21.10) with constant APC equal to κ. In the short run, years of high income will generally be years when the transitory component of income is positive. Because consumption rises only with increases in permanent income, in these high-income years the ratio of consumption to measured income [APC $= C/Y = C/(Y^p + Y^t)$] will be low. In low-income years when transitory income is generally negative, permanent income will be above measured income, and the ratio of consumption, which depends on permanent income, to measured income will be high (APC will be high).

Cross-sectional budget studies indicate that high-income families have a lower APC than low-income families, a finding that is also consistent with the permanent income hypothesis. A sample of high-income families at a given time is likely to contain more than a proportionate number of families experiencing positive transitory income flows ($Y^t > 0$). Because the consumption levels of these families depend only on their permanent incomes, the measured APCs for these families will be low, bringing down the average APC for the high-income group. On the other hand, a group of families with a low income at a given point in time will contain a disproportionate share of families with a negative transitory income component and hence a high measured APC. Consequently, the average APC for the low-income group will be pushed up.

Finally, the permanent income hypothesis is consistent with the failure of quarter-to-quarter movements of consumption to follow closely such short-run movements in income. Quarter-to-quarter income changes will contain many transitory changes to which consumption does not respond. Likewise, according to Friedman's hypothesis, there is a transitory component to consumption that is not related to income.

Policy Implications of the Permanent Income Hypothesis

The policy implications that follow from the permanent income hypothesis are similar to those of the life cycle hypothesis. With respect to fiscal policy and in particular to the Keynesian multiplier process, the crucial question again is whether consumption responds strongly to changes in *current* income. The short-run MPC, the change in consumption per unit change in current income, will be

$$\frac{\Delta C_t}{\Delta Y_t} = \kappa j \qquad (21.12)$$

that is, the long-run MPC out of permanent income ($\Delta C/\Delta Y^p$), κ, multiplied by the fraction by which the individual's estimate of permanent income is adjusted to a change in actual income, $j(\Delta Y_t^p/\Delta Y_t$; see equation 21.11). If individuals adjust their estimates of permanent income to changes in current income only slowly over time, j, and therefore the MPC out of current income, will be small. For example, if κ is 0.9 but j is 0.3, the MPC out of current income will be

$$\frac{\Delta C_t}{\Delta Y_t} = \kappa j = 0.9 \times 0.3 = 0.27$$

With a low MPC, a change in tax policy, for example, will not cause a large consumption response. In the Keynesian system, tax policy works by affecting current (disposable) income and therefore consumption (by means of the MPC). If the response of consumption to income is weak, changes in tax policy will be ineffective. However, if the estimate of permanent income is more responsive to a change in current income (j is high) or if a change in tax rates, perceived as permanent, independently causes such an estimate to be revised, tax policy, as well as other fiscal policies that depend on the Keynesian multiplier process, should be effective.

Rational Expectations and the Permanent Income Hypothesis

As formulated by Friedman, the permanent income hypothesis assumes that individual estimates of permanent income are formed in a *backward-looking* manner. This assumption is implied by equation (21.11), which states that individuals revise their estimates of permanent income on the basis of how *last* period's actual income differed from last period's estimate of permanent income. This type of backward-looking expectation is consistent with Friedman's treatment of expectations of inflation in his Phillips curve analysis (see section 11.2).

We saw in Chapter 12, however, that the new classical economists criticize the assumption of backward-looking expectations as naive. They propose instead that expectations are *rational* (or forward-looking). Expectations are formed by using all available relevant information and using it intelligently. What implications does the rational expectations assumption have for the permanent income hypothesis?

If expectations are rational, then all information available before the current period will already have been used to estimate permanent income. By implication, changes in consumption will come only as the result of *unanticipated* changes in income that cause changes in estimated permanent income.[13] Changes in consumption should come only with income surprises.

Some early research suggested that surprises in income explain changes in consumption better than actual changes in income. Later studies, however, were not favorable to this joint hypothesis. Consumption seems to respond too much to actual changes in income to be consistent with a response only to revisions in permanent income. This "excessive sensitivity" of consumption to changes in *actual* income may be due to liquidity constraints, which we discussed earlier. Households that have been unable to borrow previously, for example, will increase consumption if income increases, whether or not the increase was anticipated. On the other hand, research has shown that consumption responds less to unanticipated changes in income than is consistent with the rational expectations and permanent income hypotheses. Consumption is "excessively insensitive" to *unanticipated* changes in income.[14]

---

[13]The first to link the rational expectations hypothesis and the permanent income hypothesis was Robert Hall, "Stochastic Implications of the Life Cycle–Permanent Income Hypothesis: Theory and Evidence," *Journal of Political Economy*, 86 (December 1978), pp. 971–87.

[14]On these issues, see Alan Blinder and Angus Deaton, "The Time Series Consumption Function Revisited," *Brookings Papers on Economic Activity*, 16:2 (1985), pp. 465–521; Marjorie Flavin, "Excess Sensitivity of Consumption to Current Income," *Canadian Journal of Economics*, 18 (February 1985), pp. 117–36; and John Campbell and Angus Deaton, "Why Is Consumption So Smooth?" *Review of Economic Studies*, 56 (July 1989), pp. 357–74.

21.2 INVESTMENT SPENDING

Investment in the national income accounts includes business fixed investment (purchases of durable equipment and structures), residential construction investment, and changes in business inventories. For simplicity, our discussion of investment theory is confined to business fixed investment, the largest component of investment.

Business fixed investment is important in two respects. First, investment spending is a significant component of aggregate demand. The importance of investment to cyclical movements in income is even more than in proportion to its size as a share in GDP because it is one of the more volatile components of output. Data for (gross) business fixed investment as a percent of total output are given in Figure 21.6. The variability of business fixed investment as a share of output is evident from the figure, although in the post-World War II period this variability was considerably less than before the war. Over this postwar period, business fixed investment ranged between 9 and 13 percent of total output.

The second important macroeconomic role for business fixed investment follows from the fact that net fixed business investment measures the amount by which the stock of capital increases each period, that is,

$$K_t - K_{t-1} = I_{n,t} \tag{21.13}$$

where K is the capital stock and $I_{n,t}$ is *net* fixed investment. Business fixed investment is therefore important in the process of longer-run economic growth. In this chapter,

Figure 21.6 Business Fixed Investment as a Percentage of GDP, 1959–2002

we focus primarily on the role of investment as a component of aggregate demand. In Chapters 5 and 20, the role of investment in the growth process—the role of investment in changing aggregate supply over time—was examined.

In previous chapters, investment was assumed to depend negatively on the interest rate,

$$I = I(r) \tag{21.14}$$

Investment was also assumed to depend positively on the expected future profitability of investment projects. Here, we explain the effect on investment of changes in output. The role of the interest rate, as well as other factors that influence the cost of capital, is also discussed in more detail.

Investment and Output: The Accelerator Relationship

As just noted, net investment measures the change in the capital stock. Investment theories therefore first explain the desired stock of capital. Investment is explained as a response to deviations of the actual capital stock from the desired level. The desired capital stock depends on the level of output. Higher levels of output lead firms to demand a larger stock of capital, one of the factors used to produce output. The **accelerator model** is a simple representation of this relationship.

The accelerator model specifies the desired capital stock as a multiple of the level of output:

$$K_t^d = \alpha Y_t \qquad \alpha > 0 \tag{21.15}$$

In the simplest form of the accelerator model, net investment is equal to the difference between the desired capital stock and the stock of capital inherited from the preceding period. If we ignore depreciation of the existing capital stock, we have

$$I_{n,t} = K_t^d - K_{t-1} \tag{21.16}$$

The stock of capital inherited from the last period will be the desired capital stock based on output in the last period:

$$K_{t-1} = K_{t-1}^d = \alpha Y_{t-1} \tag{21.17}$$

Therefore, we can rewrite (21.16) as

$$I_{n,t} = K_t^d - K_{t-1} = \alpha Y_t - \alpha Y_{t-1} = \alpha(Y_t - Y_{t-1}) \tag{21.18}$$
$$I_{n,t} = \alpha \Delta Y_t$$

Investment depends on the *rate of change* in output.

This simple version suggests a crucial feature of the accelerator model. From (21.15), α can be seen to be the desired capital/output ratio:

$$\alpha = \frac{K_t^d}{Y_t} \tag{21.19}$$

accelerator model is a model of business investment that in its simplest form relates the level of investment to the rate of change in output. More complex forms take account of costs of adjustment and borrowing costs

Assume, for example, that this ratio is 2. In this case, every one-dollar change in the rate of growth in output (ΔY_t) will cause a two-dollar change in investment. Investment would then be expected to exhibit considerable instability over the business cycle. Further, recall from our discussion of the Keynesian model in Chapter 6 that changes in investment (in this case, as a result of changes in ΔY) have multiplier effects on income. Thus the simple accelerator theory, together with the multiplier process, can explain cyclical fluctuations in output.[15] A shock to output growth would cause investment to change, with resulting multiplier effects on output and therefore further effects on investment via the accelerator. As with the simple theory of the Keynesian multiplier in Chapter 6, however, considerable modification of the accelerator theory of investment is required before we can use it to explain investment in the real economy.

A first modification that makes the accelerator model more realistic is to allow for lags in the adjustment of the actual capital stock to the level of the desired capital stock. Suppose that the period to which we apply the model is a year. Also assume that, because of an increase in output, there is an increase in the desired capital stock. Investment projects will be planned to eliminate this discrepancy between the actual and desired capital stock. In addition to the direct cost of the investment projects, there will be *adjustment costs*, which, it is reasonable to assume, will rise quickly as the rate of investment is increased. Examples of such costs of adjustment include plant shutdowns or hiring of overtime labor to install equipment, extra cost of speeding plant construction (overtime, etc.), and disruption of production if management concentrates solely on expediting investment projects. If such costs of adjustment do rise as the pace of investment is quickened, it will be optimal for firms to adjust the actual capital stock to the desired capital stock slowly over time, closing only a portion of the gap between the two within one period.

To reflect this adjustment lag, we modify equation (21.16) as follows:

$$I_{n,t} = \lambda(K_t^d - K_{t-1}) \qquad 0 < \lambda < 1 \qquad \textbf{(21.20)}$$

Using (21.15), we have

$$I_{n,t} = \lambda(\alpha Y_t - K_{t-1}) \qquad \textbf{(21.21)}$$

where, because the actual capital stock is not equated to the desired capital stock in each period, K_{t-1} will *not* generally equal K_{t-1}^d. Equation (21.21) specifies a *partial adjustment* mechanism where a fraction, λ (lambda), of the gap between the desired and actual capital stock is filled each period by investment. Only a portion of the desired change in the capital stock is accomplished within one period, so in a given period investment will be responding to changes in income during a number of previous periods. Equation (21.21) implies a slower response of investment to changes in current income and hence implies that investment will be less volatile in the short run than it would be with the simple accelerator relationship [equation (21.18)]. Equation (21.21), which is termed the *flexible accelerator model* of investment, appears more consistent with the observed behavior of investment. Although investment is volatile, it is not as volatile as the simple accelerator model predicts.

---

[15]An early model of the interaction of the accelerator and the multiplier was constructed by Paul Samuelson, "Interactions Between the Multiplier Analysis and the Principle of Acceleration," *Review of Economics and Statistics*, 21 (May 1939), pp. 75–78.

The flexible accelerator model can also be modified to allow for variations in the speed with which investment is undertaken to fill the gap between the desired and actual capital stock (the λ parameter). This is a choice variable to the firm and may be influenced by credit conditions, including the interest rate, tax considerations, and other variables. For example, we would expect that, other things being equal, less investment would be undertaken to eliminate discrepancies between the actual and desired capital stock when the interest rate (cost of borrowing) was high than when the interest rate was low. Thus the flexible accelerator model is consistent with the assumption made in Part II that investment is negatively related to the interest rate. In the following subsection, we see an additional role for the interest rate, and for other factors influencing the cost of capital to the firm, in determining investment.

Investment and the Cost of Capital

Even the flexible version of the accelerator theory of investment assumes that the desired capital stock is a fixed multiple of output ($K^d = \alpha Y$). This specification ignores the fact that different levels of output can be produced with the same level of capital by varying the labor input—that is, by varying the capital/labor ratio (K/N) and therefore the desired capital/output ratio (α). The optimal choice of a capital–labor mix to produce a given output depends on the ratio of the two factor costs; the cost of capital compared to the real wage. We would expect that the amount of capital used to produce a given output would be positively related to the real wage and negatively related to the cost of capital. The relevant real wage for the investment decision is not the current real wage but the average real wage expected over the lifetime of the capital goods being purchased. If we assume that this variable does not change significantly in the short run, then the only modification we need to make to the flexible accelerator model is to take account of the relationship between the cost of capital and the desired capital stock.

In our discussion of the flexible accelerator model, we pointed out that the timing of investment would be expected to depend on credit conditions, including the interest rate. The previous argument indicates that the overall level of investment, not just the timing of investment, depends on the interest rate and, more broadly, on all factors that affect the cost of capital. This conclusion follows because the desired capital/labor ratio and therefore the capital/output ratio (α) depend on the cost of capital. We would therefore expect an investment function of the form

$$I_{n,\,t} = I(Y_t,\,CC_t,\,K_{t-1}) \qquad\qquad \text{(21.22)}$$

where CC is the cost of capital, which we now consider in more detail.

In deciding on its desired capital stock, the firm compares the marginal productivity of additional units of capital with the **user cost of capital**, the cost to the firm of employing an additional unit of capital for one period.[16] What elements make up this cost? If the firm must borrow to finance the purchase of capital goods, the interest rate is the cost of borrowing. If the

user cost of capital
is the overall cost to a firm to employ an additional unit of capital for one period

---

[16]The firm's choice of the optimal capital stock is made in a manner analogous to the firm's choice of the labor input in the short run. For the case of the labor input, the firm employs labor to the point at which the marginal product of labor is equated with the real wage—the user cost of labor. For the case of capital, the desired capital stock is the level that equates the marginal product of capital with the user cost of capital.

capital goods are purchased with previously earned profits that have not been distributed to stockholders (retained earnings), the interest rate represents the opportunity cost of the investment project, because alternatively the firm could invest its funds externally and earn that interest rate. In either case, the interest rate is an element of the user cost of capital.

So far we have assumed that investment depends on the nominal rate of interest, simply the rate observed in the market. If inflation is expected, however, we need to distinguish between the *nominal* interest rate (r) and the *real* interest rate, ϕ (phi), which is defined as the nominal rate minus the expected inflation rate ($\dot{p}^e$) that is,

$$\phi = r - \dot{p}^e \tag{21.23}$$

It is the real rate of interest on which the level of investment depends. For example, if the firm borrows at a nominal rate of 10 percent, then at the end of one year, it will have to repay $110 for each $100 borrowed. If over the year the firm expects the average price level to rise by 10 percent, then the expected real value of the sum to be repaid, its expected value in terms of goods and services at the end of the year, will be just equal to the value of the $100 the firm borrowed. The real interest rate will be zero ($r - \dot{p}^e$ = 10 percent − 10 percent = 0). Looked at slightly differently, the expected amount of output the firm would have to sell to repay $110 at the end of one year is just equal to the amount that would generate $100 at the beginning of the year if prices (including the firm's product price) are expected to rise 10 percent during the year. Therefore, real borrowing costs would be zero if the nominal rate were 10 percent.

If inflation rates are low and steady, as they have been in the United States and most other developed economies in recent years, the nominal interest rate will not be seriously misleading as a measure of the cost of capital. The real and nominal rates will differ only by a small, fairly constant amount. But when inflation rates are variable and at times very high, and when people come to anticipate inflation, it becomes important to distinguish between the nominal and real interest rates. In such circumstances, it is important to remember that the *real* interest is the relevant borrowing cost for the investment decision.

An additional element of the user cost of capital is the depreciation rate. A certain proportion, δ (delta), of the capital stock is used up (worn out) in the production process during each period, and this depreciation is a cost to the firm of using capital goods.

To this point, then, we can express the user cost of capital as

$$CC = \phi + \delta = r - \dot{p}^e + \delta \tag{21.24}$$

Equation (21.24) requires one further modification because of the effects of tax programs on the cost of capital. A number of government tax programs offset a portion of the user cost of capital. We summarize the effects of these programs by assuming that the government subsidizes investment purchases of capital goods at the rate τ (tau), where τ is a positive proportion of the cost of the investment good ($0 < \tau < 1$). The effective cost of capital to the firm is then

$$CC = (1 - \tau)(r - \dot{p}^e + \delta) \tag{21.25}$$

Perhaps the most obvious form of such a subsidy is an *investment tax credit*. The Kennedy administration, for example, instituted an investment tax credit in 1962 whereby a corporation's federal tax liability was reduced by 7 percent of the amount of its fixed investment expenditure. The government was, in effect, paying a 7 percent subsidy for investment purchases ($\tau = 0.07$). The effective user cost of capital to the firm is 93 percent of the cost without the tax credit ($1 - \tau = 0.93$).

To summarize our discussion of fixed investment to this point, we have developed an investment function of the following form:

$$I_{n,t} = I(Y_t, r_t, \dot{p}_t^e, \tau_t, K_{t-1})$$

(21.26)

Net investment (I_n) depends on income and the variables r, $\dot{p}^e$, and τ, which represent elements of the user cost of capital, where we have omitted the depreciation rate δ, which we assume to be constant over time. Given the level of the lagged capital stock, an increase in income (Y), the expected rate of inflation ($\dot{p}^e$), and the tax subsidy to investment (τ) will all increase net investment. Increases in the nominal interest rate, r, will cause investment expenditures to decline.

Monetary and Fiscal Policy and Investment

In Part II, we analyzed the effects of monetary and fiscal policies on investment. Here we consider some modifications of that analysis suggested by the investment theory in the previous subsections. First we reexamine fiscal policy effects.

The effects on investment of expansionary fiscal policies were indirect and perverse in our analysis in Part II. For example, an increase in government spending to increase aggregate demand would raise the interest rate and *crowd out* private investment. Tax cuts, where all taxes were on households, would do the same. This crowding out offset the intended effects of the policy. The analysis in this chapter suggests that by combining an expansionary fiscal policy—for example, a cut in the personal income tax—with a tax policy such as an investment tax credit to stimulate investment, these unfavorable effects on investment can be prevented. The personal income tax cut stimulates aggregate demand, pushing up both income and the nominal interest rate. The rise in the nominal interest rate increases the user cost of capital. The role of the investment tax credit is to offset this rise. In addition, our analysis suggests that tax policy toward investment (setting τ) provides an alternative tool to monetary policy as a means of stabilizing investment demand.

Another implication of our analysis in this chapter is that expansionary fiscal policy actions may, on net, stimulate rather than crowd out private investment expenditures, even ignoring changes in the tax treatment of investment. The reason is that expansionary fiscal policies will increase Y and therefore stimulate investment by the accelerator mechanism. This effect may be quantitatively more important than any negative effect resulting from a fiscal policy–induced increase in interest rates. Which effect dominates depends on the importance of output growth versus the cost of capital as determinants of investment.

Regarding monetary policy, the modification of our Part II analysis results from the distinction that we previously ignored between the nominal and the real rates of interest. Because it is the latter rate that is relevant for the investment decision, monetary policy must affect the real rate of interest in order to affect the level of investment. In the Keynesian or monetarist system, where the expected inflation rate depends primarily on the past history of inflation and, further, is assumed to change only slowly over time, changes in the nominal rate mean changes in the real rate in the short run. The expected inflation rate, which is the difference between the two interest-rate concepts, is relatively constant in the short run. Thus our previous analysis is substantively unchanged. Within the new classical view, anticipated monetary policy actions quickly affect price expectations and may not affect the real rate of interest, even in the short run. This is a further aspect of the new classical view that anticipated monetary policy actions do not affect real variables.

21.3 Conclusion

In this chapter, we examined consumption and investment in more detail to see more clearly their roles in determining the cyclical behavior of output. We also identified additional channels by which monetary and fiscal policy might influence consumption and investment spending.

Key Terms

- average propensity to consume (APC) 447
- average propensity to save (APS) 447
- life cycle hypothesis 450
- permanent income hypothesis 458
- accelerator model 463
- user cost of capital 465

Review Questions and Problems

1. Explain the essential elements of the life cycle hypothesis of consumer behavior.
2. Explain why the existence of liquidity constraints facing certain households would have an important implication for the life cycle hypothesis of consumption.
3. What are the implications of the life cycle hypothesis of consumer behavior for the effectiveness of fiscal policy actions?
4. Explain the permanent income hypothesis of consumer behavior. Compare the permanent income hypothesis with the life cycle hypothesis of consumption.
5. How do the life cycle hypothesis and the permanent income hypothesis resolve the apparent contradiction between the short-run data, which suggest a nonproportional relationship between consumption and income, and the long-run data, which suggest a proportional relationship?
6. Do the more detailed specifications of consumption in this chapter lead you to believe that monetary policy would be more or less effective than was suggested by our previous analysis? Do they indicate that fiscal policy is likely to be more or less effective, again relative to our previous analysis?
7. Explain the relationship between output and investment implied by the *accelerator* theory. How do costs of adjustment affect the model?

8. What elements are included in the cost of capital relevant to the firm's investment decision? Explain how this cost of capital can be influenced by monetary and fiscal policy actions.

9. Do the more detailed specifications of fixed business investment lead you to believe that monetary policy will be more or less effective than was suggested by our previous analysis? Do they indicate that fiscal policy is likely to be more or less effective, again relative to our previous analysis?

Chapter 22

Money Demand

Although we considered the demand for money in our discussion of the classical, Keynesian, and monetarist theories, the treatment in those chapters was limited to the simplest money demand specifications. In this chapter, we take a more detailed look at the demand for money. As a starting point, let us review our previous analysis.

22.1 REVIEW OF PREVIOUS ANALYSIS

Classical economists concentrated on money as a medium of exchange. They confined their attention to what Keynes termed the *transactions* demand for money. In the form developed by the Cambridge economists (see section 4.1), the classical money demand function can be expressed as

$$M^d = kPY \tag{22.1}$$

Money demand (M^d) was proportional to nominal income (the price level, P, times real income, Y). The proportion of income held in the form of money (k) was assumed to be relatively stable as long as we were considering equilibrium positions. In the alternative Fisherian version of the classical theory,

$$MV = PY \tag{22.2}$$

the velocity of money, equal to $1/k$, was assumed to be stable. An important feature of classical analysis is that the interest rate was not considered an important determinant of money demand.

Keynes's theory considered money a *store of value* in addition to a medium of exchange. The store-of-value function means that money is one asset in which a person can hold wealth. In analyzing the store-of-value function, Keynes was led to view money as one asset in an individual's portfolio and to consider how an individual divides wealth between money and alternative assets. Keynes lumped all assets that were alternatives to money into one category, which he termed "bonds." The important variable that Keynes believed would determine the split of an individual's portfolio between money and bonds was the interest rate on bonds. At a high rate of interest, the forgone interest payments that would result from holding money instead of bonds would be high. Further, in Keynes's view, when the interest rate was high relative to some reasonably fixed view of its normal level, the public would expect a future decline in the interest rate. A decline in the rate of interest would mean a capital gain on bonds. Because of the high forgone interest payments and the fact that at a high interest rate a future capital gain on bonds is likely, Keynes believed that a high interest rate would result in a low demand for money as a store of value. As the interest rate declined, the demand for money as an asset would increase. Thus, according to Keynes's theory, the demand for money varies inversely with the rate of interest. This is Keynes's theory of the speculative demand for money.

Keynes also considered the transactions demand for money and the precautionary demand for money. He viewed income as the primary variable determining the amount of money held because of the transactions and precautionary motives; higher values of income would increase the amount of money held for each purpose.

The Keynesian money demand function can be expressed as

$$M^d = L(Y, r) \qquad \textbf{(22.3)}$$

Money demand depends on income *and the interest rate*. The fact that in the Keynesian view money demand was a function of the interest rate as well as income is important in explaining the differences in policy conclusions between the classical and Keynesian models. If the demand for money is simply proportional to income, as in equations (22.1) and (22.2), then nominal income is completely determined by the supply of money. For example, with k fixed in equation (22.1), an increase in the money supply (M) in equilibrium must result in a proportional increase in nominal income, as can be seen by writing the equilibrium condition

$$M = M^d = kPY \qquad \textbf{(22.4)}$$

from which it follows that

$$\Delta M = k\Delta PY \qquad \textbf{(22.5)}$$

$$\frac{1}{k} \Delta M = \Delta PY$$

Note that with k fixed, nominal income can change *only* when the quantity of money changes, as can be seen from equation (22.5). Factors such as fiscal policy actions or autonomous changes in investment demand have no role in income determination. In terms of the *IS–LM* analysis, this is the classical case of the vertical *LM* schedule, where fixing the supply of money fixes the level of income, with shifts in the *IS* schedule affecting only the interest rate.

With the Keynesian money demand function, income is no longer proportional to the quantity of money. Other factors, including fiscal policy changes and autonomous shifts in investment demand, can cause changes in income. Again in terms of the *IS–LM* analysis, the *LM* curve is upward-sloping, not vertical. Shifts in the *IS* curve change the level of income. The relative importance of monetary factors and the other determinants of income (factors that shift the *IS* curve) depend on the slopes of the *IS* and *LM* schedules, as discussed previously (see Table 8.2).

In the monetarist view, the interest rate theoretically belongs in the money demand function. The monetarists do not believe that, empirically, the interest elasticity of money demand is high. They believe that the *LM* schedule, although not vertical, is quite steep. For this reason, among others, they believe that money is the dominant influence on nominal income.

The role of the interest rate in determining money demand is thus a question with important policy implications. Keynes's followers have not been satisfied with Keynes's theory of the relationship between the interest rate and money demand—his theory of the speculative demand for money. They have advanced additional reasons for the dependence of money demand on the interest rate. This modern Keynesian theory of money demand also extends Keynes's analysis of the transactions demand for money. We discuss these extensions of the Keynesian theory in sections 22.2 and 22.3. Beginning in the mid-1970s, money demand functions constructed on the basis of this theory began to "misbehave." The actual behavior of money demand began to diverge seriously from the predictions of the theory. Possible reasons for this instability in money demand are discussed in section 22.4.

22.2 THE THEORY OF THE TRANSACTIONS DEMAND FOR MONEY

Money is a medium of exchange, and individuals hold money for use in transactions. The fact that money is not only being *used* in transactions but that sums of money are also being *held* at any point in time for transaction purposes is due to the imperfect synchronization in income receipts and expenditures. Money is held to bridge the gap between receipts and expenditures. Theories of the transactions demand for money have generally assumed that income is a good measure of the volume of transactions and, as a consequence, that the transactions demand for money varies positively with income. Because the transactions motive was the major role of money considered in the classical theory, the classical money demand function ($M^d = kPY$) expressed money demand simply as a function of income.

Keynesians expressed money demand as a function of both income and the interest rate [$M^d = L(Y, r)$]; an increase in the interest rate would reduce money demand for a given income level. Keynes's theory of the relationship of money demand and the interest rate was the *speculative demand for money*, which concerned money's role as a store of value. We noted previously that the transactions demand might also be negatively related to the level of the interest rate. Individuals would economize on their holdings of transactions balances at higher interest rates. Extensions of Keynes's theory of the demand for money developing this relationship between the transactions demand for money and the interest rate are the subject of this section. In the next section, we discuss extensions of Keynes's theory of the demand for money as a store of wealth.

Before we discuss these theories, two points are worth noting. First, as explained in Chapter 17, there is no unique definition of money. For the purposes of the transactions demand, the relevant concept of money is the narrow definition confined to those assets actually used in transactions—the M1 definition. When we consider money as a store of wealth, a broader definition such as M2 or M3 will be relevant. Second, many of the theories of money demand are often stated in terms of the behavior of households. But money is also held by firms and by the government. In recent years, for example, the government and business sectors accounted for approximately one-third of money (M1) holdings.

The Inventory-Theoretic Approach to Money Demand

Extensions of Keynes's theory of the transactions demand have followed an **inventory-theoretic approach**. The transactions demand for money has been regarded as the inventory of the medium of exchange (money) that will be held by the individual or firm. The theory of the optimal level of this inventory has been developed by William Baumol and James Tobin along the lines of the theory of the inventory holdings of goods by a firm.[1]

inventory-theoretic approach
to the transactions demand for money regards money as an inventory of the medium of exchange held along the lines of a firm's holding of an inventory of goods

To explain the inventory-theoretic approach, we consider first the example of an individual who receives an income payment of Y dollars *in cash* at the beginning of the period ($t = 0$). To be concrete, suppose that the individual has a monthly income payment of $1,200. We further assume that the individual spends this income at a uniform and perfectly predictable rate throughout the period. By the end of the month ($t = 1$), cash holdings have fallen to zero. This time profile of money holdings is depicted in Figure 22.1. The average inventory of money held during the period will equal $Y/2$, in this case $600 ($1,200/2), which is also the amount that will be held at the midpoint of the period ($t = 1/2$). This relation follows from the assumption that expenditures take place at a uniform rate over the period.

Figure 22.1 shows the relationship between income and the average level of money holdings. The higher the initial income payment, the higher is the average level or inventory of money holdings. The inventory-theoretic approach also suggests that the level of the inventory holding of money depends on the carrying cost of the inventory. In the case of money, the relevant carrying cost is the interest forgone by holding money and not bonds, net of the cost to the individual of making a transfer between money and bonds, which we will call the *brokerage fee*.[2] The time profile of money holdings shown in Figure 22.1 assumes that throughout the month

---

[1]William Baumol's article "The Transactions Demand for Cash: An Inventory-Theoretic Approach" appeared in the *Quarterly Journal of Economics*, 66 (November 1952), pp. 545–56. James Tobin's article "The Interest-Elasticity of the Transactions Demand for Cash" appeared in the *Review of Economics and Statistics*, 38 (August 1956), pp. 241–47.

[2]As explained in Chapter 7, some components of M1—the definition of money relevant for transactions demand—pay interest. The interest rates paid on these M1 deposits are, however, lower than those on non-M1 assets—for example, on Treasury bills or actual bonds. The interest forgone by holding the M1 deposits that pay some interest is then the differential between the rate of non-M1 assets and M1 deposits. It will simplify our discussion, without changing our conclusions, to neglect interest payments on M1 deposits.

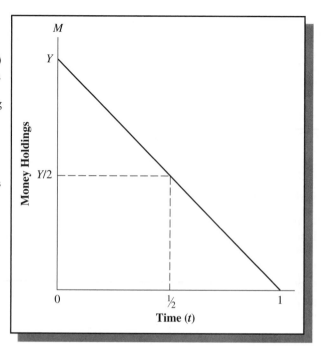

Figure 22.1

Individual Money Holdings (No Bond Market Transactions)

The individual receives income in cash of Y dollars at the beginning of the period. The income payment is spent at an even rate over the period. Average holdings of cash equal the holdings at the midpoint of the period $Y/2$.

the individual holds all the unspent income payment in the form of money. Alternatively, the person could invest a proportion of the initial income payment in bonds and then sell the bonds when additional money was needed for transactions.[3]

If the individual invested half of the income payment in bonds at the beginning of the month and then sold the bonds when cash holdings were exhausted at mid-month, the time profile of money holdings would be as depicted in Figure 22.2. At the beginning of the month, money holdings are $Y/2$ (Y minus bond purchase of $Y/2$). Money holdings are run down to zero by the midpoint of the period at a uniform rate. Average money holdings for the first half of the period are therefore $Y/4$. At the midpoint of the period, the bonds are sold. Money holdings return to $Y/2$ and are then spent at a uniform rate over the last half of the period. The average money holding for the second half of the period is again $Y/4$. Thus the average money holding for the period as a whole is $Y/4$, which is lower than $Y/2$ for the case in which no bonds are held. The average bond holding for the period is $Y/4$ (the average of $Y/2$ for the first half of the period and zero for the second). If the monthly interest rate on bonds is r percent and there is a fixed brokerage fee for each transaction in the bond

---

[3]Notice that, because money here is defined to be actual transactions balances (M1), such assets as savings deposits or money market mutual funds are *not* considered money. These assets are then included in "bonds," so the choice the individual faces can be thought of as one between holding transactions balances and, for example, holding a money market fund account that pays interest but requires periodic trips to the bank to deposit funds in a checking account. The "brokerage" cost in this case is a time cost. For the wealthy individual or business firm, the interest-earning asset, which is the alternative to holding money, might be a short-term government security, and the brokerage cost is an actual broker's fee for buying or selling the security.

Figure 22.2

Individual Money Holdings (Two Bond Market Transactions)

The individual receives Y dollars at the beginning of the period, half of which ($Y/2$) is used to purchase bonds. The other half is spent at an even rate over the first half of the period. The bonds are sold at $t = 1/2$, and the cash received ($Y/2$) is spent at an even rate during the second half of the period. Average cash holdings are $Y/4$ ($Y/2 \div 2$) for each half of the period and, therefore, for the period as a whole.

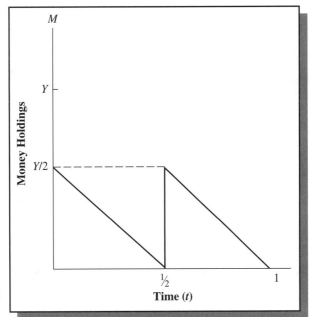

market of b dollars, the net profit (Pr) from the one bond purchase and one sale (number of transactions, n, equals 2) is

$$Pr(n = 2) = r\frac{Y}{4} - 2b \qquad \text{(22.6)}$$

The first term is the interest earning on the average bond holding. The second term is the transactions cost, which equals the brokerage fee times the number of bond market transactions.

If, instead, the individual chose to engage in three transactions ($n = 3$) in the bond market, the optimal strategy would be to buy an amount of bonds equal to $2/3Y$ at the start of the period, sell bonds equal to $1/3Y$ when initial money holdings of $1/3Y$ are exhausted at $t = 1/3$, and then sell the remaining amount of bonds, $1/3Y$, when money holdings are again exhausted at $t = 2/3$.[4] The time profile of money holdings would be as shown in Figure 22.3. The preceding example and the figure indicate that average money holdings are equal to $Y/6$ ($Y/3 \div 2$ for each third of the time period). Average bond holdings equal $Y/3$ ($2/3Y$ for the first third of the period, $1/3Y$ over the second third, zero for the last third), and net profit from the bond transactions equals

$$Pr(n = 3) = r\frac{Y}{3} - 3b \qquad \text{(22.7)}$$

---

[4]A specific strategy of purchases and sales is being considered here whereby, after the initial bond purchase, sales are evenly spaced across the time period. Such a strategy is optimal in the sense that it enables the individual to maximize the average holdings of bonds and, hence, interest earnings for a given number of transactions.

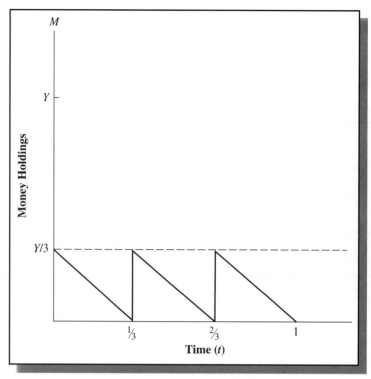

Figure 22.3 Individual Money Holdings (Three Bond Market Transactions)

In this case ($n = 3$), two-thirds of the income payment is invested in bonds at the beginning of the period. The remaining one-third Y ($Y/3$) is spent at an even rate over the first third of the period. Bond sales of $Y/3$ are made at $t = 1/3$ and $t = 2/3$, with cash receipts again spent at even rates. Average money holdings are $Y/6$ ($Y/3 \div 2$) for each third of the period and, therefore, for the period as a whole.

In general, average money holdings, average bond holdings, and net profit can be expressed in terms of the number of bond market transactions (n). Average money holdings (M) will be

$$M = \frac{1}{2n}Y \tag{22.8}$$

In the examples, for $n = 2$, money holdings were $Y/4$ [$= Y/2(2)$], and for $n = 3$ money holdings were $Y/6$ [$= Y/2(3)$]. Average bond holdings (B) can be expressed as

$$B = \frac{n-1}{2n}Y \tag{22.9}$$

For the cases considered previously, average bond holdings were

$$\frac{Y}{4}\left[= \frac{2-1}{2(2)}Y\right] \text{ for } n = 2 \quad \text{and} \quad \frac{Y}{3}\left[= \frac{3-1}{2(3)}Y\right] \text{ for } n = 3$$

The general expression for net profits is

$$Pr(n) = r\frac{n-1}{2n}Y - nb \qquad \textbf{(22.10)}$$

The first term in this expression is the interest earnings on bonds, equal to the interest rate (r) times average bond holdings $[(n-1)/2n]Y$, which is given by equation (22.9). The second term is transaction costs, the brokerage fee (b) times the number of transactions (n). By substituting $n = 2$ and $n = 3$ into equation (22.10), we get equations (22.6) and (22.7) from our previous examples.

These results show that, for a given income payment, the choice of how much money (or how many bonds) to hold is determined by the choice of n. The individual will choose n such that net profits from bond transactions (Pr) are maximized. The individual will increase the number of transactions in the bond market until the point at which the marginal interest earnings from one additional transaction are just equated with the constant marginal cost, which will be equal to the brokerage fee.

The determination of the optimal number of bond transactions is depicted in Figure 22.4. The marginal cost (MC) of an additional transaction, which is the brokerage fee (b), is assumed to be constant, hence the horizontal marginal cost schedule in Figure 22.4.

What about the marginal revenue schedule? When we previously considered going from zero bond market transactions to one purchase and sale, we found that interest earnings increased from zero to $r(Y/4)$. A further increase to three bond market transactions increased average bond holdings from $Y/4$ to $Y/3$, and therefore interest earnings rose from $r(Y/4)$ to $r(Y/3)$, a further, though smaller, increase in interest earnings of $r(Y/12)$ [note that $r(Y/12) = r(Y/3) - r(Y/4)$]. This is the general

Figure 22.4
The Optimal Number of Bond Market Transactions

The optimal number of bond transactions (n^*) is chosen to equate the declining marginal revenue of additional bond market transactions (MR) with their constant marginal cost (MC).

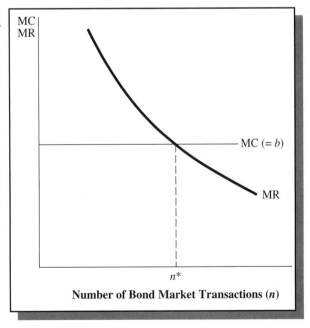

case. The increment to interest earnings from an additional bond market transaction declines as the number of bond market transactions increases. The marginal revenue schedule (MR) is downward-sloping, as shown in Figure 22.4.

The optimal number of bond market transactions is determined at the point where the marginal revenue schedule intersects the horizontal marginal cost schedule, at n^* in Figure 22.4. Beyond this point, the marginal gain in interest earned from increasing the number of bond market transactions is not sufficient to cover the brokerage cost of the transaction.

The choice of n determines the split of money and bond holdings *for a given income payment*. We can see how various factors affect the demand for money and bonds by seeing how they affect n. Factors that increase (decrease) n will, for a given income, increase (decrease) average bond holdings and decrease (increase) average money holdings. Figure 22.5a shows the effect on n of an increase in the interest rate from r_0 to r_1. This increased interest rate shifts the marginal revenue schedule upward from $MR(r_0)$ to $MR(r_1)$. At a higher interest rate, an additional bond market transaction will increase bond holdings by the same amount as before but will increase interest earnings on the bond holding by a greater amount. The individual responds by engaging in more bond market transactions; the optimal number of bond market transactions rises from n_0^* to n_1^*. The average bond holding over the period increases. The average money holding declines. This is the effect referred to in previous chapters as economizing on transactions balances at higher interest rates. The inventory-theoretic approach to the transactions demand for money provides a theoretical basis for this negative relationship between money demand and the interest rate.

The inventory-theoretic approach also suggests that the demands for money and bonds depend on the cost of making a transfer between money and bonds, the *brokerage fee* (b). Figure 22.5b illustrates the effect on the optimal number of bond transactions (n) as a result of an increase in the brokerage fee from b_0 to b_1. The brokerage fee increase raises the marginal cost of bond market transactions and consequently lowers the number of such transactions, from n_0^* to n_1^*. The increase in the brokerage fee raises the transactions demand for money and lowers the average bond holding over the period. This result follows because an increase in the brokerage fee makes it more costly to switch funds temporarily into bond holdings.

Changes in the interest rate or brokerage fee affect the split of a given income payment between money and bond holdings. What is the effect of changing the level of income (Y)? We have already mentioned one effect: For a given n that determines the split between money and bonds, a rise in Y increases the demand for both money and bonds. For the cases considered—for example, with $n = 2$—the average money and bond holdings are both $Y/4$ and clearly depend positively on Y. However, an increase in Y will *not* leave n unchanged. As Y rises, the marginal revenue from each additional bond transaction will increase, because each bond transaction will be for a greater amount and will therefore result in a greater increase in interest earnings. With the assumption of a fixed brokerage fee, the marginal cost of a transfer will be constant. The increase in income will then increase n. Graphically, this effect is the same as for the increase in the interest rate in Figure 22.5a; the MR schedule shifts to the right along a fixed MC schedule. Given the assumptions made here, the increase in n will not be so great as to cause money holdings to decline on net as income rises.

Figure 22.5
Factors Determining the Optimal Number of Bond Market Transactions (n^*)

In part a, an increase in the interest rate from r_0 to r_1 shifts the marginal revenue curve to the right from $MR(r_0)$ to $MR(r_1)$. The optimal number of bond market transactions increases from n_0^* to n_1^*. In part b, an increase in the brokerage fee from b_0 to b_1 shifts the marginal cost schedule up from $MC(= b_0)$ to $MC(= b_1)$. The optimal number of bond market transactions falls from n_0^* to n_1^*.

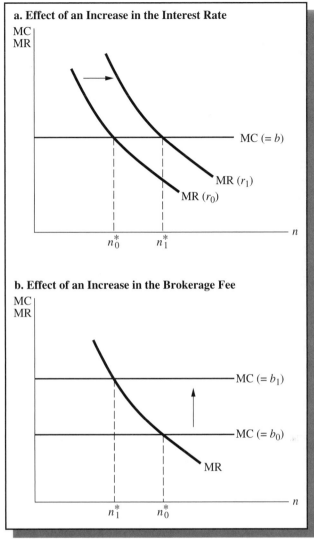

a. Effect of an Increase in the Interest Rate

b. Effect of an Increase in the Brokerage Fee

An increase in income will increase the holdings of both bonds and money. With the increase in n, the split between the two assets will move toward a higher proportion of bonds and a lower proportion of money. As a consequence, the transactions demand for money will rise less than proportionately with income.

There is one qualification to the foregoing analysis. We have so far not constrained n to be an integer, but it must be. You cannot engage in 6.89 bond market transactions and, more importantly, you cannot engage in any number less than 2. If a comparison of marginal cost and marginal revenue indicates that the optimal level of transactions is less than 2, no transactions will be undertaken. For individuals with modest incomes, this situation seems quite likely. The brokerage cost will be high enough (even if it is just a time cost of switching between savings deposits and checkable deposits) that the individual will simply hold money needed for transactions throughout the whole period. In our example of a 1-month pay period and monthly income of $1,200, if the *monthly* interest rate is one-half of 1 percent (0.005, as a decimal), then for $n = 2$, average bond holdings would be $300 ($Y/4$), and interest earnings would be $1.50 ($300 \times 0.005$). It is easy to see that the brokerage cost may exceed this amount and cause the individual to forgo any bond market transactions. For people with relatively low incomes, the transactions demand for money may, therefore, simply be proportional to income and independent of the interest rate and brokerage fee.

Summary

Our analysis to this point results in a function for Keynes's transactions demand for money expressed in the following form:

$$M^d = L(Y, r, b) \tag{22.11}$$

The demand for money depends positively on income (Y) and the brokerage fee (b). Money demand depends negatively on the rate of interest (r).

22.3 EXTENSIONS OF KEYNES'S THEORY OF MONEY AS A STORE OF WEALTH

Keynesian economists working in the 1950s followed Keynes's approach to the demand for money in that they considered money as a store of wealth (or value) in addition to its means-of-payment function. They modified and extended Keynes's analysis, however, to remedy what they saw as weaknesses in his theory of the speculative motive for money demand.

Keynes's theory had been criticized on two grounds. First, recall that Keynes's theory implies that investors would hold *all* of their wealth in bonds (other than the amount of money held as transactions balances) as long as the interest rate was above the "critical rate," a rate below which the expected capital loss on bonds outweighed the interest earnings on bonds. If the interest rate fell below this critical rate, investors would transfer all their wealth to money.[5] Keynes's theory therefore cannot explain why an individual investor holds both money balances and bonds as stores of wealth, but such *portfolio diversification* does occur.

Second, according to Keynes's theory, investors hold money as an asset when the interest rate is low because they expect the interest rate to rise and return to a "normal" level. A crucial element of Keynes's theory is the existence of a fixed or at least only slowly changing normal level for the interest rate, around which the actual interest rate fluctuates. The assumption of a normal level of interest rates is more consistent with interest-rate behavior for the period before Keynes wrote *The General Theory* in 1936 than afterward. Since 1950, there has been a generally upward trend in

---

[5]See the discussion in section 7.1.

interest rates. In such a circumstance, Keynes's assumption that investors expect a return of interest rates to some normal level requires modification. At a minimum, the normal level itself must be assumed to change over time. Keynesian economists have modified Keynes's original theory in a way that explains why portfolio diversification takes place and that does not depend on Keynes's particular assumption about investor expectations of a return of the interest rate to a normal level. The starting point of this portfolio theory of money demand is the work of James Tobin.[6]

The Demand for Money as Behavior Toward Risk

Tobin analyzes the individual's portfolio allocation between money and bond holdings. The transactions demand for money is assumed to be determined separately along the lines of the preceding analysis, and the demand for money considered here is as a store of wealth.

In Tobin's theory, the individual investor has no normal level to which interest rates are always expected to return. We can assume that the individual believes capital gains or losses to be equally likely; that is, the *expected* capital gain is zero. The best expectation of the return on bonds is simply the interest rate (r). But this interest rate is only the *expected* return on bonds. The actual return includes some capital gain or loss, because the interest rate generally does not remain fixed. Thus bonds pay an expected return of r, but they are a risky asset; their actual return is uncertain.

Money, in contrast, is a safe asset. Money's nominal return of zero is lower than the expected return on bonds, but there are no capital gains or losses when money is held.[7] Tobin argues that an individual will hold some proportion of wealth in money because doing so lowers the overall riskiness of the portfolio below what it would be if all bonds were held. The overall expected return on the portfolio would be higher if the portfolio were all bonds, but an investor who is *risk-averse* will be willing to sacrifice higher return, to some degree, for a reduction in risk. The demand for money as an asset is explained as aversion to risk.

Tobin's theory can be explained by referring to Figure 22.6. In the upper quadrant on the vertical axis, we measure the expected return to the portfolio; the horizontal axis measures the riskiness of the portfolio. The expected return on the portfolio is the interest earning on bonds, which depends on the interest rate and the proportion of the portfolio that the individual places in bonds. The total risk that the individual takes depends on the uncertainty concerning bond prices—that is, the uncertainty concerning future interest-rate movements—as well as on the proportion of the portfolio placed in bonds, the risky asset. We denote the expected total return R and the total risk of the portfolio σ_T. If the individual holds all wealth (Wh) in money and none in bonds, the portfolio will have zero expected return and zero risk. This portfolio allocation is shown at the origin (point O) in Figure 22.6. As the proportion of bonds in the portfolio increases, expected portfolio return and risk both rise. The

---

[6]Tobin's original article on this subject, "Liquidity Preference As Behavior Towards Risk," appeared in the *Review of Economic Studies*, 25 (February 1958), pp. 65–86.

[7]Again, here we are ignoring the interest rate paid on deposits. To assume a positive deposit rate, but one less than the interest rate on bonds (r) would not affect our analysis as long as we assume that, because of costs to the bank of providing deposits, as r rises the deposit rate does not rise by the same amount—in other words, as long as we assume that as r rises, the *relative* return on bonds rises.

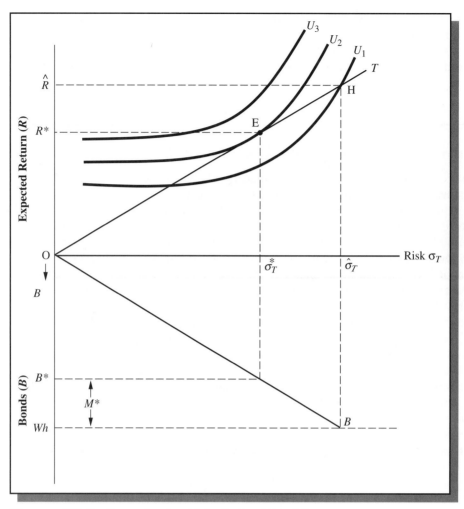

Figure 22.6 Determination of the Optimal Portfolio

The upper quadrant of the figure shows the individual's optimal portfolio allocation. At point E, the risk–expected return trade-off in the market, reflected in the slope of line T, is just equal to the terms on which the investor is willing to accept increased risk in return for an increase in expected return, given by the slope of the indifference curve (U_2). The lower quadrant shows the bond and money holdings (B^*, M^*) that correspond to this choice of risk and expected return.

terms on which the individual investor can increase the expected return on the portfolio (R) at the cost of increasing risk (σ_T) are represented by line T.[8] As the investor moves along T, more bonds and less money are being held.

The lower quadrant of Figure 22.6 shows the allocation of the portfolio between bonds and money, which results in each risk–return combination. Bond holdings (B)

---

[8]Let σ be a measure of the uncertainty about the price of a given bond. The total risk on the portfolio can be measured by $\sigma_T = \sigma B$. Total expected return is $R = rB$, so the slope of line T is $\Delta R/\Delta\sigma_T = r/\sigma$.

are measured on the vertical axis. Bonds held in the portfolio increases as we go *down* the vertical axis to a maximum of *Wh*, the total amount of wealth. The difference between bond holdings and total wealth is the demand for money as an asset (*M*). The schedule *B* in the lower portion of the graph shows the relationship between total risk of the portfolio (σ_T) and the proportion of the portfolio held in bonds, with higher levels of risk associated with higher proportions of bonds in the portfolio.

To find the optimal portfolio allocation, we consider the preferences of the investor. We assume that the investor is risk-averse; that is, the investor wishes to receive a high return on the portfolio and also wants to avoid risk. A higher level of risk will be acceptable only if compensated by an increase in expected return. Formally, we assume that the investor's utility function is

$$U = U(R, \sigma_T) \tag{22.12}$$

where an increase in expected return (*R*) increases utility, and an increase in risk (σ_T) decreases utility. On the basis of this utility function, we draw indifference curves for the investor, U_1, U_2, U_3 in Figure 22.6, showing the terms on which the investor is willing to accept more risk if compensated by a higher expected return. Each point along one of these curves represents a given level of utility. As we move from U_1 to U_2 to U_3, we are moving to higher levels of utility—higher levels of *R* and lower levels of σ_T. The curves are drawn sloping upward to represent a risk-averse investor who will take on more risk only if compensated by a higher return. Further, the curves become steeper as we move to the right, reflecting the assumption of *increasing risk aversion*; the more risk the individual has already taken on, the greater will be the increase in expected return required for the investor to accept an additional increase in risk.

We now have all the elements needed to determine the optimal portfolio allocation. The investor will move to the point along the *T* schedule at which that schedule is just tangent to one of the indifference curves. At this point the terms on which the investor is *able* to increase expected return by accepting more risk, given by the slope of the *T* schedule, will be equated to the terms on which the investor is *willing* to make this trade-off, given by the slope of the indifference curve. This is the point of utility maximization. In Figure 22.6, this tangency occurs at point E, with expected return *R** and total risk on the portfolio of σ_T^*. From the lower quadrant it can be seen that this risk–return combination is achieved by holding an amount of bonds equal to *B** and by holding the remainder of wealth *M** in money.

The demand for money is then what Tobin terms "behavior toward risk," the result of attempting to reduce risk below what it would be if all wealth were held in bonds. In Figure 22.6, such an all-bonds portfolio would incur risk of $\hat{\sigma}_T$ and earn expected return of $\hat{R}$, point H in the graph. This portfolio yields a lower level of utility than that represented by bond holdings of *B** and money holdings of *M**. The reason can be seen from the graph. As we farther along the *T* schedule past point E, the incremental expected return on the portfolio from holding additional bonds is insufficient to compensate the investor for the additional risk (the slope of the *T* schedule is lower than that of the U_2 schedule). Movement to point H takes the investor to a lower indifference curve, U_1 in Figure 22.6.

Money Demand and the Rate of Interest

Tobin's theory implies that the amount of money held as an asset depends on the level of the interest rate. This relationship between the interest rate and asset demand for money is depicted in Figure 22.7. An increase in the interest rate will improve the terms on which the expected return on the portfolio can be increased by accepting greater risk. At a higher interest rate, a given increase in risk, which corresponds to a given increase in the amount of bonds in the portfolio, will result in a greater increase in expected return on the portfolio. In Figure 22.7, increases in the interest rate from r_0 to r_1, then to r_2, will rotate the T schedule in a counterclockwise direction from

Figure 22.7 Asset Demand for Money and the Rate of Interest

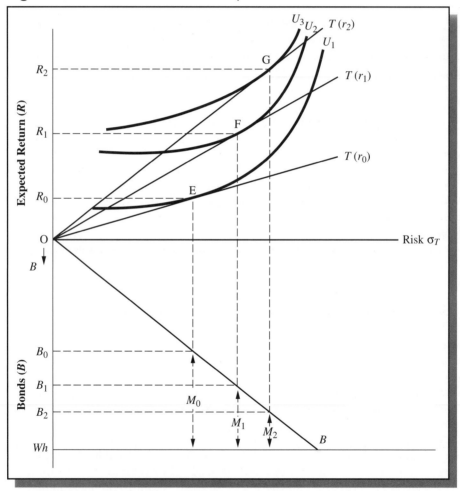

Increases in the interest rate (from r_0 to r_1 and then r_2) make the T schedule steeper by increasing the expected return that can be gained by undertaking increased risk. The individual responds by undertaking more risk and earning higher expected returns (the equilibrium point moves from point E to F, then to G). Holdings of the risky asset, bonds, increase (from B_0 to B_1, then to B_2); money holdings decline (from M_0 to M_1, then to M_2).

$T(r_0)$ to $T(r_1)$, then to $T(r_2)$.[9] The point of portfolio optimization shifts from point E to point F and then to point G in the graph. In response to the increase in the interest rate, the individual will increase the proportion of wealth held in the interest-bearing asset, bonds (from B_0 to B_1 to B_2), and will decrease the holding of money (from M_0 to M_1 to M_2).

Tobin's theory implies, as did Keynes's, that the demand for money as a store of wealth depends negatively on the interest rate.[10] Within Tobin's framework, an increase in the rate of interest can be considered an increase in the payment received for undertaking risk. When this payment is increased, the individual investor is willing to put a greater proportion of the portfolio into the risky asset, bonds, and thus a smaller proportion into the safe asset, money.

22.4 INSTABILITY OF MONEY DEMAND

Our analysis of the transactions demand for money left us with the following specification for money demand:

$$M^d = L(Y, r, b) \qquad (22.13)$$

where Y is income, r is the interest rate, and b is the brokerage cost. Our consideration of the role of money as a store of wealth—Tobin's portfolio theory—suggests an additional reason for including the interest rate in the money demand function; his analysis implies that the demand for money as a store of wealth will decline with an increase in the interest rate. Tobin's analysis also indicates that uncertainty about future changes in bond prices, and hence the risk involved in buying bonds, may be a determinant of money demand.

In practice, a simplification of equation (22.13) has become the conventional specification of the money demand function. This simple form is used in the earlier Keynesian theoretical models in Part II:

$$M^d = L(Y, r) \qquad (22.14)$$

Money demand has been taken to depend on income and an interest rate, usually a short-term interest rate. Although the preference for this specification has never been unanimous, this type of money demand function performed well in predicting actual money holdings up until 1973, and it was widely used for empirical work and in policy formation.

Beginning in 1974, equations such as (22.14) began to "misbehave." First, over the 1974–79 period, such equations, when estimated by statistical procedures and used to

---

[9]As explained in footnote 8, the slope of the T schedule is r/σ; thus an increase in r will increase the slope of the T schedule.

[10]The conclusion that an increase in the interest rate will result in a decline in money demand does require one additional assumption. As explained in the text, a rise in the interest rate on bonds improves the terms of the trade-off between risk and return, making bonds more desirable. This relationship corresponds to the usual *substitution* effect in consumer demand theory. There is also an *income* effect, however, which may work in the opposite direction. With a higher interest rate, a given return can now be achieved with a lower proportion of bonds in the portfolio. This income effect may lead the investor to lower the demand for bonds and increase the security gained from holding money. In the text we make the assumption that the substitution effect dominates any possible negative income effect.

predict the public's holding of money, began to seriously overpredict the amount of money the public was holding. At the given level of income and the interest rate, the public was holding less money than these equations predicted. Why the public reacted this way has been called the "Case of the Missing Money." Later, during the 1980s, the situation was reversed, and the conventional money demand function began to seriously underpredict the public's money demand.

The instability of money demand in the 1970s and 1980s was most pronounced for the M1 aggregate. In the early 1990s, there was considerable instability of M2. During this period, growth in M2 was very slow, even though interest rates were quite low. The later 1990s were again a period of unstable growth in M1.

Several explanations have been offered for the instability of money demand in recent decades. One of these is financial innovation, which has created many new deposit types and made it difficult to measure the transaction medium appropriate for the theory in section 22.2.

Today there are many deposits and near deposits that can be used in transactions or that are close substitutes for transactions deposits in the sense that one can move in and out of these assets with very low brokerage costs. An example is a money market mutual fund. These funds sell shares to the public, invest in short-term liquid assets, and then let shareholders withdraw funds by writing checks. There is no explicit "brokerage fee" for shifting funds from a money market account and a bank deposit.

Other financial innovations include the use of debit cards and electronic funds transfers to carry out transactions, and computerized "sweep accounts." In sweep accounts, funds in a checking account that will not be needed for transactions on a given day are automatically transferred (swept) into an interest bearing savings account near the end of the business day. Because savings account balances are not included in M1 this causes declines in that monetary aggregate that are hard to predict.

Along with difficulties in defining the transactions medium, financial market innovations have made it hard to define the opportunity cost of holding money, the relevant r in equation (22.14). Some new deposits and near deposits, such as money market mutual funds are interest bearing. They are substitutes for assets such as stocks and bonds. Their opportunity cost should then include expected returns on these assets as well as a short-term interest rate. This is consistent with Tobin's theory in section 22.3 but not with the simple money demand specification (22.14), which has commonly been used in empirical work.

22.5 CONCLUSION

In the early 1970s, a summary of the state of the theory of money demand would have approached the subject as one in which a reasonable consensus had been reached. Money demand had been shown theoretically and empirically to depend on income and the interest rate. The conventional form of the money demand function discussed in the preceding section performed well. The later failure of this conventional form has led to renewed interest in the money demand function.

Problems in predicting money demand in the post-1973 period have not led most economists to view the existing theory of money demand as fundamentally flawed. As the preceding discussion illustrates, the source of these difficulties can be found in the effects of innovations in the financial sector and in problems in measuring the opportunity cost of holding money.

Still, instability of money demand in the post-1973 years has had important consequences. One consequence has been a gradual loss of support for monetarism, a central tenet of which is a stable money–income relationship. Another, which was discussed in Chapter 18, is the Federal Reserve's deemphasis of monetary aggregates in conducting monetary policy.

KEY TERMS

• inventory-theoretic approach 473

REVIEW QUESTIONS AND PROBLEMS

1. What is the most important difference between the classical and Keynesian theories of money demand?
2. According to the inventory-theoretic approach to the transaction demand for money, how would you expect the amount of money an individual demanded for transactions purposes to be affected by:
   a. An increase in the interest rate paid on bonds.
   b. An increase in the brokerage fee for bond market transactions.
   c. An increase in income.
   d. An increase in the length of the payment period—for example, from a week to a month.
3. Show how James Tobin's theory explains the demand for money as an asset as "behavior toward risk." How does Tobin's theory differ from Keynes's formulation of the asset demand for money? In what respects are Tobin's and Keynes's theories similar?
4. Within Tobin's theory of the demand for money, explain how the optimal portfolio (the choice of money and bond demand) would be affected by an increase in uncertainty about the price of bonds.
5. Applying the analysis from sections 18.2–18.5, explain how the instability of money demand in the post-1973 period affects the choice of a monetary aggregate versus an interest rate as a monetary policy target. Illustrate this effect within the *IS–LM* curve model.

GLOSSARY

A

The **accelerator model** is a model of business investment that in its simplest form relates the level of investment to the rate of change in output. More complex forms take account of costs of adjustment and borrowing costs.

Aggregate demand is the sum of the demands for current output by each of the buying sectors of the economy: households, businesses, the government, and foreign purchasers of exports.

The **aggregate demand curve** measures the demand for total output at each value of the aggregate price level.

The **aggregate supply function** is the macroeconomic analog to the individual market supply curve, which shows the output forthcoming at each level of product price. The aggregate supply curve shows the total output firms will supply at each value of the aggregate price level.

Automatic stabilizers are changes in taxes and government transfer payments that occur when the level of income changes.

The **autonomous expenditure multiplier** gives the change in equilibrium output per unit change in autonomous expenditures (e.g., government spending).

Autonomous expenditures are expenditures that are largely determined by factors other than current income.

The **average propensity to consume (APC)** is the ratio of consumption to income.

The **average propensity to save (APS)** is the ratio of saving to income.

B

The **balanced-budget multiplier** gives the change in equilibrium output that results from a one-unit increase or decrease in *both* taxes and government spending.

The **Board of Governors of the Federal Reserve** is composed of seven members (governors) appointed by the president of the United States with the advice and consent of the Senate for a term of 14 years. One member of the board is appointed chairman.

The **Bretton Woods system** was a pegged exchange rate system set up at the end of World War II.

C

The **Cambridge approach** is a version of the quantity theory of money that focuses on the demand for money ($M^d = kPY$).

The **capital account** in the balance of payments is a record of purchases of U.S. assets by foreign residents (capital inflows) and purchases of foreign assets by U.S. residents (capital outflows).

Capital deepening is the process where capital grows at a faster rate than labor and the capital/labor ratio rises.

Capital formation is growth in the stock of plant and equipment.

A **capital gain** is the increase in the market value of any asset above the price originally paid.

Capital goods are capital resources such as factories, machinery, and railroads used to produce other goods.

A **capital loss** is the decrease in the market value of any asset below the price originally paid.

Constant returns to scale means that increasing all inputs by a certain proportion (e.g., 100 percent) will cause output to rise by the same proportion (100 percent).

The **consumer price index (CPI)** measures the retail prices of a fixed "market basket" of several thousand goods and services purchased by households.

Consumption is the household sector's demand for output for current use. *Consumption expenditures* consist of purchases of durable goods (e.g., autos and televisions), nondurable goods (e.g., food and newspapers), and services (e.g., haircuts and taxi rides).

The **consumption function** is the Keynesian relationship between income and consumption.

Corporate bonds are formal IOUs that require the corporation to pay a fixed sum of money (interest payment) annually until maturity and then, at maturity, a fixed sum of money to repay the initial amount borrowed (principal).

The **current account** in the U.S. balance of payments is a record of U.S. merchandise exports and imports as well as trade in services and foreign transfer payments.

The **cyclical deficit** is the portion of the federal deficit that results from the economy's being at a low level of economic activity.

Cyclical unemployment results from fluctuations in the level of economic activity and consequent fluctuations in industry demand for workers.

D

The **deposit multiplier** gives the increase in bank deposits per unit increase in bank reserves.

Depository institutions are financial intermediaries whose main liabilities are deposits. Depository institutions include commercial banks, savings and loan associations, mutual savings banks, and credit unions.

Depreciation is the portion of the capital stock that wears out each year.

The **discount rate** is the rate the Federal Reserve charges on loans to depository institutions.

E

Economies of scale are present when a doubling of all inputs results in *more* than a doubling of output.

The **effective tax rate** is the taxpayer's tax bill divided by her or his total income.

In **efficiency wage models**, the productivity of labor depends on the real wage workers are paid. In such models, the real wage is set to maximize the efficiency units of labor per dollar of expenditure, not to clear the labor market.

Elasticity measures the percentage change in one variable per 1 percent change in another variable: for example, the elasticity of money demand with respect to the interest rate.

The **euro** is the new currency of 12 members of the European Union (Greece joined in 2001).

An **exchange rate** is the value of one country's currency in terms of foreign currencies.

An **exchange rate system** is a set of rules organizing the determination of exchange rates among currencies.

F

Factors of production are labor, land, capital, and entrepreneurship.

The **federal funds rate** is the rate at which banks make loans to one another.

The **Federal Reserve System** (Federal Reserve, or the Fed, for short) is composed of 12 regional Federal Reserve banks and the Board of Governors located in Washington, D.C.

Financial intermediaries are institutions that accept funds from savers and make loans to ultimate borrowers (e.g., firms).

Fiscal stabilization policy is the use of government spending and tax policies to affect the level of economic activity.

Foreign exchange is a term used for foreign currencies in general.

Frictional unemployment is unemployment due to the time workers spend between jobs and to the time entrants or reentrants to the labor force need to find jobs.

G

Government purchases of goods and services are the part of current output that goes to the government sector—the federal government as well as state and local governments.

Government spending refers to government outlays for purchases, transfer payments, and subsidies.

The **Gramm–Rudman–Hollings Act** mandated a move to a balanced budget in steps over five years, by *automatic* spending cuts if Congress failed to balance the budget by legislation.

Gross domestic product (GDP) is a measure of all currently produced final goods and services.

Gross national product (GNP) is, like gross domestic product, a measure of aggregate national production. There are two differences between the two measures, both of which concern foreign transactions. GNP includes foreign earnings of U.S. corporations and earnings of U.S. residents working overseas; GDP does not include these items. Conversely, GDP includes earnings from current production in the United States that accrue to foreign residents and foreign-owned firms, whereas GNP excludes those items.

H

A **hyperinflation** is a period when the price level explodes. In the worst hyperinflation, inflation rates reach several thousand percent *per month*.

Human capital is the accumulation of investments in schooling, training, and health that raises people's productive capacity.

Hysteresis describes the tendency for a variable shocked away from an initial value to not return to that value even after the shock is over. Persistently high unemployment rates in many European countries have led economists to argue that unemployment exhibits hysteresis.

I

The **implicit gross national/domestic/deflator** is an index of the prices of goods and services included in gross national/domestic/product.

Indirect business taxes are general sales and excise taxes.

Induced expenditures are expenditures determined primarily by current income.

Insider–outsider models provide one explanation of hysteresis in unemployment. Insiders (e.g., union members) are the only group that affect the real wage bargain. Outsiders (e.g., those who want jobs) do not. Recessions cause insiders to become outsiders. After the recession, with fewer insiders, the real wage rises and unemployment persists.

Intermediate targeting on a monetary aggregate is a monetary policy strategy that aims at hitting money growth targets, with the ultimate goal of controlling the level of economic activity.

The **inventory theoretic approach** to the transactions demand for money regards money as an inventory of the medium of exchange held along the lines of a firm's holding of an inventory of goods.

Investment is the part of gross national product purchased by the business sector plus residential construction.

L

Labor comprises the physical energy, manual skill, and mental ability that humans apply to the production of goods and services.

Legal reserve requirements specify that banks must hold a certain percentage (fraction) of deposits either in the form of vault cash (currency) or as deposits at regional Federal Reserve banks. They are what are called *fractional reserve requirements*.

The **life cycle hypothesis** about consumption asserts that saving and consumption decisions of households reflect a plan for an optimal consumption pattern over their lifetime, subject to the constraint of their resources.

M

M1 is the narrowest of the money supply measures in the United States. It consists of currency plus *checkable* deposits. Two other measures, **M2** and **M3**, are broader. They include all the components of M1 plus some additional bank deposits that have no or only limited provisions for checks.

The **Maastricht Treaty** of 1991 was a key step in the move to the euro as a common currency for 12 members of the European Union. The treaty set guidelines for the economies of member countries that had to be satisfied before they could adopt the common currency.

A **managed float** for a country's exchange rate is a system in which, at some times, the exchange rate is allowed to respond to market forces while at other times the central bank *intervenes* to influence the exchange rate.

Marginal cost is the extra, or additional, cost of producing one more unit of output.

The **marginal product** of an input is the addition to total output due to the addition of an extra unit of that input (the quantity of other inputs being held constant).

The **marginal propensity to consume (MPC)** is the increase in consumption per unit increase in disposable income.

The **marginal propensity to save (MPS)** is the increase in saving per unit increase in disposable income.

Marginal revenue is the added revenue associated with the sale of one more unit of output.

The **marginal revenue product (MRP)** of any resource input is the extra revenue the firm gains by using one more unit of the input, holding other inputs constant.

The **marginal tax rate** is the rate paid on each additional dollar earned from an activity.

The **marginal utility** of a good is the additional satisfaction a consumer derives from consuming one additional unit of that good.

Menu costs refer to any type of cost that a firm incurs if it changes its product price.

The **merchandise trade balance** measures exports minus imports in the U.S. balance of payments.

The **monetary base** is equal to currency held by the public plus bank reserves.

Monetary policy is the central bank's use of control of the money supply and interest rates to influence the level of economic activity.

Money is whatever is commonly accepted as payment in exchange for goods and services (and payment of debts and taxes).

The **money multiplier** gives the increase in the money supply per unit increase in the monetary base.

N

National income is the sum of the earnings of all factors of production that come from current production.

Natural rates of output, employment, and therefore unemployment, in the monetarist model are determined by *real* supply-side factors: the capital stock, the size of the labor force, and the level of technology. In our simple model, the natural rates of output, employment, and unemployment are the classical equilibrium levels of these variables (unemployment being confined to frictional and structural forms).

Net exports are total (gross) exports minus imports.

Net national product is gross national product minus depreciation.

The **new classical policy ineffectiveness proposition** asserts that systematic monetary and fiscal policy actions that change aggregate demand will *not* affect output and employment even in the short run.

Nominal gross national product is gross national product measured in current dollars.

O

Oligopoly is closer to monopoly than to perfect competition because it is typified by few firms (as few as two or three) and by moderately difficult entry. In product-type oligopoly, markets may have either standardized or differentiated products.

The **open market** is the market of dealers in government securities in New York City.

The **Open Market Committee** is composed of 12 voting members: the 7 members of the Board of Governors and 5 of the presidents of regional Federal Reserve banks. Presidents of the regional banks serve on a rotating basis, with the exception of the president of the Federal Reserve Bank of New York, who is vice chairman and a permanent voting member of the committee.

Open-market operations are purchases and sales of government securities in the open market by the Federal Reserve. Open-market operations are the primary tool for control of the monetary base.

The **opportunity cost** of an action is the value of the best forgone alternative.

P

The **partisan theory** views macroeconomic policy outcomes as the result of ideologically motivated decisions by leaders of different political parties. The parties represent constituencies with different preferences concerning macroeconomic variables.

The **permanent income hypothesis** shares with the life cycle hypothesis the view that consumption depends on a long-term average of income earned from labor and asset holdings.

Personal income is the national income accounts measure of the income received by persons from all sources.

The **Phillips curve** is the schedule showing the relationship between the unemployment and inflation rates.

Potential GDP (output) is the level that would be reached if productive resources (labor and capital) were being used at benchmark high levels.

A **price index** measures the aggregate price level relative to a chosen base year.

The **producer price index** measures the wholesale prices of approximately 3,000 items.

A **production function** summarizes the relationship between total inputs and total outputs assuming a given technology.

Public choice is the application to macroeconomic policymaking of the microeconomic theory of how decisions are made.

Q

The **quantity theory of money** is the classical theory stating that the price level is proportional to the quantity of money. In the monetarist version, the quantity theory is a theory of nominal GNP.

R

Rational expectations are expectations formed on the basis of all available relevant information concerning the variable being predicted. Moreover, economic agents are assumed to use available information intelligently; that is, they understand the relationships between the variables they observe and the variables they are trying to predict.

Real gross national product measures aggregate output in constant-valued dollars from a base year.

The **real interest rate** is the nominal interest rate minus the anticipated rate of price inflation.

A **recession** is a period when economic activity declines significantly relative to potential output, but less severely than in a depression such as that of the 1930s.

The **required reserve ratio** is the percentage of deposits banks must hold as reserves.

S

Seigniorage revenues are the amount of real resources bought by the government with newly created money.

Sticky price models (or menu cost models) are those in which costs of changing prices prevent price adjustments when demand changes. Consequently, output falls when, for example, there is a decline in demand.

The **structural deficit** is the part of the federal deficit that would exist even if the economy were at its potential level of output.

Structural unemployment, like frictional unemployment, originates in the dynamic nature of the product and job mix in the economy, but structural unemployment lasts longer.

T

Target zones for exchange rates are ranges within which policymakers try to maintain their currency's value. The target zones are jointly set by major industrialized nations.

Technological change includes changes in technological knowledge (e.g., ways to employ robots in the production process) as well as new knowledge about how to organize businesses (managerial strategies).

A **time inconsistency** problem arises when a future policy formulated at an initial date is no longer optimal at a later date even though no new information has appeared.

The **trade deficit** is the excess of imports over exports.

U

The **unemployment rate** expresses the number of unemployed persons as a percentage of the labor force.

The **user cost of capital** is the overall cost to a firm to employ an additional unit of capital for one period.

V

The **velocity of money** is the rate at which money *turns over* in gross national product transactions during a given period: that is, the average number of times each dollar is used in gross national product transactions.

INDEX

Lowercase n denotes entry from a footnote.

Balance of trade. *See* Trade balance
Balance sheet
  for commercial banks, 367–368
  for Federal Reserve, 364, 366
Bank capital, 368n
Bank deposits. *See* Deposits
Banking system, 360–361. *See also* Commercial banks; Federal Reserve System; Money supply
  money supply and, 375–378
Bank loans, Federal Reserve balance sheet and, 366
Bank of America, balance sheet of, 370
Bank reserves, 363, 364–365, 367–375
Barro, Robert J., 90n, 274, 275n, 278, 283, 287n
Barth, James, 429n
Baruch, Bernard, 95
Baumol, William, 473n
BEA (Bureau of Economic Analysis), 28
Becker, Gary, 86n
Bernanke, Ben, 240
Bias, in CPI, 31
Blanchard, Olivier J., 297n
Blinder, Alan, 294, 399–400, 461n
Board of Governors of Federal Reserve System, 363, 382–383. *See also* Federal Reserve System
Bond market, 135, 479
Bonds, 125
  equilibrium interest rate on, 127
  government deficit bond financing and, 431
  as government funds source, 69
  government sale of, 66–67
  interest rates and, 129–132
  Keynes on, 471
  money holding and, 475–480
  relative return on, 481n
  transaction demand and, 128
  wealth and, 67
Borrowing, as government funds source, 69
BP schedule. *See* Balance of payments
"Bracket creep," 439
Bretton Woods system, 312n, 318, 329, 338
  collapse of, 320, 323–324
Britain. *See* Great Britain
Brokerage fee, 473–474, 478, 479
  for shifting funds, 486
Brumberg, Richard, 450
Brunner, Karl, 223
Bryant, Ralph, 358n
Buchanan, James M., 406n, 407

Budget (U.S.), 409–411
  automatic fiscal stabilizers and, 414–418
  under Clinton, 441
  deficit in, 7–8
  in late 1990s to 21st century, 422–423
  trade deficits and, 7–8
Budget constraint, of government, 69–70
Budget deficit, 10
Bullionism, 38, 39
Bureau of Labor Statistics, prices, quality, and, 31
Burns, Arthur, 383
Bush, George H. W., 408, 440–441
Bush, George W., 408
  budget and, 422
  economics program of, 426
  tax cuts under, 441–442
Business, interest paid to, 25
Business Cycle Dating Group, of National Bureau of Economic Research (NBER), 33
Business cycles. *See also* Real business cycle; Real business cycles
  dating of postwar, 33
Business fixed investment, GDP and, 462
Business taxes, reduction in, 439–440
Byrd, Harry, Sr., 420, 421

C

Cambridge approach, 61–62, 227–228, 229, 230, 300–301
Campbell, John, 461n
Canada
  floating exchange rates of, 321
  inflation targeting in, 398
Capital
  investment and cost of, 465–467
  use of term, 310n
Capital account, 310–311
Capital deepening, 81
Capital flows, flexible exchange rates and, 326–327
Capital formation, 87
  rate of, 84
  technology and, 88–89
Capital gains, taxation of, 432
Capital goods, 16
Capital loss, interest rates and, 132
Capital markets, perfect capital mobility and, 358
Capital mobility
  imperfect, 344–350
  perfect, 344, 350–357

Capital stock, output, labor, and, 41
Carter, Jimmy, Federal Reserve chairman and, 383
CDs. *See* Certificates of deposit (CDs)
Cecchetti, Stephen, 294
Central bank. *See also* Federal Reserve System
  changes in, 398–400
  foreign, 312
  independence and economic performance of, 384
  intervention in foreign exchange, 319–320, 321–323
  official reserve transactions and, 311
Certificates of deposit (CDs), 362
Chain-weighted real GDP, 26, 27–28
Charge accounts, 61
Checkable deposits, 134, 362, 364
Cheney, Richard, 409
Chimerine, Lawrence, 429n
Churchill, Winston, 95
Circular flow, of income and output, 98–99
Citibank. *See* Banking system; Deposits
Classical aggregate demand curve, 63–65
Classical economics, 3, 37, 38–39. *See also* Aggregate demand; Aggregate supply; Classical macroeconomics; Keynes, John Maynard; Keynesian economics; New classical economics
  aggregate demand and, 216–218, 300–301
  aggregate supply and, 193–195, 217
  economic growth and, 425
  employment and, 49
  equilibrium in, 49, 50
  interest and, 431
  intermediate-run growth in, 430
  Keynesian economics and, 303
  labor and, 43–48, 203–205
  mercantilism and, 39
  on natural levels of employment and output, 244
  output in, 49, 50, 54–55
  production and, 40–43
  real and nominal variables in, 75
  real business cycle theory and, 282
  real economic factors and, 38–39
  Robbins on, 96–97
  supply in, 49–55, 195

targeting of, 385–386,
387–390, 396
Monetary base (MB), 364–365, 372
Federal Reserve and, 365
money supply and, 379
Monetary factors
aggregate demand and, 302
classical aggregate demand
curve and, 218
Monetary policy, 32, 382–401.
See also Liquidity trap;
Money entries
classical equilibrium model
and, 69–74
consumption and, 458
effectiveness of, 170–180
of Federal Reserve, 289
fiscal policy and, 169, 170
under fixed exchange rates, 345,
351–352
under flexible exchange rates,
347–348, 354–355
implications in monetarist view,
250–251
interest rate and, 386
investment and, 467–468
Keynesians and, 93–94, 134–135,
226–227, 422
monetarists and, 245, 246–250
monetarists vs. Keynesians on,
236–238
multipliers in *IS-LM* curve
model, 185
new classical economists on,
269–270
in open economy, 341–358
process of making, 382–384
in real business cycle model,
286–287
rule-based, 240
and slope of *IS* schedule,
171–173, 180
and slope of *LM* schedule,
178–180
sources of uncertainty and, 394
strategies for, 385–386
tax policy and, 74
Taylor rule and, 398
Monetary system. See also
Exchange rate(s)
currency boards, dollarization,
and, 322
Monetary theory of aggregate
demand, in classical
model, 301
Money, 32. See also Monetarism;
Money demand; Velocity
of money
in classical economics, 38, 39, 74
creation of, 69–70
defined, 361–363, 473
demand and supply schedules
for, 376

demand for, 61–62, 190
functions of, 361
in hyperinflation, 65
interest and, 125, 133–134
interest elasticity of, 137n,
138–140
Keynesians and, 122–135,
224–227, 229
quantity theory of, 59–65,
216–217
real and nominal variables
and, 75
seigniorage and, 287
as store of wealth, 67, 472,
480–485
total demand for, 132
unstable growth of, 486
velocity of, 59–61
Money demand, 388, 470–487
instability of, 485–486
interest rate and, 484–485
inventory-theoretic approach
to, 473–480
Keynesian, 127–134, 470–472
and money as store of wealth,
480–485
risk and, 481–483
speculation and, 129–132
transactions demand for money,
472–480
uncertainty about, 393–394
zero interest elasticity of, 391
Money demand function
foreign interest rate and, 344n
shifts in, 144, 164
Money demand schedule, 376–377
Money growth, 239
rates (1961–71), 250
Money holdings, 473–480
Money hypothesis, of monetarists,
228
Money-income relationship, instability in, 238
Money market, 135
equilibrium in, 133, 135–145
Money market deposit accounts
(MMDAs), 362
Money market equilibrium, *LM*
curve and, 135–145
Money market mutual fund, 486
Money multiplier, 372–375
money supply control and, 375
Money supply, 360–361
aggregate demand and, 64, 190,
192
changes in, 142–143
components of, 361–363
control of, 375–378
deposit component of, 364
determining, 374–375
equilibrium output and, 194
Federal Reserve control of,
363–365

in Great Depression, 378–380
growth in, 133, 169, 375–376,
394–395
interest rates and, 377–378
vs. interest rate targets, 394–395
LM schedule and, 142–144,
163–164
M1 and, 125
measures of, 362–363
in new classical view, 266
price level and, 201
Money supply function, 374
Money tax cuts and, 72
Money wage, 247. See also Real
wage; Stickiness; Wage(s)
employment and, 199
fixed, 198
Keynesian theory of, 196, 197,
203–209
labor market equilibrium
and, 51
labor supply and, 203–209
new Keynesian economics
and, 291
variable, 205–206
Monopolistic firms, 292
MPC. See Marginal propensity to
consume (MPC)
MPN. See Marginal product of
labor (MPN)
MPS. See Marginal propensity to
save (MPS)
Mueller, Dennis, 405n
Multiplier(s). See also Money
multiplier
autonomous expenditures, 118
balanced budget, 114
deposit, 371
fiscal and monetary, 185–186
fiscal policy, 457–458
in *IS-LM* curve model,
184–185
tax, 112–114
Multiplier concept, equilibrium
income and, 109–112
Mundell-Fleming model, 341–344,
350
Murphy, Kevin, 86n
Muth, John, 263

N

NASDAQ, 271
National Bureau of Economic
Research (NBER), 33
National debt, projected surpluses
and, 12
National income (NI), 19–20, 21
consumption and, 449
personal income, disposable
income, and, 21–22
taxation and, 112